LEARNING AND
COMPLEX BEHAVIOR

JOHN W. DONAHOE
University of Massachusetts–Amherst

DAVID C. PALMER
Smith College

Edited by Vivian Packard Dorsel

ALLYN AND BACON
Boston   London   Toronto   Sydney   Tokyo   Singapore

Vice-President, Publisher: Susan Badger
Executive Editor: Laura Pearson
Series Editorial Assistant: Laura L. Ellingson
Editorial-Production Administrator: Annette Joseph
Editorial-Production Coordinator: Susan Freese
Editorial-Production Service: WordCrafters Editorial Services, Inc.
Manufacturing Buyer: Megan Cochran
Cover Administrator: Linda K. Dickinson
Cover Designer: Suzanne Harbison

Library of Congress Cataloging-in-Publication Data

Donahoe, John W.
    Learning and complex behavior / John W. Donahoe, David C. Palmer.
        p.   cm.
    Includes bibliographical references and indexes.
    ISBN 0-205-13996-5
    1. Learning, Psychology of.   2. Behaviorism (Psychology)
3. Cognitive psychology.   I. Palmer, David C.
II. Title.
BF318.D645   1994
153.1'5—dc20   93-22625
                                                            CIP

Printed in the United States of America

10 9 8 7 6 5 4 3   99 98 97

Excerpts on pages 154–155 and page 201 from *The Man Who Mistook His Wife for a Hat*, copyright © 1970, 1981, 1984, 1985 by Oliver Sacks. Reprinted by permission of Summit Books, a division of Simon & Schuster, Inc.

CONTENTS

PREFACE

This book draws upon basic biobehavioral processes to provide a conceptually coherent approach to understanding complex human behavior. The unity of the approach stems from its commitment to a selectionist view of the origins of complexity. Selectionism began with Charles Darwin's account of how the diversity and complexity of living organisms could have arisen by natural selection. In general, selectionism regards complexity as the emergent product of relatively simple processes whose effects endure long enough to be subjected to further selections.

Within experimental psychology, two competing views of the origins of complex behavior exist: behavior analysis, which is the most consistently selectionist perspective within psychology; and cognitive psychology. Cognitive psychology in its various forms has been the dominant approach to complex behavior for most of the past twenty years. The major goals of cognitive psychology are to investigate, through research that is well controlled *within* the experimental situation, complex behavioral phenomena in humans and to infer from these behavioral observations the unobserved cognitive processes of which complex behavior is said to be the expression. By contrast, behavior analysis has focused primarily on behavior in simplified laboratory environments using nonhuman animals as subjects. The major goals of behavior analysis are to identify, through direct manipulation and measurement of all relevant variables (i.e., through experimental analysis), the fundamental variables that affect behavior. Once the functional relations— or behavioral processes—between these variables and behavior have been described, principles are formulated that summarize those processes. These principles are then used to interpret complex human behavior. Behavior analysis and cognitive psychology share the goal of seeking to understand complex human behavior, but they differ on how best to achieve that goal.

A thorough exploration of the differences between the behavior-analytic and cognitive approaches to complex behavior and of the origins of those differences is beyond the scope of this, or any other, preface. Each approach has achieved important parts of its goals. Behavior analysis has identified many basic behavioral processes and formulated principles that describe those processes. However, the interpretations of complex phenomena have often not been persuasive to others. The failure to achieve compelling interpretations stems largely from the imprecision of purely verbal efforts to describe the effects of the many simultaneously acting processes of which any complex behavior is the expression. Cognitive psychology has been successful in revealing a host of fascinating and previously unrecognized phenomena in areas such as perception, memory, and language. In fact, these discoveries have led to what is often called "the cognitive revolution." However, little enduring consensus has been achieved concerning the underlying cognitive processes that have been inferred from observations of these phenomena.

Most recently, the confluence of a number of events has encouraged efforts to produce a comprehensive theory about complex human behavior. Within behavior analysis, a resurgence of research with human subjects has identified several phenomena—notably, the formation of equivalence classes—that have important implications for the understanding of complex behavior. In addition, applied behavior analysis has shown itself to be effective in the world of practical affairs, namely, in education and in the remediation of dysfunctional behavior. Within cognitive psychology, work on what is called "parallel distributed processing" has demonstrated that a variety of complex phenomena are not necessarily beyond the reach of relatively simple processes. Adaptive neural networks, to which parallel distributed processing is conceptually related, hold promise of providing a much more precise means for determining the cumulative effects of basic behavioral processes. Moreover, because adaptive networks may be coordinated with processes at the *neural* level, the direct experimental analysis of basic neural processes may replace the inferred processes of cognitive psychology. And, unlike the situation that prevailed at the birth of behavior analysis, advances in neuroscience have begun to identify the specific neural mechanisms that implement the behavioral processes identified by the experimental analysis of behavior.

The confluence of these events encourages the belief that the time is ripe for an integration of the experimental analysis of behavior with the experimental analysis of neuroscience to achieve a coherent interpretation of complex human behavior. A case can be made that the past thirty years have been comparable to the seventy-five-year period that elapsed between Darwin's proposal of natural selection and the general acceptance of that proposal within biology. Acceptance occurred only after biological mechanisms were identified by which natural selection could be implemented—the mechanisms of heredity—and formal means were devised whereby the implications of those mechanisms could be precisely traced—population genetics. The fusion of Darwin's functional proposal of natural selection with genetics is known as "the modern synthesis," or the synthetic theory of evolution. This book represents an effort to begin the synthesis of behavior analysis with neuroscience to produce a comprehensive and compelling interpretation of complex human behavior. The synthetic theory of evolution has shown that the cumulative effect of relatively simple biological processes can produce the tremendous complexity and diversity of the biological world. A successful synthetic theory of the origins of complex behavior would show how the cumulative effects of relatively simple biobehavioral processes lead to the equally prodigious diversity and complexity of human behavior. (See Donahoe and Palmer, 1989, and Palmer and Donahoe, 1993, for more extensive discussions of these issues.)

To the Instructor

Because the authors attempt to provide a coherent and integrated account of complex human behavior, the material cannot be read effectively in any order other than that which is presented in the book. However, it is quite possible to eliminate substantial portions of the book without impairing its intelligibility. Almost all of the first three chapters, a large portion of the seventh chapter, and all of the tenth chapter must be read. These five chapters describe the basic biobehavioral processes of which complex behavior is thought to be the cumulative product. Aside from these chapters, the last three chapters form a unit that focuses on the interpretation of complex behavior falling under the conventional headings of problem solving, memory, and language. Although the book makes use of information from the neurosciences, it is entirely self-contained. Such information is described in the text as it is needed, but only to the degree minimally necessary for present purposes. Endnotes and an extensive references section of relevant behavioral and neural research permit the advanced student to investigate these issues in much greater depth.

Preliminary versions of the book have been successfully used in three types of courses: a standard undergraduate course in learning and cognition, an honors undergraduate course, and a beginning graduate course. When only selected sections of the book are assigned, both the content and the workload are acceptable to most undergraduates. When the entire book is assigned, including the endnotes at the conclusion of each chapter, the text is suitable for an introduction to learning at the graduate level. Study Aids—a set of study questions and a list of technical terms introduced in the chapter—are appended to each chapter. In addition, a Glossary at the end of the book defines all technical terms. Finally, a booklet containing a large number of more specific questions keyed to the headings within each chapter is available at cost from the authors. These questions may be used in PSI courses or in courses employing short-answer quizzes. We have used them as the basis for frequent quizzes when earlier versions of the text were used with undergraduate students.

The following specific selections were used by the authors in a one-semester undergraduate (junior-senior) course that provided a balanced coverage of the material: Chapters 1 (all) and 2 (pages 31–35, 37–61); 4 (pages 89–99, 101–106, 109–112, 114–118); 5 (all); 6 (pages 152–157, 161–173); 7 (pages 177–180, 193–199, 200–204); 8 (pages 211–224, 226–230); 9 (pages 237–248, 256–262); 10 (all); 11 (pages 296–307, 309–312, 317–320); and 12 (pages 324–326, 330–333, 334–338, 340–347, 349–351).

To the Students

This is not an easy book. But how could it be otherwise for a book that purports to provide basic insights into that most complex of subjects, human behavior? Although not an "easy read," experience with preliminary versions of the text indicates that its main points can be mastered by most students, given a reasonable commitment of time and effort. Although there is no one "best" way to study—each of us is a product of a unique evolutionary and individual history—here are some suggestions that many students have found useful. Before reading a chapter, get an idea of the topics covered in the chapter by looking over the main subheadings listed in the Contents and the study questions listed at the end of each chapter. Then read a section of the chapter until you encounter a chapter heading. Carefully attend to any figures when you are referred to them by **boldface** entries within the text. Read the figure captions carefully; they are more complete than in most texts. After reading a section, stop and identify the main points that have been covered. Make a few brief notes with enough key phrases to serve as a prompt to your memory. After finishing a study session, look back over your notes to see if they still "make sense." If not, reread the sections that remain unclear and change your notes accordingly. Except for technical terms and portions of definitions, use your own words; it is easier to remember your own words than those of others. If your instructor distributes the detailed study questions available from the authors, make your notes with reference to these questions. When you review for an examination, read over your notes and see if they still "make sense" to you. If not, read the relevant section again. Answer the study questions at the end of each chapter. Also, go over the list of technical terms at the end of the chapter. Use the Glossary at the end of the book to check your understanding of the terms. If the tests consist of short-answer essay questions or identification items, write out at least short versions of the answers. In general, try to study in such a way that you are practicing the very behavior that will be called for on the tests.

Acknowledgments

The authors express their special appreciation to Vivian Packard Dorsel, a former graduate student and present colleague, who edited the entire manuscript and made numerous suggestions to improve its clarity and readability, and who authored the Glossary. We thank also those who participated in graduate seminars over the span of several semesters when this project was conceived. The participants included, in addition to Vivian Dorsel, Rosalind Burns, Eric Carlson, Neil Carlson, Beth Sulzer-Azaroff, and Julie Schweitzer. All made substantial contributions to our thinking, as did Andrew Barto, with whom we discussed our ideas on learning in neurally plausible adaptive networks; and Jerrold Meyer, with whom we consulted on matters of neuropharmacology. We thank also our colleagues in cognitive psychology, particularly James Chumbley and Keith Rayner, who made us aware of relevant literature in cognitive psychology even though they may have often disagreed with the purposes to which we put such information. In that regard, our apologies are extended to the many investigators whose experimental findings contributed so much to the content of the book but whose theoretical accounts were sometimes not honored. These investigators and those others whom we have specifically mentioned cannot be held responsible for what we have made of their work, of course. Great appreciation is also extended to Susan Badger, Vice-President and Publisher at Allyn and Bacon, who permitted our approach to see the light of day in the face of some advice to the contrary; and to Linda Zuk at WordCrafters, who produced the book and responded to substantial last-minute changes with good grace. Our thanks also go to Jay R. Alexander, the artist who prepared the figures and illustrations that enrich the presentation.

Our appreciation is extended to the following individuals who reviewed the text for Allyn and Bacon: Marc N. Branch, University of Florida; Dennis Cogan, Texas Tech University; Neal J. Cohen, University of Illinois; John Gabrieli, Northwestern University; Lynn Nadel, University of Arizona; Howard M. Reid, Buffalo State College; and Larry R. Squire, University of California–San Diego.

Finally, we express our gratitude to our wives—Mildred and Jill—who endured the social deprivations that too often afflict the spouses as well as the authors of books.

J. W. D.
D. C. P.

CHAPTER 1

THE ORIGINS OF LEARNED BEHAVIOR

INTRODUCTION

Everyone agrees that behavior is complex. However, there is much less agreement about how complexity comes about or how it can be understood. Consider the following account of a rather ordinary episode of behavior.

I am writing these words facing a fifth-floor window that looks out over the campus toward the White Mountains beyond. It is winter, and the snow is falling softly but steadily. Students, bundled against the cold, are trudging down the road that passes the building. The roadway is strung out along the side of a hill that slopes up to my right. At some distance, a student is climbing the hill toward the road. He slips and—because he is tall—falls rather heavily. He picks himself up, having suffered no apparent harm, and resumes his climb. Still farther off, a car backs out of a parking place onto the road and then drives away.

Seeing the car back up, I am reminded of an incident that occurred yesterday. I had been hurriedly backing out of a parking place, and shifted from reverse to first gear without coming to a complete stop. The transmission briefly protested and, in that instant, a friend from graduate-school days popped unbidden into mind. Before that moment, I doubt that I had thought of him more than once or twice in the past twenty years. I wondered why my friend had made his unexpected reappearance . . . and then I knew.

Twenty years ago, he had called me out to the parking lot of the apartment house in which we both lived. He had just bought his first car, and feared it was defective. Although he didn't yet have a driver's license, my friend hopped into the car to show me the problem. The engine started and the car shot backward, coming to an abrupt halt with a great grinding of gears. Smiling, he got out of the car, pleased that he had so successfully demonstrated the defect. He assured me that the car made the same

noise every time he shifted from reverse to first! . . . The sound of grinding gears had spanned the decades, bringing my long-ago friend to mind.

Now, as I continue to look out my window, I remember that my friend had not known how to drive because he had come from a poor family, that poverty had forced his parents to place him and his brother in separate foster homes, and that—on a snowy day much like this—he had run away from the foster home in a futile search for his brother.

There is nothing exceptional about my behavior during the few moments that I looked up to gaze out the window. If you, rather than I, had surveyed this scene, many of the same types of behavior would have occurred, although the specifics would—of course—have differed. You would likely have noticed the students walking along the road and, quite probably, have seen the student fall while climbing the hill. Although seeing the car back out of the parking place might not have triggered your memory, something you saw would probably have reminded you of an event from your own past—what happened when you saw someone fall, what happened when you walked along a road, what a friend said as you walked together, and so on. The specific events are unique to each of us, but the general types of behavior—those that come under such conventional headings as perceiving, attending, remembering, and so forth—are common to us all.

These shared behaviors are very complex, however, and we should not let their commonness obscure their complexity. When I looked out my window, I did not see mere blobs of light and shadow, but a meaningful world of people and mountains. Yet the actual stimuli striking my visual receptors were not "people" or "mountains," but complex moving arrays varying in wavelength

1

and intensity—arrays that had never before struck my receptors in precisely that pattern. I saw a tall student fall, yet the actual size of the visual image on my retina was smaller than that of shorter but more nearby students. I saw a car back out of a parking space, and this conjured up events of the day before, when I had suddenly thought of someone I had not seen in over twenty years. I then tried to discover why this memory had emerged, and found the sound of grinding gears to be the thread linking the present to the past. Finally, I wrote of these events and, in reading of them, you have experienced something akin to my reactions. And yet, what appear on these pages are not the events I had seen or recalled, nor words and phrases, nor even letters, but simply lines on paper. It is only your experience with such lines that permits them to produce reactions in you that are related to those that occurred when I looked out my window. Without a long history of learning, neither my behavior nor yours would have occurred as it did.

We hope that the example has convinced you—if any convincing were necessary—that even everyday behavior is complex. The apparently simple act of seeing a person is a complicated business in a world of varying visual energies. Moreover, the events in the environment produced their effects on my behavior through acting on a nervous system that had already been changed by earlier experiences. Seeing a car back up led me to recall events that had occurred many years before.

Difficulties in Understanding Complex Behavior

Beyond demonstrating the complexity of behavior, the example illustrates a number of general problems that we must deal with if we are to understand complex behavior. First, the behavior that is guided by the environment varies from person to person, but is highly organized. I saw people whom I recognized as students, not never-seen-before blobs. And one behavior followed another in an orderly fashion: I saw the car backing up, which reminded me of when I had backed up my car the

day before, and I then remembered my long-ago friend. What is responsible for the *organized complexity* that is so characteristic of the behavior of living organisms? How does that complexity come about? How is it acquired?

Second, understanding my behavior required information about the past. To one who did not know the relation between the sound of grinding gears and the long-ago incident with my friend, the sudden occurrence of the memory would have been a mystery. However, in many cases, information about the past is unavailable—almost always to the observer and, often, to the behaver as well. How are we to understand complex behavior if such behavior has its roots in the past but *knowledge of the past is incomplete*?

Third, much of my behavior while I was looking out the window could not have been detected by an observer. Someone watching me closely might have seen my eyes move as they shifted from one position to another, my facial expression change fleetingly as I thought of my friend's unfortunate childhood, and my hand move as I wrote. But these observed behaviors were only a part—most would say the lesser part—of what occurred. How can we understand complex behavior when *much ongoing activity is inaccessible to an observer*?

These difficulties might lead us to conclude that behavior, especially complex behavior, is beyond human understanding. How can we understand the emergence of organized yet complex behavior when it is the product of a long sequence of historical events—often inaccessible to an outside observer, and only partially accessible to the behaver himself?

APPROACHES TO UNDERSTANDING COMPLEX BEHAVIOR

Students of behavior have shown considerable agreement about the problems presented by complex behavior, but little agreement about how those problems should be addressed. In this section, we shall review some of the major approaches to one of the problems—the fact that significant parts of the organism's total activity are unobserved when complex behavior takes place. In the next section, we shall treat a related set of problems—how organized behavioral complexity comes about as the result of an incompletely known history of events.

The Status of Unobserved Events in a Science of Behavior

What is behavior? If we define behavior as all of the activities in which an organism may engage—both those that are observed by others with the unaided senses, and those that are not—then it is clear that many of the most important activities that make up complex behavior are usually unobserved. I recalled my friend's misguided effort to demonstrate the "problem" with his new car. I then wrote about recalling those events—acting in a way that was partly observable to others—rather than just recalling them silently to myself. As we have defined behavior, writing and merely recalling both qualify as behavior; the first is observed by others and the second is not. What is the place of unobserved behavior in a science of behavior?

Verbal behavior as an indirect measure of unobserved behavior. Because the activities conventionally denoted by such terms as recalling, thinking, imagining, and feeling are so salient when we observe our own behavior, these were the first behaviors studied by psychology in the late 1800s, when it became a discipline separate from philosophy.[1] The fact that others cannot observe these activities was not seen as an impediment at first, since it was assumed that what the person said— the subject's verbal behavior—reliably and validly[2] indicated the unobserved activities. And, verbal behavior *could* be observed by others.

This assumption was soon called into question, however. Similar tasks gave rise to different verbal behavior in different laboratories, even with supposedly well trained subjects. Moreover, the differences in verbal behavior often seemed to correspond to the theoretical predilections of the

investigators. For example, laboratories where certain tasks were believed to evoke visual images reported the existence of such images, while those holding that the tasks need not evoke images did not report them. At the very least, then, the subjects' verbal responses were unreliable measures of the unobserved activities evoked by the task. The alternative view—that the same task evoked different unobserved activities in different subjects—was of no help, since it meant that intersubject reliability in measuring unobserved behavior was impossible.

Still other work indicated that, as a measure of unobserved activities, verbal behavior was likely to be invalid as well as unreliable. To be a valid indicator of events unavailable to an external observer, verbal responses must be free of the influences of other events. Leaving aside the difficulties in evaluating this assumption, its tenability became increasingly suspect for two very different sets of reasons. First, Sigmund Freud's clinical observations had led him to the concepts of repression and the unconscious,[3] which implied that what we say cannot be taken at face value as an unbiased reflection of other events. Since verbal behavior, in common with all other behavior, could be influenced by many variables, it could not serve as an "uncontaminated" measure of other activities. Second, Charles Darwin's naturalistic and experimental observations led him to the view that the behavior of humans, as well as other animals, was the result of a prolonged evolutionary process during which different bodily structures had evolved at different times in the history of the species.[4] Since the structures mediating verbal behavior had evolved later than most of the other structures of the human brain, it was unlikely that those "verbal structures" were in direct contact with all other brain regions. Thus, it was unlikely that verbal behavior could be guided by the full range of unobserved events about which the subjects were asked to report.[5] In summary, Freud's work questioned whether overt verbal behavior could reflect unobserved activities in any straightforward fashion, and Darwin's work questioned on evolutionary grounds whether some unobserved activities could guide verbal behavior at all.

Methodological Approach

Faced with the unreliability and likely invalidity of verbal behavior as a measure of unobserved behavior, many psychologists in the early 1900s adopted the stance of **methodological behaviorism**. In an influential paper published in 1913, John B. Watson attempted to solve the problem of unobserved activities by arguing that scientific psychology should restrict its attention to observed behavior.[6] This approach defined the subject matter of psychology on methodological grounds—the science of behavior was to be confined to events that could be measured directly. In short, the problem of unobserved behavior was "solved" by declaring it beyond a scientific treatment. A science of behavior should restrict itself to determining the functional relations between *observed* environmental and behavioral events.

The methodologically constrained approach to the study of behavior also gave support to the study of nonhuman behavior. Because of Darwin's evolutionary arguments about the continuity of behavior and anatomical structure among species,[7] Watson and a number of his contemporaries were interested in animal behavior. If unobserved events were the focus of psychological inquiry and could be known only through verbal behavior, then animal behavior could make little contribution to the study of human behavior: Only humans are capable of speech.[8] However, if only observable responses were considered, then comparisons between humans and nonhumans could more readily be made and continuities pursued. Moreover, because genetic and environmental variables may be more tightly controlled in laboratory studies with animals, the functional relations between environmental and behavioral variables could be determined more precisely.

As viewed by the methodological approach, explanations of behavior consist of identifying the environmental conditions that affect observed be-havior, and then specifying as precisely as possible the functional relations between those variables. The diagram in **Figure 1.1** summarizes this approach, which is sometimes referred to as the "black-box" approach because no effort is made to identify the processes within the organism that intervene between the reception of stimuli and the occurrence of observed behavior. Returning to my musings as I gazed out the office window, for the methodological approach it is enough to say that seeing the car back up led me to write about my long-ago friend. No discussion of the intervening events is thought to be useful since, even if such events occurred, they were not observed by others. The car and my writing are both observable events. However, intervening events—such as remembering that the gears made a grinding noise when I backed up my car the day before, or having that sound bring my friend to mind—are unobservable to others and are therefore excluded from consideration by the methodological approach.

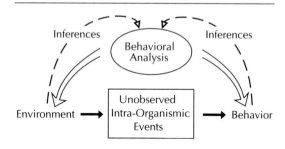

FIGURE 1.1   *The methodological approach to complex behavior*
Behavioral analysis manipulates the environment and measures the behavior that occurs as a function of changes in the environment. Which environmental events to manipulate and which behavioral events to measure are based upon inferences from the outcome of prior behavioral analyses. Although intra-organismic events undeniably mediate observed environment-be-havior relations, no attempt is made to characterize unobserved intra-organismic events on the basis of behavioral data alone.

Rationale for the methodological approach.
There are obvious practical advantages in confining accounts to observed events—such events may be measured and, perhaps, directly manipulated by experimenters in their laboratories and by applied workers in their efforts to help others. The advantages to applied work are, perhaps, most readily appreciated:[9] In order for dysfunctional behavior to be replaced by more effective behavior, the conditions that produced the dysfunctional behavior must be changed to conditions that foster more effective behavior. Since only observed conditions can be directly changed, there is little point in discussing unobserved conditions, which can only be influenced through manipulation of the observed environment. For example, if we wish to help others change their dysfunctional behavior—to enable illiterates to read, phobics to lose their fears, and so on—we must change their present environment and not the unobserved events that may have been affected by past environments, which may not be known in any case. If an adult has an unreasonable fear of dogs as the result of a bad experience with a dog when he was only a year old and unable to talk, then there are a variety of well established techniques that can be used to reduce the person's fear *without knowing anything about the specific conditions that produced the phobic behavior, or about the unobserved events that may have been a part of that early experience.* Although such information might be useful if it were available, it is not required. Skilled practitioners, guided by their clinical experience, can implement various procedures until a successful one has been identified.

A second argument for restricting the study of behavior to observable events goes as follows: Some of the unobserved events appealed to in nonfunctional accounts cannot be measured at the behavioral level. Instead, they are measurable at lower levels of analysis—the microbehavioral[10] or physiological levels. One critic of approaches to memory that do not confine themselves to observed events has put it this way: "Although entirely appropriate for students of the physical substrate of memory . . . students of memory overlook the fact that, for them, the memory trace is merely a metaphor, and in doing so they confuse psychology with physiology."[11] To us, this reservation stems from overly parochial considerations. The level of analysis at which orderly functional relations are obtained depends on the nature of the phenomena under study. The conventional distinctions between academic disciplines—e.g., between psychology and physiology—are the result of relatively arbitrary conditions, and should not be accorded the same status as distinctions that arise from scientific analysis. Complex behavior, such as remembering, is the outcome of a multitude of events occurring at the behavioral, microbehavioral, and physiological levels. Unraveling the secrets of such complex behavior may well be facilitated by interdisciplinary efforts that approach the problem at several levels.[12]

The case for unobserved events in the study of behavior.   For many applied purposes, it is not useful to consider unobserved events. Nevertheless, most behavioral scientists include such events in a comprehensive account of behavior. To begin with, an event that is unobserved during one period in the history of science becomes observed at a later period with advances in technology. Thus, the distinction between observed and unobserved events is not a distinction between *kinds* of events but between the resolving power of different technologies. An adult who is afraid of dogs not only runs away from dogs—a behavior that is readily apparent to an observer—but may also show an increase in sweat gland activity when he sees a dog. This change in activity, which is mediated by the autonomic nervous system, is observable only with technology that became available during this century. However, no one can doubt that autonomic responses occurred before the development of the special instruments required to measure them. The effects of the autonomic system on sweat gland activity were unobserved events before, are observed events now, and exist as events in the physical world whether they are measured or not.

Furthermore, if we remove from consideration all those events that are not now observed, efforts to develop technologies that permit them to be measured will come to a halt. In this way, we risk impeding the expansion of useful knowledge by placing limits on the orderliness of the functional relations that can be demonstrated at the behavioral level. For example, it may be that our "dog-phobic" runs away from only those dogs that evoke a sweat gland response. If we observe only that the person sees a dog and then *usually* runs away, we have found a functional relation between running and seeing. However, that relation may not be as orderly as the one between running and seeing a dog that evokes an autonomic response. We may be able to relate the occurrence of sweat gland responses to some observable characteristic of the stimulus, such as the size of the dog, and this should be the initial focus of our efforts to improve the precision of the functional relation. Such efforts to find correlated observed events in the contemporaneous environment may not always be successful, however, and provide an incomplete measure of the total activity occasioned by the environment in any case.

If we deny the possible contribution of unobserved events on the grounds that we cannot directly influence them with current technology, we are equating what we can directly observe and manipulate with what exists. As technology expands the range of events that can be sensed by the special instruments of science, currently unobserved events become observed and, hence, potential candidates for direct manipulation. At that point, knowledge of the formerly unobserved events may contribute directly to both practice and basic research in behavioral science. Short of that point, a consideration of the plausible candidates for such events guides the search for their experimental investigation.

B. F. Skinner, who has consistently and persuasively championed the explanatory power of careful analyses of observed environmental and behavioral events, clearly broke away from methodological behaviorism over forty years ago.[13]

Although **experimental analysis** requires that variables involved in functional relations be observed under the conditions of the experiment, unobserved events—even though they cannot be subjected to experimental analysis at that moment—are acknowledged as potential contributors to complex behavior. Indeed, to understand many complex phenomena, appeals to unobserved events are necessary. The particular circumstances under which such appeals may be made, and the form they may take, are discussed in later sections under the heading of **scientific interpretation**.

Relations between different levels of analysis. We will also describe Skinner's views of the relation between behavioral and other levels of analysis, since they—like his views about the role of unobserved events in a science of behavior—are sometimes misunderstood by otherwise knowledgeable behavioral scientists. Skinner has never objected to efforts to coordinate observations at the behavioral level with those at the microbehavioral and physiological levels. Quite the contrary, he[14] argued that coordinating observations at other levels of analysis with those at the behavioral level was desirable, *if* the functional relations defined at the behavioral level were well described. "What is generally not understood by those interested in establishing neurological bases is that a rigorous description at the level of behavior is necessary for the demonstration of a neurological correlate" (p. 422). Skinner was not opposed to efforts to establish neural correlates of behavior; he regarded differences concerning the fruitfulness of such undertakings as "a matter of tastes" (p. 426). "I am not overlooking the advance that is made in the unification of knowledge when terms at one level of analysis are defined ('explained') at a lower level" (p. 428).

In fact, Skinner believed that, ultimately, observations at the physiological level had much to offer a science of behavior. "The physiologist of the future will tell us all that can be known about what is happening inside the behaving organism. His account will be an important advance over a behavioral analysis, because the latter is necessarily 'historical'—that is to say, it is confined to functional relations showing temporal gaps. ... What he discovers cannot invalidate the laws of a science of behavior, but it will make the picture of human action more nearly complete."[15] The view that microbehavioral events are a part of a science of behavior was termed *radical behaviorism* by Skinner[16]. Such unobserved events are admissible so long as they are not accorded characteristics other than those of observed events that have been subjected to experimental analysis.

Formal reasons for considering events at the microbehavioral and physiological levels. So far, we have identified two reasons for expanding the methodological approach to include events that are unobserved at the behavioral level: (a) The distinction between unobserved and observed events is not a fixed line that separates different *kinds* of events, but a fuzzy boundary that advances as technology progresses. (b) The incorporation of subbehavioral events may improve the precision of the functional relations between events measured at the behavioral level. In this last section on the status of events that are unobserved at the behavioral level, we consider a formal argument for their consideration by a science of behavior.

Humans, and most other organisms whose behavior is of interest, possess nervous systems composed of many nerve cells, or **neurons**. These neurons mediate between the reception of environmental stimuli and the execution of behavioral responses. Neurons respond to stimulation by generating bursts of electrical activity, or nerve impulses. Nerve impulses do not begin until stimulation exceeds a certain value, called a threshold. When the threshold has been exceeded, the rate of nerve impulses soon increases in proportion to increases in the intensity of stimulation. Then, as the neuron approaches its maximum rate of firing, increases become smaller until, at high intensities of stimulation, the neuron reaches its

maximum rate of firing. (See **Figure 1.2a** for a graphic presentation of the response of a neuron to

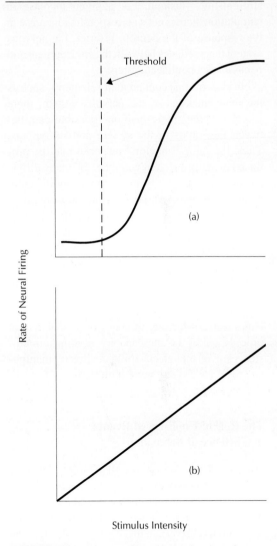

FIGURE 1.2 *Two possible relations between the rate of firing of a neuron and the intensity of the stimulus activating the neuron*
(a) The nonlinear relation characteristic of neurons, in which firing begins only after a threshold has been exceeded and then increases before slowing down as some upper limit is approached. (b) A linear relation not found in neurons, in which firing begins as soon as the stimulus occurs and increases at a constant rate as the intensity of the stimulus increases.

increasing stimulation.) The critical point, for present purposes, is that the response of a neuron to stimulation increases in a *nonlinear*—i.e., not in straight-line—fashion. For a given increase in stimulation there is not a corresponding increase in the response of the neuron. In brief, the nervous system that mediates between the environment and behavior is a nonlinear system.

In systems that contain many elements, such as the many neurons of the nervous system, there is—in general—more than one possible path between the inputs to the system and its outputs. Thus, the same behavioral response may be produced in many different ways; i.e., by many different patterns of activity involving many different neurons. Systems whose elements are nonlinear have an additional property: Even if two such systems produce identical outputs to identical inputs at one point in time and are thereafter treated identically, the two systems will not necessarily continue to respond identically to identical inputs.[17] In systems having these characteristics— and the individual organism is one such system—concern for the influence of subbehavioral processes may be inescapable in some circumstances, even though our ability to directly manipulate them is currently quite limited.

The Role of Unobserved Events in a Science of Behavior

For the above reasons—as well as simple curiosity about the processes underlying the functional relations between the environment and behavior— most workers have concluded that events at the subbehavioral level can make a contribution to the understanding of behavior, and of learning in particular. However, there is disagreement about how best to characterize these events and about their proper role in behavioral science. In this section, we consider two views. The first, which is more commonly held in psychology, is the inferred-process approach. The second, which we favor, is the biobehavioral approach.

The Inferred-Process Approach

In the inferred-process approach, the functional relations between observed environmental and behavioral events are determined first; these events and relations then serve as the basis for *inferring* subbehavioral processes that are hypothesized to underlie the functional relations.[18] These inferred subbehavioral processes are not observed at the subbehavioral level, but are inferred from observations at the behavioral level. **Figure 1.3** summarizes the logical relation between inferred processes and the behavioral observations on which they are based.[19]

An example from experimental work on memory illustrates the inferred-process approach. A visual display of a set of unrelated letters is very briefly presented to a human subject; immediately thereafter, the subject is given a retention test in which he is asked to pronounce the letters he has seen. Under these conditions, any incorrect responses that occur are apt to be those appropriate for *physically* similar stimuli. For example, if **B**

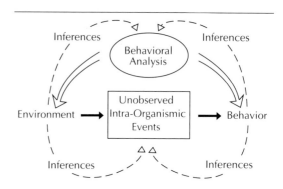

FIGURE 1.3   *The inferred-process approach to complex behavior*
As with the methodological approach, only environmental and behavioral events are manipulated and observed. However, the inferred-process approach attempts to infer the characteristics of unobserved intra-organismic events—either real or hypothetical—from the results of behavioral analysis alone. Intra-organismic events are not directly observed.

were among the letters presented, it might be mis-remembered as **R**. Thus, the vocal response "are" might occur rather than "bee."[20] If, however, the presentation and retention times are extended to a few seconds, then incorrect responses are more often of a different type.[21] Instead of being appropriate for a physically similar visual stimulus, the incorrect response is likely to resemble the *sound* of the correct letter.[22] For example, the letter **B** might lead to the vocal response "tee" even though **B** and **T** are physically dissimilar stimuli.

Experiments of this sort have discovered an important and reliable functional relation between the presentation and retention intervals of letters and the type of response evoked by those letters: At short intervals, the visual properties of the stimulus guide responding; at longer intervals, the auditory (or vocal) properties predominate. How is this reliable functional relation, based on observations at the behavioral level, accounted for within the conceptual framework of an inferred-process approach?

In the traditional inferred-process account, two different memory structures were inferred from these behavioral findings, each representing the stimulus in its own way.[23] A briefly presented stimulus is said to be stored in sensory memory, where it is represented in terms of its physical features. Thus, at short intervals, the physical features of the stimulus guide responding. If the interval is longer, then the stimulus is said to be stored in a second inferred structure, short-term memory, where it is now represented by its acoustic (sound) features or by the articulatory movements required to make the vocal response.[24] The inferred acoustic or articulatory effects of the stimulus then guide the response. In summary, the effects of presentation- and retention-time on the type of response are attributed to changes in the nature of inferred memory structures and the manner of representing the stimulus within those hypothesized structures.[25]

Evaluation of the inferred-process approach. This account of memory for letters exemplifies two general properties of inferred-process approaches.

First, the unobserved memory structures and representation processes are purely the result of *inferences* from the observed **environment-behavior relations**. As previously noted, this is why the approach is described as the inferred-process approach. In these experiments, the various memories and representations have no justification independent of the behavioral observations, and therefore cannot serve as explanations of the results. To use inferred processes and structures as explanations of the findings from which they were inferred is to engage in circular reasoning. To wit, in answer to the question "Why was a briefly presented **B** misremembered as an **R**?", one replies "Because **B** was stored in sensory memory, where it was represented in terms of its physical features." In answer to the question "How do you know that **B** was represented by its physical features?", one is tempted to reply "Because the subject responded 'are,' which is the response evoked by the physically similar stimulus **R**." Patently circular "explanations" of this sort have—to paraphrase Bertrand Russell—all the virtues of theft over honest toil.

The inferred-process approach seeks to avoid circular reasoning by attempting to use inferred processes arising from one experiment to account for findings from other experiments. To the extent that independent experimental findings may be accommodated by a common set of inferred processes, this approach may be said to escape the trap of logical circularity and to achieve—at a minimum—the worthwhile goal of summarizing parsimoniously a range of experimental findings.[26] The extent to which the inferred-process approach has realized this goal will ultimately be settled on both empirical and formal grounds. This is not the place to analyze the issue in depth, but it is appropriate to note that many investigators who previously pursued the inferred-process approach have begun to question its ultimate utility. Others have begun to express principled formal reservations as well.[27]

We believe that work carried out under the rubric of the inferred-process approach has consisted of repeated cycles of the following sequence of events. First, some interesting environment-behavior relation is discovered that may have important implications for the scientific interpretation of complex human behavior. Intervening processes and structures are then inferred that are consistent with the behavioral observations from the experiment. Next, a series of closely related experiments is undertaken. As long as the methods used in the new experiments are similar to those of the original experiment, the new results are generally consistent with the original set of inferred processes. This body of research is then taken as evidence that the inferred processes validly characterize the postulated intervening events. However, because the experimental methods are similar from one study to the next, the similarity in findings may mean only that the findings are reliable. In short, consistency is taken as evidence of validity rather than simply reliability.[28]

Ultimately, at some point an effort is made to use the same inferred processes to account for findings obtained under substantially different experimental conditions. The typical outcome of this last undertaking is that the original inferred processes are found to be inadequate. As a result, the old processes are sometimes abandoned altogether and replaced by a new set of inferred processes or, more commonly, an effort is made to salvage the old inferred processes by inferring new processes to supplement the original ones. A new program of research is then launched to evaluate the newly inferred processes, often with results that do not bear straightforwardly on the validity of the older inferred processes. The older methods and inferred processes then largely depart the theoretical scene, and the sequence of observation and inference begins afresh. Although perhaps overly harsh, we believe that the foregoing is an accurate description of much of the research that has flowed from an inferred-process approach to learning and complex behavior.[29]

The ultimate observability of intervening processes is the issue that most clearly distinguishes the inferred-process from the biobehavioral approach. In the inferred-process approach, the intervening processes are based exclusively on logical inferences from the behavioral observations with no necessary reference to observations that are or may become available at the microbehavioral and physiological levels. Indeed, some inferred-process theorists have identified the "liberation" of psychology from physiology as one of the major accomplishments of the approach.[30]

Since the unobserved structures and processes are based on conceptual and logical considerations alone, they are not easily coordinated with structures and processes identified by experimental work at the microbehavioral and physiological levels. When the inferred processes are coordinated with physical events, these events are more often the structures and processes of standard digital computers rather than living organisms.[31] For this reason, the inferred-process approach most often takes a form known as **information processing**. Like computers, organisms are said to detect, process, and act upon information. Even here, the relation is more one of metaphor than equivalence. Computers have real memories (locations within computer chips) and their memories contain real events (various electrical states). By contrast, the concepts of inferred-process approaches are seldom explicitly designed to correspond to structures and events that are even potentially observable at any level of analysis.[32]

The Biobehavioral Approach

In the biobehavioral approach, functional relations between the environment and behavior are supplemented with functional relations involving subbehavioral events. These supplementary functional relations are also the product of *independent experimental analyses*. **Figure 1.4** depicts the relation between behavioral and subbehavioral events in the biobehavioral approach to learning.

As indicated in **Figure 1.4**, because all functional relations are the result of experimental analyses, the relations involving subbehavioral events are not logically dependent on the behavioral relations—although they must be consistent with one another, of course. The independent de-

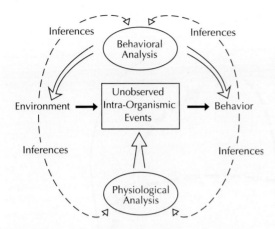

FIGURE 1.4   *The biobehavioral approach to complex behavior*
The biobehavioral approach supplements the methodological approach, which is confined to the behavioral analysis of observable environmental and behavioral events, with the physiological analysis of *observed* intra-organismic events. Like the inferred-process approach, the biobehavioral approach is concerned with intra-organismic events. Unlike the inferred-process approach, the biobehavioral approach does not attempt to infer their characteristics from observations of the environment and behavior alone. Like the methodological approach, the biobehavioral approach confines itself to the study of relations between observable events.

termination of behavioral and subbehavioral functional relations has important implications for scientific interpretation. We shall point out some of these shortly. But, first we illustrate a biobehavioral interpretation by reconsidering the previous study of the effect of the presentation- and retention-times of letters on the type of errors that occur when the letters are recalled.

Let us return to the finding that, at shorter times, errors "look" like correct responses while, at longer times, errors "sound" like correct responses. On the behavioral level, it is commonly observed that subjects rehearse vocal responses to letters and numbers when these stimuli must be recalled later. For example, during the interval between looking up a number in the phone book and dialing that number, subjects often repeat the number to themselves—either silently or out loud. Subjects rehearse responses to stimuli because, in the past, the responses were more likely to be correctly executed later. To the extent that the experimental conditions are similar to conditions in which rehearsal has been beneficial in the past, it is reasonable to conclude that the subjects in the experiment also rehearsed *if there was enough time for rehearsal to take place*. Thus behavioral observations in other circumstances provide a basis for interpreting the results of the letter-retention study. Given enough time, rehearsal occurs and errors are apt to resemble the vocal responses involved in rehearsing letters. However, if the time is too short for rehearsal, then responses are guided by the most available source—the physical properties of the visual stimuli.

These same findings are also consistent with observations at the neuroanatomical level. In general, environmental stimuli first stimulate primary sensory areas of the cortex and then sensory association areas. Activity from both these areas is communicated to the motor association and motor cortex and, finally, a behavioral response occurs. (See **Figure 1.5**.) Since time is required in order to activate successive neurons along a pathway, activity from primary sensory areas can stimulate motor areas of the cortex before sensory association areas can do so. Similarly, activity going directly to primary motor areas initiates behavior before activity coming from motor association areas. Thus, in order for errors to be affected by auditory components (sensory association area) or articulatory movements (motor association area), longer time intervals are required than when errors are affected by physical features of the visual stimulus alone (primary sensory area).[33]

The interpretation of these experimental findings illustrates two general properties of biobehavioral interpretations. First, they appeal only to behavioral and subbehavioral events and processes that have been identified by previous experimental analyses. There is ample independent experimental

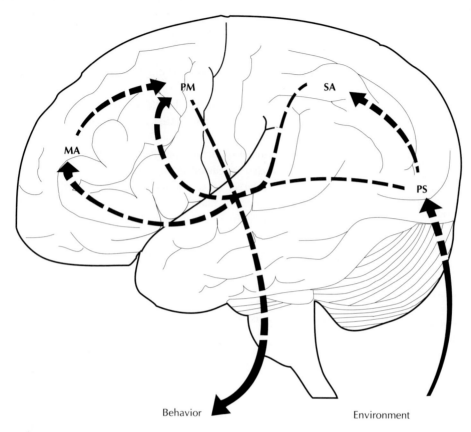

Behavior   Environment

FIGURE 1.5 *A diagram of some of the major functional regions of the cerebral cortex*
Stimuli from the environment act upon receptors to produce activity in neurons in the primary sensory
(PS) cortex. This activity leads to activity in the sensory association (SA) cortex and the motor
association (MA) cortex. Ultimately, activity is produced in the primary motor (PM) cortex causing
effector activity that results in responses measurable at the behavioral level. (Not shown are the many
subcortical structures that also participate in the mediation of relations between the environment and
behavior.)

evidence that the strength of a response is affected
by its previous consequences, and that the relevant
neuroanatomical pathways function as indicated.
Second, the conditions under which the events and
functional relations used in the interpretations
were observed are contained within the conditions
present when the experimental findings were observed. There is every reason to believe that the
subjects in the letter-retention experiments had a
behavioral history in which rehearsal previously
paid off, and that the relation among cortical areas
in their brains is the same as that in the brains of
others. Taken together, the biobehavioral processes isolated through prior experimental analyses
and the conditions present during the experiment
are sufficient to provide an interpretation of the
effects of presentation- and retention-times on errors in recalling letters.

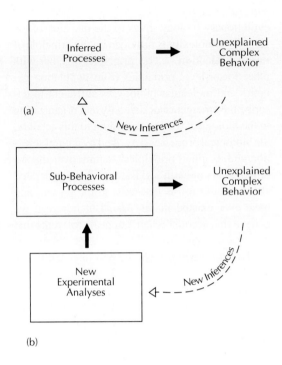

(a)

(b)

FIGURE 1.6 *Comparison of the reaction of inferred-process and biobehavioral approaches when failures to account for complex behavior are encountered*
(a) In the inferred-process approach, when previously inferred processes are inconsistent with behavioral observations, new inferences are drawn about the characteristics of either newly postulated inferred processes or modifications of previously inferred processes. (b) In the biobehavioral approach, when previously observed sub-behavioral processes are inconsistent with behavioral observations, new experimental analyses of observed intra-organismic events are conducted.

The basic difference between the biobehavioral and inferred-process approaches is best appreciated by examining what happens when the processes are *not* sufficient to account for the findings. As shown in **Figure 1.6b**, the insufficiency of a biobehavioral interpretation leads to additional ex-

perimental analyses of the processes of which the behavior is thought to be a function. However, in the inferred-process approach, a failure of the account leads to new inferences about the hypothesized processes (see **Figure 1.6a**). Since the biobehavioral approach reacts to failure of interpretation by conducting independent experimental analyses of the processes by which the behavior is interpreted, this approach avoids the logical circularity to which the inferred-process approach is—often subtly—prone.[34]

Biobehavioral interpretations may appeal only to events and the functional relations between events that result from prior independent experimental analyses. It is important to note that these events may not be observed when the behavioral phenomenon occurs. For example, in the letter-retention experiment, neither the particular subjects' history before the experiment nor the pathways active in their brains during the experiment was observed. What distinguishes biobehavioral interpretations from inferred-process accounts is not that all of the processes are observed at the time that the interpreted behavior occurs, but that all of the processes used in the interpretation have been studied in prior experimental analyses and that the conditions of those analyses were present when the interpreted behavior was observed. As Skinner has commented, "We cannot predict or control human behavior in daily life with the precision obtained in the laboratory, but we can nevertheless use results from the laboratory to interpret behavior elsewhere."[35]

We have now concluded our discussion of the status of unobserved events and their role in understanding behavior. We have seen that, unlike experimental analyses, scientific interpretations frequently appeal to processes that are the product of the subject's history. And, although those processes may not be observable when the interpreted behavior occurs, the conditions are sufficient for the occurrence of those processes. Are these appeals to historical events and to prior experimental analyses unique to the field of behavior, or are they also made in other sciences? As we asked at the beginning of the chapter, how can we understand organized complexity when the roots of behavior are in the past and our knowledge of the past is incomplete?

ORGANIZED COMPLEXITY IN HISTORICAL SCIENCE

The problem of accounting for organized complexity when we have only partial knowledge of its historical origins is not unique to the study of behavior. This same problem has been faced by those seeking to understand the development of complex phenomena in other sciences. We are not alone. In this section, we turn to another historical discipline—evolutionary biology—for guidance in our efforts to understand behavior. Our goal is not to expose the particulars of evolutionary biology, but to identify certain general themes that may help us understand organized complexity in behavior.

Organized Complexity in Evolutionary Biology

Biological man is arguably the ultimate example of organized complexity in the known universe. Our behavior systematically varies greatly from one culture to the next and from one individual to the next. The brain that mediates our behavior contains as many as 100 billion neurons. Each neuron, in turn, may communicate with thousands of its neighbors. Nor is organized complexity peculiar to our species. The earth is populated with millions of other species, most of which are exquisitely and complexly suited for their environments. There is scarcely a place on land or in the water that is not host to life. There are insects in the antarctic so suited to the cold that they die from the warmth of a human touch; there are bacteria in mid-ocean volcanic vents so suited to the heat that they die when the temperature falls below the boiling point of water.[36] How is such diversity and complexity to be understood?

Natural selection.   The primary answer that evolutionary biology gives to the question of organized complexity is provided by the principle of **natural selection**.[37] This principle, together with other lower-level principles from population genetics and molecular biology, is sufficient to describe the emergence of diversity and organization in the biological world. According to this account, the biological processes described by natural selection and its allied principles—acting over the 4.6 billion years of earth's existence—have generated all of the life forms that exist in the present and have ever existed in the past. But how can we believe this account when it appeals to events that occurred so long ago?

To begin, events from the past have left traces that can be observed in the present and serve as indirect indicators of the past. Based on observations of the other planets' atmospheres and physical processes in the laboratory, the type of atmosphere that could have existed on the ancient earth has been narrowed to only a few alternatives. Regardless of which of these is correct—and we may never know which with certainty—laboratory work has shown that all are sufficient to produce simple organic molecules found in present-day life forms.[38] (An organic molecule is composed of the elements carbon and hydrogen, and frequently nitrogen and oxygen.) Organic molecules could be built from the elements in the earth's early atmosphere, using energy from such sources as lightning, meteor showers, and intense ultraviolet light from the young sun.

These first organic molecules, interacting with clays at the bottoms of shallow seas or through other chemical processes, combined to produce larger and structurally more complex organic molecules. Within a few hundred million years of the formation of the earth, it is believed that a molecule was formed through one of these chance interactions that had a remarkable property: When it chemically reacted with surrounding molecules, it produced a second molecule like itself.[39] A molecule had formed having the ability to reproduce! These reproducing molecules were the ancestors of the genes that permit reproduction in existing life forms.

The occurrence of a reproducing molecule, or gene, permitted the process of natural selection to begin. The "offspring" of these first molecules could be expected to vary somewhat from one another depending on the organic molecules available at the time the copy was made and the accuracy of the copying mechanism itself. The more stable the reproducing molecule, the longer the time available to make copies. The more accurate the copy, the more subsequent copies would reproduce the "parent" molecule. In these ways, molecules that were stable and accurate copiers would come to predominate over their less stable and less accurate brethren. In short, stable and faithful genetic molecules would be naturally selected.

No human was there to witness the evolution of genes, and no direct trace of that process could persist into the present. Even if the ancestral genes could fossilize—and their delicate structures would not permit it—the surface of the ancient earth was in such turmoil from volcanic activity and the influx of meteorites that no rock formed at that time has endured. The most ancient rocks come from about a billion years after the earth was formed, and these rocks already contain fossilized virus-like particles and bacteria.

Experimental analyses carried out in the laboratory are needed to supply missing pieces of the puzzle, although in the case of molecular evolution, no one has yet put all the pieces together. Many of the probable steps in the chemical chain of molecular evolution have been successfully studied, however, and nothing that is now known would prevent the postulated links in the chain from being forged. Moreover, laboratory work has demonstrated how natural selection occurs once reproduction is possible. For example, if a large number of bacteria are exposed to an antibiotic (a compound that stops the making of proteins), not all of the bacteria die. Some, because of *already existing* variation in their genes, will survive. These pre-existing differences arise from changes in the genes produced by energy from the stars, by chemicals in the environment, or by variations that occur during the reproduction process. Bacteria that survive reproduce and, with time, increase in number relative to bacteria not having such characteristics. Thus the antibiotic selects some bacteria to survive and multiply, just as naturally occurring environments select other reproducing organisms.[40] The outcome of selection is an increasing preponderance of the selected life form in that environment.

Human evolution.   Natural environments contain many simultaneously acting selecting conditions, and different environments contain different combinations of selecting conditions. The outcome of these multiple and diverse selections is a continual branching of the tree of life. Once a branch has begun, it develops under the guidance of its own selecting environment—growing longer and, perhaps, branching still further. When a particular environment ends or is entered by a more efficient rival for its resources, the branch dies. The older life forms become extinct. Most species have met this fate.

One branch of the tree of life holds special interest for us—the one that leads to our own species, *homo sapiens* (thinking man). Once again, no observer was there to see the ancient process but, once again, some trace of it has persisted into the present. The earliest fossil record of the branching of the primate order from the class of other mammals is dated about 80 million years ago. The successive branchings that led from this pea-brained (1 cc) primate to the 1600 cc brain of modern humans are largely unknown. Time deals harshly with even the dense tissue of bone. However, considerable progress has been made through the field work of anthropologists exploring the fossil record and, more recently, through the laboratory work of molecular biologists exploring the genetic record.

The fossil record indicates that the hominid (manlike) family branched from the other primates at least 5 million years ago in Africa. We are all, in the first instance, Africans. That is where hominid fossils are most concentrated, where the earliest tools have been discovered, and where our nearest relatives—the chimpanzee and gorilla—are found. In the period from 1 to 3 million years ago, a hominid branch appeared along the path whose branches would lead to modern man. This early hominid, *homo erectus*, was taller—over 150 cm (5 ft)—and more robust than his predecessors and, judging from reconstructed skulls, his brain volume was about 1,000 cc. He used more complex stone tools, and examination of his campsites indicates that he constructed shelters and used fire.

The fossil record shows that the *homo sapiens* branch emerged only within the past 50–100,000 years. One subspecies, called Neandertal man after the German valley where his bones were first found, lived from 100,000 to 35,000 years ago. He stood about 170 cm (5 ft, 6 in) tall, and his skeleton was somewhat more robust than that of modern man. His forehead was sloping and his chin was not prominent, but he possessed a brain of modern volume (1600 cc)—or somewhat larger because of the more massive musculature that it controlled. Although the Neandertal people are often portrayed as less than fully human, they had a culture that included the construction of tools, such as hand-axes, and the ceremonial burial of the dead. (See **Figure 1.7**.)

Appearing 40–50,000 years ago and leading to modern man is the subspecies of *homo sapiens* called Cro-Magnon man, named for the rock shelter in France where his bones were first discovered. His brain was modern in volume and his skull was also modern in shape, having a more prominent chin and a more sharply rising forehead. The Cro-Magnon people built shelters in caves, made drawings on cave walls, and constructed flint weapons of greater penetrating power than those of their Neandertal predecessors and contemporaries. Gradually in some areas and apparently abruptly in others, the technologically more advanced Cro-Magnons replaced the more robust but less skilled Neandertals.

THE FAR SIDE   By GARY LARSON

Chronicle Features, 1983

"Neanderthals, Neanderthals! Can't make fire! Can't make spear! Nyah, nyah, nyah . . .!"

FIGURE 1.7   *Neandertals have received an undeservedly bad press*
Source: The Far Side cartoon by Gary Larson is reprinted by permission of Chronicle Features, San Francisco, CA. All rights reserved.

In addition to the traces of the past that persist in the fossil record, laboratory work in molecular biology provides insights into human evolution. Not only do bones endure, but also the genes that modern man shares with his predecessors. By comparing these genes (and the proteins whose production they control) between man and his nearest relatives among the great apes, researchers can obtain information about the time course of human evolution.

Comparisons of their genes indicate that hominids separated from the branch leading to the gorilla about 8 to 10 million years ago, and from the branch leading to the chimpanzee about 6 to 8 million years ago. When the proteins manufactured by the genes are examined, over 99% of them are the same in man and chimpanzee. In terms of proteins—which are the compounds from which our bodies are constructed—humans and chimpanzees are more alike than sheep and goats!

Emerging evolutionary themes concerning the origins of complexity.   What general themes appear in the search for the origins of organized complexity in the biological world? These are the themes that may prove most helpful in our efforts to understand the development of complexity in the behavioral world. First, faced with the problem of accounting for phenomena that arose from the unobserved past, evolutionary biology supplements laboratory observations of contemporary biological processes with whatever traces of the past have lingered into the present. Information from the study of fossil material and genes is integrated with laboratory investigations of chemical reactions occurring under conditions similar to those of the early earth. Taken together, these observations of the past and present provide the basis for formulating principles—here natural selection—that summarize the functional relations that have been uncovered.

A second general theme is that the organized complexity we see in the biological world is not the direct result of order-imposing principles. The same processes that shaped amoebas were evidently among those that shaped humans. Instead of organism-specific, higher-level processes, complexity appears to be a by-product of lower-level processes such as those summarized by natural selection. In evolutionary biology, higher-level organization is the unintended outcome of the action of lower-level processes. The cumulative action of natural selection is sufficient to account for the match between organisms and their environments, without appealing to principles that explicitly impose that correspondence.

Third, natural selection demonstrates that relatively simple processes, operating repeatedly over time, may produce great diversity as well as organized complexity. The diversity of species is testimony to the richness of which natural selection is capable. The realization that lower-level processes may lead to diversity is an important and often unappreciated insight. It is all too easy to assume that simple processes lead only to simple and uniform outcomes rather than to complexity and diversity.

Finally, the account of the origin of species through natural selection exemplifies the following approach to the understanding of historically grounded events: If lower-level processes acting on conditions that could reasonably have existed in the past are sufficient to produce present phenomena, then those processes are tentatively accepted as interpretations (explanations) of present phenomena. We have never seen either the first reproducing molecule or the first hominid, but the processes described by natural selection are sufficient to produce both when acting upon conditions that likely existed in the past.

Limitations of historical science.   Although evolutionary biology has led to principles that are sufficient to account for the development of organized complexity, the account can never be certain because we cannot know the past with certainty. Absolute truth is not to be found in any empirical science, most especially historical science. What distinguishes the historical sciences from purely laboratory sciences is their inability to know with near certainty the sequence of events that led to the complexity we see today. This characterizes historical science whether we are concerned with the origins of the universe, our species, or our individual behavior.

In particular, uncertainty about the initial conditions on which the basic processes act limits the completeness of our understanding. With only a partial knowledge of the past, historical science provides a plausible account of the present, but the present may not be the only outcome that can be accommodated. Good historical science is *sufficient* to account for the present, but the present is not a *necessary* consequence of its principles.[41] There are inescapable limits to what we can know in the historical sciences. Speaking of the imperfection of the fossil record in evolutionary biology,

Darwin commented: "We are not only ignorant, but we are ignorant of how ignorant we are." The fossil record is now more nearly complete, but it remains—and will remain—incomplete nevertheless. No less uncertainty attends the complex sequence of events that make up a single human life.

Although our knowledge of the origins of organized complexity in the biological world remains incomplete, our understanding of how it came about has been immensely deepened by evolutionary biology. Uncertainties persist, but we know much more than we did when the search began. We should be quite content if, guided by the general themes exposed in our survey of evolutionary biology, our search for the origins of complex behavior were as successful.

ORGANIZED COMPLEXITY IN A SCIENCE OF BEHAVIOR

All living organisms—including ourselves—are joint products of the processes that shape the physical, biological, and behavioral worlds. As members of the physical world, we are composed of elements forged by fusion processes in distant stars and dispersed by supernovas, only to be reunited on the earth by the forces that govern planetary formation.[42] As members of the biological world, our genes are the outcome of natural selection and the other processes that began with the ancient environments of the young earth and continued through the subsequent environments of our hominid ancestors. Thus we are made from atoms that trace their origins to the beginnings of the universe, and from genes, some of which arose at the dawning of life.

In this section, we introduce the approach that we take toward the processes that influence the behavioral world—the world of what living organisms do. The physical and biological worlds affect all living creatures, human and animal alike, but through their actions all creatures in turn affect the physical and biological worlds. We have seen some of the strategies that evolutionary biology has used to understand the origin of species. We shall

describe comparable strategies for studying the origins of learned behavior. Before doing so, however, we must make explicit the major steps in the account of organized complexity given by historical science.

Selectionist Approach to Complexity

Historical science accounts for complexity as the outcome of the three-step process of *variation, selection,* and *retention.*[43] Beginning with variation in the characteristics of the objects of selection, a selection process favors some characteristics over others, and the favored characteristics are then conserved through the action of retention processes. Repeating cycles of this three-step process are sufficient to produce organized complexity in the biological world and—we contend—in the behavioral world as well.

Many persons have contributed crucially to the development of this approach, known technically as selectionism, or evolutionary epistemology.[44] (Epistemology is the subdivision of philosophy that deals with the nature and limits of human knowledge.) Among contemporary scientists, Donald T. Campbell has applied the three-step account most generally, while Ernst Mayr[45] has explored its implications for biology and B. F. Skinner[46] has performed a similar service for the science of behavior. All such efforts can, of course, be traced to Darwin's seminal insights on evolution through natural selection.

Variation.   In organic evolution, organisms differ from one another in their structures (and the genes that guide the building of those structures). Likewise, single organisms vary in their behavior from one environment to the next (and in the states of the nervous system that regulate that behavior).

It is important to realize that variations occur without regard to the characteristics to be selected—i.e., *variation is undirected.* Structures do not vary *in order to* produce complex structures, and responses do not vary *in order to* produce complex behavior.[47] We should also emphasize that the action of prior selection and retention processes affects the variation available for subsequent selection and retention. For example, during the course of evolution, changes occurred that caused the genes producing scales in reptiles to produce feathers in birds. The environmental conditions that brought about these changes did not act in order to produce feathers. However, once that structural variation had occurred, it could then become the object of later selection.

Selection. Once variability exists, the second step in the movement toward organized complexity may be taken: The environment differentially favors some characteristics over others. In biological evolution, organisms that survive to reproduce leave greater numbers of their kind, and thereby predominate over less reproductively successful organisms. The principle of natural selection summarizes this process. By extension, understanding the emergence of complex behavior requires the identification of a selection process that describes how some responses are favored over others. The search for such a principle is the major focus of the following chapter.

Even before we have identified the specific processes described by a principle of behavioral selection, we may note certain general characteristics of all selection principles. First, although selection imposes a direction on otherwise undirected variation, it is not headed toward any enduring or ultimate destination. There is no final goal because selection is always based on conditions that exist at the moment of selection. For example, the butterfly whose color has been selected to match the bark of the species of tree on which it commonly rests may find itself suddenly conspicuous to predators if smoke belches from a nearby factory chimney and darkens the treebark.[48] Behavioral selection reveals a comparable lack of ultimate destination when, after reading a list of names like MACDONALD, MACNEILL, and MACDOWELL, we read MACHINERY as "Mac-Hinery" rather than "machinery."

A second, and related, characteristic of selection principles is that the outcome of selection is always "preparation" to live in the past (the conditions under which selection took place) and not the present, let alone the future. Only to the extent that the future is like the past does selection "prepare" us for the future. The selecting environment and the object of selection are partners locked in a perpetual dance—and the environment is always in the lead. The environment produces a finely coordinated partner when the music remains constant. But, when the music changes, the environment instructs anew or—in the case of extinct species—changes partners. When the conditions at the moment of selection remain constant, belief in the "rationality," "foresight," and "wisdom" of our species is fostered. However, when the conditions of selection change abruptly, such beliefs are revealed as only comforting illusions.

A final point needs to be made about selection principles as engines of organized complexity: Although selection is governed by conditions prevailing at the moment of selection, the outcome may importantly influence future selection by affecting the variability on which future selections act. In this indirect way, the past does influence the future. Since the products of earlier selections constitute part of the conditions on which later selections act, the course of selection shows continuity and internal coherence.[49] Thus, the objects of selection—the structure and behavior of living organisms—play an active role in channeling the development of complexity. However, they do not play an autonomous role—i.e., a role independent of the environment—because they are themselves the products of prior selections.

As an example of the active role played by prior selection, consider the evolution of feathers in birds. Feathers play an indispensable role in flying—they are light, impede the passage of air through them, facilitate the flow of air over them, and so forth. Yet feathers could not have been initially selected for these characteristics, since they first appeared on reptilian ancestors that could not fly! Because selection can occur only in the service of present and not future conditions, feathers originally must have been selected for another reason. This reason was apparently their insulating property; feathers conserve body heat, a property we exploit today in winter jackets filled with down. Once feathers had been initially selected as modifications of scales, they could undergo selection for their flight-enhancing properties. Animals better able to glide away from predators, to leap greater distances to secure food, and so forth, would have a greater chance of surviving and reproducing. To the extent that feathers facilitated such activities, they could undergo further selection for flight. Thus the subsequent course of selection was channeled and constrained by the products of prior selection.

Retention.   Once a characteristic has been selected, it must endure if it is to be available for further selection. Enduring changes in behavior are the stuff of learning, and it is from such changes that complex behavior is constructed.[50] If organized complexity is to occur, a third step—retention—must follow variation and selection. In evolutionary biology, genes—the legacy of prior selections—are passed on to the offspring, where they become the focus of further selection. Lower-level biochemical processes acting on the genes retain the earlier selections.

The processes that retain selected behaviors until they are subject to later selection are only now becoming understood. These processes involve the neurons of the central nervous system, especially the cellular and biochemical processes whereby neurons communicate with one another. We shall briefly indicate some of the possible mechanisms in the next chapter. For now, we note that much progress in understanding the effects of behavioral selection is likely without complete knowledge of the biological mechanisms of retention. Through Darwin's treatment of evolution by natural selection, giant strides were made in understanding the development of biological complexity before the underlying genetic mechanisms were known. Dar-

win had died by the time Mendel's work on genetics was rediscovered in the early 1900s.

Of course, evolutionary biology has achieved a much deeper understanding of selection since the genetic mechanisms have been identified, and a knowledge of neural mechanisms will surely have a similar effect on understanding the selection of behavior. We may also note that, while many of the implications of natural selection for evolution are logically independent of the selection mechanisms, even biologists did not generally accept Darwin's account until a plausible mechanism had been identified. If the parallel holds, the acceptance of a principle of individual selection as the origin of complex behavior may await the identification of its neural mechanisms.[51]

Implications for Complex Behavior

The historical sciences have shown that organized complexity may arise through repeated cycles of variation, selection, and retention. Indeed, the selectionist account of the emergence of complexity is so pervasive that the physicist Schroedinger described twentieth-century science as the story of how organization may arise from chaos. In the concluding section of this chapter, we identify some of the implications of selectionism for understanding the complexity of learned behavior.

Observational basis for the analysis and interpretation of behavior.   Historical sciences have progressed through integrating enduring traces of the past with experimental analyses of fundamental processes in the laboratory. Where shall we look for observations to guide our search for the origins of learned behavior, especially complex behavior?

If complex behavior is the end product of a protracted history of selection, then three complementary sources of information are particularly promising. First, we can examine the changes that occur in behavior over the life of the individual. This is the **developmental approach**. Second, we can compare the behavior of our own species with that of others, especially closely related species with whom we share a largely common evolutionary history. This is the **comparative approach**. Finally, since a history of individual selection produces enduring changes in the physiology of the nervous system, we can examine the relationship between the nervous system and behavior. This is the **neuropsychological approach**. These three approaches, together with knowledge of basic selection processes discovered through experimental analyses of behavior and the nervous system, provide the primary observational basis upon which a selectionist approach to learning rests.

Developmental approach. In principle, the developmental approach would seem to confer an advantage to the study of behavior that is not enjoyed by other historical sciences: Events occurring during an individual's lifetime are in principle observable, while the events that shaped species are not. In practice, however, pragmatic and ethical considerations impede a thoroughgoing study of the individual organism. It is impossible to follow even one person through his or her entire lifetime, recording all potentially important environmental and behavioral events. Furthermore, the attempt to achieve such a comprehensive record would so intrude on the person's life that the selection process would be altered in unknown and probably undesirable ways. Imagine recording all of the events that might influence the utterance of a child's first word, let alone an adult's entire verbal repertoire! The science of behavior is an historical science, not because the selection process spans the millennia of evolutionary biology, but because we can never completely know the initial state of the individual and his entire selection history.

Indeed, developmental observations are most often fragmentary. For example, an investigator studying language acquisition might observe the interactions between a child and its parents at weekly one-hour intervals during the first few years of life. Developmental studies in which the same individual is observed at different times are called **longitudinal studies**. A less desirable developmental method is to examine the behavior of different individuals at different times. Such studies are called **cross-sectional developmental studies**. For example, we might observe the verbal behavior of a group of 6-month-old children, a second group of 7-month-olds, and so forth.

Because the entire selection history cannot be observed in longitudinal studies and because different individuals are observed in cross-sectional methods, the selection process cannot be completely traced. Averaging observations across different individuals only complicates the interpretation of findings, since the behavior of different individuals will likely have undergone different sequences and types of selections. Different individuals of the same age will often display different behavior or, even when the behavior is the same, it may be the same for different reasons. From a selectionist perspective, averaging observations from different individuals is a bit like averaging observations from different species. Although it is mathematically possible to compute an average, it may not have any clear meaning if it does not represent the behavior of any single individual.[52] In spite of the deficiencies of longitudinal and, especially, cross-sectional studies, the developmental approach remains one of the most fruitful means for studying the emergence of complex behavior.

Whatever type of developmental study is used, observations in the natural environment must be supplemented by laboratory observations if basic selection processes are to be uncovered. The natural environment contains so many different events, appearing in so many different combinations, that disentangling the various conditions is often impossible. Consider the case in which a child says "ball" after an adult has pointed to a ball and said "ball." Did the child's verbal behavior occur because the adult said "ball" or because a ball was present? If the presence of the ball was crucial, which of its characteristics were important—its shape, its color, its manner of movement? All of these events may have occurred together in the natural environment, so an experimental analysis in the more controlled environment of the laboratory is required to tease out the important influences. Are all round objects called "ball," or only red ones? Are all bouncing objects called "ball," or only round ones? If the experimenter manipulates the environment, presenting round objects of various colors or bouncing objects of various shapes, then the crucial conditions may be isolated.

For the selectionist, observations in the natural environment are always the starting point for understanding complex behavior. Because complex behavior is the product of selection by complex environments, we must consider the behavior in the context in which it was selected if we are to understand its origins. Observations obtained under conditions in which the behavior originated are said to be **ecologically valid observations**. However, precise specification of selection processes most often requires the investigator's intrusion into the natural environment or the construction of artificial environments—i.e., experiments—that permit the various influences to be disentangled and identified. The study of learning processes by means of experiments provides the major source of information in our search for the origins of complex behavior.

Comparative approach.   The comparative approach also provides important information about the origins of complex behavior. While the developmental approach seeks to understand the selection process by studying the individual over time, the comparative approach pursues the same goal by studying species over time. For complex human behavior, the most compelling comparisons are between closely related species, such as between our species and the anthropoid (manlike) apes. Species that have shared common ancestral environments will likely have similar behaviors of partially common origins. For example, the coordinated movements of mouth and tongue required for speech could not have initially been selected for that purpose any more than feathers could have initially been selected for flight. A more primitive function, such as the efficient chewing of food, must have been the focus of events that originally selected for coordinated mouth movements.

We may never be certain that behavioral similarities in different species arose from a common origin, but the conservative nature of selection processes encourages that working hypothesis.[53] Selection processes are conservative in that, once they have produced a given capability, it may continue to be demonstrated for as long as the environment does not select against it. When the environment changes and the capability no longer benefits survival, new selections may occur but the earlier products of selection often endure. The chemical compounds that allow neurons to communicate with one another—**neurotransmitters**—are an example of this. Many of the same neurotransmitters are found throughout the animal kingdom, with humans sharing their neurotransmitters with "lowly" insects and other invertebrates that evolved over 100 million years ago. A neurotransmitter that modulates the action of the muscle that closes a clam's shell is at work in our own species, modulating the action of our muscles. Once a variation has been selected, it may be exploited for a very long time.

Among the most conserved variations of all may be those that permit individual behavior to change in response to the demands of a changing environment. Although species differences reflect the *particular* characteristics of each ecological niche, the capacity for change—the capacity to learn—is a general requirement for all species in all niches. Once the capacity to learn had been selected, it became available to act in service of later selecting environments. There is a further reason for retention of the capacity to learn: If there is time for an environment-behavior relation to be acquired in the individual's lifetime, then the focus of natural selection is on the biological processes underlying learning, and not on the specific environment-behavior relation that is learned. To the extent that the biological processes underlying learning are conserved, they may be general mechanisms present in a wide range of species. The behavioral expression of such common biological processes would vary, of course, depending on specific events in the selecting environment.[54]

Neuropsychological approach.   The third approach to the study of complex behavior—neuropsychology—is an important supplement to the developmental and comparative approaches. Underlying all human behavior, from the simplest reflex to the most profound thought, is the physiology of the organism. The selecting effects of the ancestral and individual environments change this underlying biology, most importantly the connections between neurons. Some of these changes are retained; i.e., they are learned. These learned changes in neural connections endure in the nervous system, and subsequent environments then exert their selecting effects upon a changed organism.[55]

All changes in the nervous system are observable in principle, and many are observable with present technology. Furthermore, to the extent that the neural changes underlying learned behavior are expressions of general biological mechanisms, they may be studied in nonhuman animals to the limit of our technical capabilities. Even in humans, where ethical considerations rightly limit the application of much technology, many new methods now permit us to measure indirectly neural activity in the behaving organism.[56] We shall consider evidence from some of these techniques in later chapters. For now, we will note that many neuropsychological studies have important implications for understanding complex behavior, even when the physiology and neuroanatomy underlying the behavior are imperfectly known.[57] Let us consider one such complex behavior as an example.

As the result of brain disease or accidental injury, some people have displayed the following pattern of behavior: When asked if they can see, they respond that they cannot. They do not report seeing a chair standing directly in front of them or a book held before their eyes. And yet, when asked to walk across the room, they avoid the chair. When asked to reach for the book, they position their hand to grasp it appropriately—when the book is offered vertically, the hand is oriented vertically; when it is offered horizontally, the hand orients horizontally. These persons behave nonver-bally in a way that is appropriate to the visual environment, but they do not speak appropriately. The behavioral effect of this brain damage is known as **blindsight**—although the mouths of such patients are "blind," their other organs can "see."[58]

Even without information about the precise physiological damage that produces it, this disjunction between how the visual environment guides speech and how it guides other behavior is provocative. Blindsight tells us that, under at least some circumstances, what we do and what we say may not correspond—even when we are being "truthful." Moreover, it tells us that we can engage in quite complex behaviors without any verbal awareness of the environmental events guiding those behaviors. Further experimental work must be described before blindsight can be thoroughly interpreted, but the foregoing shows that neuropsychological observations can sometimes be informative even without knowledge of their precise neuroanatomical basis.

There are complications in interpreting neuropsychological data, of course. There is no guarantee that similar behavior in an intact and a damaged organism is the result of the same biobehavioral processes—most behavior can be produced in many ways. Nor can we be certain that different behavior is the direct expression of the damage to the nervous system—damage to one region of the brain may affect the functioning of other regions. In blindsight, perhaps the behavior is the result of different processes than the ones operating in an undamaged organism. Perhaps, in the intact organism, what we say and the other things we do always correspond. Only experimental work can decide such issues. Regardless of the ultimate interpretation of blindsight and other neuropsychological observations, neurological damage shows us some of the effects of prior selection on the nervous system—effects that we might not otherwise see in behavior. Specifically, blindsight does tell us to be wary of accepting the idea that because what we say and what we do normally go together, they must go together. It tells us that what we do and what we say may be separable activities reflecting partially different neural systems and arising from partially different selecting conditions.

Principle of individual selection. If a selectionist approach is to provide insights into learned behavior, a principle must be identified that describes how the individual environment selects behavior. Such a principle would illuminate our understanding of how the individual environment affects behavior in much the same way that the principle of natural selection illuminates the effects of the ancestral environment. Uncovering a principle of individual selection depends on the experimental analysis of basic behavioral and biological processes, as well as observations in developmental, comparative, and neuropsychological studies.

Whatever the precise statement of a principle of individual selection, its function is to describe the selecting effects of the environment on the individual organism. From a selectionist perspective, behavior is the outcome of the joint effects of the ancestral and individual environments (see **Figure 1.8**). Natural selection is the province of the ancestral environment; individual selection is the province of the individual environment. The biological processes mediating the selecting effects of

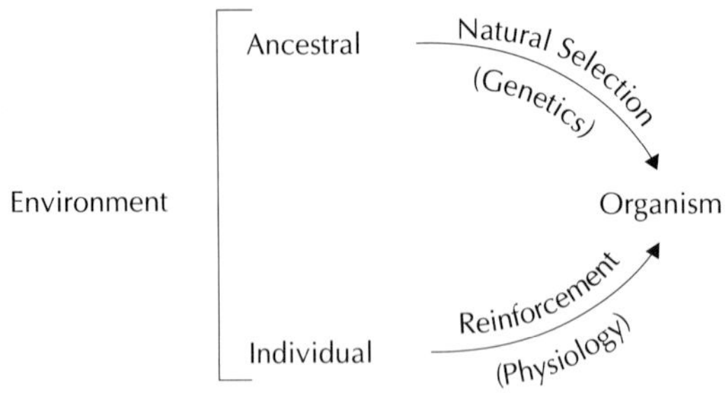

FIGURE 1.8 *All behavior is traceable to the selecting effects of the environment—the ancestral environment through the action of natural selection and the individual environment through the action of selection by reinforcement*
Natural selection is implemented by genetic mechanisms; selection by reinforcement by physiological mechanisms.

the ancestral environment are genetic mechanisms; those mediating the selecting effects of the contemporary environment are neural mechanisms. The neural mechanisms are themselves, of course, products of selection by the ancestral environment.

If a behavior, such as caring for one's offspring, benefits survival, then any genes affecting that environment-behavior relation will become relatively more frequent in subsequent generations. This increased frequency occurs both for genes manufacturing proteins that directly facilitate the specific environment-behavior relation—as with reflexes—and for those that more indirectly affect the relation through facilitating the neural mechanisms underlying learning.

Behavioral characteristics are very much the focus of selecting influences because a structure's contribution to fitness depends on its function.[59] For example, the sharp spines of the stickleback fish deter predation by larger fish only if the spines have been extended and "locked" into position.[60] Similarly, brains that think great thoughts but do not foster great deeds cannot be selected by either the ancestral or contemporary environments. Darwin's colleague and forceful defender, Thomas Huxley, commented to similar effect when he noted: "The great end of life is not knowledge but action." Once the behavioral and physiological processes underlying action have been selected, however, they may then serve those more subtle activities that we designate by such terms as "thinking," "remembering," "imagining," and the like.

The selection of behavior by the environment is only part of the story: As noted before, a selected environment-behavior relation may alter the environment, thereby influencing subsequent selection. These effects of behavior on the environment—**counterselection**s—occur in many ways and are most highly developed in our own species (see **Figure 1.9**). We cannot alter the ancestral environment itself; however, we may be able to alter the genetic processes that are the legacy of ancestral selections. This developing technology is called **genetic engineering**, and will

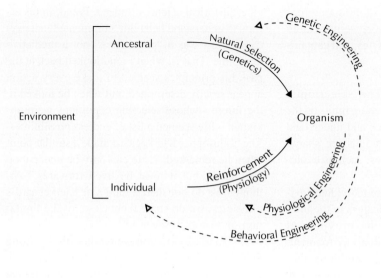

FIGURE 1.9 *Although the environment selects the behavior of organisms, behavior affects the environment and—in that indirect way—organisms affect their own behavior*
Such means of affecting behavior are called counterselections. Through genetic engineering, we are becoming able to alter our genes, the legacy of the ancestral environment. Through behavioral engineering, we are now able to alter our individual environments. Through physiological engineering, we are becoming able to alter our nervous systems.

likely become available to alleviate such genetic diseases as sickle-cell anemia. Since our knowledge of the neural processes mediating selection by the contemporary environment is less advanced, we are not yet able to alter those processes in very specific ways—although persons ingesting various "mind-altering" drugs are engaging in hazardous self-experimentation of this very sort. We do have within our technological grasp the ability to alter the contemporary environment. By doing so, we change the environment that will subsequently select learned behavior, and are engaged in **behavioral engineering**.

For some, the notion of behavioral engineering conjures up images of George Orwell's *1984* and the attendant dangers of a controlled society. However, the real issue is not whether our behavior should be influenced by the environment, but what the nature of that influence shall be. All behavior—

from the humanitarianism of a Martin Luther King to the savagery of an Adolf Hitler—is ultimately the product of selection by the joint action of the ancestral and individual environments. Thus the issue is not whether the environment shall affect our behavior, but whether we can devise a system of selections and counterselections that will allow us to more nearly attain those goals we deem worthy.

Behavioral engineering of a sort is already practiced by the various institutions of society—the family, education, government, and culture itself.[61] Such efforts have not been as effective as we might wish, as we can see from the prevalence of child abuse, illiteracy, poverty, and warfare. Effective behavioral engineering rests on an appreciation of how the contemporary environment selects individual behavior, and an informed application of techniques based on that understanding. Through knowledge of how environmental conditions select behavior, we may more nearly become "masters of our fates, and captains of our souls."[62]

Limitations of selectionism. The selectionist view forces us to acknowledge certain limits on the extent to which we can influence and understand complex behavior. These limitations are shared with the other historical sciences, such as evolutionary biology.

Because both the ancestral and individual environments influence behavior, changes in the individual environment alone—the province of behavioral engineering—may alter environment-behavior relations only within certain limits. Fortunately, these limits may often be circumvented. For example, our species evolved in the subtropical climate of ancient Africa. One legacy of that ancestral environment, the loss of most body hair, has resulted in our immense capacity to dissipate heat. This requires us to wear clothing when the temperature falls below the subtropical environment of our hominid ancestors. Selection by the individual environment, through learning to make clothes, has effectively circumvented the geographic limitations of our ancestors and permitted us to become distributed more widely than any other species. As the most striking example, we endure—with the aid of spacesuits—the frigid temperatures of the shadows cast by the mountains of the moon! We should recognize, however, that in those frigid shadows there persists next to our skin a subtropical microenvironment duplicating the macroenvironment at the dawn of our species. Something of *homo erectus* has been carried to the moon.

There are also limits to how deeply we can understand complex behavior, which is necessarily the product of an extensive history of selection in the natural environment that cannot be subjected to experimental analysis. Our incomplete knowledge of the initial conditions and the full history of selection limits the accuracy of our accounts of the present and our predictions of the future. We have confronted this limitation in our discussions of

other historical sciences. Indeed, Freud, in his efforts to understand behavior, commented that psychoanalysis was a "postdictive" not a predictive discipline. That is, when Freud looked back at the past, his principles seemed to make every action appear strictly determined, but when he looked to the future—whose selecting conditions were unknown—life seemed a list of endless possibilities. The philosopher Kierkegaard made a similar point when he remarked: "Life can only be understood backwards, but it must be lived forwards." Although we do not share Freud's or Kierkegaard's principles, we do share their views of the limitations of historical science.[63]

In laboratory environments where the selecting factors may be more completely specified, precise predictions are attainable. As in other historical sciences, the fundamental principles are isolated in the laboratory and then form the basis for interpretations of complex behavior in other experiments and in the natural environment. Although we may never be certain of the validity of our interpretations of naturally occurring behavior, we tentatively accept our interpretations if the fundamental principles are sufficient to account for the observations.

The selectionist approach to learned behavior clearly anticipates limits to our understanding, but those limitations appear to be inescapable consequences of the way in which complex behavior arises—from a complex history of selection. To us, no other approach offers more genuine insight into the origins of organized complexity while simultaneously avoiding an appeal to gratuitous order-imposing principles that postulate the very organization that we seek to understand.[64] The selecting environments that shaped our behavior contain imperfectly known conditions that guide us heedless of our concerns and independent of our purposes. Through a selectionist approach, we seek to discover the legacy of those selecting environments so that we might live in harmony with them and, by altering our present environment, better insure the survival of our species, our genes, and the counterselections that form our culture and ultimately select the behavior of ourselves and our offspring.[65]

STUDY AIDS

Technical Terms

The following technical terms were introduced in this chapter. If their meanings are unfamiliar, reread the relevant parts of the chapter and consult the glossary. The terms are listed in the order in which they were introduced in the text.

methodological behaviorism

experimental analysis

scientific interpretation

neuron

environment-behavior relation

information processing

natural selection

developmental approach

comparative approach

neuropsychological approach

longitudinal study

cross-sectional study

ecologically valid observation

neurotransmitter

blindsight

counterselection

genetic engineering

behavioral engineering

Text Questions

1. Describe the major features of the methodological, inferred-process, and biobehavioral approaches to complex behavior. What are the similarities and differences among these approaches, especially with regard to the place of unobserved (intraorganismic) processes in a science of behavior? Use the term *functional relation* in your answer.

2. What effect does the duration of presentation have on the types of errors that subjects make when recalling briefly presented letters? Indicate how each of the three approaches would discuss these findings. Indicate strengths and weaknesses of each account.

3. In what way do the accounts offered by inferred-process approaches fail to meet the definition of scientific interpretation as that term is used here? What possible difficulties arise from this fact?

4. Name and describe the major contribution to complexity of each the three steps in a selectionist approach. Use evolution through natural selection to illustrate each of the three steps.

5. In your own words, describe four main characteristics of complexity that arise from selection processes. Use examples from evolutionary biology to illustrate each characteristic. What are some limitations of a selectionist account of complexity?

Discussion Questions

6. Comment on the following statement: Although much of human behavior cannot be observed by others, e.g., thinking and feeling, the ability to talk about such behavior permits it to be studied.

7. Explain the following statement: Inferred-process theories endure, in part, because reliability is mistakenly taken as evidence of validity. (What is the relation between reliability and validity?)

8. What are some implications of a selectionist approach for the understanding of complex human behavior?

ENDNOTES

1. For a historical review of this period, see Boring, 1950. (Most of the end notes—such as this one—contain the names and dates of references that relate to statements in the text. The full citation appears in the bibliography at the end of the book. Occasionally, the end notes contain additional information about the topic. This information is not required to understand the text, but supplements it with additional information or acknowledges approaches that differ from those presented in the text.)

2. A reliable measure is one that yields the same result each time the measure is obtained. A valid measure is one that measures the event it was intended to measure. Assume, for example, that the sound of grinding gears brings my friend to mind each time it occurs. If, every time that sound occurs, I report to an observer that my friend has come to mind, then my report is a reliable and valid measure of the unobserved activity.

3. Freud, 1920.

4. Darwin, 1859, 1872. For a discussion of the delay, even within science, of the general acceptance of Darwin's ideas, see Bowler, 1988.

5. Skinner, 1945, 1963, 1974, pp. 238–239, 242, 274; see also Minsky & Papert, 1988.

6. Watson, 1913.

7. Darwin, 1871, 1872

8. But see Washburn, 1908 for an effort with nonhuman animals to infer unobserved events—the nature of consciousness—from nonverbal behavior.

9. Pavlov, 1927 lamented what he called "the practical bent of the American mind," but if science does not have some ultimate benefit to society it is unclear why society should support the enterprise. Although science is driven by the need to know (*science* comes from a Latin word meaning knowledge), that knowledge often has important societal implications—although perhaps not immediately.

10. The microbehavioral level refers to behaviors that are not observed under normal observational conditions—i.e., without the aid of devices that extend the senses—but that are observable with special procedures. For example, we can see the effects of the contraction of an entire group of muscle fibers—the movement of a limb. However, the contraction of only a few such fibers causes a slight muscle twitch, which we may not be able to detect with the unaided senses.

11. Watkins, 1990, p. 333.

12. See Skinner, 1935, 1938 for discussions of similar import concerning the factors that determine the appropriate levels of analysis for phenomena. In brief, that level of analysis is appropriate that yields orderly functional relationships.

13. See especially Skinner, 1945, 1957, 1963.

14. Skinner, 1938.

15. Skinner, 1974, pp. 236–237.

16. See Day, 1983.

17. Smolensky, 1988; Minsky & Papert, 1969. The presence of nonlinear elements in the nervous system has other important consequences. Certain functional relations between the environment and behavior that

living organisms can learn cannot be mediated by linear elements alone. We consider one such relation, stimulus patterning or the exclusive-OR problem, in Chapter 7.

18. cf. Donahoe & Wessells, 1980, pp. 63–64.

19. The inferred-process approach, which is the dominant form of theorizing in psychology, is an instance, in part, of what social psychologists call the *fundamental attribution error* (Jones & Nisbett, 1971). Studies in social psychology have found that when an observer is ignorant of the environmental determinants of behavior, the behavior is often attributed to *internal* factors. However, when the environmental history and context are known, that very same behavior is attributed to the environment. For example, suppose that you see a boy holding his jaw with a painful expression on his face. If you had seen a bee alight on the boy's face, you would attribute the behavior to a bee sting—an environmental event. By contrast, if you had not seen the bee, you would be inclined to attribute the behavior to some internal event such as a toothache—an unobserved subbehavioral event. Very often, behavioral scientists are in the position of observers who are unaware of the environmental antecedents of behavior and, in their ignorance, attribute behavior to inferred hypothetical processes.

20. Sperling, 1960. When very brief presentation and retention times are employed, the experiment is often said to be a sensory-memory procedure.

21. Procedures in which the stimulus presentation and retention intervals are longer, but still only a matter of seconds, are known as short-term memory procedures.

22. Conrad, 1964.

23. Atkinson & Shiffrin, 1968; Waugh & Norman, 1965. Those who initially propose inferred entities, e.g., the distinction between short-term and long-term memory, are often much more circumspect in their proposals than those who later employ such distinctions. See Peterson & Peterson's (1959) initial work on "short-term" memory, and Watkins's (1990) general discussion of this point.

24. For a review, see Crowder, 1976; see also Baddeley, 1986.

25. Note that in this account there is no reference to the locations within the real nervous system where the unobserved structures and representations of sensory- and short-term memory may be found. For this reason, inferred processes have been said—tongue-in-cheek—to reside within the "conceptual" nervous system rather than the *central* nervous system (CNS); Skinner, 1938, p. 421; cf. Morse, 1982.

26. cf. McCorquodale & Meehl, 1948.

27. For reservations about the inferred-process approach from empirical workers within the field, see Ades, 1981; Bransford, McCarrell, Franks, & Nitsch, 1977; Broadbent, 1973; Gibson, 1979; Jenkins, 1980; Kolers, 1973; Kolers & Smythe, 1984; Neisser, 1976; Newell, 1973a; Norman, 1986; Roediger, 1979; Rubin, 1988; Underwood, 1972; Watkins, 1990. For formal reservations, see Anderson, J. R., 1978; Townsend, 1971a, 1972, 1974.

28. Unfortunately, while reliability is necessary for validity, it is not sufficient.

29. For example, the distinction between short-term and longer-term memory has been deeply questioned (Crowder, 1982) and replaced successively by distinctions based on levels- and depths-of-processing (Craik & Lockhart, 1972; Craik & Tulving, 1975), and finally by proposals for many different types of memory stores (e.g., Sherry & Schacter, 1987)—perhaps as many as thirty (Roediger, 1990a)—and by inferred-process models of quite a different sort (e.g., Anderson, 1983, 1985; Raaijmakers & Shiffrin, 1980). Surveying the varied scene of inferred-process theories of memory, one memory researcher concluded, "Memory theorizing is going nowhere." (Watkins, 1990, p. 328).

30. Mandler, 1981.

31. Exceptions to this are increasingly frequent in some of the work carried out under the heading of cognitive neuroscience, where an explicit effort is made to coordinate inferences with structures of the nervous system.

32. Technically, the entities proposed in inferred-process theories make no existential claims. That is, they are explanatory fictions (Suppes, 1969) whose utility is determined solely by their ability to integrate functional relations observed at the behavioral level and, ideally, to suggest fruitful lines for future research.

33. The above account is by no means an exhaustive interpretation of the effects of different presentation and retention intervals on responding. A great deal more experimental work can be, and has been, directed toward understanding this type of study; e.g., see Baddeley, 1986 and reviews in Crowder, 1976 and Donahoe & Wessells, 1980.

34. Not all inferred-process approaches are equally prone to these difficulties. A common form of the inferred-process approach, other than information processing, is *associationism*. In associationism—which has its roots in the philosophical tradition of British empiricism, e.g., Locke, Mill, Berkeley and, to a lesser extent, Hume—observed environment-behavior relations are said to be the result of "associations" formed between events. These associations may be between environmental and behavioral events, as in stimulus-response associations, or between two environmental events, as in stimulus-stimulus associations (Mackintosh, 1983). If associations are assigned only characteristics that result from experimental analyses of observed environmental and behavioral events, then "associations" are simply shorthand for a relation between observable events (i.e., they have only a statistical meaning). However, if associations are held to have some independent "existence" apart from the relations they summarize and to "cause" environment-behavior relations, then they are instances of inferred processes and prey to the dangers inherent therein. In the general area covered by this book, the inferred-process version of associationism leads to the *learning-performance distinction*. Performance refers to the behavior that is observed, and learning to a hypothetical entity that is inferred and of which performance is said to be a function. Whereas performance may be variable, learning is held to be an orderly process that is imperfectly reflected by performance (cf. Skinner, 1950). From our perspective, the learning-performance distinction is reminiscent of distinctions between the pre- and post-Darwinian conceptions of species, and of the rationalism-empiricism debate more generally (cf. Donahoe, 1984; Palmer & Donahoe, 1993; Mayr, 1982). In their favor, since associations are intended to express relations between specific events, associationistic theories are more readily correlated with observations at subbehavioral levels. Indeed, several examples exist in which associationistic theories and physiological accounts have been brought into correspondence; e.g., Wagner, 1976; Wagner & Donegan, 1989; Donegan & Wagner, 1987. For the same reason, much experimental work carried out within the associationistic tradition and using animals as subjects meets the demands of experimental analysis. We shall draw heavily upon some of this work in subsequent chapters.

35. Skinner, 1974, p. 251.

36. e.g., Stetter, Lauerer, Thomm, & Neuner, 1987; see Poole, 1990 for a review.

37. The principle of natural selection was independently described by Charles Darwin and Alfred Wallace in simultaneous publications in 1859.

38. cf. Li & Graur, 1991; Wachtershauser, 1990.

39. Dickerson, 1978; Wachtershauser, 1990; see Lewin, 1986 and Waldrop, 1992 for introductions to this literature.

40. Strictly speaking, it is not the bacteria that are selected but the genes that, acting in concert with the environment, construct the bacteria, cf. Dawkins, 1976. For a particularly striking example of the selection of genes rather than organisms, see Nur, Werren, Eickbush, Burke, & Eickbush, 1988.

41. For a similar conclusion about behavioral science in the context of the information-processing approach, see Anderson, J. R., 1978.

42. cf. Wetherill, 1991.

43. Campbell, 1974.

44. Popper, 1978.

45. Mayr, 1982, 1988.

46. Skinner, 1966b, 1981.

47. Campbell, 1974; Sober, 1984; Hull, 1973.

48. Kettlewell, 1955.

49. cf. Eldredge, 1984; Gould, 1982.

50. As was true of natural selection, behavioral selection does not occur *in order to* produce complex behavior. Retained selections are necessary to produce complexity, but they are not sufficient. If subsequent environments do not select complex behavior that draws upon the products of prior selections, then complexity does not arise.

51. Donahoe, Burgos, & Palmer, 1993.

52. Sidman, 1960; Estes, 1956.

53. A related complication arises with natural selection. A structure may be similar in two species either because it was present in a common ancestral species or because of common selections by the environment after the two species had diverged.

54. At the biobehavioral level of analysis, we take the view that learning may be described by a restricted set of the same basic processes across a wide range of the animal kingdom. However, the particular outcome of these basic processes may vary greatly depending on the evolutionary and learning history of the subject. Many behavioral scientists interpret this diversity in outcome as evidence that fundamentally different learning processes are required to explain behavioral changes in different species. See the volumes edited by Lehrman, Hinde, & Shaw, 1972 and by Seligman & Hager, 1972 for critiques of the view that we hold, a view that is sometimes called *general-process learning theory*. We return to this matter briefly in the following chapter.

55. Skinner, 1953.

56. e.g., Moonen et al, 1990.

57. cf. Donahoe, 1991.

58. Weizkrantz, Warrington, Sanders, & Marshall, 1974.

59. Simpson, 1984; Wilson, 1975.

60. Tinbergen, 1952, 1964.

61. Skinner, 1953.

62. For a particularly forceful expression of this view, see Edward Thorndike's speech given on the centennial of Darwin's birth and reprinted in Joncich, 1968.

63. Not considered here are the additional uncertainties that may arise even with deterministic systems under certain sets of initial conditions. This is the province of chaos theory, cf. Gleick, 1987.

64. As we have noted earlier, there is no general agreement among behavioral scientists concerning the most fruitful approach to complex behavior, particularly human behavior. Despite this lack of agreement, we shall adhere to a consistent selectionist approach in which complex behavior is seen as the cumulative product of the repetitive action of relatively simple processes. We acknowledge that change (or, more optimistically, "progress") requires that selection be from among a variable set of alternatives. Selectionism, therefore, attends to theoretical and empirical work carried out from all conceptual perspectives. However, in our efforts to interpret empirical work, we employ a thoroughgoing selectionist approach, believing that inferred-process theories are so fundamentally different from selectionist theories that to consider them in detail would confuse rather than enlighten the reader, cf. Baars, 1986; McDowell, 1991; Morris, Higons, & Bicker, 1982; Skinner, 1977. Ernst Mayr, the evolutionary biologist, said of efforts to achieve a dialogue between selectionism and creationism in the treatment of the origin of species that no rapprochement was possible because "no two ways of looking at the facts could be more different," Mayr, 1982. Although we hope that this is not true of selectionist and inferred-process theories of complex behavior, there is little to encourage us to believe that Mayr's observation does not also apply here with equal force.

65. See Campbell, 1974; Dennett, 1984; and Skinner, 1953, 1971 for eloquent statements of the view that, paradoxically, our deepest appreciation of "free will" comes from understanding how our behavior is affected by the environment.

CHAPTER 2

SELECTION OF BEHAVIOR

INTRODUCTION

From a selectionist perspective, complex phenomena are the cumulative product of repeated cycles of the three-step sequence of variation, selection, and retention. In this chapter, we identify the basic biobehavioral processes underlying the three-step sequence that ends in complex behavior. A selectionist approach asks us to consider the possibility that even the most complex human behavior—thinking, language, memory, and the like—is the result of relatively simple biobehavioral processes acting over time. It asks us to believe about complex behavior what Darwin asked his contemporaries to believe about complex structure: The cumulative effect of simple processes can yield both diversity and complexity.

A selectionist approach to learning asks us to consider the possibility that the repeated action of the individual environment may produce the diversity and complexity of human behavior, and that this process can be described by a selection principle. The principle that summarizes the selecting effect of the individual environment is designated the **principle of behavioral selection** or, in the technical terminology of learning, the **principle of reinforcement**. This chapter describes experimental analyses that seek to identify the basic biobehavioral processes that define a principle of reinforcement. Although the statement of this principle is not yet complete, behavioral research has converged on the formulation of such a reinforcement principle and physiological research is uncovering its underlying biological mechanisms.

The reluctance of Darwin's contemporaries to accept the account of evolution offered by natural selection is quite understandable given the gaps in knowledge that existed at the time. For comparable reasons, many people today find it difficult to accept a selectionist approach to complex behavior. Indeed, we may now be in a period corresponding to the one that intervened between Darwin's proposal of the principle of natural selection and the discovery of the biological mechanisms of heredity.[1] It was only when those mechanisms were discovered that Darwin's account of evolution was generally accepted. And, it is only now that we are beginning to understand the biological mechanisms of learning.

Social Impediments to a Selectionist Account

Selectionism tells us that we must understand relatively simple biobehavioral processes in highly controlled laboratory situations before we shall be able to understand complex behavior. This suggestion is difficult to follow, for many reasons. Not the least of these is our impatience to address more compelling issues, such as "Why do people do such crazy things?", "What is consciousness, and what role does it play in human behavior?", "How do we recognize a friend's face among a sea of other faces in a crowd?", or "How can we understand a sentence whose exact wording we have never heard before?" We shall ultimately address such questions, but we must postpone them and, first, seek answers to questions about basic selection processes—often in simple laboratory situations with nonhuman subjects. In short, selectionism urges us to turn away—*temporarily*—from the very questions that most attract us to the study of behavior.

We all find the immediate goal of understanding complex human behavior more compelling than the subgoals of understanding simpler biobehavioral processes. Indeed, as we shall see, natural selection has favored the survival of organisms that seek immediate goals rather than those that postpone them in favor of more deferred goals. However, there is no route to understanding complex behavior that does not travel the more circuitous path blazed by the experimental analysis of basic biobehavioral processes.

A second major reason that many find it difficult to follow the course of action urged by selectionism is that such an approach seems to jeopardize the "specialness" of humans as a species. Are there not human-specific abilities? Does not the understanding of our behavior require new and fundamentally different processes from those we can discover by studying the behavior of (other) animals?

A selectionist approach to complex behavior does assert the uniqueness of *homo sapiens* as a species and of each person as an individual, but in the more limited and technical sense in which all species and individuals are unique. To the extent that uniqueness is a valid claim of humans, it is an equally valid claim for all species. What selectionism contends is that the "specialness" of humans—and of all other species—arises from the unique expression of a common set of biobehavioral processes, describable by a common set of principles. Whether complex human behavior can be understood in terms of principles common to all living organisms is still unclear; no one has yet provided a complete account of human behavior. Selectionism simply asks that we remain open to the possibility that the repeated action of relatively simple biobehavioral processes may be sufficient to generate complex human behavior.

The selectionist approach to complex behavior cannot diminish our "specialness" in any meaningful sense. The accomplishments of our species speak eloquently for themselves, whatever their origins. Humans are more widely distributed across the earth and our cultural heritage far surpasses that of any other species. Knowledge of how these accomplishments arose could in no way genuinely diminish them. On the contrary, a deeper understanding of the origins of complex human behavior could be the crowning achievement of our species, aiding as it must the ultimate goal of any species—its continued existence.

Uncovering the Origins of Complex Behavior

As a working hypothesis, we adopt the view that behavioral complexity arises from relatively simple processes acting over time in repeated cycles of variation, selection, and retention. How shall we uncover these processes so that the principles describing them may be formulated? Important general guidelines are provided by the central principle of evolutionary biology—natural selection. That natural selection should guide the search for a principle of behavioral selection is not surprising, since the biobehavioral processes that produce complex behavior must themselves be the products of natural selection.

Only expressed characteristics can be selected by the environment, and one of the major characteristics of living organisms is overt behavior. Selection can directly favor behavior that has actually occurred (i.e., the *behavioral phenotype*), but the microbehavioral, physiological, biochemical, and genetic processes (i.e., the *biological genotype*) of which overt behavior is a function can only be selected indirectly. Unexpressed "capabilities" and "potentialities" cannot be selected at any level of analysis: An organism possessing a structure that might benefit survival and reproduction—such as a more efficient digestive system—can realize that benefit only by behaving to attain it—in this case, foraging for food. Function, not structure, drives selection and, in that sense, is the more fundamental factor.[2]

In this chapter, we are chiefly concerned with the first two steps in the process that produces behavioral complexity—variation and selection. What are the origins of the variation upon which selection operates? In the experienced organism, the selection of environment-behavior relations clearly increases variation, but how does behavioral variation initially arise? Concerning selection, what environmental conditions are necessary for selection to occur, do those conditions change as the organism grows more experienced, and precisely what is it that is selected—i.e., what is the unit of selection? As for retention, we must postpone its full consideration until we have a more complete appreciation of the effects of selection. In truth, most of the following chapters are investigations of retention, because what is retained is increasingly nothing less than complex behavior itself.

VARIATION

Variation in the learner's behavior can be traced, ultimately, to variation in the learner's environment. Environmental stimuli have two major functions. First, stimuli and the behavior they guide vary in their biological significance during the evolutionary history of the learner's species. Some stimuli and responses consistently affect reproductive fitness throughout the ancestral environment. Consequently, organisms that responded in appropriate ways to such stimuli were more likely to leave surviving offspring. As a result, natural selection favors organisms in which these stimuli reliably activate the neural systems mediating these responses. Stimuli that reliably evoke behavior as the result of natural selection are said to function as **eliciting stimuli**, or **elicitors**. As one example, when the cheek of a human infant is touched, his head will turn toward the touch, and—if his lips then make contact with a surface—the infant will begin to suck. In addition to this **eliciting function**, a second function of environmental stimuli that contributes to behavioral variation is the **motivating function**. If, for example, a learner has been deprived of his normal contact with an eliciting stimulus, then his response to a *range* of other stimuli is altered. For example, if an infant has not been fed for several hours, a touch on the cheek will more readily elicit turning toward the touch. In addition, the infant's response to many other stimuli will be altered: A slight noise more

easily awakens him, sights and sounds that he might not otherwise respond to evoke orientation responses, and so forth. Taken together, elicitors and **motivating stimuli**, or **motivators**, contribute to the behavioral variation on which selection by reinforcement operates in the beginning learner.

The importance of variation in the acquisition of complex behavior cannot be overemphasized; it provides the raw material from which selection by reinforcement shapes successively more complex relations between the environment and behavior. Variation is thus the wellspring of behavioral creativity and novelty.[3] Indeed, evidence from evolutionary biology indicates that variation itself is a characteristic for which selection may occur.[4]

Eliciting Function: Reflexes

As expected from natural selection, the environment-behavior relations that newborn organisms bring from the womb to the world are those that contributed most to the survival of their species. These relations reflect the ancestral environment's most stable and enduring requirements. In the human infant, which is dependent for survival on its parents for longer than the young of any other species, stimuli related to feeding are among the most potent elicitors of behavior. Touching the cheek elicits head-turning; touching the lips elicits sucking. These environment-behavior relations are present even before birth; fetuses have been observed (by means of sonograms, which yield visual images from sound energy) to suck their fingers and hands while still in the uterus! A reliable relation between the environment and behavior that is largely the result of natural selection is called a **reflex**. A reflex is composed of an eliciting stimulus and an elicited response. Touching the cheek elicits head-turning, and together they constitute the *rooting reflex*; touching the lips elicits sucking and together they constitute the *sucking reflex*.[5] Reflexive eliciting relations typically involve relatively simple stimuli and responses, but chains of related reflexes—such as rooting and sucking—are not uncommon.[6]

Most human reflexes are the legacy of ancestral environments that are not unique to our species, but reflect environmental demands that are important for many other animals as well. For example, low levels of oxygen in the air (which produce high levels of carbon dioxide in the blood) stimulate an increase in breathing rate. Other reflexes trace their ancestry to more closely related species. For example, stimulation of the palm of an infant's hand will elicit a *grasp reflex* that may be strong enough to support the infant's full weight. (See **Figure 2.1**.) In related species, such as chimpanzees, the grasp reflex permits the infant to cling to the hair of its mother as she moves about the environment.

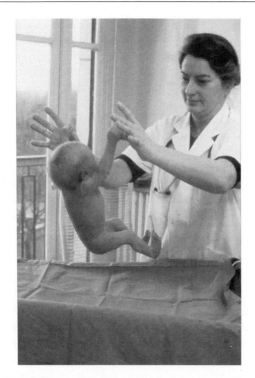

FIGURE 2.1 *The strength of the grasp reflex in the human infant may support its full weight for a few moments*
In other primates, this reflex allows the infant to maintain contact with the parent by grasping the parents' body hair.
Source: Petit Format/J. DaCunha/Photo Researchers.

Still other reflexes reveal environment-behavior relations that become important contributors to the infant's survival later in life. For example, if a newborn infant is held upright and his body is tilted slightly forward and to the side, his legs begin to move in a pattern that resembles walking. The infant's leg muscles cannot yet support his weight, but this stimulation evokes the coordinated pattern of leg movement that will occur later—in righting the infant when he falls, and in walking. This relation, called the *stepping reflex*, has been naturally selected by gravitational force, a consistent feature of the ancestral environment.

Some complications.   Although reflexive relations are the most prominent environment-behavior relations in young organisms, they are not the only means by which the environment affects behavior. Reflexive relations represent one end of a continuum of environment-behavior relations that varies along a dimension of reliability. As an example of a less reliable but appreciably strong relation, a moving object placed near an infant will evoke reaching movements. These movements will not always occur—as would blinking in response to a puff of air to the eye—nor will they be as precise as they will become with further experience. Nevertheless, stimulus-evoked reaching is an environment-behavior relation that contributes importantly to the variation available for selection. In the field of learning, responses that are reliably evoked by a specific stimulus, such as airpuff-evoked blinking, are known as **respondents**. Reflexes are a subclass of respondents. Responses that are less reliably evoked by stimuli—such as object-evoked reaching—or for which the stimulus is not well specified, are known as **operants**.[7] Respondents and operants are not two different *kinds* of environment-behavior relations, but two different regions along a continuum of relations that vary as to how precisely the stimulus can be specified and how reliably the stimulus evokes the response. For these reasons, respondents are said to be *elicited*, while operants are said to be *emitted*. On the physiological level, respondents are mediated by relatively strong synaptic connections along relatively fixed pathways, while operants are mediated by relatively weak connections along relatively variable pathways. The eye blinks for only a few reasons; it winks for many.

Although variation among operants contributes to the development of complex behavior more than respondents do, we shall see that respondents provide the initial basis for behavioral selection. At the beginning of learning, the environment-behavior relations embodied in reflexes are the basis for selection by reinforcement. As Lewis Lipsitt, a student of child behavior, has put it, "Self-regulatory behaviors are the stuff of which later learning is made."[8]

Motivating Function: Deprivation and Sensitization

As noted earlier, while the eliciting function of a stimulus refers to its effect on the strength of a single response, the motivating function refers to its effect on a *range* of responses. (See **Figure 2.2.**) In general, the motivating function may be demonstrated by either of two procedures—deprivation of contact with a stimulus or presentation of a strong eliciting stimulus. Changes in the motivating function due to the first procedure are studied under the heading of **deprivation**, those due to the second under the heading of **sensitization**.[9]

Deprivation. Technically, deprivation occurs when there is a decrease in the organism's contact with a stimulus below the level that would have occurred if the organism had been given unrestricted access to the stimulus. By this definition, we say that an infant who has not eaten in several hours is deprived of food, or that a child who interacts frequently with his parents is deprived of his parents if they are absent for a long time. Not only does deprivation result in a more vigorous response to the deprived stimulus when it is finally presented, it also affects responding to the presentation of other stimuli. That is, deprivation affects the eliciting function of not only the deprived

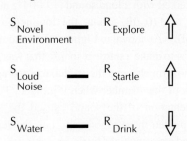

FIGURE 2.2 *The motivating function of a stimulus and its relation to the eliciting function*
(a) For an eliciting function to be demonstrated, the presentation of a stimulus must evoke a response. (b) For a motivating function to be demonstrated, the presentation of a stimulus must change the degree to which a range of other stimuli evoke other responses. The motivating function of a stimulus may be demonstrated either by presenting a stimulus such as a loud noise or a painful shock, or by presenting a stimulus of which the organism has been deprived, such as food or water.

stimulus, but of other stimuli as well. By affecting the responses evoked by many stimuli, deprivation increases the pool of environment-behavior relations available for selection by the environment.

Sensitization. Presentations of stimuli other than those affected by deprivation can also have a motivating function. Often, the presentation of any stimulus—particularly an intense stimulus—alters responding to other stimuli. For example, an infant who has just heard a loud noise may stop sucking even though food-deprived. Then, if the noise recurs, the infant may begin to cry or, if some visual stimulus suddenly appears, he may orient toward that stimulus more vigorously than he otherwise would. The presentation of intense stimuli, because of its effect on responding to a range of other stimuli, has a motivational function.[10] Stimulus presentations that alter responding to a range of other stimuli are said to *sensitize* responding, and the phenomenon itself is known as *sensitization*.

An experimental example of sensitization illustrates another phenomenon associated with the presentation of stimuli—habituation. A rat was presented with a loud sound (1,000 Hz at an intensity of 110 dB—about the loudness of a rock band).[11] As shown in **Figure 2.3**, the sound caused the rat to make a startle response that was measured by how much force the animal exerted against the floor of the chamber when it jumped. The second presentation of the sound caused the animal to jump even more vigorously, i.e., the response to sound was sensitized by the presentation of the first sound. However, with repeated presentations of the loud sound, the magnitude of the startle response declined, as shown by the falling portion of the curve in **Figure 2.3**. The decline in the strength of a response upon repeated presentations of the eliciting stimulus is known as **habituation**, and the response is said to have *habituated*. (Habituation represents the simplest form of learning in that repeated experience with a stimulus affects later responding to that stimulus.[12]) After 14 presentations, a light was briefly flashed just before the next sound presentation. The flashing light sensitized the response to the sound, as shown by the increased startle response to the fifteenth sound presentation.

Some further complications. In truth, there are probably many stimuli whose presentation has some motivating effect. Thus, like the eliciting function, the motivating function is best viewed as a region rather than a point along a continuum of motivational effects. However, substantial motivating effects are most apt to be found with intense stimuli. As an additional conceptual complication, the eliciting and motivating functions of stimuli should not be thought of as mutually exclusive. The same stimulus can function as an eliciting stimulus for one response and as a motivating stimulus for another. For example, a loud sound may elicit a startle response (evidence of the sound's eliciting function) and may also cause a light presented a few moments later to be oriented toward more vigorously (evidence of the sound's motivating function).

Finally, natural selection is not the only selection process that confers eliciting and motivating functions on stimuli. Behavioral selection, or selection by reinforcement, can have these effects as well. For example, a parent says to a child "Please pick up your toys" in order to make certain specific responses more probable. Similarly, a parent tells a child "Be careful!" so that the child's responses to many stimuli will be altered (or so the parent hopes). These learned functions of stimuli parallel the eliciting and motivating functions, respectively, and are considered elsewhere in the book.[13]

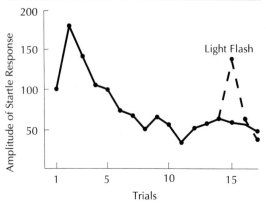

FIGURE 2.3 *Sensitization and habituation of the startle reflex in rats*

The startle reflex was measured by the amplitude of a jumping response when a loud tone (1,000 Hz at 110 dB) was presented. Greater jumping occurred with the second presentation of the tone (sensitization), then declined progressively (habituation), until a light was flashed before the fifteenth presentation of the tone for some animals. After the light flash, the jumping response increased (sensitization), thereby demonstrating a motivating effect of the light flash on the startle reflex.

Source: Groves, P. M., & Thompson, R. F. (1970). Habituation: A dual-process theory. *Psychological Review, 77,* 419–450. Copyright © 1970 by American Psychological Association. Reprinted by permission.

SELECTION

Variation in environment-behavior relations is produced by the eliciting and motivating functions of environmental stimuli and by the somewhat variable effects of those stimuli on an organism whose internal states are changing as the result of various subbehavioral processes. From this variation, selection by reinforcement begins to construct a repertoire of ever more complex environment-behavior relations—to construct, if you will, a personalized theory of the learner's environment. As selection alters the ways in which the environment guides behavior, these learned changes become progressively more important sources of variation on which later selection may act.

The need to survive in environments that are not stable over evolutionary time has selected a genetic endowment allowing organisms to learn.[14] Because natural selection favors characteristics that contribute to reproductive fitness, learning processes must have been selected initially because they benefited reproductive fitness. Thus selection processes would have been most sensitive to learning environment-behavior relations that aided mating, caring for young, and securing the necessities of life while avoiding its threats.

Indeed, there have been compelling demonstrations of the contribution of learning to reproductive fitness. Here are two examples using fish—animals that have remained in the sea, the birthplace of all life. A light was repeatedly presented to a male fish immediately before permitting him to see, but not contact, a female of his species. When the light was later presented and the male fish was permitted access to the female, he was more successful in courting the female than another male not trained with the light. Thus, courting—and, ultimately, reproductive behavior—was facilitated by experience with an arbitrary stimulus (the light) that preceded the sight of the female. Learning to respond to the light had "prepared" the male to propagate its genes, just as learning to recognize a female would do in the natural environment. Biologically important behaviors other than courting

also benefit from learning. In a related study, male fish were shown a light immediately before seeing another male. When they were later shown the light just before being given access to the other male, they were more successful fighters than males not previously trained with the light. Thus, males who learned to respond to the light were "prepared" to fight—and thereby drive off potential rivals and defend their territory.[15] In short, natural selection of the biobehavioral processes necessary for learning permitted organisms to increase their reproductive fitness. The contribution of learning is so basic to adaptation that some have spoken of the *instinct to learn*.[16]

Finally, before we begin our search for the conditions required for learning, we should remind ourselves that once the ancestral environment had selected the processes responsible for the learning of fitness-related responses, those same processes became available for learning other environment-behavior relations. Just as a feather, initially selected for warmth, later underwent selection for flight, so a learning mechanism initially selected for its contribution to mating can later be exploited for other purposes. If reflexes were the only legacy of natural selection, an organism would be ill equipped to survive in a changing environment. Instead, natural selection has provided our species—and all others as well—with that greatest of all legacies, the capacity to learn. Learning permits the environment to select environment-behavior relations that are sensitive to changing conditions.

Procedures for Studying Selection by Reinforcement

How shall we go about identifying the processes whereby the contemporary environment guides behavior and upon which a principle of behavioral selection may be based? Two types of procedures have been employed in the search, and both have taken the reflex as their starting point. In the first procedure, a stimulus that elicits a reflexive response is introduced *after an environmental event*. In the second procedure, a stimulus that elicits a reflexive response is introduced *after a behavioral event*. If the eliciting stimulus brings about a change in environment-behavior relations, then it is said to function as a **reinforcing stimulus**, or simply a **reinforcer**.

Classical procedure. The first procedure was devised by the Russian physiologist Ivan P. Pavlov in the early 1900s. The procedure in which learning is investigated by presenting an environmental stimulus followed by an eliciting stimulus is called **classical**, or **respondent**, **conditioning**. This procedure is illustrated by the well-known example in which a tone presented to a dog is followed by food-in-the-mouth, which elicits salivation. The procedure is "classical" in the sense of being the oldest well-studied procedure. The term "respondent" emphasizes that the behavioral component of the learned environment-behavior relation is the *response* to an eliciting stimulus.

Operant procedure. At about the same time that Pavlov began his work, the American psychologist Edward L. Thorndike carried out a series of experiments using the second procedure. Here, the eliciting stimulus is dependent on the occurrence of a response, and the best known example comes from the laboratory of B. F. Skinner. In a test chamber, the leverpressing response of a rat was followed by food, which evoked approach to the food, ingestion, and—ultimately—salivation. Note that in this case it is a behavioral event, leverpressing, that precedes the eliciting stimulus. Thorndike's procedure is called **instrumental**, or **operant**, **conditioning**. The term "instrumental" signifies that the response functions as an instrument to produce the eliciting stimulus. The term "operant" signifies that the response operates on the environment to produce the eliciting stimulus, and that the stimulus guiding the response may not be well specified.

Experimental examples. Both the classical and operant procedures are effective in bringing about changes in the environmental guidance of behavior, even in infants. As an example of the classical

procedure, 30-day-old infants were given paired presentations of a tone followed 1.5 sec later by a brief puff of air to the eye, which elicited a blink response. Other infants also received tones and airpuffs, but the stimuli were unpaired (i.e., not presented together in time). Within a few pairings, the infants receiving the tone followed by the airpuff began to blink during the tone *before* the airpuff was presented. The infants receiving unpaired presentations rarely blinked during the tone, showing that the airpuff had not by itself sensitized a blinking response to the tone. (See **Figure 2.4**.) By this procedure, infants as young as 10 days of age have acquired a new environment-behavior relation between tone and blink.[17]

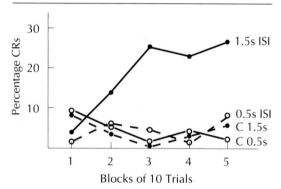

FIGURE 2.4 *Conditioned eye blink responses in human infants*

The change in the percentage of conditioned eye blink responses across blocks of paired CS-US trials is shown for 30-day-old human infants. Infants in the experimental condition were presented with a tone (conditioned stimulus) followed by a puff of air to the eye (unconditioned stimulus). For some experimental subjects, the puff followed the tone by 0.5 s and for others by 1.5 s, with acquisition occurring only for the longer interstimulus interval in this situation. In addition, the performance of two different backward-conditioning control groups are shown in which the air puff occurred *before* the tone by either 0.5 or 1.5 s. Acquisition did not occur for the subjects in either control group.

Source: Adapted from Little, 1970, described in Rovee-Collier, C. K., & Gekoski, M. J. (1979). The economics of infancy: A review of conjugate reinforcement. In H. W. Reese & L. P. Lipsitt (Eds.), *Advances in Child Development and Behavior* (Vol 13, pp. 195–225), New York: Academic Press.

As an example of the operant procedure, a 3-month-old was placed on its back in a crib with a ribbon tied loosely to each ankle. One ribbon was connected to a mobile positioned in the infant's field of view (see **Figure 2.5**), and kicking that leg caused the mobile to jiggle. The stimulus of the jiggling mobile elicited eye movements and other orienting responses from the infant. Kicking the other leg, to which the second ribbon was tied, had no effect on the mobile. Within 15 min of exposure to these conditions, there was a sustained increase in the rate of kicking the leg that jiggled the mobile. The infant had acquired a new environment-behavior relation in which the sight of the stationary

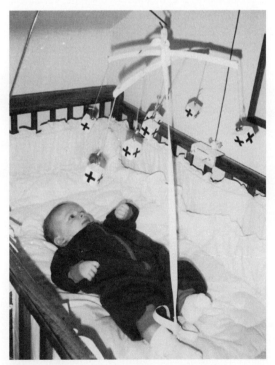

FIGURE 2.5 *Procedure for studying operant conditioning in a human infant*
Leg kicking (the operant response) pulled a ribbon, which was loosely tied to one of the infant's ankles, and the movement of the ribbon then caused a mobile above the crib to jiggle (the reinforcing stimulus). Movement of the other leg had no effect on the mobile.

mobile evoked kicking when kicking was followed by the eliciting stimulus of a jiggling mobile. In comparison, the rate of kicking the leg that was not connected to the mobile decreased after a brief initial increase at the beginning of the experiment. This control observation showed that sustained kicking was not merely sensitization of the kicking response. Other infants, who were exposed to a mobile that jiggled *independently* of kicking, showed no increase in kicking.[18]

The preceding two experiments demonstrate that the classical and operant procedures are both effective in changing environment-behavior relations, and that even infants are fully competent to acquire the new relations. Moreover, these controlled laboratory observations showed that the changed relations were dependent on the pairing of the environmental stimulus with the elicitor in the classical procedure and the pairing of the response with the elicitor in the operant procedure. In other words, the eliciting stimulus functioned as a reinforcer in both procedures. Merely presenting the eliciting stimulus was not sufficient to change the environment-behavior relations since presentations without pairing had little effect. Research with nonhuman animals, in which physiological processes are more readily studied, has shown that newborn organisms of many species can acquire environment-behavior relations with these procedures[19] and that the neural mechanisms crucial for learning are present at birth.[20] Such findings make it clear that young organisms face the world armed not only with reflexive relations selected by the ancestral environment, but also with the capacity to acquire new environment-behavior relations selected by the individual environment. Using the classical and operant methods, we now seek to discover what conditions must be present for selection by the individual environment to occur.

Conditions Required for Selection by Reinforcement

Because of ethical restrictions on the research procedures that may be used with humans, especially infants, the discovery of a principle of behavioral selection has relied heavily on work with nonhuman subjects. The capacity of all animals to learn, the conservative nature of natural selection, and the general lessons of historical science for the understanding of complexity all encourage the belief that a principle of behavioral selection may be uncovered from the study of other animals.

Research conducted under highly controlled conditions with nonhuman learners indicates that learning will occur when three conditions are met: (a) the environment that guides behavior must occur immediately before the behavior that it is to guide, (b) the eliciting stimulus must occur immediately after the environment-behavior relation that is to be selected, and (c) the eliciting stimulus must evoke behavior that would not otherwise occur in that environment. When these three conditions are met, whether in the classical or operant procedure, the eliciting stimulus will function as a reinforcer to strengthen environment-behavior relations. In the sections that follow, we will present experimental evidence bearing on each of these factors. Finally, we will describe a principle of behavioral selection that integrates the behavioral evidence with what is known about the neural mechanisms of learning.

Temporal relation between the guiding environment and behavior.   The classical procedure is best suited to study the temporal relation between the environment and behavior. This is because, in the classical procedure, the experimenter can control the time between the presentation of the environmental stimulus (e.g., a tone) and the eliciting stimulus (e.g., an airpuff to the eye)—and the eliciting stimulus then determines when the elicited response (e.g., blinking) occurs.[21] In an operant procedure, the occurrence of the instrumental response (e.g., leverpressing) is initially guided by environmental stimuli that the experimenter cannot specify and, therefore, the relation between these stimuli and behavior cannot be manipulated.

The experimental technique that has been most effectively used to study the temporal relation be-

tween an environmental stimulus and behavior uses the rabbit as the subject, a tone as the stimulus, and a type of blinking—elicited by an airpuff or brief shock to the eye—as the response. Using this method, Dore Gormezano and his students have produced a body of research with the classical procedure that is second in scope only to that of Pavlov.[22] The technique will be described in some detail because it illustrates a general theme in historical science—the use of model preparations.

In historical science, the formulation of basic principles from which complex phenomena may be derived often involves the use of artificial and highly simplified experimental situations. As noted in the previous chapter, simplified situations—or model preparations—have the advantage of clearly revealing the effects of the variables. In the **model preparation** shown in **Figure 2.6**, a rabbit is placed in a restraining device with a speaker for the presentation of a tone mounted nearby. A brief shock or airpuff is applied near the eye to evoke the elicited response. The elicited response is movement of the nictitating membrane, or "third eyelid," measured by a device attached to the membrane. The nictitating membrane is not present in humans, enduring as only a vestigial pink structure in the inner corner of the eye. However, in many other animals—e.g., dogs, cats, birds, snakes, and fish—it is a thin membrane that can be extended to cover much of the surface of the eye (the sclera and cornea). For the experimenter, the chief advantage of using the nictitating-membrane response of the rabbit is that, unlike the human eyelid, the membrane rarely moves unless elicited by specific stimuli. Thus, when a membrane response occurs, we may be quite confident that the movement was due to stimuli that were manipulated by the experimenter and not to extraneous uncontrolled stimuli. To further insure well controlled observations, the subjects are placed in the test chamber for a period of time before the experiment begins, so that any sensitized membrane responses may be habituated.

To determine the effect of the temporal interval with this classical procedure, rabbits were given a

From Air Supply

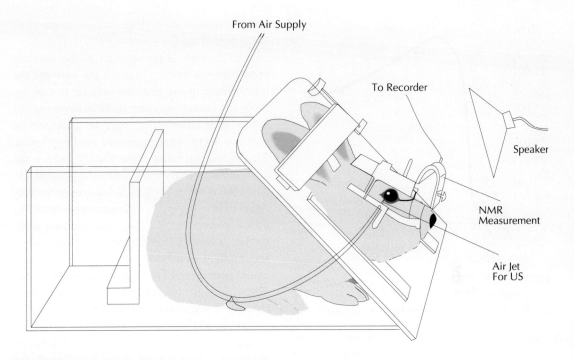

To Recorder

Speaker

NMR
Measurement

Air Jet
For US

FIGURE 2.6 *Preparation for studying learning using the classical procedure*
A tone (conditioned stimulus) is presented to a restrained rabbit followed by a puff of air (unconditioned stimulus), which elicits movement of the nictitating membrane. The movement of the nictitating membrane is monitored by a device that permits precise measurement of the extent (amplitude) of movement.
Source: Based on procedures from Gormezano, 1966, from which additional procedural information may be obtained.

number of paired trials in which a tone was followed by a mild eyeshock that elicited the nictitating-membrane response. The time interval between the paired stimuli was different for different animals. The percentages of responses that occurred during the tone at the end of training are shown in **Figure 2.7**. As you can see, the tone-membrane relation became strongest when the tone preceded the elicitation of the membrane response by an interval of about a quarter of a sec, or 250 msec (1 second = 1,000 milliseconds). When the interval was either shorter or longer, the strength of the relation declined.[23] In control conditions in which other rabbits received the eyeshock before the tone or were given unpaired presentations of the tone and eyeshock, no change occurred in the strength of responding to the tone.

The findings with nictitating-membrane conditioning agree qualitatively with those obtained under less well controlled conditions with human infants and adults: Selection is most effective when the guiding stimulus occurs a very short time *before* the stimulus that elicits the response. The finding that learning occurred only with a brief time interval between the tone and eyeshock may be summarized as follows: **Temporal contiguity** between the environment and behavior is crucial for learning environment-behavior relations.[24]

The environmental and behavioral events manipulated and measured in classical procedures are usually designated by the technical terms Pavlov used in his original experiments. The environmental stimulus (e.g., the tone) that comes to evoke behavior is known as the **conditioned stimulus,**

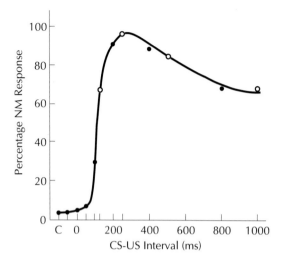

FIGURE 2.7 *Effect of the interval between a tone and a mild shock in the vicinity of the eye on the acquisition of a conditioned nictitating-membrane (NM) response in rabbits*

Different groups of rabbits received different interstimulus intervals throughout training. The final percentages of responses to presentations of the tone are shown for each group. Two control groups received either presentations of shocks unpaired with tones (C) or backward conditioning in which shocks occurred 50 ms *before* the tones.

Source: From Smith, Coleman, S. P., & Gormezano, I. (1969). Classical conditioning of the rabbit's nictating membrane response at backward, simultaneous, and forward CS-US intervals. *Journal of Comparative and Physiological Psychology, 69,* 226–231. Copyright © 1969 by the American Psychological Association. Reprinted by permission.

since its ability to evoke the response is conditional upon its being paired with the eliciting stimulus. The eliciting stimulus (e.g., eyeshock) is known as the **unconditioned stimulus** because its ability to elicit the response is not conditioned upon events within the experiment. For analogous reasons, the response evoked by the conditional stimulus is known as the **conditioned response** and the response evoked by the unconditioned stimulus is known as the **unconditioned response**. In the model preparation, the conditioned and uncondi-

tioned responses are both movements of the nictitating membrane.[25]

The increase in the strength of the environment-behavior relation between the tone and the membrane response does not indicate that an entirely new relation was formed. In all environment-behavior relations that may be changed by selection, there must be some pre-existing relation. That is, the variation must already include the environment-behavior relations to be selected. Or, described at the physiological level, from the very outset of learning some of the neurons activated by the environment must *already* lead to neural activity that to some degree contracts the muscle fibers responsible for the behavior. In short, pre-existing neural connections between the environment and behavior must be present at some minimum strength if selection by reinforcement is to be effective. In all instances of learning in which evidence of a pre-existing environment-behavior relation has been sought, it has been found. For example, before any pairing has occurred between the tone and eyeshock in the rabbit nictitating-membrane preparation, presentation of the tone by itself causes very small movements in the membrane[26] and, at the neural level, lower thresholds for activating the motor neurons responsible for membrane movement.[27]

The foregoing findings indicate that—at the neural level—the effect of behavioral selection is to strengthen connections that are already present—either through natural selection in the case of an inexperienced learner or, as we shall see in a later chapter, through prior behavioral selection in the case of an experienced learner. There are ample logical grounds for believing that there must be pre-existing connections between the neurons underlying any learned environment-behavior relation. The validity of this view is perhaps best illustrated by considering the implications of the opposite position—that pre-existing connections are *not* required. If some of the neurons activated by the environment were not already "connected" to some of the neurons responsible for the behavior, then how would the environmentally-activated neurons find the proper motor neurons?

The requirement that the neural substrate underlying an environment-behavior relation must already be present for learning to occur is not a severe constraint on what may be learned. As an illustration, we can easily respond to any of the following directions: "Turn left after you see a white house," "Turn left after you hear dogs barking," "Turn left after the road gets bumpy," or "Turn left after you smell lilacs." These directions may not all be equally helpful, but they do show that the response of turning left can be controlled by many types of stimuli—visual, auditory, tactile, or olfactory. With a human brain of 100 billion neurons, many of which are connected to thousands of other neurons, one neuron is seldom more than a few "connections," or **synapses**, away from any other neuron.

Temporal relation between behavior and the eliciting stimulus.   The classical procedure is well suited to study the relation between the environment and the behavior evoked by the eliciting stimulus. However, it does not permit us to evaluate the effect on learning of the temporal interval between behavior and the eliciting stimulus. This limitation is inherent in the classical procedure because the behavior monitored is the very behavior evoked by the eliciting stimulus. Therefore, the interval between the eliciting stimulus and the behavior is fixed and cannot be manipulated by the experimenter. In order to vary the temporal relation between behavior and the eliciting stimulus, we must observe some behavior other than that evoked by the eliciting stimulus. The operant procedure permits us to do this.

In the operant procedure, the experimenter identifies some critical response (e.g., leg-kicking in an infant) and then presents a stimulus (e.g., a jiggling mobile) that elicits a response (e.g., eye movements). As a result of this arrangement of events, the environment (perhaps the sight of the unmoving mobile) comes to guide the critical behavior (e.g., kicking). When the child next sees the unmoving mobile, kicking is likely to occur.

Besides permitting the experimenter to vary the temporal interval between behavior and the eliciting stimulus, the operant procedure has a second characteristic that is crucial to understanding complex behavior: The behavior that is guided by the environment is *not* restricted to behavior that is evoked by an eliciting stimulus. The operant procedure permits all behavioral variations, not just those due to natural selection, to be candidates for selection by reinforcement. For example, in order to use kicking as the operant response, the experimenter was not obliged to find a stimulus that evoked kicking—if, indeed, one could be found. The experimenter simply waited until the kicking response occurred—for whatever reasons—and then presented the jiggling mobile. With the operant procedure, the variation potentially available for selection by reinforcement includes the full behavioral capabilities of the learner.[28] With the classical procedure, the available variation is restricted to those behaviors whose eliciting stimuli are already known to the experimenter.

Although this discussion focuses on the study of operant procedures in the laboratory, it should be apparent that the events that define the operant procedure—behavior followed by an eliciting stimulus—are the stuff of everyday life. The infant brings a toy to its mouth, which stimulus evokes a sucking response. The older child returns his toys to the toy chest and is given a cookie and praise, which stimuli evoke salivation and those reactions we call "feeling pleased with oneself." The college student makes notes after reading a textbook and, seeing the notes, reacts to them with a "sense of accomplishment." In general, our lives are made up of responses followed by stimuli that evoke other behavior. Historical science encourages us to believe that, if we devise principles that describe learning in well controlled laboratory procedures, those same principles will allow us to interpret more complex situations that contain the types of events studied with the laboratory procedures.

A variety of laboratory techniques have been devised to determine the effect of the interval between the occurrence of a response and the presentation of an eliciting stimulus. For example, with leverpressing as the operant and food as the eliciting stimulus, the presentation of food may be delayed for different time intervals after leverpressing. The results of such studies are clear. Leverpressing is most likely to be selected if the food is presented *immediately* after leverpressing.[29] When the conditions during the delay interval are well controlled to eliminate the effects of other variables, an increase in the strength of responding does not occur with time intervals of longer than a few seconds.[30] (See **Figure 2.8**.) Thus, as in the classical procedure, the effective temporal interval in the operant procedure is extremely brief. Both sets of findings point to a similar conclusion: The processes that permit the environment to guide behavior operate over very short time intervals.

Besides demonstrating the importance of temporal contiguity between behavior and the eliciting stimulus, the operant procedure reveals an entirely new result: When an eliciting stimulus is presented, the environment comes to guide not only the behavior evoked by the eliciting stimulus, but also the behavior that preceded the eliciting stimulus. Thus, for a rat given food after leverpressing, stimuli such as the sight of the lever evoke not only salivation but leverpressing as well.

The conclusion that the operant procedure brings both the elicited response and the operant under the guidance of the environment is supported by experiments in which both responses have been measured.[31] As an example using leverpressing as the operant and salivation as the elicited response, food was produced by leverpressing if at least 90 sec had elapsed since the previous food presentation.[32] Spacing the food presentations permitted the experimenter to distinguish between food-elicited salivation and salivation evoked by other stimuli. The results obtained with this procedure are shown in **Figure 2.9**. Both salivation and leverpressing increased as the stimulus conditions approached those present at the moment when leverpressing produced food.

The fact that whatever responses immediately precede the eliciting stimulus are potentially guided by the environment presents problems for the learner. For example, when animals were presented at a choicepoint in a maze with one response that led to an immediate but small piece of food and a second response that led to a larger but slightly delayed piece of food, the first response was the one that was more strongly selected.[33] Such an outcome is "unwise" in the sense that, over the long run, more total food might be obtained by "choosing" the second response. This dilemma is not confined to organisms such as rats; there is ample experimental evidence that young children

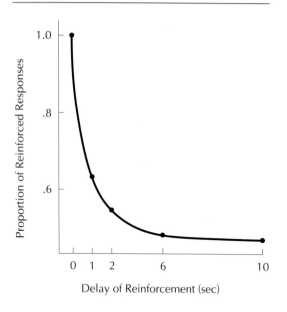

FIGURE 2.8 *Effect of delay of reinforcement between the operant and the reinforcer*
The proportion of reinforced responses relative to the total number of responses at various delay intervals between the operant response and the food reinforcer. A proportion of 1.0 indicates that all the responses that occurred were reinforced responses. A proportion of 0.5 indicates that the reinforced and unreinforced response were equally likely.
Source: Based on findings from Grice, 1948.

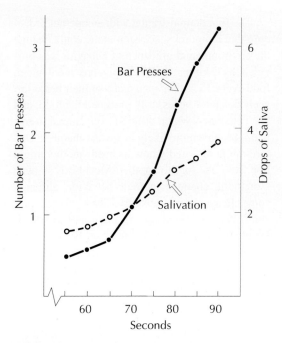

FIGURE 2.9 *Concurrent conditioning of operant (instrumental) and elicited (respondent) behavior* In the procedure, dogs pressed a lever that produced food if 90 s had elapsed since the preceding food presentation. (Technically, this procedure is known as a 90-s fixed-interval schedule, and is described more fully in Chapter 4.) The figure shows the number of leverpressing responses (operants) and salivary responses (respondents) at 5-s intervals during the final 40 s of the 90-s period for a single dog. By the end of training, lever pressing rarely occurred during the first 50-s portion of the 90-s period. *Source:* Adapted from Kintsch, N., & Witte, R. S. (1962). Concurrent conditioning of bar press and salivation processes. *Journal of Comparative and Physiological Psychology, 55,* 963–968. Copyright © 1962 by the American Psychological Association. Adapted by permission.

behave in a similar manner.[34] And, if the truth be admitted, we can all recall circumstances in which we have succumbed to the temptation of immediate reinforcers and lost sight of more important—but distant—goals. Have you ever eaten a fattening dessert even though you might not look as good in your bathing suit next summer? Have you ever gone to a party before finishing an assignment that was due next week?

Acquired reinforcement. Although selection by reinforcement can change only contiguous environment-behavior relations, we all act—at least sometimes—*as if* longer-term considerations governed behavior. How is this possible if the effects of behavioral selection are confined to short-term relations? We shall address this question in some detail in later chapters. However, three relevant factors may be mentioned here. First, responding under the guidance of momentary conditions is quite generally adaptive in the sense of benefiting Darwinian fitness. Usually, a bird in the hand is worth two in the bush. Second, the environment of the moment is often a reliable guide to the environment-behavior relations that are "appropriate" in future environments. A child who has learned to withdraw from the heat of a stove does well to withdraw from the heat of other objects—irons, fireplaces, and the like. To the extent that past environments are similar to future environments, the learner entering a given future environment will engage in responses appropriate to the stimuli in that environment. Because the environment is consistent, the short time over which selection by reinforcement operates is not as limiting as it might at first appear. Indeed, it is the relative consistency of environmental **contingencies** over substantial periods of time that has permitted natural selection to favor learning mechanisms at all.

A third factor that makes it appear as if human behavior somehow escapes the temporal constraints of behavioral selection is the increasing ability of stimuli to evoke behavior as the result of prior selection by immediate reinforcers. Such stimuli act as "acquired elicitors," or—more technically—function as **conditioned** (or **secondary**) **reinforcers**. We have seen that, when an eliciting stimulus such as food is presented, the environment that preceded the food comes to control food-elicited responses and any operants that preceded the food. Thus, by the end of the experiment, a second environmental stimulus—e.g., the sight of the lever—has acquired the ability to evoke behavior. The sight of the lever evokes both salivation and leverpressing. In short, we have established the sight of the lever as a stimulus that evokes behavior because it has been paired with an eliciting stimulus. If these environmental stimuli can function as reinforcers to select still other environment-behavior relations, then prior learning would provide a basis for later learning. That is, acquired reinforcers could supplement reflexive elicitors as the basis for behavioral selection. The cumulative effect of such a process would be an organism whose environment contained more and more stimuli that could function as reinforcers for new learning.

Superstitious conditioning.   Before moving to the third condition required for behavioral selection, we should make a final point: Although the environment-behavior relations selected in operant procedures are likely to include the response that "caused" the reinforcer, this outcome is not guaranteed. The selection process strengthens all environment-behavior relations that precede eliciting stimuli; it detects temporal contiguity, not causation. On any given occurrence of an eliciting stimulus, the environment-behavior relations that precede the eliciting stimulus may include some that are completely irrelevant to producing the eliciting stimulus. For example, a rat may press the lever as it is trying to climb out of the test chamber. Because both leverpressing and climbing precede the occurrence of food, both responses will be selected. It is important to recognize that there is nothing intrinsic to an environment-behavior-elicitor sequence that distinguishes a causal relation between the behavior and the reinforcer from a purely temporal relation.[35]

Although there is nothing that distinguishes between a temporal and causal relation, environment-behavior-elicitor sequences provide the only variation on which selection by reinforcement can operate. In the next chapter, we shall see how repeated exposures to such sequences usually restrict the environmental guidance of behavior to reliable—and, therefore, probably causal—sequences. Here, we shall consider evidence that selection can occur with sequences that are purely temporal and do not reflect a causal relation, or dependency, between behavior and the elicitor.

The first demonstration with an operant procedure that temporal succession alone could change the environmental guidance of behavior was provided by Skinner.[36] When pigeons were given food every 15 sec *independently* of their behavior, *some* behavior necessarily preceded the food, and this behavior—which differed from animal to animal—became more likely in the test chamber. One bird might repeatedly bow its head; another might hop from one foot to another. Most birds showed systematic changes in their behavior, although some changes were transitory. These changes presumably consisted of specific environment-behavior relations that happened to occur before a food presentation; because of the short temporal interval between the behavior and the food, the relations were strengthened. Since the behavior was strengthened, it was more likely to occur before the next food presentation. This process could then continue, with the behavior becoming ever more likely in the experimental environment. Because the environment-behavior relation was changed even though the presentation of the elicitor was independent of the response, this was designated **superstitious behavior**. Bowing and hopping in the pigeon and certain human behaviors, such as avoiding crossing the path of a black cat, are superstitions in that they refer to environment-behavior relations that have been selected when there are no genuine dependencies between the behavior and the eliciting stimuli.

Superstitious behavior can be demonstrated with humans as well as literal "birdbrains" like pigeons. For a four-year-old child, a piece of candy was dispensed into a food tray about every 60 sec independently of his behavior. "Early in the [session], he received several pieces of candy...while searching on the floor for a dropped piece. Subsequently, he spent the time crawling around the floor, reaching up to get each piece of candy when it was discharged into the tray."[37] Adults are not immune to selection based on purely temporal relations either. College students were seated in front of a panel on which were mounted three levers and a counter that registered points. The subjects were told to try and get as many points as possible, but not how to get them. In fact, pulling the levers had no effect; points were added to the counter every 60 sec independently of behavior. For one subject, the experimenter reported the following: "About 5 min into the session, a point delivery occurred after she had stopped pulling the lever temporarily and had put her right hand on the lever frame. This behavior was followed by a point delivery after which she climbed on the table and put her right hand to the counter. Just as she did so, another point was delivered. Thereafter, she began to touch many things in turn...About 10 min later, a point was delivered just as she jumped to the floor, and touching was replaced by jumping. After five jumps, a point was delivered when she jumped and touched the ceiling with her slipper in her hand. Jumping to touch the ceiling continued repeatedly ... until she stopped about 25 min into the session, perhaps because of fatigue."[38]

Discrepancy between ongoing behavior and the behavior evoked by the eliciting stimulus.   Let us review what we know so far about the conditions required for behavioral selection. The classical procedure has shown that a short temporal interval between the environment and the eliciting stimulus—and, therefore, between the environment and the elicited response—brings about a change in the guidance of behavior. Environmental stimuli other than the eliciting stimulus now evoke the elicited response. The operant procedure has revealed that a short temporal interval between the operant and the eliciting stimulus also produces a change in the guidance of behavior. Environmental stimuli now evoke the operant in addition to the elicited response. Is it enough that an environment-behavior sequence occur in temporal contiguity with an eliciting stimulus for selection by reinforcement to occur?

Leon Kamin conducted a series of studies in the late 1960s that addressed this crucial question.[39] Using standard classical procedures with rats, he began by determining a temporal interval that was effective in producing conditioning. Using this interval, he then gave an experimental group of rats preliminary training in which a stimulus, say a light, was paired with shock until the light was maximally effective in evoking the elicited response. Next, the same animals received further training in which a second stimulus, say a tone, was now paired with shock, *but with the light presented at the same time as the tone*. The compound tone-light stimulus was paired with shock enough times to insure that—if contiguity were all that was required for selection to occur—there was ample opportunity for a relation to be selected between the tone and shock-elicited behavior. (When an environment includes separable stimulus components, such as light and tone, it is called a **compound stimulus**.) Finally, a test was carried out to determine whether an environment-behavior relation between the tone and shock-elicited behavior had been selected. In the test, the light and tone were separately presented and conditioned responses (if any) were measured.[40]

The thinking behind the experiment was as follows: If an appropriate temporal relation is all that is required for the eliciting stimulus to function as a reinforcer, then the second stimulus—the tone—should acquire the ability to evoke shock-elicited behavior because the tone was paired with the eliciting stimulus. However, if selection also requires the eliciting stimulus to produce a *change* in ongoing behavior, then the tone should not have acquired the ability to evoke a conditioned response. The tone should fail to control shock-elicited responses because the tone was presented simultaneously with the light, *and the light already evoked shock-elicited behavior because of prior light-shock pairings*. Thus the eliciting stimulus did not produce a behavioral change.[41] Note that in all of the studies considered previously, the environmental stimulus was in an appropriate temporal relation with the elicited response and the eliciting stimulus evoked behavior that was not already occurring when the environmental stimulus was presented. With Kamin's procedure, these two conditions—temporal contiguity and behavioral change—could be separately evaluated for the first time. That is, Kamin carried out the first experimental analysis of the role of a *change* in behavior caused by the presentation of an eliciting stimulus.

The results of the experiment were clear-cut. When the tone occurred together with a light that already evoked shock-elicited behavior, the tone did *not* acquire the capacity to evoke shock-elicited behavior. The failure of the relation between the tone and shock-elicited behavior to be selected even though there was temporal contiguity between them indicated that contiguity was not enough for selection to occur. Thus, although temporal contiguity is necessary for selection by reinforcement, it is not sufficient. Experimental analysis has revealed that *both* temporal contiguity between the environment and behavior *and* a change in behavior caused by the responses evoked by the eliciting stimulus are required for selection. In the technical language of learning, the change in ongoing behavior produced by the eliciting stimulus is called a **behavioral discrepancy**.[42]

The phenomenon that Kamin discovered—called **blocking** because the first stimulus paired with the elicitor "blocked" learning with the second stimulus—has been replicated many times with both classical procedures[43] and operant procedures.[44] Further work has eliminated possible alternative accounts of the results through the use of a number of control procedures.[45] Research has consistently supported the conclusion that behavioral selection requires a discrepancy between ongoing and elicited behavior as well as an appropriate temporal relation of the environment and behavior with the eliciting stimulus.

Experimental analysis of the role of discrepancy in human learning is difficult because of the researcher's limited ability to control the subject's pre-experimental history of exposure to stimuli and to measure elicited responses, which are often subtle. Nevertheless, a number of students of human learning concur in assigning a central role to discrepancy.[46] Speaking nontechnically, an elicitor does not change the environmental guidance of behavior unless the elicitor "surprises" the organism, in the sense of causing it to act in a way that it would not have otherwise acted in that environment. Gordon Bower has put it in these terms: "The learning mechanism seems to become 'switched on' mainly when environmental events do not confirm expectations."[47]

More work remains to be done to determine the precise nature of the discrepancy that is required for behavioral selection to occur. It seems likely, however, that the relevant characteristics are quite specific to the particular behavioral responses and neural processes initiated by the eliciting stimulus. For example, using the rabbit nictitating-membrane response, if a light is paired with shock to one eye and later a tone-light compound stimulus is paired with shock to the same eye, only the light evokes a membrane response in that eye when presented alone. This is the now familiar (we hope!) blocking phenomenon. However, if the shock is switched to the other eye when the compound stimulus is paired with it, then both the tone and the light evoke a membrane response in the newly shocked eye when they are later presented separately. (This experiment makes use of the fact that membrane responses are independent in the two eyes of the rabbit, unlike the eyeblink responses of humans.) Thus blocking occurred only when the specific response evoked by the light—movement of the membrane of one eye—corresponded to the response evoked by the shock. If the shock evoked a different response—movement of the membrane of the other eye—then behavioral selection still occurred.[48]

The significance of the discrepancy requirement for individual selection is profound. Two implications are mentioned here, and others will be pointed out in later chapters. First, blocking indicates that the same eliciting stimulus may select environment-behavior relations for one person but not for another. Eliciting stimuli function as reinforcers only for persons who are not already behaving as the eliciting stimulus requires. As a hypothetical example, if a child is given "unexpected" praise for picking up toys scattered about his room, it will likely increase the chances that he will do so the next time he sees the room in disarray. However, if a second child receives the same praise from a parent who has praised him before independently of his behavior, then praise may not lead to learning. For the second child, praise was "expected" and has therefore been rendered ineffective as a reinforcer.

Second, the discrepancy requirement indicates that the same eliciting stimulus presented on different occasions to the same person may alter the environmental guidance of behavior in some situations but not others. As an illustration, a child who is given "unexpected" praise for picking up toys from the bed when only the bed is littered may be more likely to put away toys when he later sees them on the bed. If, the next time, toys are scattered on both the bed and the floor, the same praise for picking up all of the toys may not be as effective in getting the toys on the floor picked up. On the first occasion, the environment present when approval was given included toys only on the bed. Because toys are also on the bed during the second occasion, selection of the behavior of picking up toys from the floor may be blocked by the fact that praise is "expected" for just picking up the toys on the bed. Parental approval would remain effective, however, under other circumstances.

These two implications of blocking have a common theme: A given eliciting stimulus may not function as an equally effective reinforcer for all learners in all environments. The person's specific history of contact with the elicitor in earlier environments will determine whether it will function as a selector of later environment-behavior relations. Prior exposure to an elicitor in a given environment may reduce the elicitor's ability to select new environment-behavior relations *in that environment*.[49]

A Principle of Selection by Reinforcement

Based on findings from experimental analyses of conditioning experiments, we may now formulate a principle of behavioral selection. As with all principles that summarize the results of experimental analyses, a principle of reinforcement must remain open to possible modification by future findings. The findings to date indicate that a principle of reinforcement must accommodate three primary factors: (a) the temporal relation between environmental stimuli and the eliciting stimulus, (b) the temporal relation between operants and the eliciting stimulus, and (c) the evocation by the eliciting stimulus of responses that would not have otherwise occurred in that environment.

Figure 2.10 depicts a view of the relation between the environment, behavior, and the eliciting stimulus that allows these factors to be represented. An organism is immersed in a continuous succession of environmental stimuli (S_is) in whose presence a continuous succession of responses (R_js) are occurring.[50] Some of these responses are clearly evoked by stimuli from the environment and are more toward the respondent end of the continuum of environment-behavior relations. Other responses are not obviously correlated with any particular environmental stimuli and are more toward the operant end of the continuum. When an eliciting stimulus is introduced into this stream of events and an elicited response is evoked that differs from other responses occurring at that moment, then a behavioral discrepancy is produced and selection occurs. The proposed principle of selection by reinforcement holds that *whenever a behavioral discrepancy occurs, an environment-behavior relation is selected that consists—other things being equal—of all those stimuli occurring immediately before the discrepancy and all those responses occurring immediately before and at the same time as the elicited response.*

The principle of reinforcement makes no fundamental distinction between the selection process in the classical and operant procedures. For that reason, it has been called a **unified principle of reinforcement**.[51] In the classical procedure, a specific environmental stimulus must occur before the behavioral discrepancy; therefore, that stimulus is likely to become a part of the selected environment-behavior relation. The selected relation will probably include the elicited response but, since

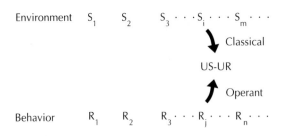

Environment S_1 S_2 $S_3 \cdots S_i \cdots S_m \cdots$

↓ Classical

US-UR

↑ Operant

Behavior R_1 R_2 $R_3 \cdots R_j \cdots R_n \cdots$

FIGURE 2.10 *Diagram depicting the introduction of an eliciting, or unconditioned, stimulus (US), and its elicited, or unconditioned, response (UR) into an ongoing stream of environmental and behavioral events*
The learner senses a series of environmental events, or stimuli (S_1, ..., S_i, ..., S_m), in whose presence a series of behavioral events, or responses (R_1, ..., R_j, ..., R_n), occur. When the eliciting stimulus is contingent upon a stimulus (a S-US contingency), a classical procedure is defined. When the eliciting stimulus is contingent upon a response (a R-US contingency), an operant procedure is defined. Clearly, regardless of whether the reinforcer is contingent on a stimulus or a response, some stimulus and some response must necessarily precede the reinforcer. However, whether a given stimulus or response *reliably* precedes the reinforcer depends upon whether the procedure is a classical or an operant procedure, respectively.

organisms are always behaving, other responses must also precede the elicitor—although these responses will vary from moment to moment. In the operant procedure, a specific response must occur before the behavioral discrepancy; therefore, that response is likely to become a part of the selected environment-behavior relation. However, since behavior always takes place in an environment, some stimulus must precede the elicitor—although the particular stimulus may vary from moment to moment. From the perspective of a unified reinforcement principle, classical and operant conditioning are not two different "kinds" of learning, but two procedures that differ with respect to the environmental and behavioral events that are reliably present when selection occurs.[52]

To see how the unified reinforcement principle accommodates the change in environment-behavior relations produced by an operant procedure, consider the following laboratory example. Suppose that food is given after a leverpress *if and only if* the leverpress occurs when a tone is sounding. Since the food elicits a response (e.g., salivation) that would not otherwise have occurred, a behavioral discrepancy is produced and an environment-behavior relation is selected. What are the stimuli most likely to be sensed before the behavioral discrepancy, and therefore to become part of the selected relation? These stimuli would be the sound of the tone and any other stimuli (such as the sight of the lever) present when leverpressing occurred. What are the responses most likely to occur in the neighborhood of the behavioral discrepancy? In addition to leverpressing, these would be any responses evoked by the tone (such as pricking up the ears), and the reinforcer-elicited response itself (salivation). According to the reinforcement principle, the selected environment-behavior relation would include all of these stimuli and responses. When the animal hears the tone and sees the lever, it is likely to prick up its ears, press the lever, and salivate (although not necessarily in that order).

These stimuli and responses are not the only candidates for inclusion in the selected environment-behavior relation, however. As the superstition experiment indicated, a response need not produce an elicitor to be selected; it need only precede the elicitor. Thus the selected relation might include response components that were not necessary to produce the reinforcer but simply accompanied the operant, e.g., sniffing the lever as it was pressed. Similarly, the sound of the tone and the sight of the lever need not be the only stimulus components of the selected relation. The smell of the lever, and any other stimuli sensed immediately before leverpressing, could be included. Thus, stimuli as well as responses can superstitiously become components of the selected environment-behavior relation.[53] (See **Figure 2.11** for a summary of the stimuli and responses that are most

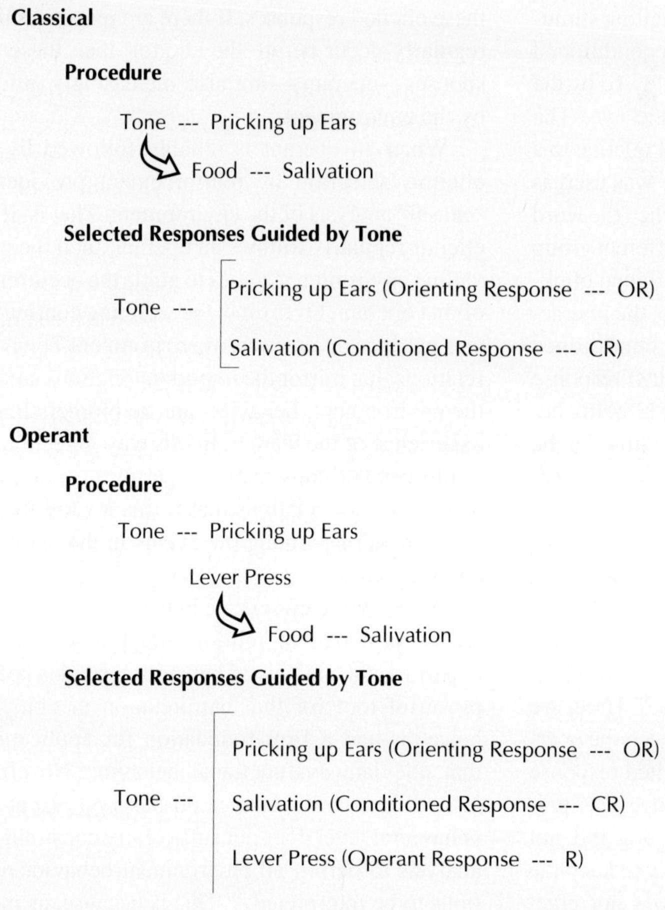

Classical

    Procedure

        Tone --- Pricking up Ears

                ⤷ Food --- Salivation

    Selected Responses Guided by Tone

                     Pricking up Ears (Orienting Response --- OR)

        Tone ---

                     Salivation (Conditioned Response --- CR)

Operant

    Procedure

        Tone --- Pricking up Ears

           Lever Press

              ⤷ Food --- Salivation

    Selected Responses Guided by Tone

                     Pricking up Ears (Orienting Response --- OR)

        Tone ---   Salivation (Conditioned Response --- CR)

                     Lever Press (Operant Response --- R)

FIGURE 2.11 *Examples summarizing the responses that are most likely to be guided by the environment as a result of the classical (upper panel) and operant (lower panel) procedures*
The wavy lines with arrows indicate the different contingencies of reinforcement that define the classical and operant procedures. The technical terms designating the various responses are shown in parentheses.

likely to become components of environment-behavior relations selected with the classical and operant procedures.)

Interactions among selected responses. The final outcome of behavioral selection depends on interactions, if any, among the stimuli and responses that are candidates for inclusion in the selected environment-behavior relation.[54] All possible types of relations—facilitating, interfering, and noninteracting—can occur and thereby affect the course of selection. We will describe several examples to give a sense of the diversity of possible outcomes.

    The first example illustrates interactions in a classical procedure between the responses evoked by the conditioned stimulus and the eliciting stimulus. College students were given as a conditioned stimulus the phrase "Don't blink," followed by the eliciting stimulus, a puff of air to the eye. The development of blinking was retarded relative to a condition in which a "neutral" phrase was used as a conditioned stimulus. By contrast, when the word "Blink" was paired with a puff for a different group of subjects, the development of conditioned blinking was hastened.[55] In the former case, the interaction between the response to the conditioned stimulus ("Don't blink") and the elicited response (blinking) interfered with selection of blinking because the two responses were incompatible. In the latter case, the relation between the two responses facilitated selection.

A second example illustrates interactions in an operant procedure. A tone was presented to a dog, and food was delivered if the dog did *not* salivate during the tone. Even though salivation prevented food delivery, the dog continued to salivate during about 50% of the tone presentations.[56] Here, we have an example of interference between the operant (having a dry mouth) and the elicited response (salivating).[57] In contrast, when a tone was presented and *water* was given if the dog did not salivate, the tone acquired the capacity to keep the mouth dry.[58] Unlike food, water does not elicit salivation, so the operant and elicited responses did not interfere with one another.

The scope of a behaviorally based principle of reinforcement. In general, the contingencies of the ancestral and contemporary environments are stable enough that natural selection and selection by reinforcement produce environment-behavior relations that are "appropriate" in future environments. As with natural selection, behavioral selection reduces the difference between the behavior that the organism brings to an environment and the behavior that is required for efficient functioning in that environment. At the beginning of learning, "unexpected" elicitors evoke responses that would not have otherwise occurred. Through selection by reinforcement, the environment comes to guide

these elicited responses. If there are responses that regularly occur before the elicitor, then these responses—operants—are also increasingly guided by the environment.

When an operant is reliably followed by an elicitor, selection by reinforcement provides a "causal" analysis of the environment. That is, if an elicitor regularly follows an operant, then the prevailing environment comes to guide the occurrence of that operant. Over time, the selecting contingencies produce diverse sets of environment-behavior relations that mirror the important relations among the environment, behavior, and reinforcers in the experience of the learner. In this way, selection by reinforcement constructs a repertoire of environment-behavior relations that forms a valid theory of the relations among the events in the learner's environment.

As we will demonstrate in the remaining chapters, a principle of reinforcement based on the experimental analysis of behavior provides both a powerful tool for the interpretation of complex behavior and a firm foundation for applications that alleviate dysfunctional behavior. Nevertheless, an exclusive reliance on observations at the behavioral level does not sufficiently constrain the analysis to permit all environment-behavior relations to be interpreted.[59] This is because, as mentioned earlier, biological mechanisms initially selected for their effects on overt behavior are then available for more subtle purposes.

We note here three types of situations that expose limitations of a principle of reinforcement based exclusively on the experimental analysis of behavior. First, selection by reinforcement may occur in situations where natural selection has biased the outcome of behavioral selection; such situations expose what are often called **biological constraints on learning.** Second, selection may occur in situations so different from those in which reinforcement evolved that behavioral measures of selection are insufficient. Such situations are *ecologically invalid*. More fundamental challenges to a behaviorally based principle of selection by reinforcement come from those situations in which there is no orderly relation between the occurrence of selection and the occurrence of an overt elicited response. Findings of this third sort require that the experimental foundation of a principle of reinforcement be expanded to include biological as well as behavioral processes.

Biological constraints on learning. The most commonly cited example of a biological constraint is provided by research on **taste aversion**. In these studies, a novel taste (or smell) was followed by a nonlethal dose of a poison that made the animal nauseated. Even when the poison was given *hours* after the gustatory or olfactory stimulus, the animal avoided future contact with that stimulus. Other stimuli paired with the poisonous elicitor—such as visual or auditory stimuli—did not become part of the selected environment-behavior relation.[60] Such findings pose two problems: (a) why did only some of the environmental stimuli become constituents of the selected relation, and (b) how did behavioral selection operate over such a long time interval between the gustatory stimulus and the elicited nausea response?

The answers to both questions reside in the evolutionary history of the relation between the stimuli accompanying ingestion and the consequences of ingestion. Unlike most other relations between environmental stimuli and elicited responses, the relation between taste and the gastric consequences of ingestion has been relatively constant over evolutionary time. The only route into the stomach is through the mouth, guaranteeing stimulation of gustatory and olfactory receptors. This has provided natural selection with the means needed to produce extensive and intimate neural connections between these sensory systems and the motor neurons involved in ingestion. Presumably, ancestral animals that avoided novel-tasting substances if they had become nauseated after ingesting them had a better chance of surviving, and such neural connections were thereby favored. Except for the tolerance of long temporal intervals and the favoring of gustatory and olfactory stimuli in relations involving nausea responses, taste aversions are affected by the same variables as other acquired environment-behavior relations. Short taste-poisoning intervals facilitate acquisition, one taste can block the acquisition of an aversion to a second taste, and so forth.[61]

Ecologically invalid situations. Although learners must behave for experimental analyses to be conducted at the behavioral level, selection by reinforcement does not require the actual occurrence of overt behavior, but merely the activity of the neural systems that produce it. Under normal circumstances, the activity of these underlying neural motor systems inevitably leads to behavior—otherwise the systems would never have been naturally selected. In the laboratory, however, the relation between motor-system activity and behavior can be surgically or chemically interrupted without eliminating behavioral selection. For example, a classical procedure can be used in which an environmental stimulus is paired with an eliciting stimulus, but the animal is paralyzed by a drug that prevents neural activity from contracting muscle fibers (and consequently blocks overt responding). Nevertheless, when the animal recovers from the drug, it can be shown that this experience has altered environment-behavior relations.[62]

As noted above, although the neural mechanisms of learning were initially naturally selected for their effects on behavior, once selected these mechanisms may serve additional functions. An animal whose muscles are paralyzed is clearly in a very different situation from the one in which its nervous system evolved; in the past, activity in a neural motor system always produced behavior. Nothing in the history of the species could have prepared the nervous system, which is where learning takes place, from distinguishing between neural motor activity and actual movement, since the two always occurred together in the ancestral environment.

Failures of an orderly relation between elicitation and selection. More fundamental questions about the adequacy of a reinforcement principle based only on the analysis of behavior are raised by cases in which eliciting stimuli cannot function as reinforcers, or reinforcers are not eliciting stimuli. Both of these phenomena have been demonstrated experimentally.

If the illumination level in a room is abruptly lowered, the pupils of our eyes will open more widely, or dilate. And yet, a tone paired with this eliciting stimulus will not become a conditioned stimulus in the classical procedure. However, if the pupil is made to dilate by shocking the subject, a tone paired with shock will become a conditioned stimulus that controls pupillary dilation.[63] How are we to understand this result? Both stimuli function as eliciting stimuli, but only one functions as a reinforcer to select an environment-behavior relation.[64] To say that one stimulus is emotion-arousing and the other is not invites circular reasoning. How do we know which stimuli arouse emotions and which do not, other than through the very observations that we seek to explain with the concept of emotion?

Although laboratory studies of this sort indicate that the analysis of some environment-behavior relations cannot be carried out at the behavioral level alone, perhaps the most compelling arguments for expanding the analysis to include the neural level comes from everyday observations of human learning. As the learner acquires an ever more extensive history of behavioral selection, stimuli that elicit few if any overt responses increasingly function as reinforcers. Although a child might receive a piece of candy for its behavior—a stimulus that elicits salivation as surely for the child as for Pavlov's dog—most reinforcing stimuli for adult behavior are not of this character. A pat on the back, a kind word, or merely a smile can be a potent reinforcer—and yet such stimuli do not elicit overt responding to an appreciable degree. In short, conditioned, or acquired, reinforcers provide the most serious challenge to a principle of reinforcement based only on the experimental analysis of behavior. It is conditioned reinforcement, which is increasingly the source of reinforcers for the selection of human behavior, as well as the scientific need to find orderly relations among variables, that drives us to supplement a behavioral

analysis of reinforcement with a physiological analysis.

A *Bio*behavioral Principle of Selection by Reinforcement

The experimental analysis of behavior provides a framework for analysis at the physiological level. That is, analyses at the behavioral level define the boundaries within which the underlying physiological mechanisms must operate. If all of the stimuli and responses in the vicinity of the behavioral discrepancy are candidates for membership in the selected environment-behavior relation, then the neural mechanisms of reinforcement—whatever they may be—must be comprehensive enough to include them. At the same time, the neural mechanisms must narrow down this large group of candidates to those that are most highly correlated with the reinforcing stimulus. To contribute to Darwinian fitness, the biological mechanisms of reinforcement must select the "right" neural pathways—i.e., the ones that are activated by environmental events, and that activate motor systems, that most reliably accompany the reinforcer. What is known of the neural mechanisms of reinforcement? Can they meet the requirements specified by analyses at the behavioral level?

One of the techniques that has been used to answer this question is the electrical stimulation of neurons. In this procedure, an **electrode**—a pair of fine wires insulated from one another except at their tips—is inserted into a brain region. A small current is then passed through the neural tissue at the tip of the wires. The stimulation produced by this current approximates that which occurs naturally when one neuron activates another. It is then possible to observe the effects of electrical stimulation on behavior and on the activity of those neurons with which the stimulated neuron makes synaptic contact.

Using this technique, James Olds and Peter Milner discovered that the electrical stimulation of certain brain areas functioned as a reinforcing stimulus for behavior.[65] Stimulating neurons in a region of the brain known as the **ventral tegmental area (VTA)** was a particularly effective reinforcer. Anatomical research indicates that there are neural cells in the VTA whose axons project (among other regions) to the motor association areas of the frontal lobes.[66] (See **Figure 2.12**.) (Neurons consist of three structures—dendrites, by means of which neurons may be activated by neurotransmitters from other neurons, a cell body, and axons, which release the neurotransmitters that activate other neurons.) In the intact animal, VTA neurons are activated by neurotransmitters released by neurons that are stimulated by biologically important stim-

uli such as the taste and smell of food.[67] The frontal lobes to which (among other areas) the VTA axons project contain many synapses between the axons of neurons coming (ultimately) from sensory and sensory association areas and the dendrites of neurons leading (ultimately) to the motor systems that produce behavior. Because the axons of the VTA neurons terminate near these synapses, they are ideally positioned to modulate the ability of neurons coming from sensory areas to activate neurons going to motor areas. Is there evidence that the activity of VTA neurons has this effect?

The VTA neurons are known to release the neuromodulator **dopamine**, so the question may be

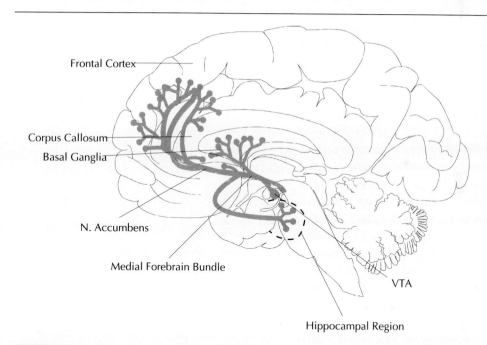

Frontal Cortex

Corpus Callosum

Basal Ganglia

N. Accumbens

Medial Forebrain Bundle

VTA

Hippocampal Region

FIGURE 2.12 *Schematic representation of the relation of axons from the ventral tegmental area (VTA) that diffusely project to various brain areas, notably the motor association cortex of the frontal lobes and subcortical motor nuclei (e.g., nucleus accumbens)*
In the frontal cortex to which VTA axons project, other axons derived ultimately from the sensory and sensory association areas of the brain make synapse upon the dendrites of neurons leading ultimately to behavior. Also shown is a projection from the VTA to the hippocampal region that plays an important role in perceptual learning and is described in later chapters.
Source: Adapted from Creese, I. (1981). Dopamine receptors. In H. I. Yamamura & S. J. Enna (Eds.), *Neurotransmitter receptors: Part 2, Biogenic amines* (pp. 129–183). London: Chapman & Hall Ltd. [Fig. 4-1, p. 132]. See also Hoebel, 1988.

rephrased as follows: Is there evidence that dopamine modulates the ability of one neuron to activate another? Experimental analysis indicates that dopamine does indeed have such an effect. To study the neuromodulatory effect of dopamine, a small piece of neural tissue was isolated from the complex influences that affect neural function in an intact brain. The activity of this tissue was monitored by means of an electrode that recorded from rather than stimulated individual neurons. Under these conditions, the axon of one neuron (the **presynaptic neuron**) occasionally released a neurotransmitter, the excitatory amino acid **glutamate,** and produced several nerve impulses in one of the neurons on which it synapsed (the **postsynaptic neuron**). When small amounts of dopamine were injected into the synapse within 200 msec *after* the postsynaptic neuron had been activated, the recordings showed long-lasting increases in the ability of the presynaptic neuron to activate the postsynaptic neuron.[68] (The experimental arrangement and results are presented in **Figure 2.13**.)

The discovery of a facilitating effect of dopamine on the ability of one neuron to activate another is a crucial finding. It demonstrates that dopamine can modulate the activity produced by glutamate, which is the major excitatory transmitter at synapses in the cerebral cortex, including those in the frontal lobes to which VTA neurons project.[69] The long-lasting effect of dopamine on glutaminergic activity provides a mechanism for altering the effectiveness, or **synaptic efficacy**, with which one neuron activates another.[70] Based on these findings, we propose the following mechanism for reinforcement at the neural level: If a presynaptic neuron activates a postsynaptic neuron and dopamine is released into the synapse immediately thereafter, then the synaptic efficacy between the pre- and postsynaptic neurons will increase.[71] Once this has occurred, glutamate from the presynaptic neuron will more readily activate the postsynaptic neuron whether or not dopamine is present in the synapse.

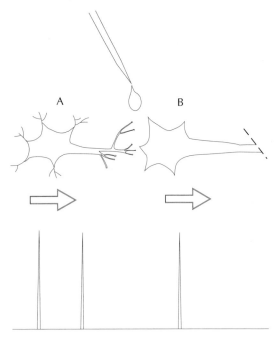

Before Applying Dopamine
Reponse of Cell B to Activity in Cell A

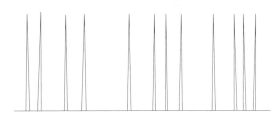

After Several Applications of Dopamine
Response of Cell B to Activity in Cell A

FIGURE 2.13 *In the upper panel, an axon from neuron A makes synaptic contact with a dendrite of neuron B*

A micropipette can inject the neuromodulator, dopamine, into the synaptic space between neurons A and B. Without the application of dopamine, activity in neuron A initiates a small amount of activity (firing) in cell B. When dopamine is injected into the synaptic cleft immediately *after* neuron B has been activated by neuron A, the response of cell B is increased.

Source: Procedure and hypothetical findings from Stein & Belluzi, 1988.

Simulations of the neural mechanisms of reinforcement. Can the proposed neural mechanisms of reinforcement accommodate the environment-behavior relations selected by the classical and operant procedures? There are too many neurons involved in most instances of learning to permit experimental analysis of the activity of all the participating neurons. To answer this question, therefore, requires some means of scientific interpretation of these complex events. As one method of interpretation, we shall use **computer simulation.** A biobehavioral simulation uses a computer program whose instructions are informed by principles derived from experimental analyses of behavior and physiology. Through its operation, the program implements these principles and produces an output that is meant to reproduce the behavior of a living organism under the simulated conditions.[72] Let us see whether computer simulations of the selection of environment-behavior relations produce outputs that correspond to the behavioral findings.

Two identical small networks of neuronal units are shown in **Figure 2.14**. The open circles are units representing neurons (or groups of neurons) in the network; the solid lines are pathways between the units, with the width of the line indicating the strength of the connection. A broken line indicates an experimental contingency, not a connection between units. (Any network of neurons

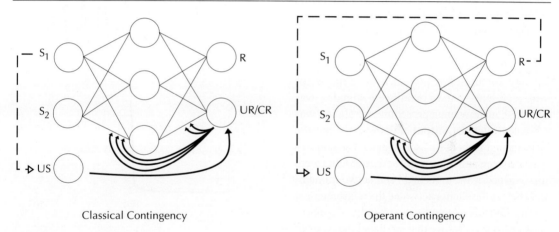

FIGURE 2.14 *Simple adaptive neural networks simulating the effects of the classical (left panel) and operant (right panel) procedures*
Units within the networks are indicated by circles; the connections between units are indicated by solid lines. The broken lines denote the environmentally mediated contingencies that define the two procedures. The input units are to the left, the interior (hidden) units are in the middle "layer," and the output units are to the right. The curved lines projecting from the UR/CR unit to the interior and output units simulate the diffusely projecting reinforcement system arising from the ventral tegmental area (VTA). When the US unit activates the UR/CR unit, the diffuse reinforcement system is activated. The lines indicating the pathways between the US and UR/CR units are heavier to indicate that the connections between these units are strong from the outset of training. In the classical procedure, after the simulation program activates the S₁ unit, the US unit is activated by the program. In the operant procedure, if the R unit is activated as a result of the program activating the S₁ unit, then the US unit is activated by the program. The R unit is activated if activation of the S₁ unit leads, at first by chance, to the propagation of activity to interior units and ultimately to the R output unit. The initial activation of the R unit represents the baseline level (or operant level) of the R unit. Note that the network and reinforcement systems are the same for both procedures; only the contingencies by which the US unit is activated differ between the two procedures.

mediating environment-behavior relations in intact animals would, of course, involve many more neurons than the small number of units used in these simulations.)

In the first network, a classical procedure is implemented; the broken line indicates that the presentation of the eliciting stimulus, or reinforcer, is contingent upon an environmental stimulus. The second network is the same as the first one, but the presentation of the reinforcer is contingent upon a response, as in an operant procedure. In both networks, the presentation of the reinforcer not only produces an elicited response but also activates a neural system that projects to each of the synapses within the network. This diffusely projecting reinforcement system simulates the dopaminergic system that projects from the VTA to the many glutaminergic synapses between neurons in the motor association cortex of the frontal lobes.

The computer simulations begin with only weak synaptic efficacies, or connections, between units in the network. In the classical procedure, the eliciting stimulus was presented after the **input unit** representing the conditioned stimulus was activated; in the operant procedure, the elicitor was presented after the **output unit** representing the instrumental response was activated. The connections between simultaneously activated units were strengthened if the units had been active immediately before the elicitor activated the reinforcement system. Did this selective strengthening of connections result in pathways that mediated the types of environment-behavior relations selected in classical and operant procedures?

The results of simulations with each procedure are given in **Figure 2.15**. The upper panel shows the results for a classical procedure, and depicts the change in activation level of the output unit corresponding to the conditioned response. The strength of activation may be interpreted as the frequency of nerve impulses in the motor neurons underlying the conditioned response. As you can see, the neural network acquired the ability to mediate the relation between the conditioned stimulus and conditioned response.

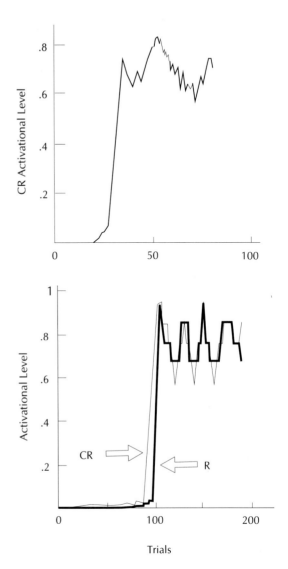

FIGURE 2.15   *The results of simulating the acquisition of environment-behavior relations with a classical procedure (upper panel) and an operant procedure (lower panel)*

For the classical procedure, changes in the activation level of the UR/CR output unit (conditioned response) by activation of the S_1 input unit are shown. For the operant procedure, changes in the activation levels of both the UR/CR and R (operant) output units by activation of the S_1 unit are shown. The activation level of an output unit indicates the strength of the simulated response, and varies from 0.0 to a maximum of 1.0.

Source: After Donahoe, Burgos, & Palmer, 1993.

The lower panel of **Figure 2.15** shows the change in activation of two output units—one representing the operant and the other the conditioned response. Consistent with behavioral observations, the simulation of the neural mechanisms of reinforcement resulted in the acquisition of both responses. That is, the pathways activated by the input unit representing the environmental stimulus mediated an environment-behavior relation that included both the operant and the conditioned response. Note that the conditioned response was acquired *before* the operant response. This is a general result in our simulations of selection by reinforcement, and occurs because the elicited response is more strongly and more recently activated by the eliciting stimulus than the operant response is activated by whatever environmental stimuli guide its occurrence at the outset of training. Increases in connection strength are greatest between units that are *strongly* coactivated; therefore, the diffuse reinforcement system initially produces greater increases along pathways mediating the environment-conditioned response relation than along those mediating the environment-operant response relation. This finding will become important in the interpretation of a number of complex phenomena in later chapters. (See **Figure 2.16** for an illustration of the changes in connection strength that occur during the simulated acquisition of environment-behavior relations in an operant procedure.) Further simulation research not described here has demonstrated that these same biobehavioral principles yield blocking, as well as other conditioning phenomena.[73]

CONCLUDING COMMENTS

Let us review the major findings and conclusions of this chapter. The learner starts the journey toward behavioral complexity with the variations in environment-behavior relations produced by natural selection and by the action of a varying environment on the organism. For some of these early environment-behavior relations, an eliciting stimulus can be identified that reliably evokes a response. These relations are called respondents. For other relations, no specific stimulus can be identified and, moreover, the initiating stimuli for the response differ from time to time. Environment-behavior relations toward this end of the continuum are called operants.

As a result of natural selection, most eliciting stimuli can function as reinforcers. That is, when an eliciting stimulus occurs and evokes a response that would not otherwise occur at that moment, whatever stimuli are present immediately before the elicitor come to guide whatever responses were occurring immediately before or at the same time as the elicited response. An "unexpected" response is said to produce a behavioral discrepancy. In the classical procedure, the experimental arrangement insures that a specified stimulus (the conditioned stimulus) is present before the behavioral discrepancy. Consequently, the environment-behavior relation selected by the classical procedure includes that stimulus and the elicited response, since both are reliably present in the vicinity of the behavioral discrepancy. In the operant procedure, the experimental arrangement insures that another response, the operant, will also occur in the vicinity of the discrepancy. Thus, whatever stimuli were present before the operant will come to guide not only the elicited response but the operant as well. The constituents of the environment-behavior relation selected in the operant procedure depend on interactions, if any, between the stimuli and responses that are candidates for membership in the relation because of their temporal proximity to the behavioral discrepancy.

Although most experimental and applied situations can be interpreted by means of a behaviorally based principle of selection by reinforcement, there are exceptions. Not all eliciting stimuli function as reinforcers; not all reinforcing stimuli elicit behavior. Because orderly functional relations do not emerge in all situations if observations are confined to the behavioral level, the biological mechanisms underlying reinforcement were explored. As a result of experimental analyses at the physiological level, it was proposed that reinforc-

Operant Contingency

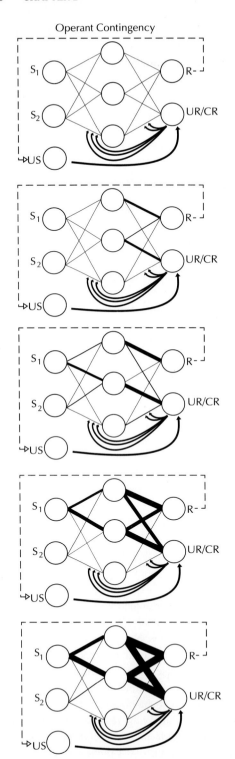

FIGURE 2.16 *Changes in the strength of connections between units in an adaptive neural network during the simulation of acquisition with an operant procedure*

The heavier the line connecting two units, the greater the connection strength between those units.

(1) The initial state of the network with lighter lines (low connection strengths) between all units except the connection between the US and UR/CR units. This connection is strong to represent the elicitation of the UR by the US, which occurs from the outset of training. When the S_1 unit is activated by the simulation program, there is only a small probability that activity will propagate through the network and activate any of the output units.

(2) After several conditioning trials on some of which the R (operant) unit was, by chance, weakly activated, the connection between the central interior unit and the UR/CR unit has become stronger. Such connections grow stronger more quickly because (a) they lead to the strongly activated UR/CR unit and (b) they are active immediately before the UR/CR unit and, hence, their activity has not had time to decay appreciably.

(3) After additional training, the connection from the S_1 to the central interior unit has now grown stronger. This makes it more likely that when the S_1 unit is activated the UR/CR unit will be activated; i.e., a conditioned response will occur. The connection strength between the central interior unit and the R unit has also increased, making it more likely that S_1 will also activate the R unit.

(4) With continued training, the connection from S_1 to the central unit has grown stronger as well as connections along pathways leading from the S_1 unit to the R unit. At this stage of training, S_1 strongly activates the UR/CR unit and weakly activates the R unit. Thus the conditioned response is being acquired more rapidly than the operant. The connections leading to R strengthen less rapidly because S_1 does not initially strongly activate the R unit, whereas US does strongly activate the UR/CR unit from the very outset of training.

(5) At the end of training, connections within the network have been strengthened to the point that S_1 strongly activates both the UR/CR unit (the conditioned response) and the R unit (the operant).

ing stimuli activate a dopaminergic system that diffusely projects to the motor association areas of the frontal lobes. There, dopamine acts as a neuro-modulator to increase the synaptic efficacies between neurons that are simultaneously active. The cumulative effect of this process is that sensory input is increasingly able to guide those motor systems that are reliably active when reinforcing stimuli are presented. Computer simulations informed by these biobehavioral principles were able to reproduce the environment-behavior relations selected by both the classical and operant procedures, using a single, unified principle of selection by reinforcement. The products of selection are always changes in the strengths of environment-behavior relations, whether the constituent stimuli are well specified as in the classical procedure or incompletely characterized as in simple operant procedures. It is these relations that increasingly make up the variation available for subsequent selection and that cumulatively lead to complex behavior.

STUDY AIDS

Technical Terms

Review the text and consult the glossary if terms are not familiar. Terms are listed in the order in which they appear in the text.

principle of behavioral selection (or principle
    of reinforcement)
eliciting stimulus (or elicitor)
eliciting function
motivating function
motivating stimulus (or motivator)
reflex
respondent
operant
deprivation
sensitization
habituation
reinforcing stimulus (or reinforcer)
classical (or respondent) procedure
instrumental (or operant) conditioning

model preparation
temporal contiguity
conditioned stimulus
unconditioned stimulus
conditioned response
unconditioned response
synapse
contingency
conditioned (or acquired) reinforcer
superstitious behavior
compound stimulus
behavioral discrepancy
blocking
unified principle of reinforcement
biological constraints on learning
taste aversion
electrode
ventral tegmental area (VTA)
dopamine
presynaptic neuron
glutamate
postsynaptic neuron
synaptic efficacy
computer simulation
input and output units

Text Questions

1. Stimuli function in two ways that have important effects on variation—as elicitors and as motivators, of which sensitization is one example. Be able to define and give an example of your own construction for each function.

2. What is the distinction between respondents and operants; i.e., how are they alike and how are they different? Give an example that illustrates each environment-behavior relation.

3. Discuss the relation between natural selection and selection by reinforcement. Indicate how natural selection contributes to selection by reinforcement. Indicate how selection by reinforcement contributes to natural selection; support your answer with experimental evidence indicating that

the ability to learn may contribute to reproductive fitness.

4. Indicate the major differences and similarities between the classical (respondent) and instrumental (operant) conditioning procedures. Describe experiments, using appropriate technical terms, that illustrate each procedure. Be able to give examples from daily life that illustrate each procedure.

5. Three interrelated conditions are required for selection by reinforcement: (a) temporal contiguity between the environment and the behavior to be guided, (b) temporal contiguity between the behavior and the eliciting stimulus, and (c) the production by the eliciting stimulus of a behavioral discrepancy. Describe each of these three conditions, citing experimental evidence to support its importance.

6. Changes in environment-behavior relations in experienced learners often appear not to be dependent on close temporal relations with reinforcers. Also, an eliciting stimulus may not function as a reinforcer in experienced learners. Interpret these apparent inconsistencies with the claimed crucial role of temporal contiguity and behavioral discrepancy. Cite evidence from studies of conditioned (acquired) reinforcement, and blocking to support your answer.

7. State the principle of reinforcement described in the text, and indicate its application to both classical and operant conditioning procedures. Indicate with examples how interactions among responses and biological constraints may affect the net outcome of the selection process.

8. Describe the neuroanatomical structures and cellular mechanisms that appear to implement the behaviorally based principle of reinforcement at the neural level. Indicate how, over time, neural connections mediating "appropriate" environment-behavior relations are strengthened by reinforcers.

9. Describe the major features of neural-network simulations and indicate how they can be used to interpret the reinforcement process. Employing technical terms, e.g., input and output units, can the

environment-behavior relations selected by classical and operant procedures be interpreted by the same behavioral and neural accounts of reinforcement?

Discussion Questions

10. The principle of natural selection is to the evolution of species as the principle of b_____ s_____, or r_____, is to the acquisition of complex behavior. Comment on the aptness and potential significance of this analogy.

11. What does it mean to say that selection is for the behavioral phenotype and not the biological phenotype?

ENDNOTES

1. Bowler, 1983.
2. Bowler, 1983, p. 46; Lehrman, 1970.
3. For a discussion of the importance of variation in Skinner's analysis of behavior, see Richelle, 1986.
4. Smith, 1978.
5. Clifton, Siqueland, & Lipsitt, 1972.
6. In nonhumans, more complex environment-behavior relations that are the result of natural selection have been identified, and they are known as *fixed-action patterns*. The best known of these is *imprinting*, whereby an attachment develops between parent and offspring. Whether fixed-action patterns occur in humans is a matter of dispute, but some have suggested similarities between aspects of "bonding" between parent and child and imprinting in other animals (Bowlby, 1969).
7. Skinner, 1938.
8. Lipsitt, 1987.
9. Donahoe & Wessells, 1980, pp. 222 ff.
10. Miller, 1959; see Donahoe & Wessells, 1980 for a more complete discussion of the motivational function of stimuli.
11. Groves & Thompson, 1970.
12. See Davis, 1970 for research exposing some of the variables that affect the retention of a habituated response.
13. When stimuli evoke specific responses as the result of behavioral selection, they are technically known as *conditioned* or *discriminative* stimuli, depending on whether classical or operant procedures were used to

produce the effect. When behavioral selection causes stimuli to change the probability of a range of responses, these stimuli are said to function as generalization stimuli, occasion-setting stimuli, or incentive stimuli, depending on the procedures used to assess the function and on the theoretical predilections of the researcher.

14.   e.g., Itzkoff, 1983, p. 54. See also Hinton & Nowlan, 1986.

15.   Hollis, 1984.

16.   Gould & Gould, 1981; Morgan, 1894; Williams, 1966.

17.   Little, 1970; described in Rovee-Collier & Lipsitt, 1983. For a summary of examples of learning of the fetus in the uterus, Kolata, 1984.

18.   Rovee & Rovee, 1969; Rovee-Collier, Morrongiello, Aron, & Kuperschmidt, 1978.

19.   e.g., Johanson & Hall, 1979.

20.   Moran, Lew, & Blass, 1981.

21.   Jones, 1962.

22.   Gormezano, Kehoe, & Marshall, 1983.

23.   Smith, 1968.

24.   For a critical review of the role of temporal contiguity in the classical procedure, see Gormezano & Kehoe, 1981. Another temporal variable affecting selection is the interval between the occurrence of conditioning trials. In general, the longer the interval between training trials, the faster selection proceeds per trial; e.g., Levinthal, Tartell, Margolin, & Fishman, 1985.

25.   In well controlled classical procedures for studying the selection of environment-behavior relations, the conditioned and unconditioned responses are highly similar. In preparations where other processes intrude, these two responses may appear to be different. Most differences arise from incomplete identification of the true unconditioned stimulus and response. As an example, consider an experiment in which a conditioned stimulus of a pinprick (produced by an injection with a hypodermic needle) is paired with the apparent unconditioned stimulus of the introduction of an opiate into the bloodstream. The opiate has the effect of making the animal less sensitive to painful stimuli (i.e., the opiate has an analgesic effect). However, after the animal has been given a number of pinprick-opiate pairings, when it is then given a pinprick that is not followed by the opiate, the animal is now *more* sensitive to pain, not less. Here, the apparent unconditioned response is a decrease in pain sensitivity while the conditioned response is an increase in sensitivity—seemingly opposite responses. However, the experimenter has mistakenly identified the unconditioned effect of the opiate. When an opiate is injected, it acts peripherally to reduce pain sensations. However, when the increased concentration of the injected opiate (exogenous opiate) is detected by the neurons that normally produce natural opiates (endogenous opiates), the production of endogenous opiates is decreased. The detection of the exogenous opiates by the nervous system is the true unconditioned stimulus and the reduced production of endogenous opiates is the true unconditioned response. These are the events mediated by the nervous system, and the nervous system is the locus of learning and must participate when learning occurs. When the pinprick is given without the exogenous opiate, the production of endogenous opiates by the nervous system is decreased causing pain sensitivity to *increase*. Thus, when the unconditioned response to an increase in circulating opiates is correctly identified, the unconditioned and conditioned responses are once again highly similar as in the rabbit nictitating-membrane preparation; Eickelboom & Stewart, 1982; cf. Siegel, 1977, 1983; Solomon & Corbitt, 1974. In general, when care is taken in identifying the stimuli actually detected and the responses actually mediated by the nervous system, the apparent differences between the conditioned and unconditioned responses disappear.

26.   Strictly speaking, the movement of the nictitating membrane in the rabbit is the indirect result of contracting the fibers in the retractor-bulbi muscle, which withdraws the eyeball further into its socket; Gormezano, Schneiderman, Deaux, & Fuentes, 1962.

27.   Cegarvske, Thompson, Patterson, & Gormezano, 1976; Disterhoft, Quinn, Weiss, & Shipley, 1985.

28.   Although there are differences among learning theories regarding the specifics of an account of learning in operant procedures, there is no disagreement concerning the importance of such learning in generating complex behavior. Consider the following comments by Daniel Dennett, a philosopher of science who has provided some of the more trenchant criticisms of Skinner's analysis of operant behavior: ". . . the Law of Effect . . . is . . . a part of . . . *any* (sic) possible adequate explanation of behavior" (p. 72); "*cognitive* (sic) psychology . . . (is) . . . bound ultimately to versions of the Law of Effect" (p. 80); Dennett, 1986. (As already noted, the defining feature of an operant procedure is that some response is followed by—i.e., has the *effect* of producing—the reinforcing stimulus. Because the emphasis is on the *effect* of the response, the principle describing how such learning takes place has often been referred to as the *Law of Effect;* Thorndike, 1932. See Coleman & Gormezano,

1979 for a critical review of the Law of Effect in relation to classical conditioning.)

29. For a review, see Donahoe and Wessells, 1980, pp. 128–132.

30. Grice, 1948.

31. e.g., Konorski, 1948; Miller & DeBold, 1965; Shapiro, 1960; Shapiro & Miller, 1965; Sheffield, 1965.

32. Kintsch & Witte, 1962.

33. Logan, 1965.

34. cf. Grosch & Neuringer, 1981.

35. This view will be recognized as equivalent to the analysis of causation by John Locke in his *Essays concerning human understanding*.

36. Skinner, 1948.

37. Zeiler, 1972.

38. Koichi, 1987. Understanding some of the effects of response-independent presentations of an eliciting stimulus requires consideration of processes in addition to the selection of environment-behavior relations on the basis of temporal contiguity with an eliciting stimulus, e.g., Staddon & Simmelhag, 1971; Staddon & Zhang, 1993; Timberlake & Lucas, 1985, 1989. It is clear, however, that temporal contiguity is one of the primary factors producing superstitious behavior; e.g., Pear, 1985, where it has most often been studied in connection with the *autoshaping procedure*, cf. Skinner, 1948.

39. Kamin, 1968, 1969.

40. In these first experiments, shock-elicited responses were not measured directly. Instead, a technique was used in which a different response was directly measured—leverpressing for food—and conditioning was indexed by the extent to which conditioned shock-elicited responses interfered with leverpressing. This technique was devised by Estes & Skinner (1941) and is known as the *conditioned suppression technique*, and the competing responses are called *conditioned emotional responses*. Although an indirect measure of conditioning is subject to methodological complications (cf. Coleman & Gormezano, 1979; Donahoe & Wessells, 1980), it has proven to be an extremely sensitive technique for studying learning with the classical procedure (cf. Rescorla & Solomon, 1967). Later work using more direct measures of conditioning, such as the nictitating-membrane procedure (Marchant & Moore, 1973), has confirmed the findings of the initial experiments by Kamin.

41. See Rescorla, 1968 for a similar interpretation of this type of experiment.

42. e.g., Donahoe, Crowley, Millard, & Stickney, 1982; cf. Rescorla, 1968.

43. e.g., Rescorla & Wagner, 1972. Consistent with the view that blocking is a ubiquitous and basic outcome of behavioral selection, the phenomenon has even been demonstrated in invertebrates; e.g., Sahley, Rudy, & Gelperin, 1981.

44. e.g., vom Saal & Jenkins, 1970.

45. For example, to eliminate the possibility that two stimuli cannot simultaneously acquire the capacity to evoke the same response, subjects in a control group received a compound stimulus paired with the eliciting stimulus from the outset of conditioning. When tested separately, both stimuli were able to evoke conditioned responses (e.g., Kamin, 1969). As another example, to control for the additional conditioning trials that subjects in the blocking group are given before compound conditioning, subjects received training with a third stimulus prior to the compound conditioning phase of the experiment. These control subjects also responded to both elements of the compound stimulus when the components were presented separately (e.g., Leyland & Mackintosh, 1978). Other studies have implicated additional processes in the occurrence of blocking (e.g., Mackintosh, 1975; Pearce & Hall, 1980), but these studies do not deny the role of discrepancy as described here. Still other studies have indicated that blocking may be affected by the environmental context present during conditioning as well as by the nominal discriminative stimuli themselves (e.g., Balaz, Gutsin, Cacheiro, & Miller, 1982; see also Miller & Matzel, 1988; Miller & Schachtman, 1985, c.f. Balsam, 1984). These findings are not necessarily inconsistent with the interpretation of blocking given later in this chapter in which selection by reinforcement is simulated with adaptive neural networks.

46. e.g., Bobrow & Norman, 1975; Bower, 1975; Rudy, 1974; Rumelhart & McClelland, 1986; see also Wagner, Mazur, Donegan, & Pfautz, 1980.

47. Bower, 1970, p. 70.

48. Stickney & Donahoe, 1983; cf. Pearce, Montgomery, & Dickinson, 1982.

49. For reviews of phenomena other than blocking that demonstrate that the ability of an eliciting stimulus to function as a reinforcer depends on the history of the learner, see Colwill & Rescorla, 1986; Rescorla, 1991. Some of these phenomena are subsequently treated in Chapter 4.

50. The metaphor of an organism immersed in a "behavioral stream" is William Schoenfeld's; e.g., Schoenfeld & Farmer, 1970.

51. Donahoe, Crowley, Millard, & Stickney, 1982.

52. Although Skinner's treatment of respondent and operant conditioning emphasized the differences between the two procedures and their outcomes, the present treatment is consistent with his emphasis on the ubiquity of what he called the "three-term contingency" (Skinner, 1938, 1953, 1981). That is, the reinforcement process always involves three elements—a stimulus, a response, and a reinforcer. There is nothing in a unified treatment of classical and operant conditioning that minimizes the crucially important differences between the *outcomes* of the two procedures for the interpretation of complex behavior. However, the unified principle does deeply question the view that classical and operant procedures produce two different "kinds" of learning or require fundamantally different theoretical treatments. Both procedures select environment-behavior relations but, because of the differences in the events that reliably occur in the vicinity of the behavioral discrepancy, the constituents of the selected relations are different. See Palmer & Donahoe (1993) for a discussion of the philosophical issues of essentialism and selectionism that lie behind the conventional version of the operant-respondent distinction, as well as a number of other conceptions in behavioral and cognitive science. See Coleman (1981, 1984) for a historical analysis of the origins of the operant-respondent distinction in Skinner's thinking.

53. Morse & Skinner, 1957. See also Herrnstein, 1966.

54. cf. Domjan, 1983, p. 264; Shettleworth & Juergensen, 1980.

55. Grant, 1972.

56. Sheffield, 1965.

57. For a similar example of interference, see Williams & Williams, 1969.

58. Miller & Carmona, 1967.

59. See Skinner, 1935, 1938 for discussions of the relation between the level of analysis and the discovery of orderly relations; cf. Palmer & Donahoe, 1993.

60. e.g., Garcia, Erwin & Koelling, 1966; Revusky & Garcia, 1970; Rozin & Kalat, 1971.

61. For reviews, see Barker, Best & Domjan, 1977; Domjan, 1980. The finding that close temporal contiguity was not necessary for acquiring taste aversions was initially taken by some as evidence that there are no general learning processes common to many learning situations and species (Seligman, 1970; Shettleworth, 1983). The view now more often held—and endorsed here—is that there are common learning processes, but that the outcome of these processes depends partly on the specific environmental and behavioral events in the learning situation and the learner's evolutionary and learning history with respect to those events (Domjan & Galef, 1983). For discussions of the special neural substrate of taste aversions, see Ashe & Nachman, 1980; Kucharski, Burka, & Hall, 1990.

62. e.g., Solomon & Turner, 1962.

63. e.g., Gerall & Obrist, 1962.

64. See Donahoe & Wessells, 1980, p. 144 for related findings.

65. Olds & Milner, 1954. It is of some interest to the history of science that this important discovery—as is not uncommon—was made while the investigators were looking for something else altogether. See Glickman & Schiff, 1967; Trowill, Panksepp, & Gandelman, 1969; Valenstein, Cox, & Kakolewski, 1969; Wise, 1989; and Wise & Bozarth, 1987 for reviews of research on reinforcing brain stimulation that are particularly relevant to behavioral treatments of reinforcement.

66. Fallon & Laughlin, 1987; Swanson, 1982. See also Parnavelas & Papadopoulos, 1989.

67. e.g., Hernandez & Hoebel, 1990. See Hoebel, 1988 for a review of the relevant literature. There are other inputs to VTA neurons from brain areas related to arousal, and that may contribute to sensitization rather than reinforcement; cf. Guan & McBride, 1989. The cellular mechanisms of arousal and reinforcement have been found to overlap considerably in invertebrate research on neural plasticity; e.g., Kandel, 1976.

68. Stein & Belluzzi, 1988, 1989.

69. The discussion of the neural mechanisms of reinforcement presented here focuses on the modification of synaptic efficacies in the motor association areas of the frontal lobes. These same dopaminergic neuromodulatory mechanisms operate in other "motor" areas, notably subcortical nuclei, with the nucleus accumbens being the most thoroughly studied, e.g., Hoebel, 1988; Imperato, Honore, & Jensen, 1990. The cellular mechanisms of plasticity have been more extensively investigated in invertebrates such as *Aplysia,* e.g., Carew, Abrams, Hawkins, & Kandel, 1984; Kandel, 1976; Gingrich & Byrne, 1987; Hawkins, Carew, & Kandel, 1986, and *Hermissenda*, Alkon, 1980, 1984, 1988. In mammals, the specific neural circuits that are modified by reinforcement have been most extensively investigated in the midbrain and cerebellum; e.g., Ito, 1984; Thompson, 1986, 1990; Thompson, McCormack, & Lavond, 1991. The selection of environment-behavior relations in these evolutionarily older organisms and structures also involves neuromodulatory mechanisms; e.g., Billy & Walters, 1989; Gimpl, Gormezano, & Harvey, 1979;

Marshall-Goodell & Gormezano, 1991. We have chosen to describe reinforcement circuits in the mammalian cerebral cortex because of the special relevance of this structure to complex behavior. In later chapters, the modification of synaptic efficacies in the sensory association areas will be considered and related to the mechanisms described here.

70.   A detailed review of the cellular mechanisms that produce long-lasting changes in synaptic efficacies is beyond the scope of this book. Nonetheless, a general overview is in order to provide a sense of what is rapidly becoming known in this extremely active area of research.

The amino-acid glutamate is the primary excitatory neurotransmitter in the cerebral cortex and basal ganglia. Glutamate is liberated by presynaptic neurons and acts upon several subclasses of receptors located in the membranes of postsynaptic neurons. For present purposes, it is important to distinguish between two subclasses of glutamate receptors. The first subclass enables glutamate to rapidly activate the postsynaptic neuron. This subclass of receptors mediates most excitatory transmission within the cortex, and is known as the non-NMDA receptor. The second subclass is critical for producing long lasting changes in the efficacy of transmission by non-NMDA receptors. The second subclass, the NMDA receptor, acts more slowly because its operation requires partial depolarization of the postsynaptic neuron. (NMDA is the acronym for N-methyl-D-aspartate, a compound that selectively activates the NMDA as opposed to the non-NMDA receptor.) When glutamate from a presynaptic neuron activates non-NMDA receptors sufficiently to depolarize the postsynaptic neuron, magnesium ions (Mg^{2+}) migrate out of the NMDA ion channel. (Many receptors control the operation of a small opening—a channel—in the cell membrane through which ions may migrate.) When the NMDA ion channel is "unblocked," calcium ions (Ca^{2+}) migrate into the postsynaptic neuron and initiate a cascade of reactions that are necessary to produce long lasting increases in the sensitivity of non-NMDA glutamate receptors. (The chain of intracellular reactions consists of what are known as second messengers to distinguish them from first messengers—neurotransmitters—that act intercellularly.)

Although activation of the NMDA receptor by glutamate is necessary to produce long lasting changes in synaptic efficacies, it is not sufficient. Long lasting changes require, in addition to glutamate, the concurrent activation of dopamine receptors on the postsynaptic neuron (Frey, Huang, & Kandel, 1993; Stein & Belluzzi, 1988, 1989). In the motor association areas of the frontal cortex, the sources of dopamine are neurons from the VTA that, because of their widespread projections, permit synaptic efficacies to be simultaneously modified throughout the frontal cortex and basal ganglia (Beninger, 1983; Donahoe, Burgos, & Palmer, 1993; Hoebel, 1988). Activation of one subclass of dopamine receptors (D1 receptors) leads to a cascade of second messengers that, together with the second messengers resulting from the action of the NMDA receptor, cause enduring structural changes in non-NMDA receptors. (In brief, activation of D1 receptors stimulates adenylyl cyclase which catalyzes the production of cyclic adenosine-monophosphate—cAMP—which, in turn, activates a Ca-dependent protein kinase that causes protein synthesis leading to enduring structural changes in non-NMDA receptors. These structural changes enable a given amount of glutamate to activate non-NMDA receptors more frequently and for longer durations (Wang, Salter, & MacDonald, 1991). In summary, as a result of the concurrent activation of NMDA receptors by glutamate and D1 receptors by dopamine, long lasting changes occur that permit non-NMDA receptors on the postsynaptic neuron to be more sensitive to glutamate liberated from the presynaptic neuron. In our view, this sequence of intracellular and receptor events provides the best present account of the neural basis of learning. Much more remains to be done, of course (cf. Bading & Greenberg, 1991; Constantine-Paton, Cline, & Debski, 1990; Cotman & Monaghan, 1988; Novak, Bregestovski, Ascher, Herbert, & Prochiantz, 1984; Salamone, 1991; Wang, Salter, & MacDonald, 1991; cf. Marder, 1991; Maricq, Peterson, Brake, Myers, & Julius, 1991; Rudy & Keith, 1990).

The cumulative effect of these changes in synaptic efficacy is that presynaptic neurons compete with one another for control over the firing of postsynaptic neurons; cf. Changeux, Heidman, & Pattle, 1984; Edelman, 1988. It is of no small interest that the NMDA receptor is also involved in synaptic changes that occur during neural development; e.g., Rabacchi, Bailly, Delhaye-Bouchaud, & Mariani, 1992. The cellular mechanisms of learning appear to have exploited pre-existing mechanisms involved in neural development. In a fundamental sense, selection by reinforcement is the continuation of neural development into the postnatal period.

Experimentally, high-frequency electrical stimulation of the postsynaptic neuron has been demonstrated to activate the NMDA receptor through depolarizing the postsynaptic neuron sufficiently to remove the Mg^{2+} "block" from the NMDA channel; Collingridge & Bliss, 1987. Changes produced in this manner have been extensively studied under the heading of long-term potentiation (Bliss & Lomo, 1973; Desmond & Levy, 1983; Iriki, Pavlides, Keller, & Asanuma, 1989; Kelso & Brown, 1986; Levy, 1985; Levy & Steward, 1979, Madison, Malenka, & Nicoll, 1991). The potential power of cellular mechanisms sensitive to coactivity in pre- and postsynaptic neurons was explicitly appreciated by Donald Hebb, 1949.

71. Beninger, 1983; Donahoe & Palmer, 1989; Donahoe, Burgos, & Palmer, 1993; Hoebel, 1988; Kety, 1970. On the neural level, implementation of a discrepancy theory requires decreases over time in the amount of neuromodulator that the reinforcer causes to be liberated and/or in the efficacy of the neuromodulator. The specific mechanisms that produce these forms of negative feedback have not been identified, although a number of plausible possibilities exist. As examples, there are limits on the rate of biosynthesis and transport of monoamines within the cell, there are inhibitory autoreceptors associated with some monoaminergic neurons (cf. Brennan, Kaba, & Keverne, 1990), and there are recurrent circuits from the prefrontal cortex to VTA that could decrease the firing of VTA neurons through overlap in the arrival times of their activity with the refractory periods of VTA neurons driven by otherwise reinforcing inputs (cf. Shizgal, Bielajew, & Rompre, 1988; cf. Deadwyler, West, & Robinson, 1981). On the behavioral level, evidence also exists for a diminution in the eliciting effects of the reinforcer following the acquisition of conditioned responses. As examples, the magnitude of the unconditioned eyelid response in the rabbit declines as the conditioned eyelid response is acquired (Donegan & Wagner, 1983), and the sniffing response elicited by reinforcing brain stimulation in the rat declines as conditioned sniffing is acquired (Clarke & Trowill, 1971). Thus the behavioral discrepancy produced by the unconditioned stimulus diminishes as acquisition progresses.

72. Donahoe & Palmer, 1989. For examples of simulating the effect of selection by reinforcement in simpler neural circuits, see Gluck & Thompson, 1987; Klopf, 1982; Sutton & Barto, 1981 among others. For discussions of general issues related to neural-network interpretation of behavior, see Hinton & Anderson, 1981; Gluck, in press; Grossberg, 1982; McClelland & Rumelhart, 1986.

73. Donahoe, Burgos, & Palmer, 1993. The method used here to change the strength of connections between units is an example of what is called *supervised* learning in the adaptive-network literature. Learning is "supervised" in the sense that changes in connection strengths depend upon feedback from the environment. This is in contrast to *unsupervised* learning in which changes in connection strengths depend only upon events within the network. The present method also exemplifies a particular subtype of supervised learning known as reinforcement learning. In reinforcement learning, feedback takes the form of a single quantity—the reinforcer—whose strength depends upon the overall performance of the network (e.g., Sutton & Barto, 1981; Widrow & Hoff, 1960). Reinforcement learning differs from other forms of supervised learning that use multiple feedback signals, e.g., a separate signal for each output unit of the network (Rumelhart, Hinton, & Williams, 1986; Werbos, 1974). These separate feedback signals may be likened to a "teacher" who provides detailed information about every aspect of the learner's performance. In contrast, reinforcement learning may be likened to a "teacher" who evaluates performance globally. The present instance of reinforcement learning also differs from other approaches in that it is constrained by what is known about the biological systems implementing reinforcement in living organisms. The simulation of a diffusely projecting system for implementing reinforcement simultaneously throughout the network addresses what has been called the *binding problem*, i.e., the need to coordinate changes in synaptic efficacies throughout the cerebral cortex (Sejnowski, 1986). Other approaches are more often guided by mathematical considerations or by analogies to physical systems. Theorists disagree about the need for simulation research to be guided by information at the neural level (e.g., Smolensky, 1988); however, to qualify as scientific interpretation in the biobehavioral approach such information is essential.

CHAPTER 3

ENVIRONMENTAL GUIDANCE
OF BEHAVIOR

INTRODUCTION

The outcome of selection by reinforcement is a change in the environmental guidance of behavior. That is, what is selected is always an environment-behavior relation, never a response alone. As studied with the classical procedure, the stimulus components of the selected relation are quite clear, since—by definition—a specific environmental event precedes the elicitor that functions as a reinforcer. For example, the tone that precedes the airpuff to the eye of the rabbit, and thereafter evokes the nictitating membrane response, is clearly part of the selected relation. However, the behavior that is guided by the environment as the result of a classical procedure is restricted to responses that are already evoked by eliciting stimuli, i.e., reflexive responses in the simplest cases. Clearly, reflexive responses alone cannot be the stuff of which complex behavior is made.

The operant procedure, in which the eliciting stimulus is contingent on an arbitrary response, does have the potential to select complex behavior. Because the response is arbitrary, any response or combination of responses is a candidate for inclusion in the selected environment-behavior relation.[1] For example, a rat might receive food for pressing a lever with either its left or right forepaw, for pulling a chain, for running a maze, or for any other responses within its capabilities. Thus operant contingencies have the potential to incorporate into environment-behavior relations the full behavioral repertoire of the learner. However, in the simple operant procedures we have examined so far, the environment in which the response occurred has not been carefully specified. The rat

might press the lever while looking at the lever or while gazing at the ceiling; leverpressing produces food in either case. Similarly, a child learning the word "ball" might be attending to the shape of the ball or to some other stimulus altogether, such as the person who threw the ball.

If we are to appreciate the full outcome of selection by reinforcement, we must understand how operant contingencies can restrict the stimulus components of the environment-behavior relation to "appropriate" stimuli. While the goal of the previous chapter was to uncover the processes whereby selection occurs, the goal of this chapter is to explore the environmental guidance of behavior that results from those processes. To achieve that goal, we use procedures that implement a **three-term contingency**, in which the response-reinforcer contingency defining the operant procedure is instituted only when a specified stimulus is present.[2] Such procedures permit an experimental analysis that combines the merits of the classical and operant procedures. That is, a three-term contingency allows the experimenter to manipulate three events simultaneously—the *stimulus* present before the elicitor, the *response* producing the elicitor, and the elicitor (*reinforcer*) itself. Only the stimulus-reinforcer relation is controlled with the classical contingency; only the response-reinforcer relation with the operant contingency.

CHARACTERISTICS OF SELECTED ENVIRONMENT-BEHAVIOR RELATIONS

Before examining specific findings obtained with procedures that implement three-term contingencies, let us identify several central issues that are at stake in these investigations.

Purpose and Selection

Environment-behavior relations provide a natural science-based account of phenomena that would otherwise be taken as evidence of the purposive or goal-directed character of behavior.[3] Consider the food-deprived pigeon that sees a disk on the chamber wall, pecks the disk, and then receives food. Instead of attributing this environment-behavior relation to the pigeon's "purposes," "beliefs," "intentions," "goals," or "intelligence," a selectionist account appeals to the learner's environmental history and the environment-behavior relations that have been selected in those environments. Disk-directed pecking occurs because, when disk-directed pecking was followed by the eliciting stimulus of food in the past, pecking was selected to come under the guidance of the sight of the disk. The outcome of the selection process is that the learner acts *as if* he had "purpose," "intelligence," and the like, but these inferred characteristics are viewed as the effects of selection rather than the causes of behavior. The selectionist account has moved the causes from within the learner—"rationality," "purposes," "beliefs," and so on—to the environment outside the learner. The causes of behavior are not within the learner, except in a technical sense: The learner is the cumulative product of the selecting effect of past environments, and it is the action of the present environment on the products of past selections that determines present behavior.[4]

On this view, living organisms behave as they do—not because of "intelligence" or "purpose"— but because of their sensitivity to selection by reinforcement. When we see behavior that corresponds to the demands of the environment, the correspondence is the product of natural and behavioral selection by the environment and not some "intelligence" or "purpose" that resides within the organism. The organism is crucially important as the arena in which environmental

selection takes place, but metaphors such as "intelligence" or "purpose"—if they are used at all—apply as much to the environment as to the organism. To the extent that the world is orderly—and to that extent only—do we act *as if* we were rational. Man is as predictable—and as unpredictable—as the environment in which he lives.

Fallibility of Selected Environment-Behavior Relations

The processes of natural and behavioral selection are not infallible, of course. Species become extinct, and learning—as shown most strikingly by the phenomenon of superstition—may also lead to error. Selection processes cannot guarantee truth: As the evolutionary philosopher Donald Campbell has put it, "Cousins of the amoeba that we are, how can we know for certain?"[5]

In principle, *any* of the stimuli occurring before any of the responses that are followed by a reinforcer could come to guide those responses. In a single occurrence of a reinforcer, there is no inherent difference between a stimulus in whose presence a response was *by chance* followed by a reinforcer and a stimulus in whose presence a response *caused* a reinforcer.[6] To illustrate, suppose that a pigeon need not peck a disk, but merely look at it, to receive food. Even though pecking is not necessary, if pecking accompanied looking then pecking would also be selected. Under such circumstances, the guidance of pecking by the sight of the disk would be "superstitious."[7]

In this chapter, we shall see how the repeated action of selection by reinforcement prunes away, or edits out, those stimuli and responses that are unreliable guides to reinforcers. The processes whereby unreliable environmental and behavioral events are eliminated from the selected environment-behavior relations are studied under the heading of **stimulus discrimination**. The eventual outcome of selection by reinforcement most often provides an accurate cause-effect analysis of environment-behavior relations, but behavioral selection can never guarantee the absolute correctness of the analysis.

Specificity of Selected Environment-Behavior Relations

The behavior of experienced learners indicates that apparently *general* relations develop between the environment and behavior—relations so general that they are characterized by terms such as "idea" or "concept." Thus we say that we have an "idea" of what a friend is like or a "concept" of what a ball is. For instance, you may recognize a friend in many ways—by her smile, the shape of her eyes, her clothes, or even her style of walking—and many responses may occur when you recognize her—speaking her name, asking what she did on the weekend, and covert responses such as remembering the last time you were together. You "know" your friend and you "know" what responses are appropriate when you see her. And yet, you may never have seen her smile, eyes, clothes, or gait under precisely the circumstances in which you now see them and react to them. In contrast to this apparently general effect of selection, reinforcers always select specific environment-behavior relations consisting of *particular* stimuli (those present immediately before the responses in question) and *particular* responses (those occurring before the reinforcer). How do the particular environmental and behavioral events that make up experience lead to the apparent generality of many environment-behavior relations?

Selectionism provides several different types of answers to this question, some of which are described in this chapter. The key insight is that a complex set of environment-behavior relations, such as that denoted by the layperson's term "concept," is the end-product of an extensive history of selection by reinforcement. It is a rare environment indeed that does not contain many stimuli from earlier environments in which many responses were selected. The many individual contributions of prior selections are often not apparent: The stimuli separately experienced in earlier environments may now be simultaneously present, and the responses guided by those stimuli often occur concurrently or in rapid succession. Thus, we almost simultaneously see both a friend's face and clothing, and say "hello," and remember the last time we met.

Occasionally, however, we catch a glimpse of the separate environment-behavior relations that make up the apparently general character of the selected relation. As an illustration, when walking across campus a few months ago, I saw a neatly dressed man approaching with hand extended, calling my name. I greeted him as warmly as I could considering that I didn't have the slightest idea who he was. It was only when I turned my eyes away from him (no doubt to hide my confusion) and heard his voice *without seeing him* that I recognized the "stranger." He was a former colleague who had occupied the office next to mine some years ago. I had not seen him since the 1960's, when he was a long-haired, self-described "Marxist-Leninist" who habitually walked barefoot and wore a purple cape. The sound of his voice had continued to guide my recalling his name, but his changed appearance lacked that power and even interfered with remembering.

The most striking examples of the separate environment-behavior relations whose cumulative effect is the generality and richness of everyday experience comes from persons who have suffered brain damage from an accident or stroke. Consider the following examples. A brain-damaged man was asked to bring together the thumb and forefinger of one hand. He could not do so. However, every morning he buttoned his shirt, which required that he make this response. Similarly, a brain-damaged man was asked to bend his hand at the wrist. He was unable to comply with the request. Yet, he readily waved good-bye as he departed, which required that he make the same response. (When brain damage causes behavioral deficits in movements controlled by verbal stimuli, these deficits are called **apraxias**, and are sometimes described as deficits in "voluntary" movement.[8])

In the preceding examples of apraxias, brain damage interrupted one set of pathways—those mediating movements controlled by verbal stimuli—while leaving intact other sets—those mediating movements guided by stimuli such as an unbuttoned shirt or a departing friend. Some of the environment-behavior relations selected by prior reinforcers were undone by brain damage, while others remained intact. These examples illustrate the point that what is selected is always a *relation* between the environment and behavior, and not a response alone. Responses are not selected or strengthened; what is selected is the ability of particular environments to guide those responses. For the brain-damaged subjects, the ability to oppose the thumb and forefinger and to bend the hand at the wrist were present in some environments but not in others. The verbal environment had lost its ability to guide these responses, but other aspects of the environment were still effective. Without specifying the environment in which selection takes place, such concepts as "strength of response" have little meaning.

Brain damage lets us glimpse the separate products of selection by reinforcement, products that are normally inseparable. Brain damage partially undoes the cumulative effect of separate selections, which is undoubtedly the primary contributor to the generality and unity of adult human behavior. There is, however, a second important contributor that is a major focus of this chapter. Although selection by reinforcement always involves particular stimuli and responses, the effects of selection extend to other environments that are *similar* to those in which selection took place. The processes whereby selection transcends the boundaries of the original selecting environment are studied under the heading of **stimulus generalization**.

STIMULUS GENERALIZATION

To isolate the processes involved in stimulus generalization, it is again necessary to carry out experimental analyses with the furry and feathered test tubes of biobehavioral science. To control the history of previous selection by reinforcement, we must begin with nonhumans; only in that way can we identify the fundamental selection processes producing stimulus generalization.

Research with animals—or research of any sort for that matter—is not necessary to demonstrate the existence of stimulus generalization. It is apparent to even casual observation that the effects of selection extend beyond the conditions of the original selecting environment. A child that has learned to catch a red ball will also catch a green one with roughly equal skill. Moreover, the ability to transcend the particulars of experience is not confined to humans, for the ball-catching behavior of a dog shows similar generality.

In the following discussion, we first focus on stimulus generalization in its simplest form—the generalization of the guidance of a single behavior by a single feature of the environment. Next, we describe the behavioral and neural processes contributing to generalization in these simple situations. Once we have identified the basic biobehavioral processes, we then proceed to more complex instances of stimulus generalization.

Gradients of Stimulus Generalization

Stimulus generalization is readily demonstrated by reinforcing a response in the presence of one stimulus, and then measuring the strength of that response in the presence of other stimuli that differ from the first stimulus along some quantifiable dimension. As an example, pecking by a pigeon of a colored disk on the test-chamber wall was first reinforced by occasional presentations of food. (See **Figure 3.1** for examples of test chambers used in operant conditioning procedures.) Following training, a test was conducted in which the color—i.e., the wavelength—of the disk was changed unsystematically every few seconds. The number of pecks contacting the disk when it was transilluminated by a test wavelength provided a measure of stimulus generalization. Food was not given during the test periods, but the training procedure had

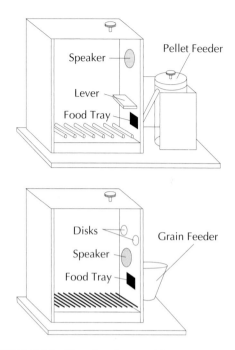

FIGURE 3.1 *Test chambers used for operant conditioning procedures*
The chamber in the upper panel is used with rats as subjects. When the rat presses the lever, a food pellet may be presented in the food tray. The chamber in the lower panel is used with pigeons as subjects. When a pigeon pecks one of the disks located on the wall, grain may be presented in the food tray. The test chambers are located inside sound and light attenuating enclosures to control unwanted stimulus variation.
Source: Adapted from Donahoe & Wessells, 1980.

made responding sufficiently resistant to change to permit extended testing.[9]

Figure 3.2 shows the frequency of pecking during the test wavelengths. Pecking had been reinforced in the presence of a disk transilluminated by a wavelength of 550 nm, or nanometers (where one nm equals a millionth of a meter). A wavelength of 550 nm appears green to a human observer. As shown in the figure, the frequency of pecking the disk was greatest when tested with the wavelength used in training, and then progressively declined as the test wavelengths departed from the training wavelength. This result indicates

that training in one environment (550 nm) affected behavior not only in that environment but also in other similar environments (the test stimuli). When an environment-behavior relation is selected, the effect may extend beyond the original selecting environment and alter relations in other environments that contain some of the same stimulus components.

When selection by reinforcement occurs in one environment and responding is affected in similar environments, stimulus generalization is demonstrated. The curve in **Figure 3.2**, which shows how the strength of responding varied as a function of the value of the stimulus dimension (here, wavelength), is a **stimulus generalization gradient**. Such gradients provide a measure of stimulus generalization when quantifiable features of the environment guide behavior. The steeper the generalization gradient around its peak, the more precise is the guidance of behavior along that stimulus

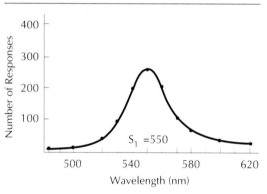

FIGURE 3.2 *Stimulus generalization after nondifferential training*
A stimulus-generalization gradient showing the effect of the wavelength of light transilluminating the disk on the number of disk-pecking responses. Prior to the generalization test, pecking S1 (a green, 550 nm disk) was reinforced with food. During the generalization test, various wavelengths of light were successively presented in an unsystematic order and responding did not produce food.
Source: Based on findings from Guttman & Kalish, 1956. Used with permission.

dimension. As shown in **Figure 3.2**, the stimulus generalization gradient was relatively flat following training in only one environment.[10] Reinforcing pecking the green disk caused pecking to occur later, when other colors appeared on the disk.

Behavioral processes in stimulus generalization.
What behavioral processes occur in an environment that is similar, but not identical, to the training environment? Experimental analysis indicates that similar environments guide the very same responses that were selected by reinforcers in the training environment, but with reduced strength. That is, the frequency of responding declines, but the response that occurs has the same form, or **topography**, as the selected response. In the pigeon example, if the selected responses included a brief glance toward the ceiling followed by a peck at the green training color, then the very same response would occur—but not as often—when the color was changed to yellow-green. Thus, environment-behavior relations selected in one environment reappear in similar environments. Without a history of selection by reinforcement in the similar environments, responding consists of variation arising from natural selection by the ancestral environment. Whether through natural selection or selection by reinforcement, only previously selected responses are found. Genuinely new responses do not occur. The observed environment-behavior relations are a **behavioral mixture** of previously selected relations.[11]

If the organism does have a complex history of reinforcement in similar environments—and this is increasingly the case—then other responses that are components of previously selected environment-behavior relations will also occur. The effect of this ever-richer behavioral mixture is an ever-greater variation on which later selection may act.

Neural processes in stimulus generalization.
Procedures employing simple, quantifiable stimuli permit us to identify the behavioral processes contributing to generalization, and some of the accompanying neural processes. In the example of stimulus generalization along the wavelength dimension, the test stimuli evoked the same responses as those guided by the green training stimulus. Because the various wavelengths stimulated some of the same visual receptors—leading to the activation of some of the same networks of neurons—responses of the same topography were evoked.

With quantifiable stimulus dimensions, it is possible to document experimentally the partial overlap in the neural networks activated by similar environments. In another experiment, cats were trained to respond to an auditory stimulus of 250 Hz (one Hertz, Hz, is a frequency of one cycle per second of sound pressure). After training, the cats were given generalization tests with auditory stimuli of higher frequencies. From physiological research, it is known that different neurons in the auditory cortex respond preferentially to different frequencies of tones. Although a given cortical neuron responds to a range of frequencies, it responds most strongly to one frequency toward the middle of that range. Also, neurons that respond to similar frequencies are located near one another in the auditory cortex. The more similar the response of two neurons to an auditory stimulus, the shorter the distance between them on the surface of the cortex. With this information, the shape of the auditory stimulus generalization gradient can be predicted if the gradient depends on the overlap in the activity of auditory cortical neurons.[12] The slope of the gradient should be relatively flat when the overlap is large, and steep when the overlap is small.

Figure 3.3 shows the results of behavioral testing along the auditory frequency dimension, and their relation to the degree of overlap in the neurons stimulated by the tones. The extent of stimulus generalization corresponded closely to the number of neurons stimulated in common by the training stimulus of 250 Hz and the three test stimuli of 500, 1,000, and 2,000 Hz. The greater the overlap between the neurons activated by the training and test stimuli, the greater the generalized behavioral response to the test stimuli.

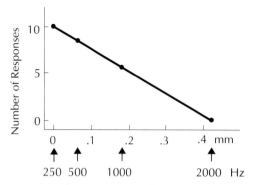

Distance Along Primary Auditory Cortex (mm)
from 250 Hz Best-Frequency Point

FIGURE 3.3 *Neural processes and stimulus generalization*
One-sided stimulus generalization gradient relating behavioral generalization with auditory stimuli to the distance along the surface of the auditory cortex between the place on the cortex activated by a 250-Hz training tone and the places most strongly activated by auditory test stimuli of other frequencies. The arrows below the horizontal axis show the distances between points on the surface of the cortex at which maximal neural responses were obtained.
Source: Adapted from Thompson, R. F. (1965). The neural basis of stimulus generalization. In D. I. Mastofsky (Ed.), *Stimulus generalization* (pp. 154–178). Stanford, CA: Stanford University Press.

Difficulties presented by complex selection histories. The correspondence between generalized responding and overlap in neural activity cannot be studied experimentally with complex environment-behavior relations. There are a number of reasons for this. First, in natural environments whose guidance of behavior is the result of a complex selection history, the underlying neural activity is correspondingly complex. Its measurement eludes the grasp of present technology, and it will defy exhaustive measurement for some time to come. Consider the following example of stimulus generalization with humans that undoubtedly involves complex interrelations among networks of many neurons, but is nonetheless a commonplace occurrence. When a response is conditioned to a

verbal stimulus such as the spoken word "farm," meaningfully related stimuli such as "barnyard" or "cow" will also evoke the learned response, although to a lesser degree.[13] The similarities between the verbal stimuli "farm" and "cow" result from the learner's experience, and are not based on physical similarities between the stimuli. No currently available physiological methods permit us to measure precisely the neural processes activated by these stimuli and, even if the technology did exist, its application to humans would probably be unethical.[14]

A further difficulty is that even tasks using relatively simple stimuli and responses actually involve a great many neurons—too many to monitor simultaneously with present methods. Consider the following study, which used sophisticated neuroanatomical techniques to determine how many neurons were involved when a learned response was performed. In the learning task, cats received food for approaching one visual stimulus and no food when they approached a second visual stimulus. The stimuli were relatively simple geometric patterns, such as triangles and circles. Following training, the cats were tested with special procedures that confined the neural activity initiated by a stimulus to neurons on one side of the brain. The other side of the brain served as a control that received equally complex stimulation, but from stimuli that were not part of the environment-behavior relation selected by the food reinforcer. The level of neural activity on the side of the brain receiving the critical stimuli was then compared to the level on the control side. The control side provided a comparison for a variety of factors common to both halves of the brain but unrelated to the learning task—such as movements of the limbs while approaching the stimuli and the motivational effects of food deprivation.[15]

To measure neural activity, both sides of the brain were injected with a form of glucose—the source of energy for neurons—that had been made mildly radioactive. Neurons that were active during task performance would take up more of the radioactive glucose, thereby labeling the brain regions mediating learned performance. By measuring the *difference* between the amount of radioactivity on the side of the brain engaged in the learned environment-behavior relation and the amount on the control side, it was possible to estimate the additional number of cells mediating the learned relation. It was found that the number of additional neurons exceeded five million, and may have been as high as 100 million! This example and others[16] make it clear that the number of neurons participating in environment-behavior relations—and in the stimulus generalization of those relations—exceeds our ability to measure them. However, there is no reason to believe that, if such measurements were possible, they would lead to conclusions appreciably different from those based on the experimental analysis of simpler relations.

The fact that selection by reinforcement routinely alters the activity of a large number of neurons is just what would be expected if reinforcers function by activating diffusely projecting neuromodulatory systems. In addition, since so many neurons participate in any given environment-behavior relation, there must be considerable overlap in the neurons mediating different relations. Consider the following: If a single environment-behavior relation may involve 100 million neurons, then the 100 billion neurons in the human brain would be capable of mediating only 1,000 different tasks without overlap among the neurons activated by the different tasks. And yet, each of us can learn many hundreds of thousands of environment-behavior relations—most of which are much more complex than those involved in a cat approaching a triangle. We are driven to conclude, then, that a single neuron must participate in the mediation of many different environment-behavior relations. The effects of learning are distributed widely throughout the brain.

STIMULUS DISCRIMINATION

The stimulus generalization of learned environment-behavior relations makes a vital contribution to our ability to function in future environments. Since some of the stimuli of past environments are common to future environments, and since the responses that produce reinforcers are often the same when the environments are similar, prior selection often "prepares" us for the future. However, not all similar environments implement similar three-term contingencies. Sometimes very different responses are reinforced in very similar environments. Thus, a teddy bear seen in your back yard and a bear cub seen in an upland meadow have many features in common, but the appropriate responses are very different. In fact, the similarity between these two environments leads to a number of maulings by female bears each year in our western National Parks. (See **Figure 3.4**.)

The processes whereby different environments, even those containing many common features, come to guide different responses are studied under the heading of stimulus discrimination. In this section, we examine how selection by reinforcement produces differential responding. As with stimulus generalization, we consider both the behavioral processes and the accompanying neural processes.

Knowing how and when to respond is so commonplace that it scarcely seems to require explanation. However, when we examine even relatively simple discriminations, such as correctly naming an object, the complexity of the process becomes apparent almost immediately. Consider again a child learning to name a ball; i.e., to emit the verbal response "ball" when viewing a stimulus that would be called a ball by an adult. Suppose that a father rolls a red ball toward his child and says "ball." From the child's perspective, even this apparently simple task is fraught with ambiguity. The problem for the child is this: Which of the many stimuli in the environment should guide the response "ball"? Do these stimuli include the shape of the object (round), its color (red), its manner of movement (rolling)? For that matter, there is no way for the child to know that stimuli provided by the ball have any special relevance at all. If the ball were rolling across a rug, perhaps characteristics

THE FAR SIDE   By GARY LARSON

11-2 Larson © Chronicle Features. 1983

And no one ever heard from the Anderson brothers again.

FIGURE 3.4   *When generalization goes awry*
Stimulus generalization usually benefits the learner because behavior often has similar consequences in similar environments. However, this is not always the case, as the Anderson brothers—who love to play with teddy bears—are about to discover.
Source: The Far Side cartoon by Gary Larson is reprinted by permission of Chronicle Features, San Francisco, CA. All rights reserved.

of the rug should guide the response "ball." If the child were looking at his parent instead of the moving ball, perhaps the features of the parent's face are relevant. In short, even if the child says "ball" and the father immediately reinforces that response with his approval, it is not clear which of the many stimuli that preceded the response should guide future occurrences of the response. A great many stimuli stand in a favorable temporal relation to the reinforcer and the verbal response "ball." How can such ambiguous circumstances provide the basis for the final performance—the guidance of "ball" by the same stimuli that guide the parent's

verbal response? (Lest this illustration be thought purely conjectural, research indicates that the naming responses of young children are, indeed, often guided by inappropriate features of the environment.[17])

The key to understanding the origin of stimulus discrimination is the realization that final performance is the cumulative effect of selection by reinforcement over *many* occasions. While on any one occasion a large variety of stimuli may precede the reinforced response, over many occasions only responses in the presence of the critical environmental features are consistently followed by the reinforcer. Thus, the child who says "ball" while looking at the rug when the ball is absent is not likely to receive parental approval. Similarly, the child who says "ball" while seeing a red fire engine rolling across the rug is also unlikely to receive approval. Receiving reinforcers for the response "ball" on some occasions, but not others, causes the child's response to be guided by only a subset of the available stimuli—those that were most often present when the response was reinforced. In this way, the child's behavior gradually comes to be guided by the same stimuli that guide the parent's behavior.

Stimulus Generalization after Discrimination Training

To see how the cumulative effect of selection by reinforcement brings about stimulus discrimination, we return to research with nonhuman animals, in which prior experience and experimental conditions may be better controlled. Since all animals must learn to respond differently to different environments, we may anticipate that many of the behavioral processes that result in stimulus discrimination are widely shared across the animal kingdom.

Differential training procedure.   As in the previously described studies of stimulus generalization, a pigeon received food for pecking a disk transilluminated by a green light of 550 nm.[18]

However, the color of the disk was occasionally changed to a yellow-green light of 555 nm and pecking the new color did *not* produce food. Thus, some stimuli in the environment (those characteristic of 550 nm) reliably preceded reinforced responses, while other stimuli (those characteristic of 555 nm and those provided by the test chamber generally) were not reliably present when reinforcers occurred. A training procedure in which the learner is exposed to different environments in which responses have different consequences is called a **differential training procedure**. A procedure in which only a single environment is presented is called a **nondifferential training procedure**. According to our understanding of the selection of environment-behavior relations, what should happen when the learner is exposed to differential rather than nondifferential training?

When a disk-pecking response occurs during the 550-nm stimulus and is followed by food, the color of the disk should begin to guide the emission of pecking. This happens because food elicits responses that would not otherwise occur, which produces a behavioral discrepancy. As a result, whatever stimuli are present should acquire control over whatever responses are occurring in proximity to the discrepancy. Thus the 550-nm stimulus, as well as any other stimuli from the test chamber that were sensed before the discrepancy, should begin to guide disk-directed pecking.

Now consider what happens when the yellow-green (555-nm) stimulus is presented. Because the yellow-green stimulus is similar to the green (550-nm) stimulus, stimulus generalization occurs— i.e., the pigeon pecks the yellow-green stimulus. The stimuli common to the two environments include both those stimuli that 555 nm shares with 550 nm and the stimuli that are common to both training environments, such as the sights and sounds of the test chamber. The stimuli that accompany the training stimuli (here, the two colors of the disk), but that are not manipulated by the experimenter, are called **contextual stimuli** or simply the **context**. Just as the child must learn to say "ball" only when balls are present, so the pigeon

must learn to peck only when the stimuli specific to 550 nm are present and not otherwise.

The weakening of responding under the guidance of stimuli that are not specific to 550 nm comes about as follows. The generalized responding that initially occurs during the 555-nm and contextual stimuli is not followed by food. When a previously reinforced response occurs in the presence of a stimulus and is no longer reinforced, the guidance of that response by the stimulus is weakened. This process is called **extinction** and the weakened response is said to be *extinguished* in the presence of those stimuli.[19] Thus—for both pecking with the pigeon and naming with the child— responding in the presence of stimuli weakens when it is not followed by reinforcers.

For the pigeon, what are the stimuli that lose their ability to guide pecking? First, there are those stimuli that the green and yellow-green disks share in common. The two colors stimulate a partially overlapping set of visual receptors, but only those pathways that are uniquely activated by the green color are consistently followed by the reinforcer. Pathways that are activated by common receptors (those sensitive to wavelengths toward the yellow end of the spectrum) lose their ability to guide the response. Second, the stimuli from the test chamber also lose their ability to guide the response as they are also not consistently followed by the reinforcer. The cumulative effect of alternating selection by the reinforcer and extinction is to confine the controlling stimuli to those that are unique to the green color. This process may be traced in **Figure 3.5**, which separately shows the rates of responding when the disk was green and when it was yellow-green. Note that the strength of responding during the green stimulus grows steadily while the strength of responding during the yellow-green stimulus increases at first (generalization from the green color) and then slowly declines (extinction).

Generalization testing.   The stimulus generalization gradient obtained following differential training is shown in **Figure 3.6**. The gradient fol-

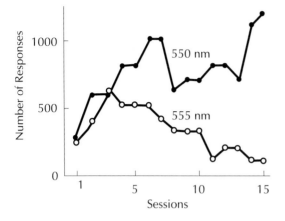

FIGURE 3.5 *Formation of a discrimination*
The course of responding to S₁—green, 550-nm disk—and S₂—yellow-green, 555-nm disk—during discrimination training. During S₁, pecking was reinforced with food; during S₂, pecking had no effect, i.e., extinction was scheduled.
Source: Based on findings from Hanson, 1959.

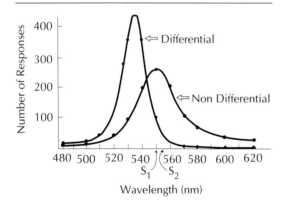

FIGURE 3.6 *Stimulus generalization after differential (i.e., discrimination) and nondifferential training for different groups of subjects*
During the training that preceded the generalization test, pecking S₁ (a green, 550-nm disk) was reinforced for both groups. For the differential training group only, training also included the presentation of S₂ (a yellow-green, 555-nm disk) in whose presence pecking was not reinforced.
Source: Based on findings from Hanson, 1959.

lowing nondifferential training is repeated for comparison. Note three differences between the gradients: (a) the gradient following differential training declines more steeply from the peak, particularly on the side nearest the yellow-green (555-nm) stimulus, (b) the peak of the gradient following differential training is shifted away from the 555-nm stimulus, and (c) the height of the gradient after differential training is greater than the height of the gradient after nondifferential training.

We describe here only the origin of the first difference—steepening. The origins of the other two differences are briefly considered later. The postdiscrimination gradient is steeper because the stimuli that are not unique to the **discriminative stimulus** (550 nm) have lost their ability to guide responding. Through extinction, stimuli shared with the yellow-green stimulus and stimuli from the context lose their control of responding. This causes the gradient to steepen between 550 and 555 nm, since colors in this region are most apt to have elements in common with the discriminative stimulus. The loss of control by contextual stimuli causes the gradient to steepen throughout its range since, by definition, contextual stimuli are present equally no matter which wavelengths are on the disk.

In summary, differential training restricts the guidance of behavior to those stimuli that reliably precede the reinforced response. Other stimuli that less reliably precede the reinforced response lose their control of the response. This outcome is the cumulative effect of the strengthening of some environment-behavior relations by reinforcement and the weakening of others by extinction.[20]

Behavioral processes in stimulus discrimination.
When examining the behavioral processes responsible for stimulus generalization after nondifferential training, we found that similar environments guided the same responses that had been selected in the training environment. Generalized responding consisted of a mixture of the environment-be-

havior relations previously selected in similar environments.

Behavioral mixing is also found after differential training. To study behavioral mixing, differential procedures are used that select responses of different topographies in the two training environments. Since the topographies are different, mixing can be directly observed when a generalization stimulus is presented. For example, suppose that a brief-duration response, such as glancing toward the ceiling between pecks, is reinforced during a 554-nm stimulus. Suppose further that a longer-duration response, such as turning around before pecking, is reinforced during a 569-nm stimulus. Responses of different durations can be selected by presenting food during the 554-nm stimulus only when a peck occurs within 1 sec of the previous peck, and presenting food during the 569-nm stimulus only when a peck occurs more than 3 sec after the previous peck. Procedures of this sort involve the reinforcement of different **interresponse times**, or **IRTs**. In the study reported here, the different IRTs were 1 sec and 3 sec, which produced a higher average rate of responding during the 554-nm stimulus and a lower average rate during the 569-nm stimulus.[21]

The behavioral processes occurring during stimulus generalization after differential training are revealed by the types of responses that occurred during an intermediate test stimulus of 561 nm. If behavioral mixing occurred, then the average rate of responding during the intermediate 561-nm stimulus would be the result of a mixture of IRTs of 1 and 3 sec. If genuinely new types of responses occurred, then the intermediate average rate would be produced by previously nonreinforced IRTs, e.g., IRTs of 2 sec.

The finding in this experiment was that the 561-nm test stimulus guided the emission of a mixture of 1- and 3-sec IRTs—the IRTs that had been separately reinforced during the 554- and 569-nm training stimuli. That is, during the test stimulus, the behavior unsystematically alternated between responses of brief duration, such as glancing toward the ceiling, and responses of longer

duration, such as turning around in the test chamber. Behavioral mixing was also found with other test stimuli, with those closer to 554 nm evoking relatively more short-duration responses and those closer to 569 nm evoking relatively more long-duration responses. (See **Figure 3.7.**) In summary, after differential training similar environments evoked a mixture of the responses that had been conditioned to the training stimuli. Although new responses did not emerge, the new environment did evoke a *new mixture* of previously selected responses.[22]

The finding that similar environments evoke new mixtures of old responses is very important for our understanding of complex behavior. This finding suggests that all instances of apparently creative responding are traceable to a history of selection in earlier environments that contained some stimuli in common with the new environment. These common stimuli cause a new mixture of previously reinforced environment-behavior relations to occur in the new environment. Strictly speaking, then, it is not the learner who is creative. Instead, creativity is the result of a new environment acting on an experienced organism to produce a new mixture of old environment-behavior relations.[23] Furthermore, other research has demonstrated that mixing of previously learned responses occurs with more "natural" stimuli, such as the shapes of leaves.[24] Behavioral mixing is not restricted to laboratory investigations; it appears to be an ecologically valid and robust outcome of behavioral selection.

In later chapters, we shall see how prior selection may lead an organism to act *as if* it were inherently creative and capable of true novelty. Nothing that has been found about behavioral mixing undermines the extraordinarily complex and apparently creative behavior of which experienced humans are capable. The issue is not whether the behavior that we call creative occurs—it does—but how it comes about. For now, we note that the limitations on novelty imposed by behavioral mixing are more apparent than real. First, since most environments have many features in common with

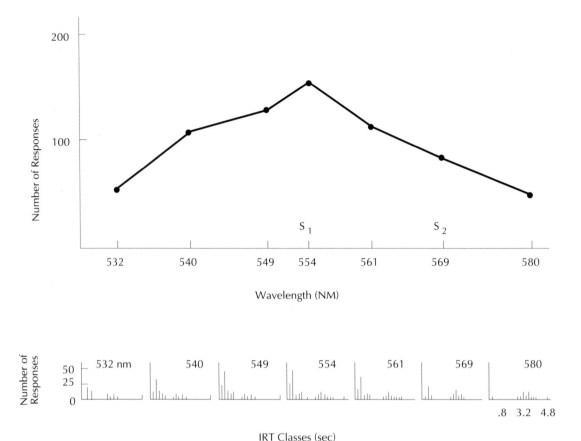

FIGURE 3.7   *Behavioral processes underlying stimulus generalization*
Stimulus-generalization gradient (upper panel) and the corresponding distributions of pecking responses that terminated interresponse times (IRTs) of various durations during the generalization test (lower panel). During prior
differential training, when S_1 (a 554-nm disk) was pecked within less than 1 sec of a preceding peck (IRT < 1), pecking
responses were occasionally reinforced with food and, when S_2 (a 569-nm disk) was pecked more than 3 sec after a
preceding peck (IRT > 3), pecking responses were also occasionally reinforced. Note how the IRTs generally fell into
the two reinforced categories for all wavelengths, with little evidence of intermediate, i.e., "new," IRTs.
Source: Based on findings from Collins, 1974.

earlier environments in which selection has taken
place, the responses that contribute to behavioral
mixing are increasingly rich and varied. The more
varied the selection history, the richer the mixture.
Second, because similar environments often contain only partially similar contingencies, the behavioral mixture provides the raw material—the
variation—upon which future selection may act.

The action of new contingencies on the mixture of
earlier behavioral selections can build behavioral
repertoires of increasing diversity and complexity.

Neural processes in stimulus discrimination.
A complete analysis of the neural processes accompanying stimulus discrimination is beyond our
present technical competence. However, there are

observations that shed some light on these processes. When a neuron is active, the movement of ions across the cell membrane produces small electrical changes. These changes may be measured by recording electrodes. When electrical changes occur in the vicinity of the several hundred neurons at the tip of the electrode, the combined effect of all of these changes can be detected.

In the following experiment, cats were given differential training in which pressing one lever was followed by food when a visual stimulus flashed at a rate of 10 per sec, and pressing a second lever was followed by food when the stimulus flashed at a rate of 5 per sec.[25] By the end of training, the two behavioral responses were reliably guided by their respective stimuli. In addition to the leverpressing responses, the light flashes evoked distinctive bursts of activity in the neurons monitored by the electrodes. This activity occurred at a rate of either 10 or 5 per sec depending on which visual stimulus was presented, and was detectable at many brain sites.

Following training, a generalization test was given in which the light flashed at an intermediate rate of 7.5 per sec—i.e., there were about 14 ms between flashes. Behaviorally, when the test stimulus was presented, sometimes one lever was pressed and sometimes the other. This variation in leverpressing is consistent with the phenomenon of behavioral mixing reported earlier. What is important here are the neural responses evoked by the test stimulus: Before a behavioral response occurred, many brain areas showed an evoked electrical response of either 10 per sec or 5 per sec—the same neural responses that were observed during training. Moreover, the evoked response corresponded to the behavioral response that was about to occur. An evoked response of 7.5 per sec—the frequency of the test stimulus—was seen only in the primary visual areas of the brain that were the first to be activated by the test stimulus. By the time neural activity had propagated to other brain areas, the evoked response often corresponded to one of the two types of neural activity characteristic of the training stimuli, and not the activity evoked by the intermediate test stimulus before training.

Although the precise relation between evoked responses from hundreds of neurons and the processes occurring in single neurons is complex, the findings do point toward two important conclusions. First, since the evoked responses were observed by electrodes in many brain areas, the neural changes accompanying stimulus discrimination and generalization were widely distributed in the brain. Second, since the neural responses during the generalization test stimulus included evoked responses observed during training, new environments produce mixtures of previously selected neural responses as well as behavioral responses. Since all behavior is mediated by physiological processes, how could it be otherwise?

Beyond Simple Stimulus Discrimination

Selectionism, in distinction to essentialism, holds that all human behavior—even the most complex—is *ultimately* traceable to selection by the ancestral and individual environments. As such, the phenomena that compose the bulk of this book—attending, perceiving, remembering, speaking, and the like—are, at heart, special instances of the environmental guidance of behavior. Although the understanding of each phenomenon involves different implications of biobehavioral principles, the principles remain the same from one phenomenon to the next. The relevant implications are considered as we address each set of phenomena in turn. However, there are two implications of selection by reinforcement that are so frequently encountered that they deserve mention here. These are: (a) the guidance of behavior by multiple discriminative stimuli and (b) the interactions among multiple discriminative stimuli.

Multiple stimuli guide behavior. The experimental studies of stimulus generalization and discrimination that we have so far considered varied only one aspect of the environment, e.g., the wavelength of light or the frequency of sound. Such relatively simple examples were chosen because they most clearly reveal the behavioral and neural processes involved in generalization and discrimination. However, the typical environment in which selection takes place is much more complex. Natural environments consist of many stimuli, a few of which are reliably present when the reinforcer occurs but many of which are not. Returning to the child learning to name a ball, a round shape is one of several reliable characteristics of balls, but its color is not a good guide for the verbal response "ball." The types of motion—rolling and bouncing—are also reliable, though not infallible, characteristics of balls. These characteristics may come to guide the verbal response. In fact, young children have been observed to call other rolling objects, such as candles, "ball,"[26] and adults react to rolling and bouncing images in video games as if they were balls.

An experiment with monkeys demonstrates the guidance of behavior by multiple stimuli.[27] The discriminative stimulus in whose presence responding produced food was a disk transilluminated with blue (497 nm), vertical (90°) lines on a black background. When a plain black disk was present, responding was not followed by food. In this differential training procedure, *both* the wavelength and the orientation of the line were in a favorable temporal relation to acquire control over the operant of pressing the disk. After the monkeys had learned differential responding to the training stimuli, two generalization gradients were measured—one along the wavelength dimension and the other along the line-orientation dimension. To obtain the wavelength gradient, the line orientation was kept constant at 90° while the wavelength was unsystematically varied from blue (497 nm) toward yellow in five steps. To obtain the line-orientation gradient, the color was kept constant at blue while the line orientation was unsystematically varied from vertical (90°) toward horizontal in five steps.

The wavelength and line-orientation gradients are shown in **Figure 3.8.** For both gradients, the number of responses progressively decreased as

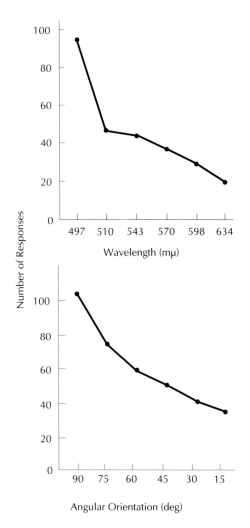

FIGURE 3.8 *Multidimensional stimulus generalization*

One-sided stimulus-generalization gradients indicating the effects of changes in the wavelength of a line projected on the disk (upper panel) and in the orientation of the line (lower panel) on the number of disk-pressing responses by monkeys. During prior discrimination training, disk-pressing responses were occasionally reinforced with food when the disk contained blue (497 nm) vertical (90°) lines, and responses were nonreinforced when the disk was black without lines.

Source: Adapted from Butter, C. M., Mishkin, M., & Rosvold, H. E. (1965). Stimulus generalization in monkeys with inferotemporal and lateral occipital lesions. In D. I. Mostofsky (Ed.), *Stimulus generalization* (pp. 119–133). Stanford, CA: Stanford University Press.

the test stimuli departed from the training stimulus. Thus, reinforcing the response when the stimulus consisted of blue, vertical lines brought behavior under the control of stimuli on both the wavelength and line-orientation dimensions. This study demonstrates that multiple characteristics of the training stimulus may acquire the ability to guide behavior if they are reliably present when responding is reinforced.[28]

The finding that behavioral selection can change the guidance of behavior along multiple stimulus dimensions extends the already far-reaching effects of selection by reinforcement. Any given training environment contains stimuli with many characteristics. For example, a single visual stimulus may vary in many respects—its wavelength, its intensity, its shape, its orientation, its location, its texture, etc. Stimulus generalization may occur along any of these dimensions. To give a more concrete sense of the potential effect of selection along multiple dimensions, suppose an environment has six discriminable characteristics and each of these characteristics has six discriminable values. Selection by reinforcement during one combination of these values could alter responding in 6^6, or 46,656 different environments! Given even a modest history of selection, the potential for new environments to generate behavioral mixing is truly staggering.

Categorical responding to multiple stimuli.   In addition to restricting ourselves to experiments in which the generalization test stimuli varied along only one dimension, we have limited the number of different stimuli used in training. For example, only one stimulus, such as 550 nm, was present when responding was reinforced and only one stimulus, such as 555 nm, was present when responding was extinguished. While this simplification helped uncover the processes responsible for differential responding, it does not represent the circumstances that exist in many natural environments. Consider again the child learning to name a ball. Not all objects conventionally named "ball" are perfectly round. A cheap baseball loses its

round shape when hit with a bat, but it is still called a ball. Footballs are round when seen from the end, but elliptical when seen from the side. In short, there is often a *range* of stimulation that guides a response, not just one particular value of the stimulus.

The effects of using a range of stimuli in differential training are illustrated by the following study using pigeons as subjects.[29] The stimuli consisted of a number of different wavelengths transilluminating a disk, presented in unsystematic order. Pecking the disk during one of 12 wavelengths in the range of 570 to 597 nm produced food on 8% of the presentations. Pecking the disk during one of 12 other wavelengths in the range of 600 to 617 nm produced food on 33% of the presentations. Thus, there were 12 stimuli in which responses were less likely to produce food and 12 other stimuli in which they were more likely. Returning once more to the child learning to use the word "ball" appropriately, these training conditions might correspond to a range of shapes that would rarely be correctly named "ball" and another range in which "ball" would often be the correct response.

Figure 3.9 shows the frequency of responding during the various wavelengths at the end of training. The stimuli have been arranged in the order of wavelength, although during training they were presented unsystematically. Several aspects of these findings require comment. First, responding was stronger during the range of stimuli in which food was more likely than it was during the range in which food was unlikely. This demonstrates that selection may occur with multiple training stimuli and when reinforcers differ in frequency, not merely in their presence or absence. Second, and most important, the change in the strength of responding between the two ranges of stimuli was very abrupt considering the very small change in wavelength. In fact, the greatest difference in response strength occurred between stimuli near the boundary between the range of stimuli during which reinforcement was less likely and the range during which reinforcement was more likely. In

Figure 3.9, the trough to the left and the peak to the right of the dividing line indicate regions in which the difference in responding was increased between the two ranges. These enhanced differences near the boundaries between regions of differential reinforcement are known as **edge effects**.

The functional significance of edge effects is very great. When the boundary between two differentially reinforced ranges of stimuli is crossed, the change in response strength—instead of occurring gradually—is abrupt and exaggerated. Stimuli adjacent to the boundary in one range are responded to least strongly; very similar stimuli— but just to the other side of the boundary—are responded to most strongly. This abrupt change in response strength even though the stimuli are

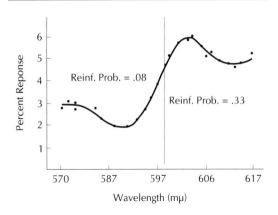

FIGURE 3.9 *Edge effects*
The percentage of total disk pecking responses as a function of the wavelengths appearing on the disk. When the wavelengths were between 570 and 597 nm, pecking responses were reinforced with a low probability of 0.08; when the wavelengths were between 600 and 617 nm, pecking was reinforced with a higher probability of 0.33. The trough to the left of the dividing line between the different reinforcement probabilities and the peak to the right of the dividing line illustrate edge effects.
Source: Adapted from Blough, D. S. (1975). Steady state data and a quantitative model of operant generalization and discrimination. *Journal of Experimental Psychology: Animal Behavior Processes, 104,* 3–21. Copyright © 1975 by the American Psychological Association. Adapted by permission.

changing gradually produces **categorical responding**. As a result of differential reinforcement with a range of stimuli, organisms tend to respond as if the environment were sharply divided into dissimilar categories that correspond to the dissimilar reinforcement conditions rather than to the highly similar stimulus conditions.[30]

How should categorical responding be understood? Consider a stimulus (e.g., 600 nm) in whose presence reinforcers are likely, but which is close to the boundary and, consequently, similar to stimuli during which reinforcers are unlikely. The generalized tendency to respond arising from these latter stimuli (e.g., 597 nm) is relatively weak because reinforcers are unlikely. This might lead us to conclude that responding during the 600-nm stimulus would be weakened—the result of a mixture of strong responding (due to the effect of frequent reinforcement during the 600-nm stimulus) and weak responding (due to the generalized effect of infrequent reinforcement during the 597-nm stimulus). However, such an analysis neglects the contribution of the behavioral discrepancy to the selection process.

Since generalized food-elicited responses from stimuli on the other side of the boundary are relatively weak, the elicitation of these responses by the presentation of food during the 600-nm stimulus creates a large discrepancy. This leads to strong selection of keypecking by food. For a stimulus well within the range of more frequent reinforcers (e.g., 610 nm), the situation is different. Because 610 nm is similar to many stimuli in whose presence reinforcers are frequent, generalized food-elicited responses are relatively strong. Thus, the discrepancy between food-elicited responses and generalized food-elicited responses is small during the 610-nm stimulus. The result is that the presentation of food does not select keypecking as strongly during the 610-nm stimulus as does the occurrence of that same food during the 600-nm stimulus. As a result, keypecking during 610 nm should be weaker than keypecking during 600 nm, even though the latter is closer to stimuli during which keypecking is less frequently reinforced. A comparable analysis can be made for the lowered responding on the other side of the boundary.

Categorical responding, then, is an implication of selection by reinforcement. No additional principles are required. The effect of selection by reinforcement is to make responding change most abruptly at the boundary between environments signaling different reinforcement conditions, the very region where—on the basis of generalization alone—behavior might be thought to change gradually. The beneficial contribution of edge effects to efficient performance should be apparent. An organism whose behavior sharply differentiates between similar stimuli, when those stimuli indicate a change in the conditions of reinforcement, is sensitive to the demands of its environment.

The behavioral processes producing edge effects also contribute to several of the phenomena associated with differential training that were described earlier. The increase in the height of the postdiscrimination gradient relative to the nondifferential gradient and the shift in the peak of the postdiscrimination gradient away from the stimulus correlated with extinction are both enhanced by the processes responsible for edge effects. If the stimuli (including contextual stimuli) that are present when responses are reinforced are similar to those present when responding is extinguished, then the effect of the reinforcer is enhanced because of the greater behavioral discrepancy. The greater discrepancy increases the height of the postdiscrimination gradient and shifts its peak away from the stimuli present during extinction. (Other processes also contribute to the outcome of differential training, but they are outside the scope of the present treatment.[31])

ENVIRONMENTAL GUIDANCE OF HUMAN BEHAVIOR

Experimental findings with nonhuman animals have been used extensively in this chapter to reveal the basic processes responsible for the environmental guidance of behavior produced by behavioral selection. These findings have led to an understanding of many phenomena associated with stimulus generalization and stimulus discrimination.

An assumption that lies behind the use of nonhumans here and elsewhere is that what a rat, a cat, a pigeon, or a monkey can do, a human can also do. This assumption—that people are as capable as other animals—is obviously conservative. People are generally more capable than other animals. The point here is that, if these simple processes can help us understand discrimination and generalization in other animals, then they can probably help us understand these phenomena in humans as well. Human capabilities are, of course, not identical to those of other species. Rats can hear high frequencies of sound to which humans are deaf, and pigeons can see ultraviolet wavelengths of light to which humans are blind. Thus the behavior of rats and pigeons can be guided by environmental events to which human receptors are insensitive. Similarly, pigeons can fly because of the movement of their feathered "forelimbs," and monkeys can easily swing through trees because of the greater relative strength of their forelimbs. Thus the environment can guide responses in birds and monkeys that cannot occur in humans because human effectors cannot support those responses.

While it is true that nonhumans acquire environment-behavior relations that humans cannot, it is even more strikingly true that humans learn relations that nonhumans do not. What factors are responsible for these differences? We shall consider several candidates as the book proceeds. For now, we note three interrelated factors. First, the upright posture of our species, which is unique among the primates, freed the forelimbs from selection for locomotion. This change allowed precise movements of the fingers to become the focus of new selecting influences by the ancestral and individual environments. The result of these altered contingencies is manual dexterity exceeding that of any other species. Second, the environment became able to guide the effectors governing the tongue, mouth, and throat movements necessary for vocal speech. These changes permitted a degree of communication between members of our species—and within ourselves—that far surpasses anything found in other species.[32] Third, selection produced organisms having extensive neural interconnections between diverse sensory and motor areas of the brain, particularly among those areas necessary for the reception and production of speech.[33] This change permitted especially complex combinations of environmental stimuli to guide human behavior.

In later portions of the book, we explore the implications of these factors and ponder their evolutionary origins. However, a note of caution should be sounded even at this early stage. Historically, man has ever been eager to find some clear means of distinguishing himself from the other animals. In earlier mentalistic approaches, man was said to possess qualities such as "reason" that were denied to the animals. The analysis of superstitious behavior in an earlier chapter revealed some of the problems in maintaining this claim. Other workers pointed to certain brain structures that man was said to possess but that were thought to be absent in other animals.[34] In Darwin's time, a brain structure called the hippocampus held this distinction. The hippocampus is now known to be generally present in mammals, and not peculiar to humans. The acknowledgement of our bias toward discovering some way—any way—of separating ourselves from the other animals should make us wary of all candidates for that honor lest our vanity tempt us to accept them uncritically.

Whatever the final answer to the question of what structural features distinguish man from other animals, they are unlikely to be anything as intuitively appealing as "reason" or as clear-cut as some distinctive neuroanatomical structure. Instead, as with other evolutionary changes, the changes responsible for "humanness" are apt to be subtle and even—at first glance—insignificant. It is not structure alone, but its impact on behavioral selection that has sweeping and far-reaching implications. The structural changes themselves, considered in isolation from their effects on selection, may well

appear trivial. For example, an axon whose growth period during the development of the nervous system is extended for only a few days could reach sensory regions with which it would not otherwise be in contact. This new contact could have substantial behavioral effects through permitting, say, the sound and sight of an object to be integrated. Just as an avalanche begins with a single snowflake or a tidal wave with a single drop of water, so the complexity of human behavior will likely trace its origins to superficially humble beginnings.

STUDY AIDS

Technical Terms

If the following terms are not familiar, reread the relevant portion of the text and consult the glossary.

- three-term contingency
- stimulus discrimination
- apraxia
- stimulus generalization
- stimulus generalization gradient
- topography
- behavioral mixture (or mixing)
- differential training procedure
- nondifferential training procedure
- contextual stimuli (or context)
- extinction
- discriminative stimulus
- interresponse time (or IRT)
- edge effects
- categorical responding

Text Questions

1. What is a three-term contingency? Give both an experimental and an everyday example. What are the advantages of procedures that use three-term contingencies relative to classical and two-term operant procedures? Referring to the three-term contingency, criticize the view that the outcome of selection may adequately be described

as a change in the strength of a response. (Hint: Do reinforcers select relations or responses?)

2. Describe the training and testing methods used to demonstrate stimulus generalization after nondifferential training.

3. Describe the basic procedure, results, and major conclusions from the study which estimated the number of brain cells involved in a simple discrimination in a cat.

4. Indicate the problems facing a child who is learning to name an object. What factors complicate this apparently simple task? In general, how does selection "solve" this problem?

5. Describe the training and testing methods used to demonstrate stimulus generalization after differential training. What are the differences between the shapes of the stimulus generalization gradients after differential and nondifferential training? How can these differences be accounted for?

6. Describe the methods and findings from experiments concerned with the behavioral and neural processes occurring during stimulus generalization. Use the terms IRT and behavioral mixing in your answer.

7. Stimulus discriminations often involve exposure to more than two selecting environments. Describe the methods, findings and significance of the study of edge effects, which is concerned with such conditions. Give an account of the biobehavioral processes responsible for edge effects, referring to behavioral discrepancies in your answer.

8. Indicate some possible reasons why human behavior is guided by the environment differently from the behavior of other animals.

Discussion Questions

9. Suppose that a hungry person salivates while looking through a restaurant window at someone eating a meal. Comment on this observation in light of the discussion of *purpose* in the reading.

(Hint: Is it the hungry person's purpose or intention to eat the meal?)

10. The constituents of any environment-behavior relation are the *specific* stimuli and responses that occurred in contiguity with the reinforcer. If this is true, then how might you account for the *general* knowledge that seems to be implied by such notions as concept or idea?

ENDNOTES

1. Whether a given response will, in fact, become a component of the selected environment-behavior relation depends, as we saw in the previous chapter, on interactions of the operant with other responses that are candidates for selection—notably the elicited response itself.

2. Skinner, 1938, 1953, 1981.

3. Tolman, 1932.

4. See Skinner, 1953, 1974, 1981 for more complete discussions of this point.

5. Campbell, 1974.

6. The realization that, on a single occasion, it is impossible for the learner to distinguish coincidence from causation logically undermines the view that basically different learning processes underlie conditioning with the classical (respondent) and operant (instrumental) procedures. The dog that pricks up its ears upon hearing a tone that precedes food in a classical procedure has no way of "knowing" that it was not the movement of its ears that produced the food. On a single trial of a classical procedure, the temporal relation between the response of pricking up the ears and the presentation of food may be identical to that of an operant contingency between the same two events. Similarly, the rat that hears a tone and receives food for pressing a lever in an operant procedure has no way of "knowing" that it was not the tone that caused the food to appear. If, on its first exposure to a sequence of events, the organism has no way of determining whether the sequence is the result of a classical or an operant contingency, then different learning processes cannot be involved in the two procedures; to "know" which processes were to be employed, the organism would have to know beforehand that which it may only learn eventually.

7. cf. Morse & Skinner, 1957.

8. See Kolb & Whishaw, 1985.

9. Guttman & Kalish, 1956. Identification of some of the factors that make responding display resistant to

change are discussed in the next chapter; cf. Nevin, 1988.

10. Here, a visual stimulus—the wavelength (color) transilluminating the disk—was varied in the tests of stimulus generalization. The steepness of the generalization gradient depends, in part, on the stimulus dimension used in training and the species of the learner. For example, if a tone is used in training with pigeons and its frequency is varied in testing, a much flatter stimulus generalization gradient is obtained than with wavelength; Jenkins & Harrison, 1960. This presumably reflects the pigeon's history of natural selection with respect to the guidance of pecking by visual as opposed to auditory stimuli—the pigeon locates its food by sight, not by sound; e.g., LoLordo, 1979. Other details of the training procedure also influence the steepness of the gradients obtained after training in only one environment, e.g., Rudolph & Van Houten, 1977; Heinemann & Rudolph, 1963. Nevertheless, the basic point is valid that, other things being equal, stimulus generalization gradients are relatively flat when training consists solely of reinforcing a response in a single environment.

11. For an experimental example of behavioral mixing after training in one environment, see Sewall & Kendall, 1965. The first study demonstrating behavioral mixing was carried out by Migler, 1964; cf. Migler & Millenson, 1969; cf. Sidman, 1969; Weiss, 1972. For reviews, see Donahoe & Wessells, 1980, and Bickel & Etzel, 1985.

12. Hind, Rose, Davies, Woolsey, Benjamin, Welker, & Thompson, 1961; Thompson, 1965.

13. e.g., Mandler, 1962.

14. What indirect evidence does exist in humans concerning the neural activity accompanying complex environment-behavior relations is consistent with the more direct observations possible with other animals. As measured by noninvasive techniques, increased metabolic activity and blood flow occur in similar regions when the nervous system mediates similar environment-behavior relations. The results of some of these types of studies are presented later in the book.

15. John, Tang, Brill, Young, & Ono, 1986.

16. e.g., LeDoux, Thompson, Iadecola, Tucker, & Reis, 1983.

17. Mervis, 1987.

18. Hanson, 1959.

19. We shall consider some of the factors that affect the extinction of environment-behavior relations in the next chapter. Here, we simply use extinction as a procedure that weakens the ability of an environment to evoke a previously reinforced response.

20. These and other cumulative effects of differential training have been confirmed by computer simulations whose instructions implement the basic biobehavioral processes isolated through experimental analysis, e.g., Rescorla & Wagner, 1972; Blough, 1975.

21. Collins, 1974; described in Donahoe and Wessells, 1980.

22. See Crowley, 1979 for especially clear-cut findings of similar import.

23. Compare this with the common view that human creativity is the result of some unanalyzable characteristic, such as "genius," that resides within the person; e.g., Aris, Davis, & Steuwer, 1983.

24. Real, Iannazzi, & Kamil, 1984.

25. John, Bartlett, Shimokochi, & Kleinman, 1973.

26. Mervis, 1980, 1987.

27. Butter, Mishkin, & Rosvold, 1965.

28. See also, Butter, 1963, for a similar study with pigeons.

29. Blough, 1975.

30. cf. Wright & Cumming, 1971.

31. More complete treatments of these and other post-discrimination phenomena are contained in Mackintosh, 1974; Terrace, 1966; Rilling, 1977. The increase in the rate of responding during the discriminated stimulus, which occurs even though the frequency of reinforcement is unchanged, is an instance of what is termed *behavioral contrast* and is probably determined by a number of relatively independent factors; e.g.; Marcucella & MacDonall, 1977; Williams, 1981, 1988, 1990b.

32. cf. Corballis, 1989.

33. Geschwind, 1965, 1972.

34. See Donahoe, 1984.

CHAPTER 4

SELECTION IN THE EXPERIENCED LEARNER

OVERVIEW

In the preceding chapters, we identified the fundamental biobehavioral processes responsible for the selection of environment-behavior relations by the individual environment. These processes were studied primarily through the use of nonhuman learners whose environmental histories could be tightly controlled. Controlled conditions enabled us to attribute changes in the environmental guidance of behavior to events that were directly manipulated and measured *within* the experiments.

Although a well-controlled pre-experimental history is required for the analysis of basic selection processes, we should not forget that environment-behavior relations are increasingly selected in learners with complex histories of earlier selections. Indeed, complex behavior can arise only as the result of such complex histories. In this chapter, we begin our consideration of phenomena that emerge as the cumulative effect of prior selection. Insofar as possible, understanding these phenomena is based on experimental analysis. However, as the complexity of behavior increases, experimental analysis must be supplemented by scientific interpretation.

We begin the chapter with an examination of what is retained as a result of selection by reinforcement. (You will recall that retention is the third step in the sequence of variation, selection, and retention that leads to complexity.) Without knowing what is retained, we cannot hope to understand the cumulative effect of selection. We then describe some of the complexities that arise when selection occurs in experienced learners. Eliciting stimuli arising from *natural* selection function as reinforcers for beginning learners, but how does selection occur in experienced learners? Adults do not learn by being given bits of food when they "do the right thing." And yet, adults learn—often with amazing speed and efficiency. What is responsible for selection in experienced learners?

Also, no two people seem to be exactly alike with respect to the specific stimuli that foster effective learning. A stimulus that functions as a reinforcer for one person may not for another. Some persons learn effectively by reading a book, while others seem to learn best through discussions or demonstrations. What is responsible for this diversity, and can it be accommodated by a single selection principle?

Finally, we examine the effects on behavior of more complex three-term contingencies than those described in the preceding chapter. For example, rarely if ever does the natural environment include only a single three-term contingency. More commonly, an environment consists of many three-term contingencies, some of which operate simultaneously. In such cases, the learner must make "decisions" regarding which behavior to "choose." Do these more complex contingencies require new principles, or do they too fall within the reach of a principle of behavioral selection?

RETENTION

In our treatment of discrimination, we found that a previously selected environment-behavior relation can be weakened if the behavior occurs later but is no longer followed by a reinforcer. This procedure—called extinction—may be demonstrated after selection with either classical or operant procedures. **Figure 4.1** depicts the acquisition, maintenance, and extinction of a nictitating membrane response (NMR) in rabbits, using a classical procedure.[1] Three findings from this study merit comment here.

First, after a tone-NMR relation was acquired by pairing each tone presentation with an eliciting stimulus of eyeshock, high levels of responding were maintained when the percentage of tone-shock pairings fell to as little as 25%. The ability of infrequent reinforcers to maintain an already acquired environment-behavior relation is a general finding: Although the intermittent presentation of reinforcers substantially impairs acquisition, maintenance of responding is much less affected.[2] The maintenance of responding by **intermittent reinforcement** (also called **partial reinforcement**) is especially likely when the percentage of reinforcers is reduced gradually, as it was in this study.

A second finding was that the tone-NMR relation was eventually eliminated after the reinforcer was omitted altogether; i.e, when an extinction procedure was instituted. As shown in **Figure 4.1**, animals that had received tone-eyeshock pairings for as many as 900 previous trials responded to less than 60% of the tone presentations after 100 unre-

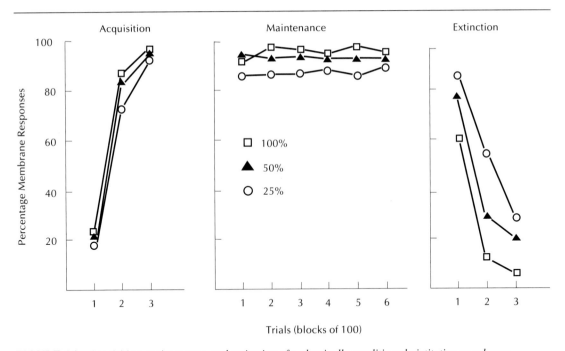

FIGURE 4.1 *Acquisition, maintenance, and extinction of a classically conditioned nictitating-membrane response in the rabbit*
During acquisition, all presentations of a tone (the conditioned stimulus, or CS) were followed by a mild shock (the unconditioned stimulus, or US) delivered in the vicinity of the eye. During maintenance, one group continued to receive 100% CS-US pairings, and the other two groups were gradually shifted to intermittent reinforcement with either 50% or 25% CS-US pairings. The remaining trials consisted of CS-alone presentations. During extinction, the CS was presented alone to subjects in all groups.
Source: Adapted from Gibbs, C. M., Latham, S. B., & Gormezano, I. (1978). Classical schedule and resistance to extinction. *Animal Learning and Behavior, 6,* 209–215. Reprinted by permission of Psychonomic Society, Inc.

inforced trials, and to less than 5% after 300 unreinforced tone presentations. The third finding of present concern was that intermittent reinforcement retarded the weakening of the tone-NMR relation. Although responding declined during extinction after all training conditions, extinction occurred *more slowly* in animals that had been trained with smaller percentages of tone-shock pairings. The less frequently the tone was paired with the reinforcer during maintenance training, the more resistant to extinction was the environment-behavior relation.

This effect of intermittent reinforcement on **resistance to extinction**, or **persistence**, is also found with operant procedures. **Figure 4.2** shows responding during the extinction of leverpressing in a rat after **continuous reinforcement** (i.e., training in which every response is reinforced) and, at a later time for the same rat, after intermittent reinforcement. (During intermittent reinforcement, leverpressing was maintained by the presentation of food only once every 12 min.)[3] Unlike previous graphic presentations of results, **Figure 4.2** is a *cumulative* record of responding. In a **cumulative record**, every response produces an *increase* in the curve with the passage of time. After continuous reinforcement for leverpressing, about 100 unreinforced responses occurred during two hours of extinction, and responding had essentially stopped by the end of testing. After training with intermittent reinforcement, the same animal made more than 200 responses during the first two hours and, moreover, responding continued largely unabated throughout the entire three hours of extinction testing.

Effects of Intermittent Reinforcement on Extinction

The increased resistance to extinction following intermittent reinforcement is puzzling if we forget what reinforcers strengthen: Reinforcers strengthen environment-behavior relations, not responses. If we see reinforcers as strengthening just responses, then the greater resistance to extinction

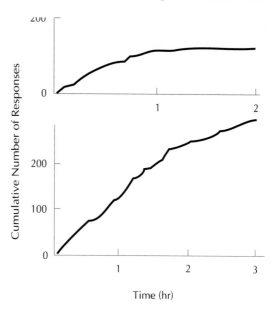

FIGURE 4.2 *Cumulative records of the extinction of lever pressing in a rat*
In a cumulative graph of responding, each response adds one count to the total; hence, the curve never declines. The slope of the curve is proportional to the rate of responding. The upper panel shows extinction after all lever presses had previously been reinforced with food (i.e., after continuous reinforcement). The lower panel shows extinction in the same animal after intermittent reinforcement of lever pressing. During intermittent reinforcement, lever presses were followed by food only once every 6 m.
Source: Based on findings from Skinner, 1938.

is paradoxical because the less frequently reinforced response appears to be stronger. However, if we keep in mind that reinforcers strengthen *relations* between the environment and behavior, then the paradox disappears. Responding occurs during extinction—as it does during any condition—to the extent that the prevailing stimuli include those that were present when selection occurred. Training with intermittent reinforcement results in greater resistance to extinction because responding is guided by more of the stimuli that are present during extinction than it is after continuous reinforcement. In short, resistance to extinction occurs to the extent that there is stimulus generalization between the training and extinction environments.

Research has supported the interpretation that greater resistance to extinction after intermittent reinforcement is an instance of stimulus generalization. During extinction, responding occurs following periods in which responding produces no reinforcer, and these are precisely the circumstances under which the response is selected during intermittent reinforcement. The more that training includes periods of unreinforced responding followed by a reinforced response, and the longer the durations of such periods, the greater the resistance to extinction.[4]

Experimental analysis has identified a number of stimuli that are present during both intermittent reinforcement and extinction. For example, if responses occur close together in time, then an eliciting stimulus of food may acquire a discriminative function with respect to the *following* response, in addition to its reinforcing function with respect to the responses that produce the food. Since the food stimulus is not present during extinction, responding after continuous reinforcement is weakened because one of the guiding stimuli—the eliciting stimulus—is no longer present. Indeed, research which varied the number of times a reinforcer *preceded* a response found that the fewer the reinforcer-response sequences, the greater the resistance to extinction. Other things being equal, responding persists to the extent that, during training, reinforced responses have been preceded by unreinforced responses.[5]

Other experimental work has isolated additional stimuli that are common to both training with intermittent reinforcement and extinction, and that therefore function as discriminative stimuli to enhance resistance to extinction.[6] Some of these common stimuli are found in the environment, and others are produced by the learner's own responses to environmental stimuli. As an example of the latter, if the environment comes to evoke conditioned (reinforcer-elicited) responses (e.g., salivation) during training, then the stimuli pro-

duced by these responses become discriminative stimuli that guide subsequent operant responses.[7]

Regardless of the specific stimuli responsible for the increased resistance to extinction after intermittent reinforcement, it is clear that training with intermittent reinforcement produces effects that would be called "motivational" in the nontechnical sense of the term.[8] As an illustration, a history of intermittent reinforcement causes the learner to behave during extinction in ways that would be described as "enduring in the face of adversity," "persistent," "stubborn," and the like. Experimental analysis indicates that persistence results, not from a history of nonreinforcement alone, but from a history of nonreinforcement followed by reinforcement—not failure, but failure followed by success. The "school of hard knocks" teaches the individual to persist only if failure has led eventually to success.[9]

Reacquisition of Extinguished Relations

After prolonged exposure to extinction, a previously selected environment-behavior relation is no longer evident—even after training with intermittent reinforcement. When responding can no longer be observed, has extinction eliminated all of the effects of prior selection, or has something of the selected environment-behavior relation been retained?

One method that may be used to determine whether there are lingering effects of the previously selected relation is to reinstitute the conditions under which it was originally acquired. If the relation is reacquired more rapidly than it was originally, then the effects of earlier selection have not been completely undone by the extinction procedure. Studies of reacquisition uniformly indicate that the environment-behavior relation is reacquired more rapidly, even after extinction has reduced responding to the point that it is no longer measurable at the behavioral level.[10] How can this finding be understood?

On the behavioral level, faster reacquisition occurs when some of the stimuli that controlled responding as the result of original learning *were not present during extinction* and are reintroduced with the onset of reacquisition. One such event is the reinforcing stimulus itself, since the stimulus-reinforcer or response-reinforcer contingency is present during acquisition but not during extinction. Consistent with this interpretation, a single presentation of the eliciting stimulus will initiate a recurrence of responding after an extinction procedure. That the eliciting stimulus often functions as a discriminative as well as a reinforcing stimulus is shown by the increased resistance to extinction that occurs when there are occasional response-independent presentations of the elicitor during extinction.[11] In summary, if the extinction procedure does not include all of the stimuli that are part of the selected environment-behavior relation, then the omitted stimulus components retain their ability to guide behavior and will do so when they reappear during reacquisition.[12]

On the physiological level, faster reacquisition is also anticipated from what is known about the cellular mechanisms of reinforcement. Recall that synaptic efficacies can be modified only between simultaneously active pre- and post-synaptic neurons (see Chapter 2). When coactivity of these neurons is accompanied by activation of the diffusely projecting reinforcing system, the synaptic efficacy between them increases. This is thought to be the cellular basis of reinforcement. However, if coactivity is *not* followed by a reinforcing stimulus—and the diffuse system is not activated—then the synaptic efficacy between coactive neurons decreases.[13] When synaptic efficacies along the pathways mediating the environment-behavior relation have been weakened to the point that one or more "links" in the neural "chain" are broken, extinction occurs on the behavioral level.

The mechanism whereby synaptic efficacies are weakened contributes to the rapid reacquisition of the response: Once the synaptic efficacies between neurons in the earlier portions of the network have been weakened, neurons in later portions of the network are no longer activated. Since *inactive* neurons are unaffected by nonreinforcement, their

synaptic efficacies are left intact. As a result of this process, the later synaptic efficacies in the network of pathways mediating the relation are relatively unaffected by extinction. (See **Figure 4.3** for an illustration of this process.) These relatively unchanged synaptic efficacies are in the more motor portions of the network, while the weakened efficacies are more toward the sensory portions.

Experimental work is consistent with this interpretation. For example, acquisition of an NMR to a new stimulus (e.g., a light) occurs more rapidly than earlier acquisition of the same response to another stimulus (e.g., a tone).[14] Rapid acquisition of the NMR to the new stimulus presumably occurs because the new stimulus activates the motor portion of the neural network that was selected when the response to the earlier stimulus was acquired. Further, as shown in **Figure 4.4**, computer simulations using biobehavioral principles of selection and synaptic modification in an adaptive neural network demonstrate the ability of this mechanism to produce more rapid reacquisition of the extinguished response.[15]

Durability of Selected Relations

Since even extinction does not eliminate all traces of a previously selected environment-behavior relation, the effects of prior selection should have enduring effects on behavior. Experimental evidence indicates that this is the case. For example, sheep that were put out to pasture after acquiring a tone-leg flexion relation flexed their legs when they were presented with the same tone three years later.[16] Similarly, a pigeon given grain for pecking different colored disks with distinctive response patterns displayed those same patterns when presented with the colored disks twelve years later.[17] Even a single presentation of an elicitor after a stimulus in a classical procedure[18] or after a response in an operant procedure[19] can produce enduring changes in the environmental guidance of behavior.

The ultimate fate of a selected environment-behavior relation depends on the later contingencies

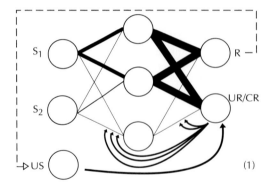

(1)

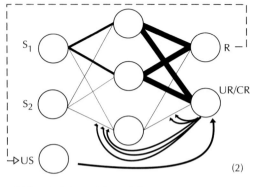

(2)

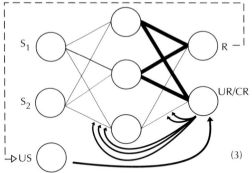

(3)

FIGURE 4.3   *Changes in the strength of connections between units in an adaptive network during extinction*
The heavier the line connecting two units, the greater the strength of the connection between them.

(1) The strength of connections at the beginning of extinction. Note the strong connections between the S_1 input unit (the discriminative stimulus) and both the R (operant) and UR/CR (conditioned response) output units. Thus, when S_1 is activated, both of these output units are likely to be strongly activated.

(2) The strength of connections after an intermediate number of extinction trials in which S_1 was activated on every trial but the reinforcing stimulus—simulated by the activation of the US unit—was not presented. The connections from S_1 to interior units weaken first because S_1 is strongly and reliably activated on every trial, thereby often activating the interior units. The connections from interior units to output units weaken less rapidly because the interior and output units are less strongly and less reliably activated than the S_1 input unit. The more strongly and reliably a unit is activated, the faster the loss of connection strength if the diffusely projecting reinforcement system is not also activated.

(3) The strengths of connections toward the end of extinction. The connections from S_1 to the interior units have become very weak, thereby preventing S_1 from reliably activating the interior units. Since the interior units are no longer activated, the remaining strengths of the connections from interior to output units can no longer change since the output units are no longer activated. And, since there is no "complete" pathway from S_1 to R, the environment-behavior relation has extinguished. However, the remaining connections in the "deeper" layers of the network permit the environment-behavior relation to be reacquired more rapidly.
Source: After Donahoe, Burgos, & Palmer, 1993.

of reinforcement to which the learner is exposed. If the same or complementary contingencies occur in later environments, then the relation may be maintained. If different responses are later reinforced in the presence of the same stimuli, then the originally selected relation may be weakened and obscured.[20] However, the original relation may

still affect the acquisition of new environment-behavior relations, and is unlikely to be undone completely for the reasons described earlier. It is rare for all of the original stimuli to lose their control of behavior and for all of the original synaptic efficacies to be altered. The effects of prior selections are retained—at least in part—and, as a result, new

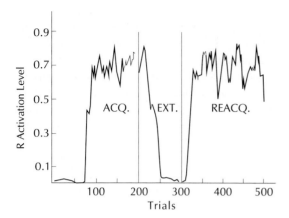

FIGURE 4.4 *Computer simulation of acquisition (left panel), extinction (center panel), and reacquisition (right panel) of responding in an operant procedure*
Changes in the level of activation of the operant (R) unit are shown as a function of the number of trials with the various conditions. Note that reacquisition of the operant is more rapid than original acquisition. The strengths of connections between units mediating the environment-behavior relation were modified by simulating the action of a diffusely projecting reinforcement system as described in Chapter 2.
Source: Based on findings from Donahoe, Burgos, & Palmer, 1993.

selections increasingly take place in the context of previously selected environment-behavior relations.[21]

ACQUIRED REINFORCEMENT

In addition to the biobehavioral processes involved in retention, previously selected environment-behavior relations also determine the stimuli that can function as reinforcers for later selection. For the inexperienced learner, only eliciting stimuli arising from natural selection can function as reinforcers. For the experienced learner, however, an increasingly large number of stimuli acquire the capacity to evoke behavior. These stimuli are the conditioned and discriminative stimuli produced by the differing contingencies of the classical and operant discrimination procedures. Can these acquired eliciting stimuli function as reinforcers to select new environment-behavior relations, and—if so—can selection by these stimuli be understood by the same principles that describe naturally selected elicitors?[22]

The implications of the answers to these questions are far-reaching, and were recognized by the pioneers of the experimental analysis of behavior—Ivan Pavlov and B. F. Skinner. If both questions could be answered in the affirmative, then the experienced learner would live in an environment where the number of potential reinforcing stimuli dramatically increased over time. Furthermore, the principles uncovered through the study of naturally selected elicitors would apply with equal force to acquired elicitors—and to the interpretation of complex behavior.

Acquired Elicitors as Reinforcers

To determine whether acquired elicitors function as reinforcers, it is first necessary to establish a stimulus that evokes behavior. This is accomplished most simply by pairing the stimulus with a reflexive eliciting stimulus in a classical procedure. After the stimulus has been established as an acquired elicitor, its ability to function as a reinforcer can be evaluated with the classical and operant procedures.

Using a classical procedure with a dog, Pavlov demonstrated that when the ticking sound of a metronome was paired with food, and then a visual stimulus was paired with the sound alone, the visual stimulus acquired the ability to evoke a salivary response. Note that the *sound* had selected an environment-behavior relation between the visual stimulus and salivation, without the visual stimulus ever having been paired with the reflexive eliciting stimulus of food. That is, the sound—an acquired elicitor—had functioned as a reinforcer.[23] When acquired elicitors are used as reinforcers to select new relations in the classical procedure, these new relations are said to demonstrate **higher-order conditioning**.

Skinner set out to demonstrate an analogous phenomenon using an operant procedure with a rat. First, a clicking sound was paired with food. Then, the sound was made contingent upon pressing a lever. Leverpressing was acquired when the response was followed by the sound, even though leverpressing was *never* followed by food.[24] Thus, acquired elicitors were shown to function as reinforcers in the operant procedure as well. As noted in an earlier chapter, when acquired elicitors serve a reinforcing function in an operant procedure, they are referred to as conditioned or secondary reinforcers. They are *secondary* only in the sense that selection by such stimuli is dependent on their having been paired with reflexive elicitors, or *primary* reinforcers. Conditioned reinforcers are by no means secondary in their importance for the selection of complex behavior, where they play a central role with experienced learners.

Acquired Reinforcers and the Reinforcement Principle

Experimental analysis indicates that stimuli may acquire the ability to function as reinforcers. But, can the reinforcing function of acquired elicitors be described by the same principles as reflexive elicitors? Determining the answer to this question is complicated by a methodological difficulty that you may have anticipated: The repeated presentation of an acquired elicitor to assess its reinforcing function weakens its ability to evoke behavior— the very ability on which the reinforcing function depends. To illustrate, suppose that a stimulus, S_1, is paired with a reflexive elicitor and then S_2 is paired with S_1 to determine if S_1 functions as an acquired reinforcer. When S_2-S_1 pairings are given, the procedure *weakens* the ability of S_1 to evoke behavior since the presentation of S_1 without the reflexive elicitor constitutes an extinction procedure. Thus, the more S_2-S_1 pairings are given to test the reinforcing function of S_1, the more the ability of S_1 to evoke behavior is weakened. Paradoxically, the more we study acquired reinforcers with these methods, the less there is to study.

Behavioral analysis.   Experimental analysis circumvents the extinction problem by interspersing within the S_2-S_1 testing procedure occasional pairings of S_1 with the reflexive elicitor. In the classical procedure, testing typically consists of an unsystematic mixture of pairings of S_2 with S_1 and of S_1 with the reflexive elicitor.[25] Likewise, operant testing typically combines instances of the operant procedure and pairings of S_1 with the reflexive elicitor. Thus both procedures attempt to maintain S_1's control of behavior by interspersing occasional pairings of S_1 with a reflexive elicitor. This arrangement parallels the circumstances that prevail in the natural environment with acquired reinforcers. For instance, if money were not occasionally exchanged for other reinforcers, it would soon cease to function as an acquired reinforcer. We get some sense of how the reinforcing value of money depends on its specific history of pairing with other reinforcers when we travel— and spend the coin of another realm more carelessly than the currency with which we are familiar.

Using the above technique, studies have been conducted to determine whether the two conditions required for behavioral selection by reflexive elicitors also hold for acquired elicitors. These conditions, you will recall, are contiguity and discrepancy. In the rabbit nictitating membrane preparation, the interval between S_2 and S_1 was varied to assess the role of contiguity in higher-order conditioning. Selection occurred only when S_2 preceded S_1 by a short time interval that closely paralleled the function obtained with reflexive elicitors.[26]

When conditioned reinforcement was studied with the operant procedure, the acquired elicitor selected an environment-behavior relation only when it followed the response by similarly short intervals.[27] With respect to temporal contiguity, the same variables that affect the ability of reflexive elicitors to function as reinforcers similarly affect acquired elicitors.[28]

For a stimulus to function as an acquired reinforcer, it is not enough that it precede a reflexive elicitor by a short interval. The reflexive elicitor must also evoke a response that causes a *change* in ongoing behavior—i.e., a behavioral discrepancy. In a study with pigeons directed at the role of discrepancy in acquired reinforcement, S_2 (e.g., a tone) was paired with food; at the same time, another stimulus, S_1 (e.g., a light) was presented that already evoked food-related responses because of prior S_1-food pairings. (You will recognize this as a blocking design.) Then the pigeons were presented with two white disks, to which pecking responses had been extinguished earlier. (Procedures in which more than one response is simultaneously scheduled for reinforcement are known as **concurrent schedules**, indicating that the various responses are available to the learner at the same time.[29]) Pecking one disk occasionally produced S_1; pecking the other disk occasionally produced S_2. Pecking never produced food during this phase of the study. Consistent with the blocking phenomenon, S_1 functioned as an effective conditioned reinforcer to increase pecking responses but S_2 did not.[30] (See **Figure 4.5**.) Thus, simply pairing a stimulus with an elicitor is not enough to enable the stimulus to later function as an acquired reinforcer. The stimulus must have control over responding if it is to select new environment-behavior relations.

Finally, as with reflexive elicitors, the effectiveness of an acquired elicitor as a conditioned reinforcer depends on interactions between the responses it evokes and the operant that produces it. If the responses evoked by the acquired elicitor interfere with the operant, then the effectiveness of the acquired elicitor as a reinforcer for that operant will be reduced or eliminated. An acquired elicitor established by a three-term contingency (i.e., a discriminative stimulus) controls both an operant and a conditioned (reinforcer-elicited) response. Thus, there are more possibilities for interaction when the eliciting function was acquired through a discriminated operant procedure than when it was acquired through a classical procedure.[31]

Physiological analysis. Behavioral research indicates that contiguity and discrepancy are essen-

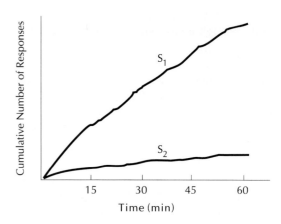

FIGURE 4.5 *Blocking of the conditioned reinforcing function*
Cumulative records of responding on a concurrent schedule in which pecking one disk occasionally produced a brief presentation of a red overhead light (S_1) that had previously been separately paired with food. Pecking the other disk occasionally produced a tone (S_2) that had previously been a component of a compound conditioned stimulus with the red light when the compound stimulus was paired with food. For other animals, the tone or light were counterbalanced as S_1 or S_2 and comparable results were obtained.
Source: Based on findings from Palmer, 1987.

tial to reinforcement with acquired reinforcers. However, just as with naturally selected reinforcers, limitations to experimental analysis arise when the analysis is restricted to the behavioral level. Acquired reinforcers, more often than naturally selected reinforcers, do not evoke responses that are readily measured on the behavioral level. We rarely if ever salivate at the sight of money, even though we may have frequently exchanged it for food. (We do sometimes speak metaphorically of drooling at the prospect of large sums of money, however.)[32] To understand the full range of biobehavioral processes responsible for acquired reinforcement, we must expand the experimental analysis to include observations at the physiological level.

As we saw in Chapter 2, our best understanding of the biological mechanisms of reinforcement is that naturally selected reinforcers activate a dopaminergic neuromodulatory system that arises from the ventral tegmental area (VTA). Axons from the VTA neurons diffusely innervate the motor association cortex of the frontal lobes (among other structures).[33] This neuromodulatory system provides a means for increasing synaptic efficacies between all recently activated neurons. The synaptic efficacies most reliably and, hence, most strongly affected are those along the pathways that mediate the reinforced environment-behavior relation.

The diffuse VTA-frontal lobe system cannot, by itself, be the biological basis of acquired reinforcement. This would require that natural selection had "anticipated" all the stimuli that might function as acquired reinforcers, and had selected functional pathways allowing all those stimuli to activate the VTA neurons. We know, however, that the stimuli that function as acquired reinforcers vary widely from one culture to another and from one individual to the next. The environmental constancy required for natural selection is not present, so natural selection must be supplemented with selection by reinforcement. How might selection by reflexive elicitors produce a neural system to implement selection by acquired reinforcers, and how might that system operate?

Although the experimental analysis of the physiological basis of acquired reinforcement is very much a work-in-progress, the basic outline of the answer is emerging. We have already seen that the cumulative effect of naturally selected reinforcers is to strengthen connections along pathways in the motor association areas of the frontal lobes. For an environmental stimulus to evoke the behavior scheduled for reinforcement, connections in the motor association cortex are strengthened along pathways that activate the motor neurons contracting the muscle fibers responsible for behavior. For the same stimulus to function as an acquired reinforcer, some of the neurons in the motor association cortex whose synaptic efficacies have been changed by the naturally selected reinforcer also activate other neurons whose axons project back to the VTA neurons. (See **Figure 4.6** for a diagrammatic sketch of such a neural system.) The pathways that feed back from the neurons in the motor association cortex and cause the VTA neurons to be activated are the pathways that mediate acquired reinforcement.

In the foregoing treatment, stimuli that function as acquired reinforcers ultimately exert their influence through the same biological mechanisms as naturally selected reinforcers. That is, as a result of selection by already effective reinforcing stimuli, acquired reinforcers come to activate the VTA-frontal lobe neuromodulatory system. The prior selection history increases the synaptic efficacies between neurons in the motor association cortex and neurons that feed back to the VTA—the source of the diffuse dopaminergic system activated by all reinforcers. Since acquired reinforcers exploit the same neural system that was naturally selected to implement reinforcement with reflexive elicitors, the biobehavioral processes and the principles used to summarize them are similar for all reinforcers—whether naturally selected or acquired.

Although much neuroanatomical and neurochemical work remains to be done, considerable evidence is consistent with this formulation of acquired reinforcement. Both electrical and chemical stimulation that affect dopaminergic neurons in motor association cortex reinforce behavioral responses that precede the stimulation. Therefore, activation of some cells in motor association cortex is sufficient to function as a reinforcer.[34] Further, if the axons that communicate between the motor association cortex and the VTA are cut, then the reinforcing effect of stimulating the motor association cortex is eliminated. Thus neural activity in the motor association cortex functions as a reinforcer through pathways leading toward the VTA. Finally, physiological research with acquired elicitors indicates that their ability to function as reinforcers is lessened if neural activity in motor association cortex is impaired or if the pathways between the motor association cortex and VTA are

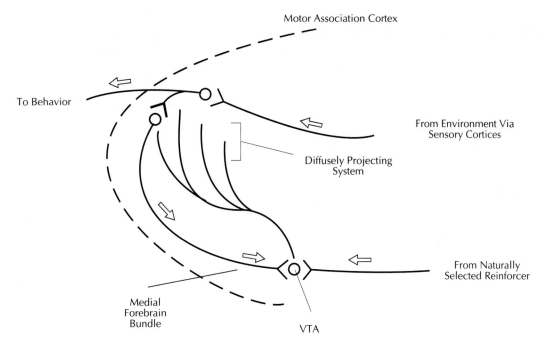

FIGURE 4.6 *Neural systems of innate (unconditioned) and acquired (conditioned) reinforcement.*
Innate reinforcement is implemented by a dopaminergic system arising from the ventral tegmental area (VTA) and projecting diffusely to synapses in the motor association cortex of the frontal lobes. When pre- and postsynaptic neurons are coactive, dopamine functions as a neuromodulator to produce long-lasting changes in synaptic efficacies, or connection strengths. Acquired reinforcement is implemented by pathways originating from neurons, in the frontal lobes and projecting to the VTA via the medial forebrain bundle. This feedback pathway then activates VTA neurons, causing further changes in synaptic efficacies in motor association cortex. The acquired reinforcement system is functional only after the innate system has selectively strengthened synapses in motor association cortex, i.e., only after the acquired reinforcing stimulus is a component of a previously reinforced environment-behavior relation.

interrupted.[35] Thus experimental analysis of physiological processes supports the view that feedback from the motor association cortex to the VTA is responsible for acquired reinforcement.

The behavioral and physiological evidence for acquired reinforcers has especially significant implications for the acquisition of complex behavior. Two general effects of acquired reinforcers are considered here: (a) their effects on the role of temporal contiguity between the response and naturally selected reinforcers and (b) their effects on the selection of complex environment-behavior relations.

Effects of Acquired Reinforcers on Temporal Contiguity

Experimental analysis has shown that environment-behavior relations can be selected only when a very brief interval—often a second or less—intervenes between an environmental stimulus, an operant, and a reinforcer. This result was obtained with both reflexive and acquired elicitors, and with both classical and operant procedures. However, the availability of acquired reinforcers enables environment-behavior relations to be selected with substantially longer intervals between the operant and a reflexive elicitor. On the behavioral level, acquired reinforcers can exert their influence through **environmental chaining** and, on the neural level, through feedback circuits implementing **internal reinforcement**.

Serial compound conditioning. Internal reinforcement and environmental chaining may both be illustrated by the procedure of **serial compound conditioning**. In serial compound conditioning, two or more stimuli are successively presented before a reflexive eliciting stimulus. For example, in the sequence S_2-S_1-elicitor, a tone and then a light might be presented before eyeshock in the rabbit nictitating membrane preparation. Note that this arrangement permits both S_1 and, eventually, S_2 to become acquired elicitors, but without the complication of extinction found in a higher-order conditioning procedure—the serial compound stimulus *continues* to be followed by the reflexive elicitor. When S_1 acquires the ability to evoke an NMR because of its close temporal proximity to the reflexive elicitor, S_2 should then also acquire the ability to evoke an NMR because of its close proximity to the acquired elicitor S_1. (See **Figure 4.7** for a depiction of the arrangement of stimuli and a record of the NMR in this procedure.)

Using a serial compound conditioning procedure in a programmatic set of well controlled experiments, James Kehoe and Dore Gormezano have shown that an S_2-NMR relation can be acquired even with a temporal interval between S_2 and eyeshock as long as 18 sec![36] This interval far exceeds the optimal interval of 250 ms, and even the few seconds over which selection is possible, in a simple classical procedure with this preparation.

As interpreted through the biobehavioral processes involved in acquired reinforcement, the S_2-NMR relation is selected in the following way.

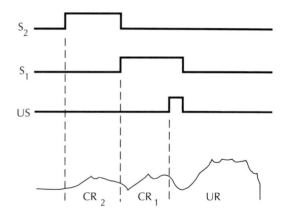

FIGURE 4.7 *Occurrence of stimuli and responding in a serial compound conditioning procedure*
The components of the compound conditioned stimulus, S_2 and S_1, were presented followed by the unconditioned stimulus, US. A light and a tone served as the component stimuli and mild eyeshock served as the US. The lower record represents the movement of the nictitating membrane of the rabbit in response to S_2, S_1, and the US after a number of compound conditioning trials.
Source: Procedure and hypothetical findings from Kehoe, 1989.

First, an S_1-NMR relation develops through temporal contiguity between S_1 and eyeshock. On the neural level, the selection of this relation depends on the direct activation of the VTA-reinforcement system by the reflexive elicitor.[37] Then, as S_1 becomes an acquired elicitor, its close temporal contiguity with S_2 selects an S_2-NMR relation even though S_2 is temporally removed from the reflexive elicitor of eyeshock. That is, S_1 functions as an acquired reinforcer for the S_2-NMR relation. Throughout this process, to the extent that S_1 and later S_2 engage feedback pathways that indirectly activate the VTA-reinforcement system, *immediate* internal reinforcement aids the selection of both the S_1-NMR and S_2-NMR relations. Immediate reinforcement is required for selection of both relations, but the reinforcement system is activated by the acquired reinforcers, S_1 and S_2, as well as by the reflexive elicitor. (See **Figure 4.8** for computer simulations comparing learning in an adap-

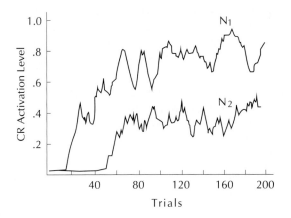

FIGURE 4.8 *Computer simulation of the effect of internal reinforcement on the acquisition of a conditioned response*
In one neural network (N₁), the connection strengths (synaptic efficacies) within the network could be modified by both the innate reinforcement system and the acquired reinforcement system implementing internal reinforcement. In the other neural network (N₂), the innate reinforcement system was intact but the acquired reinforcement system was not similarly functional.
Source: Based on findings from Donahoe, Burgos, & Palmer, 1993.

tive network with and without the internal reinforcement mechanism of acquired reinforcers.)

The relative strengths of the S_1-NMR and S_2-NMR relations depend on the interplay among a number of variables: the *particular stimuli* used in the serial compound procedure (and, therefore, the richness of the neural pathways they activate), the specific *temporal relations* among the various stimuli, and the *discrepancies* between the activation of the NMR by the various stimuli (and, therefore, the strength of the neural feedback signal mediating internal reinforcement). As an example of the role of discrepancy, to the extent that S_2 acquires the ability to evoke the NMR, the discrepancy between the evocation of the NMR by S_1 and by eyeshock is reduced, since the NMR has just been evoked by S_2. A reduced discrepancy during S_1 limits the possibility that S_1 will acquire the

ability to evoke the NMR.[38] The acquired reinforcing effect arising from the neural feedback mechanism exemplifies internal reinforcement; the acquired reinforcement arising from the reinforcing effect of S_1 on the S_2-NMR relation exemplifies environmental chaining. Through environmental chaining by means of internal reinforcement, longer sequences of environment-behavior relations can be selected that do not depend on temporal contiguity with naturally selected elicitors. As a result, to an observer the experienced learner may *appear* to learn without reinforcement—or at least without immediate reinforcement. Acquired reinforcers are often less obvious than naturally selected reinforcers because they often do not elicit readily observed responses and the critical events may be observed at the neural but not the behavioral level of analysis.

Effects of Acquired Reinforcers on Selection of Complex Behavior

In experienced learners—especially humans—acquired reinforcers are crucial determinants of most changes in the environmental guidance of behavior. The importance of acquired reinforcers has been amply demonstrated in the laboratory with both children and adults. For example, kindergarten-aged children were given 15 pairings of a colored light with candy. Then each child was allowed to press either of two levers, one of which produced the light that had been paired with candy and the other a light of a different color. By the end of a 10-min test period, the lever producing the color previously paired with candy was pressed more than 110 times, while the second lever was pressed fewer than 45 times.[39]

The ability of acquired reinforcers to assume increasing responsibility for behavioral selection makes it appear that the selection of environment-behavior relations is no longer influenced by the immediate consequences of responding. This misconception is fostered both because the observer is often unaware of the person's history of behavioral selection—and, consequently, of the stimuli that function as acquired reinforcers—and because the responses evoked by acquired reinforcers are often subtle or observable only at the neural level. However, what we know of selection by reinforcement cautions us that all learners remain forever creatures of the moment. Our species increasingly acts *as if* it were liberated from temporal constraints because the contents of the moment become ever more filled with acquired reinforcers—a legacy of prior behavioral selection.

In nontechnical terms, our actions reflect long-term goals to the extent that experience has provided us with subgoals that occur immediately after each response in the chain of environment-behavior relations that makes up much complex behavior. Consider an office worker who receives a paycheck each Friday. Can the paycheck—which is an acquired reinforcer by virtue of its pairing with many other reinforcers—be the stimulus that reinforces behavior occurring on Monday? From what we know about selection by reinforcement, an environment-behavior relation occurring on Monday cannot be selected by a paycheck that occurs on Friday; the time interval is much too long. To interpret Monday's behavior, we must examine the specific circumstances that existed on Monday when the new relation was selected, and identify the contemporaneous events that functioned as acquired reinforcers. Perhaps social stimuli from the environment—such as expressions of approval by co-workers—served as the immediate consequences that selected the environment-behavior relation. Perhaps covert stimuli—such as those provided by differentiated responses indicating that an effective response has been performed (what we might call "knowledge of a job well done")—served as the immediate consequences that selected the relation through internal reinforcement. In the natural environment, the uncircumventable limitations of historical science and our inability to analyze experimentally all relevant events usually make it impossible to identify all of the critical contemporaneous events in a particular case. Nevertheless, if the changed environment-behavior relation is to be interpreted as the product of selection by reinforcement, then the change must have been produced by reinforcers that occurred immediately after the behavior, and not by a temporally remote event such as a paycheck.[40]

Self-control.   Research on what is called "self"-control illustrates one important role of acquired reinforcers in human behavior. In studies of self-control, the learner is faced with two alternative courses of action—one that leads to an immediate but small reinforcer and the other that leads to a larger but delayed reinforcer. For instance, a student might be faced with a choice between going out for the evening or staying home to prepare for the next day's examination. When animals such as rats and pigeons are confronted with comparable situations, the response that leads to an immediate small reinforcer occurs more often.[41] Moreover, young children behave similarly in such situations.[42] This outcome is "unwise" in the sense that, over the long run, more reinforcers would be received by responding to obtain the larger, more delayed reinforcer. Although adults do not always show self-control—have you ever eaten a fattening dessert even though it would make you look less attractive in a bathing suit next summer?—they often do select the larger reinforcer even when it is delayed. How does this "wise" choice come about if environment-behavior relations are selected by their immediate consequences?

To identify the conditions under which self-control emerges, a procedure was devised to simulate self-control using concurrent schedules. As shown in **Figure 4.9**, the procedure begins with two response disks simultaneously illuminated with white light. For the pigeon subjects, pecking the left disk produced a small amount of food after a brief darkening of both disks. Pecking the right disk produced a larger amount of food, but after a delay of some seconds during which both disks were darkened. Under these circumstances, pecking the disk that was followed by the shorter delay in reinforcement occurred more frequently. In short, the pigeons showed little self-control.

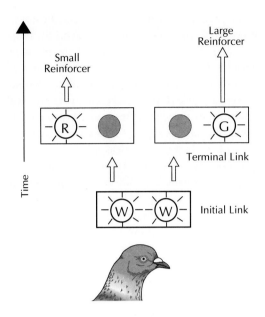

FIGURE 4.9 *Concurrent-chain procedure used in the study of self-control*
The initial link in the procedure begins with two white disks concurrently illuminated by white light. Pecking the left white disk produces a terminal link in which that disk becomes red and the other disk darkens, with a small amount of food occurring after a short delay. Pecking the right white disk produces a terminal link in which that disk becomes green and the other disk darkens, with a larger amount of food occurring after a longer delay. Self-control is said to be demonstrated if the right white disk is pecked in preference to the left.
Source: Based on findings from Rachlin & Green, 1972.

A number of studies were undertaken to isolate the variables that favor selection of the response producing the larger, delayed reinforcer. In the study considered here, instead of both white disks being darkened after a pecking response, the color of the pecked disk changed to one that differed for large and small reinforcers. For example, if the pecked disk produced the small immediate reinforcer, then the disk changed briefly to red and the other disk was darkened. If the pecked disk produced the large delayed reinforcer, then—during the longer delay period—the disk changed to green

while the other disk was darkened. This arrangement is called a **concurrent-chain procedure**, because there are two simultaneously available response options each of which consists of successive stimuli—white then red or white then green in this case. At the end of the stimulus, a further response produces a reflexive elicitor. (Note that a concurrent schedule consists of two serial compound stimuli, but with each component stimulus dependent on a response rather than merely the passage of time: A concurrent schedule exemplifies an operant rather than a classical procedure.) In this concurrent-chain procedure, the red stimulus continued until immediately before a small amount of food and the green stimulus continued until immediately before a large amount of food. Therefore, pecking the left white key was immediately followed by an acquired reinforcer for a small amount of food and pecking the right white key was immediately followed by an acquired reinforcer for a large amount of food. Under these circumstances, pecking the white key that eventually led to the delayed large food reinforcer became much more likely. In short, the availability of an *immediate* acquired reinforcer selected behavior that, were it observed in humans, would be taken as evidence of self-control. These and other related experiments have demonstrated that the same conditions that foster self-control in animals also favor the development of self-control in children.[43]

As illustrated by their effects on self-control, acquired reinforcers make crucial contributions to complex behavior. They exert their effects by providing immediate consequences for environment-behavior relations on which reflexive elicitors are too temporally remote to have an effect.[44] That is, acquired reinforcers bridge the temporal gap between the environment-behavior relation and the naturally selected reinforcer. Understanding the effects of acquired reinforcers does not require a new principle of reinforcement. If acquired reinforcers work by activating the same neural mechanisms as naturally selected reinforcers, then the reinforcement principle appears adequate to accommodate both of them.

As always, the environment is the ultimate origin of selection—whether through the feedback mechanisms of internal reinforcement or the more direct effect of naturally selected reinforcers. Self-control and self-reinforcement are simply short-hand terms for some of the effects of acquired reinforcers; the "self" is neither the origin nor the cause of internal reinforcement.[45] It is equally inaccurate to speak of the brain "reinforcing itself:" The environment, by activating the feedback pathways that implement the neural mechanisms of internal reinforcement, remains the guiding agent.

When the neural networks selected by past environments mediate environment-behavior relations that are consistent with present contingencies, then the effects of earlier selections are beneficial. The benefit is most evident when the behavioral component of the selected relation is the same in the past and present environments, as with successive stimulus components in serial compound conditioning. However, when the responses selected in the present environment differ from those of past environments, internal reinforcement may not be beneficial. The environment-behavior relations produced by selection—whether by acquired or naturally selected reinforcers—are not necessarily appropriate for all future environments. The products of past selections are appropriate for future environments only to the extent that the contingencies of reinforcement are similar in similar environments.

Behavioral chaining. Perhaps the most common contribution of acquired reinforcers to the development of complex behavior is through the chaining of environment-behavior relations. Much complex behavior consists of a sequence of relatively simple environment-behavior relations produced in a particular order. As a hypothetical example, the sight of the bathroom mirror (S_1) evokes glancing (R_1) at one's reflection, and the glance is reinforced if (say) your hair is properly arranged. Your hair is properly arranged if the sight of a hairbrush (S_2) previously caused you to pick up the brush and brush your hair (R_2). In turn, the

brush would have been sighted if, seeing the vanity drawer (S_3), you had opened it to reveal the brush (R_3), and so on. In this sequence of environment-behavior relations, each relation is maintained by the discriminative stimulus produced by the preceding response. Opening the vanity drawer was reinforced by the sight of the brush; brushing your hair established the sight of the mirror as a reinforcer; looking in the mirror was reinforced by your reflection. (See **Figure 4.10** for a diagram of this sequence of relations.) Note that the various stimuli functioned as acquired reinforcers only when the environment-behavior relations occurred in a particular order. Looking at your reflection in a mirror might not be reinforcing if your hair were not brushed. Brushing your hair might not be reinforcing if no mirror were available, and so on. When discriminative stimuli function as reinforcers for the responses that produce them, orderly sequences of environment-behavior relations are maintained. In **behavioral chaining**, discriminative stimuli are produced by responses whereas, in environmental chaining, successive stimuli occur independently of responding.

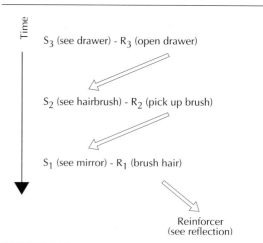

FIGURE 4.10   *A behavioral chain*
Each response in the chain is guided by a preceding discriminative stimulus and reinforced by a stimulus that functions as an acquired reinforcer for that response and as a discriminative stimulus for the next response. (See text for a more complete account.)

Very long sequences of environment-behavior relations can be maintained by discriminative stimuli serving as acquired reinforcers for the responses that produce them.[46] In the preceding example, for instance, the sequence is only part of a longer sequence that may be described as "getting up in the morning and preparing for the day." In later chapters, we describe a number of examples of behavioral chains when we interpret some of the phenomena of problem solving and remembering. Behavioral chains of substantial length may be

demonstrated in nonhumans as well. As illustrated in **Figure 4.11**, a rat was taught to execute a 10-component chain in which only the last component was reinforced with a naturally selected elicitor.[47] First, the rat was taught to press a lever for food when a light came on above the lever (a discriminated operant). Then, it was taught to get in an "elevator" and ride it to the bottom level of the test chamber, which caused the light to come on. Only then could the lever be pressed for food. Next, the rat was taught to crawl through a tunnel to gain

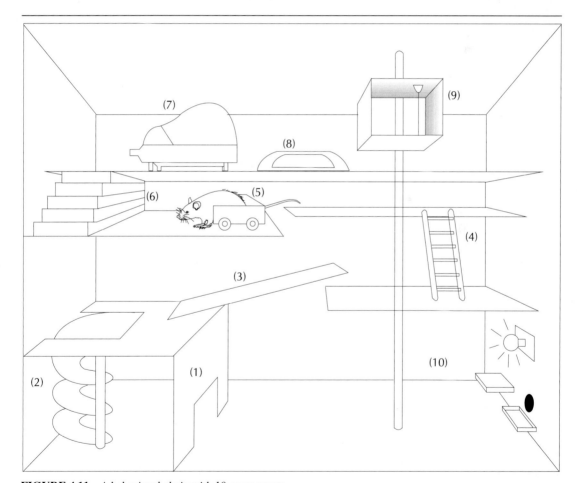

FIGURE 4.11   *A behavioral chain with 10 components*
Only the last component, pressing the lever when the light over the lever is illuminated, was followed by food. All earlier components were reinforced by the acquired reinforcer of the next discriminative stimulus in the chain.
Source: Figure from *An Introduction to Behavior Theory and Its Applications* by Robert L. Karen. Copyright © 1974 by Robert L. Karen. Reprinted by permission of HarperCollins Publishers.

access to the elevator. Gradually, earlier components were progressively added to the chain, until all 10 environment-behavior relations had been acquired. This technique, in which the components are added to behavioral chains in reverse order to the one in which they will ultimately occur, is called **backward chaining**.[48]

COMPLEX EFFECTS OF REINFORCEMENT HISTORY

So far we have identified two general effects of selection on experienced learners—the effect of retention of previously selected environment-behavior relations on the selection of new relations, and the selection of new relations by acquired reinforcers. We found that some of the effects of previously selected relations endured indefinitely, and that these retained relations caused new relations to be increasingly selected by acquired reinforcers. In this section, we consider additional effects of prior learning that are closely related to the reinforcement process itself. These are the effects of earlier selection on the behavioral discrepancies produced by eliciting stimuli and on the discriminative function of stimuli arising from conditioned responses (i.e., acquired responses similar to those elicited by the reinforcer).

Behavioral Discrepancies in Experienced Learners

The analysis of reinforcement indicated that, to function as a reinforcer, the eliciting stimulus must produce a behavioral discrepancy. As measured on the behavioral level, food functions as a reinforcer to the extent that it evokes responses—such as salivation—that do not occur in the absence of food. Selection continues until environmental stimuli evoke salivation in proportion to that evoked by the eliciting stimulus; then, since the behavioral discrepancy has been reduced, selection stops. Once an environment-behavior relation has been selected, if the reinforcer is no longer forthcoming, the relation is extinguished. At the beginning of extinction the environment guides the response originally evoked by the reinforcer; but, since the reinforcer is no longer presented, a discrepancy recurs and the environment-behavior relation weakens until the discrepancy has once again been reduced.

The foregoing account of the reinforcement and extinction of environment-behavior relations is based on controlled laboratory studies in which the learner has little or no prior history of selection in the test environment. Such a simplification is necessary to carry out an experimental analysis leading to the formulation of a principle of selection. However, in the natural environment the learner increasingly *does* have a relevant history of earlier selection, and the effects of that history must be taken into account in interpreting the effects of reinforcers. We have already considered one situation in which a prior history of reinforcement in the presence of a stimulus prevented a second stimulus from acquiring the ability to guide behavior, even when the eliciting stimulus occurred in a favorable temporal relation with the second stimulus. This is the phenomenon of blocking. Here we consider another case in which earlier selection affects the ability of an eliciting stimulus to function as a reinforcer.

Over-expectation. Suppose that two stimuli, a light and a tone, are separately paired with the same food reinforcer until performance is stable. At this point, each of the stimuli evokes a salivary response appropriate to the amount of food with which it has been paired. Next, suppose that those same stimuli are presented together in a simultaneous compound and followed by the *same* amount of food as before. If the two components of the compound stimulus evoke *more* salivation together than either one would evoke alone, then the compound stimulus will evoke more salivation than is appropriate for the amount of food. If the tone-light compound evokes an excessive conditioned response, a discrepancy occurs—the same sort of discrepancy that is produced at the beginning of an extinction procedure. That is, the responses evoked by the discriminative stimulus (the tone-light compound) are greater than those evoked by the environment (the food) that follows the stimulus. In nontechnical terms, since the learner "expects" more food than he gets, the phenomenon is commonly known as **over-expectation**. Because of the nature of the discrepancy, the ability of the light or tone to evoke salivation should decline, *even though they have received additional pairings with food during compound training*. Thus, pairing the compound stimulus with the same reinforcer should produce an effect similar to that of an extinction procedure—i.e., the environment-behavior relation should weaken.

In experimental tests[49] of this prediction of the reinforcement principle, after simple and then compound-stimulus training, the component stimuli were then presented separately. It was found that the ability of each component to evoke conditioned (reinforcer-elicited) responses had been weakened. Analogous results have been obtained with operant procedures.[50] If the environment in which a response produces an elicitor has been paired with that elicitor in the past, then giving the elicitor after the response does not strengthen responding as much as it would otherwise. In short, an elicitor is less able to function as a reinforcer of an environment-behavior relation in either the classical or operant procedure when the environment already evokes conditioned responses as a result of prior selection.

Speaking less technically, if an eliciting stimulus is already "expected," then the elicitor is undermined as a reinforcer since it produces less of a behavioral discrepancy than it normally would. The phenomenon of over-expectation, together with blocking and edge effects, supports the conclusion that, in experienced learners, the reinforcing function of an elicitor cannot be determined from its eliciting properties alone. The reinforcing function of an eliciting stimulus depends on the behavioral discrepancy it produces, and the discrepancy is, in part, a function of the responses that the environment already controls as a result of past selections. Since different learners have different

selection histories, the behavior of any two learners is likely to be affected somewhat differently by identical elicitors. As a result, in the natural environment the reinforcing effect of an elicitor is commonly modulated by the individual's history of past selections.[51] The reinforcement principle—although intended to summarize selection processes common to all organisms—implies that the effect of those common processes will vary with the unique and incompletely known experiences of the individual learner. As a consequence, behavioral engineering will forever remain, at least in part, an art in which general principles are applied to unique and incompletely known realizations of common processes.

Discriminative Function of Reinforcer-Elicited Responses

Stimuli acquire a discriminative function—i.e, the ability to guide behavior—when they occur immediately before a response that is followed by a reinforcer. In the experimental analysis of discrimination formation, we examined the discriminative function of environmental stimuli because such stimuli are readily manipulated and measured. However, any event that stimulates activity in the nervous system, whether the event occurs in the environment or within the organism, should acquire a discriminative function if the conditions for selection are satisfied. Thus, any internal stimulus that regularly precedes a reinforced response should acquire a discriminative function.[52]

In the earlier interpretation of discriminated operant conditioning by means of adaptive neural networks (see Chapter 2), a possible source of internal stimulation was identified that could provide discriminative stimuli. You will recall that conditioned responses are acquired *before* operant responses because, at the beginning of selection, reinforcer-elicited responses are evoked more strongly by the eliciting stimulus than operant responses are evoked by environmental stimuli. For instance, food initially evokes salivation more strongly than the sight of a lever evokes leverpressing. And, when reinforcement occurs, connections between more strongly activated units are changed more than connections between less strongly activated units. If conditioned responses produce distinctive internal stimuli, then—since they occur before the operant response—the internal stimuli are in a position to acquire control over the operant *in addition to* the control exerted by the discriminative stimuli from the environment. Thus an operant response can be guided by stimulation of two origins—from the environment and from the conditioned response. That is, operant responses may often be guided by a compound stimulus composed of both environmental and internal stimulus components.[53]

If operants are partially guided by internal stimuli provided by conditioned responses, then procedures that affect those internal stimuli should also affect the operant. Ruth Colwill and Robert Rescorla have carried out an extensive series of studies that bear on this issue.[54] One such study is concerned with the **devaluation** of reinforcers, and is described here.

Devaluation.   At the end of conditioning, an operant may be guided by a compound stimulus, one of whose components is a stimulus produced by the conditioned response. If, after selection has concluded, the control of the operant by stimuli from the conditioned response is altered, then the control of the operant by the nominal discriminative stimulus—the environmental stimulus—appears weakened. A weakened relation should appear because one component of the compound stimulus guiding the operant is no longer effective.

As an indirect test of the guiding role of stimuli from conditioned responses, two different operants were first selected using rats as subjects.[55] The operants were: sight of a chain—pull the chain, and sight of a lever—press the lever. One operant was selected with a food pellet as the reinforcer and the other with a sugar pellet. If distinctive stimuli are provided by the conditioned responses to food and sugar reinforcers, then chain-pulling and lever-pressing are guided by compound discriminative stimuli whose conditioned-response-produced stimuli are somewhat different. In order to alter the control of responding by the conditioned-response-produced stimuli, one reinforcer was paired with a sublethal dose of poison that caused withdrawal responses to be conditioned to these stimuli. As a result of this later training, the conditioned-response-produced stimulus paired with poison should evoke withdrawal responses. Then, when the animals were again presented with the chain and lever, the environmental stimulus controlling the conditioned-response-produced stimulus that had been paired with poison should evoke withdrawal responses that interfere with the operant response. As a result, the operant whose reinforcer had been paired with poison should occur less frequently than the operant whose reinforcer had not been paired with poison. This is precisely what occurred. If leverpressing had been reinforced with a food pellet and the animal had later been poisoned after eating a food pellet, then leverpressing occurred less frequently than chain-pulling during a test session. (See **Figure 4.12** for a diagram of this complex procedure.)

A number of other studies have been conducted in which procedures were instituted to alter the discriminative effects of conditioned-response-produced stimuli. The outcome of these studies has been consistent with the interpretation that internal stimuli of this origin are components of a compound discriminative stimulus guiding operant responses. These internal-stimulus components are well placed to guide the operant response, since their onset occurs more immediately before the operant response than does the onset of the environmental component (the nominal discriminative stimulus). Moreover, the conditioned response that produces the internal stimulus appears early in training, before the behavioral discrepancy required for selection has been reduced. The onset of this internal stimulus necessarily occurs more immediately before the operant response because the conditioned response, which produces the stimuli, is evoked by the environmental component and therefore must occur after it. Experimental analy-

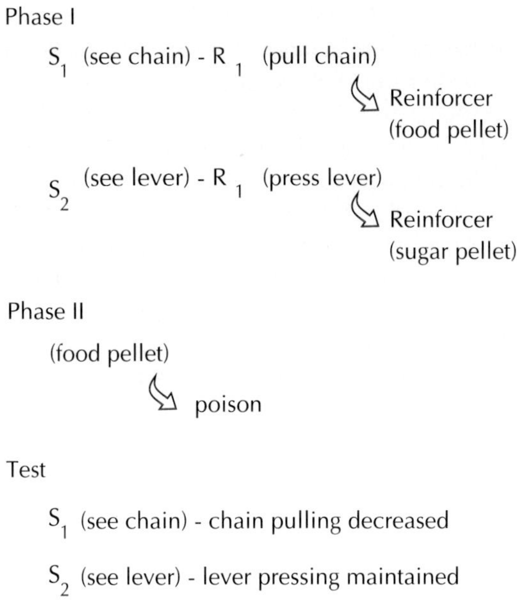

Phase I

S_1 (see chain) - R $_1$ (pull chain)

⤷ Reinforcer
(food pellet)

S_2 (see lever) - R $_1$ (press lever)

⤷ Reinforcer
(sugar pellet)

Phase II

(food pellet)

⤷ poison

Test

S_1 (see chain) - chain pulling decreased

S_2 (see lever) - lever pressing maintained

FIGURE 4.12 *Training and test conditions used to study devaluation*

In Phase 1, two environment-behavior relations are selected using different reinforcing stimuli—a food pellet and a sugar pellet. In Phase 2, one of the reinforcing stimuli, here the food pellet, is paired with an aversive unconditioned stimulus, here poison that elicits nausea and withdrawal responses. In subsequent testing, the environment-behavior relation acquired with the reinforcer that was paired with poison is weakened relative to the other relation. The reinforcer paired with poison is said to be "devalued."

Source: Based on procedures from Colwill & Rescorla, 1985.

sis—which measures the internal responses and stimuli at the microbehavioral or physiological levels—is required if these issues are to be investigated directly.[56]

This implication of the reinforcement principle—that conditioned-response-produced internal stimuli guide operant responses together with the nominal discriminative stimuli—provides an additional means by which past selections may affect present selections. An implication for behavioral engineering is that weakening dysfunctional operant behavior requires extinction—or selection of alternative responses—in the presence of the inter-

nal stimuli produced by the conditioned response. For example, the elimination of phobias would require the extinction of operants not only in the presence of the stimuli that are the object of the person's unreasonable "fear," but in the presence of those internal states conventionally called "fear" that are evoked by such stimuli. If the environment-behavior relation is to be weakened to the point that the operant no longer occurs, both components of the compound discriminative stimulus must lose their ability to guide the operant.[57]

COMPLEX CONTINGENCIES OF REINFORCEMENT

Complex behavior is jointly determined by the legacies of past selections as they are acted upon by the contingencies of reinforcement that exist at the moment. The effect of the prevailing contingencies of reinforcement—or schedules of reinforcement—is the primary focus of the final section of this chapter. Darwin spoke of the capacity of the ancestral environment "to change her species & adapt them to the wondrous & exquisitely beautiful contingencies to which every living species is exposed."[58] The contingencies provided by the individual environment are no less wonderful or exquisite.

Schedules of Reinforcement

A **schedule of reinforcement** is a complete description of the environmental and behavioral conditions that are present when a response is followed by a reinforcer. One specific type of reinforcement schedule has been explicitly encountered in this chapter—the concurrent schedule. Since there are an infinite number of different conditions under which a response might be followed by a reinforcer, concurrent schedules are but one type of schedule among an infinite number of different schedules of reinforcement.[59]

To study some of the important conditions that affect behavior in the infinity of possible schedules of reinforcement, B. F. Skinner and Charles Ferster[60] manipulated two classes of variables under which responses produced reinforcers—stimulus conditions (an important subset of which are stimuli that vary with the passage of time since a prior event has occurred) and response conditions. For example, disk-pecking might produce food if the disk were green and at least 60 sec had elapsed since a previous food presentation. These variations were chiefly studied by what may be called the *standard* schedules of reinforcement. Such schedules and their effects are described in most introductory textbooks. This work determined that organisms are extremely sensitive to the specific environmental (including temporal) and response conditions that are present when the response is reinforced. For example, when a pecking response by a pigeon produced food only after at least 60 sec had elapsed since the last food presentation, pecking occurred very infrequently after a food presentation and then grew more frequent as the 60-sec period neared its end. The pattern of responding produced by this contingency is the "scallop" of what is technically known as a **fixed-interval (FI) schedule**. When pecking produced food after a variable time since the previous reinforcer, a moderate, relatively constant rate of pecking was produced, with little pausing after the reinforcer. This schedule is called a **variable-interval (VI) schedule**. In interval schedules—whether fixed or variable—the likelihood that a response will produce a reinforcer is primarily a function of stimuli that vary as a function of time since the previous reinforcer.[61]

In ratio schedules—the other major type of standard schedule—the likelihood that a response will produce a reinforcer is primarily a function of the number of responses since the previous reinforcer.[62] For example, if pecking produced food after a fixed number of responses, say 20, then responding occurred at a high rate with little pausing except immediately after the reinforcer. This is the "break-and-run" pattern produced by what are technically called **fixed-ratio (FR) schedules**. (They are so called because the contingency insures a fixed ratio of responses to reinforcers—here, 20 to 1).[63] A

contingency during which pecking produces food after a variable number of responses is called a **variable-ratio (VR) schedule**. (See **Figure 4.13** for cumulative records showing the patterns of responding produced when a response is exposed to the contingencies manipulated in the standard schedules of reinforcement.)

Although integrated theoretical treatments have been developed for the temporal and behavioral variables manipulated in the standard schedules of reinforcement,[64] these are not our concern here. Instead, we focus on some general conceptual issues that are raised by the experimental analysis and interpretation of reinforcement schedules. These issues are discussed in our analysis of concurrent schedules—schedules in which responding is simultaneously exposed to more than one schedule of reinforcement. The effects of concurrent schedules are particularly interesting because, as noted in the earlier discussion of self-control, such schedules permit an analysis of "choice." That is, the learner is faced with several response alternatives under conditions that permit researchers to investigate the variables that determine the likelihood of responding. Concurrent schedules also more closely approximate the many possibilities for action that exist at every moment in the natural environment. As one wag has put it, "life is a bowl of concurrent schedules."

Concurrent schedules. The most commonly studied concurrent schedule has been one in which the learner is faced with two response alternatives, each of which is associated with a different stimulus and a different variable-interval reinforcement schedule. For example, a pigeon might be presented with two disks on the wall of the test chamber, with pecking one disk reinforced on a variable-interval 60-sec schedule (VI-60) and the other on a variable-interval 30-sec schedule (VI-30). Since during VI schedules reinforcers occur only occasionally and do not require the emission of more than one response, the relative frequency of responding on the two alternatives provides a sensitive measure of "choice" or "preference."

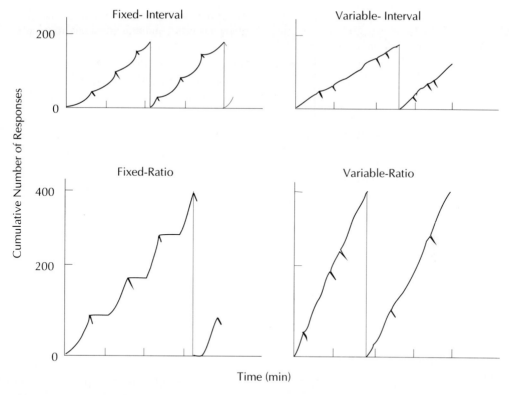

FIGURE 4.13   *Effects of different reinforcement schedules on operant responding*
Illustrative cumulative records after training in which responding was acquired and maintained on various reinforcement schedules. The occasional "tics" beneath the curves indicate the occurrence of reinforcers. Note that, other factors being equal, ratio schedules produce higher rates of responding than interval schedules and variable schedules produce more constant rates than fixed schedules.
Source: Hypothetical records based on findings from Ferster & Skinner, 1957.

The general result from the study of choice with concurrent VI schedules has been that the relative frequency of responding on an alternative matches the relative frequency of reinforcers produced by responding on that alternative. Thus, with a concurrent VI-60, VI-30 schedule, only half as many pecks would be directed at the disk associated with the VI-60 schedule as at the one with the VI-30 schedule. Over a one-hour period, only 60 food presentations would occur for pecking the VI-60 disk, while 120 would occur for pecking the VI-30 disk. Findings from concurrent schedules were described by a principle proposed by Richard

Herrnstein called the **matching principle**; i.e., the relative frequency of responding on an alternative matches the relative frequency of reinforcers for responding on that alternative.[65] **Figure 4.14**, left panel shows the outcome of an experiment which reports findings for animals exposed to a number of different pairs of VI schedules. The straight line indicates how the relative frequency of responding varies as a function of the relative frequency of reinforcement when perfect matching occurs.

The matching principle is a **molar principle**, in contrast to a **molecular principle**, because it describes the relation between two variables that

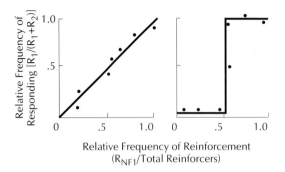

Relative Frequency of Reinforcement
(R_{NF1}/Total Reinforcers)

FIGURE 4.14 *Performance on concurrent schedules of reinforcement*
The left panel shows the relative frequency of responding after a pigeon had been exposed to a number of pairs of variable-interval (VI) reinforcement schedules in which different colors on the disks were associated with different schedules of reinforcement for pecking the disk. Various combinations of colors occurred representing three reinforcement schedules—VI 30 s, VI 60 s, and VI 90 s. The relative rate of responding on a disk closely matched the relative frequency of reinforcement for pecking that disk. The right panel shows the relative frequency of responding under the same test conditions, but when the pairs of reinforcement schedules to which the subjects were exposed prior to testing were restricted to pairs of the *same* variable-interval schedules—i.e., VI 30 s - VI 30 s, VI 60 s - VI 60 s, and VI 90 s - VI 90 s. Without prior exposure to different concurrent schedules, matching did not occur. Instead, responding was directed almost exclusively toward the disk whose color was associated with the more frequent reinforcement.
Source: Based on findings from Crowley, 1981.

are defined over an appreciable time interval—the frequency of responses and the frequency of reinforcers over a test session. A molecular principle, such as the reinforcement principle, describes the relation between variables that are defined over a brief time interval—the interval between the occurrence of a single response and the occurrence of its reinforcer.[66] In the following section, we examine the distinction between molar and molecular principles, since it is central to the difference between the contingencies responsible for selection by the ancestral and individual environments.

Molar and Molecular Accounts of Selection

The principle of natural selection describes the effects of the ancestral environment on the frequency of genes in populations of living organisms. It summarizes a selection effect that emerges over substantial periods of time when summed over many individuals. There is no guarantee that on every occasion natural selection will favor any particular structure (and the behavior that utilizes that structure) or any particular individual. For example, George and Martha Washington left no children of record (i.e., they had zero reproductive fitness), yet many of the characteristics that they possessed are surely favored by natural selection *over the long run*. Natural selection can favor changes that benefit reproductive fitness over the long run because, in a population of individuals, changes in gene frequency do not occur immediately but only after reproduction. In contrast, a principle of selection by reinforcement describes the immediate effect of the contemporary environment on the population of environment-behavior relations from a single individual.[67] There is no guarantee that selection by reinforcement will favor any particular environment-behavior relation on all occasions, but if a particular relation is selected it must be because of events that existed *at the moment of selection*. Although changes in gene frequency do not appear immediately upon the selecting action of the ancestral environment, the synaptic changes accompanying behavioral selection must occur immediately upon the selecting action of the individual environment. The effects of selection by reinforcement are not postponed until the individual organism has been exposed to hundreds of three-term contingencies.

Although selection by reinforcement must be based on conditions that exist at the moment of selection, there is an important interdependence between the principles of natural and behavioral selection—between the selecting effects of environments that endure for long periods and those that exist for a moment. The ancestral environment selects reinforcement processes that, acting *at the moment of selection*, favor reproductive fitness *over the long run*.[68] From this perspective, molar principles are appropriate to describe the outcome of natural selection and, perhaps sometimes, the *cumulative* effect of selection by reinforcement. However, molecular principles are needed to describe the processes responsible for selection by reinforcement. A molar principle appears to describe the effects of reinforcement accurately only to the extent that it is equivalent to the cumulative effect of a molecular principle.[69]

In keeping with this general expectation, the molar relation between response frequency and reinforcer frequency described by the matching principle has been shown to be derivable, under certain conditions, from the cumulative effects of the processes described by a molecular reinforcement principle.[70] Not surprisingly, matching and other molar accounts [71] have been most helpful in summarizing relations between variables that are heavily influenced by natural selection—a process that does operate over long time intervals. For example, animals vary in how they allocate their behavioral resources in the natural environment, depending on the availability of food in various "patches." Thus an insect-eating bird may find more insects in one patch within its range in the morning and more in another patch at twilight.[72] The proportion of time and other resources allocated to traveling between and searching the various patches is reasonably well described by the matching principle, which takes much the same form as corresponding principles from evolutionary biology.[73]

Limitations of molar principles. However, since a molar principle describes the *effect* of selection by reinforcement rather than its cause, the correspondence between molar principles and the functional relations between variables produced by behavioral selection is often imperfect.[74] As one example of a limitation of a molar matching principle, consider the following study. During training, pigeons pecked either of two disks with each of three colors on the disks associated with a different VI schedule—VI-30, VI-60, and VI-90 sec.[75] Only one response-disk was illuminated at any one time. After training with each of the three schedules on each of the two disks, the pigeons were tested with two disks illuminated simultaneously. Note that before the test with the concurrent schedule, a number of different environment-behavior relations had been selected, with each color on both disks controlling pecking at three different rates. If performance on concurrent schedules is simply a function of "choice" or "preference" among the schedules, then the subjects should match their relative response frequencies to the relative frequencies of reinforcers received during training with each color. Instead, the subjects did not match, but distributed their responses in an all-or-none fashion: Pecking was directed almost exclusively at the color associated with the more frequent reinforcer. (See **Figure 4.14**, right panel.)

If, however, performance on concurrent schedules is a complex mixture of several operants—including the operant of "switching" from one disk to the other—then matching would not be expected on the first exposure to a concurrent schedule: The animals' selection histories did not include reinforcement for switching behavior.[76] To assess this interpretation of the failure to obtain matching, the pigeons were given additional training with a special concurrent schedule. Each trial consisted of the simultaneous presentation of a pair of *identical* colors on the two disks—one of the three colors, with its associated VI reinforcement schedule, used in the original training. This procedure added switching behavior to the operants that were reinforced in the training procedure. After this training, when the pigeons were again tested with *different* colors on the two disks, pecking was distributed in a manner that was well described by the matching principle. (Again, see **Figure 4.14**, left panel.) That is, the birds approximately matched the relative frequency of pecking a particular color to the relative frequency of reinforcement produced by pecking that color.

The experimental analysis of concurrent schedules demonstrates that performance is the result of a complex mixture of different operants, and not a simple reflection of the relative strengths of pecking operants alone. Thus the relative frequency of pecking is not a measure of a unitary quantity—choice, or preference.[77] All of the environment-behavior relations occurring in a complex situation must be taken into account if the behavior is to be interpreted. Since complex situations often do not permit an experimental analysis of all of the relevant relations, understanding complex behavior must often take the form of interpretations based on biobehavioral principles grounded in prior experimental analyses. Since a complete experimental analysis is often foreclosed in complex situations, interpretation often provides the only road we may travel toward understanding. The experimental analysis of even the relatively simple case of concurrent schedules remains partially incomplete, but its interpretation seems to fall well within the reach of a molecular principle of reinforcement.[78]

Contingencies with Aversive Stimuli

Until this point, we have considered contingencies in which the eliciting stimuli were *appetitive*. An **appetitive elicitor** is a stimulus that evokes an approach response; i.e., a response that brings the learner into contact with the stimulus. For example, an animal approaches environmental locations in which food is presented. In this section, we briefly consider *aversive* elicitors. An **aversive elicitor** is a stimulus that evokes withdrawal, or **escape**, **responses**.[79] A learner escapes from locations in which shocks are presented. In addition to naturally selected aversive stimuli, such as those that stimulate pain receptors, learners withdraw from stimuli that have been paired with aversive elicitors.[80] Thus there are *acquired* aversive elicitors as well as naturally selected aversive elicitors. The question of present interest is: Can the principle of

behavioral selection accommodate the effects of aversive elicitors as well as those of appetitive elicitors?

Punishment.   According to the unified principle of behavioral selection, when aversive elicitors are contingent on responses, they produce interactions between operants and conditioned escape responses. Recall that when a behavioral discrepancy occurs, whatever responses occur in the vicinity of the discrepancy come under the guidance of whatever stimuli preceded the discrepancy. If the operant and the elicited response are incompatible, then the strength of the operant declines because the eliciting stimulus evokes an escape response that prevents the operant from occurring. If the elicitor reduces the strength of the operant that produces it, then the eliciting stimulus is said to function as a **punishing stimulus**, or **punisher**, and the procedure is termed a **punishment procedure**.[81] Aversive elicitors function as punishers because, according to the unified reinforcement principle as implemented in adaptive neural networks, conditioned responses are acquired before operants. Since the conditioned response—an escape response—is acquired before the operant, the operant does not occur and is therefore not among the responses available to be selected by the discrepancy.[82]

As a specific experimental example of punishment, leverpressing that was maintained by the occasional presentation of food was then sometimes made to produce a shock.[83] The effect of introducing the shock was to reduce or eliminate leverpressing. Under these circumstances, the aversive eliciting stimulus of shock functioned as a punisher with respect to the operant of leverpressing. That is, shock-elicited escape responses were guided by the some of the same stimuli that formerly guided leverpressing and, as a result, conditioned shock-elicited responses interfered or competed with leverpressing. The most salient effect of introducing the shock was to decrease the likelihood of leverpressing, but this was the indirect result of increasing the strength of incompatible conditioned shock-elicited responses. Punishers act by causing conditioned responses to interfere with operants.

Aversive stimuli as reinforcers.   If the responses elicited by an aversive elicitor are *not* incompatible with the operant, then the elicitor does not function as a punisher but as a reinforcer! An all-too-common example is provided by the parent who spanks a child for crying. The operant is crying and one of the responses elicited by spanking is crying. Crying quietly is about the "best" that this procedure can produce. Of course, spanking also elicits a number of responses other than crying—escape, biting, etc.—and we may expect these responses to increase in strength as well.[84]

Paradoxical effects of aversive elicitors occur in situations in which an operant is chosen that is not incompatible with the responses elicited by the "punisher." As one example, shock to the tail of a restrained rat elicits extension of the hind legs—i.e., "running away." If an operant procedure is instituted in which "spontaneous" extension of the hind leg occasionally produces shock to the tail, then shock will function as a reinforcer for leg extension. The rat extends its leg and, under these circumstances, shocks itself forever.[85] The operant is leg extension, the elicited response is leg extension, and—because the two responses are compatible—shock functions as a reinforcer. Lest it be thought that only the "lowly" rat falls victim to such arrangements, the effect was first demonstrated in monkeys.[86] This example also illustrates the fallacy of equating reinforcers with stimuli that are "liked" and punishers with stimuli that are "disliked." The rat in the above experiment did not "like" electric shock. The effect of presenting an elicitor after an operant depends on the specific interaction between conditioned responses and the operant.

Shaping

The final contingency of reinforcement considered here, and one that makes an important contribution to the emergence of complex behavior, is *shaping*.

In **shaping**, a response-reinforcer contingency is gradually changed to select environment-behavior relations that progressively approach some criterion response topography.

When selection begins, stimuli guide the occurrence of only a small fraction of the responses of which the organism is capable of emitting. For example, consider a child learning to catch a ball. Initially, the sight of a rapidly approaching object, such as a ball, might evoke escape and protective responses. Thus the child might jump to the side to escape the oncoming ball or extend his hands to fend it off. Extending the hands to make contact with the ball is a component of the more complex behavioral skill required to catch it, but the escape and protective components of the initial behavior interfere with catching the ball. Accordingly, a parent might begin by slowly rolling the ball toward the child instead of throwing it, and using a ball made of foam rubber rather than some harder and heavier material. In this way, the escape and protective responses would extinguish while contacting the ball with the hands would be maintained. Next, the parent might vary the speed and path of the ball as it rolled toward the child. At first, merely intercepting the rolling ball would be praised by the parent, but gradually grasping the ball would be required. After the child had developed skills in moving his hand toward the approaching ball and grasping it, the same ball might be thrown slowly though the air with praise first being given merely for contacting it and later for grasping the ball. Once again, the speed and path of the ball could then be varied so that many different response topographies of "catching" were reinforced. Finally, the foam rubber ball might be replaced by a hard rubber ball and, ultimately, by a baseball with a glove used on the catching hand. Through these gradual changes in the topography of the response required for reinforcement, a full repertoire of "catching" behavior would be acquired. Note that if the parent had insisted upon using a baseball from the outset, the child might never have learned to catch it—and, indeed, would probably have learned quite different responses upon sight of the parent approaching with the baseball in hand.

Shaping is often used in laboratory situations—as when leverpressing is shaped in a rat or disk pecking in a pigeon—and in applications of biobehavioral research—as when a child is taught to "sound out" the letters of an unfamiliar word. Although shaping plays an absolutely crucial role in the emergence of complex behavior, the experimental analysis of shaping has been difficult to carry out because the topography of the responses are so varied and the criteria for the occurrence of reinforcers so changeable. However, with the recent development of computer-controlled video systems, it is now possible to subject the process of shaping to experimental analysis. In one example, [87] the behavior of three pigeons was automatically tracked by a video system when each was placed in a test chamber. From preliminary observations, one point within the space of the chamber was identified into which the pigeons *never* moved their heads. The computer then defined an imaginary sphere surrounding this point and an effort was made to shape the behavior of moving the head into this region. At first, the radius of the imaginary sphere was made large enough so that the head of the pigeon would occasionally enter the sphere. When the head entered the sphere, the computer delivered grain to the pigeon as a reinforcer. Following the reinforcer, the radius of the imaginary sphere was gradually reduced in 10-mm steps and delivery of the next reinforcer required a closer approximation to the designated point in space. If the bird's head failed to enter the smaller sphere within 10 s, the sphere was gradually expanded in 2.5-mm steps until the bird again moved its head into the imaginary sphere.

The findings from this study of shaping are shown in **Figure 4.15**. As you can see, the position of each of the three pigeons' heads initially moved within the imaginary sphere only when its radius was very large (150–300 mm). However, upon continued exposure to the shaping contingency, the radius of the imaginary sphere progressively contracted—with occasional expansions following

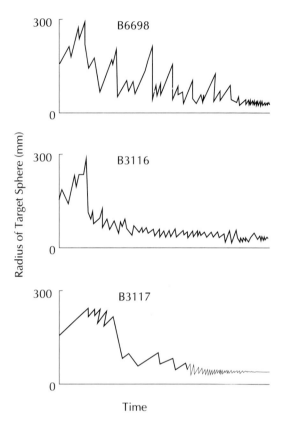

FIGURE 4.15 *Shaping an environment-behavior relation*

The shaped response was the movement of a pigeon's head into an "imaginary" target sphere within the test chamber. The pigeons never moved their heads into this region during an observation period prior to shaping. The panels depict changes in the radius of the target sphere during the shaping of head movement by a computer-controlled video tracking system. The criterion radius of the target sphere into which movements were reinforced was gradually decreased until a radius of 30 mm was reliably attained for each bird. Criterion responses were reinforced with food. By the end of training, all three birds moved their heads into the 30-mm criterion region. The horizontal axes indicate a total shaping time of approximately 122 m for bird B6698, 138 m for bird B3116, and 30 m for bird B 3117.

Source: Adapted from Pear, J. J. & Legris, J. A. (1987). Shaping by automated tracking of an arbitrary operant resonse. *Journal of the Experimental Analysis of Behavior, 47,* 241–247. Copyright 1987 by the Society for the Experimental Analysis of Behavior, Inc.

10-s periods without food—until each pigeon reliably moved its head into a target sphere with a radius of only 30 mm. The topography of the reinforced head movement was a "bowing" response that ended about 160 mm above the floor of the chamber. Control experiments in which food was delivered independently of the birds' behavior showed that the target response never occurred in the absence of the shaping contingency; i.e., it was not produced by the presentation of food alone.

The experimental study of gradually changing the criteria for the reinforcement of a head-movement response elegantly illustrates the shaping process. Still, it provides only a glimpse of the extensive shaping history that predates the complex behavior of which experienced learners are capable. Much of the remainder of the book is concerned with an examination of that history and its consequences. Because we are usually unaware of the extensive history on which later selection depends, human behavior often appears too complex to be the result of a selection process. Occasionally, when we observe efforts to shape environment-behavior relations in children or in adults having behavioral deficits, we are forced to appreciate the extensive history on which most adult behavior depends.

Consequences of shaping.   Although overly simple, the laboratory study of shaping illustrates two important points about the process. First, note that the target response was not in the learner's behavioral repertoire at the beginning of the shaping process; the learner never moved its head into the target region of the chamber. Thus the shaping process can produce behavior that is novel. In the laboratory, the contingencies that produce the novel behavior are the result of the experimenter's intervention into the environment of the learner. It is the experimenter that provides direction to the selection process. But we can learn without a human "teacher;" how then can shaping be the basis for novelty and complexity in the world outside the laboratory? This question is reminiscent of the question posed to Darwin when he appealed to selective breeding experiments to support natural selection as the basis for direction in evolution. While Darwin's critics agreed that dairy cattlemen and pigeon fanciers could bring about progressive changes as the result of their breeding programs, these changes could be attributed to the intentions of the animal husbandryman and not to a blind selection process.

What Darwin pointed out, and what is equally true of shaping, is that the environment imposes natural contingencies that yield directed change without the need for explicit human intervention. Breeding programs simply permit the evolutionist to study the selection process under controlled circumstances; they do not introduce contingencies in an otherwise contingency-less environment. Even a simple leverpressing example can illustrate the role of natural contingencies in selection by reinforcement. Although a rat can produce reinforcers by pressing a lever with either its snout or its forepaw, it is likely that the rat will eventually confine its responses to the forepaw *without the intervention of an experimenter*. Pressing a lever with a forepaw take less time—to say nothing of being less painful—than pressing with the snout. The environment teaches the rat this lesson—how to respond efficiently—without the intervention of an experimenter.

Second, the reinforcer did not completely specify the topography of the response that was selected. In the shaping example, any topography of response that resulted in movement of the pigeon's head into the imaginary target sphere produced the reinforcer. Thus, the contingency implemented by the shaping schedule defined a class of response topographies rather than a response of a single form. The contingency did not distinguish between various "styles" of head movement as long as all met the criteria of a target response. In general, a variety of response topographies meet the criteria for selection, and any of these topographies may come under the control of the environment. Hitting a baseball is reinforced for all baseball players, but the contingency between swinging and hitting does not completely specify the stance from which the bat is swung. Differences in the topography of the selected behavior determine the members of the response class, and unnecessary restrictions on class membership limit the variability available for future selection.

Similarly, just as the response-reinforcer contingency does not completely restrict the response topographies that are components of the selected environment-behavior relation, so the contingency may not completely restrict the stimulus components of the selected relation. Whether the pigeon was looking toward the floor or toward the chamber wall as it "bowed," if head movement entered the target sphere, then food was delivered.

Thus, the stimulus components of the selected environment-behavior relation often vary as well. In short, an environment-behavior relation typically consists of variable components and, for that reason, is a relation between *classes of stimuli and responses*.[88] In the next chapter, the characteristics of those classes are examined for their contribution to complex behavior.

STUDY AIDS

Technical Terms

intermittent reinforcement (or partial reinforcement)
resistance to extinction (or persistence)
continuous reinforcement
cumulative record
higher-order conditioning
concurrent schedule
environmental chaining
internal reinforcement
serial compound conditioning
concurrent-chain procedure
behavioral chaining
backward chaining
over-expectation
devaluation
schedule of reinforcement
fixed-interval (FI) schedule

variable-interval (VI) schedule
fixed-ratio (FR) schedule
variable-ratio (VR) schedule
matching principle
molar principle
molecular principle
appetitive elicitor
aversive elicitor
escape response
punishing stimulus (or punisher)
punishment procedure
shaping

Text Questions

1. Four general types of effects of reinforcement on selection in experienced learners are discussed. (These are described in the four main (capitalized) headings.) After reading the chapter, be able to identify these types of effects and to describe an experimental example of each.

2. In general, what is the effect of intermittent reinforcement on the acquisition and extinction of environment-behavior relations? What biobehavioral processes contribute to these effects?

3. Does extinction completely undo the effects of prior selection? How may this finding be interpreted? What is the evidence regarding how long the effects of prior selections are retained?

4. Describe procedures and results which indicate that acquired reinforcers can select environment-behavior relations in both the classical and operant procedures.

5. Is the reinforcement principle that describes unconditioned reinforcers useful in describing conditioned reinforcers? How are the neural mechanisms of unconditioned and conditioned reinforcers (internal reinforcement) related?

6. Distinguish between environmental chaining and behavioral chaining. Describe experimental procedures for the study of each. Indicate some of their contributions to the emergence of complex behavior.

7. How does prior experience with eliciting stimuli affect their ability to function as reinforcers? Illustrate your answer with findings from the studies of over-expectation and devaluation.

8. Indicate why reinforce-elicited responses should be selected before operant responses. What are the implications of this for the nature of the stimuli that guide operant responses?

9. What is a schedule of reinforcement? Illustrate your answer with several of the commonly used schedules and the behavioral effects they produce.

10. Comment on the following: Even though the *cumulative* effects of selection by reinforcement may be describable by a molar principle, the reinforcement principle itself must be a molecular principle.

11. Under what conditions may an eliciting stimulus function as a punisher? As a reinforcer? What are the implications of these findings for the view that reinforcers are stimuli that the learner "likes" and punishers are stimuli that the learner "dislikes"?

12. What is a shaping procedure? Does shaping always require a "shaper"? Explain.

Discussion Questions

13. Comment on the following statement: As the complexity of behavior increases, experimental analysis must increasingly be supplemented by scientific interpretation.

14. Why is it important for the selection of complex behavior that reinforcing stimuli are not restricted to unconditioned (naturally selected) elicitors? Do conditioned reinforcers permit learners to reinforce themselves? Explain.

15. Critique the following statement: Other species require immediate reinforcement for their behavior, but our behavior can be affected by remote consequences. Include information on "self-control" in your answer.

ENDNOTES

1. Gibbs, Latham, & Gormezano, 1978.

2. For the effects of intermittent reinforcement on acquisition, maintenance, and extinction in classical and operant procedures, see Gibbs, Latham, & Gormezano, 1978 and Amsel, 1958. The cellular mechanisms involved in changing synaptic efficacies also appear to differ from those involved in maintaining them; cf. Cotman & Monaghan, 1988.

3. Skinner, 1938, p. 135.

4. Capaldi, 1966, 1971.

5. Spivey, 1967.

6. See Mackintosh, 1974 for a review of this literature.

7. cf. Amsel, 1958, 1972.

8. The effect of intermittent reinforcement on resistance to extinction is one aspect of the more general area of *schedules of reinforcement*. Additional implications of schedules of reinforcement will be considered in later sections of this chapter. With regard to the relation between schedules of reinforcement and "motivational" effects, consider the following: "By the manipulation of schedules, a wide range of changes in behavior can be produced, most of which would previously have been attributed to motivational and emotional variables," Ferster & Skinner, 1957, p. 2.

9. As with most behavioral phenomena, the persistence of a selected environment-behavior relation is significantly influenced by a number of variables; i.e., most responses are multiply determined. The variable emphasized in the present treatment—the discriminative stimuli correlated with specific sequences of nonreinforced and reinforced responses—is, perhaps, the most important one. Another important variable is the frequency with which the environment-behavior relation has been reinforced. The more often a relation has been reinforced, the greater its persistence—other things being equal; cf. Amsel, 1972; Capaldi, 1966. With more frequent reinforcers, the likelihood is increased that all of the stimuli that can potentially reliably occur before a response in that situation will become discriminative stimuli for the response. The greater the number of stimuli that guide a response, the more likely that any given environment will contain at least some of those stimuli and, hence, that the response will occur and/or persist. Also, with more frequent reinforcers, the greater the likelihood that conditioned-response-produced stimuli will occur prior to the operant and acquire a discrimination function with respect to the operant as discussed in the interpretation of the over-expectation effect later

in this chapter. Environment-behavior relations that are resistant to change are said to display *behavioral momentum*, Nevin, 1988, 1992; Nevin, Mandell, & Atak, 1983.

10. For evidence with classical procedures, see, e.g., Hoeler, Kirschenbaum, & Leonard, 1973. For evidence with operant procedures, see, e.g., Spear, 1973.

11. e.g., Lattal, 1972.

12. Consideration of all of the stimuli present during acquisition and extinction, and of the consequences of any changes in stimulation between these conditions, permits an interpretation of a number of extinction-related phenomena. For example, responding is typically strongest at the beginning of each extinction session, even after prolonged extinction. This phenomenon, known as *spontaneous recovery*, can be attributed to stimuli that occur only at the beginning of the extinction session. Since such stimuli occur only briefly, they guide responding for many sessions and produce spontaneous recovery; cf. Estes, 1955; Skinner, 1938; cf. Welker & McAuley, 1978.

13. The conditions under which synaptic efficacies are modified are consistent with observations at the neural level, e.g., Desmond & Levy, 1986; Levy & Steward, 1979. Most information about these conditions comes from studies of what is called *long-term potentiation (LTP)* of activity in cells of the hippocampus; e.g., Bliss & Lomo, 1973. Long-term potentiation refers to a long-lasting increase in synaptic efficacy as the result of high frequency of stimulation by a presynaptic cell. Although LTP has been most extensively studied in the hippocampus, it is known to occur generally in neurons throughout the cerebral cortex.

14. Holt & Kehoe, 1985.

15. Donahoe, Burgos, & Palmer, 1993. See also Kehoe, 1988 for recognizing this implication of reinforcement principles when implemented in multi-layer networks; cf. Sutton & Barto, 1981. The variables affecting reacquisition discussed here—stimulus generalization and the partial preservation of synaptic changes—should not be viewed as the only ones affecting subsequent learning, cf. Harlow, 1959. A number of other variables will be described in later portions of the book.

16. Liddell, James, & Anderson, 1935.

17. Donahoe & Marrs, 1982.

18. e.g., van Willigen, Emmett, Cotte, & Ayres, 1987; Levinthal, Tartell, Margolin, & Fishman, 1985.

19. Skinner, 1938.

20. When different responses are selected in the presence of the same stimuli, interference effects are produced. The nature of interference effects and an analysis of the conditions under which they occur in adaptive networks is a matter of intense current interest, and will be considered at a later point in the text; e.g., Lewandowsky, 1991; McCloskey & Cohen, 1989.

21. In the application of behavioral principles to the remediation of dysfunctional behavior, a central problem is to insure that a favorable environment-behavior relation—once selected—will endure; cf. Stokes & Baer, 1977. If the training and later environments are similar, and if the contingencies of reinforcement for the response are similar, then the trained relation will endure. As an example, a group of hospital caregivers tending disabled patients suffered from back injury as a common job-related health risk. Back injuries occurred when they were transferring patients from wheelchairs to beds. Research had shown that simply instructing caretakers about safer lifting behaviors had little effect. Accordingly, an operant procedure was implemented in which verbal praise (i.e., a learned reinforcer) was given after execution of correct lifting behavior. The desired behavior included such responses as standing in front of the patient rather than to the side, lifting by hugging the patient rather than holding him at arm's length, and so forth. The caregivers' behavior rapidly changed to the safe practices and training was then discontinued. Follow-up observations one year later indicated that the environment-behavior relations selected by the training contingencies remained at undiminished strength; Alavosius, 1987.

However, if the training and subsequent environments are similar and the contingencies of reinforcement are different, then the previously selected environment-behavior relations will not endure and new relations will emerge. There are no remedial procedures that "immunize" the learner against the potentially undesirable selecting effects of all later environments. Such procedures, were they to exist, would contradict the very principle upon which any remedial procedure is based—that environment-behavior relations are selected by the contingencies of reinforcement to which the learner is later exposed. The continued sensitivity of behavior to selection poses a serious threat to the durability of any therapeutic procedure when the learner is returned to the environment in which the dysfunctional behavior was originally selected, and undoubtedly plays a major role in "relapses" and recidivism generally.

22. Throughout this discussion, the phrase *acquired elicitor* refers to a stimulus that controls behavior as a result of either the classical or operant contingency. Thus acquired elicitors include both conditioned stimuli and discriminated stimuli. Similarly, the phrase *acquired reinforcer* refers to an acquired elicitor that functions as a reinforcer in either the classical or operant procedure. Thus acquired reinforcers may be studied with either higher-order or conditioned-reinforcement procedures.

23. Pavlov, 1927.

24. Skinner, 1938.

25. Rescorla, 1980.

26. Gormezano & Kehoe, 1981; Kehoe, Feyer, & Moses, 1981.

27. e.g., Bersch, 1951. For a review of much of the earlier literature, see Hendry, 1969.

28. Williams & Dunn, 1991a, 1991b.

29. Ferster & Skinner, 1957.

30. Palmer, 1987. See also Dinsmoor, 1950, and Thomas & Caronite, 1964, for related experimental work and Keller & Schoenfeld, 1950 for the proposal that a stimulus that functions as conditioned reinforcer for one response also functions as discriminative stimulus for a second response.

31. For an early study of response interactions, when a discriminative stimulus was *approached* to secure food during initial training, that stimulus functioned as an effective conditioned reinforcer for a different response during a subsequent task in which the stimulus was also approached (Saltzman, 1949). However, when the discriminative stimulus was *withdrawn from* to secure food (but also signaled the availability of food), it did not function as a reinforcer for an approach response in a subsequent task (Long, 1966). Interactions of this sort are probably at the root of many findings purporting to demonstrate fundamental differences between the learning processes associated with conditioned stimuli in classical procedures and discriminative stimuli in operant procedures (e.g., Rescorla, 1988, 1991).

32. Nonhuman animals do sometimes respond toward acquired reinforcers in ways that are ordinarily directed toward the reflexive elicitors with which they have been paired. For example, monkeys put tokens that have been paired with food in their mouths (e.g., Kelleher, 1958a, b). See Breland & Breland, 1961, for other examples.

33. In addition to the motor association cortex of the frontal lobes, the dopaminergic VTA system also innervates various motor nuclei lying beneath the frontal lobes. Because of the concentration of cell bodies in nuclei, much of the physiological research on neural mechanisms of reinforcement has focused on these structures for technical reasons, e.g., Hoebel, 1988; Kelley & Delfs, 1991. Other projections of the VTA to structures involved in the processing of sensory input also play an important role in selection, but we have postponed their consideration until the chapter on perceiving.

34. Studies have shown that electrical or chemical stimulation that affects dopaminergic synapses in the motor association cortex can function as a reinforcer; e.g., Goeders & Smith, 1983; Hill, 1970; Roberston, 1989; cf. Cohen & Branch, 1991.

35. e.g., Shizgal, Bielajew, & Rompre, 1988; Yeomans, 1975, 1982, 1988, 1989; Yeomans, Kofman, & McFarlane, 1988. Additional experimental work is required to specify precisely the neural circuitry and neurotransmitter systems involved in the projections from the prefrontal cortex and the ventral tegmental area.

36. Kehoe, Gibbs, Garcia, & Gormezano, 1979.

37. This account is not necessarily intended to apply to the neural mechanisms of acquired reinforcement in the rabbit nictitating membrane preparation. Simple NMR conditioning can occur in the absence of a functioning cerebral cortex, although more complex conditioning procedures do involve the cortex; Berger, Berry, & Thompson, 1986. Physiological research in the rabbit on the role of the cortex in serial compound conditioning has not yet been conducted. However, dopaminergic mechanisms are known to affect NMR conditioning in the rabbit; Gimpl, Gormezano, & Harvey, 1979; Marshall-Goodell & Gormezano, 1991.

38. Because the effect of serial compound conditioning is a dynamic process depending on the complex interplay between these biobehavioral processes, computer simulations are required to interpret the outcome of such complex procedures; cf. Kehoe, 1988; Kehoe & Napier, 1991.

39. Myers & Myers, 1965. See Wolfe, 1936 for an early experimental study of conditioned reinforcement in chimpanzees.

40. For clear early statements of the dependence of behavior on immediate acquired reinforcers, see Skinner, 1953 and Spence, 1956.

41. e.g., Logan, 1965; Rachlin & Green, 1972.

42. e.g., Mischel & Bakler, 1975.

43. e.g., Grosch & Neuringer, 1981; Logue, 1988.

44. cf. Spence, 1947.

45. cf. Catania, 1975; Gewirtz, 1971; Goldiamond, 1976; Hayes, Rosenfarb, Wulfert, Munt, Korn, & Zettle, 1985.

46. For surveys, see Gollub, 1977; Kelleher, 1966, and Nevin, 1973.

47. Karen, 1974.

48. Skinner, 1953; cf. Richardson & Warzak, 1981; Weiss, 1978.

49. Kremer, 1978; Rescorla, 1970.

50. Engberg, Hanson, Welker, & Thomas, 1972; Konorski, 1967.

51. For other phenomena of this type, such as *super-conditioning*, see Rescorla, 1971, 1985b. Although behavioral discrepancies—and the physiological mechanisms underlying them—modulate the effects of selection, they are not the only means by which prior selection affects present selection. A learner has a history of selection with respect to relations *between environmental events* as well as between environmental and behavioral events. The analysis of environment-environment relations is postponed until the chapter on perceiving, but these relations also modulate the effects of selection—especially in response to complex stimuli such as stimulus compounds. The study of complex stimuli in basic conditioning procedures is often carried out under the heading of *configural conditioning* (cf. Rescorla, 1973, 1976; Wagner, 1981; Krieckhaus, Donahoe, & Morgan, 1992).

The present discussion does not include an analysis of effects that are usually discussed under the heading of *inhibition*. On the behavioral level, no concept of inhibition appears in the present treatment; cf. Donahoe & Palmer, 1988; Weiss & Schindler, 1985. Most phenomena in which "inhibition" is appealed to by other formulations are viewed here as instances of stimulus discrimination (Skinner, 1938). For example, when S_1 is paired with a reinforcer and an S_1-S_2 compound is nonreinforced, the control of responding exerted by S_2 is the result of extinction as interpreted by the standard discrepancy account of extinction and interference from the selection of competing environment-behavior relations, cf. Staddon, 1977. There is no separate construct of inhibition (cf. Wagner & Rescorla, 1972) and, hence, there is no inhibition to be extinguished (cf. Zimmer-Hart & Rescorla, 1974; Witcher & Ayres, 1984). In general, decreases in responding that are attributed to inhibition (or negative association values) in other formulations are here attributed to the addition to the behavioral mixture of other and competing environment-behavior relations that interfere with, and hence reduce the strength of, the measured behavior; cf. Bickel & Etzel, 1985; Donahoe & Wessells, 1980; Miller & Schachtman, 1985; Miller & Matzel, 1988; Weiss, 1972.

52. On the physiological level of analysis, of course, all events that immediately precede a reinforced response are internal. That is, environmental stimuli that are discriminated necessarily produce distinguishing internal events; cf. Skinner, 1938.

53. This view resembles two-factor accounts of operant conditioning in which stimuli from conditioned responses are assumed to have a motivating (Rescorla & Solomon, 1967) and/or a mediating function (Dickinson, 1988; Trapold & Overmier, 1972) for the operant response. The role of conditioned responses in operant conditioning, according to the unified reinforcement principle, differs in several respects including the following: (a) The adaptive-network interpretation of conditioned responses is based on experimental analyses of both behavior and physiology. (b) The distinction between classical and operant conditioning is not one of two different "types" or "kinds" of learning, but procedural only. (c) The stimuli from conditioned responses do not necessarily play a mediating role with respect to the operant response. They simply provide a potential additional source of stimuli that may, when such stimuli occur before the operant, acquire a discriminative function with respect to the operant. (d) The occurrence of conditioned responses not only serves a potential discriminative function for the operant response, but also a reinforcing and motivating function through the internal reinforcement mechanism described in the previous section of this chapter. All efforts that exploit the stimulus consequences of conditioned responses in operant conditioning may be traced to the earlier work of Guthrie, 1935, and Hull, 1934.

54. See Colwill & Rescorla, 1986 and Rescorla, 1991 for reviews.

55. Colwill & Rescorla, 1985.

56. With a number of notable exceptions—e.g., Shapiro, 1962; Kintsch & Witte, 1962; Konorski, 1948; Sheffield, 1965—technical difficulties in simultaneously measuring reinforcer-elicited responses and operant responses have impeded the experimental analysis of response interactions. Accounts of the effects of reinforcer-related events (sometimes called *outcomes*) on operant conditioning have recently proceeded along a different line from that described here and previously (e.g., Trapold & Overmier, 1972). Briefly, these accounts have appealed to interactions between different "kinds" of associations—e.g., stimulus-response, stimulus-outcome, and response-outcome associations—and to "higher-order" associations—e.g., between a stimulus and a response-outcome association (Mackintosh &

Dickinson, 1979; Rescorla, 1991). Some efforts have been made to differentiate between the interpretation given here and alternative associationistic accounts (e.g., Rescorla & Colwill, 1989), but they do not compel acceptance of the alternative accounts.

57. The behavioral technique called *flooding* may exert its beneficial effect on the extinction of "fear" in this way. In a flooding technique, the learner is not permitted to avoid the feared stimulus but must remain in its presence while the eliciting stimulus that evokes the "fear" is omitted. For example, a rat that received shock after a tone might be held in the chamber while the tone was repeatedly presented, but without the shock. Under such conditions, subsequent testing indicates that escaping from the tone declines in strength more rapidly and more completely than if a simple extinction procedure had been instituted; Mineka, 1979; cf. Solomon & Wynne, 1953.

58. From a letter written by Charles Darwin to Asa Gray, a botanist who was among Darwin's more stalwart American supporters. Reprinted in Dupree, 1988.

59. Because there are an infinite number of schedules of reinforcement, some have questioned the importance of understanding the specific schedules investigated by Ferster and Skinner (1957). In our view, this reservation misses the central point. Investigating ratio and interval schedules per se may not be required, but understanding the effects of the contingencies of reinforcement embedded in these standard schedules is both central and unavoidable if the selection of behavior by complex contingencies is to be understood. The standard schedules were constrained by the technical limitations inherent in electromechanical switching circuits of the time and are, therefore, limited as instruments for the experimental analysis of contingencies of reinforcement. These problems are now better addressed with computer-controlled procedures that implement contingencies of reinforcement with greater specificity and precision; e.g., Platt, 1979.

60. Ferster & Skinner, 1957.

61. Ferster & Skinner, 1957.

62. For a careful analysis of the temporal and behavioral variables that are manipulated in the conventional schedules of reinforcement, see Morse, 1966.

63. For a full presentation of the effects of the standard schedules of reinforcement, singly and in combination, as well as a variety of other schedules, see Ferster & Skinner, 1957.

64. See Morse, 1966; Schoenfeld, 1970; and Schoenfeld, Cole, Blaustein, Lachter, Martin, & Vickery, 1972

for theoretical treatments of the standard schedules of reinforcement.

65. Herrnstein, 1970. See Baum, 1974 for a more general statement of the matching principle and Killeen, 1972 for a theoretical discussion of such principles. Much of the research related to the matching principle is summarized in de Villieurs, 1977. Alternative molar principles have been developed, e.g., Killeen & Fantino, 1990, and the analysis has been extended to acquired reinforcers as well; Williams & Dunn, 1991b.

66. The use of the term "molecular" to differentiate moment-to-moment accounts of behavior from more global accounts was first introduced in Skinner, 1938.

67. The view that a population of environment-behavior relations from a single individual is the focus of selection by reinforcement has important implications for the manner in which research should be conducted in biobehavioral science. While averaging findings from different individuals is appropriate in the study of natural selection, it is inappropriate (and potentially misleading) in the study of the behavioral selection. For discussions of this matter, see Sidman, 1960; Estes, 1955; and Donahoe & Wessels, 1980.

68. Staddon & Hinson, 1983.

69. The distinction that is being made here corresponds to the distinction made in evolutionary biology between selection *for* and selection *of* a characteristic; Sober, 1984. A given characteristic (or gene) may be selected *for* and have the cumulative effect of increasing the frequency *of* some characteristic that is correlated with the characteristic for which selection occurs.

70. Shimp, 1969. See also Hinson & Staddon, 1983; Donahoe, 1977, among others.

71. For other molar theories of performance on concurrent schedules, see Timberlake, 1980.

72. On the relation between matching and foraging theory, see Dallery & Baum, 1991.

73. Biological models commonly assume that natural selection has led to behavior that leads to optimality of some quantity; e.g., the number of calories ingested relative to the number of calories expended in securing food (Dallery & Baum, 1991; Stephens & Krebs, 1986; Roberts, 1991). A number of papers have pointed out the relationship between such theories and molar principles such as matching; e.g., Dallery & Baum, 1991.

74. For example, see Hinson & Staddon, 1983; Silberberg, Hamilton, Ziriax, & Casey, 1978; Silberberg & Ziriax, 1982. However, the appropriate level at which to evaluate the matching principle continues to be debated; e.g., Herrnstein & Loveland, 1975; Williams, 1991.

Increasingly, various forms of molecular theorizing are replacing the more molar formulations, e.g., Herrnstein, 1982; Vaughn, 1981. See Marr, 1992 for a general discussion of this and related issues.

75. Crowley, 1981.

76. Skinner, 1950.

77. cf. Skinner, 1938.

78. The relative merits of molar and molecular accounts of behavior remain a controversial topic within biobehavioral science. References on this topic include Arbuckle & Lattal, 1992; Hinson & Staddon, 1983; Mazur, 1981; Rachlin & Burkhard, 1978; Shimp, 1969; Silberberg, Thomas, & Berendzen, 1991; and Williams, 1990a, 1991, among many others.

79. Because the escape responses evoked by aversive stimuli vary with the evolutionary history of the species, such responses are also known as *species-specific defense reactions*; Bolles, 1970.

80. Aversive elicitors may result from natural selection—e.g, stimuli that activate pain receptors such as electric shock—and from behavioral selection. These last are termed acquired aversive elicitors—e.g., stimuli paired with shock or with extinction (Hearst & Franklin, 1977).

81. The likelihood of an operant can also be decreased by reinforcing a second operant that competes with the first. For example, reinforcing pecks to one disk decreases pecks to a second disk. This procedure, called an *alternative-response procedure*, decreases an operant without punishing it, and is often used in applied work because it does not require the use of an aversive elicitor to reduce a dysfunctional operant. Reducing responding by means of an alternative-response procedure is one of the important implications of the matching principle.

82. Whether the frequency of the operant upon which the aversive elicitor is contingent continues to be reduced depends on several factors. First, the aversive elicitor must continue to evoke escape responses; i.e., habituation of the aversive elicitor must not occur. Second, the environment to which the escape response takes the learner should not resemble the environment to which the escape response has been conditioned. If the environments are similar, then the learner may "escape" back to the environment in which the aversive elicitor is presented. Third, if the learner is to minimize contact with the aversive elicitor, then the escape response must either be reinforced or lead to an environment in which other responses are reinforced. All of these factors are important if contact with the aversive elicitor is to be minimized; i.e., if an *avoidance response* is to be selected (cf. Donahoe & Wessells, 1980, pp. 207–210).

83. e.g., Church, 1969; cf. Mackintosh, 1974.

84. Skinner, 1953.

85. Donahoe & Burns, 1986.

86. See Morse & Kelleher, 1977.

87. Pear & Legris, 1987. For other experimental examples and discussions of shaping, see Eckerman, Hienz, Stern, & Kowlowitz, 1980; Platt, 1979; Skinner, 1953; and Staddon, 1983.

88. Skinner, 1935.

CHAPTER 5

CLASSES OF ENVIRONMENT-BEHAVIOR RELATIONS

The legacy of experience is the accumulation of an ever-larger repertoire of environment-behavior relations. These relations are selected by reinforcers that are themselves increasingly the product of previous selections—of behavioral, rather than natural selection. The selected relations include variable stimulus and response components. The stimuli sensed by the learner inevitably vary from moment to moment, producing variation in responses, and a range of these variations is tolerated by the prevailing contingencies of reinforcement. Since the stimulus and response components of environment-behavior relations are variable, a *class* of environmental events comes to guide behavior and a *class* of behavior is, in turn, guided by the environment. In this chapter, we examine the processes that affect membership in *stimulus classes* and *response classes*.

Although human experience consists of a series of *specific* environmental and behavioral events, the cumulative result of experience commonly has general effects. For example, after a child has said "dog"—and received reinforcement for doing so—in the presence of many particular dogs, he is likely to respond "dog" when asked to identify a dog that he has never seen before. His ability to do this is described in everyday language as "having a concept." (Note that, for present purposes, it is not critical that the "concept" be correct. The issue is a person's competence to respond at all, which is basically the same whether he calls a Bedlington Terrier a lamb—which it resembles—or a dog—which is the conventionally correct response.) The term **stimulus class** denotes that a response is guided by a *range of stimuli*, whose members are not restricted to the specific stimuli present when selection took place.[1] (See **Figure 5.1a**.) How does the cumulative effect of selection bring behavior under the control of a class of stimuli? Or, in everyday language, "How are concepts formed?"

The cumulative effect of selection also causes a stimulus to guide a class of responses. A baby who has only crawled to get to the pots and pans in the kitchen cabinet makes a dash for the "toys" as soon as he can walk. Walking toward the cabinet door is guided by the sight of the door, even if walking has never before occurred in its presence and, therefore, never been followed by the potent elicitors behind the door—shiny pots that make wonderful noises when banged together. How may selection lead to a **response class**, a *range of behaviors* not necessarily confined to the specific responses that were previously selected by reinforcers in that environment? (See **Figure 5.1b**.)

ANALYSIS AND INTERPRETATION

Both stimulus classes and response classes are the *cumulative* products of selection. That is, neither phenomenon may emerge or be fully understood on the basis of a single occasion on which an environment-behavior relation is selected. A child that "recognizes" dogs does not do so by having the same dog repeatedly pointed out to him. Instead, the child's experience typically consists of sensing the sights and sounds of specific dogs on many occasions when the verbal response "dog" is followed by acquired reinforcers.

Because the emergence of stimulus and response classes results from a prolonged history of selection—usually incompletely known to an observer—experimental analysis must be supple-

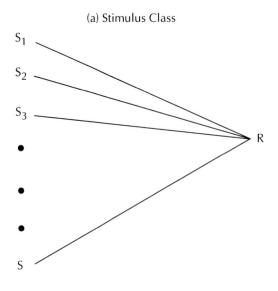

(a) Stimulus Class

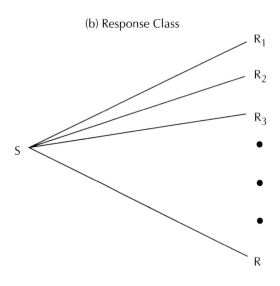

(b) Response Class

FIGURE 5.1 *Relation between the environment and behavior with (a) stimulus classes and (b) response classes*
With a stimulus class, multiple stimuli (S) guide the occurrence of a single response (R). With a response class, a single stimulus guides the occurrence of multiple responses. A given stimulus may be a member of more than one stimulus class and a given response may be a member of more than one response class.

mented by the *interpretation* of behavior. As in other historical sciences, understanding complex behavioral phenomena requires both experimental analysis, which uncovers fundamental processes largely through laboratory work, and interpretation, which explores the implications of those processes as rigorously as circumstances permit. Understanding stimulus and response classes requires us—for the first time—to make extensive use of interpretation. For that reason, we shall examine some of the general approaches to interpretation before using them to understand stimulus and response classes.

Although experimental analysis is applied to the study of complex behavior, two major factors limit its use. The first limitation—our incomplete knowledge of the learner's full selection history— has been noted before. The second is, perhaps, less obvious: If complex behavior requires a complex selection history, then conditions that allow us to assess all the relevant variables may be too impoverished to permit complex behavior to emerge. Thus, in our effort to control and measure variables precisely, we may unintentionally prevent the occurrence of conditions that foster complex behavior. For this reason, understanding complex behavior almost always requires interpretation as well as experimental analysis. Indeed, it could be argued that the central purpose of science is interpretation, because it is through interpretation that we understand our behavior in the natural environment.[2]

Strategies of Interpretation

Three general interpretive strategies supplement the experimental analysis of complex behavior. These complementary strategies are verbal interpretation, organismic interpretation, and formal interpretation.

Verbal interpretation.   **Verbal interpretation** is the most familiar interpretive strategy because we engage in something very much like it when we try to make sense of our daily lives. Consider this example of verbal interpretation, based on the science of physics: When a boulder rolls down a hillside and blocks the road below, we attribute that outcome to variables that may have dislodged the boulder (perhaps a heavy rain), thus permitting gravitational forces to cause the boulder to roll. We are quite comfortable with this interpretation because it appeals to processes, and the principles that summarize them, that are well known and generally agreed upon. Note, however, that we are ignorant of the precise sequence of events that occurred as the boulder moved down the hillside to its resting place on the road. Moreover, although physics has identified all of the relevant processes thought to operate in this situation, even a skilled physicist could not predict the boulder's final resting position with certainty. First, the physicist does not know the values of all of the relevant variables. Second, even if he tried to determine these values, exact prediction would still elude him. There are simply too many variables—the boulder's irregular shape, which changes as it bumps against other rocks while rolling downhill; the irregular grade of the hillside; the irregular composition of the materials making up the hill, and so forth. Even when experimental analysis has identified all of the relevant processes, understanding complex phenomena usually requires interpretation.

What, then, distinguishes verbal interpretation—or, indeed, interpretation generally—from mere speculation? As illustrated by the example of the boulder, interpretation relies solely on principles established through experimental analysis. The physicist is not free to postulate principles of any other origin. While earlier cultures might have attributed the boulder's movement to a spirit of nature residing in the rock, or to divine will, the physicist may not appeal to such entities. His interpretation is restricted to principles that have been identified by experimental analysis. Similarly, students of complex behavior must confine themselves to principles based on experimental analyses of biobehavioral processes. New processes, and principles that describe those processes, are never

discovered through interpretation; interpretation is a consumer, not a producer of principles.[3]

The reliance of interpretation on experimental analysis is what chiefly distinguishes between, for example, biobehavioral and psychoanalytic accounts of complex behavior. Psychoanalytic accounts may be every bit as intricate as biobehavioral accounts, but in psychoanalysis the principles are inferred from the very types of observations that they seek to explain. In biobehavioral science the principles arise from independent experimental analyses. Unless a principle is the result of an independent experimental analysis, it is difficult to identify the origins of any problems that arise in interpreting the complex phenomenon. Do the problems result from a failure to trace all of the implications of the principles, a failure to identify all of the relevant principles, or an inadequacy in the principles themselves? When the principles arise from an independent experimental analysis, their adequacy is knowable apart from the complex behavior they are used to interpret.

Although verbal interpretation provides a very useful method for understanding complex phenomena, it has distinct disadvantages. Very often, so many processes are involved—many of them acting simultaneously—that a purely verbal account cannot keep track of them all. Too much is happening at once for a sequence of words to faithfully describe the interrelations of the processes. For example, verbal interpretation might provide an acceptable account of a rock bouncing down a hill, but it would not provide an equally satisfying account of the formation of a planetary system—although many of the same principles are involved. Verbal interpretation will always play an important role in understanding complex phenomena, particularly in the early stages of inquiry, but biobehavioral science ultimately seeks more precise means of interpretation.

Organismic interpretation. **Organismic interpretation** is the second strategy for understanding complex behavior. In this approach, an investigator provides a learner with the experience that experimental-analytic principles indicate is sufficient to produce the complex behavior.[4] We have already come upon several examples of this strategy in previous chapters. For example, everyday experience teaches us that a given stimulus will not function as a reinforcer for all learners. Experimental analyses of phenomena such as blocking and over-expectation indicate how some of these individual differences could have come about. In keeping with the general practice of historical science, if the principles are sufficient to account for the phenomenon, they are tentatively accepted as explanations of how the complex behavior arose.

Organismic interpretation attempts to simulate in the laboratory the naturally occurring history of selection that produces complex environment-behavior relations. When based on an experimental analysis using methods that permit manipulation of many relevant environmental variables, organismic interpretation is a powerful tool. Most research with human subjects falls into the category of organismic interpretation because, with very few exceptions, not all of the variables affecting human behavior are under the investigator's control. Although research with human subjects may very carefully control the variables *within* an experiment, the subjects' differing pre-experimental histories *outside* the study cannot be completely controlled or, often, even described.

In spite of these limitations, research—particularly developmental and comparative research—is very helpful in interpreting complex behavior. Although each of us has a unique history, as members of the same culture we share a partially common history of behavioral selection and as members of the same species we share a largely common history of natural selection. To the extent that aspects of complex behavior are unique to our species, understanding them requires research with human subjects. However, research with other species—particularly closely related species—can aid interpretation because our greater ability to control individual history partially offsets the lesser similarity in evolutionary history. As noted in Chapter 1, both the developmental and comparative methods have much to offer the interpretation of complex human behavior.

Formal interpretation.   **Formal interpretation** is the third interpretive strategy. Computer simulation is the most common type of formal interpretation in modern biobehavioral science.[5] In computer simulation, a computer is given a set of instructions, called a *program*, that embodies principles established by experimental analysis. As expressed in the program instructions, the principles are repeatedly applied to determine if they are sufficient to generate the complex behavioral phenomena observed in nature. As with other forms of interpretation, no new principles may be introduced; the principles informing the program are restricted to those that are derived from research on the relevant biobehavioral processes. This use of computer simulation should be distinguished from that in which the goal is simply to devise a program whose output mimics some aspect of complex behavior, but whose instructions are not constrained by biobehavioral principles. Efforts of this second type fall within the field of *artificial intelligence*. Biobehaviorally constrained simulations should also be distinguished from those that use principles based on inferences from the complex behavior itself.[6]

We have encountered examples of computer simulations in our interpretations of selection by means of adaptive neural networks; e.g., of reacquisition after extinction. This method of interpretation is also used in other historical sciences. In studies of the origins of the universe, for example, galaxy formation and planetary formation are often interpreted through computer simulations based on Newtonian principles. Similarly, many examples exist in evolutionary biology, as when the natural selection of adaptive behavior is simulated by computer programs informed by the principle of natural selection.[7]

In comparison to purely verbal interpretations, computer simulations have the advantage of being precisely stated in the program's instructions and of being able to keep track of many simultaneously acting processes. In comparison to organismic simulations, computer simulations have the advantage of exhaustively describing the history of the complex behavior from the beginning of the program's execution to its final state when the simulation is ended. Moreover, an individual selection history that might encompass many months or years in a human learner may be simulated in a computer in a matter of minutes or hours.

A major disadvantage of computer simulations is that the program's designer is often only partially knowledgeable of the initial state from which the simulation should begin. That is, information comparable to the evolutionary history of the learner is often unknown. The inherent limitation of all historical sciences—incomplete knowledge of the entire relevant selection history—may also occur with computer simulations.[8] In this respect, organismic simulations have an advantage over computer simulations of complex behavior. Man and other animals, especially closely related species, share a partially common evolutionary history. To the extent that this history is similar, organismic simulations of human behavior with nonhuman animals begin from similar initial conditions.

As should now be clear, there is no one uniformly "best" approach to the interpretation of complex behavior; this formidable challenge requires all the forces we can muster—verbal interpretation, organismic interpretation, and formal interpretation.

DISCRIMINATIVE STIMULUS CLASSES

The cumulative effect of selection produces a discriminative stimulus class if a range of stimuli is able to guide a common response *and* if the members of the class are not restricted to the particular stimuli present when selection occurred. After enough experience, the child says "dog" when a dog is present that he has never seen before. (See **Figure 5.2**.) The technical term stimulus class denotes environment-behavior relations that are often referred to by the nontechnical term concept.

Although the terms *stimulus class* and *concept* denote some of the same types of environment-behavior relations, they are by no means synonymous. Technical terms, such as stimulus class, are the products of experimental analyses while related nontechnical terms, such as concept, arise from the give-and-take of everyday experience. As a result, technical terms are applied to environment-behavior relations that are produced by a common set of well-defined biobehavioral processes. Nontechnical terms, on the other hand, group together phenomena that bear some similarity to one another but that may result from a variety of diverse processes. Put briefly, technical terms are **theoretically coherent**, whereas nontechnical terms are commonly **theoretically incoherent**—they are not the product of a consistent set of basic processes. As an example of the distinction, consider the nontechnical term *flying*. Many different objects can be said to fly, but the particular combination of physical processes responsible for flying can vary widely. A blimp flies because it is lighter than air, a glider flies because of the pressures created by the flow of air over its wings, a rocket flies because of the forces generated by its exhaust gases, a stone flies because someone threw it, and so on. If an aeronautical engineer were to treat these different cases of flying identically, problems would immediately arise. To say that a nontechnical term, such as concept, is theoretically incoherent is not to deny that it identifies an important set of phenomena. It is to say that these phenomena are likely to be the products of different combinations of selection processes.

Consider concept as a nontechnical term. We say that a person has a concept of *dog*, and we also say that a person has a concept of *triangle*. Although it is conventional to use the term concept to refer to both, the environmental guidance of the verbal responses "dog" and "triangle" are likely to involve quite different biobehavioral processes. As already noted, a person ordinarily acquires the stimulus class to which "dog" is an appropriate verbal response as a by-product of the selection of "dog" in the presence of many different dogs. In

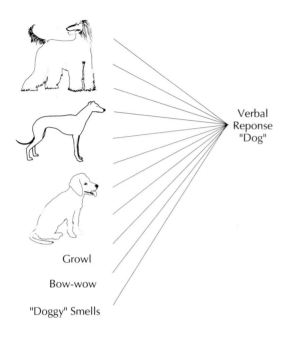

Verbal
Reponse
"Dog"

Growl

Bow-wow

"Doggy" Smells

FIGURE 5.2   *An example of a specific stimulus class in which a common verbal response, "DOG," is guided by a number of different stimuli*
Some stimuli involve the same sensory modality; e.g., the appearance of various breeds of dog ranging from an Afghan to a mutt; and other stimuli involve other sensory modalities; e.g., the sounds and odors emanating from dogs. Under appropriate circumstances, all of these stimuli are capable of guiding the same response, "DOG."

contrast, the response "triangle" is more likely to be the result of verbal instruction in which the response is partly guided by a verbal stimulus commonly called a definition—e.g., "a triangle is a three-sided plane figure." Lumping together "dog" and "triangle" as examples of concepts would lead to problems when the emission of "dog" and "triangle" were later found to be affected differently by similar variables. For example, a stroke victim who is unable to say "triangle" when shown a triangle might still say "dog" in the presence of dogs.

To further complicate matters, the behavior of a stroke victim who acquired the verbal response "triangle" through exposure to many different triangles and one who acquired "triangle" only through a definition in a geometry class might be differently affected by damage to the same brain area. Different environment-behavior relations are involved when the verbal response "triangle" is guided by the spatial stimuli provided by particular triangles than when it is guided by the verbal stimuli provided by a definition. This difference further illustrates that the form of a response— here, the word "triangle"—provides an inadequate basis for experimental analysis. Behavioral selection changes environment-behavior *relations*. Any construct sensitive only to response topography, and not to the stimuli guiding the response and the processes leading to that guidance, creates confusion. Constructs that are insensitive to the guiding stimulus and the selection history are usually theoretically incoherent.[9]

Because nontechnical terms, such as concept, lump together many different types of environment-behavior relations of many different origins, they often appear richer than technical terms. However, their apparent richness is achieved at the cost of theoretical incoherence. This incoherence ultimately leads to confusion when behaviors purporting to be the same are affected in different ways by the same variables. Experimental analyses, and interpretations based on such analyses, must make a place for the full richness of human behavior. But, it is unlikely that a single technical term can capture all of the environment-behavior relations implied by an incompletely analyzed nontechnical term. To regard the illusory richness of nontechnical terms as a virtue is to mistake obscurity for profundity.

Varieties of Stimulus Classes

Two distinguishable sets of phenomena fall under the heading of stimulus classes—*discriminative* stimulus classes and *functional* classes.[10] **Discriminative stimulus classes** are composed of stimuli that bear some *physical similarity* to one another and that control common responses. Stimulus classes of this sort are exemplified by the "concept" *dog*. **Functional classes** are composed of stimuli that may not be physically similar but bear some *functional similarity* to one another and, like any stimulus class, control common responses.[11] Functional classes are exemplified by the "concept" *toy*. Toys differ widely in appearance, but all support the kind of behavior we call playing. Because all toys guide playing, they may be said to have a common function.

Stimulus classes, whether based on physical or functional similarity, do not exhaust the environment-behavior relations that conventionally fall under the heading of the nontechnical term concept. Both discriminative stimulus classes and functional classes are products of the cumulative effect of differential reinforcement on a number of environment-behavior relations. That is, both stimulus classes are instances of **contingency-shaped behavior**. Other stimulus classes, such as *triangle*, may result from the guidance of behavior by verbal stimuli in the form of definitions, instructions, and the like. Environment-behavior relations that are established by verbal stimuli are instances of **rule-governed behavior**, and are treated in later chapters when verbal behavior is examined.[12]

Interpretation of Discriminative Stimulus Classes

The biobehavioral processes producing selection by reinforcement and stimulus generalization are the starting points for understanding discriminative stimulus classes. Experimental work described earlier demonstrated that reinforcers bring the behavior that precedes them under the control of the environments in which those behaviors took place. This is selection by reinforcement, or contingency-shaping. Other experimental work showed that environments that were not identical to those present during selection, but that contained some of the same stimulus elements, also acquired the capacity to guide behavior. This is stimulus generali-

zation. Finally, when differential reinforcement occurred in which responses had one consequence during one range of stimuli and a different consequence during an adjacent range, different responses were evoked by stimuli within the two ranges. This is stimulus discrimination, and the phenomenon of edge effects indicated that differential responding was *greatest* near the boundary between stimuli correlated with different reinforcement contingencies.

Organismic interpretation.   Taken together, selection by reinforcement, generalization, and discrimination provide a strong foundation for interpreting discriminative stimulus classes. Consider the following study of the formation of a discriminative stimulus class with human subjects.[13] One group of subjects was successively exposed to 30 pairs of items, e.g., VVTRXR - DETROIT. The first member of each pair (e.g., VVTRXR) served as a stimulus to guide the response with which it was paired (e.g., DETROIT).[14] The subjects' task was to produce each response when its stimulus was presented. The stimulus of each pair consisted of a letter sequence constructed according to either of two sets of rules, although the subjects were not told this when they were asked to learn the task. Thus, the letter sequence VVTRXR simply provided the stimulus for the response DETROIT, VVTRVV for GIRAFFE, MRMRTV for BABOON, XMVRXR for BOSTON, and so forth. Training with the 30 pairs of items continued until the set had been completed one time without error. Although it was not pointed out to the subjects, all the responses to one range of stimuli were the names of cities, while all the responses to the other range were the names of animals.

To determine whether a stimulus class had formed, the subjects were tested with 30 letter sequences *that had never been presented before.* (Recall that all the members of a stimulus class need not appear during selection.) One-third of the test stimuli were constructed according to one of the rules used to construct the training stimuli, one-third according to the other rule, and the remaining third according to neither rule. As is clear from the preceding examples of the letter sequences used as stimuli, the two sets of sequences were quite similar and the construction principles were not obvious.[15] The subjects were asked to sort the novel test stimuli into one of three categories—category A, category B, or neither—although the test stimuli used in training had never been described as belonging to two categories. When the new letter sequences were sorted, 60% of them were placed in the correct categories, although only 33% correct categorizations were expected by chance alone. These results occurred despite the subjects' protests that they did not know how to sort the test stimuli and could not describe the basis on which they made the sorting!

Compare the sorting behavior produced by the conditions just described with the performance of a second group of subjects trained with the same 30 letter sequences, but using a different training procedure. During training, the second group was given instructions that were intended to encourage categorization of the letter sequences by means of verbal stimuli, or rules. Specifically, the subjects were told that each letter sequence belonged to one of two categories—either category A or B. The 30 letter sequences were then presented one at a time and the subjects assigned each of them to either category A or B, and were told if the categorization was correct. The stimuli were presented repeatedly until each subject had sorted all 30 letter sequences once without error. Following training, the subjects in the second group were asked to sort the same novel test stimuli that had been given to the first group. The second group of subjects, who had known from the outset that their task was to categorize the stimuli, sorted only 46% of the test stimuli correctly.

This study demonstrates that contingency-shaping is sufficient to produce a discriminative stimulus class. That is, a stimulus class may emerge as a by-product of selection without any "conscious effort" on the part of the learner to form a stimulus class.[16] As a result of a stimulus dis-

crimination procedure, the subjects in the first group responded similarly to stimuli within the class, or category, and differently to stimuli outside the class. This pattern of responding was found with the stimuli used in training and with *novel* stimuli as well. Subjects in the second group were less successful in categorizing the new stimuli. The weaker evidence for the formation of a stimulus class in the second group indicates that a stimulus class may sometimes develop more readily through contingency-shaping than through rule-governance.

The finding that contingency-shaping produces a discriminative stimulus class without the explicit participation of verbal behavior, or rules, suggests that nonhuman learners may also acquire environment-behavior relations that exemplify stimulus classes. Indeed, the evidence supports this expectation.[17] Pigeons were presented a series of more than 1,500 photographic slides without repetition. Half the slides showed naturalistic scenes that contained different examples of the critical stimuli—e.g., trees for some pigeons, people for others, and water for still others. The remaining half of the slides showed otherwise comparable scenes that did not include the critical stimuli. Pecking a disk was occasionally reinforced with food if the slide contained an example of the critical stimuli. Following training, tests were conducted with occasional presentations of unreinforced test photographs that differed from any previously shown in training.

The results were essentially the same whichever type of critical stimulus—trees, people, or water—was used in training. When the novel test stimuli were presented, the percentage of total responses when the slides contained the critical stimuli ranged from 72 to 94% correct for individual pigeons, with an average of 84% correct. Clearly, differential reinforcement had produced a discriminative stimulus class. Moreover, when human subjects were asked which slides they found particularly easy or difficult to categorize, their responses were in general agreement with the pigeons'. For example, an easily categorized slide might show a lone tree in silhouette at the crest of a hill, while a more difficult slide might show a single branch, with the remainder of the tree obstructed by a building. (See **Figure 5.3** for examples of some of the stimuli used in this experiment.)

The preceding organismic simulations indicate that discriminative stimulus classes are produced as an emergent consequence of the differential reinforcement of responding in the presence of a range of stimuli. Such stimulus classes were demonstrated with both people and pigeons. Of course, the entire selection history that is potentially relevant to the formation of stimulus classes has not been specified by these studies. The human sub-

jects had extensive experience with letters of the alphabet before the experiment and undoubtedly had previously sorted other stimuli. The pigeon subjects, although reared under laboratory conditions, had extensive histories of seeing and pecking. Thus, as in all historical sciences, the complete selection history contributing to the complex phenomenon remains only partially identified. Nevertheless, these studies clearly indicate that—with prior selection histories that are likely to exist in many cases—differential reinforcement is sufficient to produce discriminative stimulus classes.

Formal interpretation. Formal interpretation may also be used to interpret complex environment-behavior relations, such as discriminative stimulus classes. As in earlier treatments of reinforcement, the formal interpretations use adaptive neural networks that implement biobehavioral processes identified in independent experimental analyses.

When the learning of a complex environment-behavior relation is simulated by an adaptive network, a computer program is written that represents the units and the initial connection weights between them. Then, environmental stimuli activate various input units, which in turn activate various hidden units and, ultimately, the output units. At first, which output units are activated depends on the initial connection weights between the units in the network. In the nervous system, the initial strengths of the connections reflect the cumulative effects of natural selection and, as the organism grows more experienced, of earlier selection by reinforcement. In an adaptive-network simulation, the initial weights are typically assigned small, randomly assigned values at the beginning of learning. Thereafter, the connection weights change based on the degree of correspondence between the activation of the relevant output units by the environment and the activation required for the reinforcer. A large discrepancy between the output of the network activated by the training stimuli and the output required for the reinforcing stimulus produces large changes in the

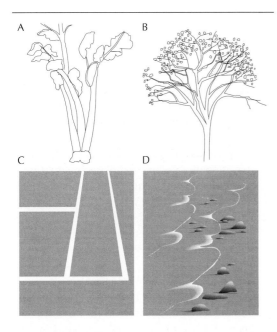

FIGURE 5.3 *Renderings of photographs rejected or accepted as instances of two stimulus classes—TREES and WATER*
The upper left drawing of celery was rejected and the upper right was accepted as TREE by pigeons. The lower left drawing of the lines on a tennis court was rejected and the lower right was accepted as WATER by pigeons. Acceptance was indicated by pecking a disk on which the image was projected (see text).
Note: See also Herrnstein, Loveland, & Cable, 1976.

connection weights within the network. Conversely, when the discrepancy between the output produced by the environment and the required output is small, the weights change very little. This is consistent with selection by reinforcement in that the change in connection weights reduces the discrepancy between the output produced by the environment and the target output required for the reinforcing stimulus.[18]

An example.   Consider the following example of the use of an adaptive network to simulate the formation of a discriminative stimulus class. Suppose that a child sees a number of dogs that differ somewhat from one another, but share certain features in common. Some dogs are brown, but there are occasional black dogs and white dogs; some dogs have a tail, but others do not, and so on. In the adaptive network used to simulate these conditions, there were 16 features, each represented by an input unit. An input unit was activated if the feature was present, but not if it was absent.[19] Suppose further that the child's parents reinforce the verbal response "dog" in the presence of the *canine* input patterns of features provided by particular dogs, but reinforce other responses in the presence of *non-canine* input patterns. In the simulation, there were 8 output units, with a particular pattern of activation representing the verbal response "dog." Output patterns representing other verbal responses, e.g., "cat," might be strengthened in the presence of other input patterns.

The first goal of the simulation was to determine whether reinforcement could change the connection weights in the network so that the input patterns containing the features of dogs could evoke the output pattern representing the verbal response "dog." The effect of reinforcement was simulated by adjusting each connection weight in proportion to the discrepancy between the activation levels of the output units produced by the training stimulus and the levels required for reinforcement. The network was repeatedly exposed to 50 different dog input patterns and 100 input patterns corresponding to other stimuli. The dog input patterns were variable, consisting of random combinations of the various features of dogs. After each stimulus presentation, the connection weights were adjusted so that the *canine* stimulus (input) patterns progressively produced the "dog" response (output) pattern, and the *non-canine* patterns produced other output patterns. The cumulative effect of this selection process was that the various *canine* input patterns activated the same output pattern—the one corresponding to "dog"—and the other input patterns did not. Thus, the cumulative effect of discrimination training changed the connection weights so that the network distinguished between *canine* and *non-canine* input patterns. In short, the network "recognized" dogs.

The competence of the network to produce a "dog" output when any of 50 *canine* inputs activated the network is illustrated in **Figure 5.4**. For each of the 16 features represented by the 16 input units, a filled circle indicates that the feature that activated the unit was present and an open circle indicates that it was absent. For example, the first feature, which is present, might represent having a brown color, and the second feature, which is absent, might represent having feathers. The alternating pattern of strongly and weakly activated output units represents the verbal response "dog." The relative strength of activation of each output unit by the *canine* input patterns at the end of training is shown by the bar graph in **Figure 5.4**. Only the output units that produced the pattern corresponding to a "dog" response were appreciably activated by the *canine* input patterns.

Characteristics of simulated stimulus classes. Three characteristics of a discriminative stimulus class simulated by adaptive networks merit special comment. First, a stimulus class produced by selection has what are called *fuzzy* boundaries.[20] The term **fuzzy boundary** indicates that no single feature need be present in an input pattern to evoke the output pattern corresponding to the correct response. For example, suppose that one of the input features corresponded to *has four legs*. Although the connection weights linking this feature with the output pattern for "dog" might be relatively strong, input patterns not containing this

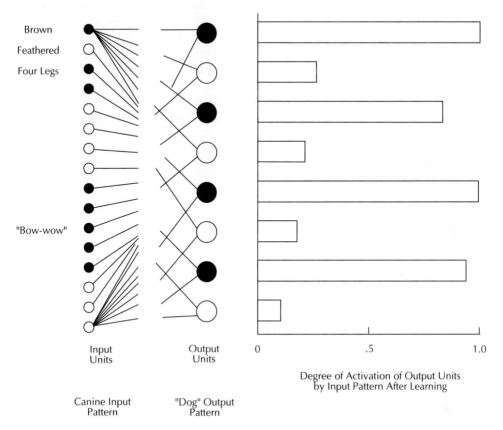

FIGURE 5.4 *The 16 input units and 8 output units of an adaptive network with the connections between units indicated by the lines emanating from the units*

When the input units indicated by filled circles were activated, some of the output units were activated. The activated input units correspond to various characteristics of dogs, e.g., "has four legs." The inactivated input units correspond to characteristics not possessed by dogs, e.g., "has feathers." The connection strengths between the input and output units were modified by learning until activation of the filled input units caused only the filled output units to be reliably activated. The pattern of filled output units represents the target output pattern, and corresponds—for example—to the verbal response "DOG."

Source: Adapted from procedures and findings of McClelland & Rumelhart, 1986.

feature would also be able to evoke the "dog" response. Thus a dog unfortunate enough to have lost a leg through an accident, but possessing other *canine* features, would still be called a dog.

Second, the values of the connection weights depend on the particular examples of dogs and nondogs that were used to train the network, and on the order in which the inputs were presented during training. Thus, the strengths of the connec-

tions are **path-dependent**—i.e., influenced by the particular sequence of events during the network's selection history. Connections in networks, like synaptic efficacies in the nervous system, reflect their unique selection histories. To illustrate, the pathways activated by the feature "has legs" would have large connection weights in a network that had been trained to distinguish dogs from fire hydrants, but would have smaller and more complexly arrayed weights in a network trained to distinguish dogs from cats. Fire hydrants do not have legs, but cats do; hence, the feature "has legs" would be helpful in distinguishing dogs from hydrants but not from cats.

Third, selection of the verbal response "dog" in the presence of the particular 50 *canine* input patterns would change the way the network responded to input patterns on which it had not been trained. The network would respond correctly to input patterns that had features overlapping with the patterns to which it had been exposed; i.e., a stimulus class would be formed, and not merely a series of particular discriminations. Moreover, the network might respond most strongly to an input pattern to which it had never been exposed! This would be the input pattern that shared the most features in common with the 50 specific input patterns used in training. The input pattern shown in **Figure 5.4**, which was not used in training, is the pattern of features to which the "dog" response was greatest. (Recall that the training input patterns were random variations of the *canine* input pattern.) Thus, selection of environment-behavior relations with particular *canine* stimuli produced a network that responded most vigorously to a *typical* dog, and not to any of the particular input patterns to which it had been exposed. This characteristic, commonly observed with trained networks, is denoted by saying that the network responds most strongly to a prototype of the input. A **prototype** may be thought of as the most typical combination of the environmental features that were present when the response was selected.[21]

Several comments should be made about the term prototype as it is used in the context of selection in adaptive networks and living organisms. First, the prototype is an emergent property of selection. No additional processes are required for the network to respond maximally to a stimulus having the most features in common with the stimuli used in training. No central agency, as implied by terms such as "intelligence" or "reasoning," is necessary to oversee the changes that permit the network to function in this way. The extraction of

a prototype arises as an emergent consequence of selection. Second, the prototype emerges from the functioning of large portions of the network, as determined by the connection weights. The prototype is not a *thing* stored at some one place within the network; it is not an *ideal representation of reality* waiting to be retrieved by a stimulus. Networks, and the living organisms whose functioning they simulate, act *as if* there were prototypes, but what exist are sets of connection weights and synaptic efficacies, respectively. Responding *as if* there were a prototype is simply how a trained network or an experienced organism functions after selection.

In summary, adaptive networks simulate the formation of discriminative stimulus classes that share three characteristics with classes formed by humans and other organisms: (a) the boundaries of stimulus classes are fuzzy in that no single feature is required to distinguish one class from another, (b) the formation of stimulus classes is path-dependent in that the final properties of the class vary with the details of the learner's selection history, and (c) the cumulative effect of selection causes the network to function *as if* a prototype has been formed. We now consider one last important respect in which networks mimic the environment-behavior relations formed by living organisms—their reactions to a procedure known as *fading*.

Fading

When learners acquire new environment-behavior relations, the initial requirements for successful performance are usually quite modest. A child just beginning to read is not given a copy of James Joyce's *Finnegan's Wake*. Instead, a new skill such as reading begins with simpler tasks—single letters are discriminated and then single words are "sounded out." More demanding tasks are introduced only gradually. One way of simplifying a complex task has already been identified—shaping. In shaping, the response on which the reinforcer is contingent is gradually made more complex or the sequence of responses is gradually made longer. Simplifying the initial exposure to complex tasks is not confined to work with animals or formal instruction. When parents speak with their young children, they use a simplified grammar and vocabulary.[22]

Another important way in which complex tasks may be simplified is through the use of a **fading** procedure. In fading, the stimuli to be discriminated initially differ substantially from one another and then, as the learner begins to respond differentially, the training stimuli are progressively and gradually changed to their final and more similar values.[23] For example, a learner might be taught to discriminate between two very different colors, such as red and green, as the first step toward acquiring a final discrimination between two more similar colors, such as red and orange. Fading denotes a gradual change during training in the stimulus components of environment-behavior relations; shaping denotes a gradual change in the response components.

Fading the training stimuli has been shown to facilitate discrimination formation in many studies with both human and nonhuman learners. Consider the following experiment, in which children acquired a discrimination between two forms—circles and ellipses—using a fading procedure for some learners and a nonfading procedure for others.[24] The children were shown eight stimuli, each displayed on a small panel. (See **Figure 5.5**.) When a child pressed the center panel, the various stimuli were displayed and touching the circle produced candy, a small toy, or the sounding of chimes as reinforcers. Touching one of the ellipses caused the display to darken until the next trial began. The final discrimination was between a circle and a very similar elliptical form displayed on the other panels.

Of the nine children exposed to the nonfading procedure, in which training was begun with the circle and the most similar ellipse, only one child learned to confine his presses to the panel displaying the circle. Of the ten children exposed to the

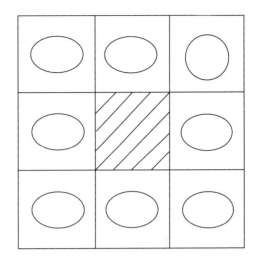

FIGURE 5.5 *The display of nine stimulus panels used to train a stimulus discrimination between circles and ellipses*

A trial began when the subject pressed the center panel (shown here as shaded). Pressing the center panel caused eight panels to be illuminated with a circle on one panel, whose position varied from trial to trial, and ellipses on the other 7 panels. The similarity of the ellipses to the circle could be varied. Pressing the panel containing the circle produced a reinforcer.

Source: Adapted from procedures of Sidman & Stoddard, 1967.

fading procedure, seven successfully confined their presses exclusively to the circle.

The fading procedure consisted of the following steps. First, only the panel containing the circle was illuminated, and touching it was reinforced. Next, the other panels were gradually brightened but remained blank. Responding to the circle continued to be reinforced. Then, ellipses were dimly illuminated on the incorrect panels and gradually brightened and made more similar in shape to the circle. Fading the ellipse-circle discrimination enabled the subjects to discriminate highly similar ellipses from the circle.

Adaptive-network simulations of discrimination formation also show the beneficial effects of fading. In one such simulation, very many trials were required for the network to make a particularly difficult discrimination between two patterns on its input units. However, when four steps of fading from an easy to the final discrimination were used, the same discrimination was acquired with less than one-quarter of the training![25]

Before concluding the discussion of adaptive networks as a means for interpreting discriminative stimulus classes, note that our presentation has left several important problems untouched. For example, the simulations assumed that different stimuli may be represented by different patterns on the input units and that different responses may be represented by different patterns on the output units. Clearly, perceiving a stimulus and executing a response require analysis as challenging problems in their own right. The simulations do indicate, however, that selection with adaptive networks produces many salient aspects of the complex environment-behavior relations of discriminative stimulus classes.

FUNCTIONAL CLASSES

Stimulus classes form not only when stimuli within the class are physically similar—as in discriminative stimulus classes—but also when stimuli within the class guide similar responses. To the extent that the stimuli in a class guide similar responses, the stimuli are *functionally equivalent*.

Functional Stimulus Classes

In animals, functional stimulus classes have been demonstrated with the following procedure.[26] Pigeons were successively presented with 80 different slides of trees projected on a small screen. When a *random* half of the slides were presented, pecking the screen was intermittently reinforced with food. When the remaining half were presented, pecking was nonreinforced. The slides were presented in a mixed order that varied from day to day. Thus the subjects received discrimination training with multiple stimuli in the reinforced and nonreinforced classes, and with no simple physical basis on which to distinguish between the

stimuli in the two classes—all stimuli were pictures of trees.

Testing for the formation of functional stimulus classes was carried out as follows. After the two sets had been discriminated, the reinforcement contingency was reversed. Slides to which pecking had previously been reinforced were now nonreinforced, and *vice versa*. If a functional stimulus class had been formed, then—after experiencing the first few reversal trials—subjects should respond appropriately to the reversed contingency on the *initial* presentations of the other stimuli in the class. The subjects were given repeated cycles of discrimination training followed by reversal training. After 20 to 30 cycles, five of the 6 subjects began to respond appropriately to the reversed contingency on their initial exposures to stimuli in the newly reinforced or nonreinforced class. (See **Figure 5.6**.) That is, if the reinforcement contingency had changed for a few members of the class, subjects responded as if it had changed for the other members of the class as well.[27]

The analysis and interpretation of the formation of functional classes in animals remains largely a task for the future. However, the stimulus consequences of conditioned responses probably play an important role in this phenomenon. Recall the phenomenon of devaluation, in which pairing a reinforcer with an aversive stimulus reduced the strength of the responses that had previously produced that reinforcer, but not the strength of other responses that had produced different reinforcers.[28] Devaluation experiments demonstrate the formation of functional classes on the basis that responses to all stimuli in the same class produce the same reinforcer.[29]

Equivalence Classes

The most striking examples of functional classes are found in verbal behavior, although they are not restricted to such behavior. For example, a Cocker Spaniel, a Siamese cat, a goldfish, and a parakeet—although physically dissimilar—are alike in that they all guide the common response "pet." More-

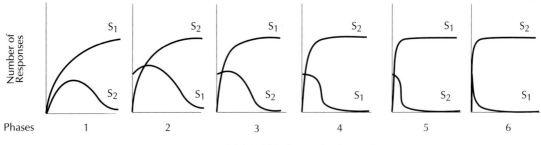

FIGURE 5.6 *Formation of functional stimulus classes with sets of arbitrary stimuli, S_1 and S_2*
The stimuli were 80 pictures of trees arbitrarily subdivided into two sets of 40 pictures. During any one phase of the study, responses to members of one stimulus class were reinforced and responses to members of the other stimulus class were nonreinforced (extinguished). Between different phases of the study, which are shown in separate panels of the figure, the reinforced stimulus class was reversed. That is, S_1 was the reinforced class in the leftmost panel, S_2 in the next panel, and so forth.
Source: Hypothetical findings based on data from Vaughn, 1988.

over, if a never-before-encountered stimulus, such as a new breed of dog, is called a "pet," we immediately engage in pet-appropriate behavior without the need for that behavior to undergo selection by reinforcement in the presence of the new stimulus. Some behavior is common to all pets; e.g., approach responses occur and withdrawal responses do not occur because pets are "safe." Other behavior, of course, is influenced by the particular features of the stimulus—and, therefore, the discriminative stimulus class of which the new stimulus is also a member. Thus we might call both a Cocker Spaniel and a parakeet a pet, but throw a ball to one and not to the other.[30]

In this section, we identify the conditions under which stimuli become members of a particular type of functional class known as an *equivalence class*. **Equivalence classes** are the cumulative products of selection after a learner has been exposed to a series of differential training procedures called *contextual discriminations*. In a **contextual discrimination**, a stimulus guides one response in one stimulus context and the same stimulus guides a different response in a second stimulus context.

That is, the environment-behavior relation selected by the reinforcer depends on the context in which the guiding stimulus appears. Equivalence classes play a crucial role in the development of complex environment-behavior relations, and their modern study was initiated by Murray Sidman and his colleagues.

Contextual discriminations.   When carefully examined, most discrimination procedures involve contextual discriminations. It is rare that a response is appropriate in all circumstances when a given stimulus is present. For instance, it is quite appropriate to speak to a stranger at a party, but not on the street. Talking to strangers at parties is often reinforced; talking to strangers on the street is not.

In the laboratory, contextual discriminations are studied with a procedure called *matching-to-sample*. In a **matching-to-sample procedure**, a single stimulus, the **sample stimulus**, is presented followed by two or more other stimuli, the **comparison stimuli**. Which response to a comparison stimulus is reinforced depends on the value of the sample stimulus. For instance, suppose that the sample stimulus is a triangle and the comparison stimuli are a triangle and a circle. Under these circumstances, a response to the triangular comparison stimulus might be reinforced. However, if the sample were a circle, a response to the circular comparison stimulus might be reinforced. Note that reinforcement of responding to the triangular or circular comparison stimulus depends on the context provided by the sample stimulus. (This particular type of contextual discrimination is known as **identity matching** in that the response is reinforced if the comparison stimulus is the *same as*—i.e., matches—the sample stimulus. Other types of contextual discriminations will be considered shortly.)[31]

To illustrate equivalence classes, consider a study in which eight children, between five and seven years of age, were successively taught three contextual discriminations.[32] The study is complex, but complex experience is necessary to produce the important environment-behavior relations known as equivalence classes.

During a trial, each child was presented six displays arranged as shown in **Figure 5.7**. The stimulus that appeared in the central display was the sample stimulus; the stimuli in the five peripheral displays were the comparison stimuli. A trial began with a stimulus on the central display only. When the child pressed the central display containing the sample stimulus, the comparison stimuli then appeared in the peripheral displays. Reinforcers occurred when the child pressed the comparison display containing the stimulus that was appropriate for the sample stimulus on that trial. Reinforcement consisted of the ringing of chimes after a correct response, and the occasional presentation of pennies.

The three contextual discriminations taught to each child are depicted in **Figure 5.8**. The stimuli used in all three tasks were letters of the Greek alphabet. Since the children were unfamiliar with these stimuli, the conditions required to produce the contextual discriminations—and, subsequently, equivalence classes—could be more

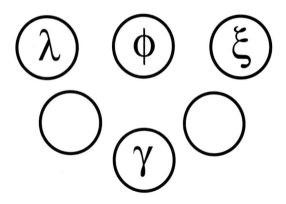

FIGURE 5.7   *Display of six stimulus panels used to train a contextual discrimination by the matching-to-sample procedure*
The center display contains the sample or contextual stimulus, here φ. Pressing the center display caused three comparison stimuli—here λ, ξ, and γ—to be presented in three of the remaining five positions. The positions occupied by the comparison stimuli varied from trial to trial. When the panel was pressed containing the correct comparison stimulus for that contextual stimulus, a reinforcing stimulus was presented.
Source: Sidman, M. & Tailby, W. (1982). Conditional discrimination vs. matching to sample: An expansion of the testing paradigm. *Journal of the Experimental Analysis of Behavior, 37,* 5–22. Copyright 1982 by the Society for the Experimental Analysis of Behavior, Inc.

nearly confined to the variables manipulated in the experiment.

In the first contextual discrimination, hereafter termed the A-B task, reinforcement was contingent on pressing the comparison display containing the visual stimulus (an upper-case Greek letter) corresponding to an auditory sample stimulus (a repeatedly presented, tape-recorded word).[33]   An auditory sample stimulus was presented to begin each trial, and the comparison stimuli were then presented after the central display was pressed. For instance, if the sample word "lambda" was presented, then pressing the peripheral display containing the comparison stimulus was reinforced. The five comparison stimuli presented on each trial

Contextual Discriminations	Sample Stimuli	Comparison Stimuli Correct	Incorrect
A-B	"Lambda" "Xi" "Gamma"	$\underset{\equiv}{\Lambda}$ $\underset{\equiv}{\equiv}$ Γ	$\underset{\Lambda}{\equiv}$ $\underset{\Lambda}{\Gamma}$ Γ $\underset{\equiv}{\Lambda}$
A-C	"Lambda" "Xi" "Gamma"	$\underset{\gamma}{\underset{\xi}{\lambda}}$ $\underset{\lambda}{\xi}$ γ γ ξ	
D-C	$\underset{\delta}{\underset{\sigma}{\phi}}$	$\underset{\gamma}{\underset{\xi}{\lambda}}$ ξ γ λ γ λ ξ	

FIGURE 5.8 *Sample and comparison stimuli used in the three contextual discriminations, A-B, A-C, and D-C*
The first letter of each contextual discrimination refers to the set of sample (contextual) stimuli and the second letter refers to the set of comparison (discriminative) stimuli for those sample stimuli. For each contextual discrimination, there were three sample stimuli and three comparison stimuli—one of which was the correct stimulus to which to respond for a given sample stimulus. The A stimuli consisted of tape-recorded spoken words, the B and C stimuli were upper and lower case Greek letters. *Source:* Sidman, M. & Tailby, W. (1982). Conditional discrimination vs. matching to sample: An expansion of the testing paradigm. *Journal of the Experimental Analysis of Behavior, 37,* 5–22. Copyright 1982 by the Society for the Experimental Analysis of Behavior, Inc.

hereafter termed the D-C task, the sample stimuli consisted of three new, visually presented Greek letters and the comparison stimuli were the same visually presented Greek letters used as comparison stimuli in the A-C task. All three contextual discriminations are examples of **arbitrary** or **symbolic matching**, rather than identity matching, since the sample and comparison stimuli bore no physical similarity to one another. **Figure 5.9** summarizes the relationships among the three contextual discriminations.

The foregoing contextual discriminations—A-B, A-C, and D-C—were acquired through the use of fading techniques. First, one component of the A-B task was acquired (e.g., "lambda" - Λ), then its other components were progressively intro-

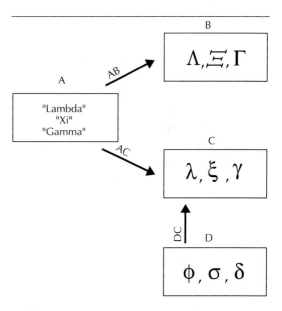

FIGURE 5.9 *Summary of the three trained contextual discriminations—A-B, A-C, and D-C—showing the relations between the stimuli used in the various discriminations*
The A, B, C and D stimuli are enclosed in boxes.
Source: Sidman, M. & Tailby, W. (1982). Conditional discrimination vs. matching to sample: An expansion of the testing paradigm. *Journal of the Experimental Analysis of Behavior, 37,* 5–22. Copyright 1982 by the Society for the Experimental Analysis of Behavior, Inc.

consisted of three possible upper-case Greek letters and two blank displays, the position of each stimulus varying unsystematically from trial to trial. In the second contextual discrimination, hereafter termed the A-C task, the sample stimuli were the same auditory stimuli (spoken words) as the A-B task and the visual comparison stimuli were the corresponding lower-case Greek letters (see **Figure 5.8**). In the final contextual discrimination,

duced. This was followed by the successive introduction of components of the A-C and D-C tasks,
with a gradual intermixing of components from all
three tasks. Before moving from one task to the
next, each child was required to perform the contextual discrimination to a criterion of over 95%
correct. Final performance, with intermixed presentations of all components of all three contextual
discriminations, was at least 97% correct for each
child. While this experiment may seem complex,
the total number of environment-behavior relations is trivial compared to the number acquired by
children in the course of their daily living.

Derived relations.   Environment-behavior relations that are strengthened by a training procedure
but not directly reinforced within the procedure are
called **derived relations**. Among the derived relations produced by contextual discrimination procedures are those that document the formation of
equivalence classes. An equivalence class is a type
of functional class having the distinctive characteristics described below.

Consider first the A-C and D-C tasks. These
tasks require panel-pressing responses to be guided
by common stimuli (C) in the presence of different
contextual stimuli (A or D). A and D are equivalent
in the sense that A and D both provide the context
for responding to the C stimuli. In order to evaluate
their functional equivalence, nonreinforced A-D
probe trials were occasionally introduced among
the training trials. If A and D contained equivalent
stimuli, then matching should occur between their
corresponding components *without additional
training*. When A stimuli were presented as samples and D stimuli as comparisons, the children did
indeed press the D display that corresponded to the
C response that was common to both A and D. For
instance, when the spoken word "lambda" was the
sample and ϕ, σ, and δ were the three comparison
stimuli, the children pressed the display containing
ϕ. (Refer to **Figure 5.9.**) All children showing the
A-D relation responded with the common response
to C on at least 85% of the probe trials. To appreciate the full significance of these findings, recall

again that the A-D relation occurred as the by-
product of selection for the A-C and D-C relations,
without explicit training.

The derived A-D relation is only one of the
environment-behavior relations that occur as by-
products of contextual discrimination training.
Figure 5.10 shows the full range of relations found
in this experiment through probe trials. Several are
of particular interest. Consider the derived B-C and
C-B relations. Here, prior A-B and A-C training
caused responses to B and C to be guided by the
same contextual stimulus (A), and this common
stimulus produced the new relations. As an illustration of the derived B-C relation, when Λ was
presented as the sample, λ was responded to rather

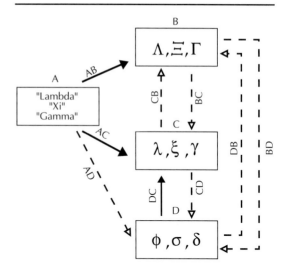

FIGURE 5.10   *Summary of the three trained and six
derived contextual discriminations*
The three directly trained contextual discriminations—
A-B, A-C, and D-C—are indicated by the solid lines. The
six derived relations that testing revealed after training
with the three contextual discriminations are indicated by
the dashed lines.
Source: Sidman, M. & Tailby, W. (1982). Conditional
discrimination vs. matching to sample: An expansion of the
testing paradigm. *Journal of the Experimental Analysis of
Behavior, 37,* 5–22. Copyright 1982 by the Society for the
Experimental Analysis of Behavior, Inc.

than ξ or γ as the comparison stimulus. While the A-D relation indicates an equivalence class *based on a common response* to the C stimuli in the A-C and D-C tasks, the B-C and C-B relations indicate an equivalence relation *based on a common contextual stimulus* in the A-B and A-C tasks.

Consider also the B-D and D-B relations. All three contextual discriminations contribute to these derived relations. For example, when D is presented in the context of B (i.e., D is the comparison and B is the sample), a sequence of covert processes guiding the appropriate D response might be as follows. (Refer to **Figure 5.10** throughout the following account.) Because of prior A-B training, the presence of B makes the appropriate A processes more likely. Given the occurrence of A processes, prior A-C training in turn makes appropriate C processes occur. Finally, given the occurrence of C processes, prior D-C training makes the appropriate D processes occur. Since the D stimuli are present in the B-D task, the appropriate response to D then occurs. By this *behavioral chain* of previously established relations (B to A, A to C, C to D), the derived B-D relation may be mediated. For example, in the context of Λ as the sample stimulus, φ was responded to when it appeared with σ and δ as comparison stimuli.

Significance of equivalence relations. The above study and many others[34] indicate that the selection of multiple contextual discriminations produces a large number of derived environment-behavior relations *without direct reinforcement of those relations*. In the experiment just described, a series of contextual discriminations yielded two types of equivalence relations (one based on common comparison stimuli and the other based on common sample stimuli) and a chaining relation. Since there were three contextual discriminations, each consisting of three components, there were nine directly selected environment-behavior relations. As the result of these nine direct selections, a substantial number of derived environment-behavior relations were produced. Considering only the relations tested in **Figure 5.10**, 18 derived rela-

tions—six types, each having three components—were found. In short, twice as many derived environment-behavior relations were produced as were directly trained! Other work indicates that all of the reciprocal relations, including the untested D-A, C-A, and B-A relations, also occur. If additional contextual discriminations are directly trained, with each discrimination consisting of many components, then the increase in the number of derived relations is even greater.[35]

The practical significance of derived equivalence relations is better appreciated when they are illustrated with commonplace stimuli rather than Greek letters. As a component of the A-C task, suppose that in the presence of the spoken word "pet," responding to a picture of a parakeet is reinforced and responding to a lion is nonreinforced. As a component of the D-C task, suppose that in the presence of the printed word BIRD, responding to a picture of a parakeet rather than a chair is reinforced. In this case, the derived A-D relation is demonstrated by presenting the spoken word "pet" and the learner responding to BIRD rather than to other printed words as comparison stimuli. The spoken word "pet" and the printed word BIRD are members of the same equivalence class *without ever having been presented together*. Such derived relations can guide appropriate behavior in new environments—a bird would be responded to as a pet without the need for direct reinforcement. Indeed, such derived relations are the beginnings of "reasoning" by metaphor and analogy.

On the average, environment-behavior relations derived from contextual discriminations greatly affect responding in environments in which direct selection has not yet occurred.[36] A beneficial result is not inevitable, however. Consider a child that has acquired three contextual discriminations consisting of the following components: "pet" - Cocker Spaniel, Cocker Spaniel - "dog," and "dog" - pit bull. Through the derived chaining relation, if the child were given the word "pet," he would select a pit bull in preference to other objects! Hearing "pet" and responding to dogs is very often reinforced, but not necessarily. Derived environment-behavior relations are no more guaranteed to be reinforced in future environments than are relations that were directly reinforced in past environments.

The fact that derived relations are not necessarily maintained in future environments indicates that these relations must often undergo further modification by direct selection, as do all other relations. Nevertheless, derived relations greatly extend the effects of direct selection and thereby enrich the variation available for later selection. The practical benefits of derived relations arising from multiple contextual discriminations are now being realized in the design of efficient procedures for teaching children such skills as reading and counting.[37]

Basic relations. Experimental work indicates that the derived relations of equivalence and chaining are dependent on three basic relations—*reflexivity*, *symmetry*, and *transitivity*. A **reflexive relation** is demonstrated when, after learning identity matching with one set of stimuli, e.g., A-A, the subject matches a different set of stimuli, e.g., B-B, without additional training. That is, when B is the sample, the subject responds to B as a comparison stimulus after A-A training alone. The reflexive relation demonstrates **generalized identity matching**. In the previous experiment, before the study began the children were given training for identity matching with colors. When tested for generalized identity matching on their first exposure to the Greek letters, the children responded appropriately. That is, if Λ was the sample stimulus and Λ, Ξ, and Γ were the comparison stimuli, the children responded to Λ.

The second basic relation, the **symmetric relation**, is demonstrated if, after contextual discrimination training, the sample and comparison stimuli are interchangeable. That is, after training on an A-B task, when the sample is changed to B the subject responds to A as a comparison stimulus. During the experiment, the performance of six of the eight children showed all of the derived relations described previously. However, two of the children did not show evidence of either equiva-

lence classes or chaining. The behavior of the same two children also failed to show symmetry. After all contextual discriminations (A-B, A-C, and C-D) were completed and all derived relations were tested, symmetry was assessed in probe trials. For example, appropriate matching performance did not occur on D-C probe trials although these two children had completed the C-D task. If symmetry is not demonstrated when the sample and comparison stimuli are interchanged, then the derived relations dependent on symmetry cannot occur.

The final basic relation, the **transitive relation**, is demonstrated if, after A-B and B-C training, appropriate matching performance occurs on an A-C task. That is, when A is the sample, the subject responds to C as a comparison stimulus. The transitive relation is required for the occurrence of chaining. Appropriate performance on an A-C task after A-B and B-C training involves transitivity alone. Appropriate performance on an A-C task after A-B and C-B training requires both transitivity and symmetry of the C-B relation.

Origins of the basic relations. To date, equivalence classes have been demonstrated experimentally in only one species—our own. Only in humans have multiple contextual discriminations consistently and unequivocally produced the full range of derived relations. What is responsible for this crucial difference? Which of the basic relations—reflexivity, symmetry, or transitivity—are absent from the repertoire of nonhumans? And, what are the reasons for their absence?

Experimental analysis has yet to provide complete answers to these questions. Humans and nonhumans differ in their evolutionary histories, and also in their pre-experimental histories of selection by reinforcement with the stimuli used in contextual discrimination tasks. Although the children in the previous experiment probably had little prior experience with Greek letters, they almost certainly had experience with other types of letters. Also, they probably had earlier experience with contextual discriminations using letter-like stimuli. Research indicates that such factors facilitate the occurrence of derived relations with both normal and retarded children.[38] Even when simple nonverbal stimuli are used, e.g., triangles instead of letters or words, such stimuli are also more likely to have been used in earlier differential training with humans than with nonhumans. For many children, a triangle is seen as a unitary "figure." For a nonhuman—particularly one without the relevant experience—the same visual stimulus may be seen as a number of unintegrated "lines" or "corners."[39] In general, more experimental analysis is needed to determine which specific aspects of the sample and comparison stimuli are guiding behavior.[40] The guiding features of the "same" stimulus may be different for humans and nonhumans in what appear to the experimenter to be identical contextual discriminations.

Whatever the differences in individual or ancestral selection history, experimental work has yet to find evidence for all of the basic relations in species other than humans. Reflexivity (i.e., generalized identity matching) has been demonstrated in monkeys,[41] as has transitivity.[42] However, despite considerable effort, no evidence has been found for symmetry and the equivalence relations that depend on symmetry.[43] Can a history of selection by reinforcement be found that produces in nonhuman animals the full range of basic relations and the equivalence classes that those relations generate? This remains to be determined.

Equivalence classes and verbal behavior. In the search for the critical variables affecting equivalence classes, the ancestral and individual selection histories with respect to verbal behavior—less technically, language—are prominent candidates. Indeed, equivalence relations were first studied, though from a different theoretical perspective and with different methods, in research on verbal behavior.[44] Some research has been interpreted to mean that equivalence relations are restricted to verbally competent organisms.[45] Other work indicates that verbal responses to the stimuli used in the contextual discriminations need not precede the emergence of equivalence classes. For example, in the experiment using Greek letters, probe

trials indicated that most—but not all—of the children could emit the appropriate verbal response, e.g., "lambda," when shown the corresponding Greek letters from the B, C, or D stimuli, e.g., Λ, λ, and ϕ. That is, most of the children could orally name, or read, the letters even though naming had not been directly reinforced. Sometimes, however, the derived relations were present even though naming had not yet occurred.[46] These findings are consistent with the view that both verbal behavior and equivalence classes are dependent on *common* prior selections that are not unique to verbal behavior. Some of these earlier selections may be found in the individual history of the learner, but others may eventually be traced to the ancestral selection history—i.e., to species differences.

Internal reinforcement. One factor that probably makes an important contribution to the development of equivalence classes is internal reinforcement. Internal reinforcement occurs, you will recall, when activity from neural networks selected in motor association cortex by prior reinforcers feeds back to the reinforcement system in the ventral tegmental area (VTA). The activity caused by feedback to the VTA then projects diffusely to the motor association cortex and modifies any active connections there. Internal reinforcement is implicated in the formation of equivalence classes because the probe trials used to assess equivalence relations often show the relations growing stronger with repeated probes, *even though no reinforcers are delivered during probe trials!* According to the internal-reinforcement interpretation of these observations, the stimuli presented on the probe trials activate networks in motor association cortex to which connections have been strengthened on previously reinforced trials with those stimuli. The feedback from the activation of these networks then strengthens the connections that mediate equivalence relations.

The neural mechanisms implementing internal reinforcement may be more extensive in humans than in other species, but this difference alone would not be enough to account for a species difference—if one exists. For internal reinforcement to strengthen the connections mediating equivalence relations, those connections must already exist and the neurons using the connections must already be activated. Put simply, such connections may exist in our species but not (or not as abundantly) in other species.

Polysensory integration. The species difference that may be linked most persuasively to equivalence classes is the capacity for *polysensory* or *cross-modal integration.*[47] Polysensory integration may be illustrated by the phenomenon of **cross-modal generalization**. Cross-modal generalization occurs when selection of an environment-behavior relation in one modality enables stimuli in a second modality to guide the same behavior, without specific reinforcement of the second relation. For example, if a response is selected by food reinforcement when a triangular object is *seen* and the same response later occurs when the object is *touched*, cross-modal generalization has occurred.[48]

In the experiment on equivalence classes using Greek letters, *auditory* stimuli (the spoken letter "names") were used as samples to provide the context in which responding was guided by different *visual* stimuli (the printed letters). Successful performance on this task clearly requires a convergence somewhere in the nervous system of pathways activated by auditory and visual stimuli. Behavioral data indicate that connections of this sort exist in even very young infants. As an experimental example, infants were placed in front of a speaker which emitted the sounds of a series of words. Two video monitors, one on each side of the speaker, displayed images of the same person talking. (See **Figure 5.11**.) One monitor showed a face whose mouth movements were synchronized with the words; the other showed the same face mouthing different words. When simultaneously confronted with these visual and auditory stimuli, the infants turned their heads toward the monitor whose visual stimuli were synchronized with the auditory stimuli! Thus the temporal characteristics of visual and auditory stimuli *jointly* determine head orientation in the human infant.[49] Clearly,

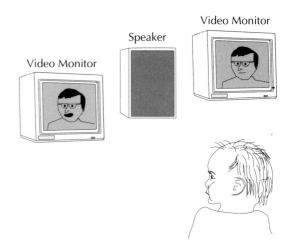

FIGURE 5.11 *Procedure for testing the effects of combined auditory and visual stimuli on head orientation in human infants*
The auditory stimulation came from a central loudspeaker that presented a series of speech sounds. Two television monitors were used, with one displaying a picture of a person speaking the words presented by the loudspeaker. The other monitor displayed a picture of the same person speaking different words.
Source: Adapted from procedures of Kuhl & Meltzoff, 1982.

auditory and visual stimuli are both crucially important for the verbal skills involved in speaking and writing, and polysensory integration may contribute to the formation of equivalence classes as well.

Research with nonhuman animals indicates that selection by the ancestral environment importantly contributes to cross-modal generalization and thereby, perhaps, to equivalence classes. Only our near relatives among the primates have demonstrated matching across modalities. For example, chimpanzees and perhaps some species of monkeys can match a tactile (i.e., touched) comparison stimulus with a visual sample stimulus.[50] Further comparative work on species differences in cross-modal generalization is required before its origins and possible contribution to equivalence classes can be fully evaluated. Work on perceiving, to be discussed later in the book, explores further the possible contribution of polysensory integration to equivalence classes and other complex environment-behavior relations.

RESPONSE CLASSES

In our treatment of classes of environment-behavior relations, we have focused on stimulus classes. Through the formation of discriminative stimulus classes, a range of *physically* similar stimuli come to guide responding. Through the formation of equivalence classes arising from contextual discriminations, a range of *functionally* similar stimuli may also guide responding. Since most discriminations qualify as contextual discriminations, the most common result of selection is that behavior is guided by both physically and functionally similar stimuli. In short, most stimuli come to be components of both discriminative stimulus and equivalence classes.

The discussion of stimulus classes should have made it clear that the same selection history that produces stimulus classes often produces response classes as well. (A response class, you will recall, is a range of responses guided by a single stimulus.) By definition, when an equivalence class is formed, any stimulus within that class may evoke all of the responses that have been separately conditioned to the individual members of the class. For example, in the study using Greek letters, a single contextual stimulus, e.g., ϕ, guided not only the children's response to the comparison stimulus for which selection took place, e.g., λ, but also their response to the corresponding comparison stimulus, e.g., Λ, as well as the corresponding verbal response "lambda." (Refer again to **Figure 5.10**.) The cumulative effect of selection is not simply that a single stimulus guides a single response, but more typically that a *class* of stimuli guides a *class* of responses.[51]

Although response classes do not emerge independently of stimulus classes, we consider response classes separately to simplify the presentation. In this last section of the chapter, we consider the origins of *response* classes in the selecting effects of both the ancestral and individual environments. We make use of experimental work on biobehavioral processes, supplemented by interpretations based on adaptive networks.

Origins of Response Classes

Some response classes in humans owe their existence to natural selection. For the cumulative effect of natural selection to produce a response class, the selecting influences must be relatively constant over long periods of time. One of the most compelling examples of a response class of this origin is movement through the environment, or locomotion. All of the various forms of human locomotion—crawling, walking, running, and even swimming—depend on much the same parts of the motor system[52] and develop their basic topographies largely independently of specific experience. The general conditions of life required for survival are adequate for the emergence of a class of locomotor responses. A stimulus that causes a young child to crawl toward an object will later evoke walking toward that same object without the need for the separate reinforcement of walking. Nonhuman animals display a similar class of locomotor responses: A rat that has learned to run a complex maze to find food will swim the same maze correctly when it is later filled with water.[53]

Selection by reinforcement and response classes.

By far the most common origin of response classes is the selecting effect of the individual environment. The specific circumstances of the learner's selection history largely determine which responses "go together." The particular responses that make up the classes vary from one culture, situation, and person to the next. Such changing circumstances require the more rapid action of selection by reinforcement.

As a normal outcome of their functioning, the biobehavioral processes involved in selection by reinforcement automatically bring a range of responses under the control of the environment. Any response topography that satisfies the prevailing contingencies of reinforcement becomes a member of the response class. On the neural level, when a behavioral discrepancy occurs, the diffusely projecting reinforcement system is activated and all connections between active neurons are modified. Since there are generally a number of possible paths between the relevant input and output units, and since the active pathways mediating the selected input-output relation are likely to vary over time, the selected pathways include a number of alternative paths between the input and output units. Within the network—and that portion of the nervous system the network is intended to simulate—an input unit evokes activity in a *class* of pathways between the input and output units. At the end of selection, the discriminative stimulus that activates the input units does not so much elicit the response as permit the response to be mediated by one or more of the selected pathways in the network. The discriminative stimulus does not elicit the response; it permits the response to be emitted by the organism.[54]

The class of selected pathways resulting from a diffuse reinforcement system allows a network to mediate input-output relations with great reliability. If some of the pathways in the class are not activated by the input, then others are capable of mediating the relation. The selection of a class of pathways also allows the functioning of a network to be relatively resistant to disease or aging processes that cause the loss of some connections. When connections along one pathway are lost, others are available to mediate the input-output relation. The behavior of humans and other animals demonstrates this relative insensitivity to damage. Damage within a region of the network typically produces a general lessening of the functions served by that region; the loss becomes substantial only with extensive damage. Damage to pathways that communicate between regions usually produces more severe losses, unless there are alternative pathways whose connections can be modified by later selections.[55] Computer simulations using adaptive networks display these properties also. In a highly trained network, almost half the connections may be lost before it suffers a substantial decline in its ability to mediate input-output relations reliably. Moreover, if the losses occur slowly with the opportunity for relearning between losses, then performance shows even less deterioration.[56] Since humans lose brain cells almost from birth, we should be thankful to natural selection for this property of nervous systems and the adaptive networks that simulate them.

STUDY AIDS

Technical Terms

stimulus class

response class

verbal interpretation

organismic interpretation

formal interpretation

theoretically coherent

theoretically incoherent

discriminative stimulus class

functional class

contingency-shaped behavior

rule-governed behavior

fuzzy boundary

path-dependent

prototype

fading

equivalence class

contextual discrimination

matching-to-sample procedure

sample stimulus

comparison stimulus

identity matching

arbitrary (symbolic) matching

derived relations

reflexive relation

generalized identity matching

symmetric relation

transitive relation

cross-modal generalization

Text Questions

1. What are meant by the technical terms *stimulus class* and *response class*? Give laboratory and everyday examples of each.

2. Indicate the similarities and differences between experimental analysis and scientific interpretation. How does interpretation differ from mere speculation? Describe and give an example of each of the following forms of interpretation—verbal, organismic, and formal. What are the strengths and weaknesses of each?

3. The environment-behavior relations defining discriminative stimulus classes bear some similarities to those phenomena grouped together by the nontechnical term "concept." In what ways are they similar; in what ways are they different? Indicate how discriminative stimulus classes are acquired, and their major characteristics, as illustrated by formal interpretations using adaptive neural networks. Are only humans capable of demonstrating discriminative stimulus classes? Explain.

4. Indicate the selection history that produces functional stimulus classes. How do such classes differ from discriminative stimulus classes?

5. Describe, using technical terms, the selection history that produces equivalence classes. Indicate the basic relations that appear to be necessary for the emergence of the derived relations defining equivalence classes. Be able to illustrate with an example each of the basic relations and their role in the interpretation of equivalence relations.

6. What factors have been identified that may contribute to the emergence of equivalence classes and to their appearance thus far only in humans?

Discussion Questions

7. What basic biobehavioral processes contribute to fading? [Hint: How might the processes that lead to blocking also affect fading?]

8. Why may it be said that the neural mechanisms of reinforcement select *classes* of pathways?

What effect does this mechanism have on the ability of the brain to function with unreliable components (neurons) and in some instances of brain damage?

ENDNOTES

1. cf. Goldiamond, 1962.
2. Skinner, 1957; Donahoe & Palmer, 1989; Palmer & Donahoe, 1993.
3. Donahoe & Palmer, 1989; Skinner, 1957.
4. Epstein, 1984.
5. Computer simulations are used rather than "closed-form" mathematical formulations because the behavior to be interpreted is often too complex to permit such formulations. This situation is by no means unique to the interpretation of behavior. In the physical sciences, complex situations such as many-body problems in astronomy or turbulent flow of liquids defy precise mathematical analysis even though all of the relevant physical principles are known.
6. Not all computer simulations of human behavior qualify as interpretations as the term is used here. For example, a computer simulation could implement principles that are based on inferred processes rather than independent experimental analyses. The considerations that should inform computer simulations is a matter of current controversy; e.g., Donahoe & Palmer, 1989; Marr, 1992; McClelland & Rumelhart, 1986; Smolensky, 1986.
7. e.g., Dawkins, 1986; Maynard-Smith, 1982.
8. This problem may be addressed by what is called *genetic programming*. In genetic programming, the structure of an adaptive network is generated by principles that reflect natural selection. The connections between elements of the network can then be modifed by principles that reflect selection by reinforcement. In such simulations, both genetic and learning principles inform the simulation just as the processes described by these principles affect living organisms; cf. Ackley & Litman, 1991; Hinton & Nowlan, 1986.
9. For a review of concept formation that makes a similar point, see Farah & Kosslyn, 1982, p. 161; Medin & Smith, 1984. See also Harzem, 1986.
10. For a related a distinction arising from a different theoretical perspective, see Mervis & Mervis, 1988; Rosch, Mervis, Gray, Johnson, & Boyes-Braem, 1976.
11. Functional classes are closely related to James Gibson's concept of *affordance*, Gibson, 1979. The affordance of a stimulus refers to the behavior that the

stimulus is capable of evoking. For example, chairs differ in their physical characteristics but they share in common the behavior that all may be sat upon. All chairs *afford* sitting.

12. See Skinner, 1966a for the distinction between contingency-shaped and rule-governed behavior.

13. Brooks, 1978.

14. Complex stimuli and responses of the sort involved in this study present complications not encountered when stimuli such as simple lights and tones or responses such as leverpressing are used. Issues related to differences in the interpretation of the effects of such stimuli are discussed in the treatment of verbal behavior in Chapter 11. The present discussion disregards such differences.

15. The principles used in this study form what is called a *phrase-structure grammar*. Grammars of this type have been used by linguists to characterize language, and consist of sets of rules which state how elements, in this case letters, may be combined to form sequences. The particular phrase-structure rules are not of concern here.

16. Similar results have been obtained with children as well as adults, e.g., Kossan, 1981.

17. Herrnstein & Loveland, 1964. For other examples, see Bhatt, Wasserman, Reynolds, & Knauss, 1988; Herrnstein, 1984; Herrnstein, Loveland, & Cable, 1976; Holmes, 1979; Malott & Siddall, 1972; Roberts & Mazmanian, 1988.

18. Donahoe & Palmer, 1989; Donahoe, Burgos, & Palmer, 1993.

19. McClelland & Rumelhart, 1985, 1986; cf. Knapp & Anderson, 1984. This simulation used a technique for changing the connection weights called the *delta rule*. The delta rule is closely related to discrepancy theories of reinforcement, e.g., Sutton & Barto, 1981. With the delta rule, the discrepancy is a function of the difference between the activation levels of *each* of the output units and the target activation levels for those units. With the unified reinforcement principle, the discrepancy is a function of the activation level of only those output units activated by the reinforcer; Donahoe, Burgos, & Palmer, 1993. However, since the reinforcing stimulus only activates its output units when the target activation levels occur on the output units corresponding to the operant, the two methods for changing connection weights can be closely related. The discussion that follows does not depend on which method is used for changing the connection weights within the adaptive network.

20. Rosch & Mervis, 1975.

21. cf. Posner & Keele, 1968.

22. Snow, 1972; see also Reeve, Reeve, Brown, Brown, & Poulson, 1992.

23. Fading was introduced in the technical literature as a means of facilitating discrimination formation by Skinner, 1938. Subsequently, fading was investigated by a number of investigators in connection with "errorless" learning; e.g., Terrace, 1966; Rilling, 1977. Perhaps the most extensive work using fading to facilitate the acquisition of difficult discriminations has occurred with handicapped humans; e.g., Sidman & Stoddard, 1967; Stoddard & Sidman, 1967. There are differences in terminology, with fading sometimes called *stimulus shaping* or, more recently, *stimulus control shaping*; e.g., McIlvane & Dube, 1992. Different terms are used because changes in the procedure have included gradual alterations in aspects of training other than the stimuli to be discriminated, e.g., changes in the interval between sample and comparison stimuli in the matching-to-sample procedure.

24. Sidman & Stoddard, 1967.

25. Jacobs, 1988. See also Selfridge, Sutton, & Barto, 1985.

26. Vaughn, 1988.

27. Work on the formation of functional stimulus classes is related to earlier work on the development of *learning sets*; Harlow, 1959.

28. For several examples of this and related phenomena, see Rescorla, 1991.

29. Urcuioli, 1991.

30. Saunders, Wachter, & Spradlin, 1988.

31. Contextual discriminations are also known as *conditional discriminations*; Lashley, 1938. The appropriate response to the comparison stimulus is conditional upon the value of the sample stimulus. Also, the sample stimulus is sometimes said to exert *instructional control* over the response to the comparison stimuli; Cumming & Berryman, 1965. The sample stimulus *instructs* the learner which comparison stimulus to respond to.

32. Sidman & Tailby, 1982.

33. The symbolization A-B task, in which both upper case letters represent sets of *stimuli* in a matching-to-sample procedure, should not be confused with a similar and more common symbolization used in paired-associate verbal-learning procedures. In paired-associate learning, A refers to the set of stimuli in the pairs and B refers to the set of corresponding *responses*. In matching-to-sample procedures, the response of interest is controlled by the stimuli symbolized by the second

upper-case letter but is not indicated in the symbolization.

34. e.g., Dube, McIlvane, Mackay, & Stoddard, 1987; Spradlin & Saunders, 1984. See Lipkens, Kop, & Matthijs, 1988, for a summary of this work.

35. Saunders, Wachter, & Spradlin, 1988.

36. Sidman, 1986.

37. Sidman & Cresson, 1973.

38. Stromer, 1986.

39. Other animals without prior experience with line drawings of objects may have such "piecemeal" and "fragmentary" perceptions; e.g. Cerella, 1980; Watanabe, 1988.

40. e.g., Cohen, Looney, Brady, & Aucella, 1976; Kohlenberg, Hayes, & Hayes, 1991; Santi, 1978; Sidman, 1980; Sidman, Rauzin, Lazar, Cunningham, Tailby, & Carrigan, 1982.

41. e.g., Wright, 1989.

42. e.g., D'Amato, Salmon, Loukas, & Tomie, 1985.

43. e.g., Sidman, Rauzin, Lazar, Cunningham, Tailby, & Carrigan, 1982; cf. McIntire, Cleary, & Thompson, 1987 in which the relations were directly trained. Although most studies of equivalence classes have employed visual stimuli, equivalence classes have been found using auditory stimuli as well, e.g., Dube, Green, & Serna, in press; Fields, Adams, Verhave, & Newman, 1990. For a discussion of the relation of functional stimulus classes and equivalence classes, see Sidman, Wynne, Macguire, & Barnes, 1989. For a discussion of the failure to find equivalence classes in nonhumans, see Hayes, 1989. For discussions of methodological issues, see Fields & Verhave, 1987; O'Mara, 1991.

44. Jenkins, 1965; Osgood, 1953; e.g., Horton & Kjeldegaard, 1961.

45. e.g., Devaney, Hayes, & Nelson, 1986; Spradlin, Cotter, & Baxley, 1973.

46. Sidman, Cresson, & Willson-Morris, 1974.

47. See Geschwind, 1965.

48. Cross-modal formation of equivalence classes has been reported using the visual and tactile modalities, e.g., Feniello, 1988.

49. Kuhl & Meltzkoff, 1982. It is important not to overinterpret this finding to mean that the infants were doing anything as complex as "lip-reading." For a review of cross-modal relations in infants, see Rose & Ruff, 1987; and Spelke, 1976.

50. Davenport, Rogers, & Russell, 1973; Jarvis & Ettinger, 1977; Mishkin, 1979.

51. Skinner, 1935.

52. Kolb & Whishaw, 1985.

53. MacFarlane, 1930.

54. On the level of the nervous system, this is the counterpart of Skinner's distinction between elicited responses (respondents) and emitted responses (operants); Skinner, 1937.

55. Cowley, Green, & Braunling-McMorrow, (in press); Green, 1991.

56. Anderson, 1984.

CHAPTER 6

ATTENDING

Because human behavior is the cumulative product of an extensive selection history, it cannot be understood solely by appeals to the environment of the moment. The environment of the moment directly guides behavior, but the behavior of the moment is the result of the present environment acting on an organism that has been changed by an ever-richer history of selection. The same environment evokes different responses from the same person at different moments, and different responses from different persons at the same moment. The outcome of selection is diversity, not sameness.

INTRODUCTION

When—in the same environment—we observe differences in behavior among persons, we often use the everyday term "attention" in discussing those differences. For instance, we might describe a student who is taking notes during a lecture as "paying attention" to the lecturer, and her neighbor who is not taking notes as not "paying attention." However, attention and other terms from the everyday vocabulary are prone to theoretical incoherence. That is, nontechnical terms usually refer to a diverse and varying assortment of biobehavioral processes. Different histories of selection lead one student to take notes and another student not to take notes, even though both are in the same classroom. Our purpose in this chapter is to identify some of the differences in selection history that produce the behavioral differences conventionally grouped under the heading of attention. However, we interpret those differences without appealing to a separate process of "attention."

We avoid using attention as a technical term for several reasons. First, because "attention" is theoretically incoherent, using the same term to discuss phenomena of different origins misleads us into treating superficially similar phenomena as if they were identical. Behavior *does* differ among individuals in the same environment, but it is unlikely that all or even most differences are the result of a common set of biobehavioral processes acting in the same manner. There can be no one account of "attention" because there is not one phenomenon of attention. Persons of diverse theoretical persuasions agree that attention should not be thought of as a single entity, but as a field of study.[1]

Second, the noun "attention" lends a unitary and thing-like quality to the diverse expressions of a number of different biobehavioral processes. Treating "attention" as a thing tempts us to use it as an explanation of behavior rather than—at best—a heading under which a set of superficially similar phenomena may be grouped. When "attention" is used to describe the differing behavior of the two students, for example, it is easy to slip into statements such as "The first student took notes *because* she was attending, but the second student did not *because* he wasn't attending." To use attention in this way is to fall prey to the **nominal fallacy**; i.e., to treat the name of a phenomenon as if it were an explanation. Further, the nominal fallacy encourages circular reasoning. To wit— Question: Why did the first student take notes? Answer: Because she was attending. Question: How do you know that the student was attending? Answer: Because she was taking notes. When misused in this way, "attention" deludes us into believing we have explained behavior when we have merely classified it.

Although there is no technical justification for the term attention, the rejection of the term as scientifically useful in no way denies the importance of the phenomena conventionally grouped under that heading. Questions about why different people behave differently on the same occasion are fascinating, and the answers are important for the interpretation of complex human behavior. On this point, investigators of different theoretical persuasions can agree.[2] Because of the importance of interpreting individual differences in behavior, we treat many of them in one chapter even though the differences are expressions of a diverse set of processes. However, we use the verb, attending, rather than the noun, attention, to emphasize that these differences arise from diverse *processes*, not a unitary *thing*. By emphasizing process, we hope to minimize the temptations of the nominal fallacy. The evolutionary biologist Ernst Mayr commented on the progress made in biology when nouns were replaced by verbs, and the study of behavior would benefit from the same practice.[3]

An Approach to Attending

A common characteristic of the diverse phenomena that exemplify attending is the failure of environmental stimuli to guide behavior even when they are apparently adequate to do so. Viewed in this way, attending is part of the more general field of the environmental guidance of behavior, a topic we have examined in some detail. The environment comes to guide behavior through the selecting effects of the ancestral environment (natural selection) and the individual environment (selection by reinforcement). According to a selectionist account, behavior can fail to occur in an environment for one of several reasons: Selection has never brought behavior under the control of stimuli in that environment, the discriminative stimuli are present but are not sensed by the organism, or the biobehavioral processes evoked by other stimuli interfere with the control of behavior by the discriminative stimuli.

Failure to sense the stimulus.   Four major and interrelated sets of biobehavioral processes involved in attending are identified here. Each is explored in later sections. First, although the environment may contain all of the required stimuli and selection has occurred with those stimuli, the learner does not sense them.[4] Perhaps the learner does not sense *all* of the controlling stimuli, or does not sense them in the required temporal order. Most behavior, especially complex behavior, is guided by multiple stimuli. If some of these stimuli are missing, or if they appear in an order different from that in which selection took place, the "appropriate" (i.e., selected) response may not occur.

Difficulties in environmental guidance caused by the absence of some of the required stimuli are illustrated in the following diary entries by college students who kept records of their own lapses of "attention:"[5] (a) "I had decided to cut down on my sugar consumption and wanted to have my cornflakes without it. However, I sprinkled sugar on my cereal just as I had always done." (b) "I meant to take off only my shoes but took off my socks as well." What these examples have in common is the absence of *some* of the discriminative stimuli when the response failed to occur. Sugar was mistakenly sprinkled on the cornflakes because the stimuli guiding the "sprinkling" response were present (e.g., the sight of the cornflakes and the sugarbowl), but the stimuli that had guided the decision to go without sugar were no longer present (e.g., the sight, a few moments earlier, of the student's weight on the bathroom scale). Similarly, the socks were removed because the stimuli that guided their removal were present (e.g., the stimuli accompanying removing one's shoes while sitting on the side of the bed), but those that had guided the earlier decision to remove only the shoes were not (e.g., painful stimuli from a pebble in the shoe).

Discrimination history.   A second source of failures in environmental guidance is the specific history of selection with respect to the stimulus. Consider an example from the laboratory. If a stimulus (e.g., a tone) is present when an environment-behavior relation is selected and then a second stimulus (e.g., a light) is presented with the first stimulus while the response continues to produce the reinforcer, the second stimulus does not acquire the ability to evoke the response. The second stimulus has been sensed, the critical response has occurred in its presence, and a known reinforcer has followed the response, but the supposed discriminative stimulus (the light) does not guide the response. In the language of "attention," the learner has failed to attend to the second stimulus. You will recognize this as an instance of blocking.[6] Some attentional phenomena are the outcome of the same processes that produce blocking.

Context.   A third—and frequent—source of attentional phenomena is a change from the context in which the environment-behavior relation was originally selected to the context in which the discriminative stimulus now appears. As noted before, almost all discriminations are contextual discriminations. Thus, a stimulus that has been sensed and discriminated may fail to guide behavior when it occurs outside the context in which the discrimination was acquired. Many everyday examples of failures to attend are probably of this origin. Have you ever walked past someone at a shopping mall whom you had previously met only at work, and—for a moment, at least—not been able to place him? Have you ever been introduced to someone at a party, and then failed to recognize the same person the very next day on seeing her in another setting? Most of us have had experiences of this sort, and they illustrate the important role of the context in which the discriminative stimulus appears.

Concurrent stimuli.   A fourth source of attentional phenomena is the simultaneous occurrence of discriminative stimuli guiding biobehavioral processes that interfere or compete with one another. Although each of the stimuli is sensed and each is an effective discriminative stimulus in that environmental context, the responses normally

evoked by those stimuli do not occur. In such cases, several outcomes are possible—the responses occur successively, some mixture of the two responses occurs, or one response occurs and not the other. The student diaries also provide illustrations of these outcomes: "I unwrapped a candy, put the paper in my mouth and threw the candy into the wastepaper basket."[7] Here, the simultaneous presence of two stimuli—the wrapper and the candy—guided two incompatible responses by the same hand—throwing away the wrapper and placing the candy into the mouth. Each response occurred, but guided by an inappropriate stimulus. Thus, the same example also illustrates a mixture of two environment-behavior relations. Lest it be thought that only students are afflicted by such lapses, the same study describes a professor whose work had been frequently interrupted by visits from colleagues and students: "During a morning in which there had been several knocks on my office door, the phone rang. I picked up the receiver and bellowed 'Come in' at it."

Interfering processes are dramatically illustrated by a neuropsychological disorder known as Tourette's syndrome.[8] This disorder reveals the multitude of environment-behavior relations that can be evoked by stimuli in the natural environment. Tourette's syndrome—named for its first describer, Georges Gilles de la Tourette—is a hereditary disorder affecting subcortical motor systems of the brain. This disorder results from a deficit in the brain's normal ability to inhibit simultaneously activated responses. The deficit is described by a neurologist in the following report of events he observed on a busy city street.

> My eye was caught by a grey-haired woman in her sixties, who was apparently the centre of a most amazing disturbance . . . As I drew closer, I saw what was happening. She was imitating the passers-by—if 'imitation' is not too pallid, too passive, a word. In the course of a short city-block, this frantic old woman frenetically caricatured the features of forty or fifty passers-by, in a quick-fire sequence of kaleidoscopic imitations, each lasting a second or two . . . And there were ludicrous imitations of the

second and third order; for the people in the street. . . took on these expressions in reaction to her; and these expressions, in turn, were re-flected, re-directed, re-distorted, by the Touretter, causing a still greater degree of outrage and shock . . . . Suddenly, desperately, the old woman turned aside, into an alley-way which led off the main street. And there, . . . she expelled, tremendously accelerated and abbreviated, all the gestures, the postures, the expressions, the demeanours, the entire behavioural repertoires, of the past forty or fifty people she had passed . . . . And if the taking in had lasted two minutes, the throwing-out was a single exhalation—fifty people in ten seconds, a fifth of a second or less for the time-foreshortened repertoire of each person.[9]

For this unfortunate woman, the responses by which we all mirror the expressions of others—smiling when they laugh, frowning when they cry—were expressed in exaggerated form as rapidly as their incompatibility permitted.

The final resolution of the dilemma posed by the concurrent presence of multiple discriminative stimuli is usually the emission of only one of the possible responses. This can be illustrated in the laboratory with the Stroop task.[10] In the Stroop task, subjects are asked to speak the names of various colors as quickly as possible, but the colors are presented in the form of letters that spell the names of other colors; e.g., the word BLUE, printed in yellow ink. Under these conditions, subjects often say "blue" rather than "yellow." That is, in spite of the contextual stimuli provided by the instructions, the letters that spell the word BLUE guide the verbal response "blue" more strongly than the yellow ink guides the verbal response "yellow."

In the sections that follow, each of these four sources of attentional phenomena is considered further. The interpretations are based primarily on findings obtained with laboratory methods, but use a range of approaches—developmental, comparative, and neuropsychological—and a range of interpretive strategies—verbal, organismic, and the formal interpretations provided by adaptive neural networks.

SENSING AND ATTENDING

Regardless of the selection history of the individual, a stimulus must be sensed if it is to guide behavior.[11] But, since two persons in the same environment cannot simultaneously occupy the same point in space, no two people can ever sense the environment identically at the same instant. The light energy reflected from a surface differently stimulates the visual receptors of two persons—or even the two eyes of the same person—because the visual receptors are located at different points in space. Thus, each eye has a slightly different view of the world from that of every other eye, whether the eyes are located in the same or different heads. Similarly, the sound energy emitted by an object differently stimulates the auditory receptors of two persons—and the two ears of the same person—because the auditory receptors also occupy different points in space. When one person sees or hears what another does not, the two persons may respond differently in what, to an observer, appears to be the same environment. The observer, who is sensing still a third view of the "same" environment, may describe one person as attending and the other as not.

It would be a mistake, however, to regard the individual as simply a passive recipient of whatever physical energies happen to fall on his receptors. Individuals, through their own behavior, profoundly influence the environmental events they sense. Responses that affect the sensing of environmental events are the joint products of selection by the ancestral and individual environments. We have already come across one product of ancestral selection that affects the sensing of stimuli, the orienting response. When a dog pricks up its ears at the sound of a tone, the response enhances hearing the tone. Similar environment-behavior relations are found in human infants. For example, in the first few weeks of life, a visual stimulus presented to one side of an infant elicits rapid and increasingly coordinated movements of the head and eyes that cause the stimulus energy to fall on the center of the retina, where vision is most acute.[12] Likewise, a sound presented to one side of the infant elicits turning the head toward the side of the more intensely stimulated ear. The turning response stops when the ears are equally stimulated by the sound energy. When the sound energy falls equally on the receptors of the two ears, the infant is directly facing the source of the sound and, therefore, is likely to see the source of the sound as well.[13] Even in infancy, behavior exerts an important influence on the sensing of stimuli.

Observing Responses

The processes by which behavior affects what we sense begin with the maturation of reflexive environment-behavior relations, such as those just described. However, these relations are soon supplemented by acquired relations that reflect individual experience. Acquired environment-behavior relations whose primary function is to affect the sensing of stimuli are called **observing responses**.[14]

Consider an everyday example of an observing response. Suppose you wanted to speak with someone who lives in your house. For a conversation to take place, the person must be within easy speaking distance and preferably within sight. If you urgently wanted to speak with her, you would not wait until she happened to walk by. Instead, you might call out her name and, when you heard a reply, move toward its source. The conversation could then take place. In this example, calling out the person's name and moving to the source of the reply are observing responses. Their function is to make it more likely that a stimulus will occur—here, the sight of a friend—in whose presence a response—here, talking—will be reinforced. In this case, the reinforcer might consist of an answer to a question or a sympathetic hearing of a personal problem.

Observing responses can be demonstrated under the more controlled circumstances of the laboratory, with both animals and humans. In a study using pigeons as subjects, a disk located on one wall of the test chamber appeared in two alternating colors—red when pecking the disk produced food and green when pecking had no effect. However, the red or green color appeared *only if the bird depressed a pedal on the floor near the disk.*[15] Otherwise, the disk remained white even though periods during which pecking produced food still alternated with those in which pecking had no effect. In this study, depressing the pedal served as an observing response since it produced the discriminative stimuli. Note that pedal-pressing itself was never followed immediately by food but, rather, by a discriminative stimulus. As shown in **Figure 6.1**, the pigeon acquired the observing response, and pedal-pressing occurred more frequently when it produced the red disk than the green disk.

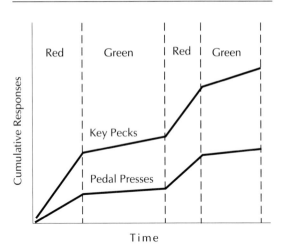

FIGURE 6.1   *Observing responses*
Maintenance of an observing response (pedal-pressing) and another operant (disk-pecking) in the pigeon. The disk was transilluminated with white light and pecking the disk produced food during some intervals and had no effect during others. When the pigeon pressed a pedal during the intervals in which pecking produced food, the disk was briefly transilluminated with red light. Pressing the pedal during intervals in which pecking was ineffective caused the disk to be briefly transilluminated with green light. Thus pedal-pressing was immediately followed by discriminative stimuli but not food.
Source: Hypothetical cumulative records based on findings from Wyckoff, 1962.

How is the observing response of pressing the pedal acquired and maintained? According to the analysis of selection by reinforcement, a stimulus guides a response if the response is followed by a reinforcer. Since food did not immediately follow pedal-pressing, we must look to a stimulus other than food for the reinforcer. Although food did not follow pedal-pressing when the disk was white, one of two stimuli *did* immediately occur—a change in the disk's color to either red or green. Could the presentation of either of these colors function as a reinforcer? The answer is clearly "yes." Since red was paired with food, the red disk would acquire the capacity to function as an acquired, or conditioned, reinforcer. In contrast, since the green disk was never paired with food, it should not become an acquired reinforcer and, therefore, should not maintain the observing response of pedal-pressing.

Later research has confirmed this interpretation of the origin of observing responses. When an observing response produces a stimulus that has been paired with a reinforcer, it is acquired and maintained. When the observing response produces only the stimulus that has not been paired with the reinforcer, the observing response is not acquired. This result has been obtained with both animals[16] and humans.[17]

It is important to note that the interpretation of observing responses does not require any new principles. Observing responses are not a new *type* of response. They are responses having a particular *function*—that of producing discriminative stimuli that serve as acquired reinforcers for the observing response. Observing responses are one of the many means by which past selection produces ever more complex environment-behavior relations. In the case of observing responses, the result of earlier selection is an organism whose own behavior partially determines the environment that will guide its later behavior.

The cumulative product of selection is not a passive organism that is a "slave" to its present environment, but an active organism whose behavior increasingly affects its future environments.

STIMULUS DISCRIMINATION AND ATTENDING

Although some instances in which people behave differently in the same environment are due to differences in what they sense, many differences cannot be interpreted in this way. Many lapses of "attention" are due to straightforward differences in the history of discrimination training. For example, at the sound of a fire bell, the volunteer fireman rushes to the firehouse while his neighbor continues behaving much as before. Both people heard the bell, but their different selection histories caused the bell to guide different responses. To an observer who is ignorant of the different histories, the fireman "attended" to the bell but his neighbor did not.

Selective Attending

Different selection histories also have more subtle effects on attending than those produced by simple discrimination training. For example, in complex decision making, or judgment, behavior is guided by the combined effects of many stimuli, and there may be differences among decision makers in the stimuli to which they "attend." The phenomenon of blocking provides a means by which some of these differences can be interpreted. Blocking, you will recall, occurs when a stimulus fails to guide a reinforced response because the stimulus is accompanied by another stimulus in whose presence the reinforcer has already occurred. To the extent that the reinforcer is already "predicted" (or, more technically, to the extent that conditioned reinforcer-elicited responses are already evoked by the other stimulus), the ability of the first stimulus to guide behavior is reduced, or blocked.

Blocking ordinarily benefits the efficient selection of environment-behavior relations in the sense that it prevents new relations from being formed when the learner's behavior is already "appropriately" guided by other stimuli. However, in complex discriminations in which multiple stimuli are reliably correlated with reinforced responses, the processes that produce blocking can lead to the selection of less than optimal environment-behavior relations. The effect of these processes can lead us to devote more "attention" to some stimuli than is warranted by their true correlation with the reinforced response. Consider the following hypothetical example: The enrollment in a class studying Shakespeare's tragic plays is almost entirely composed of students majoring in English; however, a few science majors are taking the course to satisfy a university humanities requirement. Suppose you see that one of the students in the course takes extremely orderly notes, neatly arranged in strict outline form. Is this student an English major or one of the few science majors? When asked this question, many people guess that the student is a science major, weighing heavily his orderliness and giving insufficient weight to the overwhelming odds that he is an English major. Our preconceptions (prejudices?) about the note-taking habits of science and English majors override the information about the much greater likelihood that this student is an English major.

Base-rate neglect.   Experimental findings indicate that "paying too little attention" to the overall likelihood of an event is a common failing of human judgment. We tend to overvalue a stimulus when we believe it is characteristic of an infrequent event.[18] This bias in judgment is called **base-rate neglect**, since the decision maker has not taken into account the overall likelihood—the base rate—of the event. How can the processes involved in blocking allow base-rate neglect to be interpreted?

To simulate the contribution of blocking to base-rate neglect, a study was conducted in which college students were given an artificial medical diagnostic task.[19] The multiple discriminated stimuli were various symptoms—fever, stomach ache, and the like—and the responses were diagnoses of either of two diseases—disease A or B. In the cases that the students were given, disease A occurred three times as often as disease B. In other words, of every 100 cases, 75 had disease A and 25 had disease B. Thus, the base rates for disease A and B were .75 and .25, respectively. One of the symp-

toms—say, fever—was present in 40% of the cases of the more common disease (disease A) and in 60% of the cases of the rare disease (disease B). Three other symptoms were equally or more likely to be present in the more common disease. The base rates and the percentages of the symptom for the two diseases were such that, given the fever symptom, the probability of the rare disease was only .15 ($.25 \times .60 = .15$). However, when the fever symptom was present, the subjects diagnosed the rare disease about 25% of the time. (See **Figure 6.2.**) This greatly overvalues the fever symptom in diagnosing the rare disease, and illustrates base-rate neglect.

How is base-rate neglect to be interpreted by means of the processes involved in blocking? When the more frequent disease was diagnosed correctly, the fever symptom was often accompanied by other symptoms. Moreover, the other symptoms also occurred more often by themselves when the diagnosis of disease A was correct (i.e, reinforced). Because the fever symptom was frequently accompanied by other symptoms when disease A was the correct diagnosis, control of the disease-A diagnosis by the fever symptom would be blocked. Thus, relative to disease A, the stimulus of the fever symptom would more strongly control the rare disease-B diagnosis than the more common disease-A diagnosis.

This interpretation of base-rate neglect is consistent with the results of the diagnostic-judgment study, and may be simulated using an adaptive network. In the computer simulation, four input units corresponded to the four symptoms, two output units to the two diagnoses, and the strengths of connections between the input and output units to the degree to which each symptom guided each diagnosis. Whenever an input pattern of symptoms generated a diagnosis, the connection weights were changed in accordance with a discrepancy-based reinforcement principle. After the adaptive network had been trained with the same cases presented to the college students, the performance of the network corresponded closely to that of the students. Like the students, the network overval-

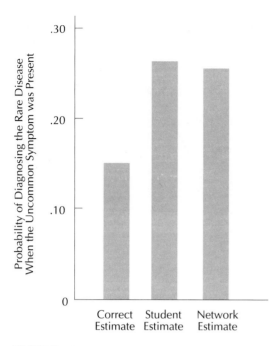

FIGURE 6.2 *Base-rate neglect illustrated by the probability of diagnosing the rarer of two diseases when an uncommon symptom was present*
The actual percentage of cases of the rare disease when the symptom was present was 15%. However, the uncommon symptom influenced the diagnosis of the rarer disease more strongly. When the symptom was present, about 25% of the cases were diagnosed as having the rarer disease. A computer simulation of the diagnostic responses, which implemented a reinforcement principle, also revealed the tendency for the diagnosis to be overly influenced by the symptom.
Source: Gluck, M. A. & Bower, G. H. (1988). From conditioning to category learning: An adaptive network model. *Journal of Experimental Psychology: General, 117*, 227–247. Copyright © 1988 by the American Psychological Association. Reprinted by permission.

ued the fever symptom in diagnosing the rare disease.[20] (See **Figure 6.2**.)

"Selective attention" is nontechnically used to describe behavior that is guided by only some of the stimuli present when a response is reinforced. Through earlier discrimination training and the action of the biobehavioral processes involved in blocking, the behavior of an experienced organism may be strongly guided by some stimuli and only weakly by others. However, since "selective attention" is a phrase from the everyday vocabulary, and likely to be theoretically incoherent, we may anticipate that there are other means by which organisms respond selectively. Before indicating some of these other means, let us first see how the same processes—when realized in a different way— may enhance rather than restrict the range of discriminative stimuli.

Heightened Attending

Through their effect on contextual stimuli, the biobehavioral processes involved in reinforcement and stimulus discrimination may enhance rather than restrict the range of stimuli that guide behavior. As noted before, almost all discriminations are specific to some context; i.e., almost all discriminations are contextual discriminations. Here, we consider how contextual stimuli affect discriminations later acquired in the same context. Under certain conditions, acquiring a discrimination in one context facilitates the formation of new discriminations in that context. That is, earlier discrimination training may produce "heightened attention" to new stimuli in the same context.[21]

When acquiring any new environment-behavior relation, a major task for the learner is to determine which aspects of the situation are relevant to effective performance and which are not. Consider a driver whose car refuses to start even though it has gas (the fuel gauge reads full) and the battery is charged (the starter turns over the engine). When mechanically inexperienced drivers raise the hood to view the jumble of parts that make up a modern engine, they are uncertain where to look to isolate the problem. If the engine is not getting fuel, then which parts might be malfunctioning? If the spark plugs are not getting electricity, then which parts might be at fault? The unskilled person is as likely to examine the window-washer pump as the fuel pump or the electronic windshield-wiper controls as the ignition system. For the skilled mechanic, however, the irrelevant stimuli provided by windshield-washer pumps and controls do not guide behavior. Consequently, behavior is more likely to be guided by those stimuli that are relevant to locating and repairing the true problem. What are the processes responsible for heightened attention to the relevant stimuli, in comparison to the many irrelevant stimuli present in most situations?

Although several processes are involved in most everyday examples of "heightened attention," we focus here on one source—the effect of earlier discrimination training on the control exerted by contextual stimuli during later training in the same context. When earlier selection affects selection in a later task, a **transfer effect** of the first task on the second task is said to occur. Heightened attending is thus a type of transfer effect. As an experimental example, we return to the use of animal subjects since their prior selection history may be better controlled.

The experiment[22] was conducted in two phases. In the first phase a discrimination was acquired in a particular context; then in the second phase a new discrimination was acquired in that same context. If earlier discrimination training facilitates the guidance of behavior by a new discriminative stimulus *in the same context*, then "heightened attention" is demonstrated.

Pigeons in the experimental group were placed in a test chamber in which pecking a disk on the wall occasionally produced food when the disk was blue, but not when the disk was green. Thus, the birds received discrimination training with respect to the color of the disk. After the blue color had come to guide pecking, the birds were returned to the same test chamber, but now the stimulus on the disk was a vertical line on a white background. Pecking the vertical line produced food, and no other lines were presented during this phase. Thus, discrimination training did not occur during the second phase. When pecking the vertical line had been acquired, the precision with which the vertical line guided pecking was assessed by presenting lines of other orientations on the disk. As shown in **Figure 6.3**, for pigeons in the experimental group, pecking was rapid when the line was vertical but decreased as the orientation varied.

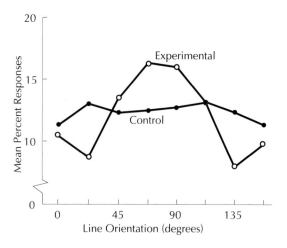

FIGURE 6.3 *General attentiveness produced by prior discrimination training in the same context*
Shown are the percentages of disk-pecking responses that occurred during a stimulus generalization test in which various line orientations were projected on the disk. Pecking a disk on which a 90° (i.e., vertical) line was projected had previously been reinforced with food for both groups. For pigeons in the experimental group, differential training between two wavelengths on the disk had been given prior to line-orientation training. For pigeons in the control group, nondifferential training with the same two wavelengths on the disk had been given prior to line-orientation training.
Source: Honig, W. K. (1969). Attenuational factors governing stimulus control. In R. Gilbert & N. S. Sutherland (Eds.), *Discrimination learning* (pp. 35–62). New York: Academic Press.

A control group of other pigeons was also trained to peck blue and green disks but was *not* given discrimination training on the wavelength dimension. Then they too were trained to peck the vertical line. When tested with various line orientations, the control pigeons pecked all of the line orientations equally. In the language of "attention," the experimental animals, which had received prior discrimination training, showed "heightened attention" to line orientation in comparison to the control animals that had not received discrimination training.[23]

To interpret this example of "heightened attention," it is crucial to recognize that, in addition to being exposed to the blue and green disks during discrimination training, the experimental subjects were also exposed to a large number of other stimuli at the same time. When responding was reinforced, the disk was not only blue, it was round, of a particular brightness, located at a particular place on the wall, and so forth. Each of these stimuli and many others from the experimental chamber were simultaneously present when pecking the blue disk was reinforced. Consequently, each of these stimuli was eligible to become a component of the compound stimulus guiding pecking. Every learner—whether pigeon or person—faces the same problem at the beginning of discrimination training: Which of the many stimuli being sensed are relevant to the guidance of the response? Discrimination training addresses this problem by initiating processes that restrict the guidance of behavior to those stimuli that are most highly correlated with the reinforcer.

In the pigeon experiment, restriction of control to the blue stimulus was accomplished as follows. Since the blue stimulus was always present when pecking was reinforced, the blue color increasingly guided behavior. However, when the disk was not blue and pecking was guided by stimuli from the experimental context—e.g., the shape of the disk—pecking was not reinforced. The cumulative effect of this process was that the color of the disk rapidly acquired the capacity to guide pecking and, as a result, the ability of the other stimuli to guide pecking was increasingly blocked. Since blue rapidly and increasingly came to evoke food-related responses, the behavioral discrepancy required to select other environment-behavior relations was eliminated, thereby blocking the inclusion of other stimuli as components in the selected environment-behavior relation.

For the control subjects, guidance of pecking by these other stimuli was not blocked since the subjects had not received prior *discrimination* training. Thus, stimuli from the context could continue to guide responding. Later, when pecking the vertical line produced food during the second phase of training, the contextual stimuli could continue to control responding and block acquisition of control by the vertical line. The lack of control by line orientation is indicated by the "flat" generalization gradient. (See **Figure 6.3**.) Because some of the controlling stimuli—those from the context—remained constant during the test, responding remained constant.[24]

The preceding interpretation indicates that the same biobehavioral processes that produce "selective attention" are capable, under other circumstances, of producing "heightened attention." Although "selective attention" diminishes the control acquired by new stimuli and "heightened attention" enhances their control, each may be understood as a different expression of the same biobehavioral processes.[25]

CONTEXTUAL DISCRIMINATIONS AND ATTENDING

Discriminations probably give rise to most of the environment-behavior relations to which the term "attention" is commonly applied. And, since most discriminations are contextual discriminations, most of the attentional language in everyday discussions of behavior may be traced to this source.

The context in which a discriminative stimulus appears comes about in a variety of ways. For example, the context may be the result of observing responses. If, while at home, you hear someone call "Open the door!" your response to this request is quite different depending on whether you see a friend or a stranger when you look out the window. The same auditory stimulus ("Open the door!") occasions very different responses depending on the visual context (the sight of the speaker) produced by the observing response (looking out the window).

In this section, the examples of "attention" focus on instances where the contextual stimuli are provided by the environment relatively independently of overt observing responses. For example, the admonition "Listen carefully to what I am about to say" makes it likely that the speaker's next words will guide the listener's behavior more effectively. Contextual discriminations of this sort are the cumulative effect of a selection history in which the words spoken after such admonitions are especially highly correlated with reinforcement.

Dichotic Listening

Listening to the words of another is, indeed, a human behavior with an extensive selection history. Moreover, we must sometimes listen in noisy environments where many people are talking at the same time. At a noisy party, effective listening is aided by observing responses, such as looking toward the speaker while directing an ear toward his mouth. But listening is primarily guided by the auditory stimuli provided by the speaker's words themselves. To simulate listening under such conditions, an experimental procedure was devised called *dichotic listening*.

In the **dichotic listening procedure**, the listener wears stereophonic earphones that permit the experimenter to vary the characteristics of the stimuli, i.e., the messages, that are simultaneously presented to the two ears.[26] The contextual stimulus is provided by the experimenter's instruction to attend to only one of the messages (e.g., auditory stimuli presented by the left earphone) and to ignore other messages (e.g., stimuli presented by the right earphone). To insure that the context provided by the instructions is effective, the listener is asked to repeat aloud, as soon as they are heard, the words in the attended message. For example, if a discussion about adaptive networks is presented in one earphone and a discussion about baseball in the other, the person might be asked to repeat word for word everything heard in the ear sensing the adaptive-network message. The words in both messages appear at high rates, typically over 100 per min.

This technique for measuring the effectiveness of the instructional context is called **shadowing**, and the listener is said to *shadow* the attended message. Since the subject is asked to emit vocal responses whose sounds are similar to those of the shadowed message, the shadowing task is said to require the subject to emit **echoic responses**.[27] How are echoic responses to words in the shadowed message affected by the instructional context? Are echoic responses affected by the words in the unshadowed message?

During a shadowing task, any stimuli that allow the shadowed message to be discriminated from the unshadowed message contribute to the accuracy of echoic responses. If the two messages are presented separately to different ears rather than together to both ears, if they are spoken by different voices rather than the same voice, if they are concerned with different topics rather than the same topic, and so forth, then shadowing is more accurate.[28] As is true of discriminations generally, the more the two sets of stimuli differ from one another, the more effectively the contextual discrimination is maintained.

Guidance of verbal responses. The instructions implementing the contextual discrimination are particularly effective in restricting the guidance of *verbal* responses to stimuli in the shadowed message. If, while shadowing one message, subjects are asked to detect specific words occasionally appearing in the unshadowed message, they are often unable to do so.[29] Also, if subjects are tested for their recall of unshadowed words only a few minutes after completing the shadowing task, they generally cannot remember them.[30]

Since stimuli in the unshadowed message do not guide verbal responses, we might conclude that they do not guide *any* behavior. This would be too strong a conclusion, however. It assumes that everything we know—i.e., every environment-behavior relation—is reflected in our verbal behavior. This assumption—that knowledge may be equated with verbal behavior—is called the **verbal bias**. Most persons in our culture are predisposed to this bias and, because it is so pervasive, we must be on constant guard against it.[31]

Guidance by stimuli from the unshadowed message.   Later research showed that stimuli from the unshadowed message may affect the guidance of other responses and of the echoic responses themselves. To demonstrate the guidance of a nonechoic response by a stimulus from the unshadowed message, galvanic skin responses were conditioned before the shadowing task by pairing certain words (e.g., the names of towns) with an electric shock.[32] Later, when these words, or even similar words, occurred in the *un*shadowed message, they sometimes evoked a galvanic response. However, even though galvanic skin responses were guided by the unshadowed words, the subjects did not emit echoic responses to these words during the shadowing task or recall them at the end of the experiment.

The earlier findings indicate that stimuli in the unshadowed message can guide behavior. Other research indicates that pre-experimental histories acquired in the natural environment can have the same effect. For example, when commands such as "Stop it!" appear in the unshadowed message, they are detected, especially if preceded by emotion-arousing words such as curses.[33] Also, whether instructed or not, subjects often detect certain other stimuli in the unshadowed message—e.g., their own names being spoken, or a change in the gender of the speaker.[34] Stimuli that are characteristic of commands, one's name, and—apparently—the speaker's gender are reliable guides to behavior *in many different contexts*. Hence, these stimuli guide behavior in many contexts—including the context provided by instructions to shadow the other message.

Additional evidence for the influence of stimuli in the unshadowed message is provided by the echoic response itself. When two sets of words are separately presented to the two ears, a word in the shadowed message (e.g., "couch") is echoed more promptly when it is preceded in the unshadowed message by a related word (e.g., "sofa") than by an unrelated word.[35] A more dramatic effect of the unshadowed message on the echoic response is found when connected discourse is presented separately to the two ears. When the shadowed message contains a standard English phrase (e.g., ". . . crept out of . . .") and the unshadowed message next contains a phrase that is a natural continuation of the shadowed phrase (e.g., ". . . the swamp . . ."), the echoic response is often guided by the unshadowed continuation. That is, the echoic response is "crept out of the swamp." The subject has echoed the continuation in the unshadowed message rather than the next words in the shadowed message![36] The phrase "crept out of" reinstates an environmental context in which the unshadowed phrase "the swamp" guides the echoic response. Thus, for a few moments, the new context overrides the instructions and the words in the unshadowed message control the echoic response.[37]

Findings from the dichotic listening task, when taken as a whole, indicate that multiple response measures must be used to reveal the full effects of selection. Verbal responses, although crucially important for the understanding of human behavior, provide an incomplete and potentially misleading appreciation of the richness of selection. The findings from dichotic listening also re-emphasize that a response is often guided by multiple discriminative stimuli. When subjects echo a word as specified by the experimenter's instructions, the instructional context and the shadowed word itself are not the only sources of stimulation that guide behavior. Much of the person's selection history—not just the conditions present when the observation is made—affect responding in the experienced learner.[38]

Interpretation of the Role of Context on Attending

Interpreting the contribution of contextual stimuli to attentional phenomena does not require an appeal to unique "attentional" processes. Instead, the joint guidance of behavior by contextual and discriminative stimuli allows us to interpret these phenomena as the cumulative product of the biobehavioral processes involved in the selection and environmental guidance of behavior. Through these processes, the stimuli in the shadowed message, when accompanied by the contextual stimuli provided by the shadowing instructions, restrict the guidance of *echoic* responses to the stimuli in the shadowed message. Such contextual discriminations are, therefore, another way—in addition to blocking—to produce selective attending. The restriction in the environmental guidance of behavior is, however, specific to echoic responses. The unshadowed stimuli may continue to guide nonverbal responses, e.g., galvanic skin responses, and some verbal responses as well; e.g., when the subject's own name appears in the unshadowed message.

These conclusions are not confined to simultaneously presented auditory stimuli. A study was conducted to determine if a contextual discrimination produced by instructions to attend to one *visual* stimulus produced results analogous to those obtained in the dichotic listening situation.[39] Videotapes were prepared of two activities—e.g., playing catch or pat-a-cake. Then, subjects were shown images of the two activities superimposed by means of a mirror arrangement. The subjects were instructed to follow one of the activities (e.g., throwing a ball or handclapping), and to press a button whenever they saw it. In agreement with the finding in the auditory shadowing task, there was little or no evidence from the subjects' verbal behavior that they had seen the "unshadowed" activity.[40]

Adaptive-network interpretations. Contextual discriminations, and the "selective attention" they produce, can be simulated by adaptive networks. Consider the case in which two sets of messages (A and B) are presented simultaneously to different inputs of a network, with a third input (C) for the instructions to respond to only one of the messages, e.g., message B. (See **Figure 6.4**.) Examples of the A and B messages might be the simultaneous auditory stimuli "tree" and "yard." Output unit Y represents the response system to which the instructions apply, e.g., the speech system responsible for echoing the auditory stimuli. As a result of the selection history of the network, the connec-

tions between the A and B inputs and the Y output unit are assumed to be moderately strong at the outset of the experiment, but not strong enough by themselves to activate output unit Y reliably. (Without this limitation, whenever the A and B inputs were stimulated the output units would be activated at the same time. Such a network would behave like the unfortunate victim of Tourette's syndrome at the beginning of the chapter—it would "try" to do everything at once.)

The function of the third input unit (C)—the instructions to respond to message **B** only—is to activate some of the same pathways activated by the message **B** input. When the **B** and **C** inputs are stimulated simultaneously, their combined effect activates the common paths strongly enough to activate output unit **Y** reliably. (See **Figure 6.4**.) Thus, in the context of the instructions, output **Y** is guided by input **B** and not by input **A**. However, other output units, e.g., **X**, could still be activated

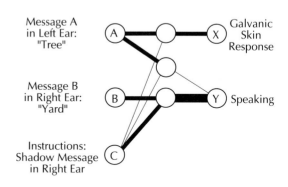

FIGURE 6.4 *Simultaneous guidance of the behavior of two different response systems mediated by the same neural network*
The network has three input units (A, B, and C), three interior units, and two output units (X and Y). The widths of the lines indicate the strengths of connections between the units. In the context of the shadowing instructions, only acoustic stimuli presented to the right ear guide speaking, but a galvanic skin response is guided by the acoustic stimulus to the left ear since the two response systems do not interfere with one another. (See discussion in the text.)

by input **A** if the initial strengths of the connections between **A** and **X** were great enough, and if there was no interference between these pathways and those leading from input **B** to output **Y**. A network with these characteristics would respond to the simultaneous presentation of the stimuli "tree" and "yard" with the echoic response "tree," and with a galvanic skin response to "yard," if "yard" had previously been paired with shock.

Other "attentional" phenomena, such as responding to one's name or to a command even though these stimuli appear in the unshadowed message, can also be interpreted through an adaptive network. If the connections between some input and output units are strong *independent of context*, then the stimuli that guide those responses will activate their outputs whatever the context. It is reasonable to believe that hearing one's name spoken would be such a stimulus. Unlike the responses to most stimuli, responding to one's name would have been reinforced in almost every environment. Similarly, responding to commands is reinforced in a wide variety of environments. The difficulty of the game *Simon says* depends on this. When the leader of the game commands "Raise your hand!" many players do so, in spite of the instructional context to follow only commands preceded by the phrase "Simon says."

Networks and neuroscience.   Before moving to the final section of the chapter, a few comments are in order about the adaptive networks discussed here. The units in these networks are more functional than structural; i.e, their characteristics are determined primarily by experimental work at the behavioral level. The units in the networks discussed in earlier chapters were more clearly neuron-like; i.e., their characteristics were more closely tied to experimental work at the neural level. For example, the command "Raise your hand!" is an extremely complex, time-varying acoustic stimulus that activates a large number of receptors, and then neurons in the auditory system. Moreover, the response to such a command is an equally complex pattern of neuronal activity producing coordinated contractions of many muscle fibers. At the neural level, to represent such a stimulus by a single input unit or such a response by a single output unit is a great simplification, even a great oversimplification. Nevertheless, at the behavioral level of analysis, the simplification is justified to the extent that orderly environment-behavior relations are found when the stimulus and response are so defined.[41] When a stimulus defined as "Raise your hand" occurs, a response defined as *raising the hand* is reliably observed. Defining the complex acoustic stimulus as the command and the complex muscular contractions as the response permits an orderly environment-behavior relation to be described at the behavioral level.

Of course, processes at the behavioral and neural levels must ultimately be consistent with one another, and each level of analysis potentially aids the experimental analysis of the other. The interrelation between levels of analysis may be illustrated with the previous network interpretations of selective attending produced by contextual discriminations. In the network interpretation, a stimulus may simultaneously guide one response (e.g., a galvanic skin response) and not another (the verbal response of echoing the stimulus). We have already seen evidence from neuropsychology that such disassociations between response systems may occur. In the phenomenon of blindsight, a person who has suffered damage to brain regions involved in complex vision may be able to point to objects in the visual field but not to talk about them.[42] In that case, a stimulus guides manual responses but not verbal responses.

The network interpretation of selective attending as a contextual discrimination also proposed that the context selectively strengthens connections leading from the shadowed stimulus input to the designated response output. Work at the neural level is consistent with this proposal. Monkeys were trained with a contextual discrimination in which the correct response to tones simultaneously presented to different ears depended on the context provided by a visual stimulus. In the presence of one visual stimulus, the response appropriate to the tone in the left ear was reinforced; in the presence of the other visual stimulus, the response appropriate to the tone in the right ear was reinforced. Thus, the animals were trained on a contextual discrimination in which the visual stimulus provided the context that specified the tone that was to be "shadowed." When the activity of neurons in the auditory association cortex was monitored, an enhanced neural response to the auditory stimulus was found *when the visual context indicated that the auditory stimulus was correct.*[43] The observed neural events are consistent with network interpretations that some "attentional" phenomena are instances of contextual discriminations.

CONCURRENT GUIDANCE AND ATTENDING

The environment usually contains many concurrently sensed discriminative stimuli (i.e., stimuli capable of guiding responses because of the learner's selection history). Accordingly, there are many possibilities for interference among the biobehavioral processes initiated by these stimuli. We have already seen an illustration of such interference effects in the shadowing experiment. As illustrated by the adaptive network in **Figure 6.4**, the words in either the shadowed or unshadowed message are capable, under different conditions, of evoking echoic responses. However, the instructions to echo only one of the messages causes shadowing to be guided by one message to the exclusion of the other. To the extent that some of the processes necessary for shadowing are devoted to shadowing one message, the other message cannot be shadowed. That is, the processes required for the two echoic responses interfere with one another. The most obvious source of interference in the shadowing task is that there is only one set of articulators available for the emission of a vocal response, so only one echoic response may occur at a time.[44]

In general, shadowing and other environment-behavior relations involve many biobehavioral processes. Some of these processes may be observed at the behavioral level and others require observations at microbehavioral and physiological levels. Interference can occur at any point in the sequence that begins with sensing the discriminative stimulus and ends with emitting the differentiated response. If the processes involved in one ongoing environment-behavior relation are needed by a second relation, then the second relation cannot occur. Laboratory procedures that produce interfering interactions are commonly called **divided-attention tasks**.

Divided "Attention"

Interference in divided-attention tasks can arise in many ways.[45] In the shadowing task, at least part of the interference occurred in the emission of the vocal response: The subject could not say two things at once. In other divided-attention tasks, interference occurs when the stimuli are being sensed. When the discriminative stimuli are in the same modality, e.g., both visual or both auditory stimuli, interference may occur at an early stage in the sequence. For example, if a visually presented letter of the alphabet is followed within 100 msec by a circle to the same portion of the retina, subjects do not report seeing the letter.[46] In this case, the interfering biobehavioral processes occur peripherally in the retina, and perhaps in other portions of the visual system.[47]

Interference effects may also involve biobehavioral processes that occur between sensing the stimulus and emitting the response. For example, if subjects are told to visually scan an array of stimuli for the letter "O" and press a button when they see it, the "O" is detected more rapidly if it appears among a group of numbers than if it appears among a group of letters. Conversely, when the experimenter describes the identical stimulus as the *number* zero rather than the letter "O," it is now more readily detected among a group of letters than among a group of numbers.[48] Since the visual stimulus (O) and the response (pressing a button) are the same in both cases, this effect of context on search behavior clearly involves the interaction of processes intervening between sensing the stimulus and executing the response.

While interactions among biobehavioral processes may facilitate as well as interfere with environment-behavior relations, we focus here on interactions that produce interference in divided-attention tasks. Our goals are to identify some of the conditions that produce interference, and to consider whether and how experience with the task may modulate interference effects.[49]

Interference in Divided-Attention Tasks. The Stroop task may be used to study interference effects. In this task, you recall, subjects are instructed to name a color, but the color is presented in the form of a word that is the name of another color. Under these conditions, the name of the color is spoken with hesitancy—perhaps 50% more slowly than would otherwise occur—and with more errors—perhaps 15% errors when the word is the name of a color different from that of the ink in which the word is printed.

Performance in the Stroop task may be interpreted as the result of interference between two strong pre-existing environment-behavior relations: The letters of the word guide speaking one color name, and the color of the ink guides speaking another color name. The contextual discrimination implemented by the experimenter's instruction that speaking should be guided only by the color of the ink sets the stage for interference between these two relations. From this perspective, any change in conditions that weakens the relation between the letters of the word and speaking its color name should reduce the amount of interference.

Several findings support the above interpretation. Children in first or second grade, who name colors faster than they read color words, do not show interference effects on the Stroop task.[50] Similarly, children who are poor readers, no matter what their grade, also show less interference.[51] The interfering effects of the pre-existing environment-behavior relation should also be reduced if a nonvocal response is required: *Speaking* the word is

the previously selected response guided by the sight of the color name. This conjecture has also been supported: When subjects are required to *press a button* designating the color, rather than speak the name of the color, interference declines.[52] Finally, any change that increases the guidance of behavior by the instructional context should also lessen interference. This follows because the processes initiated by the instructions strengthen the color-naming relation relative to the word-naming relation. In keeping with this expectation, extended practice reduces interference on the Stroop task.[53]

To summarize, circumstances that favor interference are as follows: Interference between two environment-behavior relations is likely when (a) the stimuli guiding the environment-behavior relations are in the same modality and occur simultaneously, (b) the responses guided by the stimuli involve the same effectors, (c) the contingencies of selection that produced the two environment-behavior relations are similar, and (d) as a result of selection, both of the relations are strong. In the Stroop task, the stimuli were both visual (the color of the ink and the letters of the word), the responses were both vocal (naming the color and speaking the word), the contingencies of selection were similar (both relations were likely the product of similar schedules of acquired reinforcers), and the different vocal responses were strongly guided by the color and the letters of the word, respectively.

Network interpretations of interference. Interference effects in divided-attention tasks may be interpreted using neural networks. A network description also suggests the means whereby experience may reduce interference effects. The upper panel of **Figure 6.5** shows a neural network with three input units (A, B, and C), two output units (X and Y), a number of interior units, and various connections between the units. Suppose that one environment-behavior relation involves the S_1 stimulus (which stimulates both input units A and B) and the R_1 response (output unit X). For example, S_1 might be a musical chord consisting of the simultaneous presentation of two notes—one

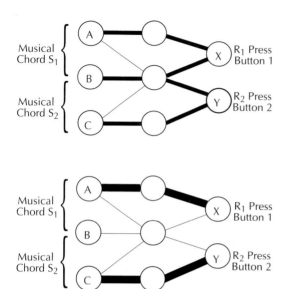

FIGURE 6.5   *Effect of fading on concurrent performance*

Different interference effects mediated by two neural networks having the same connectivity but different strengths of connections. The widths of the lines connecting the units indicate the strengths of connections between units. The network in the upper panel shows much interference; the network in the lower panel shows less interference. In the upper panel, because S_1 and S_2 both stimulate input unit B—which is the origin of moderately strong pathways to both output units X and Y—either R_1 or R_2 (or both) may be produced by either stimulus. In the lower panel, a fading procedure was used in which pretraining with inputs A and C preceded training with S_1 and S_2, thereby reducing interference effects by blocking the ability of input unit B to acquire the ability to guide either response. (See text for additional information.)

which stimulates input unit A and the other input unit B. The R_1 response might consist of pressing a button. Suppose that portions of the same network mediate a second environment-behavior relation involving S_2 (input units B and C) and R_2 (output unit Y). S_2 might be a second musical chord consisting of the simultaneous presentation of two notes, one which also stimulates input unit B and the other input unit C. R_2 might consist of

pressing a different button. In this situation, the network performs "correctly" if stimulation of the inputs by S_1 alone activates only R_1, stimulation by S_2 alone activates only R_2, and stimulation by S_1 and S_2 simultaneously activates both R_1 and R_2. Thus the network is able to carry out either task separately or both together.

With the network whose strengths of connections are shown in the upper panel of **Figure 6.5**, when S_1 and S_2 stimulate the inputs of the network—either separately or simultaneously—the two input-output relations can interfere with one another. When S_1 is presented alone, R_1 generally occurs because output unit X is more strongly activated than output unit Y. There are two moderately strong pathways from S_1 units to the R_1 unit and only one to the R_2 unit. However, the "wrong" response, R_2, can sometimes occur because S_1 activates one moderately strong pathway leading to R_2. Contrary to what is desired, when S_1 is presented, both responses may occur, depending on which pathways are activated and the degree of incompatibility between the responses. Comparable problems arise when S_2 is presented alone. The source of potential interference is that both S_1 and S_2 potentially activate a common interior unit, and that unit is the origin of pathways to both R_1 and R_2.[54]

Is interference, or "divided attention," a necessary result if the stimuli to be discriminated can activate interior units giving rise to pathways that lead to different responses? When the implications of behavioral selection are fully considered, it is apparent that interference effects are possible but not inevitable in such cases. Since selection occurs only so long as there is a behavioral discrepancy, and since fading may be used to facilitate discrimination formation, interference effects can be reduced or avoided altogether—even with highly similar tasks involving many potentially common pathways.

To illustrate the effect of selection with a fading procedure, consider again the two environment-behavior relations, S_1-R_1 and S_2-R_2, mediated by the network in the upper panel of **Figure 6.5**. The source of interference is that both S_1 and S_2 stimulate input unit B. When input unit B is stimulated, pathways are activated that lead to both output units X and Y—and, hence, to R_1 and R_2, respectively. This source of interference may be minimized if a fading procedure is used when the S_1-R_1 and S_2-R_2 relations are being selected. First, the network is trained to activate output unit X when only input unit A is stimulated and output unit Y when only input unit C is stimulated. The success of this training depends on the presence of *multiple* pathways leading from A to X and from C to Y, some of which do not lead to both output units. The pathways that meet this requirement are indicated by the heavy lines between units, denoting the existence of very strong connections along the pathways leading from the input units to the appropriate output units. Once pathways had been selected for each of these components of S_1 and S_2, the network could be presented with the complete stimuli that stimulate input unit B in common. At this point, the reinforcer is already fully "predicted" by input units A and C; i.e., there is no longer a discrepancy. Consequently, no increases can occur in the strength of connections along the pathways leading from input unit B to the output units. That is, even though input unit B is stimulated by both S_1 and S_2, further learning is blocked. After such training, the same network can mediate the S_1-R_1 and S_2-R_2 relations either separately or simultaneously without interference.[55]

Experience and divided-attention tasks.   A biobehavioral interpretation of "divided attention" indicates that, with appropriate training, fading should permit the learner to perform two activities simultaneously that would otherwise be incompatible. What is the evidence?

Strong suggestive information from everyday observation indicates that, with extended practice, a person may engage in several complex environment-behavior relations at the same time. Do you recall how, when you first learned to drive, you were unable to "pay attention" to anything else? Indeed, research confirms this impression. As novice drivers become more skilled, they are increasingly able to accurately carry out arithmetical calculations posed to them as they drive.[56] (No mention is made of whether arithmetical calculations interfere with driving, an effect of perhaps greater interest to other drivers sharing the road!) Similar work has found that experienced secretaries can type while shadowing a telephone message, and experienced piano-bar musicians can sight read while listening to patrons.[57] In the laboratory, subjects with prolonged experience in a dichotic listening task can reliably detect stimuli appearing in either the attended or unattended ear.[58] Not surprisingly, an exception occurs when the same response system is used to report simultaneous detections. As the subject responds to one stimulus, the other stimulus has no measurable effects on the same response system.[59]

Although the above findings are consistent with the view that several environment-behavior relations can occur at the same time, some of the concurrent tasks were relatively undemanding— simple addition problems and detecting single words. These tasks could have been carried out in rapid succession rather than simultaneously. The best indication of the ability of experienced learners to perform complex tasks at the same time comes from a remarkable series of experiments conducted by Ulrich Neisser and his colleagues, Hirst, Spelke, and Reaves.

Simultaneous complex behavior.   The two complex tasks to be performed simultaneously were copying dictated words while reading, with the subjects required to comprehend both sets of verbal material. In the copying task, the stimuli were auditorily presented words and the behavioral responses were the hand movements required to write the words. In the reading task, the stimuli were visually presented words and the behavioral responses were the eye movements required to read the words. Because the stimuli were from different sensory modalities and the behavioral responses used different effector systems, the tasks avoided peripheral interference from sensing the stimuli and executing the responses. The remaining sources of interference included the processes mediating the environment-behavior relations, including those required for comprehension. Since both copying and reading involve verbal relations, they are likely to share partially common biobehavioral resources.

In an initial study, two college students were asked to copy novel three-word and four-word sentences while reading prose material.[60] As soon as they had copied one sentence, they were given the next new sentence to copy. Reading speed was continuously measured, and tests for remembering and comprehending both sets of materials were given intermittently. After over 100 hours of experience on these two tasks, none of the subjects were able to read at normal speed while understanding and remembering both the sentences they had copied and the sentences they had read. Note that in this first study, practice had begun with both of the complex tasks introduced at the beginning of the experiment. The investigators speculated that the two tasks had been introduced too rapidly.

In a second experiment, a fading procedure was used to more gradually train copying while reading.[61] This experiment began with a simple copying task that was made progressively more demanding as the study went on. Subjects were first trained to copy single unrelated words, and then progressed gradually to three- and five-word sentences. Longer copying tasks were introduced only after the subjects' reading speed and comprehension had reached levels comparable to those achieved when they were just reading. During this phase, no tests were given for comprehension of the copied sentences.[62] To give some appreciation of the length of training, normal reading speed and comprehension—while copying three-word sentences—was reached after either 28 or 71 one-hour sessions for the two subjects in the study. Interestingly, the subject who required less training had been a secretary before becoming a college student, and she reported being able to type while talking on the telephone.

Comprehension of the copied material was assessed only after the subjects were reading and comprehending the prose passages with normal speed and accuracy while copying the dictated sentences at the same time. Comprehension was measured in several ways with tests administered between training trials. As one test of comprehension, subjects were given a list of sentences and asked to judge which ones they had copied and how confident they were in the accuracy of their judgments. Although it had not been pointed out to the subjects, some sets of three successive copied sentences were related to one another; for example, "Cookbooks contain recipes," "Susan owns several," and "Mary hates cooking." The list of sentences presented in the memory tests included some that were identical to copied sentences (e.g., "Cookbooks contain recipes"), some that were implied by the copied sentences although they had not been copied (e.g., "Susan owns cookbooks"), and some that were unrelated to the meaning of the copied sentences (e.g., "Susan hates cooking"). Implied sentences were included because other research had shown that, under normal reading conditions, subjects often judge implied sentences to have actually been read.[63] This result is taken as particularly strong evidence for comprehension of the verbal material because it requires that information be integrated across different sentences.

The results of the comprehension test are shown in **Figure 6.6** for the two trained subjects, Arlene and Mary, and for a group of four control subjects who had copied the sentences *without* simultaneously reading. The trained and control subjects showed the same pattern of results: They most confidently judged the copied sentences as having been copied, followed by the implied sentences, and then the unrelated sentences. In short, both experimental subjects correctly remembered the copied sentences and drew correct implications about them. While Arlene and Mary were somewhat less confident of their judgments than the control subjects, the differences among the three types of test sentences were reliable for all subjects. Moreover, this pattern was obtained on the very first test, when the subjects were unaware that they would be tested on the copied material.

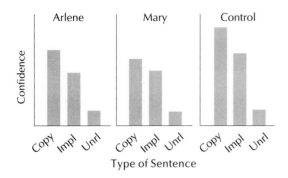

FIGURE 6.6 *Effect of extended practice and fading on concurrent performance*
Shown are the confidence ratings that various sentences had occurred during a prior task in which sentences were copied. The rated sentences were of three types: (a) those that had actually been copied (Copy), (b) those that had not been presented but were implied by the copied sentences (Impl), and (c) those that had not been presented and were unrelated to the copied sentences (Unrl). Arlene and Mary were the experimental subjects who had copied the sentences while simultaneously reading other sentences. The control subjects had copied the same sentences but not while engaged in any other task.
Source: Hirst, W., Spelke, E., Reaves, C. C., Caharack, G., & Neisser, U. (1980). Divided attention without alternation or automaticity. *Journal of Experimental Psychology: General, 109*, 98–117. Copyright © 1980 by the American Psychological Association. Reprinted by permission.

It is well to re-emphasize that Arlene and Mary comprehended and remembered the copied sentences while, at the same time, they read and comprehended the prose passages at normal levels! Moreover, they comprehended the copied material even though they were surprised to be told, at the end of the study, that any of the successive sentences were related to one another. Thus, as in the shadowing task, stimuli of which the subjects were unaware were nevertheless able to influence verbal behavior.

Limits on Attending

Given the remarkable finding that two independent verbal messages can—with a prolonged history of selection using a fading procedure—be comprehended and remembered, the authors of these studies concluded: "The limits of mental performance at any given time are determined by an individual's history rather than by fixed cognitive structures . . . People can learn to do indefinitely many things indefinitely well."[64] Indeed, this conclusion seems much closer to the truth than the conventional wisdom that our ability to carry out multiple environment-behavior relations at the same time is limited to one or, at most, a few simple relations. A major contributor to the conventional wisdom is the verbal bias by which we equate what we know with what we can talk about. Because we can talk about only one thing at a time, we mistakenly believe we can do only one thing at a time.

As interpreted by adaptive networks, a history of selection with fading strengthens different pathways that mediate otherwise interfering environment-behavior relations. From this perspective, the subjects in the above studies were reading and copying *in qualitatively different ways after training with the fading procedure* than they were at the beginning of the study. The original environment-behavior relations were not simply made stronger by prolonged selection; they were to some degree replaced by other relations using new pathways.[65]

Note, however, that adaptive-network interpretations do not necessarily indicate that any two tasks can be carried out simultaneously. There are limitations beyond our obvious physical inability to sense all stimuli or to execute all responses simultaneously. Some tasks, by their very nature, involve components that must be carried out sequentially; e.g., you cannot say whether two stimuli are similar until *after* you have sensed both of them.[66] Other tasks, because of unavoidable interactions within regions of the brain, cannot be performed at the same time.[67] The ability of selection to produce two simultaneous environment-behavior relations depends on the prior existence of alternative neural pathways between the relevant receptors and effectors.

The extent to which alternative pathways are found depends on many factors. Here, we emphasized the contribution of fading during the training procedure. Another factor is the presence of stimuli having a motivating function; i.e., stimuli whose presentation changes the strength of a range of environment-behavior relations. The simplest example of a motivating function is the sensitization of reflexive relations by eliciting stimuli, but acquired environment-behavior relations can be enhanced as well. As applied to adaptive networks, motivating stimuli increase the activation of many pathways within the network. The effect of this indiscriminate increase is to make it more likely that one or more alternative pathways between the critical input and output units will be activated, and thereby become eligible for selection by the diffuse reinforcing system. In the "divided attention" literature, the motivating function of stimuli is commonly referred to as "effort."[68] The general finding in studies of "attention" is that simultaneous tasks require the greatest "effort" at the beginning of training and then progressively less "effort" as training goes on. For example, the subjects in the experiment on simultaneous reading and copying reported just such a result.

Since environment-behavior relations involving similar stimuli, responses, and contingencies of reinforcement are most apt to involve overlapping pathways in an adaptive network, tasks having these characteristics are most apt to interfere with one another. For example, when simultaneous tasks involve different environment-behavior relations, e.g., spelling vs. addition[69] or speech vs. music,[70] interference is less likely. However, when the tasks are similar, e.g., multiple color discriminations[71] or word detections,[72] interference is more likely. Whether extensive training with fading procedures would eliminate interference even in such cases is unknown.

Ultimately, of course, the limits on simultaneous performance are imposed by the availability of potential alternative pathways in the nervous system. Without alternative, partially non-overlapping neural pathways between receptors and effectors, two simultaneous environment-behavior relations cannot be mediated. Research employing tasks likely to vary in the degree of involvement of overlapping areas in the nervous system confirm the view: Tasks requiring different brain areas are less prone to interference effects.[73] Until we have detailed knowledge of the potential connectivity within and between brain areas, questions about limits on concurrent performance cannot be fully answered.[74]

CONCLUDING COMMENTS

We have encountered a number of examples of behavioral phenomena that—in everyday language—are taken as evidence of "attention." Selective-attention and divided-attention procedures provide examples of such phenomena. Several interrelated themes emerged in our efforts to interpret "attention." First, "attention" is not a theoretically coherent field of study; i.e., no single interpretation can be given for all such phenomena because they involve *different* realizations of basic biobehavioral processes. For example, selective attending can have several origins, including blocking and the interference produced when several stimuli compete for control of a single effector system. Of course, to conclude that "attention" does not constitute a theoretically coherent field of study in no way detracts from the importance of such phenomena in the interpretation of complex behavior.

Second, the behavior of the learner plays an increasingly active role in determining the environmental events that guide behavior. As a cumulative effect of past selection, the environment evokes observing responses and these responses, in turn, affect the stimuli that are sensed.[75] The experimental analysis of some observing responses, such as the movement of the eyes from one fixation point to another, can be carried out on the behavioral level. The analysis of other observing responses, such as attending to a message in one ear while simultaneously sensing a different message in the other ear, requires supplementation by measurements on the microbehavioral and physiological levels. At whatever level they are measured, observing responses appear to originate from and to be maintained by the same biobehavioral processes that select other environment-behavior relations—notably those required for selection by reinforcement and discrimination formation.

Third, as with historical sciences generally, an interpretation of attentional phenomena requires an intimate knowledge of the full history of selection. The interpretation must be sensitive to the effects of both the individual and ancestral environments. Consider the question of an organism's ability to mediate simultaneous environment-behavior relations. This ability depends on both the specifics of selection by reinforcement, e.g., discrimination through fading; and the specifics of natural selection, e.g., the potential connectivity of the nervous system. Furthermore, the interpretation must take into account a number of the learner's response systems, and not—in the case of human learners—just the response systems mediating verbal behavior. On the issue of simultaneous environment-behavior relations, we would have formed an inadequate appreciation of our abilities if our conclusions had been based on verbal responses alone. The verbal bias leads us to underestimate the full complexity of selection.

Last, the interpretation of attentional phenomena did not require the introduction of a uniquely attentional process or entity. Instead, attentional phenomena seem to arise as the emergent consequences of an extended history of selection. Although we must remain open to the possibility that other processes may ultimately be required, the various phenomena included under the heading of "attention" appear to be within the reach of basic biobehavioral principles identified by experimental analysis and interpreted by adaptive networks. If simple processes identified by experimental analysis are sufficient to interpret complex phenomena, then historical science tentatively accepts those interpretations as explanations of the complex phenomena.

STUDY AIDS

Technical Terms

nominal fallacy
observing responses
base-rate neglect
transfer effect
dichotic listening procedure
shadowing
echoic responses
verbal bias
divided-attention tasks

Text Questions

1. In the introduction to the chapter, four general accounts of attending are described. Identify each type of account and give an experimental and everyday example of each.

2. Sensing a stimulus is necessary for it to guide behavior. What is the role of observing responses in attending? How are they acquired and what maintains these responses?

3. Many attentional phenomena may be interpreted as the direct outcome of the subject's history of discrimination learning. Indicate how some instances of both selective attending and heightened attending can be produced by the biobehavioral processes responsible for blocking.

4. Describe the dichotic listening situation as an example of a contextual discrimination. Summarize the major findings with this procedure with regard to both the shadowed and unshadowed messages. How may these results be interpreted?

5. Describe the divided-attention procedure as an example of a concurrent discrimination. In general, when should concurrent environment-behavior relations interfere and when should they occur independently of one another? Indicate experimental evidence from the Stroop task that is consistent with your interpretations.

6. Describing the work of Ulrich Neisser and his associates, indicate the conditions under which

prolonged experience with concurrent tasks may affect interference between environment-behavior relations. Refer to fading in your answer.

Discussion Questions

7. Is the fact that different people behave in different ways in the same environment inconsistent with the idea that behavior is guided by the environment? Explain.

ENDNOTES

1. cf. Posner, 1978; Kinchla, 1980.
2. e.g., Kahneman & Triesman, 1984a, b; Posner, 1984.
3. Hineline, 1980. See Mayr, 1982 for a similar point about biology; cf. Neisser, 1976.
4. To say that an event is sensed, i.e., that it is a stimulus, means that the event constitutes a change in the physical energy falling on a receptor and that the change initiates neural activity that is propagated to the central nervous system.
5. Reason, 1984.
6. Kamin, 1969. See also Mackintosh, 1975.
7. Reason, 1984. This paper also contains a historical example of a similar lapse of "attention." Of the 17th century Comte de Brancas it was said: "He plays at backgammon and asks for something to drink; it is his turn to play, and having the dice-box in one hand and the glass in the other, being very thirsty, he gulps down the dice, and almost the box as well, throwing the liquor on the board and half drowning his antagonist." (Pritchard, 1953, pp. 363–366, cited in Reason, 1984, p. 518.)
8. Friedhoff & Chase, 1982.
9. Sacks, 1987, pp. 122–123.
10. Stroop, 1935.
11. Of course, stimuli not sensed at the moment indirectly affect behavior through the enduring effects of earlier exposure to those stimuli. The effects of past selections are retained and, thus, present stimuli act on an organism that has been changed by earlier selections.
12. Banks & Salapatek, 1983.
13. Clifton, Morrongiello, Kulig, & Dowd, 1981; Wolff & White, 1965.
14. Wyckoff, 1952, 1969. See also Spence, 1936; Sutherland & Mackintosh, 1971.
15. Wyckoff, 1969.

16. e.g., Kelleher, 1958a; Mueller & Dinsmoor, 1984, 1986.
17. Case, Fantino, & Wixted, 1985. See also Case, Ploog, & Fantino, 1990, and Frazier & Bitetto, 1969.
18. Kahneman & Tversky, 1973; Kahneman, Slovic, & Tversky, 1982.
19. Gluck & Bower, 1988.
20. For a discussion of some of the difficulties in genuine diagnostic judgments, see Dawes, Faust, & Meehl, 1989.
21. cf. Staats, 1968, p. 394.
22. Honig, 1969.
23. For related work, see Reinhold & Perkins, 1955; Thomas, 1970; and Thomas, Miller, & Svinicki, 1971. For reviews, see Lubow, Weiner, & Schnur, 1981 and Thomas, 1985.
24. For theoretical analyses of this and other attentional phenomena, see Mackintosh, 1977 and Rescorla & Wagner, 1972.
25. In order for heightened attention to occur in the manner just described, the contextual stimuli must remain similar during both phases of discrimination training. If the context changes when the discrimination changes, then new contextual stimuli are not as effectively blocked. In addition, the discriminative stimuli from the first training condition must not be present during the later discrimination training, or the old discriminative stimuli will block the guidance of responding by the new stimuli. For representative work with animals on the role of context in stimulus discrimination, see Balsam, 1984; Gibbon & Balsam, 1981; Grau & Rescorla, 1984; Miller & Matzel, 1987; and Miller & Schachtman, 1985.
26. The dichotic listening procedure was developed by Cherry, 1953 and Broadbent, 1958. Dichotic listening is an ecologically valid procedure in that it simulates an environment in which the subject has an extensive selection history in the natural environment; cf. Neisser, 1976.
27. Skinner, 1957, p. 55.
28. e.g., Broadbent, 1952, 1958.
29. Moray and O'Brien, 1967. But see Shiffrin, 1975.
30. Norman, 1969.
31. The idea that behavior may be guided by events that are not reflected in speech was, perhaps, Freud's great contribution to a science of human behavior. Although many readily accept the place of what Freud called the "unconscious" in pathological behavior, Freud argued for the much more general influence of such events (Freud, 1904). Among contemporary work-

ers, Neisser has put it well: "Information pickup is not entirely under voluntary control; we would be too absentminded to survive if it were." (Neisser, 1976, p. 94.) In the "attention" literature, the verbal bias is most apparent when "attention" is equated with awareness, or consciousness. The treatment of awareness is postponed until a later chapter.

32. Corteen & Wood, 1972; Corteen & Dunn, 1974; von Wright, Anderson, & Stenman, 1975.

33. Moray, 1959.

34. Triesman, 1960.

35. Lewis, 1970; see also MacKay, 1973 and Treisman, Squire, & Green, 1974.

36. Triesman, 1960.

37. Stimuli from the unshadowed message may also affect the recall of the shadowed message; Lachner & Garrett, 1972. For example, if the shadowed message contains a sentence with an ambiguous verb, e.g., "The spy put out the torch as our signal to attack," when the unshadowed message simultaneously contains the sentence "The spy *extinguished* the torch in the window," the shadowed sentence might be remembered as "The spy *turned off* the torch in the window." (In Great Britain, where this study was conducted, the word "torch" is used to designate a flashlight as well as a flaming object.) Here, the stimuli in the unshadowed message, although not themselves echoed or remembered, have influenced remembering the shadowed message.

38. For reviews of research using the dichotic listening task and related methods for the study of attention, see Broadbent, 1982; Hirst, 1986; Kahneman & Treisman, 1984a, b; and Posner, 1982. The contribution of context to discriminative performance is by no means restricted to humans; see Balsam & Tomie, 1985 for representative examples of this work.

39. Neisser & Becklen, 1975.

40. Littman & Becklen, 1976. See also Neisser, 1976; Stoffregen & Becklen, 1989.

41. Skinner, 1931, 1938.

42. Weizkrantz, Warrington, Sanders, & Marshall, 1974.

43. Hocherman, Benson, Goldstein, Heffner, & Hienz, 1976. For related work of similar import, see Hubel, Henson, Rupert, & Galambos, 1959; Wurtz, Goldberg, & Robinson, 1980; Moran & Desimone, 1985; and Petersen, Robinson, & Keys, 1985.

44. Marcel, 1983a, b.

45. Norman & Bobrow, 1975.

46. Averbach & Coriell, 1961.

47. DiLollo, Lowe, & Scott, 1973. See also Sakitt, 1975 and Turvey, 1978.

48. Jonides & Gleitman, 1972.

49. For alternative approaches to the analysis of interfering interactions, see Allport, 1980; Deutsch & Deutsch, 1963; Kahneman & Treisman, 1984b; and Posner, 1978.

50. Ehri, 1976. See also Geffen & Sexton, 1978.

51. Gibson, 1971.

52. Pritchatt, 1968.

53. Stroop, 1935. For work that uses the Stroop task to implement a visual analog of the auditory shadowing experiment, see Kahneman & Henik, 1981 and Kahneman & Chajczyk, 1983. This research shows that when two simultaneous Stroop problems are presented, instructions to respond to only one of them do not entirely eliminate the guidance of responding by stimuli in the other problem. Thus, as with auditory shadowing, responding may be affected by the entire ensemble of stimuli and is not restricted to those specified by the instructions that institute the contextual discrimination.

54. This treatment of interference within an adaptive network is overly simple, especially because the effects of inhibitory connections between units are not considered. The activity of some neurons exerts an excitatory effect on the neurons with which they synapse; i.e., the postsynaptic neuron is *more* likely to be activated. The activity of other neurons has an inhibitory effect; i.e., the postsynaptic neuron is *less* likely to be activated by its excitatory inputs. Inhibitory interactions are very important to the functioning of the nervous system and to the adaptive networks that simulate its functioning. The contribution of inhibitory neural interactions to the functioning of neural networks is considered in later chapters.

55. The foregoing discussion focuses on the contribution of fading to the selection of non-interfering environment-behavior relations. Other factors contribute to this outcome as well. When two environmental stimuli guide different responses, and the stimuli are composed of partially common components, the cumulative effect of selection reduces the guidance of behavior by the common components relative to the unique components (e.g., Blough, 1975; Rescorla & Wagner, 1972)—although not so completely as with fading. As an example, in a visual search task, an array of letters was scanned to detect letters such as B, C, D, G, J, O, P, Q, R, S, and U (Gibson & Yonas, 1966). With extended practice, performance improved—presumably because the target letters were distinguished from the others by the presence

of curved lines. The ability of the common straight lines to affect behavior was reduced by selection. A second factor is that, since most discriminations are contextual discriminations, the role of contextual stimuli should be included in interpretations of "divided attention." The context in which environment-behavior relations are separately selected is often different from that in which they are jointly selected. This difference in contextual stimuli can also facilitate the formation of non-interfering pathways in the network through the biobehavioral processes involved in discrimination formation. "Divided attention" refers to a theoretically incoherent set of phenomena and is an expression of a number of different realizations of a common set of processes.

56. Brown & Poulton, 1961.

57. Shaffer, 1975; Allport, Antonis, & Reynolds, 1972.

58. Underwood, 1974; Kahneman, 1973; cf. Shiffrin, 1975.

59. Ostry, Moray, & Marks, 1976.

60. Spelke, Reaves, Hirst, & Neisser, 1977.

61. Hirst, Spelke, Reaves, Caharack, & Neisser, 1980.

62. Previous work had shown that, when comprehension of the copied material was not required, reading while copying was able to occur at normal rates with extended training; Spelke, Hirst, & Neisser, 1976.

63. Bransford & Franks, 1971.

64. Hirst, Spelke, Reaves, Caharack, & Neisser, 1980, pp. 99, 114.

65. cf. Hirst, Spelke, Reaves, Caharack, & Neisser, 1980, p. 115. This interpretation is consistent with animal research that has shown fading to be a very effective procedure for producing discriminations. However, as noted elsewhere, behavior selected in this way differs in a number of respects from environment-behavior relations produced by other procedures, e.g., Terrace, 1966.

66. Several tasks conventionally studied under the heading of attention involve sequential behavioral processes and, for that reason, are not considered here. These include tasks in which there is no consistent relation between the stimuli and responses appearing in the task; e.g., Fisk & Schneider, 1983; Shiffrin & Grantham, 1974; Schneider, Dumais, & Shiffrin, 1984; Shiffrin & Schneider, 1977; Schneider & Shiffrin, 1977; as well as those in which a stimulus may be responded to only after a second stimulus has been detected; e.g., Reeves & Sperling, 1986; Weichselgartner & Sperling, 1987. The behavioral processes involved in these tasks require additional interpretations of the sort described in a later chapter on problem solving, cf. Hunt & Lansman, 1986.

67. Holtzman & Gazzaniga, 1982.

68. Kahneman, 1973.

69. Hirst & Kalmar, 1987.

70. Allport, Antonis, & Reynolds, 1972.

71. Treisman & Davies, 1973.

72. Friedman, Polson, Dafoe, & Gaskill, 1982.

73. Kinsbourne & Hicks, 1978.

74. cf. Friedman, Polson, Dafoe, & Gaskill, 1982; Hirst & Kalmar, 1987; Navon, 1977; Neisser, 1976, p. 99; Wickens, 1980, 1984.

75. To aid experimental analysis, observing responses that are measurable on the behavioral level have been emphasized in this chapter. However, observing responses may occur at the microbehavioral and neural levels as well—as when a stimulus falling on the periphery of the retina is "attended to" in the absence of overt eye movements that fixate the stimulus on the fovea; e.g., Posner, 1978; Posner & Petersen, 1990. Research of this sort is considered in the chapter on perceiving. Whether the observing responses are overt or covert, the same basic processes seem to permit their interpretation.

CHAPTER 7

PERCEIVING ENVIRONMENT-ENVIRONMENT RELATIONS

Although environmental and behavioral events are forever changing, the changes often bear orderly relations to one another. The orderly relations that we have so far considered are between environmental and behavioral events. For example, stimulation of receptors in the mouth by food elicits salivation, the sound of a tone evokes salivation if the tone has been followed by food, the sight of a lever evokes lever pressing if food has occurred after lever pressing, and the sight of a friend evokes saying "hello" if such greetings have been returned in the past. Each of these environment-behavior relations is a product of selection processes—the first of natural selection, and the last three of selection by reinforcement. In this chapter, we consider the significance of orderly relations between environmental events alone—i.e., **environment-environment relations**. Are biobehavioral processes sensitive to environment-environment relations? If so, what are these processes and under what conditions are they selected?

INTRODUCTION

The relation between some environmental events is relatively constant over long periods of time. Consider perceiving an object.[1] One characteristic that distinguishes one object from another is that parts of the same object tend to look more alike than parts of different objects. When we look at a tree, we sense its leafy green appearance at many points, and this helps to distinguish it as a single object from the sky or house behind it. The selection of biobehavioral processes that are sensitive to

relations among similar stimuli from adjacent parts of the environment would facilitate the discrimination of objects, which would clearly benefit reproductive fitness. Relations between environmental events that are constant over evolutionary time—such as the relatively greater similarity of stimuli from different parts of the same object—are known as **perceptual invariants**. When one location in the environment has a leafy green appearance, it is more likely that an adjacent location is also leafy and green because trees—and all other objects—are extended in space. Biobehavioral processes that are sensitive to perceptual invariants can be favored by natural selection.

Other environment-environment relations change over evolutionary time but are relatively constant within the lifetime of an individual. For example, consider the relation of the visual stimuli provided by a tree to the auditory stimuli of the spoken word "tree" or the visual stimuli of the written word TREE. These relations are relatively constant within an English-speaking community, but vary over the evolutionary history of our species and from one contemporary verbal community to the next. Environment-environment relations that are relatively constant only within an individual's lifetime are here known as **perceptual regularities**. Biobehavioral processes that are sensitive to perceptual regularities can also be selected.[2] However, the formation of perceptual regularities cannot be guided by natural selection alone because they are not constant over evolutionary time. Perceptual regularities also cannot be the products of selection by reinforcement alone, since environment-environment relations do not include a behavioral component on which the reinforcer is contingent. If environment-environment relations are to select perceptual regularities, natural selection and reinforcement must be supplemented by other processes.

Perceiving as the Product of Selection Processes

If perceptual invariants and regularities are the cumulative outcomes of a history of selection, then understanding them presents the same difficulties as does all historical science. For one, knowledge of the full history of selection is likely to remain incomplete. For another, perceptual invariants and regularities will not be infallible guides in every environment. Like all products of selection, they bear the marks of the environments that selected them, and are valid in other environments only to the extent that the other environments are like those in which selection took place. For example, a newly hatched duckling forms an attachment, called **imprinting**, to members of its own kind. The duckling forms this attachment by following a moving object that is present shortly after hatching. In the history of the species, the moving object was most often the duckling's parents. However, in other environments, such as the animal behavior laboratory, the moving object may be an electric train (or even a duck hawk), and still the duckling imprints to the environment-environment relations provided by motion.[3] Selection has taught ducklings to recognize motion, not their mothers. In the evolutionary history of ducklings, motion has been enough. (See **Figure 7.1**.)

A history of selection cannot guarantee that we will perceive the world with perfect accuracy. Nevertheless, the relative constancy of the physical environment, the long exposure of life to that environment, and the obvious benefits of accurately perceiving the environment all argue for a close relation between the world we perceive and those aspects of the world that are important for our

THE FAR SIDE By GARY LARSON

When imprinting studies go awry

FIGURE 7.1 *One effect of imprinting is that the young animal follows whatever moving stimulus happens to be sensed shortly after hatching*
Source: The Far Side cartoon by Gary Larson is reprinted by permission of Chronicle Features, San Francisco, CA. All rights reserved.

survival. As Jerome Bruner has put it, "The senses tell us, on the whole, what we need to know. . . ."[4]

Direct Perceiving

For selection to produce perceptual invariants and regularities, the organism must be able to sense biologically relevant portions of the environment and to behave appropriately with respect to them. Thus, the environment must contain patterns of physical energy that *specify*—i.e., are correlated with—biologically important events, and this energy must be detected with sense organs that are properly positioned by the behavior of the organism. In short, the environment must be rich enough to guide perceiving, and perceiving must be selected in coordination with other biobehavioral processes.

The view that environmental stimuli *specify* the environment has been most fully developed by James J. Gibson. This view is known as **direct perception**,[5] to distinguish it from the common view that what is sensed specifies the environment only indirectly and incompletely. Indirect, or **constructionist**, views of perceiving postulate various inferred processes—mental operations—that are intended to compensate for the incomplete and impoverished stimuli provided by the environment. These mental operations are said to *construct* an accurate representation from the inadequate environmental stimuli. For example, if an observer views a circular form with a small gap in its circumference, he sometimes reports seeing a complete circle. A constructionist view of perceiving might attribute the "completion" of the circle to a tendency to see "good form." How appropriate mental operations can be evoked unless the environment initiates them—and therefore contains stimuli that specify the environment—is unclear. Instead of postulating inferred mental operations, direct perception seeks to identify characteristics of stimulus patterns that are competent to specify the environment. Perceptual invariants and regularities are derived from such characteristics. The direct-perception theorist counsels the constructionist: "Ask not what's inside the head, but what the head is inside of."[6]

Perceiving and Its Relation to Other Biobehavioral Processes

Uncovering the environment-environment relations that select perceptual invariants and regularities presents special problems when pursued only at the behavioral level of analysis. Some of the stimulus patterns that specify the environment do so relatively independently of the topography of the behavior that allows us to sense those patterns. As an illustration, whether an object moves toward us or we move toward it, that object will occupy an increasingly larger portion of our visual field. Although other concurrently available stimuli almost always allow us to discriminate these two situations from one another, an increase in the area of the visual field occupied by an object is correlated with the approach of an object *independently* of whether we are moving. Other things being equal, the larger the portion of the visual field an object occupies the nearer it is to the observer, and the smaller the portion the more distant it is.[7]

The correlation between environmental stimuli—such as how much of the visual field an object occupies at successive moments—provides the basis for the selection of perceptual invariants and regularities. Biobehavioral processes sensitive to such correlations may be selected without necessarily having specific behavioral components. This is not to say that selections relevant to perceiving are seldom evident in behavior, or that behavior seldom participates crucially in the selections relevant to perceiving. Unless perceiving ultimately affects behavior at some point, it can have no effect on fitness. Without an effect on fitness, there is no basis for natural selection or, ultimately, selection by the individual environment. Indeed, many of the stimuli that specify the environment require behavior—such as observing responses—for their very occurrence. However, to the extent that there is *any* correlation between environmental events, biobehavioral processes mediating environment-environment relations may be selected *in addition to* the processes mediating environment-behavior relations.

PERCEIVING INVARIANTS

Because changes in environment-environment relations are not as completely or directly reflected at the behavioral level as changes in environment-behavior relations, the analysis of perceiving uses more observations at the physiological level. Although the field of "perception" is not a major focus of this book, we must consider some of its aspects to appreciate the basic processes by which environment-environment relations are selected.[8]

Environment-environment relations contribute to the environmental constituents of environment-behavior relations. However, we will confine our consideration of physiological processes to those involved in one aspect of perceiving—discriminating variations in visual texture. Texture discriminations are crucial for perceiving objects, and for many other discriminations, such as distance.

Confining our analysis to the perceptual invariants involved in discriminating visual texture is enough to expose a number of general characteristics of the selection of perceptual invariants. For our species, light specifies the world more importantly than any other form of energy.[9] Visual stimuli activate fully half of the total sensory neurons entering the central nervous system—some two million axons. By contrast, the next most important sense, hearing, involves "only" about sixty thousand axons.[10] Natural selection would not have made such a heavy investment in light if the visual environment were not vitally important to survival.

In this section on perceptual invariants, we first describe the major structures in the visual system. Without such knowledge, it is impossible to discuss the biobehavioral processes involved in the selection of textural invariants, or of environment-environment relations in general. As a part of the discussion, the concept of *sensory channel* is introduced. Sensory systems contain a number of sensory channels; in the visual system, one of these is texture discrimination. We conclude the section with a discussion of how perceptual invariants are selected when they require integration of activity from different sensory channels. Perceptual invariants that integrate the activity of different sensory channels are called *polysensory invariants*.[11] Throughout the presentation, the functional significance of neuroanatomical structures and the pervasive role of selection are emphasized.

Structure of the Visual System

Reception of visual energy.   The visual receptors that react to light and initiate neural activity contain **photopigments**—chemical compounds sensitive to visible electromagnetic energy. Through the effect of light on photopigment molecules, energy is *transduced* (literally, "carried across") from the environment to the nervous system. The visible portion of the electromagnetic spectrum for humans, and most other species, falls roughly in the range of wavelengths between 400 and 700 nm (i.e., between blue and red).[12] However, the full spectrum of electromagnetic energy is much wider, extending from shorter wavelengths—such as the ultraviolet—to longer wavelengths—such as the infrared. Why are we sensitive to only a relatively small portion of the spectrum?

Light in the range of 400 to 700 nm, unlike shorter and longer wavelengths, *cannot pass through objects*, but is absorbed by them. An organism that could see beyond the visible spectrum would not be able to see objects because they block the transmission of electromagnetic energy only within that range.[13] In other words, objects cast shadows only in the visible spectrum. Thus, an organism that is capable of appreciating variations in the intensity of visible light can sense the presence of objects. To an organism that must move through the environment, the biological advantage of sensing objects is obvious.

Major visual pathways.   The visual receptors that contain the photopigments are located in the **retina**, a network of complexly interconnected receptors and neurons that cover the back interior surface of the eyeball. From ganglion cells in one layer of the retina, axons extend up the **optic tract** toward two major destinations in the brain—the **superior collicular nuclei** and the **lateral geniculate nuclei**. (See **Figure 7.2a** and **b**.) The superior collicular nuclei are located in an evolutionarily ancient portion of the brain, the hindbrain, and contain cells that respond differentially to movement and the orientation of objects, among other characteristics.[14] The destinations of other ganglion-cell axons are neurons in the lateral geniculate nuclei of the thalamus.

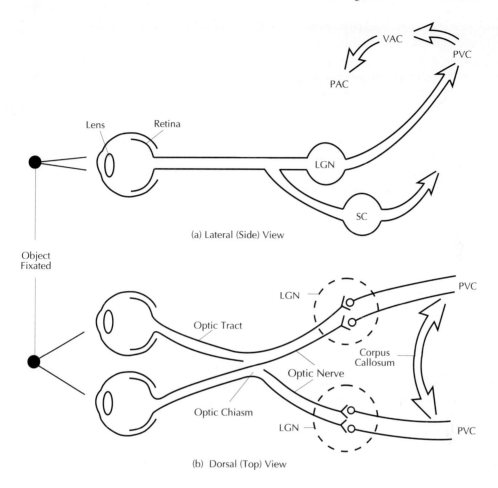

FIGURE 7.2   *Schematic diagram of major neural pathways in the visual system*

(a) Lateral view showing the two ultimate destinations of activity from retinal ganglion cells—the collicular pathway to the superior colliculus (SC)—and the geniculo-cortical pathway to the lateral geniculate nucleus (LGN) and, thereafter, to the primary visual cortex (PVC). Also shown is the relation of the PVC to the visual association cortex (VAC) and polysensory association cortex (PAC). The PAC receives inputs from sensory channels in addition to those of the visual system.

(b) Dorsal view of the geniculo-cortical pathways showing crossing of the ganglion-cell axons at the optic chiasm and the pathway interconnecting the association cortices of the two hemispheres via the corpus callosum.

Although an analysis of the development of the nervous system is beyond the scope of this book, one pervasive factor should be noted. The development of synapses, or neural connections, often depends on concurrent activity in pre- and postsynaptic neurons. When multiple presynaptic neurons are activated, their combined activity is more likely to activate the postsynaptic neurons next to them. The activation of these pre- and postsynaptic neurons at the same time causes functional connections to develop between them.

In general, **activity-dependent mechanisms** play the dominant role in the formation of connections in the mammalian nervous system. You will recall that, in learning, coactivation of pre- and postsynaptic neurons was necessary for the diffuse reinforcing system to strengthen existing connections. At the cellular level, the mechanisms of learning and development would appear to have much in common.

As one example of activity-dependent mechanisms in visual development, bursts of activity in neighboring ganglion cells play an important role in forming connections to lateral geniculate neurons.[15] Because *neighboring* ganglion cells are active, the connections in the lateral geniculate preserve the spatial relations between the ganglion cells in the retina—and therefore the relations between the receptors on which light falls and, most importantly, between the parts of the object from which the light originated. In other words, lateral geniculate cells that are next to one another are connected to ganglion cells that are next to one another, which are connected to visual receptors that are next to one another, which receive stimulation from parts of the environment that are next to one another.

The neurons in the lateral geniculate nuclei give rise to axons that project to the forebrain, the evolutionarily more modern region of the brain. The forebrain region to which these axons project is the visual cortex. Once again, activity-dependent mechanisms make it more likely that coactive lateral-geniculate neurons will form connections with the same or neighboring cortical neurons.[16] Longer-range lateral connections also develop between neurons in the primary visual cortex, and these also tend to interconnect cells that are simultaneously active.[17] Since light originating from adjacent portions of the retina is apt to stimulate cells located close together in the visual cortex, coactivity occurs when the cells are responding to similar aspects of an extended object, e.g., the visual texture, or grain, of the object.

Texture is not the only aspect of the visual environment to which natural selection has made the geniculo-cortical system responsive. Cells in the visual cortex are also sensitive to variations in color, depth,[18] and motion.[19] Although the neural circuits mediating sensitivity to these aspects of visual stimuli are not entirely separate, their selection at different times in evolutionary history has led them to be independent enough to constitute different **sensory channels**. A sensory channel is a neural circuit that is activated by one aspect of environmental stimulation. Sensory channels can be entirely within one modality, such as the various channels involved in seeing, or in different modalities, such as seeing and hearing.

From neurons in the primary visual cortex, axons project to **visual association cortex** and **polymodal association cortex**. (See **Figure 7.2a** and **b**.) Cells in visual association cortex are activated by neurons from different sensory channels in the visual cortex. Cells in polymodal association cortex are activated by inputs from different sensory channels from multiple sensory modalities— e.g., auditory and tactile stimuli in addition to visual stimuli. The area of the cerebral cortex that can be activated by visual stimuli is very large, extending well beyond those regions commonly labeled as "visual."[20] The cortical regions that respond to visual stimuli include neurons that respond differentially to the fine visual details required for texture discriminations, to colors, to movement, and to a wide variety of complex combinations of inputs from visual and other sensory channels.[21]

Blindsight and visual subsystems. Ordinarily, the collicular and geniculo-cortical visual subsystems function together to guide seeing. However, when one of them is damaged, their separable functions become apparent. We have encountered an example of just such damage in the phenomenon of blindsight (see Chapter 1). In blindsight, a person's verbal behavior indicates that he is blind—e.g., talking can no longer be guided by visual stimuli—yet he is able to navigate through the environment without bumping into things. Blindsight occurs when the geniculo-cortical subsystem is damaged, but the collicular subsystem is left intact.[22] Such damage prevents outputs from the visual cortex from activating the motor systems that control speaking. However, since outputs from the collicular subsystem are intact, they continue to activate nonverbal motor systems, such as those controlling eye movements, reaching, and walking. To a very rough approximation, the person with blindsight is seeing in the evolutionarily more ancient manner of nonmammalian species that do not have a geniculo-cortical subsystem.[23]

Those of us who have not suffered the damage that produces blindsight can catch a glimmer of the separability of the collicular and geniculo-cortical subsystems. If you have ever ducked to avoid a ball thrown rapidly and without warning, you have likely done so before you had any verbal recognition of the object. Similarly, if you have ever closed your eyes to avoid an oncoming insect while pedaling a rapidly moving bike, you have probably blinked without any verbal awareness of the object. In both cases, the neural circuitry of the collicular subsystem has guided nonverbal responses (ducking or blinking) *before* the geniculo-cortical subsystem could guide the verbal responses needed for you to recognize the object as a "ball" or a "bug."

Relation of the retina to the visual cortex. We shall describe one final aspect of the neural pathways mediating seeing before we consider the selection of the perceptual invariants responsible for texture discrimination. This information will also prove useful in the interpretation of consciousness in a later chapter. As shown in **Figure 7.2b**, the ganglion cells from half of each retina send axons to *different* lateral geniculate nuclei, and then to different visual cortices. The axons from each retina move together up the **optic nerve** and then half of them cross to the other side of the brain in a

region called the **optic chiasm**. From there, the axons move up the optic tract to one of the two lateral geniculate nuclei. Why might the ancestral environment have selected this arrangement of pathways?

As with all questions about selection, the answer may be traced to the environment. Consider an object shown to the left of the fixation point in **Figure 7.2b** and, more particularly, where the light from that object falls on the two retinas. For the right eye, the stimulated receptors are located in the outside (temporal) half-retina, their ganglion-cell axons do not cross at the optic chiasm, and neurons in the right visual cortex are ultimately activated. For the left eye, the stimulated receptors are in the inside (nasal) hemi-retina, the activated axons *do* cross at the optic chiasm, and neurons in the right visual cortex are activated. Because half of the ganglion-cell axons cross before they reach the lateral geniculate nucleus, the light originating from the *same* half of the visual field ultimately produces neural activity in the *same* visual cortex. Light from the left visual field activates cells in the right visual cortex; light from the right visual field activates cells in the left visual cortex. This arrangement insures that the light from an object is brought together in the same region of the primary visual cortex, no matter where the object lies in the visual field.

The crossing of half of the ganglion-cell axons at the optic chiasm has a second consequence: Receptors lying near the vertical midline of the retina directly activate cells in *different* visual cortices. This produces a complication since, when we fix our eyes on an object, the light from the object falls on a retinal area called the **fovea**, which is crossed by the vertical midline. Therefore, light from a fixated object stimulates receptors that are ultimately connected to cells in both the right and left visual cortices.

In spite of this complication, light falling on the fovea is most acutely seen; i.e., gradations in texture are most readily discriminated.[24] This is possible because the activity from the two visual cortices is integrated by connections between the right and left hemispheres. The cortical cells activated by receptors near the vertical midline of the two retinas are interconnected by axons that make up a very large bundle of fibers called the **corpus callosum**. (See **Figure 7.2b**.) In animals with frontally placed eyes, such as humans, these connections are very extensive.[25]

Selection of a Sensory Invariant

Perceptual invariants are selected when there are correlations between environmental events over time. Some of these correlations do not depend on any *particular* response topography, but movement of some kind—either by the perceiver or by the object—is often required for the correlations to appear. For example, suppose that a human face passes across your visual field. Under such conditions, there are relatively invariant relations among the facial features—the two eyes are symmetrically placed above the nose, the nose is above the mouth, and so on. However, if you never saw these facial features except in one stationary context, e.g., a striped background, then the relations among the features of the face would be no more stable than the relations between the features and the background stripes. It is only because the facial features move together through different background environments that the features "go with" each other, rather than with the stripes. The correlation among facial features depends on the features moving together. As remarked by Ulrich Neisser, echoing James J. Gibson, "Each of our perceptual systems has evolved to take advantage of the special kinds of information that motion makes available."[26]

We shall trace some of the processes by which perceptual invariants are selected. The analysis focuses on the selection of neural connections in sensory cortex by visual stimuli. Because of the importance of activity-dependent mechanisms in the formation of connections between neurons, the selection of sensory invariants is affected by the individual environment as well as the ancestral environment.[27]

Textural Invariants in the Structure of Light

As a result of environmental selection, living organisms are constant explorers of their environments.[28] Beginning with the guidance of behavior arising from selection by the ancestral environment, and increasingly through observing responses selected by the individual environment, we sense stimuli that specify the environment in which we (and our offspring) must survive.

Observing the structure of light. In seeing, observing responses take the form of coordinated head and eye movements that position our visual receptors so that we can observe variations in the light. In short, seeing allows us to appreciate the structure of the light.[29] Different observing responses cause us to sense the "same" environment in different ways; this is strikingly demonstrated when the same picture is looked at under different viewing instructions.[30] The picture is in the upper left panel of **Figure 7.3**, and the patterns of eye movements produced by different viewing instructions are shown in the other panels. Different instructions guide different patterns of eye movements and, consequently, the sensing of different visual stimuli. For example, when subjects were asked to determine the financial circumstances of the people in the picture, light from furniture and clothing was fixated (see **Figure 7.3c**); when they were asked to determine the people's ages, the light from faces was fixated (see **Figure 7.3d**).

In infants, eye movements are not precisely guided by visual stimuli, let alone by instructions. Eye movements themselves are the products of an extensive selection history. As a result of selection by the ancestral environment, the infant's collicular visual subsystem controls eye movements that cause light from objects that moves across the retina to be fixated on the fovea. Selection by the individual environment soon comes into play as well; the eye movements of infants as young as four months begin to follow the gaze of their mothers.[31] However, unlike adults, infants do not

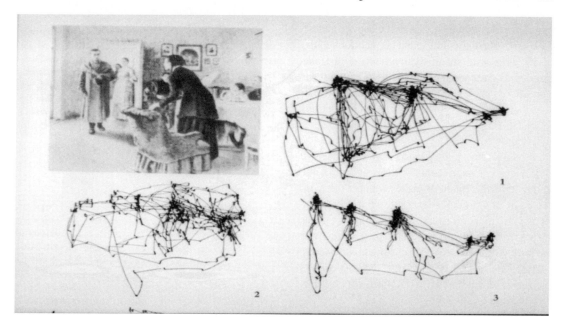

FIGURE 7.3 *Eye movements as observing responses*
The painting was viewed by subjects under different instructions. The lines shown in the other portions of the figure trace the course of eye movements when a subject was instructed: (1) simply to look at the painting, (2) to determine the financial circumstances of the people depicted in the painting, and (3) to determine the ages of people.
Source: From Yarbus, A. L. (1967). *Eye movements and vision.* New York: Plenum.

accurately fixate light from an object in one step. Fixation requires a series of movements that increasingly approximate foveal placement of the light.[32] The rapid eye movements that fixate objects detected in the periphery of the visual field are called **saccadic eye movements** or **saccades**. These eye movements—which ultimately play an important role in such complex behavior as reading[33]—are controlled by neural circuits that were naturally selected long before humans evolved.

The selection of sensory invariants begins with the movement of light across the receptors of the retina. We shall consider only one of the relations selected by the structure of light—the variations in light and dark that produce visual texture. For us to see texture, the structure in the light must differentially strengthen connections between neurons in the primary visual cortex that permit the light-

dark variations in objects to be specified. How is this accomplished?

Texture: Spatial frequency analysis.   Objects, and the backgrounds across which they move, are characterized by distinctive invariants in light and dark. An object moving nearby, such as a face, produces relatively slow variations in lightness and darkness corresponding to the considerable spacing between facial features. A background against which the face might be seen would likely have different variations in the spacing of light and dark—slower variations for a uniformly illuminated wall, more rapid variations for an intricate wallpaper pattern. If variations in the pattern of light and dark were about the same for both face and wall, then the face would be more difficult to detect—until it moved, which would cause the features to move together across the background.[34] If the environment could select connections in the visual cortex that specified invariants in the patterning of light, then the sensory invariants implemented by those connections would benefit reproductive fitness. How might such connections be selected?

Interconnections among cells in primary visual cortex. Each axon coming from a cell in the lateral geniculate nucleus makes connections with hundreds of cortical neurons. Located between these cortical neurons are intermediate neurons that receive inputs from nearby cortical neurons and have outputs to other cortical neurons.[35] These intermediate neurons reduce the activity of the neurons to which they have outputs. (For a simplified diagram of this arrangement, see **Figure 7.4**.) The intermediate neurons are **inhibitory neurons**, and the neurotransmitter that they release is called an **inhibitory neurotransmitter**. Inhibitory transmitters make it *less* likely that a postsynaptic neuron can be activated by its excitatory inputs. The inputs to cortical cells from geniculate cells release **excitatory neurotransmitters** into the synapse. Excitatory neurotransmitters tend to activate the cortical neurons on which they synapse. Thus, whether a given cortical neuron is activated depends on the balance between the excitatory input from the geniculate cells and the inhibitory input from the intermediate inhibitory cells. Can interactions between the inhibitory and excitatory inputs to the cortical cells produce differential sensitivity to the texture of light?

Receptive fields of cortical cells. To study how cortical cells respond to patterns of light and dark, visual stimuli are presented to an anesthetized animal, such as a monkey, while the activity of a cortical cell is monitored with a recording electrode.[36] A visual stimulus commonly used in these studies is a **grating** made up of parallel bands of light and dark. The grating is moved across the animal's visual field until the cortical cell is activated. The region of the visual field in which light from the grating activates the cortical cell is called

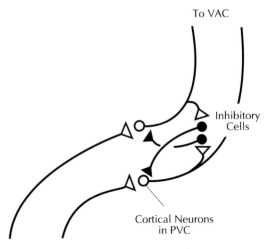

To VAC

Inhibitory Cells

Cortical Neurons in PVC

From LGN

FIGURE 7.4 *Excitatory-inhibitory interactions between cortical neurons*

Axons from the lateral geniculate nucleus make excitatory synapses (open triangles) on cells in the primary visual cortex (PVC). Axons from these cortical cells make excitatory synapses on cells in the visual association cortex (VAC). In addition, axons from cells in the PVC synapse on intermediate neurons whose axons then make inhibitory synapses (filled triangles) on other cells in the PVC. (See text for a description of the functional significance of these interactions.)

the **receptive field** of the cell. As long as the grating *moves* within the receptive field, the cell remains active.[37]

Once the receptive field of a cortical neuron has been identified, the characteristics of the grating are varied. Here, we shall consider only two characteristics—the orientation of the grating and its spatial frequency. **Figure 7.5a** shows a grating with a vertical orientation—light "fuzzy stripes" run up and down on a dark background. **Figures 7.5b** and **c** show gratings with the same number of fuzzy stripes, but oriented 45° and horizontally, respectively. These gradients differ in *orientation* but not in **spatial frequency**—i.e., they do not differ in the number of stripes per grating. Once a spatial frequency to which the cortical cell re-

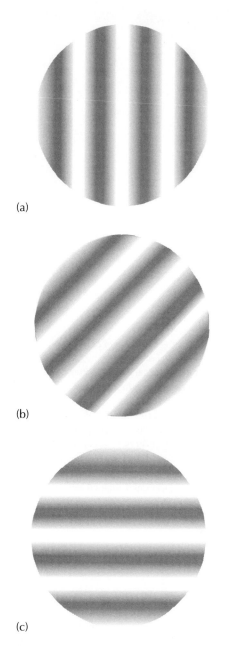

(a)

(b)

(c)

FIGURE 7.5 *Spatial frequencies of different orientations*
Stimuli provided by spatial-frequency gratings are commonly used to determine the receptive fields of cells in the visual cortex. The gratings shown here have the same spatial frequency—i.e., the same number of "fuzzy" stripes per degree of visual angle. However, they differ in their orientation—(a) 90°, (b) 45°, and (c) 0°.

sponds has been found, the orientation of the grating is varied. When the orientation of a grating is changed, individual cortical cells are most responsive to one orientation of stripes and become progressively less responsive as the stripes move away from that orientation. Thus different orientations of patterns of light on the retina produce differential responding of individual cortical neurons.

Individual cortical neurons are also sensitive to the spatial frequency of the grating. **Figure 7.6** shows a series of gratings that have the same orientation of stripes, but differ in their spatial frequency. As with orientation, a given cortical cell responds most strongly to a particular spatial frequency and becomes less responsive as the stripes depart from that frequency. Moreover, when the activity of neighboring cortical cells is monitored, they are found to respond maximally to the same spatial frequency, but to slightly different orientations. The primary visual cortex consists of clusters of cells within which individual cells respond maximally to the same spatial frequency, but to different orientations. As shown schematically in **Figure 7.7**, the cells in different clusters, which sample light in partially overlapping receptive fields, respond maximally to different spatial frequencies. The outcome of this arrangement is that the spatial frequency and orientation of light patterns are specified at many points in the observer's visual field.[38]

Selection of spatial-frequency clusters. We can get some sense of how the structure of the light selects clusters of cortical cells if we consider the arrangement of inhibitory connections. Suppose that a given cortical cell receives an input from a geniculate cell that was, in turn, activated by a ganglion cell in a particular place on the retina. Given that objects are extended in space, and that adjacent parts of the same object tend to have similar textures, neighboring cortical cells will—on the average—have similar geniculate inputs.[39] However, because neighboring cortical cells have inhibitory connections between them, the stimulation of one cell should somewhat decrease the response of its neighbors. Because of these inhibi-

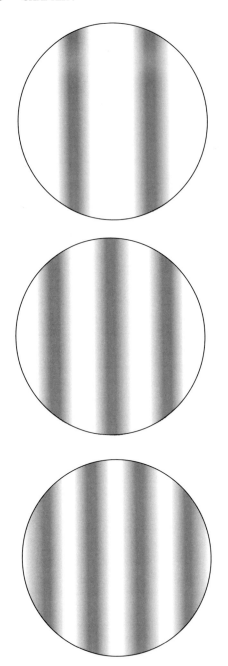

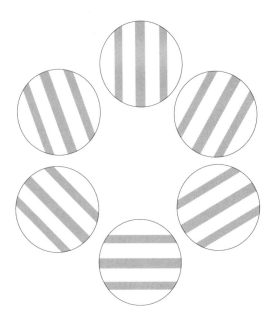

FIGURE 7.7 *Arrangement of cells within spatial-frequency columns*
The surface of the primary visual cortex contains clusters of cells, with all cells within a cluster responding to the same spatial frequency but at different orientations. Within a cluster, different cells in the same column respond to the same orientation of that spatial frequency. Cells in different clusters respond to different spatial frequencies. Indicated here is the arrangement within a cluster of the orientations to which the cells maximally respond. Several thousand such clusters exist in the human primary visual cortex, each specifying the spatial frequency and orientation of light within a region of the visual field.

FIGURE 7.6 *Different spatial frequencies—i.e, number of "fuzzy" stripes per degree of visual angle*
The spatial-frequency gratings shown here have the same orientation—90°. Such gratings stimulate cells in different spatial-frequency columns in the primary visual cortex.

tory interactions, the cortical cells with momentarily stronger geniculate inputs will become most active and the activity of neighboring cells will be suppressed. Thus, if one cortical cell is activated strongly by a stripe of a given orientation, and a neighboring cell is less strongly activated, the first cell will inhibit the activation of the second. Through activity-dependent mechanisms, the strengths of the inhibitory connections are selected in keeping with the competition between cortical neurons for responding to variations in the texture of light. The outcome of this competitive process is that neighboring cells within the same cluster come to respond maximally to different orientations of the same spatial frequency and neighboring clusters to different spatial frequencies.[40]

In this interpretation, the differential responsiveness to orientation within a spatial-frequency cluster, and to spatial frequency between clusters, arises as a by-product of the selection of inhibitory connections among cortical cells. The inhibitory neurons whose outputs are strengthened are those that synapse with simultaneously active cortical neurons. Since neighboring cortical neurons are activated by stimuli from neighboring parts of the visual field, and since neighboring parts of the visual field tend to be stimulated at the same time by light from the same object, and since neighboring parts of the same object tend to have similar patterns of light and dark, strong reciprocal inhibitory connections are formed between cortical cells that are activated by similar visual stimuli. In this way, the structure of light from the individual environment—acting on the neural substrate selected by the ancestral environment—produces clusters of cortical cells that respond maximally to different orientations of the same spatial frequency. This complex process, which is difficult to describe verbally because so many selections are going on at the same time, has been simulated with computers. **Figure 7.8** shows the result of one such simulation,[41] which illustrates the clustering of orientation-sensitive units as an emergent product of a selection process.[42]

The end products are of the selection process are clusters of cells that respond to different spatial frequencies. Consider a cortical cell (cell A) that receives a geniculate input activated by light from a fuzzy stripe in a grating. Under these circumstances, cell A tends to become active. However, if an adjacent stripe in the grating simultaneously stimulates a neighboring cortical cell (cell B), then B will also tend to become active and its activity will, in turn, reduce the activation of A because of an inhibitory connection from B to A. How much the response of cell A is reduced will depend on

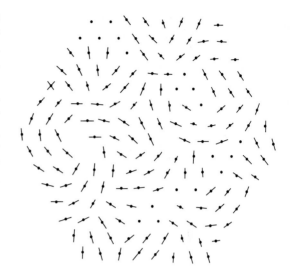

FIGURE 7.8   *Computer simulation of the formation of orientation clusters*
As the emergent outcome of interactions among units in an adaptive network that simulates interactions among neurons in the primary visual cortex, clusters form in which adjacent units respond to different, but similar, orientations of lines. The orientation to which a unit responded most strongly is indicated by lines whose midpoints are the locations of the units on the surface of the cortex. Units without lines did not develop orientation specificity by the end of training.
Source: From von der Malsburg, C. (1973). Self-organizing of orietation sensitive cells in the striate cortex. *Kybernetik, 14,* 85–100. Heidelberg, Germany: Springer-Verlag.

two factors—the degree to which B is activated by the adjacent stripe in the grating, and the strength of the inhibitory synapses from B to A. If both of these values are high, then the stripe *next* to the one activating cell A will strongly inhibit cell A. As a result, cell A would respond only to widely spaced stripes, or low spatial frequencies. Conversely, if the strength of the inhibitory synapses from B to A is low, or the adjacent stripe does not activate cell B strongly, then the activation of A by its stripe will not be inhibited. In this case, cell A will respond even when the stripes are closely spaced, i.e., to a higher spatial frequency. In short, through differences in the mutually inhibitory interactions among cortical cells, different clusters of cells are able to respond selectively to different spatial frequencies.[43] See **Figure 7.9** for a graphic representation of the processes by which different cortical cells respond to different spatial frequencies.[44]

Perceiving and awareness. The functioning of individual cortical cells to analyze portions of the visual field into their component spatial frequencies—i.e., into local patterns of light and dark—occurs without our being aware of it. Spatial frequencies help to specify objects and are important for that reason, not in themselves. Although we "see" them, we do not "know" that we do. Because individual spatial frequencies do not directly guide our verbal behavior, spatial-frequency analysis is inconsistent with the verbal bias that we bring to most situations. However, there is direct evidence at the physiological level,[45] and indirect evidence at the behavioral level,[46] that a local spatial-frequency analysis of the environment is being carried out.

It is apparently not important that we be able to discriminate the individual spatial frequencies that allow us to discriminate objects from one another.[47] The analysis of local parts of the visual field into their constituent spatial frequencies specifies the environment well enough to permit environment-behavior relations to be selected. What we perceive are the objects specified by the spatial frequencies, not the individual frequencies themselves.[48]

Illusions. Although the specific neural processes that allow us to appreciate the texture of light are not available to our awareness, the results of those processes nevertheless affect the way we see. Examine the light and dark grid pattern shown in **Figure 7.10**. Compare the brightness of the white space between any two black squares with the brightness of the white space at any intersection of four black squares. For most people, the first white space appears brighter than the white space at the intersections. Why is this so? The answer lies in

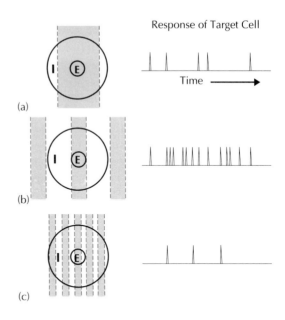

Response of Target Cell

Time ⟶

(a)

(b)

(c)

FIGURE 7.9   *The effects of different visual stimuli on the activation of target cells in primary visual cortex*

The inner circle indicates the portion of the receptive field of the target cell from which a visual stimulus has an excitatory (E) effect on the target cell. The outer circle represents the portion of the receptive field from which a stimulus has an inhibitory (I) effect on the target cell. Stimuli in this latter portion of the visual field activate adjacent cells in the primary visual cortex that exert lateral inhibitory effects on the response of the target cell. (a) A target cell that responds weakly to low spatial frequencies. A wide "stripe" activates both the target cell and adjacent cells whose lateral inhibitory connections suppress the response of the target cell. (b) A target cell that responds most strongly to intermediate spatial frequencies. One "stripe" activates the cell but the adjacent stripes, because they are widely spaced, do not activate adjacent cells that have lateral inhibitory connections with the target cell. (c) A target cell that responds weakly to high spatial frequencies. The many "stripes" that fall within the receptive field activate both the target cell and adjacent cells that laterally inhibit the response of the target cell. The above illustrates the operation of a so-called "center-on" cell, since a stimulus falling in the center of the receptive field activates the target cell. Other arrangements of excitatory and inhibitory connections can produce "center-off" cells and more complex responses, such as to the end of a "stripe."

FIGURE 7.10 *Illusory brightness contours produced by excitatory-inhibitory interactions*
Most viewers see faint gray squares in the white spaces at the intersections between the large black squares.

between two squares. Yet most of us see the former area as darker than the latter. How can such illusions occur if perceiving is the outcome of selection processes that enable us to see the world as it is—i.e., a world of objects? The answer comes when we recall that the ancestral environment selects biobehavioral processes that, *on the average over the long run*, benefit reproductive fitness. The same processes that occasionally produce illusions more often benefit perceiving the natural environment. The inhibitory processes producing the illusion in **Figure 7.10** enhance the discrimination of the boundaries between light and dark, and boundary detection facilitates the discrimination of objects. Light reflected from the brighter side of a boundary activates neurons that inhibit the neurons stimulated by light from the darker side of the boundary. The typical effect of these lateral inhibitory processes is, therefore, to increase our ability to detect variations in brightness between and within objects.[50]

Contributions of the ancestral and individual environments.   The sensory invariant that specifies the spatial frequency of light is selected by the combined actions of the ancestral and individual environments. A combination of genetically controlled and activity-dependent mechanisms determine the connectivity of the visual system. A particularly striking demonstration of the ability of the individual environment to organize connections in the brain comes from an experiment with young weasels. In this work, a surgical procedure caused retinal ganglion cells to synapse on cells in the *medial* geniculate nucleus instead of the lateral geniculate nucleus. Cells in the medial geniculate nucleus normally receive inputs from the auditory system, and their axons then project to the auditory cortex. After surgery, the structure of light was able to select connections in the auditory cortex using activity-dependent mechanisms. When the responses of cells in the auditory cortex were monitored, the "auditory" cells displayed differential sensitivity to the orientation of *visual* stimuli.[51] Thus cells in the primary auditory cortex are capa-

the net inhibitory effects exerted by cells responding to light from the sides of the white spaces. In the first case, the white space has white on only two sides. Light reflected from the two white sides somewhat inhibits activation of the cells stimulated by light from the central white space. Less inhibition is produced by light reflected from the two black sides. (A surface is seen as black if it reflects relatively little of the ambient light.) However, the white spaces at the intersections are surrounded by white space on *all four sides*. The total inhibition exerted by light from all four sides causes the white space in the intersection to appear less bright. Because the inhibitory effects are produced by the stimulation of cells to the *side* of the intersection, the phenomenon is known as **lateral inhibition**.[49]

The less bright appearance of the white area at the intersections is an **illusion**. That is, physical measurements show that the amount of light reflected from the area at the intersection of four squares is identical to the amount from the area

ble of analyzing local regions of the visual field into their spatial-frequency components when acted upon by the structure in the light. The individual visual environment exerts its effect through selecting the inhibitory connections that interconnect the cortical cells.[52]

In the individual environment of all species, the action of gravity causes most variations in light and dark to be oriented either vertically or horizontally. Objects, such as trees and houses, stand vertically because gravity would otherwise pull them down and cause them to lie horizontally. The proportion of cortical cells sensitive to various orientations is consistent with this feature of the environment. More cortical cells are activated by lines of vertical or horizontal orientation than by lines of oblique orientation.[53]

The relative sensitivity to particular spatial frequencies also reveals the combined effects of the ancestral and individual environments. Organisms that view the world from short distances—such as cats, which move close to the surface of the ground—are most sensitive to low spatial frequencies.[54] When an object is viewed from nearby, it has fewer variations in light and dark per degree of visual angle (i.e., a lower spatial frequency) than when it is viewed from a greater distance. Humans, who tend to view objects from a greater distance above the ground than cats, are sensitive to higher spatial frequencies. Finally, birds of prey—such as falcons, which see objects from great distances—are most sensitive to still higher spatial frequencies. (See **Figure 7.11** for the relative sensitivities of several species to different spatial frequencies.)

Differential sensitivity to different spatial frequencies occurs within species as well as between species. For example, human infants are maximally sensitive to lower spatial frequencies than adults. (See **Figure 7.12**.) Sensitivity is typically assessed by allowing the infant to view one grating for some time, and then later presenting the grating at the same time as one with a different spatial frequency. If the infant looks preferentially at one of the two gratings, then she has discriminated the difference in spatial frequencies. When tested, in-

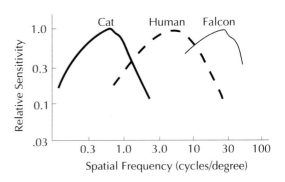

FIGURE 7.11   *Differing relative sensitivity to spatial frequencies in different species*
(Maximum sensitivity is defined as a sensitivity of 1.0.) Cats respond most to low, humans to intermediate, and falcons to high spatial frequencies.
Source: Adapted from De Valois & De Valois, 1988. *Spatial Vision.* New York: Oxford University Pess.

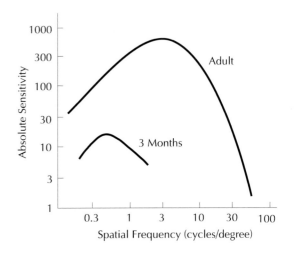

FIGURE 7.12   *Absolute sensitivity to spatial frequencies in infant and adult humans*
Three-month-old infants are generally less sensitive to spatial frequencies than adults, and are especially insensitive to higher spatial frequencies.
Source: Adapted from Aslin, R. N., & Smith, L. B. 1988. Perceptual development. In A. R. Rosenzweig & L. B. Smith (Eds.), *Annual Review of Psychology, 39,* 435–473. Adapted, with permission, from the *Annual Review of Psychology,* Volume 39, © 1988 by Annual Reviews Inc.

fants look more often at the new spatial-frequency grating; the observing response to the old grating has habituated.[55]

Experimental analysis. The sensitivity of cortical cells to orientation and spatial frequency can be altered experimentally as well as by the natural environment. Rearing kittens with goggles that permit only vertical lines to be presented to one eye and only horizontal lines to the other changes the responses of cells in the visual cortex.[56] When various orientations of stripes are later presented to such animals, the part of the cortex that received geniculate inputs activated by vertical lines contains a greater number of cells that respond only to vertical lines. Similarly, the part of the cortex that was activated by inputs from horizontal lines responds preferentially to horizontal lines. In another study, in which kittens' visual experience eliminated exposure to stripes altogether, cortical cells did not respond to stripes of any orientation, but only to symmetrical spots of light.[57] For even the "lowly" fly, exposure to variations in light and dark is required for the development of sensitivity to patterns.[58]

Visual experience also plays a critical role in selecting the cortical connections that mediate environment-environment relations in our close relative, the monkey. Monkeys deprived of experience with high spatial frequencies as infants show deficits in their responsiveness to those frequencies as adults.[59] Further, human infants who suffer blurred vision because of astigmatism have deficits in perceiving high spatial frequencies when they become adults.[60] Since high spatial frequencies (i.e., closely spaced alternations in light and dark) are required to discriminate printed letters, the failure to detect astigmatism and other visual problems early in life may adversely affect a person's later ability to read.[61]

There are many experiments supporting the notion that seeing in humans has much in common with seeing in nonhuman organisms. When pigeons are taught to discriminate between visually presented letters of the alphabet, the errors—such as "confusing" **O** with **Q** or **P** with **R**—are the same as those made by children first learning the alphabet or by adults shown letters for very brief time intervals.[62] Similarly, procedures known to affect other types of discriminations also affect discriminations between letters of the alphabet. When a fading procedure is used to train letter discriminations in children, the discrimination is facilitated. For example, if the portion of a letter that distinguishes it from similar letters is printed in red ink (e.g., the "leg" that distinguishes **R** from **P**), and then is gradually changed to the black ink in which the rest of the letter is printed, children with reading difficulties come to discriminate the letters more easily.[63]

Selection of a Polysensory Invariant

Environment-environment relations are not restricted to correlations between events within a single sensory channel, such as the spatial-frequency channel. Correlations between environmental events in *different* sensory channels are referred to as **polysensory invariants**. Here, we consider a *poly*sensory invariant involving the relation between auditory and visual stimuli.

We have already encountered several cases that exemplify the selection of polysensory invariants. For one, when an object to the side of an infant emits a sound, the infant's head turns toward the sound, and increases the likelihood that he will observe light from the object.[64] For another, an infant presented with two television monitors—each displaying a talking face, but only one of which is speaking in synchrony with the auditory stimulus—looks at the face whose movements are synchronized with the sound.[65] In both cases, the invariant relation was between properties of sound and light—the intensity and temporal pattern of sound with the intensity and temporal pattern of light.

The correlation between these environmental events is relatively constant over evolutionary time; sound almost always arrives first at the ear closest to the sounding object, and turning toward the ear that first hears the sound most often allows the object to be seen. Because of this constancy, selection by the ancestral environment can contribute directly to the selection of a polysensory invariant involving sound and sight. Indeed, evidence of such a polysensory invariant appears in very young organisms without benefit of extensive individual experience.[66] However, just as with sensory invariants, the selection of polysensory invariants is the joint expression of the selecting effects of the ancestral and individual environments. Natural selection produces the proximity between neurons that permits individual selection to strengthen neural connections through activity-dependent mechanisms.

To analyze the joint contribution of the ancestral and individual environments to the selection of polysensory invariants, nonhuman animals are used for greater experimental rigor. The owl, an animal that hunts its prey under the low-light conditions that exist at night, must integrate visual and auditory stimuli if it is to accurately localize its quarry. Even without substantial experience, the young owl—like the human infant—tends to turn its head toward the source of sound in its environment; i.e., to localize sound.[67]

The owl confronts a more formidable localization problem than the infant, however. The owl moves in a three-dimensional world (i.e., it flies), the light levels are low, and its prey is usually moving when it makes a sound. For the owl to localize its prey accurately under these demanding conditions, neural activity arising from its visual and auditory systems must be integrated in the brain. This integration takes place in polysensory cells that are found in the inferior collicular nuclei, located in the hindbrain. When the auditory and visual inputs to a polysensory neuron are *both* active—making it more likely that the polysensory neuron is activated—the connections between the polysensory neuron and its inputs are strengthened. Different combinations of visual and auditory stimuli activate different combinations of polysensory cells, which then specify the location of the prey.

The selection of these neural connections is further complicated by the fact that, when the owl is growing, the pattern of activity specifying location must change to compensate for the changes produced by growth. As the owl's head grows larger, the distance between its ears increases; this changes the relation between the prey's location and the sound's intensity and time of arrival at the owl's two ears. The growth of the owl's head also increases the distance between its eyes and, therefore, the places on the retina stimulated by light from the prey.

Auditory changes similar to those produced by growth can be simulated in the laboratory by plugging one ear of a young owl, reducing the intensity of sound in that ear. Owls with one plugged ear develop an altered pattern of activity in their polysensory cells, but one that accurately specifies the location of sound.[68] When the earplug is removed, the pattern of activity specifies location incorrectly at first, but then adjusts to respecify location if the owl is less than 40 weeks old. After 40 weeks, the time at which growth normally stops, readjustment no longer occurs. The effect of the individual environment on the selection of sensory and polysensory invariants is commonly restricted to circumscribed time periods called **sensitive** or **critical periods**. The specific genetic, neural, and behavioral processes that determine sensitive periods are beyond the scope of this book, but they are often related to factors that affect growth,[69] and probably reflect the time periods during which inhibitory connections can be modified by activity-dependent mechanisms.

PERCEIVING REGULARITIES

The correlation between some properties of auditory and visual stimuli permits the selection of those environment-environment relations known as polysensory invariants. The relation between the time that a sound arrives at the two ears and the location at which the sounding object can be seen is relatively constant over evolutionary time because of the constancy of the physics of sound and light. However, other relations between stimuli are relatively constant only within the lifetime of an individual. Thus the sound and sight of a *particular* barking dog may be reliably related to one another and, if their conjunction is experienced often enough, consitutes an environment-environment relation. Relations of that sort select **polysensory regularities**.

Polysensory regularities are especially important for complex behavior. They are selected as a result of arbitrary but nevertheless reliable relations among environmental events that are specific to an individual's experience. These environment-environment relations are relatively constant within a local portion of the environment, but may vary from one environment to the next. That is, polysensory relations may be conditional on the value of other environmental events. An important human example of such relations is the relation between the sight of an object and the sound of its "name." There is no necessary relation between the sight of a dog and the sounds produced when the following words are spoken—"dog," "perro," "chien," or "hund." The relation of one of these sounds to the sight of a dog is quite reliable within a given verbal environment, but varies from one verbal community to the next. Saying "dog" is reinforced in the United States; saying "perro" is reinforced in Venezuela (or Miami for that matter); and so forth.

Polysensory Regularities

As an example of a polysensory regularity, consider an organism localizing *itself* in an environment. At first glance, this resembles the earlier situation in which an object was localized in relation to the organism, but on further consideration, it differs fundamentally. The laws of physics insure a constant relation between the properties of the sound and light reaching our senses from an object as a function of the object's location. However, there are no comparable invariances between the stimuli from the environment and the location of an individual. *Within any single environment—*

e.g., a room in your house—you regularly sense certain stimuli depending on your location. Between different environments, however, there are no specific stimuli that reliably specify your location. Consider an animal, or a young child, that is learning its way around a new environment. In such a situation, the learner has no "map" to consult. Maps, when they exist at all, are the outcomes of selection processes and are not available to guide the learner's behavior when he is first exposed to an unfamiliar environment. Organisms have no absolute frame of reference—no "organ" that indicates latitude and longitude, and directly specifies location, or place.[70]

Place learning. Each location in a navigable environment is specified by a unique *combination* of stimuli. From any given position in the environment, our senses are distinctively stimulated—our eyes by particular combinations of spatial frequencies and wavelengths, our ears by particular combinations of auditory stimuli, and so on. As our position changes, so do these combinations of stimuli. The environment uniquely specifies our location to the extent that available stimuli give rise to unique patterns of neural activity, and that we are sensitive to these patterns. In mammals, integration of the activity initiated by combinations of stimuli occurs in the sensory and polysensory association areas of the cortex, and is critically influenced by environment-initiated activity in another brain structure, the hippocampus.[71] See **Figure 7.13** for an overview of the neural circuitry relating the hippocampus and association cortex.

Several pieces of evidence indicate that the hippocampus plays a crucial role in the integration of neural activity in sensory association cortex. If a rat is placed in a tank of water and allowed to swim about until it finds a slightly submerged platform on which it can rest, it rapidly learns the location of the platform.[72] No matter where the rat is placed into the tank, it swims rather directly toward the location of the submerged platform. The rat cannot see the submerged platform because the water has been made opaque by the addition of

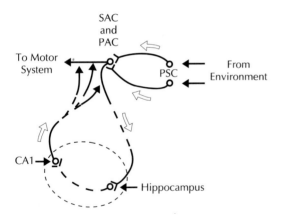

FIGURE 7.13 *Schematic diagram of the relation of sensory and polysensory association cortex (SAC and PAC) to the hippocampus*
Stimuli from various sensory modalities initiate activity in primary sensory cortex (PSC), such as the primary visual cortex. Axons from cells in the PSC communicate that activity to motor systems of the brain and to cells in SAC and PAC. These cells, in turn, send axons to motor systems and to pathways that lead after several synapses to the hippocampus. Within the hippocampus, after interactions among cells within that structure, CA1 hippocampal cells give rise to axons that diffusely project to cells in SAC and PAC after several synapses. Thus the multi-channel sensory input into the hippocampus is diffusely projected back on the association cortex from which those inputs arose. The diffuse feedback from the hippocampus is postulated to strengthen connections to recently active SAC and PAC neurons.

a substance, but it can see landmarks in the room containing the tank. Since behavior is guided by stimuli that immediately precede the reinforced response, the rat's performance tells us that the combinations of stimuli that specify its location and that of the submerged platform have come to guide the appropriate swimming movements. If, however, the hippocampus is nonfunctional due to surgical damage or chemical treatment, the rat can no longer learn to navigate efficiently about the tank. Normal **place learning** is prevented.[73]

Configural conditioning, or patterning.   Further experimental work indicates that the selection of polysensory regularities other than those involved in place learning is dependent on a functioning hippocampus. Consider a rat confronted with the following task: When a light and tone occur together (a simultaneous compound stimulus), lever pressing is reinforced with food. However, when the light or tone component occurs alone, lever pressing has no consequences. Under these circumstances, rats acquire the response when the compound stimulus is presented, but lever pressing is ultimately extinguished when the light or tone component is presented alone. This type of discrimination task, which is known as **configural conditioning**, is not acquired without a functioning hippocampus.[74] Since the light-tone combination guides behavior differently from either the light or tone alone, some set of neural events must differentiate the joint occurrence of the light and tone from their separate occurrences.[75] In summary, a functioning hippocampus appears to be necessary to select polysensory regularities in mammals, whether the stimuli activate sensory channels within the same sensory modality, as in place learning, or channels in different sensory modalities, as in configural discriminations.[76]

Interpretation of Polysensory Regularities

What biobehavioral processes implement the selection of polysensory regularities? How does the hippocampus contribute to the selection of this class of environment-environment relations?

Neuroanatomical studies indicate that neurons in the sensory association cortex send axons that ultimately initiate activity in the hippocampus. Once these axons enter the hippocampus, interactions occur among the hippocampal neurons; these interactions are also affected by inhibitory neurons within the hippocampus. The final neurons in this chain of activity are the so-called CA1 neurons, whose axons constitute the major output of the hippocampus. The CA1 axons initiate activity in multi-synaptic pathways that project diffusely back *to the very same regions of association cortex that gave rise to the inputs to the hippocampus.* Because of this neuroanatomical arrangement, interactions among hippocampal cells are in a position to modulate the functioning of cells in the sensory association cortex. (Refer to **Figure 7.13** for a summary of these neuroanatomical relations.[77])

The interactions within the hippocampus that affect the activity of CA1 cells are not fully understood; additional experimental analysis is required. However, the nature of the neural circuitry is such that several types of integration are neurally plausible.[78] For example, the activity of CA1 cells could reflect *changes* in the activity level of the polysensory inputs to the hippocampus, *co-occurrences* of multiple polysensory inputs to the hippocampus, or *novel* patterns of polysensory input to the hippocampus.[79] The important point is that, whatever the nature of the interactions in the hippocampus, they are in a position to affect synaptic efficacies in the sensory association cortex by means of the pathways originating from the CA1 neurons. Because the diffuse output from the hippocampus to the polysensory association areas is initiated by neural activity in those same association areas, the feedback from the hippocampus necessarily occurs in close temporal contiguity with neural activity in the sensory association areas.

What we propose here is that the diffuse feedback from the hippocampus has an effect on synaptic efficacies in sensory association cortex that is functionally equivalent to the effect of the diffuse reinforcing system on the motor association cortex.[80] That is, diffuse hippocampal feedback strengthens the synaptic efficacies between coactive cells. If this is the case, then the most reliably affected synapses are those whose activity is correlated with the output of the CA1 cells. For example, suppose that a tone and light occur together, and that their co-occurrence causes a hippocampal output. The change in the diffusely projected output of the hippocampus would increase synaptic

efficacies between the cells in the visual and auditory cortices and the tone-light polysensory cells in sensory association cortex.[81] The cumulative effect of this process is to strengthen the connections from auditory and visual cells that converge on polysensory cells. These polysensory cells then become more strongly polysensory; i.e., they become reliably activated by the co-occurrence of stimuli from different sensory channels.

For example, in the configural conditioning experiment during which reinforcers occurred after the tone-light compound stimulus, some cells in polysensory cortex to which connections are strengthened become, functionally, "tone-light" cells. The result of this selection process is to change the connectivity to cells in sensory association cortex so that their activity reflects the structure of the environment—here, the correlation between tone and light. In short, diffuse feedback from the hippocampus to the sensory association cortex selects connections that reflect the regularities in the individual environment of the learner. As the correlations between environmental events change, the connectivity of the sensory association cortex is altered to reflect those changes. That is, new polysensory regularities are selected. As one investigator put it: ". . . what a [neuron] does is temporary and . . . , in fact, its role in the network depends on its history in that network."[82]

Stimulus-selection network. The relation between cells in polysensory association cortex and the hippocampus may be simulated with a **stimulus-selection network**, which selects connections that mediate environment-environment relations. To distinguish a stimulus-selection network from the previously described network that selects connections mediating environment-behavior relations (see Chapter 2), the earlier network is designated a **response-selection network**. The outputs of units in the stimulus-selection network serve as the inputs to the response-selection network. The relations between these two networks will be described in greater detail shortly.

Figure 7.14a shows a simplified stimulus-selection network. This network consists of two input units, which represent neurons in primary sensory cortex for different sensory channels, and one interior unit, which represents polysensory neurons in sensory association cortex. An output of the polysensory unit goes to a change-detection circuit that simulates the action of the hippocampus. When a change occurs in the input to the hippocampal circuit, the diffusely projecting output of the circuit is fed back to the polysensory units. Just as in the response-selection network, the feedback acts as a neuromodulator to increase the connection weights between all recently active units.[83]

Figure 7.14b indicates the simulated increase in activation of the polysensory unit by the simultaneous stimulation of the two input units representing different sensory channels. If the two channels represent visual and auditory stimuli, then the polysensory unit functions as a tone-light unit. The increased connection strengths to the tone-light unit mirror the environment-environment relation to which the stimulus-selection network was exposed, and exemplify the selection of a polysensory regularity. Once these connections have been strengthened, the inputs to the response-selection network indicate not only the presence of a tone or a light, but also the presence of a tone-light compound stimulus. The polysensory unit thus provides a basis for the acquisition of configural conditioning.[84]

Relation of the stimulus- and response-selection networks. The parallel between the functioning of the stimulus-selection and response-selection networks is clear. In both cases, a diffusely projecting signal acts to strengthen all connections between recently active units.[85] The cumulative effect of this process differentially strengthens certain connections—those that reflect the relations between environmental events, and between environmental and behavioral events, *in the experience of the individual organism.* In the stimulus-selection network, the relations between environmental events select connections between stimulus units

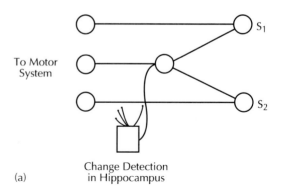

(a)

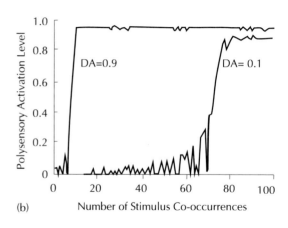

(b)

FIGURE 7.14 *Network architecture and simulation results illustrating the functioning of a stimulus-selection network for the selection of polysensory regularities*

(a) An adaptive network whose architecture contains two primary sensory units (S_1 and S_2) converging on a polysensory unit that, in turn, is connected with the hippocampus. (b) Simulation results show increases in the levels of activation of the polysensory unit with repeated simultaneous presentations of S_1 and S_2. The change in the activation of the polysensory unit is shown for two different amounts of dopamine (DA) at CA1 synapses. The source of DA is the ventral tegmental area, the origin of the reinforcing signal for the response-selection network. If S_1 were activated by light and S_2 by tone, then the polysensory unit would function as a light-tone unit and become reliably active only when both stimuli occurred together.

and polysensory units when they are coactive; i.e., when the stimulus inputs occur together. In the response-selection network, response-reinforcer relations select connections between the input units to the network and the response units that are active when the reinforcer is presented. The net effect of the stimulus-selection and response-selection networks is to change the connectivity of the overall selection network to mirror the correlations between environment-environment and environment-behavior events, respectively.[86]

In the living organism, the selection processes simulated by the stimulus- and response-selection networks—and postulated to occur in the sensory and motor association cortices, respectively—must function as a coordinated whole. What is the relationship between the two neural systems, and what does it imply for the relationship between the stimulus- and response-selection networks that are intended to simulate them?

Physiological analysis. Physiological and neuroanatomical evidence indicates that the relationship is intimate. The CA1 hippocampal cells—whose activity determines the output of the hippocampus to the sensory association cortex—are activated by the excitatory neurotransmitter glutamate released by other hippocampal neurons.[87] Next to these glutaminergic synapses are axons from other neurons that release dopamine, *and these dopaminergic axons arise from cells in the ventral tegmental area (VTA)—the source of the reinforcement system for the motor association cortex.*[88] The reinforcement system that is thought to select connections in the motor association cortex is also in a position to modulate the selection of connections in sensory association cortex!

Recording electrodes monitoring the activity of the CA1 hippocampal cells indicate that dopamine does indeed modulate the response of CA1 cells to their inputs from other cells in the hippocampus.[89] Under the conditions of the experiment, the activity level of CA1 cells was found to vary somewhat from moment to moment. After an atypically high level of activity occurred in a CA1 cell, the experi-

menters introduced a small amount of dopamine into the input synapses of that cell. After several pairings between a higher-than-average activity level and dopamine, the activity level of the CA1 cell increased still further. That is, the cells that synapsed on the CA1 cell showed an enhanced ability to activate the CA1 cell. The study was carried out with an isolated slice of hippocampal tissue—an *in vitro* preparation. If dopamine was not presented immediately after the heightened CA1 activity, no increase was observed. In short, the activity level of CA1 cells was reinforced by the immediate presentation of dopamine. Whatever interactions in the hippocampus normally affect the activity of CA1 cells, the effects are modulated by the introduction of dopamine from the VTA reinforcing system into the synapse. Selection in both the sensory and motor association cortices appears to be coordinated by a common reinforcing system.

The effect of a coordinated reinforcing system on the selection of connections in sensory association cortex may be summarized as follows. When the level of dopamine in the CA1 synapses is at the resting or baseline level, a relatively weak signal is diffusely projected to the sensory association cortex, and polysensory connections are therefore only weakly selected. In contrast, when a reinforcing stimulus occurs—i.e., when the VTA system is activated—the diffusely projected feedback from the CA1 cells is amplified, and polysensory connections are now selected more strongly. Thus if there are regularities in the relation between environmental events, synaptic efficacies between simultaneously active neurons in sensory association cortex are somewhat strengthened. But, if these regularities are followed by reinforcing stimuli, then the synaptic efficacies are much more intensely strengthened.[90]

Implications of stimulus selection. According to the above interpretation, mere exposure to the co-occurrence of environmental events selects polysensory regularities to some degree. However, exposure supplemented by reinforcing consequences for responding in that environment selects polysensory regularities more strongly.

Latent learning.   Consistent with this account, rats that were allowed simply to roam about a maze later learned the maze more rapidly when food was given as a reinforcer, compared to animals not given earlier exposure to the maze.[91] However, this facilitating effect—which is known as **latent learning**—is neither large nor robust.[92] The efficient selection of environment-environment as well as environment-behavior relations requires the occurrence of reinforcing stimuli.

Equivalence classes.   The selection of polysensory regularities by the biobehavioral processes that are simulated by a stimulus-selection network also provides a basis for the formation of equivalence classes. During a contextual discrimination when the sample and comparison stimuli are occurring together, a polysensory regularity can be selected that mirrors the correlation between these environmental events. In the stimulus-selection network, the polysensory regularity is represented by interior units that are activated by the joint occurrence of the sample and comparison stimuli, and whose outputs are available to guide responding. That is, these units are components of the selected environment-environment relation. Over time, depending on individual selection history, patterns of unit activity corresponding to many polysensory regularities are selected and are then available to serve as components of many environment-behavior relations. According to this view, equivalence classes do not depend on verbal behavior; instead, equivalence classes and verbal behavior both depend on a neuroanatomy that permits the selection of complex polysensory regularities.[93]

Perceptual learning.   The contribution that the consequences of responding make to the selection of polysensory regularities is demonstrated by other experimental findings. Animals that are passively carried through the environment—rather than allowed to move "under their own power"—show deficits in the polysensory regularities that

are selected. In one well-known study, a visually naive kitten was permitted to walk around the periphery of a small circular arena whose walls were painted with stripes. A second visually naive kitten was restrained in a sling and passively moved through the same environment in a manner identical to that of the first. Thus both kittens sensed the same sequence of environmental stimuli, but for the second kitten the stimuli were not coordinated with its own movements. When the two kittens were later tested, the second kitten showed many deficiencies in perceiving the relation between itself and objects.[94] Although mere exposure to environmental regularities may select some environment-environment relations, exposure is much more effective when the organism behaves and experiences the consequences of its behavior.[95]

EFFECTS OF ENVIRONMENT-ENVIRONMENT RELATIONS

Selection by the ancestral environment produces an organism that can appreciate the relation between environmental events *after* it has been acted upon by the selecting effects of its individual environment. Some environment-environment relations are constant over evolutionary time and involve only a single sensory channel. Such relations select sensory invariants; e.g., spatial-frequency clusters. Other relations are also constant over evolutionary time but involve multiple sensory channels. These relations select polysensory invariants; e.g., localization of sights and sounds.

Finally, many environment-environment relations are stable only within the lifetime of an individual. Such relations select sensory and polysensory regularities. Polysensory regularities integrate environmental events that produce activity in different sensory channels and that, in combination, specify objects and "tie together" the diverse stimuli correlated with their occurrence. These stimuli include both the discriminative stimuli provided by objects and the contextual stimuli provided by the environments in which the objects appear. The selection of polysensory regularities that integrate the sight of an object with the sound and sight of the word for the object is crucial for verbal behavior.[96]

For perceptual invariants, the biobehavioral processes that implement selection involve relatively local interactions among cells in primary sensory cortex. For perceptual regularities, the biobehavioral processes that implement selection arise from more widely distributed interactions among cells in sensory and polysensory association cortex. In the latter case, the integration of activity appears to require feedback from the hippocampus, and the intensity of this feedback is modulated by the same reinforcement system that selects the connections in motor association cortex that mediate environment-behavior relations.

Perceptual Invariants and Regularities Guide Behavior

The selection of neural connections that are sensitive to environment-environment relations allows an extremely rich and varied combination of environmental events to contribute to environment-behavior relations. A sense of the complexity of behavioral guidance is provided by studies of persons who have suffered damage to sensory association areas.[97] For some of these persons, behavior is guided by only simple features of the environment, e.g., the color of an object. In other cases, complex features guide behavior, but the person no longer appreciates relatively simple features; e.g., he can identify an object as a chair, but cannot describe its color. Still others may recognize parts of an object, but not the object as a whole.[98]

Consider the following description of a neuropsychological patient shown a picture in a magazine.

His responses here were very curious. His eyes would dart from one thing to another, picking up tiny features, individual features, as they had done with my face. A striking brightness, a colour, a shape would arrest his attention and elicit comment—but

in no case did he get the scene-as-a-whole. He failed to see the whole, seeing only details, which he spotted like blips on a radar screen. . . . [At the end of the examination] He . . . started to look around for his hat. He reached out his hand and took hold of his wife's head, tried to lift it off, to put it on. He had apparently mistaken his wife for a hat! His wife looked as if she was used to such things."[99]

Perhaps some similarity between the color of his wife's hair and the color of his hat had prompted the man's bizarre behavior. In any case, damage to his sensory association areas had left intact his behavioral responses to individual sensory events, but prevented the integration of neural responses into the patterns of activity that normally specify objects.[100]

Selectionism and constructionism. This chapter began by exposing the differences between the approach of direct perception, which holds that the environment is sufficiently complex and stable to provide stimuli that specify the environment, and constructionism, which holds that the environment consists of an impoverished and chaotic array of stimuli that must be supplemented by inferred processes if a meaningful and orderly world is to be perceived. The experimental analysis and interpretation of perceiving encourages us to believe that relations between environmental events select connections in the nervous system that are sufficient to specify the world in which we live. Of course, much remains to be done before that belief may be comfortably accepted, but so far we have encountered no difficulties that demonstrate that perceiving is beyond the reach of basic biobehavioral processes of selection.

Construction as a product of selection. There is no doubt that the outcome of perceiving *appears as if* it involved construction. We catch a brief glimpse of part of a friend's face and recognize the friend; we see only part of an object and recognize the entire object. From a selectionist perspective, any "construction" is a *product* of the biobehavioral processes involved in perceiving, and not the cause of perceiving. From an earlier discussion of concept formation in adaptive networks, we know that only a subset of the stimuli with which a network was trained is required for the network to generate the appropriate response. No single stimulus must be present, and many combinations of stimuli are adequate to specify its output.

In addition to behavioral responses, adaptive networks "construct" environment-environment relations—i.e., "percepts"—when their guiding stimuli are not complete. For example, in another computer simulation a network that had undergone selection with an input pattern was then presented with only portions of the trained pattern. The question of interest was: Will a partial input pattern produce a complete "perceptual response" from the network? The input pattern used in training corresponded to the pattern of light and dark in a picture of a person's face. The output pattern that the network was trained to produce was the same pattern of light and dark that occurred in the input pattern. Speaking nontechnically, the network was trained to "recognize" the face.[101]

The faces in the left column of **Figure 7.15** illustrate the incomplete or degraded input patterns that were presented to the adaptive network after it had been trained with complete input patterns for each of the two faces. The right column contains the corresponding output patterns that were "constructed" by the adaptive network from the degraded input patterns. Whether it was presented with an unclear picture or a picture with a portion missing, the adaptive network "reconstructed" outputs that closely resembled the complete input pattern with which it had been trained. "Reconstruction" is an *emergent* property of the functioning of an adaptive neural network after selection; it is a by-product of lower-level selection processes, and an effect rather than a cause of perceiving.[102]

The production by trained neural networks of relatively complete perceptual regularities from only partial inputs should not be overinterpreted. It does not mean that they have somehow transcended their selection histories. If these networks, which were trained with only frontal views of faces, were presented with side views—even complete side views—their performance would be very poor. Indeed, they would not "recognize" the faces at all. For the networks to "recognize" side views, they would have to be trained with side views. After such training, they would then "recognize" even partial side views.

Studies using neuropsychological subjects with damage to their sensory and polysensory association areas provide insights into the reconstructive functions of these areas. In one study, subjects with damage to *one* hemisphere were presented with sequences of 4 to 6 letters, with their eyes fixated at the middle of the visual display.[103] The display was presented so briefly (100 ms) that their eyes were unable to move before it vanished. Because of the relation between the two hemi-retinas and the visual cortex, one half of each sequence initiated activity in the undamaged hemisphere and the other half in the damaged hemisphere. If the letter sequence made up a familiar word, then the subjects reported seeing the entire word. However, if the letter sequence did not make up a word, the subjects reported seeing only the letters that initiated activity in the undamaged hemisphere. In short, a pattern of neural activity that specified the remaining letters in the sequence was reconstructed only when the sequence had been a part of the learner's selection history.[104]

As another example, recordings were made from cells in the sensory association cortex of sheep while pictures of the faces of various other sheep were presented.[105] Certain cells responded reliably to pictures of sheep faces—particularly familiar or salient (e.g., large-horned) sheep. However, when the pictures were inverted so that the same faces were upside down, the cells no longer responded. The sheep had not had a selection history that included experience with upside-down faces. In monkeys, however, functionally similar cells in the sensory association cortex *do* respond to upside-down faces. Monkeys, in contrast to sheep, are likely to have a selection history that includes upside-down faces—monkeys hang from tree branches.[106] The perceptual invariants and

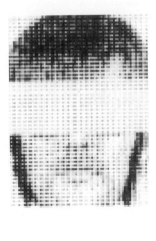 

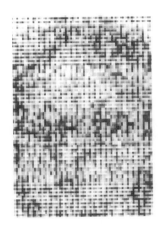 

FIGURE 7.15 *Simulation of the ability of a neural network to "construct" an output pattern from an incomplete input pattern after the connection strengths between units within the network are changed by selection*

Input patterns corresponding to clear and complete pictures of these two faces were presented to the input units of the network during training. Connections within the network were selected so that the network produced the same pattern on its output units; i.e., the network "recognized" the faces. (a) In the top pair of pictures, the much degraded pattern on the left was applied to the input units of the trained network. The network "constructed" the more complete pattern shown on the right. This simulates recognizing a familiar person's face in dim light. (b) In the bottom pair of pictures, the input pattern on the left contains only a portion of the trained pattern. Nevertheless, the network "constructed" the more complete pattern shown on the right. This simulates recognizing a familiar person's face from only a partial view of the face.

Source: Adapted from Kohonen, T. (1977). *Associative memory–a system-theoretical approach.* New York: Springer-Verlag.

regularities selected by consistent relations between environmental stimuli guide behavior in wondrous ways, such as by reconstructing neural patterns that were originally selected by complete arrays of stimuli. However, the guidance they provide reflects the history of selection.

STUDY AIDS

Technical Terms

environment-environment relation
perceptual invariant
perceptual regularity
imprinting
direct perception
constructionism
photopigments
retina
optic tract
superior collicular nuclei
lateral geniculate nuclei
activity-dependent mechanisms
sensory channels
visual association cortex
polymodal association cortex
optic nerve
optic chiasm
fovea
corpus callosum
saccadic eye movements (or saccades)
inhibitory neuron
inhibitory neurotransmitter
excitatory neurotransmitter
grating
receptive field
spatial frequency
lateral inhibition
illusion
polysensory invariant
sensitive (or critical) period
polysensory regularity
place learning

configural conditioning
stimulus-selection network
response-selection network
latent learning

Text Questions

1. The chapter is concerned with two major classes of environment-environment relations—perceptual invariants and perceptual regularities, of which polysensory invariants and polysensory regularities are important subclasses. What is meant by an environment-environment relation? In general, what is the difference between the selection histories of perceptual invariants and regularities? Give examples that illustrate each of these classes of environment-environment relations.

2. What is direct perception, and how does it differ from the constructionist view of perceiving? Discuss some perceptual phenomenon from the perspectives of both direct perception and constructionism. What are the implications of the computer simulations at the end of the chapter for this distinction?

3. Describe the major neuroanatomical structures of the visual system in the order in which they are activated by visual stimuli.

4. Regarding perceiving visual texture: (a) Describe the procedures used to determine the stimuli to which individual cortical cells are most responsive. Include the terms receptive field, grating, electrode, and spatial frequency in your answer. (b) Cortical cells are grouped in clusters. What do cells within a cluster have in common, and how do they differ from cells in other clusters? Referring to lateral inhibitory interactions, indicate the process by which spatial-frequency clusters form.

5. How can the occurrence of illusions be reconciled with the view that selection processes generally produce adaptation to the demands of the environment?

6. Describe evidence that illustrates the contributions of both natural selection and individual

selection to perceiving, using sensitivity to spatial frequencies as an example.

7. Using the example of specifying the location of prey in the owl, describe evidence which illustrates that both natural selection and selection by the individual environment produce this polysensory invariant.

8. The hippocampus plays a crucial role in the selection of polysensory *regularities*. (a) Describe evidence that supports this view, using localization of oneself in space and configural conditioning as examples. (b) Indicate the process whereby connections to cells in sensory association cortex are strengthened to produce sensitivity to polysensory regularities.

9. Describe the major features and interrelations between the stimulus-selection and response-selection components of the selection network that simulates the acquisition of environment-environment and environment-behavior relations, respectively. Does selection occur independently in the two components?

Discussion Questions

10. Comment on the following: If the environment contains enough information to tell the "mind" when to construct a complete "percept" from incomplete sensory information, then the environment contains enough information to construct a complete "percept" in the first instance.

11. Comment on the relative contribution of experimental analyses at the behavioral and physiological levels to the interpretation of environment-environment relations and environment-behavior relations.

12. What does this statement in the text mean: "What we perceive are the objects specified by spatial frequencies, not the individual frequencies themselves." Refer to the verbal bias in your answer.

ENDNOTES

1. We prefer to speak of "perceiving" rather than "perception" to emphasize the *processes* involved in responding to complex arrays of stimuli. We resist using nouns such as "perception" or "percept" for the same reasons that we avoided the use of nouns to designate processes in the earlier discussion of "attention." The emphasis on process is especially important because perceiving—by its very definition—involves *complex* stimuli. And, as with all complexity, selectionism holds that perceiving can only be understood by reference to the *history* of interaction of individual organisms and species with their environments; cf. Goldiamond, 1962. Without an extended history of selection by the ancestral and individual environments, perceiving cannot occur: Complex relations are selected when there are complex selection histories.

Some have been especially critical of efforts to study perceiving using simple stimuli. Regarding the briefly presented, relatively simple stimuli displayed on computer monitors in much laboratory research on perceiving, Ulrich Neisser (1976) has wryly observed: "Such displays come very close to not existing at all. ... Most psychologists do not believe in ghosts, but they often experiment with stimuli that appear just as mysteriously," pp. 35, 41. Commenting on a survey of 59 laboratory tasks intended to study complex behavior, he continued in the same vein: "... the only [tasks] with any shred of ecological validity are playing chess and looking at the moon. ... A satisfactory theory of human cognition can hardly be established by experiments that provide inexperienced subjects with brief opportunities to perform novel and meaningless tasks," pp. 7–8. We would note, however, that, whereas the *establishment* of complex stimuli as guides to behavior does require an extensive selection history with respect to those stimuli, less complex stimuli—assuming that appropriate precautions are observed—may be employed with great profit to identify the products of that selection history.

2. cf. Campbell, 1966, 1974.

3. Peterson, 1960. For a review, see Hoffman & Ratner, 1973.

4. Bruner, 1988.

5. See Gibson, J. J., 1950, 1966, 1979. See also Brunswik, 1956; Campbell, 1966; Costall, 1984; and Turvey & Shaw, 1979.

6. Mace, 1977.

7. The correlation is not perfect, of course: A balloon that is being inflated also occupies an increasingly larger portion of the visual field but without an appreciable

change in its distance from the eye. It is pertinent to note, however, that under restricted viewing conditions that eliminate other sources of stimulation, an expanding balloon is perceived as coming nearer rather than as expanding; Ittelson, 1952. This result likely reflects the greater frequency of rigid as opposed to deformable objects in the selection history of the observer.

8.   cf. Hall, 1991.

9.   Julesz, 1980.

10.   De Valois & De Valois, 1988.

11.   Gibson, E. J., 1982, 1988; Gibson, E. J. & Spelke, 1983; Spelke, 1976; and Aslin & Smith, 1988.

12.   Fish, insects, and birds show sensitivity into the ultraviolet range, due to differences in the accessory organs of vision as well as in photopigments; cf. Harasi & Hashimoto, 1983; Wright, 1972.

13.   Campbell, 1974.

14.   Stein & Gordon, 1981.

15.   Mesiter, Wong, Baylor, & Shatz, 1991.

16.   Miller, Keller, & Stryker, 1989.

17.   Jagadeesh, Gray, & Ferster, 1992; Lowel & Singer, 1992.

18.   Depth or binocular cells are activated by simultaneous inputs from corresponding portions of the two retinas, and their connections are also formed as the result of activity-dependent mechanisms, e.g., Hubel & Wiesel, 1962; Wiesel, 1982. See also Bear & Cooper, 1989; Bienstock, Cooper, & Munro, 1982; Blakemore & Cooper, 1970; and Pettigrew, 1974.

19.   Hubel & Livingstone, 1987.

20.   Macko, Jarvis, Kennedy, Miyako, Shinohara, Sokoloff, & Mishkin, 1982.

21.   We have concluded our brief overview of the neural system for seeing. The overview has been necessarily incomplete, but two major omissions may be noted here. First, we have emphasized those neural pathways leading from the environment into the brain; e.g., from the retina to the lateral geniculate and then the primary visual cortex. We have not mentioned the extensive pathways leading in the reverse direction; e.g., from the cortex to the lateral geniculate nucleus. The neural systems mediating seeing and, indeed, the systems mediating all behavior, are highly integrated networks with many reciprocal connections; e.g., Merzenich & Kaas, 1980.

Second, the presentation has stressed those inputs and outputs that are most directly related to seeing. However, no perceptual system operates in complete isolation from other systems. There are substantial *inputs* from other systems to the neural system mediating seeing,

such as inputs to the lateral geniculate nucleus from the neural circuits controlling eye movements; e.g., Lal & Friedlander, 1989. (See Spillman & Werner, 1990 for a presentation of the various neural processes involved in seeing.) The existence of inputs from other systems was briefly acknowledged in describing polymodal association cortex. In addition, there are substantial *outputs* from the visual system to other systems, such as from the superior colliculus to the motor neurons controlling eye movements. In short, although one sensory channel may function in relative isolation from others, the various channels are by no means independent of one another. Each channel influences—to some degree—the functioning of the others and each is, in turn, influenced by them.

22.   Stein & Gordon, 1981; Tranel & Damasio, 1985; Weiskrantz, 1986.

23.   Outputs of the geniculo-cortical system that do not activate the motor systems of speech may also remain intact in cases of blindsight.

24.   Among other reasons, seeing in the foveal region is acute because the receptors are smaller and more closely packed than in the periphery. In addition, each foveal receptor activates a single ganglion cell, while several peripherally located receptors may "share" a common ganglion cell.

25.   cf. van Hof & van der Mark, 1976. Frontal eye placement is common in predators, animals that catch and eat other animals, and in primates, for whom seeing the hands is important. Frontal eye placement facilitates nearby distance discrimination, an ability important to both predators and primates. The corpus callosum also contains many axons that are activated by nonvisual stimuli. Neural activity stimulated by these environmental events is also communicated between the left and right cortices, but is not of concern here.

26.   Neisser, 1976; cf. Gibson, J. J., 1966, 1979. See also Michaels & Carello, 1981.

27.   The theme that selection reflects the coordinated action of both the ancestral and individual environments should be quite familiar by this time. Both environments contribute to even the most basic structures and processes. For example, in some animals the very *shape* of the eyeball, and therefore the occurrence of visual abnormalities such as nearsightedness (myopia), may be affected by visual experience early in life; Wallman, Gottlieb, Rajaram, & Fugate-Wentzek, 1987.

28.   Gibson, E. J., 1988.

29.   By "structure" is meant the variation in the physical properties of light reflected from or emitted by

objects in the environment—variations in wavelength, intensity, and spatial distribution. Again, it was James Gibson (1979) who most fully appreciated the need to explore the competence of variations in the light to specify the environment.

30. Yarbus, 1967.

31. Scaife & Bruner, 1975. For reviews, see Gibson, 1988, and Banks & Salapatek, 1983. On this point, the pygmy chimpanzee, whom many believe to be the species most closely related to man, is unique in having the "whites" of its eyes (i.e., a white schlera) readily visible to an observer. An unpigmented schlera provides a salient discriminative stimulus to guide the eye movements of an observer.

32. Aslin & Smith, 1988.

33. Saccadic movements are to be contrasted with *pursuit movements* that smoothly maintain fixation on light from moving objects. Pursuit movements do not appear in infants until after about 8 weeks of visual experience, and then only when the objects are moving slowly. Both saccadic and pursuit movements require selection by the individual environment to shape their speed and accuracy. For reviews and recent behavioral and physiological work on the development of eye movements, see Aslin & Smith, 1988; Berthoz & Jones, 1985; Lisberger & Pavleko, 1988; and Colombo, Mitchell, Coldren, & Atwater, 1990.

34. A coherently moving pattern stands out against a stationary background, even when the moving and stationary patterns of light and dark are identical; e.g., Dick, Ullman, & Sagi, 1987; Frost & Nakayama, 1983.

35. Colonnier, 1968. See also Ramoa, Campbell, & Shatz, 1987.

36. This method was originally developed by David Hubel and Torsten Wiesel in their pioneering research on the visual system, for which they received a Nobel Prize; e.g., Hubel & Wiesel, 1959, 1962, 1968, 1972.

37. If the grating ceases to move, the activity soon declines to the baseline level; e.g., Albrecht & De Valois, 1981. If the position of a visual stimulus with respect to the retina is held constant (a so-called stabilized retinal image), the stimulus pattern fades in and out of view—portions becoming invisible within only a few seconds, Ditchburn & Ginsborg, 1952; Riggs, Ratliff, Cornsweet, & Cornsweet, 1953. Movement is critical to seeing.

38. It is estimated that there are perhaps 2,000 spatial-frequency clusters in the monkey primary visual cortex; De Valois & De Valois, 1988.

39. Cortical cells are innervated by fibers arising from adjacent portions of the retina; Tootell, Silverman, Switkes, & De Valois, 1982. See also Guthrie, 1989.

40. The general principle that the connectivity of the nervous system is importantly influenced by competition among potential inputs to a cell has been extensively applied to the visual system—e.g., Blakemore & Tobin, 1972; von der Malsburg, 1973; Sillito, 1975; Miller, Keller, & Stryker, 1989—and to the connections in adaptive networks generally—e.g., Rumelhart & Zipser, 1986.

41. von der Malsburg, 1973.

42. For other computer simulations of this process in sensory cortex, see Ambros-Ingerson, Granger, & Lynch, 1990; Edelman, 1987.

43. For work of similar import concerning the organization of motor cortex, see Jacobs & Donoghue, 1991.

44. For example, the cortical cells with the smallest excitatory areas in their receptive fields—and, therefore, those capable of responding to the highest spatial frequencies—receive their inputs from the fovea where the receptors are most closely packed. Because the receptive fields of cells in the primary visual cortex are often excitatory in their centers and inhibitory in the surrounding area, these cells are called center-on cells. The exploration of the ability of these cells to carry out a spatial-frequency analysis of local regions of the environment is primarily due to the work of Campbell and the De Valoises; e.g., Campbell & Robson, 1968 and De Valois & De Valois, 1988. This work is to be distinguished from that which uses a global spatial-frequency analysis of the entire visual field; e.g., Weisstein & Harris, 1980. For related theoretical analyses of the visual system, see LaBerge & Brown, 1989. The issues are further complicated by recent work suggesting that the time intervals between successive activations of cortical cells are appreciated by the visual system, see Optican & Richmond, 1987; Richmond & Optican, 1987.

45. De Valois, De Valois, & Yund, 1979; Maffei, Morrone, Pirchio, & Sandini, 1979; Pollen & Ronner, 1982; De Valois & De Valois, 1988.

46. Campbell & Robson, 1968; Graham & Nachmias, 1971.

47. For a discussion of the similarities and differences between the visual and auditory sustems in this regard, see Julesz, 1980.

48. The inability of verbal responses to be directly guided by all biobehavioral processes is anticipated both on evolutionary grounds—e.g., the verbal system was

selected after the basic perceptual systems had already been selected; cf. Skinner, 1974—and on neuroanatomical grounds—e.g., direct connections do not exist between all units in a network of neurons; cf. Minsky & Papert, 1988, pp. 270, 280.

49. Hartline & Ratliffe, 1957.

50. For discussions of possible relations between illusions and the detection of spatial frequencies, see Ginsburg, 1971 and De Valois & De Valois, 1988. For a comprehensive treatment of illusions, see Gregory & Gombrich, 1973. For some demonstration of illusions in animals other than humans, see Fujita, Blough, & Blough, 1991; Rilling & LaClaire, 1989.

51. Sur, Garraghty, & Roe, 1988.

52. For other examples, see Roe, Pallas, Hahn, & Sur, 1990 and Schlaggar & O'Leary, 1991.

53. Campbell, Kulikowski, & Levison, 1966.

54. If the distance of a grating from an observer is held constant, as has so far been assumed, the spatial frequency of the grating is simply a function of the number of fuzzy stripes in the grating. However, if the distance is allowed to vary, then the spatial frequency of the grating must be expressed as the number of stripes per degree of visual angle for the observer. The spatial frequency of a grating increases—i.e., there are more stripes per degree of visual angle—as the distance of the observer from the grating increases. As an illustration, when held at arm's length a typical ruled pad of paper has about one line per degree. At a distance of ten feet, the same pad has about 4 lines per degree of visual angle.

55. Aslin & Smith, 1988; Aslin, Alberts, & Peterson, 1981.

56. Hirsch & Spinelli, 1970; Stryker, Sherk, Leventhal, & Hirsch, 1978; cf. Blakemore & Cooper, 1970; Blakemore & Mitchell, 1973. See Banks & Salapatek, 1983 for a review.

57. Pettigrew, 1974.

58. Mimura, 1986.

59. Boothe, 1981.

60. Mitchell, 1980, 1981.

61. Hein, Held, & Gower, 1970; Held, 1981; Mitchell & Ware, 1974; Movshon, Chambers, & Blakemore, 1972; and Hein, 1980. Although the visual stimuli required for reading and writing figure prominently in complex human behavior, these stimuli were absent from the ancestral environment of humans—the environment in which seeing was selected. For instance, changing visual fixation from one point in the environment to another—which occurs in reading—was selected by an environment populated with moving objects, not stationary words on a printed page. When the individual environment selects for the biobehavioral processes involved in reading, these selections exert their effects upon an already rich legacy from the ancestral environment. Reading is not an expression of only these more ancient processes, of course, but reading does not occur independently of them either.

62. Blough, 1985, 1989, 1991; cf. Neisser, 1964; Gibson, Schapiro, & Yonas, 1968; Townsend, 1971b.

63. Egeland, 1975.

64. Wolff & White, 1965.

65. Kuhl & Meltzoff, 1982. For other studies and reviews, see Starkey, Spelke, & Gelman, 1983; Gibson & Spelke, 1983; Shepard, 1984.

66. See Gibson & Spelke, 1983 and Rose & Ruff, 1987 for reviews of this literature.

67. Knudsen, 1984; Knudsen & Knudsen, 1985; see also Knudsen & Brainard, 1991. For work of similar import with mammals, see King, Huthings, Moore, & Blakemore, 1988; Meridith & Stein, 1986; Stein, Honeycutt, & Meridith, 1988.

68. Knudsen, 1983.

69. Mitchell, 1980; see also Munro, 1986.

70. This characterization of localizing oneself applies when there is no selection history within that or highly similar environments and when there are no technical aids by which the senses are augmented; e.g., a device that uses satellite information to determine absolute latitude and longitude. When an organism is experienced in an environment, then other processes—such as those considered in later chapters on problem-solving and remembering—become relevant; cf. Kosslyn, Pick, & Fariello, 1974; Acredolo, 1979.

71. e.g., Nadel, Willner, & Kurz, 1985.

72. Morris, 1983.

73. O'Keefe & Nadel, 1978.

74. Sunderland & Rudy, 1989. Configural discriminations may be studied with either classical (Kehoe, 1986; Kehoe & Gormezano, 1980) or operant (e.g., Woodbury, 1943) procedures. Configural discriminations can involve either positive patterning, in which reinforcers occur only during the compound stimulus, or negative patterning, in which reinforcers occur only during the components. For other theoretical treatments of configural discriminations, see Hull, 1943; Kehoe, 1988; and Rescorla, 1973, 1985a.

75. In the technical language of adaptive-network theory, or linear algebra, such discriminations are instances of *nonlinearly separable* problems; cf. Rumelhart, McClelland, & the PDP Group, 1986.

76. cf. Olton, 1983; Rasmussen, Barnes, & McNaughton, 1989; Rawlins, 1985. For recent reviews of the literature on the effects of the hippocampus on "memory," see Eichenbaum & Otto, 1992; Squire, 1992; Sutherland & Rudy, 1989.

77. Amaral, 1987; Krieckhaus, Donahoe, & Morgan, 1992.

78. Sharp, 1991.

79. cf. Krieckhaus, Donahoe, & Morgan, 1992; Ambros-Ingerson, Granger, & Lynch, 1990; Squire, Shimamura, & Amaral, 1989; Trehub, 1977, 1987, 1991. Since the origins of inputs to hippocampus appear to be restricted to cells in polysensory association cortex in primates (Amaral, 1987), the inputs to hippocampus *already* reflect the conjunction of activity in multiple sensory channels. Thus interactions within the hippocampus involve higher-order conjunctions of neural activity arising from multiple environmental events (see also Deadwyler, West, & Robinson, 1981).

80. Donahoe, Burgos, & Palmer, 1993; Krieckhaus, Donahoe, & Morgan, 1992.

81. In the motor association cortex, the diffusely projecting neural system of reinforcement uses dopamine as the neuromodulator (see Chapter 2). If the diffusely projecting neural system originating from the hippocampus provides a similarly functioning neuromodulator of synaptic efficacies in sensory association cortex, it has not been specifically identified—although it is probably a monoamine other than dopamine, such as norepinephrine; cf. Fallon & Laughlin, 1987. The view that changes in the synaptic efficacies of cells in sensory cortex require a neuromodulator is not without precedent. Changes in the synaptic efficacies of neurons in *primary* visual cortex have been shown to be dependent on monoaminergic neuromodulators that are present when the animal is alert; Singer & Rauschecker, 1982. Thus, the neuromodulatory system for primary sensory cortex is *tonic*, i.e., continuously active in a normal animal. What we propose here is that a *phasic* neuromodulatory system controlled by the hippocampus serves sensory association cortex.

In both the sensory and motor association cortices, the primary neurotransmitter is the excitatory amino acid glutamate. Long-term changes in the synaptic efficacies of glutamate receptors require activation of a subset of these receptors, the NMDA (N-methyl-D-aspartate) receptor complex. The neuromodulator is postulated to act through its effects on this receptor complex. The cellular mechanisms through which these effects may act are beyond the scope of this book.

82. Merzenich, 1984, quoted in Fox, 1984, p. 821.

83. cf. Gray, Konig, Engel, & Singer, 1989.

84. Donahoe, Burgos, & Palmer, 1993; Krieckhaus, Donahoe, & Morgan, 1992. In the technical language of adaptive-network interpretations, a stimulus-selection network implements a type of *unsupervised* learning; cf. Rumelhart & Zipser, 1986. Unsupervised learning occurs independently of feedback from the environment. Alternatively, the hippocampal feedback to polysensory association cortex may be viewed as implementing *self*-supervision based upon environmental input to the network. The stimulus-selection network selects, on-line, *higher-order units* that permit "difficult" (e.g., nonlinear) discriminations to be acquired; cf. Maxwell, Giles, & Lee, 1986. A response-selection network implements *supervised* learning, although the supervision is not necessarily identical to that implemented by algorithms such as the delta rule; cf. Rumelhart, Hinton, & Williams, 1986.

85. The use of diffuse projection systems to modulate the synaptic efficacies between recently activated neurons appears to be a general evolutionary "strategy." For example, diffusely projecting systems, in addition to those postulated here, modulate the selection of connections in other cortical areas; Fallon & Laughlin, 1997; Kety, 1970; Miller, Keller, & Stryker, 1989; Pettigrew, 1985; Singer, 1985; Singer & Rauschecker, 1982.

86. cf. Stone, 1986.

87. e.g., Lyford & Jarrad, 1991.

88. e.g., Swanson, 1982.

89. Stein & Belluzzi, 1988, 1989; cf. Kitai, Sugimori, & Kocsis, 1976.

90. One of the most important consequences of a mechanism that coordinates the selection of connections throughout the cerebral cortex is that it addresses what has been called the *binding problem* (Hinton, McClelland, & Rumelhart, 1986; Smolensky, 1987). A coordinated reinforcing signal "binds together" all those connections that were reliably active before the occurrence of a reinforcer. The potential power of a mechanism that simultaneously modifies synapses between synchronously active neurons was apparently first recognized by von der Malsburg, 1981, 1987; and subsequently and apparently independently by a number of other investigators (e.g., Crick, 1984; Donahoe, Burgos, & Palmer, 1993; Strong & Whitehead, 1989). Mechanisms of this general type are currently being applied to complex problems in perceiving (e.g., Hummel & Biederman, 1990) as are conditioning mechanisms generally,

such as those involved in blocking (e.g., Siegel, Allan, & Eisenberg, 1992).

91. Tolman & Honzik, 1930.

92. Latent learning, like all complex behavior, is influenced by many variables; cf. Osgood, 1953.

93. In the primate brain, more so than in the brains of other mammals such as the rat, inputs to the hippocampus and outputs from the hippocampus arise from sensory association rather than primary sensory cortex; Amaral, 1989.

94. Hein & Held, 1962; Hein, 1980; Held, 1980; Harris, 1980; Hein & Jeannerod, 1983; Held & Hein, 1958.

95. The important relation between perceiving and responding has been emphasized by Gibson in his concept of *affordance*. Environments are said to afford, i.e., to permit, actions. Thus a floor affords walking, a chair affords sitting, and so forth; Gibson, 1979; Johansson, von Hofsten, & Jansson, 1980; Turvey, Yosel Solomon, & Burton, 1989; Yonas & Granrud, 1984; Yonas & Owsley, 1987.

96. cf. Sussman, 1989.

97. Damage that changes the sensory input to the cortex also profoundly affects its connectivity, even in the adult organism; e.g., Pons, Garraghty, Ommaya, Kaas, Taub, & Mishkin, 1991.

98. Luria, 1976; Teuber, 1963. For a review, see Brown, 1988.

99. Sacks, 1987, pp. 10–11.

100. For physiological work related to the integration of activity from different sensory channels, see Hubel & Livingstone, 1987; Livingstone & Hubel, 1987; and Ungerleider & Mishkin, 1982. For further comments on such work see Blake, 1989; Logothetis, Schiller, Charles, & Hurlburt, 1990; and De Valois & De Valois, 1988, p. 238; cf. Mignard & Malpeli, 1991.

101. Kohonen, 1977; Kohonen, Lehtio, & Oja, 1981; Kohonen, Oja, & Lehtio, 1985.

102. cf. Ambros-Ingerson, Granger, & Lynch, 1990.

103. Sieroff, Pollatsek, & Posner, 1988.

104. For related work, see Sieroff & Michael, 1987; Sieroff & Posner, 1988.

105. Kendrick & Baldwin, 1987.

106. Bruce, Desimone, & Gross, 1981; see also Bruyer, 1986 and Whitely & Warrington, 1977. It would be a mistake to conclude from such studies that a complex stimulus, such as a face, is recognized by a single "face" cell. Instead, complex stimuli activate small subnetworks of cells whose extent is determined by the selection history with respect to the stimulus and constrained by lateral inhibitory interactions that limit the excitatory cells in the network to those that are most strongly activated by the stimulus; Young & Yamane, 1992.

CHAPTER 8

MEMORY: REMINDING

Throughout most of the earlier chapters, the focus has been on the *selecting* role of the environment. When stimuli are sensed and responses occur in their presence followed by reinforcing stimuli, environment-behavior relations are selected. When stimuli are sensed concurrently, especially when they are followed by reinforcing stimuli, environment-environment relations are selected. Together, the coordinated selection of environment-behavior and environment-environment relations enables our actions to become exquisitely guided by the environment. This guidance is based exclusively on brief sequences of events. However, the cumulative effect of such sequences of stimuli, responses, and reinforcers produces environment-behavior relations that, in general, accurately reflect the overall structure of our world and the consequences of our behavior in that world.

INTRODUCTION

In this chapter, and throughout the remainder of the book, our focus shifts from the selection of environment-behavior and environment-environment relations to the *effects* of selection—how the learner functions after selection has taken place. The nontechnical term "memory" is conventionally used when the focus is on the effects of past selections on present behavior. We treat "memory" as we did "attention" and "perception" before it. That is, we view "memory" as an emergent product of past selections, not as an independent field requiring a different set of basic principles. No uniquely "memorial" principles are needed to summarize the action of uniquely "memorial" processes. Furthermore, as with other nontechnical terms, "memory" is unlikely to denote a single combination of basic biobehavioral processes acting in a specific fashion. Instead, the field of "memory"—like the field of "attention"—consists of a diverse set of phenomena having certain features in common. In the case of "memory," these features are that the behavior of interest is importantly influenced by selections that have occurred in previous environments and, often, considerable time has elapsed between these earlier selections and their effects in the present environment. Because "memory" depends on the history of selection, and the relevant history usually varies from one person to the next, considerable individual differences are to be expected.[1]

We begin our efforts to understand "memory" by exploring some implications of the principles that have emerged from our study of behavior. This framework enables us to provide interpretations for such puzzling questions as: How can a person answer questions on any of a wide range of topics in a fraction of a second, while even a powerful computer may take many seconds to search its memory for the answer? How can we recall the name of an acquaintance in one situation and then forget it in another, and where did the "memory" go when it was not recalled? Why are some "memories" very detailed even after a single experience, while others require many repetitions? Why do some "memories" endure indefinitely while others are quickly forgotten?

MEMORY AS ENVIRONMENTALLY GUIDED BEHAVIOR

Memory as a Cumulative Product of Selection

Experimental analyses of the biobehavioral processes involved in variation, selection, and retention indicate that the "appropriate" response occurs when the environment contains stimuli that have acquired the ability to guide the response. At the behavioral level, if such stimuli are present, the response occurs.[2] At the neural level, if these stimuli activate networks of pathways in the nervous system that contract the appropriate muscles, observable behavior occurs.

What is selected?   The cumulative effects of selection by reinforcement are environment-behavior relations whose environmental components have been enriched by concurrently selected environment-environment relations. At the neural level, enough synapses have been strengthened throughout the networks to permit reliable mediation of the relation between the environment and behavior. The number of selected pathways and the synaptic efficacies mediating the relation depend on the initial connectivity of the nervous system and the co-occurrence of activity between connected units during selection. In a neural network with the number of units and rich connectivity of the human brain, the number of pathways mediating a given environment-behavior relation is, in general, very large. What do the behavioral and neural accounts of the effects of selection suggest about the nature of "memory"?

First, note that what is selected is not properly described as a response but as a *relation* between the environment and behavior or, on the neural level, a set of connections between receptors and muscles. In general, the same response, or pattern of muscular contractions, can be produced in many different ways. There are different pathways by which activity in one brain region may affect activity in another brain region, and different patterns of contraction of individual muscle fibers may

produce the "same" behavioral response. Variability in the specific circumstances at the moment of selection causes the specific pathways mediating a given environment-behavior relation to vary from moment to moment. Selection does not forge a single chain of invariable links between the receptor and the effector; it creates a functional network whose constituent units vary somewhat with the environmental and organismic conditions of the moment. Even when we engage in such relatively simple behavior as flexing an index finger to scratch an itchy nose, the flexion response likely involves the contraction of different muscle fibers on different occasions.[3] And, when we flex our index finger under the control of different stimuli—to scratch an itchy nose, to press a key on a typewriter, or to keep time to music—the "same" movement of our finger results from the contraction of different individual muscle fibers. Selection leads to reliable environment-behavior relations, but the specific neural elements that mediate those relations are likely to be quite variable.

By appreciating that what is selected is a large and variable set of connections, we can avoid a dilemma that often arises when we mistakenly equate the occurrence of a response with the existence of a "memory." Consider the following otherwise problematic example. When asked to state the word for a sweet-tasting substance that begins with "s," a patient who had suffered brain damage was unable to answer. However, when she was asked to complete the rhyme "Roses are red, violets are blue . . ., " she immediately replied "sugar is sweet and so are you."[4] Did the patient have a "memory" for sugar or not? When we appreciate that the product of selection is an environment-behavior relation and not a response alone, such observations are not troublesome. The vocal response "sugar" was no longer guided by the auditory stimulus provided by the question, but was still guided by the auditory stimulus of the first part of the rhyme.[5] This result undoubtedly reflects the conditions under which the vocal response "sugar is sweet and so are you" was originally selected; most children acquire this verbal behavior immediately after hearing "Roses are red, violets are blue."

Appreciating that selection changes the strength of environment-behavior relations and the neural connections mediating them has a second benefit: It provides a way to conceptualize the status of "memories" when we are not recalling them. If a "memory" is a pattern of activation in a network of neurons, then the "memory" does not exist when the pattern is not present. And, the pattern is not present unless some event activates it. Technically speaking, what is retained as a result of selection is not a "memory" or a set of active pathways, but changes in connection strengths between neurons that allow the network to be activated under certain conditions. In short, when we are not having them, "memories" do not exist. "Memories" are not stored away in a metaphorical filing cabinet; what are stored—if the storage metaphor is to be used at all—are the connection strengths needed to create the appropriate pattern of activity when the appropriate environmental and organismic events occur.[6]

Under what conditions do "memories" occur?
If "memories" are interpreted as environment-behavior relations mediated by the activation of a network of pathways in the nervous system, then "memories" occur only when the network is activated. And, the network is activated only when present conditions reproduce the conditions under which selection took place. That is, stimuli guide "memories" just as they do other responses.[7]

The stimuli that guide "memories" are sometimes said, metaphorically, to *retrieve* them. This is misleading. The use of the retrieval metaphor to describe the processes by which "memories" occur implicitly assumes that "memories" exist when they are not occurring—as a written record exists both when it is being read and when it is in a file drawer waiting to be read. Retrieval also implies that the "memory" is being retrieved *by someone*, rather than resulting from the environment acting on the organism. If we speak of people retrieving "memories," then we must also speak of dogs

retrieving salivary responses when they hear tones, and pigeons retrieving pecking responses when they see colors on a disk. We can avoid the problems implicit in the use of retrieval if we do not treat "memories" as a different *kind* of behavior, but simply as a cumulative product of previously selected environment-behavior relations.

When viewed as environment-behavior relations, much of what falls under the conventional heading of "memory" becomes part of the more general field of the environmental guidance of behavior (see Chapter 3). Accordingly, the variables that experimental analysis has identified as bringing behavior under the control of the environment should prove useful in interpreting "memory." For example, we expect a response to recur at a later time to the extent that the stimuli that guide the response are present at that later time.[8] Let us briefly review some of the variables that determine whether the environment guides behavior.

To begin with, behavior is most strongly guided by the particular stimuli that were present when selection occurred. These stimuli include not only the nominal discriminative stimuli—or **cues**, as such stimuli are often called in memory research—but also the contextual stimuli in whose presence the discriminative stimuli occur. As selection proceeds, those stimuli that most reliably precede the reinforced response guide the response ever more strongly, and stimuli that are less reliably present lose their ability to guide the response. The more reliable stimuli increasingly block the ability of the less reliable stimuli to guide behavior. To insure that the guidance of behavior is restricted to a given set of stimuli, differential training is usually required. That is, the response must be reinforced when a particular subset of stimuli is present, and not reinforced (or differently reinforced) when other stimuli are present. For example, if a tone is present in an experimental chamber when a response is reinforced, but not when the response is unreinforced, then the contextual stimuli provided by the chamber gradually lose their ability to guide the response. The response becomes increasingly guided by the stimuli provided by the tone, as the tone acts on a nervous system that is affected by the context in which it occurs. That is, the same tone presented in two different contexts is likely to activate somewhat different sets of units in the neural network. Thus, although contextual stimuli lose their ability to guide behavior by themselves, the nominal discriminative stimulus—acting on a nervous system that is affected by the context—determines which specific connections are strengthened by the reinforcer.[9]

What determines the constituents of "memories"?   What we know about discrimination formation leads us to expect that different "memories" will vary greatly in the number and type of stimuli that guide them, and in the number and type of responses that are guided. For example, suppose that you pressed a button on a vending machine and got a bar of candy without putting any money in the machine. Under these circumstances, you are likely to recall the details of the situation—the particular button you pressed, the particular machine you used, the building where the machine was located, and so forth. Similarly, if a knowledgeable friend told you a surprising fact, e.g., that scientists had made a mouse as big as a dog through genetic engineering, you would likely recall both that fact and the person who told it to you. When events are surprising and occur in only one context, a "memory" that includes the specifics of the context is likely to be formed. Based on your earlier history of selection in unusual situations, you are apt to engage in behavior that causes your responding to be guided by many aspects of the situation. Speaking nontechnically, when your experience indicates that the likelihood that a response will be reinforced in future environments depends on the particular features of the current environment, you behave in ways that bring the response under the control of many features of the selecting environment. Thus, at the time of the unusual event's occurrence you might note the location of the vending machine, or the origin of the statement about giant mice.

When the environment-behavior relation constituting the "memory" includes responses guided by many of the stimuli in whose presence selection occurred, such a relation is sometimes said to be an instance of **episodic memory**.[10] Although some students of memory believe that different processes are required to understand episodic as opposed to other memories, we—among others—do not.[11] If we apply the information we have gained from the experimental analysis of discrimination formation, we can account for the observed variation in the stimuli and responses that make up those environment-behavior relations known as episodic memories.

Differences in the specificity and number of stimuli that guide a response are primarily the result of two variables. First, if behavior has occurred and been reinforced on only a few occasions, then many specific stimuli and responses are candidates for inclusion in the selected relation: Differential reinforcement has not had an opportunity to narrow the range of stimuli and responses to those that most reliably precede the reinforcer. Second, if the reinforcer that selects the environment-behavior relation is a potent elicitor, then many of the particular stimuli that happen to be sensed at the moment of selection—even if they are present on only a single occasion—may acquire the capacity to guide many of the responses. As interpreted by selection networks, a potent reinforcer may substantially strengthen connections between all active units even on a single occurrence. If the connections along many pathways are sufficiently strengthened, then many stimuli can potentially guide the response. However, if differential training occurs, some of these stimuli—those least reliably preceding the reinforced response—would not be components of the selected environment-behavior relation.

Recalling the detailed circumstances surrounding some dramatic event provides the most striking example of episodic memory. For persons of the authors' generation, the assassinations of President Kennedy and Martin Luther King are unfortunate examples. For others, witnessing the explosion of the space shuttle *Challenger*, or hearing of the death of a friend or parent, may qualify as such events. Many claim to recall the precise circumstances under which they learned of such dramatic events. Because the specifics are sometimes so well recalled, these particularly rich episodic memories are known as **flashbulb memories**.[12] They are so called because it is as if a flashbulb had gone off, illuminating the entire situation at the moment of the event. As interpreted through a selection network, such "memories" are the result of selection by very potent elicitors that strongly activate the diffuse reinforcing system, greatly strengthening connections along all pathways that happen to be active at that moment.[13]

Finally, there are those "memories"—probably the majority—in which a narrower range of stimuli and responses make up the selected relation. In inferred-process approaches to "memory," the term **semantic memory** comes closest to encompassing such relations—especially when the behavior includes verbal responses.[14] (The term semantic refers to meaning—a concept that is interpreted in a later chapter on verbal behavior.) A semantic memory might be exemplified by responding to the question "What color is the sky?" with the answer "The sky is blue." Answering "blue" in response to this and similar inquiries has been reinforced on many specific occasions. Yet, it is a rare person who recalls even one of those occasions. Semantic "memories" are commonly the product of a prolonged history of selection. In the "blue sky" case, the response "blue" has been reinforced on many different occasions in which the only common stimulus has been the dominant wavelength of light coming from the sky—that which we call "blue." The response "blue" has been reinforced whether the person asking the question was a parent or a stranger, whether there were mountains on the horizon or trees, whether the sky was clear or flecked with clouds, and so on. The net effect of differential training is to restrict the guiding stimulus to a narrower range of wavelengths.[15]

Simulation research has demonstrated that the connection strengths in a single adaptive network can be modified in such a way that the same network mediates both episodic and semantic memories.[16] Thus the same stimulus pattern may produce a very specific output pattern in one context and a categorical output pattern in another context. The context may be simulated by the state of input units other than those activated by the discriminative stimulus. To illustrate, if a given input pattern represented the features of a particular person, then in one context that pattern could produce an output pattern representing some person-specific characteristic—e.g., the person's name—while in another context it could produce an output pattern of a categorical response—e.g., the person's gender.

As with many environment-behavior relations, semantic "memories" have multiple origins. Much adult human behavior does not result only from shaping by the contingencies of reinforcement. Particularly since the beginning of verbal behavior, many responses result partly from guidance by stimuli provided by the behavior of others—instructions and the like. (Of course, the ability of verbal stimuli to guide behavior is ultimately traceable to the contingencies of reinforcement with respect to verbal behavior.) Verbal stimuli can take many forms—vocal speech, written speech, diagrams, etc. Many semantic memories originate from behavior whose initial occurrence is the result of verbal stimuli. For example, you may recall the Pythagorean theorem about the relation between the length of the hypotenuse of a right triangle and the lengths of the other two sides, but it is unlikely that you recall the specific occasion on which you first acquired this behavior. As noted in an earlier chapter, such behavior is best understood on its first occurrence as rule-governed rather than contingency-shaped.

To summarize, "memory" refers to the enduring effects of the selection of environment-behavior relations. In experienced learners, acquired reinforcers play an increasing role in the selection process. Selected responses occur to the extent that the stimuli—or cues—guiding them are present.

And, finally, the stimuli and responses that constitute the "memory" depend on the specific contingencies of selection. We turn now to a consideration of factors that determine how long "memories" last.

The Durability of Memory

As interpreted by biobehaviorally informed adaptive networks, a "memory" endures as long as the stimuli present during original selection can be re-presented to the network's input units, and the connection strengths along the pathways that mediate the input-output relations remain relatively unchanged. What is the evidence regarding the durability of the environment-behavior relations that adaptive networks are intended to simulate?

Autobiographical "memories."   Anecdotal evidence abounds that memories may endure for a very long time. Systematic naturalistic observations of what are called **autobiographical memories** confirm this impression. In one of a series of studies conducted by Harry Bahrick and his colleagues, subjects were shown either the names or pictures of former high-school classmates intermingled with those of other persons.[17] Subjects who had left high school 14 years earlier could pick out the names of their classmates with 90% accuracy, a performance as good as that of newly graduated subjects. Subjects who were shown pictures picked out those of former classmates with 90% accuracy as much as 34 years after graduation! Thus, the subjects discriminated familiar from unfamiliar stimuli—whether printed words or pictures—for a *very* substantial period. Further, when subjects were given pictures of their former classmates and asked to recall their names, naming responses were about 70% accurate immediately after leaving high school, and only declined to about 30% after 34 years. Thus almost a third of the naming responses were still guided by the pictorial stimuli after a lapse of 34 years—an impressive performance. (See **Figure 8.1**.)[18]

A second study provides additional information on the relation between the strength of the response evoked by a stimulus—i.e., its familiarity—and the topography of the response.[19] Subjects were shown pictures of persons who had been well known to the public in past years. The subjects were then asked to indicate how strongly they believed that they had seen the person before—i.e., how familiar the face was—and, if possible, the person's name. The pictures that seemed most familiar were correctly named with over 80% accuracy; those that seemed least familiar were correctly named with somewhat less than 50% accuracy. Two aspects of these findings merit particular attention. First, the more familiar the picture, the more likely the subjects were to correctly name the person depicted. This suggests that, as a result of our selection history, we may come to discriminate the strength of the response evoked by a stimulus as one indication that the response is correct. Second, the relation between the strength of a response and its accuracy was by no means perfect. Under the conditions of this experiment, even though the subjects did not believe they knew the names of some of the persons pictured, they still named these persons correctly almost half the time. Thus the strength of the response evoked by a stimulus, while correlated with the correctness of the response, is almost certainly influenced by additional variables.[20]

As interpreted by adaptive networks, the findings with autobiographical "memory" suggest that the connection strengths along pathways mediating environment-behavior relations—and the synaptic efficacies that the connections are intended to simulate—may endure for a very long time. We should not be surprised that the effects of selection on neural networks are robust. As noted earlier, one characteristic of selection networks is that the effects of selection are often distributed over many pathways. As a result, the input-output relations that the pathways mediate are resistant to damage to parts of the network. On any one occasion, the stimulus need not activate all of the modified pathways for the output pattern to be produced. Even

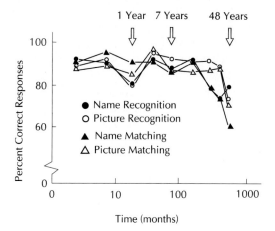

FIGURE 8.1 *Changes in the accuracy of autobiographical "memory" over time*
Measures were the recognition of names and pictures of former high-school classmates when interspersed among the names and pictures of strangers, the matching of pictures of classmates with their correct names, and the recall of their names when shown their pictures.
Source: Adapted from Bahrick, H. P., Bahrick, P. C., & Whittlinger, R. P. (1975). Fifty years of memories for names and faces: A cross-sectional approach. *Journal of Experimental Psychology: Human Perception and Performance, 1,* 35–47. Copyright © 1975 by the American Psychological Association.

when some units are lost, which occurs as neurons die during the aging process, the network continues to function quite well.

Do "memories" weaken over time?   Although research on autobiographical "memory" clearly indicates that selections of environment-behavior relations have enduring effects, it also indicates that the effects can change over time. After a period of years, the subjects were less accurate in picking out their former classmates' names or pictures. The most obvious possibility for the weakening of environment-behavior relations is that they simply decay over time. Can the mere passage of time change "memories"?

The possibility that changes in environment-behavior relations are produced by internal factors alone—what is called **decay theory** in the memory

literature—seems unlikely and, in any case, cannot be experimentally analyzed on the behavioral level. To evaluate the effect of the passage of time alone, time must be allowed to pass between selection and the retention test, without the occurrence of either environmental or behavioral events in the interim. Since some environment is always stimulating the organism and some behavior is always occurring, the required state of "suspended animation" is impossible to attain. However, these conditions may be approximated. In a classic experiment,[21] subjects who had learned a list of nonsense syllables immediately before falling asleep recalled more of the syllables when awakened than they did when tested after a waking period of equal length. (See **Figure 8.2**.) The high retention level, together with evidence of accurate

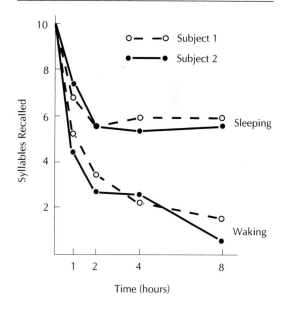

FIGURE 8.2 *Effects of intervening activity on retention*
Recall of nonsense syllables by two subjects after comparable periods of sleeping and of waking.
Source: From Jenkins, J. G., & Dallenbach, K. H. (1924). Oblivescence during sleep and waking. *American Journal of Psychology, 35,* 605–612. © University of Illinois Press, Champaign, IL.

autobiographical memories extending over many years, makes a convincing case against internal factors—i.e., decay—making an important contribution to most cases of "memory" loss. It is the environmental events that occur as time passes, not time itself, that change selected environment-behavior relations.[22]

Stimulus Change and Retention

Given that deterioration of the physical substrate of "memory" is unlikely to be a major cause of the weakening of environment-behavior relations, we turn now to a second factor that contributes to retention losses—the absence of the stimuli that were present during selection from the environment in which retention is assessed.

Returning to studies of autobiographical "memory," the stimuli present during the retention tests were almost certainly somewhat different from those present when the environment-behavior relations were originally selected. The subjects did not learn the names of their classmates while looking at black-and-white photographs of their faces. We may speculate that the subjects' naming responses would have been even more accurate if, for example, they had been shown color motion pictures of their former classmates taken in the contexts in which they had seen their classmates in the past.

Studying the effects of stimulus change on retention in the natural environment is difficult because the same response is often selected in the presence of many different stimuli. Thus, we might speak a person's name whether we see that person from the side or the front, alone or with others, or in one setting or another. Indeed, such variation is critical to the formation of stimulus and response classes (see Chapter 5). Although naturalistic observations reveal the cumulative products of selection in their full richness and complexity, they are often ill-suited to isolating the variables that produce the emergent complex products of selection. For that reason, we return to the laboratory to

investigate how stimulus change contributes to the weakening of environment-behavior relations.[23]

In one such study, special reading materials were prepared in which the words were printed upside down, so that the stimuli used during selection were unlikely to be encountered in other situations. Subjects were presented with 200 pages of this inverted text and asked to practice reading it. Needless to say, they read very slowly at first. With continued practice, however, they came to read the inverted text about as rapidly as normal text. Moreover, when tested a year later, they continued to read inverted text readily, thus showing good evidence of retention. However, when the inverted text was changed so that the letters were printed in a slightly different typeface, the reading rate dropped considerably.[24] A relatively minor change in the stimulus in whose presence reading had been selected was sufficient to reduce the rate of reading. The subjects had not learned to read upside-down letters in general, but upside-down letters in a particular typeface.

In another investigation of similar import, subjects were shown a sequence of still photographs of a person engaged in a series of movements, e.g., going from one place to another in a cluttered room.[25] When they were later shown a number of photographs of this action and asked whether they had seen them before, the subjects readily distinguished the ones they had seen from photographs of the same action taken from a *different* vantage point in the room. The particular stimuli produced by the action, and not the general "sense" of the action, guided recognition of the photographs. Interestingly, other photographs taken from the *same* vantage point, but never seen before, were not discriminated from the photographs that the subjects had seen previously. This latter phenomenon is related to the ability of adaptive networks to produce a trained output pattern in response to an input pattern similar to the one in whose presence selection occurred. Thus, when the stimuli provided by the photograph were similar to those of a previously presented photograph, they evoked a strong enough response for the subject to incorrectly classify the photograph as familiar. These and other findings suggest that many apparent losses of "memory" result from failures to reinstate the precise stimuli that were present when the environment-behavior relation was selected.

Effects of Later Learning on Retention: Retroaction Effects

Selection is an ongoing process in the natural environment, and newly selected environment-behavior relations may affect the retention of earlier selections. With autobiographical "memory," for instance, a subject might have contact with a former classmate after graduation, and this contact could alter the "memory." Suppose that a female former classmate married, and thereafter went by her married rather than her maiden name. Under such circumstances, knowledge of her married name might interfere with recalling her maiden name. Two naming responses would have been selected in the presence of similar stimuli—e.g., the appearance of the woman during and after high school.

It is difficult to study the interfering effects of new selections on old selections in the natural environment because the experimenter cannot control the learner's environment. Such control can be achieved in laboratory situations, especially with nonhumans, because the original training can occur in a distinctive test chamber and the animal can then be excluded from the chamber throughout the retention interval. When such methods are used to prevent new selections from occurring in the training environment, we have seen that the original environment-behavior relations appear to last indefinitely. For example, a classically conditioned leg flexion response in sheep remained intact after years grazing in the field,[26] and an operantly conditioned keypecking discrimination in pigeons endured after years spent in the loft.[27] Environment-behavior relations do not decay as a function of time, and they need not be affected when new relations are selected in different environments. The sheep and pigeons almost certainly acquired

new environment-behavior relations during those years spent outside the experimental chambers. What happens, however, when new selections take place in environments similar to those in which earlier selections occurred?

Retroactive interference and facilitation. In humans, the effect of later learning on the retention of earlier environment-behavior relations has been most extensively studied using a procedure called **paired-associate learning**. In paired-associate learning, pairs of words are sequentially presented to the subject. When the first word of a pair is presented, the subject attempts to speak the second word before it too is presented. For example, the stimulus word might be a nonsense syllable and the response word a meaningful word, e.g., *PEM-big*. Word pairs are presented in random order until the subject can go through the entire list responding to each stimulus word with the correct response word.[28]

To investigate the effect of later learning on retention of the responses from the first list, subjects learned a second list of word pairs in which the similarity of the stimulus and response words to those on the first list was varied. For example, the second list might contain among its word pairs *PEM-bright*. In this case, the stimulus word is the same on the two lists, but the response words are different. This arrangement impairs retention of the first word pair because the stimulus PEM now guides two responses, *big* and *bright*. When retention of the first set of word pairs is impaired by the acquisition of the second set, the phenomenon is known as **retroactive interference**, since *later* learning has interfered with the retention of earlier learning. When later learning benefits the retention of earlier learning, it is known as **retroactive facilitation**. For example, if the second list contained the word pair *PEM-large*, then retention of the response word *big* might be enhanced by its meaningful similarity to *large*.[29]

Interpreting the various findings obtained with the paired-associate procedure formerly received a great deal of experimental attention in the field of human learning.[30] For present purposes, the major conclusion from that work may be summarized as follows: The similarity between the stimuli and responses appearing in the first and second tasks greatly affects retention of the environment-behavior relations selected in the first task. This conclusion is of general significance, applying to selections in the natural environment as well as in the laboratory. On the behavioral level, the effects of similarity are interpreted by the use of stimulus generalization and response differentiation, and the biobehavioral processes responsible for these phenomena.[31] From the perspective of adaptive networks, similarity relations can be simulated by overlapping activation patterns of input, interior, and output units. The greater the overlap in the patterns, the greater the possibility for interfering or facilitating effects, depending on the specific nature of the overlap.

Although the study of paired-associate learning made important contributions to our understanding of retention, a number of the variables affecting performance in such tasks were specific to the nature of the task and the type of materials used. For example, if "memory" is an emergent product of a prolonged history of behavioral selection, then, to the extent that nonsense syllables successfully eliminate the effects of that history, they prevent some "memorial" phenomena from occurring. In short, if nonsense syllables are truly nonsense, then their use precludes studying some of the very phenomena that we seek to understand.[32] In addition, many variables important to retention in the natural environment cannot be studied with separate word pairs, e.g., the organizational characteristics of natural language. For these reasons, we shall not describe the study of paired-associate learning in detail.

One area that is of great current interest, however, is the interpretation of interference effects by adaptive networks. If adaptive networks are to simulate the cumulative effects of selection, then questions arise about their capacity to mediate multiple environment-behavior relations, and the conditions that affect the degree of interference

between different relations.[33] The initial work with some techniques for modifying connections in adaptive networks suggested that large interference effects—much larger than those observed in human learners—were inevitable.[34] Later work has demonstrated that interference effects on a human-like scale can be reproduced in adaptive networks.[35] For example, the upper panel of **Figure 8.3** shows the amount of retroactive interference found in the retention of one experimental task as a function of the number of intervening tasks that were acquired.[36] The lower panel shows the amount of retroactive interference found when this experiment was simulated with an adaptive network. Clearly, adaptive networks are capable of simulating interference effects, but much more remains to be done on this problem. In future work, one of the central concerns should be the role of inhibitory connections in interference effects. As we found in the study of perceiving, inhibitory connections act to restrict the number of active pathways to those that are most strongly activated. Such lateral inhibitory interactions would tend to reduce interference when multiple pathways mediating different environment-behavior relations were activated by similar stimuli.

Context and retroaction.   In the natural environment, retroaction effects produced by similarities between the stimuli guiding different responses are greatly reduced by contextual discriminations. Even when the discriminative stimuli are similar, if the responses are selected in otherwise different environments, *and those different environments have been discriminated from one another*, then the contextual stimuli differentiate the selected environment-behavior relations.[37]

The differentiating effects of contextual discriminations can be demonstrated experimentally. In one such study,[38] subjects first learned a set of 45 paired associates in a distinctive context, e.g., a cramped office. In a second session, the same subjects learned another set of paired associates in different context, e.g., an outside patio. Some of

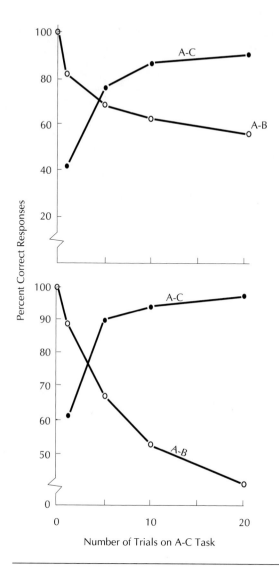

FIGURE 8.3 *Retroactive interference of subsequent learning on the recall of prior learning*

The upper panel shows performance on the present task (A-C) and the past task (A-B) as the present task was acquired. (From Barnes, J. M., & Underwood, B. J. [1959]. "Fate" of first-trial associations in transfer theory. *Journal of Experimental Psychology, 58,* 97–105. Copyright © 1959 by the American Psychological Association. Reprinted by permission.) The tasks were paired-associate learning in which the first letter represents the set of stimuli (A) and the second letter represents the set of responses (either B or C). Thus, the stimuli in the two tasks were identical but the responses were different, a condition producing substantial interference. The lower panel shows the result of a computer simulation by an adaptive network of performance on these tasks. (From Lewandowsky, S. [1991]. Gradual unlearning and catastrophic interference: A comparison of distributed architectures. *Cognitive Processes Laboratory Technical Report.* Norman, OK: University of Oklahoma.) Both the experimental data and the computer simulations show gradual deterioration of recall of the past task (A-B) as the present task (A-C) was acquired.

the stimulus words in the second set were the same as those in the first set, but the response words paired with them were different. This arrangement would ordinarily produce strong retroactive interference for the responses selected in the first session. Finally, in a retention test the subjects were given stimulus words from the first session and asked to produce a response for each. Half of the subjects were given the retention test in the first context and half in the second context. The findings were that the stimulus words evoked responses appropriate to the context in which they were tested. For example, if the first session occurred in the cramped office and the retention test also occurred in the cramped office, then the stimulus words evoked the response acquired in the first session about 50% of the time. However, if the retention test occurred in the outside patio, then the same stimuli evoked responses learned in the first session only about 35% of the time. Thus, retroactive interference was substantially reduced by the contextual discrimination. Some interference continued to occur, of course. When stimuli were presented that had appeared in only one session and the retention test was carried out in that context, the percentage of correct responses was over 60%.[39] (See **Figure 8.4** for a full presentation of these results.)

In addition to the environmental context, the internal or intraorganismic context may also affect retention of environment-behavior relations. For example, if learning occurs in one hypnotically induced mood-state (e.g., feelings of sadness) and is then tested in the same state, retention is better than when it is tested in a different mood-state (e.g., feelings of happiness).[40] More robust examples of this effect come from animal research in which the internal context is more precisely controlled through drug injections (e.g., alcohol or morphine) during acquisition or retention. Retention is uniformly better when testing occurs in the same drug-induced context that was present during acquisition.[41] The contextual effect of drugs on retention was exploited in *The Moonstone*, written in 1868 by Wilkie Collins. In this story, which is regarded as the first full-length detective novel, a man who had been given laudanum (tincture of opium) as a cure for insomnia takes his cousin's valuable diamond for safekeeping during the night. In the morning, the diamond is nowhere to be found and the man is suspected of stealing it. It is only when his drugged condition is reinstated a year later that he is able to recall what he did with the Moonstone! (It is of no small relevance that Collins was himself addicted to opium and had personally experienced the effects of drugs on retention.)[42] When performance is impaired because of differences between the internal context during acquisition and retention, the phenomenon is referred to as **state-dependent forgetting**. Both intraorganismic and environmental contextual stimuli enter into the selected environment-behavior relation, and interference effects on "memory" are therefore affected by stimuli of both origins.

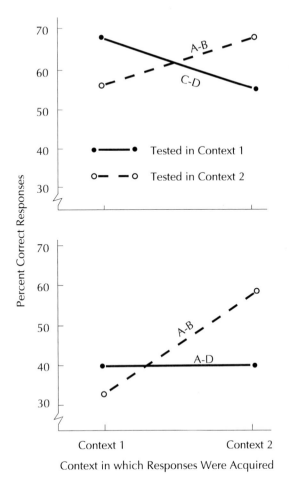

FIGURE 8.4 *Effect of context on the recall of responses in a paired-associate task*
The upper panel shows the recall of responses when the stimuli in the two tasks were different and the test context was varied. Recall was generally good, but was better when the test context was the same as the training context. The lower panel shows the recall of responses when the stimuli in the two tasks were the same and the test context was varied. Recall was generally lower when the stimuli were the same in the two tasks, demonstrating a retroactive interference effect. Once again, recall was better when the test context was the same as the training context.
Source: Adapted from findings of Smith, Glenberg, & Bjork, 1978.

REMINDING AND REMEMBERING

Until this point, we have treated the field of "memory" as if all of its phenomena could be interpreted as straightforward examples of the environmental guidance of behavior. Indeed, we have deliberately restricted our discussion almost exclusively to such examples. In studies of autobiographical memory, naming responses may be thought of as having been selected in the presence of visual stimuli provided by the faces of classmates. And, in paired-associate learning, response words may be thought of as having been selected in the presence of stimulus words. Does "memory" involve nothing more than the guidance of behavior by present stimuli that were part of the environment in which the relations were originally selected?

Something more is needed to interpret many instances of "memory," as the following example illustrates. Suppose someone asked you "When was the last time you went to the shopping mall?" You might reply "Let's see . . . Oh, yes, I went to the mall last Tuesday to buy a new pair of running shoes. The last time I went to the mall was Tuesday." Can this example of "memory" be successfully interpreted as a case in which a response (the answer) previously occurred in the presence of a stimulus (the question) and was reinforced? Clearly not. Not only is it unlikely that this response was ever reinforced before in reply to *this* question, but—more fundamentally—the same question might be the occasion for an entirely different response at another time. The response to the question changes as our trips to the mall change. The same stimulus is the occasion for different responses at different times, and the process cannot be interpreted as a straightforward case of the environmental guidance of behavior.

In order to separate those cases of "memory" that can be understood as instances of the guidance of behavior by the immediate environment from those that cannot, we make a distinction between two types of situations in which the nontechnical term "memory" is used.[43] In the first type, the present environment *does* contain stimuli that, as a result of past selections, guide the behavior cur-rently scheduled for reinforcement. Present stimuli guide behavior because the response has previously occurred, and been reinforced, in their presence. In such situations, later occurrences of behavior may be interpreted as the product of enduring environment-behavior relations. Such instances of "memory" are the outcome of selection resulting from the three-term contingency of stimulus, response, and reinforcer. From now on, we use the term **reminding** to refer to such instances. The present environment *reminds* the learner of responses that were selected in past environments. It should be clear that reminding is not the name of a special "memorial" process, but a procedural distinction that signifies similarity between the stimuli present during acquisition and retention.

We reserve the term **remembering** for all other instances of "memory;" i.e., those cases in which present behavior is determined by previously selected environment-behavior relations, but for which the present environment does *not* contain stimuli sufficient to guide the behavior now scheduled for reinforcement. The interpretation of remembering must await discussions of awareness, problem solving, and verbal behavior—subjects for later chapters. The reminding-remembering distinction is related, although not identical, to several other proposals.[44] One of the differences between the view offered here and alternative views is that, very often, the latter base their distinction on whether or not the subject is aware of—i.e., able to speak about—the retention process. Where retention is accompanied by verbal behavior related to the retention process, it is common to speak of "memory" as *explicit* rather than *implicit*.[45] Retention without awareness of the retention process is also sometimes described as *passive memory*.[46] Our interpretation recognizes that "memories" differ in these respects, but denies that these differences require postulating the existence of different *kinds* of "memories." Instead, we interpret these differences as the outcome of different realizations of a common set of biobehavioral processes.

Before we resume the analysis and interpretation of reminding, some additional comments should be made about the reminding-remembering distinction. First, it is well to repeat that the distinction is not between two different *kinds* of "memory." The terms are intended to distinguish between two different situations, in *both* of which the interpretation of present behavior depends on an appreciation of the effects of past selections. In situations to which the term reminding is more appropriately applied, the present environment contains at least some stimuli in common with past environments and it is reasonable to believe that, as a result of selection in those past environments, these common stimuli are sufficient to guide the behavior in question. Thus when someone recalls the German word for *dog*, i.e., *hund*, 50 years after taking a high-school German class in which *dog* was a vocabulary word,[47] this may reasonably be regarded as a case of reminding and interpreted as an instance of the environmental guidance of behavior.

Second, behavior that occurs under conditions of reminding or remembering does not require new principles for its understanding. The fundamental principles of a selectionist approach to complexity apply equally to the interpretation of reminding and remembering. However, the same principles have different implications for the interpretation of remembering, because the relation of the present environment to the one in which selection took place is more complex. In reminding, the responses scheduled for reinforcement are guided by contemporaneous environmental stimuli. In remembering, the responses scheduled for reinforcement are guided by other stimuli—sometimes covert—that are produced by the subject's own behavior. These other responses and the stimuli that control them may be collectively referred to as remembering processes, but they are viewed as particular expressions of general biobehavioral processes.

Finally, it is rare that any situation—particularly in the natural environment—provides a "pure" instance of either reminding or remembering. Almost all environments contain some stimuli

in common with earlier environments, and some of the responses guided by those environments are likely to be scheduled for reinforcement in the present environment. This is particularly true as the learner's history of selection grows ever richer and, to that extent, "memory" exemplifies the direct environmental guidance of behavior characteristic of reminding. However, many environments do not contain stimuli sufficient to guide the behavior scheduled for reinforcement. To that extent, "memory" exemplifies remembering. For example, recalling the German word for *dog* might not be an instance of reminding if the person recalled the answer by going through something like the following process: "Now, what is that word? I used to know it. Could it be *hound*? . . . No, *hound* is an English word. . . But the word I'm looking for is something like *hound* . . . Oh, I know! It's *hund*."[48] Here, the response "hund," which is the one scheduled for reinforcement, is not guided by the stimulus of the question; rather, the question guides the occurrence of other processes that lead eventually to the stimulus controlling "hund."

Methodological Implications of the Reminding-Remembering Distinction

Although an experimenter has no way of guaranteeing that a given retention procedure is a "pure" reminding procedure for all subjects, two circumstances make this more likely. First, and most obviously, the stimuli present during the retention test must include some of those that functioned as discriminative stimuli when the response in question was originally selected. This increases the likelihood that present stimuli are sufficient to guide the response whose retention is being assessed. Two methods are used to insure that the stimuli used in the retention test are sufficient to guide the response: (a) The stimuli are events from the natural environment that are likely to have been encountered under similar circumstances by most subjects; e.g., they are common meaningful words. (b) The stimuli used in the retention test include discriminative stimuli from an earlier learning task specifically arranged by the experimenter. Either of these methods increases the likelihood that previous discriminative stimuli are present during the retention test.

A second way to favor a "pure" reminding procedure is to employ methods that prevent or severely restrict the occurrence of remembering processes. Again, two methods are used with human learners, often together, to approximate this goal: (a) The interval between the presentation of the stimulus whose response is to be recalled and the occurrence of the retention test is made very short—a few seconds at most. (b) The retention interval is occupied by activities that interfere with any remembering processes. Shortening the retention interval and filling it with other activities are both intended to prevent remembering processes from occurring. With some learners, an additional means is available: The opportunity for remembering may be controlled by using subjects—such as young children or animals—who have not had a selection history in which they have acquired remembering processes.

REMINDING

Here, we consider findings from several procedures that approximate conditions that restrict "memory" to instances of reminding; i.e, cases in which the environment directly guides the response scheduled for reinforcement.

Reminding in Short-Term Memory Procedures

In one typical short-term memory procedure, the experimenter presents a visual stimulus consisting of three familiar letters, e.g., RLQ, and after a brief interval asks the subject to pronounce the name of each letter. During the interval, the subject is required to engage in some task, e.g., counting aloud backwards by 3's from a randomly determined number such as 541. At the end of a variable and brief retention interval, the subject is asked to recall the three letters. This basic sequence of events is repeated many times for a variety of letter combinations, until a number of observations are obtained at several different retention intervals. Although recalling a just-pronounced set of three letters would normally be trivially easy, when a **distractor task** such as counting backwards by 3's is introduced, performance typically falls to chance levels in less than 20 seconds![49]

The inability of visually presented letters to guide vocal responses only a few seconds after the letters were presented demonstrates retroactive interference by the distractor task. Among other factors, the vocal responses of counting backwards by 3's may compete with remembering by preventing the subject from subvocally rehearsing the names of the letters, which would otherwise occur during the retention interval.[50]

Proactive effects. Events that occur *before* the stimuli whose responses are measured in the retention test also affect performance in short-term memory procedures. In the preceding experiment, each subject was given multiple trials in which a letter combination was presented and recall was required. Thus, except for the first trial, each letter combination was preceded by the distractor task and the presentation of other letters. The result of this sequence of events is that the different letter combinations and the stimulus context in which they appear become increasingly similar as the experiment goes on.

Consistent with the above interpretation, the subjects' retention performance on successive trials progressively declined.[51] On the first trial, retention was perfect in spite of the distractor task. However, as the number of previous trials increased, retention became progressively worse. (See **Figure 8.5**.) When meaningful words were used as stimuli, further evidence was obtained supporting the interfering effects of previous trials on retention. If at some point during the experiment the types of stimuli are changed, e.g., from the names of fruits to the names of professions,[52] or the circumstances of the retention test are

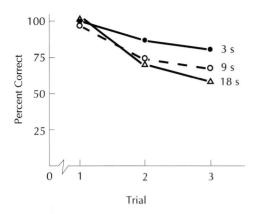

FIGURE 8.5 *Changes in recall with a short-term memory procedure after 1, 2, or 3 trials of the procedure*
The results are shown for three different retention intervals—3 sec, 9 sec, and 18 sec. Note that recall declined as the number of preceding trials increased, demonstrating a proactive interference effect.
Source: From Keppel, G., & Underwood, B. J. (1962). Proactive inhibition in short-term retention of single items. *Journal of Verbal Learning and Verbal Behavior, 1,* 153–161.

multiple lists of paired-associates. Benton Underwood gathered together the findings from many different experiments and examined retention as a function of the number of lists the subjects had previously learned.[54] The findings are summarized in **Figure 8.6**. Subjects who had learned only one list recalled about 75% of the response words; those who had learned more than five lists (pity the poor subjects!) recalled less than 20%.

Reminding in Serial-Recognition Procedures

A second type of task that approximates the defining conditions of a reminding procedure is similar to the matching-to-sample procedure described in an earlier chapter. In the **serial-recognition procedure**, a sequence of stimuli is rapidly presented and then, after a short retention interval, a **probe stimulus** is presented. The subject's task is to

changed,[53] retention markedly improves. Effects on retention produced by events that occur *before* the presentation of the stimuli to be recalled are known as **proactive effects**. As with retroactive effects, proactive effects can either interfere with or facilitate retention, depending on the specifics of the situation. For instance, improved retention following successive learning trials on the same task—simple acquisition—exemplifies proactive facilitation.

The natural environment contains a massive potential for proactive effects. The longer we live, the greater is the opportunity for such effects to occur. Indeed, older persons sometimes find it difficult to "stick to" a story because events in the story keep reminding them of other stories. The problem arises, not because their "memories" are bad, but because they are so good. Everything reminds them of something else. This situation can be simulated in the laboratory when subjects learn

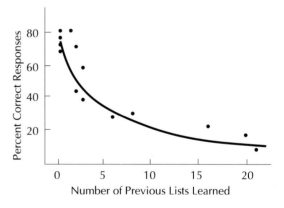

FIGURE 8.6 *Changes in recall of responses on a paired-associate task as a function of the number of preceding paired-associate tasks*
Recall of the present task decreased as the number of preceding tasks increased, demonstrating a proactive interference effect.
Source: From Underwood, B. J. (1957). Interference and forgetting. *Psychological Review, 64,* 48–60, in which the individual studies are cited that produced the various findings. Copyright © 1957 by the American Psychological Association. Reprinted by permission.

indicate whether or not the probe stimulus was among the set of sequentially presented stimuli, often called the **target stimuli**. In contrast to the matching-to-sample procedure, multiple sample stimuli (the target stimuli) are presented and the subject's response indicates whether or not the probe stimulus "matches" the enduring effect of one of them. Findings obtained with this procedure illustrate both proactive and retroactive interference effects, and suggest that the biobehavioral processes involved in reminding are the same in both humans and nonhumans.

In one of a sophisticated series of experiments conducted by Anthony Wright and his colleagues,[55] the responses of a human and a rhesus monkey were studied in the same serial-recognition procedure. On each trial, a series of 20 pictures of a variety of items such as flowers, people, and animals was flashed on a screen—each target picture for a duration of 1 sec, with a .8-sec period between stimuli. Then, after an interval of 1 sec, the probe stimulus was presented. The subject moved a lever to the right if the probe stimulus was the "same" as one of the target stimuli and to the left if it was "different." As **Figure 8.7** indicates, the overall percentage of correct "same" responses was very similar for the human and monkey subjects. Moreover, the percentage of correct "same" responses was similarly affected by the serial position of the target stimulus. As shown in **Figure 8.7**, the percentage of correct "same" responses was about 90% when the stimulus appeared first in the target set, declined somewhat for the middle stimuli, and then rose to high levels for the last few stimuli. The function relating the percentage of correct responses to the serial position of the target stimuli is called a **serial-position curve**. The higher retention of the earlier stimuli is known as a **primacy effect**, and for the later stimuli it is called a **recency effect**.[56]

Serial-position curves. The similarities between the performances of humans and nonhumans on serial-recognition tasks are even more striking. **Figure 8.8** shows serial-position curves

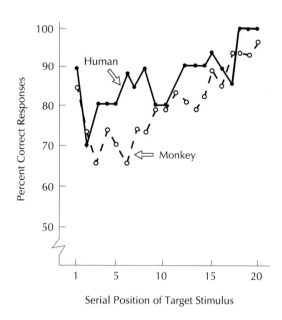

FIGURE 8.7 *Serial position curves obtained with a serial-recognition procedure*
Shown is the accuracy of recognition of a probe stimulus as a function of the position of that stimulus in the set of target stimuli. For both human and monkey subjects, recognition was high for the initial stimulus in the target set (primacy effect), lower for middle stimuli, and increased for later stimuli (recency effect).
Source: Adapted from Sands, S. F., & Wright, A. A. (1980). Serial probe recognition performance by a Rhesus monkey and a human with 10- and 20-item lists. *Journal of Experimental Psychology, 6,* 386–396. Copyright © 1980 by the American Psychological Association. Adapted by permission.

from pigeons (top panels), monkeys (middle panels), and humans (bottom panels) at different intervals between the end of the target set and the presentation of the probe stimulus. For all species, the serial-position curves show only a recency effect at a 0-sec retention interval, both primacy and recency effects at intermediate retention intervals, and only a primacy effect at the longest retention intervals.[57] Note, however, that these changes in the serial-position curves occurred at shorter retention intervals for pigeons, somewhat longer intervals for monkeys, and still longer intervals for humans.

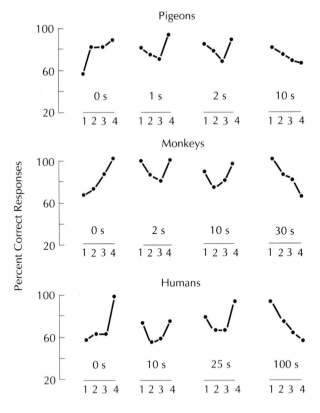

Serial Position of Target Stimulus

FIGURE 8.8   *Serial position curves obtained with a serial-recognition procedure at different retention intervals between the last stimulus of a four-stimulus target set and the presentation of the probe stimulus*
The top panel shows serial-position curves for pigeons at retention intervals of 0, 1, 2, and 10 s. The middle panel shows serial-position curves for monkeys at retention intervals of 0, 2, 10, and 30 s. The bottom panel shows serial-position curves for humans at 0, 10, 25, and 100 s.
Source: Adapted from Wright, A. A., Santiago, H. C., Sands, S. F., Kendrick, D. F., & Cook, R. G.(1985). Memory processing of serial lists by pigeons, monkeys, and people, *Science, 229,* 287–289. Copyright 1985 by the AAAS.

What is responsible for changes in the shape of the serial-position curve as the retention interval increases? First, note that within each trial, the processes initiated by earlier-appearing stimuli have an opportunity to alter the reaction to later-appearing stimuli—a proaction effect. Similarly, the processes initiated by later-appearing stimuli can alter reactions to earlier-appearing stimuli—a retroaction effect. Reactions to stimuli toward the middle of the target set can be altered by effects of both origins.[58]

Primacy and recency effects.   Let us examine the origins of primacy and recency effects more closely. To interpret these effects, the relation between the length of the retention interval and the length of the intertrial interval between successive serial-recognition trials is crucial. In these experiments, the length of the intertrial interval ranged from 4 to 10 sec in various studies. The first stimulus in the target set appeared after the intertrial interval, and therefore—unlike all other stimuli—was not immediately preceded by other stimuli. Thus, when the retention interval was long, the context in which the probe stimulus appeared and the context in which the first stimulus in the target set appeared were most similar; i.e., neither stimulus was immediately preceded by any other stimulus. If the context in which a stimulus appears partially determines the effect of that stimulus, then primacy effects should occur when there are longer retention intervals between the last stimulus of the target set and the probe stimulus. This is precisely what was found. (See the rightmost panels of **Figure 8.8**.)

An examination of the context in which the target and probe stimuli appeared also permits an interpretation of the recency effect. The last stimulus in the target set was presented immediately after other stimuli. The probe stimulus was presented in such a context only when it appeared immediately after the last stimulus of the target set. That is, the contexts of the last target stimulus and the probe stimulus were most similar at short retention intervals. And, as shown in the leftmost panels of **Figure 8.8**, recency effects were confined to the shorter retention intervals.

In summary, primacy and recency effects appear to be instances of context effects, and therefore interpretable by means of the basic biobehavioral processes identified in experimental analyses of the guidance of behavior. Of course, it is logically possible—although unparsimonious—that similar functional relationships between variables may result from dissimilar biobehavioral processes. Thus, it is possible that the origins of primacy and recency effects in humans may be different from their origins in other species. For example, inferred-process theories have postulated alternative accounts of the primacy and recency effects with human subjects in related procedures.[59] Specifically, it has been postulated that human subjects rehearse verbal stimuli when they are presented and that, since there is more opportunity to rehearse the earlier stimuli, the primacy effect is the result of rehearsal. However, serial-recognition studies with humans in which the stimuli were complex and unfamiliar kaleidoscope pictures—and, therefore, unlikely to be rehearsable—also showed a primacy effect. The occurrence of primacy effects with kaleidoscopic stimuli, which are not rehearsable, and with nonhuman species, whose selection history does not produce rehearsal behavior, indicate that rehearsal is not necessary for the primacy effect.[60]

Remembering in serial-recognition procedures.
When the conditions that restrict remembering processes are relaxed, the serial-recognition procedure no longer approximates a "pure" reminding procedure. And, if remembering processes can occur, then something other than a quantitative difference emerges between retention in humans and other species. For example, when the stimuli were color slides of everyday objects such as flowers, trees, and cars, *and* the time between presentations of stimuli in the target set was increased to 4 sec, the retention of humans improved while that of monkeys did not. The use of familiar stimuli and increased time between stimuli permitted remembering processes to affect retention. The familiarity of the stimuli permitted them to evoke discriminated responses (e.g., the sight of a tree could evoke the verbal response "tree"), and the increased time permitted the subjects to rehearse those responses.

To evaluate the contribution of rehearsal to retention, another serial-recognition experiment was conducted using kaleidoscope stimuli with human subjects. In this study, however, the subjects were first given a paired-associate task in which they acquired a distinctive verbal response to each of the kaleidoscope pictures. For example, if a kaleidoscope picture looked a bit like an insect, the reinforced verbal response was "bug." Although the primacy and recency effects continued to occur, overall retention performance *improved* as the time between presentations of the target stimuli increased from 0.8 sec to 4.0 sec.[61] In a control condition in which the subjects had not acquired distinctive verbal responses to the kaleidoscope stimuli, increasing the time between target stimuli had no effect on retention. A closer analysis of behavior during the retention test indicated that subjects whose retention improved most rehearsed the verbal responses in the intervals between presentation of the target stimuli, and matched the verbal response evoked by the probe stimulus to the set of rehearsed verbal responses. Thus, when stimuli are meaningful (i.e., are discriminative stimuli) and there is enough time to permit remembering processes to occur, retention in the serial-recognition procedure is no longer a "pure" measure of the direct environmental guidance of behavior; i.e., reminding.[62] It is not yet known how retention in monkeys is affected when stimuli are used that have been discriminated before the serial-recognition procedure, and when behavior analogous to rehearsal has been acquired—assuming that were possible.

Reminding in Cued-Recall Procedures

Cued-recall procedures provide the final experimental example in which "memory" can sometimes be interpreted as a case of the direct guidance of behavior by the environment during the retention test. However, as with most phenomena denoted by the nontechnical term "memory," retention in cued-recall procedures is often the expression of other biobehavioral processes as well. In one *cued-recall procedure,*[63] subjects were given a series of lists of word pairs to study. After each list of 24 word pairs, a retention test was given in which the first word of each pair—the cue—was presented, and the subject was asked to recall the second word of the pair—the target. As a result of the subjects' pre-experimental experience, some of the cue words strongly guided the target words, e.g., *SKY-blue*, while others guided

them only weakly, e.g., *BOY-blue*. In the retention test following the third list, cue words frequently evoked correct responses. Retention was about 80% correct when the cue word had guided the response strongly before the experiment, and over 70% when the cue word had initially guided the response only weakly. Thus, if the cue word appeared both when the lists were studied and when the retention test was conducted, retention was high. The beneficial effects of cue words on retention could not be attributed to pre-experimental relations alone. Cue words that guided target words equally strongly on the basis of pre-experimental experience, but that had not been presented during the study session, evoked correct target words with a frequency of only 30% for strongly guiding cues and only 4% for weakly guiding cues. For a cue to effectively facilitate retention, it had to be present during *both* the study and retention periods.

In a second cued-recall study,[64] subjects studied a list of word pairs in which all of the cue words weakly guided the target words, e.g., *GLUE-chair*. Then, the subjects were given two types of retention test in succession. In the first test, target words were embedded in a set of new words that had *not* appeared in the study session, e.g., *desk, top, chair, table*. Subjects were asked to recognize the target word among the new words. The second test was a standard cued-recall procedure in which the cues were those that had appeared in the study session, e.g., *GLUE*. The subjects recalled more target words in the cued-recall test than they recognized in the test without the cues. Although a "common-sense" view suggests that it would always be easier to merely recognize a word than to recall it, retention was once again better when the environment during the test was similar to the study environment in which the target response was strengthened.

Remembering in cued-recall procedures. Major aspects of findings obtained with cued-recall procedures allow them to be interpreted as reminding procedures: The target response was previously selected in the presence of the cues, and the presence of the cues during the retention test improved retention. However, biobehavioral processes other than those directly initiated by the cues are almost certainly involved as well. The cues were meaningful stimuli, i.e., they already guided many responses because of their extensive selection history before the experiment. Also, the procedure did not severely restrict the opportunity for remembering processes during the study and retention periods, allowing ample time for their occurrence.

Complex human behavior—even in well-designed laboratory studies—can seldom be unambiguously interpreted as the result of only one biobehavioral process. Our selection histories are so rich, and the experimental conditions are insufficiently controlled to eliminate all the effects of that history. As an illustration, consider another example of retention in a cued-recall procedure. Subjects studied several lists, each consisting of groups of words from various conceptual categories, e.g., *apple, orange, pear, . . ., house, cottage, hotel*, etc. The category names—fruits and buildings in the example—were *not* mentioned to the subjects during the study periods. After studying and then recalling each of a number of such lists, the subjects were given a final retention test for words from all the lists. Some subjects were asked to recall the words with the aid of the category names; others were simply asked to recall as many of the words as possible without the category names. The retention test indicated that the subjects given the category names recalled many more words than the subjects who had studied the lists to the same degree but were not given the category names.[65]

How should these findings be interpreted? One possible account is that—during the study sessions—the target words evoked the category names because of the subjects' selection histories before the experiment. The category-name responses, which are unobserved on the behavioral level, could then provide distinctive stimuli that acquired an increased ability to guide the target words because of selection *taking place during the study sessions.* Thereafter, when the category names were presented by the experimenter during the retention test, they could facilitate the occurrence of the target words because category-name stimuli strongly guided the target words. In short, unobserved biobehavioral processes are assumed to provide covert stimuli that function in the same manner as the observed cue words in the earlier cued-recall procedures. According to such an account, the occurrence of the target words during the retention test is simply another instance of the guidance of behavior—even though some of the critical stimuli are unobserved. (See **Figure 8.9a** for a summary of this interpretation.)

Other accounts of these same findings are equally plausible, however. Perhaps covert stimuli provided by the unobserved category-name responses did not acquire an increased ability to evoke the target words during the study session. Instead, the improvement in retention may be attributed to unobserved processes occurring exclusively within the retention test. To be specific, when the category names were presented during the retention test, they may have evoked unobserved responses because of the subjects' pre-experimental selection history. For example, in the context of instructions to recall as many words as possible, a category name such as *fruit* may evoke covert responses such as *apple*, among others. Since *apple* was presented during the study session, the subject might recognize *apple* as more "familiar" than some of the other fruit words evoked by the category name—e.g., *grape*—and therefore respond *apple* in the retention test. This second interpretation is an instance of remembering rather than reminding, since the environment during the retention test did not contain stimuli sufficient to guide the emission of the target words. (See **Figure 8.9b** for a summary of this account.)

Both interpretations are plausible: Both appeal to biobehavioral processes—behavioral selection, discrimination, generalization—that are well understood from earlier experimental analyses. Moreover, both the study and retention sessions contain stimuli that may reasonably be thought

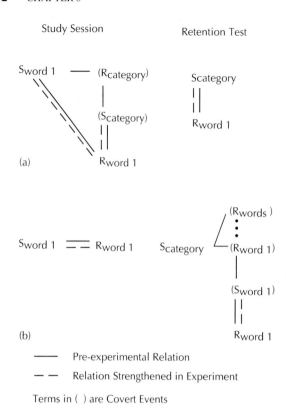

Study Session   Retention Test

(a)

(b)

——   Pre-experimental Relation

— —   Relation Strengthened in Experiment

Terms in ( ) are Covert Events

FIGURE 8.9   *Two interpretations of the results from cued-recall procedures*
(a) During the study session a stimulus-word is assumed to evoke the category name as a covert response and the covert stimulus produced by the category name is assumed to acquire an increased ability to evoke the response-words that occurred in its presence. Then, during the retention test when the stimulus of the category name is presented, response-words are evoked because the category name acquired control of these words within the study session. (b) During the study session the stimulus-word acquires an increased ability to evoke the response-word. Then during the retention test, the stimulus of the category name is assumed to evoke various words as a covert responses and some of these responses are recognized as the overt responses that occurred during the study session. In this interpretation, enhanced performance is interpreted as the result of events occurring within the retention test.

sufficient to initiate the various processes. However, some of the events invoked in the interpretations were unobserved under the conditions of the experiment. What is clear is that, when retention involves stimuli and responses that have been subject to a prolonged history of pre-experimental selection, and the time intervals between the presentation of stimuli or between study and retention are long, the retained responses cannot be understood solely as instances of direct guidance by the contemporary environment.

How can we evaluate the cogency of these and other interpretations of complex behavior when they appeal to events that are unobserved with present technology? When appeals are made to processes that cannot be directly observed, as with complex patterns of activity among neurons in the brain, we have left the domain of experimental analysis and entered the realm of interpretation. Our efforts to understand "memory" have reached (perhaps exceeded) the boundaries of our ability to directly manipulate all of the variables that guide behavior, and to measure all of the biobehavioral processes affected by those variables. The first is an uncircumventable characteristic of all historical science. In such circumstances, historical science provides interpretations that are sufficient to encompass the observations, but the observations may not be necessary consequences of processes resulting from experimental analysis. The second is a technical problem that is increasingly remedied as biobehavioral science develops ever more sensitive techniques for measuring microbehavioral and physiological processes.

In the next chapter, we explore adaptive neural networks as means of interpreting complex behavioral phenomena that are expressions of unobserved subbehavioral processes and prolonged histories of selection. As long as our interpretations are constrained by principles that summarize findings obtained through experimental analysis, we need not lose our way. Experimental analysis together with scientific interpretation provide a powerful means for understanding complexity, as other historical sciences amply demonstrate.

STUDY AIDS

Technical Terms

cue
episodic memory
flashbulb memory
semantic memory
autobiographical memory
decay theory
paired-associate learning
retroactive interference
retroactive facilitation
state-dependent forgetting
reminding
remembering
distractor task
proactive effect
serial-recognition procedure
probe stimulus
target stimulus
serial-position curve
primacy effect
recency effect

Text Questions

1. From a procedural perspective, in what circumstances is the nontechnical term "memory" used? Why is "memory" likely to be a theoretically incoherent term?

2. If the outcome of behavioral selection is the selection of environment-behavior relations, then what must be present in order for a "memory" to occur? When the same "memory" occurs, must the stimulus be the same; must the neural pathways activated by the stimuli be the same? Explain your answer using information from both the behavioral and neural levels.

3. What are the similarities and differences between those environment-behavior relations that are referred to as episodic, semantic, and flashbulb "memories"? Do these terms refer to different types of "memories" arising from different biobehavioral processes?

4. Summarize the evidence from research on *autobiographical memory* and on animal memory concerning the retention of environment-behavior relations. Comment on any advantages and disadvantages of the methods used to study autobiographical memory. Comment on the relevance of

the verbal bias for the interpretation of these findings.

5. Summarize findings concerning the effects of environmental and intra-organismic context on "memory." Interpret these results as complex instances of the environmental guidance of behavior.

6. What is the distinction between reminding and remembering? Be able to give likely examples of each. Can you determine from the response alone whether it exemplifies reminding or remembering? Explain.

7. Describe the methods and findings from research using *short-term memory procedures*. Use the term *proactive effect* in your answer.

8. Using technical terms, describe the procedures and major findings obtained with the *serial-recognition procedure*. Include a presentation of serial-position effects and interpret these findings as instances of reminding and/or remembering. Do these studies indicate that remembering occurs only in humans? Explain.

9. Describe the major findings obtained with the *cued-recall procedure*. Interpret these findings in view of the distinction between reminding and remembering. Comment on the distinction between recognition and recall measures in the light of this distinction.

Discussion Questions

10. Inferred-process theories, such as those in cognitive psychology, refer to "memories" as being "stored" (either in some hypothetical structure such as long-term memory or, less often, in the real brain). From a biobehavioral perspective, where are "memories" when we are not having them? Explain your answer.

11. Under laboratory conditions, what are the circumstances that favor the occurrence of reminding? Of remembering? Under everyday conditions, are there apt to be responses that are "pure" instances of either reminding or remembering? If not, is there any point to making the distinction?

ENDNOTES

1. As with other nontechnical terms, "memory" has potentially undesirable effects other than simply grouping together phenomena that are only superficially similar. The noun "memory" confers a static *thing*-like quality to what is a process, and encourages unhelpful practices such as ascribing individual differences in behavior to differences in "memory capacity" rather than to differences in selection history. Thus people are often said to have good or bad memories and their different histories of selection are not considered. The objection to "memory" is not a mere philosophical quibble since, when we attribute deficiencies in "memory" to deficient histories, we are encouraged to provide the missing history rather than to passively accept a difference in capacity.

Clearly, we do not regard the behavior studied under the heading of "memory" as different in kind from other environment-behavior relations. The arbitrariness of distinguishing the study of "memory" from the study of selection is apparent when we consider that the selection process necessarily involves "memory"; If the effect of one trial of a learning experiment were not retained, performance on the subsequent trial could not be affected; i.e., acquisition could not occur without "memory." The term "memory" is customarily reserved for the effects of other environment-behavior relations on the retention of prior relations. However, it is also clear that other environment-behavior relations can affect the acquisition as well as the retention of present relations. The term "transfer" is commonly used to denote such effects; the effects of prior selection are said to "transfer" to the learning of new selections. The variables that influence retention affect "transfer" as well since, as noted above, the distinction between "memory" and acquisition does not refer to a difference in kind but to a difference in the focus of the investigation (cf. Osgood, 1949). The processes involved in stimulus generalization contribute to both "memory" and "transfer"; similar environments guide similar responses. But robust "memory" and "transfer" require more than the naturally occurring outcome of generalization. Robust effects require explicit training for "transfer" and "memory," and are particularly important if behavioral therapies are to prove effective beyond the therapeutic environment (cf. Stokes & Baer, 1977). Training for "memory" is explicitly addressed in Chapter 12.

2. When the present conditions include such stimuli—both environmental and intra-organismic (cf. Estes, 1958)—this constitutes *sufficient* conditions for

the control of responses by these stimuli. However, responses may also reliably occur under other conditions; i.e., such conditions are not *necessary* for their occurrence. The general circumstances under which responses may reliably occur when present conditions do not contain stimuli that control them are considered in a later chapter on problem solving, and are acknowledged later in this chapter as instances of *remembering*.

3. e.g., Georgopolous, 1990; Georgopoulos, Schwartz, & Ketner, 1986; Kalaska & Crammond, 1992.

4. Geschwind, Quadfasel, & Segarra, 1968.

5. This example will be recognized as yet another demonstration of the inadequacies of response topography as an index of selection, cf. Skinner, 1957.

6. cf. Rumelhart, Smolensky, McClelland, & Hinton, 1986, pp. 20–21; Skinner, 1977.

7. Consistent with this view, some working within the inferred-process approach speak of "guided memories;" e.g., Malpass & Devine, 1981.

8. The inferred-process theory of encoding specificity (Tulving & Thomson, 1973; Tulving, 1974) is recognized as closely related to this general view, and studies motivated by that theory are discussed later in this chapter.

9. The view that the connections that are strengthened within a network are a joint function of the units activated by the nominal discriminative stimulus and those activated by the stimulus context is closely related to Clark Hull's principle of *afferent neural interaction* (Hull, 1943). Donald Hebb said that this principle "had the smell of brimstone about it" (Hebb, 1949, p. 79) because, unless the precise nature of the interaction was specified, precise prediction could not be achieved. We concur with Hebb's concerns, but regard the problem as only a particular instance of the more general problem faced by all historical sciences—incomplete knowledge of the full history of selection. Experimental analysis clearly demonstrates that the thresholds of some neurons are affected by inputs in several sensory channels; interpretations of behavior must accommodate that fact.

10. Tulving, 1972.

11. e.g., Anderson, J. R., 1983; Jacoby, 1988; Snodgrass, 1989.

12. Brown & Kulik, 1977.

13. There is controversy about the validity of flashbulb memories and, again, some investigators believe that they require special principles for their understanding, while we and others do not; cf. Schmidt & Bohannon, 1988; McCloskey, Wible, & Cohen, 1988.

14. cf. Tulving, 1972, p. 386.

15. Note that response topography is not a reliable indicator of whether a "memory" is best viewed as toward the episodic or semantic end of a continuum of environment-behavior relations. For a person reared in a cave and first emerging into the daylight as an adult, the response "blue" would likely be one of the responses making up an *episodic* memory. The specifics of the individual's selection history determine which stimuli guide what responses; the topography of the response alone is insufficiently informative.

16. cf. McClelland & Rumelhart, The PDP Group, 1986.

17. Bahrick, Bahrick, & Wittlinger, 1975.

18. For related findings, see Bahrick, 1979, 1983, 1984; Pillemer, Goldsmith, Panter, & White, 1988; Squire, 1989.

19. Bahrick & Phelps, 1988.

20. For more on this point, see Hart, 1965; Nelson, Gerler, & Narens, 1984.

21. Jenkins & Dallenbach, 1924.

22. cf. McGeoch & Irion, 1952. Among the most important events that occur as time passes are those that select environment-behavior relations relevant to the original selections. For example, in studies of autobiographical "memory" for high-school classmates, it is likely that some of the classmates were seen or thought about during the interim. Adaptive-network simulations have shown that environment-behavior relations can be mediated by the network even with substantial losses of connections *especially if additional selections occur throughout the period of loss.* This simulation result parallels experimental findings which indicate that the deleterious effects of a given surgically-produced brain lesion are diminished if the lesion is produced by the cumulative effect of successive smaller lesions than by a single complete lesion; Anderson, J. A., 1984.

23. For a discussion of the relation between laboratory methods of studying retention in humans and more ecologically valid procedures, see Winograd, 1988.

24. Kolers, 1979; cf. Hunt & Elliott, 1980.

25. Franks, described in Jenkins, 1980.

26. Liddell, James, & Anderson, 1935.

27. Skinner, 1950.

28. To designate words as stimuli or responses is a great oversimplification since words are much more complex events than those designated by the same terms in the animal learning laboratory—events such as tones and leverpresses. Clearly, words themselves are products of substantial histories of behavioral selection. Complications arising from considering a word as a

simple stimulus or response are considered in later chapters, but do not affect the main thrust of the present discussion.

29. To avoid the nominal fallacy, recognize that retroactive interference and retroactive facilitation are simply the names of phenomena and not their explanations.

30. For surveys of this literature, see Crowder, 1976; Postman & Underwood, 1973.

31. cf. Postman, 1971.

32. For a discussion of some of the conceptual problems in work using standard verbal learning procedures, see Donahoe & Wessells, 1980, pp. 210–216. The generality of all experimental findings is limited by the methods used to produce them, and paired-associate learning provided an inadequate inductive basis for understanding many of the phenomena of memory and verbal behavior in experienced leaners.

33. cf. Anderson, J. R., 1983; Hinton & Anderson, 1981; Smolensky, 1986.

34. e.g., McCloskey & Cohen, 1989; Ratcliff, 1990.

35. Lewandowsky, 1991.

36. Barnes & Underwood, 1959.

37. cf. Greeno, James, DaPolito, & Polson, 1978; Martin, 1971.

38. Smith, Glenberg, & Bjork, 1978.

39. For an early demonstration of the effects of context on retroaction, see Bilodeau & Schlosberg, 1951. For overviews of some of the factors that affect context effects in humans see Bjork & Richardson-Klavehn, 1989; Davies & Thomson, 1988; and in nonhumans see Balsam & Tomie, 1985. See Rudy, 1974 for the contribution of blocking to contextual and other retroaction effects.

40. Bower, 1981.

41. For a review, see Overton, 1985.

42. See Siegel, 1985 for a fascinating account of the background of these events.

43. Palmer, 1991.

44. e.g., Kolers & Roediger, 1984; Newell, 1973b; Tulving, 1985; Roediger, 1990a; see also Jacoby, 1988.

45. Schacter, 1987.

46. Spence, 1988.

47. cf. Bahrick, 1984.

48. This example, in which the "same" response, *hund*, is the result of a different sequence of biobehavioral processes, is another illustration of the general point that response topography by itself does not provide a basis for the analysis or interpretation of behavior. The "same" response may occur under the guidance of many different stimuli and, as such, cannot be considered the same in any useful sense. Thus, different procedures for studying "memory" do not study the same "memory," but—at most—responses of similar topography guided by a partially common set of stimuli.

49. Brown, 1958; Peterson & Peterson, 1959.

50. Crowder, 1976; Johnson, 1980.

51. Keppel & Underwood, 1962.

52. Wickens, 1972.

53. Gardiner, Craik, & Birtwistle, 1972.

54. Underwood, 1957.

55. Sands & Wright, 1980.

56. The results described here were from the final condition following a very extended period of pretraining for the monkey subject. The human subject's behavior was established by instructions and maintained by the consequences of performing satisfactorily, which included an hourly wage. The monkey's behavior was maintained by such reinforcers as orange juice and banana pellets for correct responses. Before being tested with a 20-item target set, the monkey had received extensive training with target sets of gradually increasing size—a fading technique. Most importantly, the monkey had first received training in which only two stimuli were presented and moving the lever to the right was reinforced when the stimuli were the same and to the left when they were different. Speaking nontechnically, a "same/different concept" was first established.

57. Wright, Santiago, Sands, Kendrick, & Cook, 1985; cf. Wright & Watkins, 1987.

58. cf. Postman & Underwood, 1973.

59. e.g., Glanzer & Cunitz, 1966; Atkinson & Shiffrin, 1968; Waugh & Norman, 1965.

60. cf. Wright, Cook, Rivera, Shyan, Neiworth, & Jitsumori, 1990.

61. See Wright, Cook, Rivera, Shyan, Neiworth, & Jitsumori, 1990 for further analyses and interpretations of such findings.

62. These studies are summarized in Wright & Watkins, 1987; Wright, 1989.

63. Thomson & Tulving, 1970.

64. Tulving & Thomson, 1973; cf. Watkins & Tulving, 1975.

65. Tulving & Psotka, 1971.

CHAPTER 9

FUNCTIONING OF
THE EXPERIENCED LEARNER

As selection by the individual environment proceeds and the products of selection accumulate, the functioning of the learner becomes increasingly difficult to understand solely in terms of the stimuli sensed at the moment and their relation to ongoing behavior. The present environment increasingly acts on an organism that has been changed by the selecting effects of past environments. Although the environment of the moment remains necessary for the interpretation of complex behavior, it becomes increasingly insufficient as the selection history grows more extensive. The view that contemporary events provide an incomplete basis for understanding complexity should be neither novel nor surprising at this point; it is inherent in all historical sciences, of which the science of behavior is one.[1]

We begin this chapter by summarizing the biobehavioral processes initiated when the environment acts on a learner with an extensive history of behavioral selection. This sequence of events, which begins with the sensing of the environment and ends with the guidance of behavior, is largely a product of behavioral selection. The effects of behavioral selection are not confined to events that are observable at the behavioral level, but include subbehavioral events as well. Subbehavioral events also trace their lineages to the action of the environment because, without their ultimate effects on behavior, they would not have been selected. Subbehavioral events—notably changes in synaptic efficacies between neurons—are the means by which environment-behavior relations are mediated. However, once selected for their effects at the behavioral level, subbehavioral events are available to mediate more subtle activi-

ties of experienced learners such as problem solving, verbal behavior, and remembering. Later chapters provide interpretations of such complex behavior; this chapter describes some of the major biobehavioral processes mediating that behavior.[2]

ENVIRONMENTAL GUIDANCE IN
THE EXPERIENCED LEARNER

The outcome of selection is that the learner's behavior is guided by environmental events—especially by stimuli and combinations of stimuli that were sensed before the occurrence of reinforcers. Stimuli that function as reinforcers, or selectors, of environment-behavior relations are initially limited to reflexive elicitors. However, other stimuli increasingly become able to function as reinforcers as they acquire the ability to evoke behavior as a result of prior behavioral selection. Together, innate and acquired reinforcers act on the organism to select new environment-behavior relations and environment-environment relations. New relations allow the learner to be sensitive to both correlations between environmental events and between environmental and behavioral events. The precision of the selected relations is sharpened through stimulus discrimination and response differentiation, narrowing the membership of stimulus and response classes to those stimuli and responses that most reliably precede reinforcing stimuli.[3]

On the neural level, environment-environment and environment-behavior relations are selected through the modification of synaptic efficacies between neurons. Synaptic efficacies are modified by influences of two general types—local influences and more widespread influences involving broadcast neuromodulatory systems. First, the concurrence of environmental stimuli activates neighboring neurons in sensory systems. This coactivity strengthens excitatory synapses between neighboring neurons and lateral inhibitory synapses between coactive excitatory neurons. The structure of the environment, acting through these mechanisms, selects sensory invariants.[4] Second, the concurrence of reinforcing stimuli with activity in different sensory channels—or with motor-system activity produced by inputs from one or more sensory channels—selects polysensory regularities and environment-behavior relations, respectively. Polysensory regularities, which integrate activity from different sensory channels, are selected by a diffusely projecting neuromodulatory output from the hippocampus to the sensory association areas. When polysensory neurons are activated by coactive inputs from different sensory channels, the neuromodulator increases the synaptic efficacies between those neurons and their inputs. Environment-behavior relations, which integrate sensory activity with motor activity that precedes reinforcing stimuli, are selected by a diffusely projecting neuromodulatory output from the ventral tegmental area (VTA) to the motor association areas. This neuromodulatory output is activated by reinforcing stimuli. When pre- and post-synaptic neurons in the motor association areas are coactive, the neuromodulator increases the synaptic efficacies between them. The VTA-derived neuromodulator also amplifies the output of the hippocampus to sensory association areas when a reinforcing stimulus occurs. Through these mechanisms, pathways in the brain mediating environment-environment and environment-behavior relations are selected in a coordinated fashion.[5] (See **Figure 9.1** for a schematic diagram of the neural mechanisms of selection.)

Given this account of the effects of selection on the behavioral and neural levels, we now explore its implications for the biobehavioral processes initiated when stimuli act upon an experienced learner.

➤

FIGURE 9.1 *Neuroanatomy of selection (upper panel) and its simulation in the architecture of a selection network (lower panel)*

As shown in the upper panel, stimulation from environmental stimuli (S$_1$ and S$_2$) activates neurons in different primary sensory areas of the cortex. Axons from these neurons propagate activity to neurons in the sensory association cortex and, ultimately, to neurons in the motor cortex. Axons from neurons in the sensory association cortex are the source, via several intervening neurons, of inputs to the hippocampus. After interactions among neurons within the hippocampus, the output of the hippocampus is diffusely projected via several intervening neurons back upon neurons in sensory association cortex. The diffusely projecting hippocampal output is proposed to cause a neuromodulator to be liberated that changes synaptic efficacies between recently coactive pre- and post-synaptic neurons in sensory association cortex. The polysensory neurons (e.g., S$_1$-S$_2$ neurons) then provide additional inputs to the motor association cortex that supplement the inputs coming more directly from sensory areas. When a reinforcing stimulus occurs, the ventral tegmental area (VTA) is stimulated. Stimulation of the VTA has two effects. First, VTA neurons diffusely project to neurons in the motor association cortex and liberate a neuromodulator, dopamine. The neuromodulator changes synaptic efficacies between recently co-active pre- and post-synaptic neurons. Among the synapses in motor association cortex that are affected are those leading to pathways that project back to the VTA via the medial forebrain bundle (MFB). The MFB pathway mediates internal reinforcement. The second effect of activating VTA neurons is to amplify the diffuse output from the hippocampus to neurons in sensory association cortex, thereby facilitating the modification of synaptic efficacies in sensory association cortex. The VTA-hippocampal pathway coordinates the selection of connections in the motor and sensory association cortices—i.e., the connections that mediate environment-behavior and environment-environment relations, respectively. Finally, neurons in the motor systems of the brain give rise to axons that produce behavior by innervating the cells of muscles and glands.

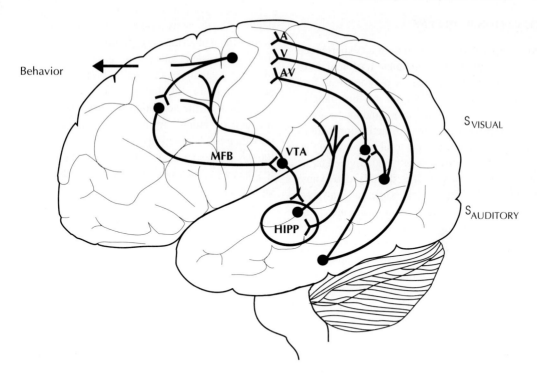

Selection Network

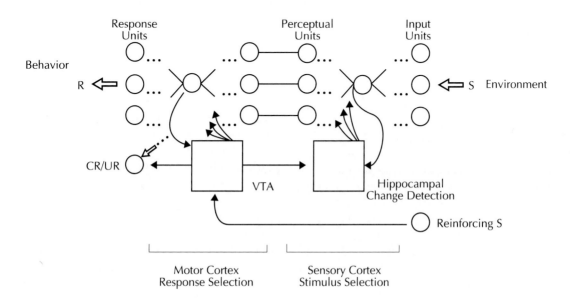

ACTIVATION PATTERNS

Stimuli applied to the receptors of an experienced learner initiate a widespread pattern of neural activity in the brain that may or may not lead to a behavioral response. We refer to this pattern, which can extend to both sensory and motor areas, as an **activation pattern**.[6] An activation pattern meets the criteria for a behavioral response in that it is guided by the environment and affected by its consequences; however, it is directly observable only at the neural level of experimental analysis.[7]

An activation pattern is not a static entity. The particular neurons whose activity makes up an activation pattern vary from moment to moment as changes occur in the organism's environment and in the local chemical environment of the constituent neurons.[8] This varying population of neuronal activity results in measurable responses at the behavioral level only if the contingencies of reinforcement in that environment have selected such responses. For example, speaking one's innermost "thoughts" might be reinforced when the audience is a friend, but not an enemy. However, the environment might evoke an activation pattern corresponding to having those "thoughts" in either case. Let us outline how an activation pattern emerges in an experienced learner.

Sensory Component

The sensory component of an activation pattern consists of the neurons in the sensory systems that are activated after the learner has sensed an environmental stimulus. Which neurons are activated depends on the synaptic efficacies in the primary sensory and sensory association cortices.[9] The synaptic efficacies depend, in turn, on the learner's cumulative selection history to that moment—both natural selection and behavioral selection. In the case of seeing, a visual stimulus initiates cortical activity that analyzes the environment into its constituent spatial frequencies. At the same moment or milliseconds later, other neurons in the visual system are analyzing other aspects of the same visual stimulus—e.g., its color, movement, and depth.[10] As the activation pattern grows with the involvement of an increasing number of neurons in the visual system, other aspects of the environment—e.g., auditory and tactile stimuli—are initiating activity in still other portions of the sensory component of the activation pattern. The activity initiated by stimuli from all sensory modalities may then produce activity in still other neurons in the sensory association areas, if synaptic efficacies to polysensory neurons have been strengthened by earlier selection.

Measurement of activation patterns.   We cannot directly measure the responses of the hundreds of thousands of neurons that constitute the sensory component of an activation pattern. However, the activity of some of the individual neurons may be monitored by microelectrodes—as we noted in earlier discussions of perceiving—and the general extent of an activation pattern may be determined. One of the methods for determining the extent of an activation pattern is positron-emission tomography, or PET. When a neuron is activated, the required energy comes from the "burning" of glucose, a simple sugar. When glucose is metabolized in the activated neuron, charged particles are emitted that can be measured from outside the head with appropriate detectors. When a stimulus is presented to a human subject, those brain areas that are most activated emit the most particles. A PET-scan detects these particles. An example of the record produced by a PET-scan is shown in the top panel of **Figure 9.2**. This record shows the brain region—the primary auditory cortex of the temporal lobe—that was active when an unfamiliar auditory stimulus (i.e., not a discriminative stimulus) was presented.[11]

If activity in different sensory channels has been correlated in the learner's experience, then the sensory component of the activation pattern includes not only neurons in the primary sensory cortex, but also neurons in the sensory association areas. These neurons mediate polysensory regularities. For example, certain combinations of auditory stimuli, and not others, appear in spoken

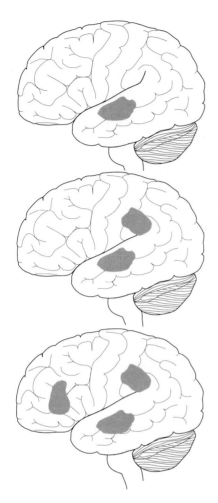

FIGURE 9.2 *Reconstructions of PET-scans in which the most strongly activated cortical regions are indicated by shaded areas*

In the upper panel, an auditory stimulus (e.g., a pure tone) was presented that was not a discriminative stimulus (i.e., did not guide behavior, was not "meaningful"). The primary auditory area was most strongly activated. In the middle panel, an auditory stimulus was again presented but now the stimulus was a speech sound (phoneme) that occurred in English, the language of the listener. With this stimulus, the auditory association area was strongly activated in addition to the primary auditory area. In the lower panel, a discriminative stimulus (a "meaningful" word) was presented and the activated areas now included the motor association cortex in addition to the primary auditory and auditory association cortices.

Source: Schematic depictions of findings from Petersen, Fox, Snyder, & Raichle, 1990.

language, and these combinations have been present when verbal behavior was differentially reinforced. The sequence of auditory stimuli that produces the /ch/ sound of "child," "choose," and other verbal stimuli occur together in the experience of listeners of English. The middle panel of **Figure 9.2** shows how familiar sequences of stimuli affect the activation pattern. A PET-scan from the subject who previously responded to unfamiliar sounds with activity only in primary auditory cortex now showed activity in auditory association cortex.

Motor Component

The primary sensory and sensory association cortices provide inputs to the motor areas of the brain through various subcortical and cortical pathways, or tracts.[12] These inputs can recruit a motor component of the activation pattern, *if* environment-behavior relations have been previously selected in the presence of the stimuli that activate the stimulus component. Thus a history of behavioral selection changes synaptic efficacies in motor areas, so that a stimulus evokes an activation pattern that includes a motor component as well as a sensory component.

The lower panel of **Figure 9.2** depicts the brain regions that were activated when speech sounds that occur in English were presented to the same subject. Now, a region of the motor association area was activated in addition to the sensory cortices. For example, if a series of the following speech sounds was presented—/ch/ /i/ /l/ /d/—a motor component was produced. This series of sounds makes up the word "child," which is a discriminative stimulus for which the English-speaking subject has an extensive selection history. Consequently, hearing this sequence of sounds causes a motor component to be added to the activation pattern evoked by the auditory stimulus. When the same subject was presented with the same speech sounds, but in an order that does not appear in English—e.g., /ch/ /l/ /d/ /i/—the activation pattern was once again confined to a sensory component.

The motor component did not appear because no behavior had ever been selected in the presence of this particular sequence of stimuli. Since the speech sounds were not "meaningful," a motor component did not emerge.[13]

Inhibitory Processes in Activation Patterns

Both the sensory and motor components of activation patterns are affected by inhibitory as well as excitatory interactions between neurons. Throughout the nervous system, the activity of individual neurons is determined by the interplay of excitatory and inhibitory processes in a fashion similar to that described in the earlier discussion of visual spatial-frequency analysis. In general, inhibitory neurons lie between neighboring excitatory neurons. The connections of inhibitory to excitatory neurons strengthen when the excitatory neuron that activates the inhibitory neuron and the excitatory neuron to which the inhibitory neuron connects are activated at the same time.[14] On this view, the selection of inhibitory connections is subordinate to the selection of excitatory connections and requires relatively little specific guidance by the genes, over half of which are already concerned with guiding the development of the nervous system. When the diffuse reinforcing systems of the sensory and motor association cortices selectively strengthen excitatory connections, inhibitory connections between coactive excitatory neurons are automatically selected. Inhibitory interactions of this sort occur at every level of the nervous system—from neurons activated by receptors to motor neurons—and limit the neurons participating in an activation pattern to those that were most reliably and strongly active when selection took place.[15]

BEHAVIORAL EFFECTS OF ACTIVATION PATTERNS

In the natural environment, activation patterns are in a constant state of flux. As behavior occurs and the environment changes, one activation pattern flows into the next, with each pattern generated by the environment depending on the state of the nervous system at that moment—and, therefore, on the state of the environment immediately before that moment. Verbal stimuli provide especially clear examples of the interdependence of successive activation patterns. For example, suppose you heard a friend say "I wanted toast for breakfast so I went to the refrigerator to get a loaf of . . . ," and a loud noise then occurred to prevent you from hearing the next word. Under such circumstances, you would "know" what your friend had said; you might even have "heard" him say the missing word even though you had not sensed the appropriate auditory stimulus.[16] In the experienced learner, the activation pattern evoked by a stimulus depends on the learner's history of selection *in the context in which the stimulus occurred*. The beginning of your friend's statement provided a context in which the missing word could be understood, or even "heard." The earlier part of the sentence *primed* you, the listener, to hear the missing word.

Priming Procedure

Although experimental analyses of activation patterns can be carried out only at the physiological level, the functioning of activation patterns may be used to interpret observations at the behavioral level. Indeed, without behavioral consequences, the neural mechanisms that implement activation patterns would not have been selected in the first place. A procedure that permits the behavioral effects of activation patterns to be studied is a **priming procedure**.

In a priming procedure, the **priming stimulus** is presented, followed shortly thereafter by the **target stimulus**. For example, the priming stimulus might be the phrase *loaf of* and the target stimulus might be the word *bread*. Or, the priming stimulus might be a single word, *butter*, and the target stimulus *bread*. The subject's task is to respond to the target stimulus according to the experimental instructions. The response evoked by the target stimulus is called the **target response**. For instance, the target response might be to pronounce the target stimulus *bread*. If some characteristic of the target response is affected by the priming stimulus, then the priming stimulus is said to **prime** the target response. For example, the target response "bread" might be spoken with a shorter latency[17] when *bread* is preceded by a priming stimulus such as *butter* rather than by an unrelated word such as *letter*.[18] (See **Figure 9.3** for a depiction of this procedure.)

Priming and Activation Patterns

From the perspective of activation patterns, if the response to a target stimulus is affected by the priming stimulus, then the activation pattern generated by the target stimulus must have been affected by the activation pattern previously generated by the priming stimulus. This can occur only if the two patterns involve some of the same neurons. Priming occurs to the extent that the activation patterns generated by the priming and target stimuli "overlap."

Possible regions of overlap in activation patterns. The activation patterns generated by priming and target stimuli may overlap in one or more brain regions, depending on the subject's history of selection with respect to those stimuli. The overlap may begin in primary sensory areas, extend to sensory and motor association areas, and conclude in motor areas. On the behavioral level, research on reminding reveals the potential richness of the guidance that stimuli can exert on responding. On the neural level, PET-scans and recordings from individual neurons indicate the potential richness of the activation patterns generated by stimuli.

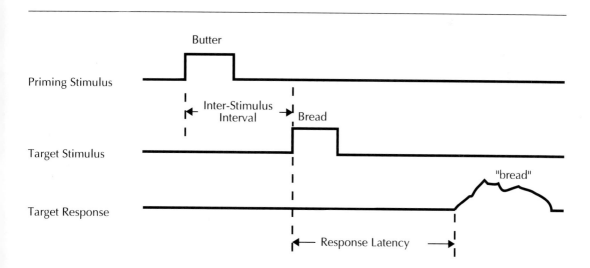

FIGURE 9.3 *Arrangement of events in a priming procedure*
A priming stimulus is presented—here the visual stimulus BUTTER—followed, after an interstimulus interval specified in the experiment, by the target stimulus—here the visual stimulus BREAD. The subject is instructed to emit a target response to the target stimulus as rapidly as possible—here the *name* of the target stimulus, the verbal response "bread." The latency of the target response is the time between the presentation of the target stimulus and the occurrence of the target response. If the latency of the target response is affected by the priming stimulus, then the priming stimulus is said to prime the target response.

Verbal stimuli, because of their rich selection histories, can evoke particularly extensive responding and activation patterns. When a subject learns lists consisting of a mixture of words printed in upper-case (e.g., *FARM*) and lower-case letters (e.g., *book*), retention tests indicate that words are more apt to be recognized when they are printed in the same case in which they were learned.[19] Thus, specific visual features of verbal stimuli may be retained, and activation patterns may be generated in sensory areas of the brain. Studies also indicate that auditory and articulatory aspects of visually presented verbal stimuli may be retained. When a subject learns a list of paired-associates composed of items such as 27-*tacks* and is later asked to learn a second list of paired-associates with the same stimuli but different responses, the new responses are learned more rapidly if they evoke similar vocal responses (e.g., 27-*tax*).[20] Thus, activation patterns generated by verbal stimuli may involve auditory association and motor association cortex as well as visual cortex. Finally, retention tests indicate that when responses in the paired-associate procedure are similar in meaning (e.g., *sofa* and *loveseat*), that similarity also affects retention. Even when stimuli do not "look alike" or "sound alike," their activation patterns may overlap in the motor association areas of the brain. (See the lower panel of **Figure 9.2**.)[21] In summary, the activation patterns generated by priming and target stimuli may overlap in a number of regions in the sensory and motor areas, depending on the learner's history of selection with respect to those stimuli. Where the overlap occurs, and when it occurs, affects the nature and degree of priming.[22]

Extent of Priming

Given the abundant behavioral evidence that selection can produce very complex relations involving verbal stimuli and responses, let us see what priming procedures reveal about the activation patterns that mediate these relations. In priming procedures, many different types of priming stimuli, target stimuli, and target responses have been used. We largely restrict ourselves to conditions that resemble those under which selection takes place in the natural environment. When more ecologically valid procedures are used, stimuli are more apt to evoke activation patterns that the selection history has, in fact, produced.[23]

Verbal stimuli undeniably have rich selection histories. Do priming stimuli evoke activation patterns that reflect that extensive history? The results of priming procedures suggest that they do. Under some conditions, a verbal stimulus may be shown to exert complex priming effects on the response to the target stimulus, presumably as a result of correspondingly complex interactions between their activation patterns.

In a procedure known as a **naming task**, the subject is presented with a priming stimulus and then a visually presented target word that is to be named aloud, i.e., that requires a **textual response**. Textual responses—reading written or printed words—are environment-behavior relations for which adults have extensive selection histories. The behavioral measure most often used in naming tasks is the latency with which the target response occurs following the presentation of the target stimulus. If the latency of the target response varies with characteristics of the priming and target stimuli, this is interpreted as the result of overlapping activation patterns generated by the two stimuli.

When the priming stimulus is a phrase that is meaningfully related to the target word, the naming response is facilitated—i.e., the latency of the target response is decreased—compared with when the priming and target stimuli are unrelated.[24] For example, if the priming stimulus is the phrase *If Joe buys the straw* and the target stimulus is either *HAY* or *SIP*, the naming response is facilitated. Note that, in the context of this phrase, the meaning of *straw* is ambiguous because the word guides two relatively common responses, and both are potentially appropriate. The facilitation of naming responses to both *HAY* and *SIP* may be interpreted as indicating that the activation pattern generated by the phrase included components corresponding to both meanings of the word *straw*. A different result is obtained when the priming phrase provides a context in which the last word is related to only one target stimulus. For example, when the phrase is *If Joe buys the wheat*, only the response to the target word *HAY* is facilitated. Thus the component of the activation pattern that affects the naming of *HAY* need not affect the naming of *STRAW*. Work of similar import has been carried out with naming tasks using single words as priming stimuli.[25]

Other experiments using a different type of procedure have produced results that converge on the same interpretation. A sentence containing a word of ambiguous meaning was presented on a video monitor, and the subjects were asked to read it. Through a sophisticated experimental technique, it was possible to determine which words the subject was looking at, and for how long. It was found that when the subject came upon an ambiguous word, the word was fixated for a longer time than unambiguous words of comparable length. In addition, the subject's gaze frequently returned to the ambiguous word after later parts of the sentence had clarified its meaning.[26] For example, in the sentence *The records were carefully guarded after they were scratched*, the word *records* was fixated for a relatively long time. *Records* is ambiguous in meaning, as indicated by the following sentence that begins identically: *The records were carefully guarded after the political takeover*. The conclusion reached from these and other findings is that a stimulus can evoke an extremely complex activation pattern that reflects the subject's entire selection history with respect to that stimulus.

This conclusion holds not only for the motor components of the activation patterns guided by verbal stimuli—i.e., their meanings—but also for the sensory components. Priming effects have been demonstrated for the physical features of verbal stimuli, for their spelling (orthography), and for their auditory/articulatory characteristics. Moreover, priming effects also occur between priming and target words that are unrelated, but evoke common responses. For example, *lion* may serve as a priming stimulus for the target stimulus *stripes*

even though the first word does not evoke the second in a "free"-association test. Here, priming may occur through the mediation of the activation pattern for *tiger*, which is a common response evoked by *lion* in a "free"-association test, and to which *stripes* is a response.[27] However, one cannot infer intervening processes with certainty from behavioral observations alone. Depending on their unique selection histories, *lion* may have primed the response to *stripes*, not through the mediation of *tiger*, but through direct activation by *lion* (some persons erroneously "believe" that lions have stripes). Alternatively, *lion* may have been misperceived as *line*, and then *line* primed *stripes*. As always, the activation pattern mediating environment-behavior relations depends on the specifics of the individual's selection history; different persons may show the "same" response for different reasons.

Restrictions on the extent of priming. An ambiguous verbal stimulus may prime responses to many stimuli, because it generates an extensive activation pattern due to a diverse selection history. However, the extent of priming is often restricted by the context in which the stimulus appears. Consider one of the ambiguous sentences mentioned before. If the word order in the sentence is changed so that it now reads *After they were scratched, the records were carefully guarded*, the subjects did not fixate *records* for a longer time, and did not glance back after reading later words in the sentence.[28] Similarly, when an ambiguous word has a clearly dominant meaning rather than two meanings of approximately equal strength, priming occurs only for target words related to the dominant meaning.[29] Some evidence can be interpreted to indicate that a more extensive activation pattern begins to emerge, but the components that are inappropriate in that context are rapidly inhibited.[30] Finally, if the instructions provide a context that favors the guidance of one response by the target stimulus, then priming will be restricted to that response. For example, if the subject is instructed to detect whether the target stimulus contains a certain letter (e.g., *h*), then a priming stimulus such as *straw* does not prime the response to a meaningfully related target stimulus such as *hay*.[31]

Inhibitory processes in priming. Priming effects may be interpreted as the outcome of excitatory and inhibitory interactions among units in the activation patterns generated by the priming and target stimuli. As an illustration, the failure of a priming stimulus to prime subordinate responses to target stimuli can be interpreted as follows: The priming stimulus begins to evoke an extensive activation pattern that includes a motor component for both dominant and subordinate meanings of the priming stimulus. However, the more strongly activated units for the dominant meaning soon inhibit the continued activation of units for the subordinate meanings. Thus the activation pattern generated by the priming stimulus affects only target responses corresponding to the dominant meaning. In contrast, if the priming stimulus has two equally strong meanings, then the activation pattern it generates will include units for both of them. These two sets of units will inhibit one another to some extent, depending on the strength of inhibitory interactions between them. Thus two strong but related meanings would inhibit each other more than two equally strong but unrelated meanings.

Consistent with these interpretations, PET-scans indicate that when subjects are instructed to think of the meaning of words, regions of the motor association cortex are activated. (See **Figure 9.4**.) Unfortunately, PET-scans are not yet sensitive enough to provide moment-to-moment records of the growth and decline of activation patterns, and they do not distinguish between the activity of excitatory and inhibitory neurons. However, what experimental analysis has revealed about excitatory and inhibitory interactions between individual neurons supports these interpretations.

The facilitating effect of the priming stimulus on the latency of the response to the target stimulus may also be interpreted. When the priming stimulus is presented, it generates an activation pattern; the activity of the units in that pattern inhibits nearby units activated less strongly by other con-

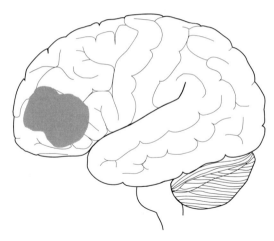

FIGURE 9.4 *Reconstruction of a PET-scan showing the most strongly activated region of the cortex when the subject was asked to* think about *a meaningful word* Note that the activation pattern involved the motor association cortex.
Source: Schematic depictions of findings from Petersen, Fox, Snyder, & Raichle, 1990.

current stimuli. If a related target word is then presented, its activation pattern overlaps somewhat with that of the priming stimulus. The target activation pattern is generated more rapidly than it would be otherwise, because the priming stimulus has just inhibited the activity of nearby units that might have laterally inhibited the recruitment of units in the target activation pattern. Because the activation pattern of the target stimulus is generated more rapidly, the behavioral response produced by that pattern occurs sooner—i.e., its latency is decreased.

An analogy may be useful in understanding this process. The priming stimulus acts like a person bulling his way through a crowd, all of whose members are pushing and shoving each other. The target stimulus follows closely on the heels of the priming stimulus and takes advantage of the path cleared by the priming stimulus before it has time to close up. Meeting less resistance, the target stimulus moves through the crowd more rapidly than it would if it had to clear its own way. Of course, verbal interpretations of complex interacting processes such as those involved in priming must be supplemented by specific neural network simulations before the interpretations can be considered compelling.[32]

Temporal Effects on Priming

So far, we have considered the nature of the priming and target stimuli and the context in which priming takes place. What are the effects of the other variable that is easily manipulated in the priming procedure—the time interval between the priming stimulus and the target stimulus? What effect might this variable have on priming and the activation patterns of which priming is a function?

An activation pattern generated by a stimulus consists of a set of interconnected neurons, some in the sensory areas and others—for discriminative, or meaningful, stimuli—in the motor areas of the brain. This pattern cannot be activated all at once. The environment first activates receptors, and then a subset of neurons that, in turn, activates another subset, and so on. Several tens of ms are required to activate the relevant receptors, several more to activate sensory neurons, and still more to activate the other neurons to which they are connected. The activation pattern may require hundreds of ms to be completely generated, and it changes over time as "deeper" units in the network are recruited.

Since it takes time to generate a complete activation pattern, the degree of overlap between two successive patterns should also depend on the interval between the stimuli that evoke those patterns. Accordingly, the effect of the priming stimulus on the response to the target stimulus should be affected by the interval between the two stimuli.[33] Consider an activation pattern that is just emerging because of the presentation of the priming stimulus. If the target stimulus is presented immediately after the priming stimulus, then only the initial units of the priming activation pattern are available to interact with the units of the emerging

target activation pattern. Thus, only priming effects that depend on interactions between the early units of the two activation patterns should be present. However, if the interstimulus interval between the priming and target stimuli is longer, then interactions are possible among units throughout both activation patterns. Are behavioral observations consistent with this interpretation?

The results of varying the interstimulus interval in priming procedures are consistent with the interpretation of priming as a result of overlapping activation patterns. The earlier-activated units of an activation pattern are those in the primary sensory areas and, as such, are sensitive to the physical features of the stimulus, e.g., spatial frequencies for a visual stimulus. Even with brief priming-target intervals, responses to the target stimulus should be affected when there are physical similarities between the priming and target stimuli—and this is what is found.[34] With somewhat longer priming-target intervals, there is enough time for the priming stimulus to activate polysensory neurons in the sensory association cortex. Visually presented words activate patterns that are particularly rich in polysensory units because, in English, a visually presented letter or word is correlated with an auditory stimulus—the sound of the letter or word. For example, the visual stimulus P is correlated with the speech sound /p/. Consistent with this expectation, priming effects are observed when an auditorily presented word serves as the priming stimulus and the same visually presented word is the target stimulus. This illustrates **cross-modal priming**, because the target response is primed even though the priming and target stimuli are in different sensory modalities.

At even longer priming-target intervals, priming occurs between words that are meaningfully related but bear no other relation to one another. When the interstimulus interval is brief, a meaningful relation between the priming and target stimulus should not affect the target response because not enough time has elapsed for the priming stimulus to activate the later motor units of the pattern, which constitute the meaning of the priming word. This expectation is also confirmed. With brief interstimulus intervals, the target response is not affected by a meaningfully related priming stimulus. However, with interstimulus intervals of several hundred ms, priming stimuli meaningfully related to the target stimulus do facilitate the target response.[35] Further, even when meaningfully related priming and target words are presented in different sensory modalities (e.g., visual and auditory), priming effects occur.[36] Of course, cross-modal priming does not occur for physical features of the priming and target stimuli since there can be no overlap in the early, more sensory components of activation patterns generated by stimuli in different modalities.[37]

Contributions of Priming to Complex Behavior

The behavioral effects of priming procedures reveal some of the rich possibilities for interplay between the activation patterns initiated by successive stimuli and by different stimuli acting concurrently. Such interactions undoubtedly occur extensively in the natural environment as environment-behavior relations are mediated by the nervous system. As remarked by Endel Tulving and David Schacter, "Priming is a ubiquitous occurrence in everyday life."[38] Indeed, priming provides yet another indication that the cumulative effects of relatively simple biobehavioral processes operating over time can produce extremely complex relations on both the neural and behavioral levels.

The view that emerges is one in which the behavior occurring at any given moment is the outcome of constantly changing activation patterns involving many units acting at the same time—in *parallel*. As contrasted with conventional digital computers, many processes occur simultaneously in the brain, implementing the **parallel processing** of environment-environment and environment-behavior relations. Even though a single neuron operates much more slowly than an electronic circuit in a computer, the brain can mediate complex relations very rapidly because many units are act-

ing at one time, not just one after the other. When processes occur successively, they exemplify **serial processing**. Serial processing also occurs in the brain, of course: The sensory component of an activation pattern must occur before the motor component can be recruited.

An ever-changing activation pattern is produced by ever-changing events in the environment, acting on a learner who has been changed as the cumulative result of selection. All contemporaneous stimuli potentially affect the activation pattern generated by a stimulus; in that way, an activation pattern is constrained by both the environment of the moment and the cumulative effects of selection from all previous moments.[39] To complicate matters still further, when an activation pattern includes enough motor units to produce responses at the behavioral level, these responses may cause changes in the environment. Such changes, in turn, stimulate the receptors of the neural network afresh and bring an altered activation pattern into existence. The complexity and diversity of these shifting activation patterns seem competent to mediate a vast array of environment-behavior relations.

In the natural environment, shifts in activation patterns are produced by stimuli less easily characterized than the single words or simple phrases used in priming procedures. For instance, if a friend refers to an earlier statement that we made but have momentarily forgotten, we may ask her to remind us where and when the conversation took place, who else was there, and so forth. As interpreted by a selection network, the friend's replies to these inquiries serve to prime the "memory" that we are trying to recall.[40]

Schemata.   As another example of a complex priming environment, suppose that you go to a party and discover that the men are dressed in tuxedos and the women in evening gowns, champagne is being served, and Lester Lanin's society orchestra is playing Broadway show tunes. This environment would prime a largely different set of "party responses" than one where people are dressed in jeans, drinking beer, and listening to

Grateful Dead records. Complex discriminative stimuli serve as contexts in which the same stimulus—e.g., seeing a friend—initiates very different responses mediated by very different activation patterns. In inferred-process approaches to complex behavior, complex contextual discriminations are sometimes referred to as *schemata, scripts, or plans.*[41] As conceived here, such terms do not refer to inferred structures or require new biobehavioral processes for their interpretation. Instead, they refer to the effects of complex discriminative stimuli on the functioning of the organism. As David Rumelhart, Paul Smolensky, James McClelland, and Geoffrey Hinton—major contributors to adaptive-network accounts of complex behavior—have put it: "Schemata are not 'things.' There is no representational object which is a schema. Rather, schemata emerge at the moment they are needed from the interaction of large numbers of simpler elements all working in concert with one another."[42]

Enduring effects of priming. In our discussion of priming, we have so far considered only the transitory effects of the priming stimulus on the activation pattern initiated by the target stimulus. To simplify the discussion, we have acted as if selection were no longer taking place and the initiation of an activation pattern would have no effect on the connectivity of its active units. This is probably never correct; any time a pattern is activated there is the opportunity for additional selections to occur. For example, suppose that an infrequently encountered word is used as the target stimulus in a naming procedure. Under these conditions, it is likely that the textual response of reading the word aloud will be strengthened. Experienced learners can discriminate when they correctly pronounce a word, which permits the auditory stimuli produced by their naming response to function as an acquired reinforcer. Acquired reinforcers further strengthen the connections that were active when the target stimulus was present (see Chapter 4). Thus priming may produce enduring effects on the ability of the target stimulus to guide the target response.[43]

Multiple Determinants of Priming

Priming is a behavioral phenomenon measured by the effect of an immediately preceding stimulus on the response to a subsequent stimulus. Priming is not a fundamental biobehavioral process, but, rather, a product of such processes. As such, priming—like phenomena such as retroactive interference and recency—cannot provide an explanation of other phenomena but is itself a phenomenon to be explained. Because priming is not a fundamental process, it is likely to be produced in a number of different ways. So far, we have considered only one way in which priming effects can be produced—as the outcome of interactions between common units in successive activation patterns. Are there other processes that can produce priming?

Recurrence and reafference. Until this point, interpretations of priming have been restricted to neural networks in which the activity of a unit could only be influenced by the activity of "earlier" or "upstream" units in the network. Such networks are technically called **feed-forward networks**. Activity initiated at the input units "feeds forward," activating units ever "deeper" in the network. In the specific case of the nervous system, sensory units activate polysensory units which, in turn, activate motor association units. However, motor association units do not affect polysensory units except indirectly, through changes in environmental stimulation produced by behavior. That is, changes in behavior change the environment sensed by the organism and, in that less direct way, change the activity of units in the sensory component of the activation pattern.

This account of the propagation of activity in a neural network is overly simple. The nervous system is more richly interconnected than a feed-forward network. In general, pathways that convey activity from one brain region to another are complemented by other pathways that convey activity in the reverse direction.[44] For example, while there are tracts that carry activity from sensory association to motor association areas, still others carry activity from motor association to sensory association areas. In general, there are reciprocal connections between most brain regions—either directly or through various intervening nuclei.[45]

An adaptive network that can simulate the effects of these "backward" pathways is said to have **recurrent connections**. (See **Figure 9.5**.) Functionally, the effect of activity conveyed by recurrent connections is similar to the effect of changes in behavior that produce changes in the environment. That is, both behavior—through changes produced in the environment sensed by the organism—and recurrent connections—through activity carried in "backward" pathways in the nervous system—alter the activity of units in the sensory component of the activation pattern. While the environment may be said to "afferent" the organism, activity carried by recurrent connections may be said to "reafferent" the organism.[46] What are the implications of **reafference** for some instances of priming?

As interpreted by selection networks, even when there is little overlap in the feed-forward

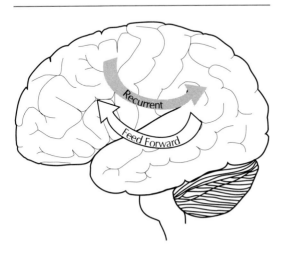

FIGURE 9.5   *Schematic representation of feed-forward and recurrent connections between the sensory and motor association areas of the cerebral cortex*

activation patterns initiated by the priming and target stimuli, priming may occur if recurrent activity induced by the priming stimulus alters the activation pattern initiated by the target stimulus. If the activation pattern generated by the target stimulus is altered, then the behavioral response to the target stimulus may be affected. However, priming effects produced through recurrent connections would take longer to occur: The activation pattern of the priming stimulus must recruit units in later portions of the network before the recurrent or feedback pathways that reafferent the earlier units can be activated. Priming effects mediated by recurrent connections should require longer interstimulus intervals between the priming and target stimuli than priming effects of other origins.

In an experiment that bears on this interpretation of some priming phenomena, subjects were instructed that when the priming stimulus was a particular category name, such as *building*, the target word would be an instance of another category, such as a part of the body—e.g., *leg*. This procedure implements an arbitrary, but systematic, relation between priming and target stimuli. That is, the relation is not one that has been selected by the pre-experimental environment. With nonarbitrary relations between category names and instances—e.g., the relation of *building* to *door*—priming of instances by category names is known to occur.[47] But does priming occur when the relation between the priming category and the target instances is systematic but arbitrary? If so, what interstimulus interval is required to produce priming effects of this sort?

Experimental work indicates that nonarbitrary relations between category names and instances (e.g., *building-door*) reduces the latency of the target response when the interstimulus interval is 250 milliseconds. Priming of this origin occurred even though the relation was not described in the instructions given to the subjects before the experiment. Thus category names were demonstrated to prime instances. An arbitrary priming-target relation also produces priming, but requires an interstimulus interval of almost 1,000 milliseconds before it appears![48] As interpreted by selection networks, the priming of the nonarbitrary relation occurred quickly because the priming and target activation patterns overlapped during the feed-forward phase of the activation patterns. The priming of the arbitrary relation took longer to emerge because units in "deeper" regions of the network had to be activated before recurrent connections from them could alter the activity of earlier units. Speaking nontechnically, it is as if the subject first had to say to himself "The priming word *building* means that the target word is some part of the body," before the target response *leg* could be primed.

An implication of this interpretation is that extended practice with arbitrary relations should eventually produce rapid priming through feed-forward connections, and the evidence supports this expectation.[49] Once again, the cogency of neural network interpretations awaits direct observations at the neuroanatomical/physiological level and the implementation of specific computer simulations. However, these verbal interpretations do indicate that a considerable range of priming effects is within the competence of basic biobehavioral principles.[50]

Priming and Awareness

Whatever the ultimate fate of neural-network interpretations of priming, evidence indicates that the priming stimulus need not evoke verbal behavior for priming to occur. Some hint of this conclusion was provided by the earlier observation that category names prime instances even when such relations are not mentioned in the experimental instructions. More to the point, research has shown that priming can occur when the subject is unaware of the priming stimulus—i.e., when the priming stimulus does not guide a textual response. In fact, priming can occur when the subject has no awareness that a priming stimulus has even been presented![51]

In an experiment directed at this issue,[52] a modification of a matching-to-sample procedure

was first used to assess awareness of words presented for different durations. These durations were then used in a later study of priming. A word was presented on some trials as a sample stimulus followed within a few ms by a **masking stimulus**, e.g., XXX. The subject was asked to indicate whether or not a word had been presented. An average stimulus duration of about 20 ms before the introduction of the masking stimulus was necessary for the subjects to accurately judge that a word had been presented. Even though their judgments were accurate, the subjects had no awareness of the nature of the word at these brief intervals, and described their responses as merely "guesses." The duration at which a subject could accurately judge that a word had been presented—called the **threshold of detectability**—was determined individually for each subject. Next, the same subjects were presented a sample word and then the masking stimulus, followed by two words as comparison stimuli. Their task was to indicate which of the two comparison words was identical to the sample word. When the interval between the sample word and masking stimulus was increased to about 30 ms, the subjects selected the correct comparison word with reasonable accuracy. This duration defined the **threshold of semantic detection**. However, the subjects were still unable to give a textual response to the sample stimulus, and reported that their choices of the comparison stimuli were "guesses."[53]

In later testing, when the priming stimulus was presented to these subjects for a duration equal to the detectability threshold, priming occurred for identical but not for meaningfully related target stimuli. However, when the duration of the priming stimulus was increased to the semantic threshold, priming also occurred with meaningfully related target words. Note that *both* priming effects—the first based on physical similarity and the second on similarity of meaning—occurred without awareness of the priming stimulus. The priming stimulus influenced the activation pattern of the target stimulus, even when the subject was unable to give a textual response to the priming stimulus.

Speaking nontechnically, we need not be "aware" of a stimulus for it to influence our reactions to other stimuli.

IMAGINING

Priming experiments indicate that stimuli generate activation patterns that can be sensitive to the individual's entire history of selection, and not just the physical properties of the initiating stimuli. A familiar verbal stimulus activates, at least briefly, all of the motor components of the activation pattern—i.e., all of the "meanings" of the verbal stimulus. So far, we have demonstrated the potential richness of activation patterns almost exclusively with verbal stimuli and the verbal responses that they guide. Can environment-behavior relations involving nonverbal events also be sensitive to the entire selection history? For example, can pictorial stimuli activate extensive activation patterns that include motor components? The answer to this question bears ultimately on such matters as the interpretation of imagining. In imagining, a stimulus evokes an activation pattern that includes components that are ordinarily evoked by a stimulus in another sensory modality. For example, when smelling a food that was a childhood favorite, you may visualize the kitchen where you last smelled it. In short, under some conditions a subject "sees" in the absence of stimuli that usually guide seeing, "hears" in the absence of stimuli that usually guide hearing, and so on.

Priming procedures demonstrate that nonverbal stimuli can generate extremely rich activation patterns. Moreover, some of the components of these patterns may be described as perceptual. For example, when a line drawing of a geometric figure is presented as a priming stimulus, the response to a target stimulus of the same figure is facilitated—but only if the priming and target figures are perceptually possible. That is, priming occurs only when the line drawings depict figures that have the characteristics of real objects, and have therefore been subject to behavioral selection. (See **Figure 9.6**.) In these experiments, the response that was

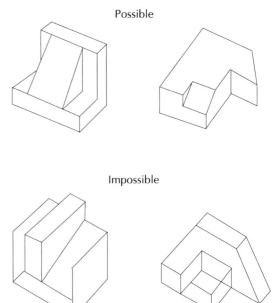

FIGURE 9.6   *Priming and target stimuli used in the study of perceptual priming*
The line drawings in the upper portion of the figure are examples of three-dimensional renderings of objects that are "possible." The line drawings in the lower portion are examples of "impossible" objects—i.e., objects that could not exist in three-dimensional space. Only prior exposure to "possible" drawings reduced the latency of classifying a drawing as "possible" or "impossible" when those drawings were later used as target stimuli.
Source: Adapted from Schacter, D. L., Cooper, L. A., Delaney, S. M., Peterson, M. A., & Tharan, M. (1991). Implicit memory for possible and impossible objects: Constraints on the construction of structural depositions. *Journal of Experimental Psychology: Learning, Memory, & Cognition, 17,* 3–19. Copyright © 1991 by the American Psychological Association. Adapted by permission.

primed was the speed of classifying the figure as either a perceptually possible or impossible three-dimensional form. If the figure was perceptually impossible—that is, if it could not have been sensed during the selection history of the learner—then priming did not occur.[54]

Priming procedures can also be used to demonstrate that the activation patterns evoked by verbal stimuli include components that are ordinarily evoked by pictorial stimuli. In the previous study with three-dimensional line drawings, priming occurred when the figures approximated stimuli provided by real objects. The results of this study were analogous to earlier work with verbal stimuli in which a priming stimulus facilitated naming an identical target stimulus. Can priming of responses to nonverbal target stimuli occur when the priming and target stimuli are presented in different sensory modalities? This is analogous to using an auditorily presented word to prime a naming response to a visually presented word. The results indicate that cross-modal priming does occur in such circumstances. For example, when the priming stimulus is a word—e.g., *boat*—detection of a picture of a boat is primed to about the same degree as it is when the priming stimulus is a picture of the same boat.[55] The word *boat* and a picture of a boat generate activation patterns that have components in common. Among these components are sets of units in the sensory association cortex—what may be called a *perceptual component*—and sets in the motor association cortex—what may be called a *meaning component*.

A nonexperimental example also suggests that perceptual components can be evoked by stimuli in modalities other than those that ordinarily activate them. Take a moment to answer the following question: How many windows are on the front of your house? . . . Unless you have answered this question before and now recall the answer, you are likely—speaking nontechnically—to conjure up an image of your house as it would appear if you were facing it, and then count the windows that you "see." Moreover, when you count the windows, you are apt to proceed in a systematic fashion, e.g., from left to right. In short, you are likely to engage in activity—largely unmeasurable at the behavioral level—that seems similar to the activity you engage in when you actually see the house and count its windows.

Behavioral Observations

As measured on the behavioral level, **imagining** occurs when a stimulus that is not physically similar to the one that usually guides perceiving evokes behavior similar to the behavior guided by the customary stimulus.[56] For example, when asked to imagine the windows on the front of your house, you may make certain eye movements as if scanning the front of your house, count aloud the windows as you "see" them, count more rapidly when the windows are close together than when they are far apart, and so on. Under the guidance of verbal instructions, you engage in behavior that is similar to that which occurs when you are, in fact, in front of your house counting its windows. Further, you may shut your eyes as you engage in this behavior, as if sensing current visual stimuli would somehow interfere with visualizing your house.

Considerable experimental work is consistent with the view that visual imagining involves many of the same biobehavioral processes as seeing. For example, an older literature indicates that, when subjects were asked to imagine the Eiffel Tower, their eyes often moved upward as if they were looking at a tall structure. Or, when a subject is asked to imagine hitting a nail twice with a hammer, two subtle contractions occur in the muscles of his forearm.[57] These studies demonstrate—to the extent that it can be measured on the behavioral level—that the topography of our behavior when we are imagining an activity is similar, although much diminished in magnitude, to the topography of our behavior when we are actually engaging in that activity.

More recent research indicates that there are also striking functional similarities between imagining and seeing. That is, variables that affect seeing affect imagining in similar ways. Just as you cannot look at two objects at the same time, you cannot visually imagine one object and look at another simultaneously. For example, when subjects were asked to imagine a visual stimulus while responding to another visual stimulus, they showed more interference in responding than when they were asked to imagine an auditory stimulus during the same task.[58]

Among the more compelling demonstrations are those in which subjects are shown pairs of line drawings of complex objects and asked if the drawings are of the same object.[59] The two drawings are three-dimensional line drawings of objects from different vantage points. Sometimes the two drawings are of the same object (upper panel of **Figure 9.7**), sometimes of different objects (middle panel of **Figure 9.7**). The subjects quite accurately indicated whether or not the drawings were of the same object. More importantly for present purposes, the time they required to make the judgment increased with the angle through which real objects of that shape would have to be rotated to view them both from the same vantage point! That is, the time varied in much the same fashion as if the subject had made the judgment by rotating one object in her hand until it corresponded visually to the other object. As shown in the lower panel of **Figure 9.7**, the greater the degree of rotation necessary, the more time it took to make the response. Note also that the time it took to judge the drawings was quite long compared with the time it takes to obtain priming with meaningful verbal stimuli—over 1,000 ms when the drawings were made from the same vantage point, and over 4,000 ms when they were 180° different.[60]

Physiological and Neuropsychological Observations

The interpretation of imagining using only behavioral data is dangerous business. To begin with, on the behavioral level no independent evidence can confirm that the subject is "having an image;" only the experimenter's instruction to form an image and the subject's verbal response that an image has formed can be observed.[61] Imagining is a biobehavioral process observable—if at all with present technology—largely on the neural level. Observations at the behavioral level provide only intermit-

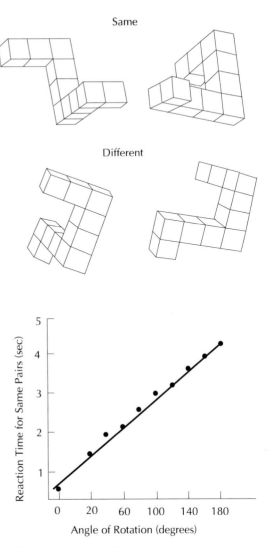

FIGURE 9.7   *Pairs of drawings that are or are not renderings of the same object drawn from different vantage points*

The upper panel contains pairs of drawings of the same object. The middle panel contains pairs of drawings that are not of the same object. The lower panel depicts the effect on the latency of the response indicating that the drawings were of the same object as a function of the number of degrees by which the vantage points differed or, equivalently, the number of degrees by which one object would have to be rotated to make the renderings identical.

Source: Adapted from Shepard, R. N., & Metzler, J. (1971). Mental rotation and three-dimensional objects. *Science, 153,* 642–654. Copyright 1971 by the AAAS.

tent and incomplete access to the activities that occur during imagining. Most fundamentally, behavioral observations provide an inadequate basis for inferring neural processes, just as they do for inferring hypothetical processes. The same environment-behavior relation may occur as the result of different neural processes. Is there any evidence at the neural level that similar activation patterns occur during seeing and imagining?

Two lines of evidence support the conclusion that the activation patterns involved in visualizing and seeing overlap considerably. First, when neural activity is monitored after subjects have been instructed to imagine an activity such as taking a walk through the neighborhood,[62] various measurements[63] indicate that similar brain regions are involved in imagining the activity and engaging in the activity. These regions include sensory association areas and extend to motor association areas.[64]

The second line of evidence comes from behavioral observations of persons who have damage in brain regions known to be involved in seeing. In general, if the damage affects seeing, it also affects visual imagining, or visualizing—and in similar ways. For example, because of the neuroanatomical relation between the two halves of each retina and the visual cortex, damage to the visual association area of the right visual cortex selectively impairs seeing the visual world to the left of the fixation point. (Refer back to **Figure 7.2** if you need to refresh your memory of the anatomy of the visual system.) Persons who have suffered damage to the right visual association area—and, hence, to the polysensory neurons located in that region—cannot respond appropriately to the visual world to the left of the point in space toward which their gaze is directed. The activation pattern that would normally be initiated by stimuli to the left of the fixation point does not emerge, so the motor components of the activation pattern cannot occur. A drawing of a clock face by a person with damage to the right visual association area is shown in **Figure 9.8**. Note the omissions from the left side of the drawing. Persons with these deficits do such remarkable things as shave or put makeup on only

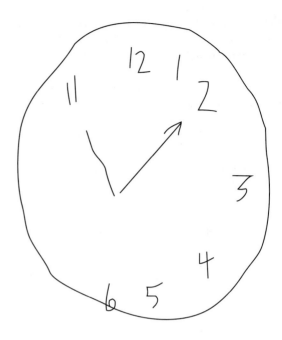

FIGURE 9.8 *A sketch of a clock face by a person with damage to the right visual association cortex*
Note that the right half of the clock face is somewhat larger than the left half and that the numerals are generally confined to the right half of the clock face. Light reflected from the left half of the clock face normally activates neurons in the damaged right parietal cortex and, consequently, is "neglected."
Source: From findings of Kaplan, E., & Velis, D. C. The neuropsychology of 10 after 11. Paper presented at the International Neurological Society Meeting, Mexico City, 1983.

the right side of their faces, and eat food from only the right side of their plates! Only by reinforcing glancing toward the left—thereby allowing the patient to sense stimuli farther to the left—can we partially overcome these deficits.

Damage to the right visual association areas affects not only seeing the left visual world, but imagining that part of the world as well. Persons with this damage not only fail to describe the left visual world, they act as if it did not exist—and, for them, it does not.[65] For example, a man with damage to the right visual association area was asked to describe the buildings surrounding a plaza in a city that was well known to him. When he imagined looking in a southerly direction, he described only the buildings on the western side of the plaza (i.e., those to the right of his imagined line of sight). This was not because he lacked knowledge of the buildings on the eastern side of the plaza since, when he imagined looking in a northerly direction, he described only the buildings on the eastern side of the plaza![66]

Interpretation of Imagining

The major conclusion from research on both the behavioral and neural levels is that many of the same variables affect imagining and perceiving in much the same way. The interpretation of imagining does not appear to require the postulation of any biobehavioral processes that are unique to imagining.[67] Returning to the earlier illustration, we may anticipate that imagining the windows in a house would reflect the specific selection history of seeing those windows. If you have walked around a house by daylight and it is not obscured by trees, you will count the windows by imagining the outside of the house. However, if you have visited the house only at night or it is obscured by trees, you might imagine the interior of each room and count the windows as you walk through the house. The activation patterns involved in imagining, just as those involved in other environment-behavior relations, have both sensory and motor subcomponents. James Gibson's concept of **affordance**, by which the observer is said to perceive the behavior that the stimulus affords as well as its sensory aspects, foreshadows the present interpretation of perceiving.[68]

AWARENESS

As indicated earlier, when a person makes verbal responses with respect to a stimulus, the person is said to be aware of the stimulus.[69] For instance, if a child says "ball" when a ball is present and does not say "ball" when it is absent, we may say that the child is aware of the ball. Thus awareness refers to environment-behavior relations in which the guided behavior includes verbal behavior.[70] However, since the environment began guiding vocal responses and other verbal behavior late in the evolutionary history of our species, verbal behavior is likely to be an expression of the same basic biobehavioral processes that affect other responses.

The occurrence of priming without awareness of the priming stimulus indicates that, to affect behavior, stimuli need not generate activation patterns that include motor components concerned with speech. The implementation of environment-behavior relations does not require verbal behavior. Moreover, other research indicates that environment-behavior relations can also be acquired without awareness.[71] Nevertheless, because verbal behavior rightly occupies an important place in the interpretation of human behavior, we devote special attention to activation patterns that mediate verbal behavior.

Neuroanatomical Basis of Verbal Behavior

Although techniques such as PET permit indirect measurements of neural activity correlated with perceiving and producing speech, studies of the effects of brain damage on verbal behavior provide the richest source of information. Before considering these effects, let us review some relevant behavioral and neuroanatomical findings. The stimuli entering into verbal environment-behavior relations often activate more than one sensory channel. For example, a visual stimulus, such as an object or printed word, is often accompanied by an auditory stimulus that is the "name" of that object or word. In general, because verbal behavior often involves polysensory integration,[72] the hippocampus plays an important role here. You will recall that a diffusely projected neuromodulatory signal from the hippocampus to polysensory association cortex was proposed as the means by which connections to polysensory units are strengthened. Recall also that there are extensive connections between the right and left halves, or **hemispheres**, of the brain by means of several fiber tracts—most notably the corpus callosum.

The brain regions that play an especially important role in perceiving and producing speech are located—for most persons—in the cortex of the left hemisphere. In the sensory areas of the cortex, the regions receiving visual and auditory inputs are located in the **occipital lobe** and **temporal lobe**, respectively. (See **Figure 9.9**.) Between these two regions, and bounded by the **parietal lobe** that receives inputs from senses such as touch, is the sensory association cortex. The polysensory neurons of the sensory association cortex that are

involved in the integration of visual and auditory activity are especially important for the perception of speech. These polysensory neurons provide inputs to the hippocampus, and then receive back from the hippocampus a diffuse projection that is postulated to strengthen connections to recently activated polysensory neurons. In the motor portion of the cortex, subregions of the motor association cortex and motor cortex control muscles whose coordinated action produces verbal behavior—vocal speech and writing. The motor regions for verbal behavior are located in the **frontal lobe** of the left hemisphere.[73]

We now examine the effects of two types of brain damage on the functioning of the verbal system—damage to the corpus callosum that con-

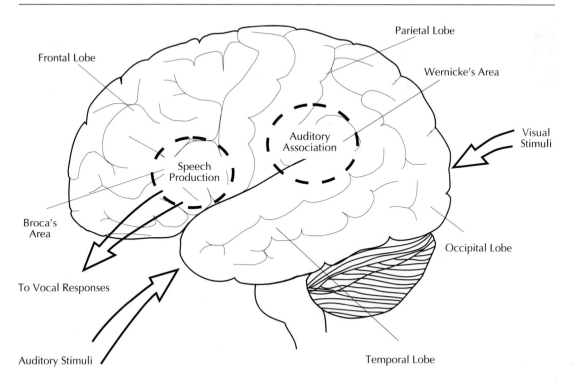

FIGURE 9.9 *Cortical regions in the left hemisphere of the cerebral cortex that play important roles in mediating environment-behavior and environment-environment relations involved in verbal behavior*

nects the two hemispheres, and damage to the pathways that connect regions within the left hemisphere.

Effects of Damage to the Corpus Callosum

Because the corpus callosum is the major tract connecting the left and right hemispheres, damage to this structure allows us to observe the functioning of each hemisphere relatively independently of the influence of the other hemisphere. In nonhuman animals, damage to the corpus callosum can be produced experimentally.[74] However, for obvious reasons, such damage occurs in humans only accidentally or in the course of treating certain illnesses in medical patients. Those very few patients who have had the corpus callosum surgically interrupted have all suffered from rare forms of epileptic seizures that could not be controlled by drugs. Seizure activity would begin in one hemisphere and then propagate through the corpus callosum to the other hemisphere, disrupting the functioning of large portions of the brain. Because such seizures prevent the person from living a productive life—and produce severe neurological impairment if permitted to continue—the corpus callosum was severed.

How should interrupting the corpus callosum affect verbal behavior? Because of the special role of the left hemisphere in mediating verbal behavior, sensory input to the left hemisphere will continue to initiate activation patterns that mediate verbal behavior. However, sensory input confined to the right hemisphere will not be able to evoke verbal behavior, because the pathways to the left hemisphere through the corpus callosum are no longer functional. Disrupting the corpus callosum enables us to study the ability of the right half of the brain to mediate environment-behavior relations without awareness.

To assess the capabilities of the right hemisphere, a procedure originally devised to study the effects of callosal damage in animals was modified for humans. In one such experiment, a verbal stimulus, e.g., *key case*, was briefly visually presented while the subject's eyes were fixated on the space between the two parts of the compound word. Under these conditions, the right half of each retina "sees" only the word to the left of the fixation point—*key*. Most importantly, stimuli confined to the right half of each retina activate neurons in only the right visual cortex. As a result, subjects report no awareness that any visual stimulus has been presented to the left of the fixation point—let alone the word *key*. The word *case*, which activates the left visual cortex, is the only word they name.

Clearly, visual stimuli that generate activation patterns in only the right hemisphere do not guide verbal responses. But can such stimuli guide other responses without awareness? To answer this question, a response system was used that—unlike the vocal system—could be activated by neurons in the right visual cortex. Since movements of the left arm and hand are controlled by motor components in the right frontal lobe, and since pathways connecting right sensory areas to right motor areas were intact, movements of the right arm were used. Now, when *key case* was flashed, the subjects were instructed to search behind a screen with the left hand and select—by touch alone—the object named by the visual stimulus. With this procedure, although the subjects did not report seeing the word, they were able to pick out a key with the left hand! However, they could not report the name of the object that they had picked out. The stimulus *key* initiated an activation pattern that mediated the manual response, even though the lesion to the corpus callosum prevented generation of a motor component for a vocal response.[75]

Thus, in at least some instances, responding does not require mediation by verbal processes. Speaking nontechnically, the environment does not first "give us an idea," which then causes the action. Persons in whom the corpus callosum has been interrupted have no "idea"—i.e., no awareness of the stimulus—but can sometimes respond appropriately nevertheless. However, it would be too much to conclude from this research and from priming experiments that verbal components of activation patterns are never required for a stimulus to guide behavior. In general, whether verbal components play a role in activating other components depends on the specifics of the learner's selection history.

Effects of Damage to Intrahemispheric Pathways

If a stimulus generates an activation pattern in the left hemisphere, verbal components may still not be recruited if lesions interrupt pathways that interconnect "verbal" regions with other regions. **Figure 9.10** depicts two types of pathways that carry information relevant to verbal environment-behavior relations. First, pathways communicating between the sensory association cortex and the hippocampus may be damaged. (See line **A** in **Figure 9.10**.) This interruption prevents further strengthening of connections to polysensory units that are important for the mediation of verbal and other polysensory relations.

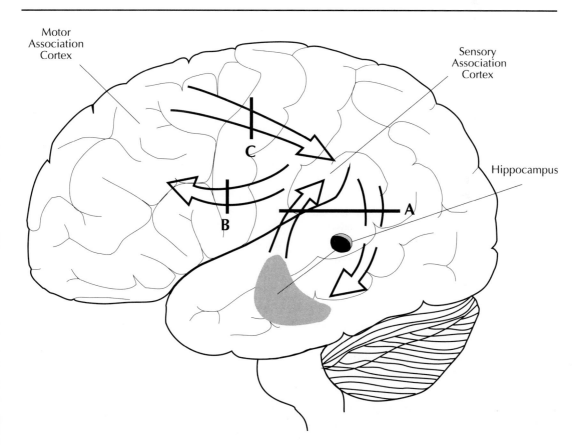

FIGURE 9.10   *Critical points of interruption of cortical pathways involved in selecting and mediating polysensory integrations*
Interruptions at **A** prevent neural activity occurring in the sensory association cortex and hippocampus from affecting one another. Interruptions at **B** prevent polysensory integrations from being communicated to motor association areas and, hence, from guiding behavior. Interruptions at **C** prevent the reafference of sensory association cortex by activity in motor association cortex.

Second, pathways communicating between the sensory association cortex and the motor areas of the frontal cortex may be damaged. If the pathways *from* the sensory areas *to* the frontal cortex are damaged (see line **B** in **Figure 9.10**), then output from the sensory cortex cannot activate the motor components mediating verbal behavior. If the recurrent pathways *to* the sensory association cortex *from* the frontal cortex are damaged (see line **C** in **Figure 9.10**), then the sensory cortex would be deprived of reafferent stimulation from motor components mediating verbal relations.[76]

Damage to the pathways indicated in **Figure 9.10** impairs the selection and/or maintenance of verbal environment-behavior relations. When the environment can no longer evoke verbal behavior with respect to past stimuli, a "memory" impairment known as **amnesia** occurs. Here, we consider only the form of amnesia produced by interruption of pathways communicating between the sensory association cortex and hippocampus, i.e., **hippocampal amnesia**.[77]

Hippocampal amnesia.   Connections to polysensory neurons in sensory association cortex are held to be strengthened by diffuse neuromodulatory feedback from the hippocampus. If this feedback is interrupted, further changes in the synaptic efficacies between neurons in primary sensory areas and polysensory neurons are prevented. (See the interruption indicated by line **A** in **Figure 9.10**.) If connections to polysensory neurons can no longer be modified, then environment-environment and environment-behavior relations dependent on the strengthening of new polysensory connections cannot be selected. However, previously selected relations requiring polysensory input would endure, because the required connections in sensory association cortex have already been selected.[78]

Pathways between the sensory association cortex and the hippocampus are never intentionally interrupted in humans, of course. However, such damage has occurred either through misadventure during surgery or, more commonly, through accident involving carbon monoxide poisoning or cerebral hemorrhage (stroke). Interpreting lesions of such origins is often difficult because other structures or pathways are often damaged, and the effects of this damage produce variation from case to case. In spite of this, the accumulation of observations from diverse human cases, together with the development of model preparations with monkeys and with rats, to a lesser extent,[79] now yields a consistent picture.

Perhaps the clearest evidence of the effects of hippocampal lesions on awareness comes from a patient who suffered brain damage due to oxygen deprivation during open heart surgery.[80] Extensive behavioral testing was conducted in the months following surgery and, at the patient's request, the precise location of the damage was determined after his death. The damage was found to be confined almost exclusively to the CA1 neurons of the hippocampus, the origin of the pathways that diffusely project from the hippocampus to the polysensory association cortex. Thus the lesion interrupted communication between the sensory association areas and the hippocampus, and little else. The general outcome of behavioral testing with this patient, and others with functionally similar lesions, is that new environment-environment relations—and, hence, the environment-behavior relations dependent on the selection of those environment-environment relations—cannot be acquired. Thus, guidance of verbal responses and other expressions of polysensory integration are severely impaired. Although new verbal relations can no longer be selected, those selected before the damage remain essentially intact. (See endnote 78 for additional information on the occurrence of retrograde amnesia with hippocampal damage.) Finally, new environment-behavior relations *not* requiring new polysensory integrations can still be acquired.

Among the observations that support the foregoing conclusions are these: As measured by their verbal behavior, patients with interruptions in the pathways between the sensory association cortex and the hippocampus cannot recall events that have occurred since the lesion. For example, if they are introduced to a stranger and explicitly asked to remember his name, they cannot do so even a few minutes later. This occurs even though they clearly understood the name, since they were able to repeat it immediately after hearing it.[81] Laboratory studies confirm these clinical observations. When persons with hippocampal damage are presented with new sentences or pictures to remember—both of which require new polysensory integrations—their verbal retention falls to very low levels within only a few minutes.[82]

Although performance is deficient on tasks requiring new polysensory integrations, performance making use of existing polysensory integrations endures. For patients with hippocampal amnesia, when *num* is used as the priming stimulus for the target stimulus *number*, the naming response "number" is primed. However, when the target response is a novel word such as *numdy*, priming does not occur.[83] Clinical observations reveal a similar result. Verbal "memory" for events *before* the damage remains relatively intact (i.e., there is minimal **retrograde amnesia**), but "memories" for events occurring *after* the damage are not formed (i.e., there is **anterograde amnesia**). A particularly poignant example of this phenomenon occurred recently when a professor of physics suffered hippocampal damage after eating shellfish containing a toxin produced by algae that the shellfish had consumed. The professor can still teach physics (these "memories" were formed before the damage), but he cannot remember teaching the class after it is over! At the end of every day, he is plagued by the thought that he has not accomplished anything, because he cannot verbally remember anything. He keeps a notebook in which he writes all he has done and all he needs to do each day, but reading a notebook is not the same as remembering the past and anticipating the future by means of the vast "notebook" of the human brain.

Behavioral deficits produced by failures in polysensory integration also appear with relations other than those involving verbal behavior. Behav-ior guided by the conjunction of stimuli required to specify location are also impaired by damage to the hippocampal-cortical system. Spatial deficits have been reported in both humans[84] and monkeys.[85] In contrast, environment-behavior relations not requiring new polysensory integrations are readily acquired. Learning occurs for perceptual-motor skills, such as hand-eye coordination,[86] for reading words reflected in a mirror,[87] for classically conditioned eyelid responses,[88] and for emotional responses to pictures.[89] In all of these cases, the subjects learn the new environment-behavior relations without any verbal "memory" that they have ever encountered either the stimuli or procedures before. For example, subjects that learned to read words reflected in a mirror improved from session to session, but began each session claiming that they had no prior experience with the task.[90]

In summary, research on hippocampal amnesia provides additional evidence that the activation patterns initiated by stimuli need not include components that mediate verbal behavior for old environment-behavior relations to be carried out or for new relations to be acquired. However, relations requiring new polysensory integration by units in the sensory association cortex—including those required for verbal behavior—depend on intact pathways interconnecting the hippocampus and sensory association cortex.[91] A final caution must be repeated, however: Behavioral observations by themselves do not sufficiently constrain inferences about the underlying neural processes. Polysensory integrations, and the proposed role of the hippocampus in bringing them about, require additional analysis on the neuroanatomical and cellular levels. The interpretation of verbal behavior presents particularly formidable obstacles to experimental analysis, since verbal behavior is conventionally present only in humans—and our ability to experimentally analyze polysensory integrations in our own species is severely limited.

The findings described in this chapter further encourage the belief that even extremely complex behavior is not beyond the interpretive power of fundamental biobehavioral processes. Moreover, environment-environment and environment-behavior relations mediated by the human brain do not appear to be driven exclusively or even primarily by verbal processes. As Marvin Minsky has put it: "It is because our brains primarily exploit [neural networks] that we possess such small degrees of consciousness, in the sense that we have so little insight into the nature of our own conceptual machinery. What appear to us to be direct insights into ourselves must be rarely genuine and usually conjectural. Reflective thought is the lesser part of what our minds do."[92] This conclusion offends belief in the rationality of our species—if such a belief could survive Freud—and is contrary to the verbal bias that pervades our culture. Nevertheless, the weight of experimental evidence and theoretical analysis points strongly in that direction.

STUDY AIDS

Technical Terms

activation pattern
priming procedure
priming stimulus
target stimulus
target response
prime
naming task
textual response
cross-modal priming
parallel processing
serial processing
feed-forward network
recurrent connection
reafference
masking stimulus
threshold of detectability
threshold of semantic detection
imagining
affordance
hemispheres
occipital lobe

temporal lobe
parietal lobe
frontal lobe
amnesia
hippocampal amnesia
retrograde amnesia
anterograde amnesia

Text Questions

1. After reading the entire chapter, summarize the general outcome of the selection process on the functioning of the experienced learner. Describe the outcome at both the behavioral and neural levels.

2. What is an *activation pattern*? Include a description of the development of both sensory and motor components of the pattern and its function, using a specific example as an illustration.

3. Describe the *priming procedure,* using technical terms and a specific example in your answer. Indicate how some results obtained with this procedure can be interpreted as the outcome of interactions between activation patterns. Indicate the possible contribution of inhibitory processes to these interactions.

4. Indicate why the activation patterns of meaningless auditory stimuli, phonemes, and words are different in the experienced learner. Indicate why the interstimulus interval at which priming occurs varies with the nature of the priming and target stimuli, giving specific examples to illustrate your answer.

5. Under what circumstances might priming depend on the presence of recurrent connections? Illustrate your answer with a specific example. Use the term *reafference* in your answer.

6. Indicate the major conclusions of research at both the behavioral and neural levels for the interpretation of *imagining*. Refer to experimental findings to support your answer.

7. Is awareness required for complex behavior? Refer to specific information from studies in which

the corpus callosum has been interrupted and in which damage has occurred to the pathways communicating between the hippocampus and sensory association cortex.

8. Describe the major features of hippocampal amnesia. Indicate why selection by reinforcement is impaired for some contingencies following damage to the hippocampal system and not for others. Illustrate your answer with examples and use technical terms, such as *anterograde* and *retrograde amnesia*.

Discussion Questions

9. Describe an everyday example of complex behavior that illustrates how behavior may be influenced by the biobehavioral processes studied in priming experiments. Make reference to the possible contributions of internal reinforcement to the behavior.

10. How should the relative dependence of complex behavior on environmental feedback and re-afference change with continued experience (exposure to the contingencies of behavioral selection)? Why should this occur? What are the implications of this change for the apparent lack of dependence of complex behavior on the environment of the moment?

11. Comment on our ability to use experimental analysis to investigate verbal behavior. What are some of the implications of this state of affairs?

ENDNOTES

1. See Chapter 1; cf. Skinner, 1957; Smolensky, 1986, pp. 422-424.

2. In the inferred-process approach, which is pursued by most workers in psychology, unobserved mediating processes are commonly called *cognitive processes*. Cognitive processes are the functional counterpart of the subbehavioral processes considered in a biobehavioral approach. However, as noted in the first chapter, unlike biobehavioral processes, cognitive processes are inferences from behavioral observations and not the products of independent experimental analyses at the subbehavioral level. The adjective *cognitive* is a

term from the everyday vocabulary and denotes "the process of knowing," where knowing refers to "understanding gained by actual experience" (Merriam-Webster). According to the dictionary definition, all products of selection would seem to qualify as cognitive processes, since all environment-behavior and environment-environment relations may be said to contribute to knowledge. For example, even a dog who salivates to a tone that has been paired with food may be said to demonstrate a gain in its knowledge of the world. However, when used as a technical term within the inferred-process approach, cognitive processes are unobservable in principle, not merely unobserved because of current technical limitations. Cognitive processes are inferred constructs constrained primarily by logical considerations and, as such, cannot be the object of experimental analysis since they are not events in the physical world.

Most inferred-process theories make no claim that the cognitive processes that they postulate can be coordinated with observations at the subbehavioral level. Instead their goal is to develop an account that is sufficient to accommodate all and only all of the observations obtained at the behavioral level. Cognitive theories, because of the complex relations that they attempt to accommodate, typically postulate many inferred processes that interact in complex ways. John R. Anderson's ACT* model (Anderson, J. R., 1983) and Allen Newell's SOAR model (Newell, Rosenbloom, & Laird, 1989) are among the most highly developed theoretical treatments of this sort. In such models, a given complex behavior is said to be the result of the formation of extensive sets of "condition-action-consequence" sequences. (The resemblance of this cognitive structure to Skinner's ideas of three-term contingencies and behavioral chaining is apparent, except that—as inferred processes—the characteristics of these sequences are not constrained by experimental analysis.) By the end of training, the computer program that implements the series of condition-action-consequence sequences is able to produce an output that corresponds to the complex behavior. For this reason, models of this sort are said to be *production systems*. (For other examples of general cognitive models, see Gillund & Shiffrin, 1984; Raaijmakers & Shiffrin, 1980, 1981; Murdock, 1982, 1987; cf. Eich, 1985.) Inferred-process models designed to accommodate complex behavior have sometimes been criticized because they are so complex that they are often difficult to reject. (The ability of a theory to be falsified by experiment is one of the standard criteria by which scientific theories are evaluated; Popper, 1978.) This criticism, even if valid, misses the mark in our view. The primary goal of inferred-process theories is to generate input-output relations that mimic complex environment-behavior relations observed in a wide variety of situations. The sufficiency of the model to accomplish this task is its chief goal (Anderson, 1978, 1983). Direct testability of the validity of the intervening processes and their correspondence to processes within the organism are largely beside the point. Our most fundamental reservation about such models is not that they approach untestability at the level of the complete model—this is likely to be an unavoidable characteristic of any comprehensive effort to accommodate complex behavior—but that the intervening processes are not firmly grounded in independent experimental analyses at the behavioral and subbehavioral levels of analysis. If experimental analyses of the intervening processes are possible—and this can only occur if the intervening processes are physical processes, and not just logical inferences—then the falsifiability criterion can be met. In that way, interpretations of complex behavior may be evaluated through means other than the sufficiency of the complete model.

3. The present description of the selection of relations on the behavioral level, and the neural mechanisms that mediate them, is stated in a declarative form to simplify the exposition. Of course—as indicated at numerous points when these proposals were first introduced—much experimental analysis and scientific interpretation remain before the account may be accepted with even the usual tentativeness that accompanies all conclusions in science.

4. e.g., Yuste, Peinado, & Katz, 1992. The selection of neural connections in motor systems, where activity-dependent mechanisms are also very much in evidence, is beyond the scope of this book. Their inclusion would not undermine the present treatment but importantly supplement it; cf. Gallistel, 1990; Rosenbaum, 1991.

5. The coordinated diffusely projecting neuromodulatory systems proposed to strengthen connections throughout the sensory and motor association cortices address what has been called the *binding problem* in adaptive-network research (e.g., Sejnowski, 1986). Among the pathways that are active in the neural network immediately before the reinforcer must necessarily be those responsible for mediating the reinforced input-output relation. The proposed mechanism selects *all* such connections throughout the entire network, and thereby binds together the required pathways.

6. In the inferred-process approach, the construct of *working memory* is most similar to the present notion of activation pattern, cf. J. R. Anderson, 1985.

7. cf. Goldiamond, 1962; Skinner, 1953, 1945, 1964.

8. In the inferred-process approach, a stimulus is said to evoke some *representation* of itself. To refer to the activation pattern as a representation is misleading. According to the dictionary definition, a representation is an entity such as "a picture or image" that "represents something else," where represent means "to serve as a symbol of" or "to stand in the place of" the entity (Merriam-Webster). But an activation pattern does not have the dimensions of a stimulus, and thus is unlike a picture or an image. In addition, the notion of representation does not include the motor component of the activation pattern. Finally, and most fundamentally, representation is too static a conception. The same stimulus may evoke somewhat different activation patterns at different times and in different contexts. An activation pattern specifies a variable but distinctive pattern of neural activity—a probabilistic ensemble of unit activity and not a "thing."

9. On this account, the contribution of neurons in subcortical structures to an activation pattern is not explicitly considered. The basic thrust of the present account is not changed by their inclusion, however.

10. Hubel & Livingstone, 1987; Ungerleider & Mishkin, 1982.

11. The PET-scan procedure has been employed to depict differential neural activity in the brains of both animals (e.g., Petersen, Robinson, & Keys, 1985) and humans, using stimulation with simple visual stimuli (e.g., Fox, Mintun, Raichle, & Miezin, 1986) and with verbal stimuli (e.g., Petersen, Fox, Snyder, & Raichle, 1990).

12. Fuster, 1989.

13. For overviews of this work, see Montgomery, 1991; Posner, Petersen, Fox, & Raichle, 1988.

14. cf. Swindale, 1979.

15. Within the inferred-process approach, some treatments of inhibition can be made commensurate with the present analysis, e.g., Roediger, Neely, & Blaxton, 1983; Roediger & Neely, 1982; Rumelhart & Zipser, 1986; whereas others appear to be concerned with quite different processes; e.g., Dagenbach, Carr, & Barnhardt, 1990. If the term inhibition is used to refer to a decrease in performance independent of the processes that produce that decrease, then the term is being used in a theoretically incoherent fashion; cf. Donahoe & Palmer, 1988.

16. You will recognize this as another instance of the capability of a neural network to "construct" an output when presented with only part of the input with which it has been trained.

17. The *latency* of a response is the time between the presentation of a stimulus and the occurrence of the measured response to that stimulus.

18. Although many different characteristics of behavioral responses have been used in an attempt to study the effects of subbehavioral events, response latencies—and the temporal characteristics of sequences of responses in general—have been used most often. Efforts to use temporal characteristics of behavior to indirectly assess subbehavioral processes, or inferred processes in the case of cognitive theories, may be traced to the beginning of scientific psychology with Donder's subtraction method. For modern evaluations of such methods, and of the many difficulties associated with them, see Townsend, 1972; Townsend & Evans, 1983 and Luce, 1991.

19. e.g., Jacoby & Hayman, 1987.

20. e.g., Nelson & Rothbart, 1972.

21. For other examples of the ways in which retention may be affected by various characteristics of stimuli, see D'Agostino, O'Neill, & Paivio, 1977; Durso & Johnson, 1980; Morton, 1980. For summaries of work of this sort, see Ashcraft, 1989; Donahoe & Wessells, 1980 and Glass & Holyoak, 1986.

22. The present interpretation of priming in terms of overlapping activation patterns can be contrasted with the account of priming in inferred-process or cognitive approaches. In inferred-process approaches, studies that document the characteristics of stimuli that affect retention are usually discussed under the heading of encoding. That term is not used here, both because it emphasizes the stimulus to the relative exclusion of the responses guided by the stimulus and because it implies—by the introduction of a new technical term—that encoding processes differ from those biobehavioral processes already identified through studies of stimulus discrimination and response differentiation. The biobehavioral approach views stimuli and responses as scientifically meaningless apart from the environment-behavior relations in which they participate, and seeks to interpret verbal behavior according to the same types of processes involved in the interpretation of other environment-environment and environment-behavior relations.

23. One commonly used priming technique, a *lexical decision task*, presents a word as a priming stimulus and a group of letters as a target stimulus. Some letter groups form words, others do not. The subject's task is to indicate—often by pressing one of two buttons—whether the target stimulus is a word or nonword; Meyer & Schvaneveldt, 1971. Although the lexical decision task was the first priming procedure studied systematically and has produced interesting findings, we shall generally not consider it further here since performance on this task is likely not to be the product of an extensive pre-experimental selection history.

24. Seidenberg, Tanenhaus, Leiman, & Bienkowski, 1982.

25. e.g., Meyer & Schvaneveldt, 1976; cf. Conrad, 1964; Onifer & Swinney, 1981.

26. Frazier & Rayner, 1990; Rayner & Frazier, 1989.

27. Balota & Lorch, 1986; cf. McNamara & Healy, 1988.

28. Frazier & Rayner, 1990.

29. See Simpson, 1984 and Carr, 1986 for reviews; cf. Kintsch & Mross, 1985.

30. e.g., Onifer & Swinney, 1981.

31. Bowles & Poon, 1985; cf. Henik, Friedrich, & Kellogg, 1983; Neely, 1977.

32. cf. McClelland & Elman, 1986.

33. In the priming literature, this interval is usually called the Stimulus Onset Asynchrony (SOA) interval. We shall refer to it simply as the interstimulus interval.

34. cf. Posner & Snyder, 1975.

35. cf. Freedman & Loftus, 1971; Neely, 1977; Posner & Snyder, 1975; Ratcliff & McKoon, 1988.

36. cf. Graf, Shimamura, & Squire, 1985.

37. Jacoby & Witherspoon, 1982.

38. Tulving & Schacter, 1990, p. 302.

39. On the behavioral level, we noted in Chapter 3 that responses are most commonly guided by multiple discriminative stimuli. The importance of this factor in interpreting complex behavior was explicitly recognized by B. F. Skinner in *Verbal behavior* (1957), in a chapter entitled "Multiple Causation." In the technical literature of adaptive networks, this factor has more recently been recognized by noting that the strength of connections must satisfy *simultaneous constraints*, cf. McClelland, Rumelhart, & Hinton, 1986.

40. This is an example of remembering rather than reminding as that distinction was introduced in Chapter 8, and is discussed in Chapter 12. We regret continued references to topics not yet discussed, but postponing some topics is unavoidable. The organism functions simultaneously as a cohesive whole, but our descriptions of that functioning must necessarily be sequential.

41. Shank & Abelson, 1977; cf. Smith & Graesser, 1981; Bower & Morrow, 1990.

42. Rumelhart, Smolensky, McClelland, & Hinton, 1986, pp. 20-21.

43. cf. Foss, 1988; McKoon & Ratcliff, 1980; Roediger & Challis, 1989; McDaniel & Masson, 1985.

44. Crick & Asanuma, 1986.

45. e.g., Fuster, 1989.

46. There are potentially important differences between the effects of afference and reafference on selection. For example, if reafference produces more rapid changes in earlier components of the neural network than does behaviorally mediated afference and if the reinforced behavioral response thereby occurs more rapidly, then connections mediating reafference will be more immediately (and hence more strongly) strengthened than connections involved in the less rapid behavioral mediation. When temporal factors favor the selection of reafferent inputs to interior units over inputs to output units, covert rather than behaviorally expressed processes may be preferentially selected. This possibility has important consequences for the interpretation of such complex behavior as problem solving, but its further consideration is deferred until the next chapter.

47. cf. Freedman & Loftus, 1971.

48. Neely, 1977; cf. Ratcliff & McKoon, 1988.

49. cf. Shiffrin & Schneider, 1977.

50. In the inferred-process literature, fast-occurring effects are commonly described as *automatic processing* whereas slower-occurring effects are described as *strategic processing*. From the biobehavioral perspective, it is not helpful to conceive of effects as differing along a dimension of automaticity. One effect is as automatic (or as nonautomatic) as another. Effects that require different times for their occurrences are simply produced by different combinations of the same fundamental processes expressed in different ways.

51. Balota, 1983; Marcel, 1983a, b.

52. Carr & Daggenbach, 1990.

53. For some subjects, the duration at which a stimulus exceeded the detectability threshold was greater than the duration of the semantic threshold for other subjects. These large individual differences between subjects indicate once again the importance of research methods that permit the study of biobehavioral processes with single subjects. Different subjects have such different selection histories that averaging results across subjects often obscures rather than clarifies our understanding of those processes.

54. Schacter, Cooper, Delaney, Peterson, & Tharan, 1991; cf. Dagenbach, Carr, & Barnhardt, 1990, Experiment 2.

55. e.g., Potter, 1975.

56. Note that, according to this definition, imagining involves largely similar biobehavioral processes to those evoked by the customary environmental stimuli that guide the perceptual responses. However, instead of perceptual responses being initiated by the direct action of the environment, these responses are now instigated by the effect on sensory association areas of neural activity arising in motor association areas. As interpreted by selection networks, imagining consists of activation patterns with particularly rich participation of the stimulus-selection component through the action of recurrent connections from the response-selection component.

57. For a summary of early work on behavioral accompaniments of imagining and thinking, see Humphrey, 1951. Much of this work was carried out as a part of what was called the "motor theory of thinking." Modern behavioral research regards the overt motor accompaniments of imagining and thinking as incomplete and nonessential components of these responses; but see McGuigan, 1978.

58. Segal & Fusella, 1970; see Logie & Baddeley, 1990 for a review.

59. Shepard & Metzler, 1971; Cooper & Shepard, 1973.

60. The activation patterns required for imagining take considerable time to develop and are affected in similar ways by the variables that affect seeing. In general, the long latencies of responding are probably due to the need for a number of cycles of reafference of the sensory association cortex by feedback from motor components of the activation pattern involved in the imagined rotation of the objects; cf. Moyer, 1973; Kosslyn & Pomerantz, 1977; Kosslyn, 1983.

61. Not unexpectedly, since verbal responses are not necessarily correlated with the covert activity of imagining, there have been difficulties in replicating some behavioral research on imagining; e.g., Broerse & Crassini, 1984; Intons-Peterson, 1983. A related problem plagued an earlier period in psychology when the issue was whether thinking was necessarily accompanied by images; see Boring, 1950 for a discussion of the work of the Wurzburg school.

62. Roland & Friberg, 1985.

63. A number of different procedures can be used to determine the general level of activity in various brain regions in fully conscious human subjects. For example, radio-opaque dyes and weakly radioactive materials can be injected into the bloodstream and their concentrations determined in different brain regions by external de-

vices. For another, the electrical changes produced by neural activity in a brain region may be detected by electrodes placed on the scalp. Or, the rate of metabolism of the fuel used by nerve cells—glucose—can be measured by PET-scans, and so on. See Farah, 1985, 1988, 1989 for reviews of this research. Of course, such measures provide very gross indications of the activity of the single units that make up activation patterns. There is, as yet, no technique for measuring single-unit activity in conscious humans except briefly during brain surgery conducted to alleviate a pathological condition, but for related work with animals see Georgopoulos, Lurito, Petrides, Schwartz, & Massey, 1989.

64. e.g., Farah, Peronnet, Gonon, & Giard, 1988; cf. Teuber, 1963.

65. e.g., Sacks, 1987.

66. Bisiach & Luzzatti, 1978; cf. Bisiach, Luzzatti, & Perani, 1979. For general reviews, see Brown, 1988; Friedman & Weinstein, 1977; Heilman & Valenstein, 1979; and Stiles-Davis, Kritchevsky, & Bellugi, 1987. For information regarding the effects of this type of brain damage on perceiving faces, see Bruyer, 1986.

67. See Haber, 1983 for a critique of alternative views; cf. Parsons, 1987.

68. Gibson, 1979. As one type of evidence implicating motor components in imagining, sighted subjects who have learned the locations of objects by looking around an environment, blind subjects who have learned the locations of objects by moving around the environment, and blindfolded sighted subjects who have learned the locations of objects in a miniature environment by hand movements all show similar behavioral effects when imagining these environments. For instance, when subjects are asked to imagine an object located in one part of the environment and then to imagine another object at another location, the time before they report imagining the new object increases as a function of the distance between the two objects. Whether the environment has been sensed through eye movements, leg movements, or finger movements, the greater the distance between objects in space the greater the movement—and, therefore, the time—between imagining objects in different locations; e.g., Carpenter & Eisenberg, 1978; Marmor & Zaback, 1976; Zimler & Keenan, 1983.

69. Since awareness is a term from the everyday vocabulary, it is commonly used in nontechnical senses as well. Often, an organism is said to be aware of any stimulus to which it responds by means of any response

system. When used in this nontechnical sense, to say that an organism is aware of a stimulus is simply to say that the stimulus is a discriminative stimulus. Here, awareness is restricted to the guidance of verbal behavior by a stimulus.

70. There is a related technical term, *self-awareness*, in which the stimuli that guide verbal responses are not found in the environment but within the organism; cf. Skinner, 1945, 1964. We postpone an interpretation of self-awareness until the chapter on remembering.

71. e.g., Hefferline & Bruno, 1971; Rosenfeld & Baer, 1970. See Donahoe & Wessells, 1980 for a discussion of some of the conceptual difficulties confronted by this research area.

72. cf. Geschwind, 1972.

73. Additional information concerning the neural mechanisms involved in perceiving and producing speech is given in Chapter 11 in which verbal behavior is more fully discussed. The right hemisphere also makes important contributions—for example, to the stress patterns, or prosody, of vocal speech. Although there are brain regions that play a special role in verbal behavior, it should be clear that the brain functions as a richly interconnected whole and that, although the effects of specific regions may be especially apparent for certain functions, many regions contribute importantly to most environment-behavior relations.

74. Animal research on the effects of the corpus callosum on brain function was undertaken by Roger Sperry, 1968, 1974, for which he shared a Nobel Prize.

75. For reports of other findings, see Gazzaniga, 1970; LeDoux, 1978; Sperry, 1974.

76. See Horel, 1976; Mishkin, 1978.

77. Amnesia produced by a combination of damage to the sensory-hippocampal pathways and pathways to and from the sensory and frontal cortices has more complex behavioral consequences. The clinical syndrome that approximates this condition is *Korsakoff's amnesia*. This type of amnesia is most commonly produced by prolonged excessive ingestion of alcohol (ethanol), in conjunction with a thiamine vitamin deficiency. For general reviews of amnesia, see Cermak, 1982; Squire & Cohen, 1984.

78. This presentation assumes that damage has occurred to the hippocampal systems of *both* hemispheres. If damage is only unilateral, even if in the left hemisphere, then environment-behavior relations requiring new polysensory integrations—including those mediat-

ing verbal behavior—can be maintained through pathways interconnecting the two hemispheres via the corpus callosum.

Quite general agreement exists that the hippocampus is necessary for modifying synaptic efficacies in polysensory association cortex, although complex interconnections of the hippocampus with other brain regions implicate contributions of these structures as well; cf. Eichenbaum & Otto, 1992; Krieckhaus, Donahoe, & Morgan, 1992; Milner, Corkin, & Teuber, 1968; Squire, 1992; Squire & Zola-Morgan, 1988; Squire, Shimamura, & Amaral, 1989; Sutherland & Rudy, 1989; cf. Squire, Cohen, & Nadel, 1984; Warrington & Weiskrantz, 1982; Weiskrantz, 1988. A biological mechanism for implementing this function is what is contributed here.

Because lesions of the neural system interconnecting the hippocampus with sensory association cortex prevent the formation of new polysensory integrations, experience following the lesion cannot select new polysensory regularities (i.e., anterograde amnesia occurs with respect to such regularities). However, this is not the only effect of lesions to the hippocampal system. Such lesions can also impair the consolidation of polysensory integrations selected in the period *prior* to the damage (a form of retrograde amnesia); Zola-Morgan & Squire, 1990. Retrograde amnesia for recently selected regularities is consistent with the present account of the functioning of the hippocampal system. To illustrate, a given CA1 hippocampal cell—which cells give rise to the pathways that diffusely project to polysensory association cortex—has presynaptic inputs carrying information from the polysensory cells that serve as inputs to the hippocampus. Assume that a given polysensory input to the hippocampus indicates the conjunction of two stimuli—e.g., A and B—and that their conjunction must be detected in order for behavior to be appropriately guided under the prevailing contingencies of reinforcement. For example, suppose that A and B are visual and auditory stimuli and that the task is configural conditioning (see Chapter 7). Through the mechanisms described in the text, the diffuse output of an intact hippocampus would differentially strengthen synaptic efficacies between cortical cells carrying A and B information and any polysensory cells on which they converge in sensory association cortex. This effect is dependent, in turn, on the differential strengthening of synaptic efficacies between polysensory inputs to CA1 cells within the hippocampus. For example, a given CA1 input might specify the conjunction of A and B and other

inputs to that same CA1 cell might specify the stimulus context in which the conjunction occurs. Once the intrahippocampal polysensory connections to CA1 are strengthened, then any subsequent activity of a polysensory cell in sensory association cortex that has inputs from A and/or B stimuli has the potential to further strengthen its cortical connections through the action of the hippocampus. In short, once hippocampal mechanisms are in place to strengthen connections to a given polysensory cell in sensory association cortex, then those mechanisms may continue to operate until the intrahippocampal connections to CA1 have been modified by subsequent selection. This lingering effect of prior selection continues until subsequent experience has altered the synaptic efficacies to CA1 cells because of new reliable and reinforced conjunctions of sensory information. However, until the effects of prior experience on the inputs to CA1 cells have been "overwritten," sensory inputs that activate polysensory cells in association cortex can continue to have a *differential* strengthening effect on the synaptic efficacies of inputs to the polysensory cells, *even if the sensory input is relatively unrelated to that which produced the polysensory integration in the first instance.* In short, once connections to CA1 cells have been modified, these connections enable later experiences to further strengthen, or consolidate, the previously selected polysensory regularities. Then, if the hippocampal system is damaged, not only anterograde amnesia should occur but also retrograde amnesia for regularities selected before the damage—especially those selected immediately prior to damage.

(For possible contributions of hippocampal damage to Alzheimer's disease, see Van Hoesen & Damaisio, 1987.)

79. Mishkin, 1982; Squire, 1992; Squire & Zola-Morgan, 1983.

80. Zola-Morgan, Squire, & Amaral, 1986.

81. Milner, Corkin, & Teuber, 1968.

82. e.g., Milner, 1972.

83. Diamond & Rozin, 1984; cf. Schacter, 1985; Shimamura & Squire, 1984. Priming, even of pictorial stimuli, is dependent upon the similarity of the target stimulus to previously experienced components and not merely of overlap in physical features, e.g., Biederman & Cooper, 1990.

84. Hirst & Volpe, 1984.

85. Parkinson, Murray, & Mishkin, 1988.

86. Brooks & Baddeley, 1976; Milner, 1962.

87. Cohen & Squire, 1980, 1981.

88. Weiskrantz & Warrington, 1979.

89. Tranel & Damaisio, 1985.

90. For other examples, see El-Wakil, 1975.

91. Some classify tasks that require polysensory integration and those that do not as instances of *declarative memory* and *procedural memory* (or simply *nondeclarative memory*), respectively; e.g., Squire, 1992. Since the term declarative connotes verbal behavior, but the deficit appears to be a general failure of polysensory integration of which the verbal deficits are but one manifestation among many (e.g., spatial deficits), we prefer to describe the deficit as a failure of polysensory integration.

92. Minsky & Papert, 1988.

CHAPTER 10

PROBLEM SOLVING

No behavior seems to require more "higher mental processes" than problem solving. We are delighted when the family dog figures out how to open the screen door, we are fascinated by chimpanzees that have learned to use tools, and we are eager to be duped by showmen who demonstrate mathematical genius in horses, goats, or pigs. It is not that we think these skills are commonplace; it is that we want to believe that these animals, too, can think and reason. We take problem solving to be the surest sign of intelligence and the best tool for evaluating it.

Part of the charm of problem-solving behavior is its unpredictability. We revere Archimedes, Galileo, and Newton not simply for their remarkable accomplishments but for the poverty of their tools. We are bombarded daily by the advances of modern science, by the announcement of new vaccines or the identification of a gene responsible, perhaps, for some congenital disorder, but we reserve our highest esteem not for the teams of scientists with the latest tools of genetic engineering at their disposal, but for pioneers such as Jenner and Pasteur who toiled in unexplored fields without established and proven procedures. Their discoveries seem to have sprung from their genius alone. Similarly, while we nod our approval to a student who successfully solves a problem in geometry using principles that have been covered this week in school, we stand in awe of Euclid and other ancients, who discovered the principles in the first place. The more a discovery seems to arise from insight rather than from obedience to precedent, the finer the example of problem solving, and the more we are inclined to appeal to the operation of higher mental powers.

No doubt we can explain mere computation and the following of prescribed rules by appealing to the reinforcement principle, to contingencies arranged, deliberately or not, by schools, parents, employers, siblings, and tutors. After all, a formula is a discriminative stimulus, or a complex sequence of discriminative stimuli, and following a formula is typically reinforced by success of some sort.[1] Computation smacks of chains of responses learned by rote. But can intuition, insight, and flashes of genius be explained without appealing to more complex and irreducible cognitive functions? Let us see how far selectionist principles can take us, and what phenomena remain as an intractable and inexplicable residue.

"PROBLEM" DEFINED

We must begin by defining what we mean by a problem and what it means to solve one. As a first approximation, we note that we have a problem whenever an important consequence is contingent, at least in part, on conditions that are not currently in effect. If we want a garden tractor, but have no money, we have a problem. If we want a job as an accountant, but have studied botany, we have a problem. If we want an A on the botany exam, but have *not* studied botany, we have a problem. But when we speak of problem solving, we typically are concerned with difficulties that we can overcome through special efforts. The following criteria define the domain of interest:

First, the behavior which constitutes or brings about a solution must be possible for us (or for the other organism of interest). No doubt we would like to take back that embarrassing slip of the tongue, to turn a lump of coal into a diamond through the force of our grip, to bring peace to the Middle East, to determine once and for all why Kennedy was shot, to sing the role of the troubadour in Verdi's opera, and so on. We are not concerned here with problems for which we lack the strength, the ability, or the propitious circumstances for a solution, problems that are insoluble to us regardless of our efforts. Nor are we concerned here with global problems, however important, that can be solved only by teams, groups, or whole societies. A different level of analysis is required for such problems.

Second, we must somehow recognize that we are faced with a problem. We must know that some behavior is required, and that it will pay off in some way; that is, there must be some motivation for emitting the solution as such. A boy who finds his mother's earring while digging for nightcrawlers has solved a problem, but such accidents are of little interest as examples of problem solving. Often problems are presented by teachers, parents, employers, or peers, and a correct solution is followed by a modicum of approval, recognition, respect, or prestige. The statement of the problem specifies that a solution is required, and past consequences usually insure that we will try to oblige. For someone with a history of successfully solving such problems, the activity can be intrinsically enjoyable, as legions of puzzle solvers will attest, and an extrinsic "payoff" is unnecessary. In some cases, a desired object is in sight, or an unpleasant event is annoying us; we may spot a ten-dollar bill through a sewer grate, or we may have inadvertently triggered our neighbor's burglar alarm when we went to borrow a rake. Here, the payoff is conspicuous and not socially mediated.

Finally, there must be some obstacle to our simply emitting the solution directly. A problem is not a problem to us if we have encountered it before and already know the solution. In everyday usage we typically call something a problem if it has certain formal properties. Math problems, word problems, etc., are so called regardless of whether we have encountered them before. As we have had many occasions to remark, however, the formal

properties of a stimulus or an event do not, by themselves, provide appropriate criteria for classification; we must consider, as well, the organism and its history relative to the stimulus. Problem solving calls for a special analysis only when we confine ourselves to behavior that has not already been reinforced in the presence of the problem as a stimulus.

In providing a behavioral account of problem solving it will be helpful to translate these criteria into technical terms:

1. A *target response*, or set of responses, is in the organism's repertoire and can be evoked by one or more stimulus conditions.

2. Discriminative stimuli are present indicating that the response is scheduled for reinforcement.

3. The current complex of discriminative stimuli is not sufficient to evoke the response directly, or stimuli are present that evoke prepotent competing responses.

For example, the response "67" is in our repertoire under the control of a variety of stimulus conditions. It is a response evoked by the written or auditory stimuli "64 . . . 65 . . . 66 . . ." (called an **intraverbal response** in Skinner's classification of verbal operants[2]); it is a response to the printed stimulus "67" (a textual response); if we are repeating the words of another, it is a response to the auditory stimulus "67" (an echoic response); it is a response to "66 + 1"; and so on. For most English-speaking adults the response is occasioned by a very wide variety of stimuli or stimulus complexes. In contrast, leaping a five-foot hurdle or uttering an echoic response to many foreign words are not responses in our current repertoire under any stimulus conditions.

If we are asked to name the smallest prime number that is greater than 61, the response "67" is scheduled for reinforcement. The form and intonation of the utterance and the context in which it occurs identify it as a question and indicate that a particular response (the target response) will be followed by reinforcement.[3]

Unfortunately, the question and its context do not control the response directly, unless, of course, we have heard the question before and have correctly responded to it. When asked "What is nine times seven?" most of us will promptly reply "63." However, when asked for the smallest prime larger than 61, few of us can reply immediately, though if given a few minutes, we will come up with the correct answer. It is not a matter of latency, with the second response being more weakly evoked by the question and hence having a longer latency; we simply never have encountered the three-term contingency necessary to condition the response as a discriminated operant to the question. Uttering the target response must be explained in other terms.

Similarly, if we want to get in out of the cold but have dropped the apartment key in the snow, we have a problem. The act of unlocking the door, opening it, and entering the apartment is a well-practiced chain of responses in our repertoire. The closed door, the stoop, the brisk air, are part of a stimulus complex in the presence of which we have successfully entered this door, or similar doors, in the past. Unfortunately, a crucial stimulus is missing: the key. The inventive reader will think of dozens of solutions to this problem: ringing the doorbell, jimmying the lock with a credit card, climbing in a window, trying the back door, phoning the manager, waiting for one's spouse, calling a locksmith, knocking the door down, and, of course, looking for the key.

Solving a problem, then, requires emitting a response in a context that does not directly evoke that response. The task of a behavioral analysis is to explain how this is possible. If the context does not evoke the target response, it must evoke, presumably in conjunction with other variables, some other responses. If the target response eventually occurs, that is, if we solve the problem, then additional variables must have been brought to bear, variables that were sufficient to evoke the response. Problem solving is the process of marshaling these additional variables.

MARSHALING SUPPLEMENTARY STIMULI

There are many techniques by which we bring additional variables to bear on a problem. Often we simply change our orientation. If we kneel down, turn our head, cup our hands behind our ears, shade our eyes, or stand on our toes, we alter our contact with environmental stimuli. Simply turning one's head alters control by countless visual stimuli and perhaps auditory stimuli as well. Just as importantly, it reduces or eliminates control by many other stimuli. Effective looking behavior can be helpful in a wide variety of problems, from finding a contact lens to spotting errors in a manuscript or a mathematical proof.

Sometimes we solve problems by physically manipulating environmental variables. We alphabetize our papers or highlight important passages, we turn up the volume on the television or shut the door, we arrange cards by suit or gather necessary tools. A particularly helpful strategy, familiar to every algebra student, is to translate a problem into symbols. This reduces the control by irrelevant properties of a problem, and may emphasize obscure relationships.

In some cases we don't simply manipulate variables, we supplement them—for example, by asking advice, looking in a cookbook, or consulting an encyclopedia. Often we supplement environmental variables with stimuli produced by our own behavior. This is perhaps best illustrated with arithmetic or algebra problems where there are formal procedures that generate stimuli that are usually sufficient, along with the stimuli arising from the problem itself, to occasion the target response and identify it as the answer. Consider the arithmetic problem 362×784. We undoubtedly have never encountered this particular arrangement of stimuli before, and consequently have no unique response conditioned to it. In a suitable context the form of the stimulus—the numerals, the spacing, the "times" sign—identifies it as a multiplication problem. (In another context we might assume it to be a license plate number, a serial code, a phone extension number, etc.) We have learned codified strategies for solving such problems. We begin by physically manipulating the stimuli:

362
784

The new arrangement is merely a convention, but, depending on our educational history, the arrangement may be helpful or even necessary to evoke the sequence of subsequent responses. We still have no unitary response conditioned to this particular stimulus configuration, but we have responses conditioned to components of the stimulus complex. We must execute them in a particular order, however, an order we presumably learned in grade school. We orient toward the 4, then the 2; the 4, then the 6; and so on. As we do so, we emit discriminated operants under the control of these stimuli: "Four times two is eight; four times six is twenty-four. . ." Each response provides stimulation that controls looking at the next number in the sequence. As we emit responses we write them down: Vocal, or subvocal, stimuli rapidly cease to control our subsequent behavior as they recede in time (as we saw in Chapter 9 in our discussion of short-term memory procedures); textual stimuli will continue to control our behavior as long as we continue to orient toward them. As we step through the pairs of numbers in an orderly way we reach the leftmost pair, 7 and 3. This evokes a new sequence of responses, orienting toward the textual stimuli we have produced and adding them in a particular order.

362
 784
1448
2896
2534

When we have added the leftmost column, we know that the new textual stimulus we have created, the number below the bottom line, is the answer. The step-by-step control of our behavior by procedural conventions, the configuration, the lines, etc., may not be obvious, so natural do they seem to us now. However, we can demonstrate

their importance by simply disregarding convention. Suppose we choose to write our products to the side, vertically, and not staggered:

		1	2	2
362		4	8	5
784		4	9	3
		8	6	4

We now have to "think," to struggle, to check and recheck our work.

Unless we have independent corroboration of our work, we will not know if we have reached the correct answer to an arithmetic problem. The answer only rarely has distinctive properties.[4] Procedural conventions provide us with a technique for identifying the answer as such; the answer is usually set apart by a line, a division symbol, a square root sign, etc. When we have finished the last response in the procedure we can read the answer as a simple textual response, and no further behavior evoked by the problem or the response-generated stimuli is strong.

Most problems have no codified solutions, and the steps from the presentation of the problem to the target response are by no means so certain. However, we solve, or attempt to solve, such problems in analogous ways. We generate responses, producing changes in stimuli that supplement those of the problem itself. These stimuli evoke new responses that serve to evoke still further behavior. As the solution progresses, some stimuli become increasingly remote, some are more recent. We repeat important terms or write them down in order to reinstate their control in full force. The cumulative effect, if one is successful, is to strengthen the target response and weaken competing responses. Eventually the target response becomes the **prepotent response** and is emitted, satisfying the contingency posed by the problem.[5]

The target response must be identified as such to halt further problem-solving behavior. Often the response is followed by reinforcement—we find the lost glasses, the lawnmower starts, the teacher says, "That's right," and so on. Sometimes it satisfies some corroboratory test. If we are asked to think of a word in which all five vowels and "Y" occur in alphabetical order, we can put our candidate words to the test.[6] However, there are problems for which the target response is difficult to identify. "Why does a spinning gyroscope not fall when you let go of one end?" It is hard to say what an acceptable answer would be. Or consider the following problem (see **Figure 10.1**):

A large cube is divided into thirds in each plane, yielding 27 smaller cubes, like rooms in a large house. A snake crawls through the house, going from room to room. The snake can only enter and leave a room at right angles through one of its six sides, always makes a right angle turn in the center of each room, and can never re-enter a room that he has left. What is the largest number of rooms that the snake can enter before he emerges to the outside?

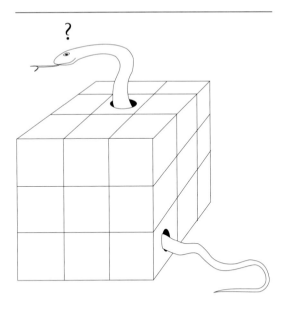

FIGURE 10.1.   *In every room the snake must make a right-angle turn and cannot return to a room he has entered*
How many rooms can he visit before he must emerge to the outside? Unlike most puzzles, but like many questions in science, it is difficult to be sure when one has arrived at the best answer.

Here, it is hard to be sure when one has arrived at the "largest number" of rooms.

To illustrate how a subject solves a problem without using codified strategies, consider the behavior of a subject asked to solve the following problem without using a calculator or paper: "The square root of 1764 is an integer. What is it?" The subject paused for a while, then replied, "Well, it's more than 40 . . . It can't be 41 because it has to end in '4' . . . It can't be 42 . . . Wait! Yes it can . . . No. No, it isn't 42 . . . Oh, I give up! I can't solve that kind of thing in my head!"[7]

Much of the behavior of this subject was covert, but the overt responses suggest that he began by squaring round numbers to "close in" on the answer, presumably an acquired strategy: "10 times 10 is 100. Too small. . . 50 times 50 is 2500. Too big." And so on. Eventually the subject emitted the target response, but failed to recognize it as such. Perhaps it failed a corroboratory test. The response "42" was undoubtedly weak with respect to the initial statement of the problem, but by the time the target response was emitted we can assume that the subject had generated a constellation of intermediate response-produced stimuli including the following: "Less than 50. . . More than 40 . . . Forty-something . . . Ends in 4 . . . Closer to 40 than 50 . . . 2 times 2 is 4." Each stimulus increased the probability of a wide variety of responses including "42." In the presence of this sequence of stimuli, the response "42" may well have been prepotent, even if it was only weakly controlled by each stimulus.

To summarize, problem solving is the behavior of supplementing or manipulating discriminative stimuli until a particular response in the organism's repertoire becomes prepotent over the many other responses that are changing in probability. These manipulations are terminated when the original contingency (the problem) is satisfied, i.e., when reinforcement is delivered, either by another person or agent, by some natural consequence, or by a corroboratory test indicating that the target response has been emitted. The responses may be overt, but they may also be covert, i.e., below the threshold of observability under normal conditions. Thus, we solve many problems "in our head," much as we would solve them overtly, by emitting responses that provide supplementary stimuli. When asked for the smallest prime number larger than 61, one may give the correct answer after a moment or two, apparently with little relevant overt behavior.[8] The response does not just appear spontaneously; there is no doubt that most of us simply count upward from 61, testing each number in turn, to arrive at 67. It is equally clear that the chain of responses is usually observable, at best, only to the subject.

The Status of Covert Responses

The status of covert responses in a science of behavior, and the notion that they provide stimuli, may seem doubtful to the reader. However, we should recall that the observability of a response is not determined by its intensity or magnitude, but by the characteristics or tools of the observer. Many venerable dependent variables in psychology, such as changes in skin conductivity, blood pressure, heart rate, etc., are measurable only through instrumental amplification. As Hefferline and Keenan[9] have shown, minute muscular movements detectable by an electromyograph device may be unobservable even to the subject. We must avoid the temptation to think of covert behavior as a *kind* of behavior, with properties essentially different from overt behavior. Rather, all behavior lies on a continuum of observability. The whispering of a school child is not intended to reach the front of the room, while the bellowing of the Town Crier or the yodeling of a shepherd can be heard for miles.[10] Our subject matter—behavior—is not defined by its magnitude or by the ability of observers to agree on its occurrence. Rather it is any activity of the organism that can enter into orderly relationships with environmental events. We have already had occasion to consider the role of perceptual responses (Chapter 7) in our interpretation of behavior; we must now consider the role of other covert behavior.

Let us consider **Figure 10.2**. This is an example of a simple adaptive network, like many that we have already encountered in this book, that we assume models a part of the nervous system. Individual units represent populations of not-necessarily-adjacent neurons. An output unit represents the population of neurons controlling a particular behavior, say, blinking an eye. In a real organism the eyeblink is an overt behavior and, as such, can be measured, recorded, and agreed upon by disinterested observers. However, the activity of the unit (the output neurons) is observable, if at all, only by the most intrusive of neurophysiological techniques. Since the activity of the unit determines the activity of the eyelid there is no reason to distinguish the two events: They are two dimensions of a single response. However, the two events play different roles. The environment only sees the overt response, and so can arrange contingencies of selection only for the eyeblink. However, the enduring changes brought about by the contingency surely happen at the unit, and elsewhere in the network. The probability of overt responses is altered by contingencies of reinforcement only because the nervous system is. The overt response is no more the "real" response than its neural precursors are.

The relationship between an overt response and its neural precursors is analogous to the relationship between the phenotype and genotype in biology. Contingencies of natural selection operate only on the phenotype. A favorable gene, if not expressed, will not contribute to fitness. However, it is the genes that are modified and the genes that endure. A physical feature will occur more frequently in future generations only because the genes have been selected as well.

When we make an overt response, we often alter the stimulating environment in some way, and the new stimuli can enter into orderly relationships with subsequent behavior. For example, when we reach for a dime on a countertop our behavior results in a change in tactile stimulation (we feel the dime or the countertop); the tactile stimuli then help guide the behavior of adjusting our fingers to

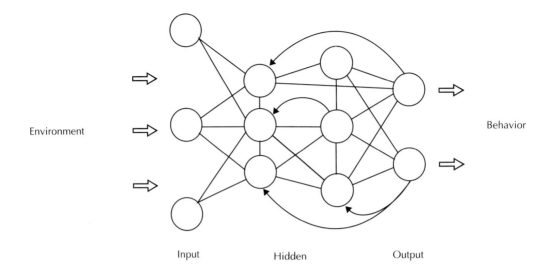

FIGURE 10.2   *A simple adaptive network*
Output units driving behavior may feed back to earlier elements and consequently influence subsequent activity of the network. The activity of an output unit, like the response it drives, depends upon environmental input, the physical structure of the network, and a history of reinforcement, and will have all of the orderly properties of the overt behavior.

pick up the coin. When we make an overt response we also typically experience proprioceptive feedback that can serve a similar function. For example, we can learn a sequence of responses in a relaxation exercise, responses that are paced largely by proprioceptive feedback. "Take a deep breath; clench your fists; now slowly let your fingers loosen up; now your forearms;" etc. Each response is guided, at least in part, by the internal sensations arising from preceding responses.

Similarly, if there are fibers from output units that feed back to earlier elements in a network, the output can serve as input for subsequent activity of the network. This is an instance of *reafference,* introduced in Chapter 9. Again, there appears to be no reason, in principle, to distinguish between the output unit (or even any earlier units that are served by the diffuse reinforcement signal) and an overt response. Under some conditions a unit may be active without a corresponding change in overt

behavior—say, if incompatible behavior is strong, or if the neuronal activity of effectors has been blocked by a toxin such as curare. Yet, if there are recurrent fibers, activity in that unit will influence subsequent activity in the network. The unit is affected by the same stimulus events as the overt response and is modified by the same diffuse reinforcement signal; in the absence of reinforcement, it presumably undergoes extinction just as an overt response would. If activity in the unit could be observed by the naked eye, we would not hesitate to call it a response. The fact that conditioning phenomena at the neural level can only be studied with instrumental intrusion poses overwhelming practical problems to our attempt to provide a complete experimental analysis of human behavior, but it does not pose problems in principle. We believe that we are justified in considering covert events—thoughts, images, unexpressed feelings—in our interpretation of complex behavior provided that we do not introduce *ad hoc* principles, principles that are not founded in the experimental analysis of overt, measurable, quantifiable behavior. We must reiterate that most analysis of complex human behavior is interpretation and not basic science.

Postulating a role for covert behavior in our interpretation of problem solving is not an invitation for unconstrained speculation. Covert responses must be plausible in the context in which they are inferred, and the three-term contingencies necessary to establish these responses as behavioral units must plausibly have occurred in the history of the organism. Since some responses are, in practice, unobservable, and since they undoubtedly influence the course of subsequent observable behavior, we must sometimes make inferences about them if we are to provide a complete account of behavior, but behavioral laws must not be violated when we do so. Inferences about covert events should *follow from* behavioral laws, not serve to mask their inadequacy.

THE EXPERIMENTAL ANALYSIS OF PROBLEM SOLVING

We are faced with dozens, perhaps hundreds, of problems every day, though few of them seem noteworthy: We can't find our keys, the dog is howling, the postage stamp has lost its "stickum," we're cold, we have to make something for supper that the kids will eat but that isn't loaded with fat and salt. Such problems are personal, idiosyncratic, and often poorly defined, and consequently have received scant attention from experimental psychologists. Problems encountered in industry and science are often better defined but are usually too formidable for an experimental analysis. However, problems encountered on IQ tests, in the schoolroom, in puzzle books, and so on, are often both well-defined and relatively straightforward. It is these problems, trivial though they are, that have been studied most extensively. We cannot review the immense literature on even this restricted class of problems here; rather we shall briefly consider a few well-studied examples of problem solving,

but we will interpret them from a behavioral perspective, a perspective that is often somewhat different from that assumed by the original researchers. We will then consider one problem-solving phenomenon—insight—in more detail. We leave to the reader the exercise of extrapolating the interpretive technique to other classes of problems—problems, perhaps, in his or her own experience.

The Role of Response Variability in Problem Solving

What one is doing at the time a problem arises is inadequate to solve the problem—otherwise there would be no problem. It is necessary to do something else; in this sense, response variability is intrinsic to problem solving. In some cases fostering response variability is, by itself, central to a problem's solution. A metallurgist, for example, may need to test systematically a wide variety of alloys to discover one with particular physical properties; likewise, a horticulturist may need to conduct a systematic program of plant breeding to produce a strain of lilac with a particular hue and fragrance. Activities of this sort have been called **trial-and-error problem solving**. The term is misleading, but it survives for historical reasons. The early Gestalt psychologists[11] used the term mainly to contrast with "insightful" problem solving, which, they held, requires perceiving a problem in a special way that cannot be reduced to demonstrated principles of behavior. We do not endorse this conclusion, but it cannot be denied that some examples of problem solving are more complex than others. At a minimum, trial-and-error problem solving, like natural selection, requires only blind variation, selection (in the form of a solution to the problem) and, if the problem recurs, retention.

Consider one of Thorndike's early experiments in instrumental conditioning. A hungry cat was placed in a cage that could be opened by stepping on a treadle. Food was available outside the cage, posing a problem for the cat. Thorndike[12] reports that the cat would typically try to squeeze through various openings in the cage, would bite and claw the bars, would thrust its paws through the bars and claw anything within reach. It might then paw or bump the treadle and, in so doing, trip the latch holding the door. The problem, so far as the cat was concerned, was solved. True to the law of effect, on subsequent trials the cat tended to escape more quickly; once the cat had been exposed to the three-term contingency of stimulus-response-reinforcer, the problem was no longer a problem.

Let us consider this performance from moment to moment in time. A cat has a vast repertoire of responses, some acquired, some innate, many of which can be executed in Thorndike's box, and many of which are mutually incompatible. Owing to the cat's having been deprived of food, a wide variety of responses will be strong.[13] For some reason, unknown to us, one response is prepotent—say, thrusting its paw and nose through the bars of the cage. This response is not reinforced—indeed, the consequences may be mildly aversive—and it loses strength. At some point in this extinction procedure the response ceases to be stronger than competing behavior, and some other response occurs, say, biting the bars. This too is scheduled for extinction and loses strength. The behavior of the cat varies as a necessary consequence of the extinction of prepotent responses; in a novel setting such as Thorndike's puzzle box many responses in the cat's repertoire may be of roughly equal strength, contributing to the variability. Eventually a response that operates the treadle becomes prepotent, and the door drops open. The stimulus configuration is now quite different and the prepotent response is to escape from the cage. The critical response is strengthened and becomes more probable on subsequent occasions.

While this may be a satisfactory account of the acquisition of an instrumental response, it seems a bit threadbare as an example of problem solving. We are accustomed to thinking of problem solving as goal-directed, and this account makes no reference to the food, apart from its reinforcing effect on prior behavior and perhaps a general motivating

effect. The initial operation of the treadle was "accidental" and might have occurred even if the cat had been quite content in its cage. It is true that many examples of problem solving require a more elaborate analysis, but these analyses typically apply only to experienced problem solvers. The naive organism has no repertoire of problem-solving skills; blind variation appears to be its only tool.[14] Moreover, the present account applies quite aptly to many examples of problem solving in humans who are faced with a problem about which they know practically nothing.

For example, consider the behavior of a friend of ours who could not start his car one evening. Knowing nothing about cars, and being in a hurry, he did what anyone else would do: He fiddled and poked and pumped and jiggled every knob, wire, and pedal within reach. He finally started the car shortly after he had slammed the hood with particular vigor. Whether the slammed hood had any effect on the starting of the car is doubtful, but the coincidence had a powerful effect on our friend: His first response to a balky automobile, be it his own or anyone else's, was to slam the hood, a behavior that took an annoyingly long time to extinguish. There is little in our account of Thorndike's cat that cannot be applied to this example.

In the naive organism variability appears to be, at least in part, a by-product of extinction. In the experienced problem solver, variability may be the result of a deliberate strategy. When deciphering a hastily scrawled note we are often reduced to going through the alphabet, letter by letter, supplementing the textual stimuli with intraverbal prompts; the intraverbal cues provided by the recited alphabet exhaust the possibilities for any given letter. Similarly, when solving anagrams—arrangements of letters that must be unscrambled to form words—we often systematically try short sequences of letters, searching for promising candidates for the initial sound. For example when faced with the following sequence of letters

A C S O H T E K

we might proceed by mumbling "SOCK-SACK-SECK-SCOT-SCAT-STOCK-" and so on. The variability here is again more or less systematic, an indication that it is a product of our individual histories. Exhaustive variability is feasible only with short anagrams, of course—there are some 40,000 permutations of an eight-letter anagram—so other strategies must be employed as well. Some letters "go together"—CH, SH, TH, CK, ST, ATE, AKE, etc.—so we will tend to use these combinations as elements in our systematic variations. Without the use of such devices, the anagram might be unsolvable. This anagram is relatively difficult since most of the obvious combinations of letters are not found in the word. Avid puzzle solvers may also wish to try their luck with the more formidable problem of finding the word formed from the letters in ROAST MULES.[15]

Some problems can be solved, then, simply through varying one's responses in an undirected way; others can be solved most expeditiously if the variability is constrained in some way. Let us consider in more detail the origin of variability and factors that limit response variability.

Stereotypy and Variability

When one considers the neural substrate of behavior it is not response variability that needs explaining, it is response stereotypy. Our behavior at any moment is the product of the integrated action of billions of neurons, most of which fire at an appreciable resting rate (perhaps ten times per second for a typical neuron). This cauldron of activity is constantly stirred up by the simultaneous bombardment of thousands of stimuli in several modalities. The orderly relation between stimulus classes and response classes observed in the laboratory emerges from a substrate of enormous variability. It is safe to say that no response is ever precisely replicated. Even at the level of stimulus and response classes in the naive organism there is great variability. A naive pigeon in an experimental chamber will engage in a wide variety of exploratory responses. Staddon and Simmelhag[16] re-

corded the rate of 16 well-defined baseline responses in naive pigeons (raising the head, walking in circles, putting head in the feeder, etc.), and their list was presumably not exhaustive. Experimental psychologists discover principles of behavior by using greatly simplified experimental preparations in which it is usually possible to identify discrete response classes, but ordinarily behavior is fluid, interactive, and novel, with response classes continuously overlapping and blending with one another.

Reinforcement and stereotypy. The effect of a sustained contingency of reinforcement is to strengthen the contingent response relative to other behavior. While the contingency is in effect, behavior may appear stereotypic. Certainly the behavior of a pigeon pecking a key on a variable interval schedule is less variable than its behavior during baseline. Even when a variety of responses satisfies a contingency, an organism may engage in only a single response (or sequence of responses). This was demonstrated in an experimental paradigm pioneered by Vogel and Annau[17] and extended by Schwartz.[18] Pigeons were reinforced for pecking exactly four times on each of two keys, but there was no constraint on the order or sequence of pecking the keys. Schwartz found that, while there were some 70 sequences that satisfied the contingency (e.g., LRRLLLRR or LLLLRRRR, where L = left key and R = right key), all pigeons developed stereotyped sequences that they displayed most of the time. In subsequent experiments using the same paradigm, Schwartz[19] found similar results with college students, with some subjects reporting that a particular stereotyped pattern of responses was not merely sufficient for reinforcement but necessary.

Effective behavior is selected by contingencies of reinforcement, and this has obvious adaptive significance; however, the perseverance of a response when variability is required may be detrimental. When Schwartz subsequently asked his subjects to return to the apparatus and discover the general rule for earning reinforcement (with a slightly altered rule in this phase of the experiment), only one out of four subjects was able to do so, given some 750 trials. In contrast, four naive subjects were all able to do so within 600 trials. The persistence of previously acquired behavior in the experienced group interfered with the kind of variability in response topography necessary to solve the problem.

Extinction and variability.   Consistent with our account of Thorndike's cat, Schwartz found that an extinction procedure increased response variability in both pigeons and college students.[20] Within the first extinction session there was an increase in the variability of response sequences; when the original contingency was reintroduced, stereotyped responding emerged anew. Other studies of extinction have found similar effects.[21] Notterman[22] studied extinction and discrimination procedures in the rat and found that the force of lever-pressing responses was more variable and, on the average, greater during extinction and the extinction phase of a discrimination procedure than during reinforcement phases. Mechner[23] found a similar effect of extinction for the length of consecutive response runs, while Carlton[24] observed that both satiation and decreased magnitude of reinforcement increased response variability. (See **Figure 10.3**.)

The effect of extinction on response variability may be particularly important in problem solving, since, by definition, the response scheduled for reinforcement is not directly evoked by the problem or its context. Prepotent responses that do not lead to a solution will presumably extinguish, leading to greater variability in responding, which, by itself, may contribute to the solution of the problem.

Selecting for variability.   It should not be concluded that reinforcement contingencies necessarily stifle variability and creativity. Cole,[25] for example, found that response force for pigeons pecking a key was actually more variable during a reinforcement condition than during extinction,

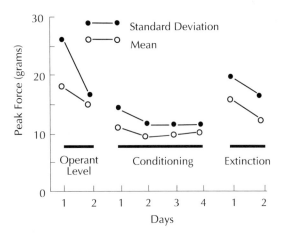

FIGURE 10.3   *The variability of bar-pressing under three experimental conditions*
The force with which a bar was pressed during a baseline phase was relatively great and variable. When bar-pressing produced food, the force stabilized at a relatively low and steady level. During extinction the response became more forceful and more variable again.
Source: From Notterman, J. M. (1959). Force emission during bar pressing. *Journal of Experimental Psychology, 58,* 341–347. Copyright © 1959 by the American Psychological Association. Reprinted by permission.

suggesting that the effect may vary from one preparation to the next. More to the point, when reinforcement is made contingent on response variability itself, responding indeed becomes more variable.[26] Consider the results of an experiment by Pryor, Haag, and O'Reilly on creativity in two trained porpoises. In each experimental session, the porpoises received reinforcement for engaging in some identifiable maneuver that the experimenters had not previously seen. The porpoises obliged them by displaying a wide variety of novel patterns of behavior, such as spinning, corkscrew dives, inverted flips and some stunts not seen before in this species of porpoise.[27] Neuringer and his colleagues have found response variability in both pigeons and people approaching that produced by a random number generator when reinforcement was made contingent specifically on novel patterns of responding.[28] Moreover, they found that variability, like other dimensions of responding, could be brought under the control of a discriminative stimulus. However, their results, when considered together with those of Schwartz, suggest that, with pigeons, prolonged response stereotypy arising from one contingency can reduce response variability when the contingencies change to select for variability.

The deleterious effect of instructions on response variability.   The control of human behavior by rules or instructions vastly extends our ability to act effectively in the world, for we can profit, vicariously as it were, from the nonverbal contingencies of reinforcement experienced by other people.[29] If an approaching jogger warns us not to take the River Road because there is a yard full of furious Rottweilers down there, we will wisely seek another route. If we buy a new coffee-maker or camera, we can be confident that a pamphlet of instructions will enable us to use it correctly without a prolonged period of experimentation. Behavior under the guidance of instructions is typically richly reinforced—considerably more so, for the naive subject, than the nonverbal contingencies that the instructions supplement. Any patron of pirated computer software will confirm that there is virtually no point in having a software package if you cannot also copy the instructions for its use—blind variation at the computer keyboard would be fruitless. The purpose of instructions is precisely to solve problems for us; they provide stimuli, supplementing the stimuli from the problem, that guide our behavior from the problem context to an effective target response. Not coincidentally, much problem-solving behavior in the experienced subject involves seeking out instructional stimuli in the form of reference books, manuals, or advice from other people.

So richly reinforced is instructed behavior, that instructions commonly exert more powerful control than incompatible nonverbal contingencies. For example, if the manual tells us to use a 24-to-1 ratio of gas to oil in our chainsaw, we will continue to do so despite the fact that it happens to run better at a 32-to-1 ratio. If we have been taught to solve a particular class of problems by finding the lowest common denominator, we are apt to do so even when there is a faster way of getting the answer. Instructions tend to restrict or even eliminate variability in response topography, an effect that can impair performance when contingencies change. Experimental analyses of behavior under such conditions indicate that behavior often continues to be guided by the inappropriate instructions rather than by the actual contingency of reinforcement.[30] In a typical experiment, a human subject is given points or money for pressing a key on a particular schedule of reinforcement. The subject is told the optimal pattern of behavior for that schedule or is asked to discover it. After the schedule has been in effect for some time, the schedule changes without warning. Subjects typically persist in the pattern appropriate to the original schedule.

How can we limit such inappropriate persistence in instructed behavior? Studies by Chase and his colleagues indicate that providing subjects with a varied repertoire facilitates effective responding when contingencies change unpredictably. Subjects who were given instructions on eight different schedules of reinforcement subsequently adapted relatively quickly to unsignaled changes in reinforcement schedule,[31] as did subjects who, during a baseline phase, were given instructions to vary their pattern of responding.[32]

Stereotypy and mental set.   The deleterious effect of a dominant response on problem-solving behavior underlies the classic notions of **functional fixedness** and **mental set.** Functional fixedness is the tendency to neglect secondary properties or uses of a familiar object. For example, one might not think of using an inverted umbrella to carry water from a stream to an overheated automobile, but, in the absence of a better container, it would serve the purpose. The term mental set is more general and refers to a tendency to approach a problem in a particular way—usually a way that has recently proven successful in similar circumstances—even if another approach would be more fruitful. Consider the following problems in which it is your task to determine the next number in the series:

```
1   2   4   7   11   16   22   ?
1   3   7   15   31   63   ?
1   2   6   21   88   ?
1   12   16   8   1   2   5   ?
```

The first three problems are straightforward number series problems, progressing in complexity. Solving them in order makes it more difficult to solve the fourth problem.[33]

Several classic studies on functional fixedness and mental set (or *Einstellung*) can be interpreted as illustrating stereotypic responding. Dunker[34] presented subjects with an array of objects on a table—matches, a candle, a small box and some tacks. The subject's task was to mount the candle on the wall in such a way that wax would not drip on the floor. In one condition the box was empty; in other conditions it held the candles, matches, or tacks. The problem could be solved by tacking the box to the wall and using it as a shelf for the candle. Subjects who were presented with an empty box were more likely to solve the problem than those to whom the box was presented as a container. Presumably the latter group persisted in using the box as a container or "thinking of the box as a container" and were therefore slow to consider orienting it in such a way that it would serve as a shelf and not a box.

We saw above that providing subjects with a varied repertoire inoculated them against the tendency to persevere with old patterns of behavior when contingencies changed. Brown and her colleagues have found similar benefits of a varied repertoire in the study of functional fixedness.[35] Children, ranging from three to nine years of age, were presented with scenarios that posed a problem, specifically, how to transport small round objects (cherries, eggs, or jewels) past an obstacle without actually carrying them across. Children had a variety of everyday objects available to them to use as tools, one of which was a piece of paper. The target solution was to form the paper into a

tube and roll the objects through it. One group of children (the functional fixedness group) had previously used paper in this context only for drawing. A second group (the varied training group) had used it in three ways: drawing, making paper houses, and in a communication game. A third group had no relevant experience with paper in the experimental setting. As expected, more of the children in the varied training group suggested the target solution than did those in the other groups. (See **Figure 10.4**.) In a related experiment, chil-

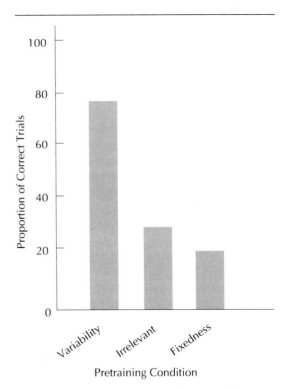

FIGURE 10.4   *The proportion of correct solutions by kindergarten children to a novel task in which paper could be rolled into a tube to transport round objects over a barrier*
Children in the variability condition had used paper in a variety of ways; those in the "functional fixedness" condition had used it only in drawing. Other children had no relevant experience. Similar results were found for fourth graders.
Note: See Brown, 1989.

dren were told about curious adaptations that have evolved in various animals and then were asked to propose a solution for another species faced with a difficult struggle for survival. For one group, the examples all illustrated a common device: Make yourself look like a dangerous animal. The capricorn beetle reveals wasp-like markings when attacked, the hawkmoth caterpillar has a pattern on its underside like that of a poisonous snake, and the crested rat, when attacked, parts its hair to reveal a skunk-like stripe on its back. The second group was given examples that illustrated a variety of adaptations: The hoverfly makes a buzzing sound like a bee, the opossum plays dead, and the walking stick looks like a twig. When the children were told about white moths that could easily be spotted against the mottled bark of trees by predators, the group that had received varied examples proposed far more kinds of solutions (5.3, on average) than the other group (1.7, on average). The children in the latter group almost invariably suggested imitating a dangerous animal.[36] Thus, as with the adults studied by Chase and his colleagues, a varied repertoire appears to be a crucial ingredient in problem solving in children.

Maier's Two-String Problem

Although Maier[37] was the first to study the now-famous **two-string problem**, it has served as a paradigmatic problem in many subsequent studies, and so can serve as an example to illustrate the main points discussed above. The critical features of the problem are as follows: A subject is shown into a room in which some objects, such as a pair of pliers, a screwdriver, or a clamp, are lying about. Two strings are hanging from hooks on the ceiling, and the subject's task is to tie the ends of the strings together, using any materials at hand as needed. The problem can be solved by tying the pliers, or some other object, to one of the strings, setting it swinging like a pendulum, going over to the second string and catching the pliers when they swing within reach. The prepotent response is invariably to grab the end of one string and walk toward the

other, only to find, of course, that the second string is out of reach. (See **Figure 10.5**.) The next response is to repeat the performance with the other string, to the same effect. When something is out of reach one naturally looks about for something to extend one's reach, and subjects usually next try to use the pliers as a hook or to extend their grip on the first string. Typically, only after these responses have extinguished do subjects begin to cast about for other solutions to the problem.

The probability of solving the two-string problem depends, in part, on the relative strength of various responses in the subject's repertoire in this particular complex context. This can be demonstrated by altering the probability of various responses by altering the stimuli in the room. Maier observed, for example, that of 23 subjects who were unable to solve the problem 19 were able to do so after the experimenter unobtrusively brushed against one of the strings and set it swinging. The sight of a swinging string presumably increased the probability of actively setting the string in motion, and thus facilitated the solution.

The effect of the pliers cannot be neglected in interpreting this experiment. One uses pliers to grip something with great force, and for little else. The

FIGURE 10.5 *A subject's strongest response when asked to tie two strings together is invariably to try to bring the two ends together by reaching*
Only when this response extinguishes do alternative responses become prepotent.

behavior evoked by the sight of pliers is quite stereotypic and does not include tying them to a string. Birch and Rabinowitz[38] demonstrated the importance of this variable by manipulating subjects' prior experience with the objects that were available in the room. Each subject was presented with two relatively unusual objects that could serve as weights to make a pendulum: an electrical switch and an electrical relay (a special kind of switch, but different in appearance from a typical switch). Some subjects had been given pretraining in which they used the switch to complete electrical circuits; other subjects had been given similar training with the relay. Of the 19 subjects who eventually solved the two-string problem, 17 used the unfamiliar object to serve as a weight; that is, those for whom the relay evoked "circuit-board behavior" used the switch as a weight, and those who were familiar with the "correct" use of the switch used the relay as a weight. In subsequent interviews, subjects in the relay group maintained vehemently that the switch was obviously a better weight; the subjects in the switch group maintained the opposite opinion with equal fervor. Clearly, the pretraining had established responses incompatible with the response necessary to solve the problem.

Epstein[39] provided subjects with only a single object as a potential weight, but found that solution times depended on the functional properties of the object. For one set of subjects the object was a short heavy cylinder with a small hook at the top; for the other subjects it was the same cylinder with a 15-inch rod extending from it, terminating in a large hook. (See **Figure 10.6**.) Typical responses evoked by the objects were assessed by asking an independent panel to suggest uses for them. Over 80% suggested using the first object as a weight; an even greater percentage suggested using the second to extend one's reach. No one suggested the alternative use for either object. As expected, subjects who were provided the small cylinder solved the problem quickly (2.75 minutes average); no one in this group tried to use it to reach the second string. About a fourth of the subjects given the

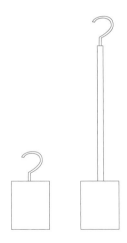

FIGURE 10.6   *When faced with the two-string problem, subjects who were provided with the object on the right tried to use it to extend their reach, presumably reflecting prior history with similar objects* Only after this response extinguished were subjects able to solve the problem. Subjects provided with the object on the left typically "treated it as a weight" and tied it to one of the strings. The pendular motion, however slight, that occurred when the object was released typically occasioned a rapid "solution": Subjects promptly set the weight swinging in a long arc.

other object failed entirely to solve the problem, and solution times for those who did solve it were much longer than in the first group. Moreover, part of the difference could be attributed to futile attempts to hook the second string with the object.

Epstein[40] found that performance on the two-string problem could be simulated with a computer by tracking the probability of each of five responses commonly observed in subjects who successfully solved the problem. The probabilities were determined from just three linear equations specifying the effects of extinction, **resurgence** (the emergence of alternative responses as a dominant response undergoes extinction),[41] and **automatic chaining** (the emergence of an integrated sequence of responses in which each response brings about conditions that evoke subsequent elements of the chain), with parameters estimated from the data. Initially, the probability of pulling one string to the other was quite high. As this response extinguished, other responses increased in probability, including tying something to the string. As this became more probable, setting the pendulum in motion became likely, after which the solution was virtually certain. (See **Figure 10.7**.)

The Role of Acquired Reinforcers in Problem Solving

Many problems cannot be solved feasibly simply by fostering variability in response topography, for

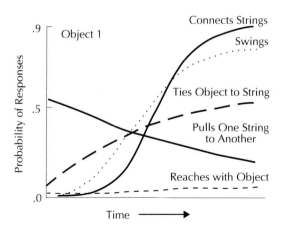

FIGURE 10.7 *A computer simulation of a solution of the two-string problem*
The baseline probability of five behaviors relevant to the solution was derived from observation of subjects; these baseline probabilities were then modified, moment-to-moment in time, according to simple equations describing extinction, reinforcement, resurgence, and chaining. As reaching extinguishes, other relevant responses are more likely to become prepotent. Once the object is tied to one of the strings, swinging becomes much more likely and a solution quickly follows. The simulation closely approximates the probabilities of actual responses observed in Epstein's subjects.
Source: From Epstein, R. (1991). Skinner, creativity, and the problem of spontaneous behavior. *Psychological Science, 2,* 362–370. Copyright © 1991 Cambridge University Press.

the terminal performance may be too complex or may depend on the products of intermediate responses. The task of checkmating one's opponent in chess, for example, usually cannot be executed by merely considering variations systematically; the terminal position is too distant and the possible variations too numerous. Similarly, one cannot usually solve a cryptogram or a long anagram by an exhaustive search of the possibilities. Many problems are complex and are best solved in steps. Solving problems of this sort usually requires the use of acquired strategies. As mentioned above, some strategies have been codified, such as algorithms for doing long division, multiplication, square roots, and so on. These strategies typically are instructed, since they are useful for an unlimited range of problems. Many problems cannot be solved with codified strategies; nevertheless general strategies are often helpful. Whether a general strategy is helpful or not depends largely on how much one knows about the domain in question. A strategy in the hands of an expert will quickly lead to a solution; the same strategy employed by a novice may lead nowhere.

Being an expert at something means, in part, that many aspects of the domain are familiar; that is, they serve both a discriminative function, evoking behavior, and a conditioned reinforcing function that can strengthen other behavior. Acquired reinforcers play an important role in many acquired strategies, for they can serve to select variations that lead to partial solutions.

In the game of chess, for example, an experienced player recognizes many stable properties of a given position: an open line, a particular pawn structure, a weak king-side, a material advantage, and so on. Some of these properties have tended, in the past, to lead to victory, others to defeat; consequently they can serve a conditioned reinforcing or punishing function. For the expert, an enormous number of properties of chess positions can serve these functions, and while the novice is moving his pieces virtually at random, the expert is systematically exploring variations that will lead to a reinforcing position. Novices are often astonished to learn that, most of the time, a grand-master will calculate no more than a few moves ahead. It is the novice who must exhaustively explore variations, for intermediate positions have little meaning to him.

Means-end analyses.   Some strategies that are quite general depend on acquired reinforcers for their effectiveness. A **means-end analysis**, for example, is a strategy of minimizing the difference between the present situation and the target situation.[42] If you are locked out of your car, you may consider trying to slip a coat-hanger through the window to jimmy up the locking knob. But of course you have no coat-hanger with you; you will have to set about to find one, or to find something equivalent. A long piece of wire serves a conditioned reinforcing function for someone in this situation, as can be seen by the alacrity with which a wire is picked up, purchased or borrowed. It also "reduces the distance" between the present situation and the target situation and so conforms to a means-end strategy.

Working backward.   Working backward from the solution is a general strategy that can establish partial solutions as events that can serve a conditioned reinforcing function. If you book a hotel room in an unfamiliar city—say, London—it would be a wise policy to learn the way to the hotel from a nearby landmark—say, Trafalgar Square. Then you could easily find your way back to the hotel from any point in the city, since you have identified a way-station far easier to locate than your terminal goal. Trafalgar Square would then serve a conditioned reinforcing function; any behavior that brought you to Trafalgar Square would be strengthened.

Working backward is often a useful strategy in mathematical proofs, solving mazes, trying to reconstruct the sequence of events leading up to an accident or a crime, and, in general, any problem in which the target is known but the path to the target is obscure. Working backward provides us with subsidiary goals or way-stations that we can more easily reach from our initial conditions. These way-stations will select variations that lead to them, evidently serving a conditioned reinforcing function.

Breaking a problem into parts.   When faced with a complex problem, it is often a useful strategy to break up the problem into its constituent parts and work on each part separately. We often solve jigsaw puzzles in this way, particularly if it is a group project, with one person working on sky pieces, another on "that red thing, whatever it is," and so on. When writing a complex computer program it is standard practice to write separate procedures for different components of the task. For example, when writing a program to compute the area of land encompassed by a survey, one might begin by writing a procedure to convert rectangular coordinates into polar coordinates. One might not even know, at the outset, how to solve the larger problem. It is often the case that scientific research is directed at a subordinate part of a problem whose solution remains a distant promise. A cure for AIDS eludes us, but researchers have been working feverishly for a decade on small but essential parts of the problem: isolating the virus, describing its molecular architecture, testing antigens, and so on.

When parts of a problem have been identified, they serve as acquired reinforcers that select and maintain the behavior that produces them. Even if we have erred in our analysis of the larger problem and have identified a part that in fact plays no role in the ultimate solution, it will serve as an acquired reinforcer. It may be, for example, that polar coordinates are useless to our surveying program, or that a particular compound tested by a pharmacology laboratory has no effect on the AIDS virus. The conditioned reinforcing function of an event presumably arises from the initial analysis of the problem into its component parts, not on its proven relevance.[43]

Evidence from the animal laboratory.   A complex problem can be discouraging; we say, "I just can't get started," or "I'll get up early tomorrow and work on it." Animals responding on very high ratio schedules act the same way. For example, chimpanzees reinforced only for every 4000 button-pressing responses paused for long periods—sometimes falling asleep—after each reinforcer before "getting back to work" and pressing the button. However, on alternate trials an acquired reinforcer (the food hopper light) was presented after every 400 responses; on these trials the long pauses were virtually eliminated.[44] (See **Figure 10.8**.) Moreover, when the chimpanzees were given an opportunity to choose between the two conditions they invariably chose the condition that provided acquired reinforcers. We can think of the task as a problem broken into ten parts, each part comprising 400 responses. The acquired reinforcer maintained performance on the subordinate parts of the problem, thus expediting solution of the larger problem.

Chained schedules of reinforcement help illuminate the role of acquired reinforcers in maintaining behavior on a difficult task. As an illustration of a chained schedule, a pigeon might respond on a variable interval (VI) schedule in the presence of a red light, only to have the light change to blue. Responding in the presence of the blue light changes the light to green. Responding in the presence of the green light finally produces food.

Here, the only consequence of responding to the red light is that the blue light comes on. Responding to red will be maintained only to the extent that the blue light has become an acquired reinforcer. Similarly, responding to blue will be maintained only if the green light is reinforcing. In chained schedules of this sort it is commonly found that responding in early links of the chain is weaker than in later links.[45] Responding on early links tends to be interrupted by long pauses. This stands to reason, as the stimuli signaling the early links are temporally removed from the final reinforcement and presumably acquire a conditioned reinforcing function only weakly. However, when the stimulus order is varied from trial to trial so that each stimulus is occasionally paired with food, responding is strong in all links of the chain, and

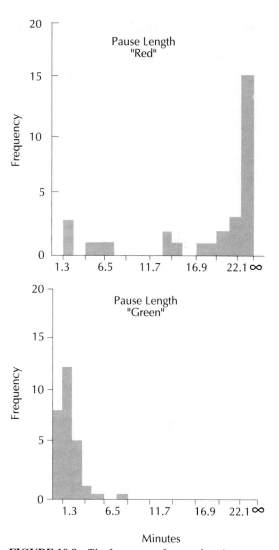

FIGURE 10.8 *The frequency of pause durations when conditioned reinforcers were omitted (top panel) and when they were provided (bottom panel)*

In the presence of the red light reinforcement followed the 4000th response; long pauses between responses were common. In the presence of the green light, every 400th response was followed by the sound of the feeder, but food occurred only after the 4000th response. In this condition the chimpanzees responded rapidly with few long pauses.

Source: From Findley, J. D., & Brady, J. D. (1965). Facilitation of large ratio performance by use of conditioned reinforcement. *Journal of the Experimental Analysis of Behavior, 8*, 125–129. Copyright 1965 by the Society for the Experimental Analysis of Behavior, Inc.

long pauses are eliminated.[46] The frequency of reinforcement in the terminal link of the chain is also important. For example, Findley[47] found with rats that the rate of chain-pulling responses in the first link of a two-link chain decreased as the rate of reinforcement in the terminal link decreased. (See **Figure 10.9**.)

Thus, mastering the components of a problem will serve a conditioned reinforcing function provided that doing so has indeed been correlated with successful solution of the problem, or similar problems, in the past. A common weakness of educational contingencies is that students are required to work on skills and problem components that have never been paired with successful performance of a larger problem. Students often learn about fractions and memorize Spanish vocabulary, not be-

cause these activities have led to effective action, but to avoid the censure and gain the approval of parents and teachers.

The Role of Insight in Problem Solving

According to allegory, Archimedes was pondering, as he settled into his bath, how to determine the density of the crown of the King of Syracuse, so that the King might be assured of its purity. "Eureka!" he cried, in history's most famous moment of insight. The displacement of the bathwater had suggested a way to determine the crown's volume; the rest of the calculation was a simple matter.

Insight remains the most mysterious problem-solving phenomenon. We tend to use the term whenever an organism faced with a problem abruptly rouses itself from relative inactivity and swiftly, smoothly, and energetically emits the target response. It is relatively rare and unpredictable, and hence very difficult to analyze experimentally. Most of our understanding of insight comes, curiously, from work with animals.

Among the most thoroughly studied examples of insight are the spontaneous and novel use of tools to achieve some practical consequence. Wolfgang Köhler[48] was one of the first to study this sort of problem solving in chimpanzees. In a typical problem, a bit of food, such as a banana, hung in the cage, out of reach of even a leaping chimpanzee. Lying about the cage were boxes of various sizes. Köhler reported that after long gazing and futile attempts to reach the banana, a chimp would suddenly run over and push one of the boxes toward the banana, vault off the box, and seize the fruit.

In another experiment, Köhler placed a bit of food *outside* a cage. Sultan, the chimp, was adept at pulling in food with sticks, but, in this case, the two available bamboo rods were too short. However, they could be fit together like tent poles to make a stick sufficiently long. Köhler describes Sultan's behavior thus:

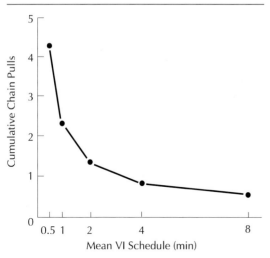

FIGURE 10.9 *In Findley's experiment, a rat's chain-pulling responses turned on a light; in the presence of the light, lever-pressing produced food on a variable interval (VI) schedule*
Chain-pulling was more likely when the average interval in the schedule was relatively short and consequently reinforcement was relatively immediate and more predictable than when the average interval was long.
Source: After Findley, J. D. (1962). An experimental outline for building and exploring multi-operant behavior repertoires. *Journal of the Experimental Analysis of Behavior, 5,* 113–166. Copyright 1962 by the Society for the Experimental Analysis of Behavior, Inc.

He takes great pains to try to reach it with one stick or the other, even pushing his right shoulder through the bars. When everything proves futile, Sultan commits a "bad error," or, more clearly, a great stupidity, such as he made sometimes on other occasions. He pulls a box from the back of the room towards the bars; true, he pushes it away again at once as it is useless, or, rather, actually in the way. Immediately afterwards, he does something which, although practically useless, must be counted among the "good errors": he pushes one of the sticks out as far as it will go, then takes the second, and with it, pokes the first one cautiously towards the objective . . . and actually touches the objective with its tip . . . and Sultan visibly feels (we humans can sympathize) a certain satisfaction. . .

[After an hour of this] Sultan first of all squats indifferently on the box, which has been left standing a little back from the railings; then he gets up, picks up the two sticks, sits down again on the box and plays carelessly with them. While doing this, it happens that he finds himself holding one rod in either hand in such away that they lie in a straight line; he pushes the thinner one a little way into the opening of the thicker, jumps up and is already on the run towards the railings . . . and begins to draw a banana towards him with the double stick.[49]

The chimp's solution was insightful. He had never encountered the problem situation before. After direct attempts to reach the banana failed, he appeared to be puzzled and discouraged. Suddenly the chimp "changed tactics;" he swiftly and smoothly executed a new pattern of behavior which was successful in obtaining the fruit. Apparently the chimp had had a "brainstorm," a "flash of insight," that enabled him to solve the problem. He "saw" the solution and then carried it out.

We are inclined, at first, to accept this interpretation of the experiment. After all, we have had similar experiences ourselves, and we remember with satisfaction the euphoria that attends a flash of insight. We remind ourselves that chimpanzees are close relatives, and wonder if other animals are capable of similar feats of ingenuity.

We must admit to a certain dissatisfaction, however. Attributing the sudden solution of a problem to insight is to give it a name, not to explain it. The above account may be correct, so far as it goes;

but an analogy with our own behavior is not an explanation unless we understand our own behavior better than that of the chimpanzee. What exactly is insight, and why do we sometimes have it and sometimes fail? The term insight suggests spontaneity and unpredictability. If behavior is lawful it should be possible, at least in principle, to predict behavior that is commonly attributed to insight.

Although Köhler and others apparently accept insight as an irreducible psychological concept, some researchers have attempted to provide an experimental analysis of insightful behavior. Birch[50] showed that the ability of a chimpanzee to solve problems with tools could be predicted, in part, by knowing the animal's prior history with the tool. Birch posed the following problem to six chimpanzees, all five to six years old: A bit of food lay outside the animal's cage, just out of reach. Available to the chimp was a stick with which the food could be pulled or raked within reach. Of the six chimpanzees, one had had prior experience manipulating sticks, while one other had had prior experience reeling in bits of food tied to a string. The remaining four animals had not had any specific training that was directly relevant to the problem, though the behavior of reaching for and manipulating objects was presumably well established. Birch found that the four naive animals were unable to solve the problem. However, the animal experienced in manipulating sticks solved it almost immediately (in 12 seconds), while the one that had retrieved food with a string was able to solve it in five minutes. Birch then allowed the four naive animals to manipulate sticks for three days, after which they were again presented with the problem. All of them solved the problem virtually immediately.

Schiller[51] showed that the amount of specific experience with sticks that a chimpanzee requires to solve this problem depends, in part, on its age. Two-year-old chimpanzees did not improve their problem-solving skills after three days, but after one year in a compound with sticks to play with and several platforms to climb on, they improved dramatically. They not only solved the simplest form of the problem, in which the stick and food were both on the same platform positioned so that a single sweeping motion would pull in the food; they were also able to retrieve the stick from another platform, out of view of the food, return to the food and rake it in with the stick. However, they were not as skilled with tools as experienced older animals (seven- to nine-year-olds), who could solve more complex problems, such as one that required them to fit two sticks together to form a long rod.

The findings of Birch and Schiller indicate that whatever insight is, the organism must have an appropriate repertoire of operants to serve as components of a possible solution to the problem at hand. Insight seemed to escape those chimpanzees that did not have such a repertoire. Note, however, that these findings do not explain the problem-solving behavior of the chimps. We know that successful chimpanzees had used sticks before to rake, poke, and push objects around, but what exactly is the relationship between these operants and their integration into a solution of the problem? The problem itself was a novel arrangement of stimuli for the animals, and the solution required a particular sequence of responses that had never been practiced. We have not yet shown the term insight to be superfluous. What is the lawful relationship between the experience of the chimps and their solution of the problem? Can we predict that a chimpanzee will solve the problem if it has had a chance to play with sticks? If so, what behavioral principles do we invoke?

Schiller reports considerable variability in the performance of his animals. The mere acquisition of component operants was not sufficient to insure that the problem would be solved at all, and some animals took considerably longer than others to solve it. A science of behavior must, as an ideal, explain the solution of the successful animals, the failure of the unsuccessful ones, and the variability among animals in each category. We can appeal to extinction, response generalization, multiple determinants of response strength, and so on. It should be possible to give a *post hoc* account of each

animal's behavior using only familiar behavioral principles. However, since we know little about the moment-to-moment behavior of the chimps in the problem-solving task, and even less about the fine-grained interactions with the environment in the animals' past, there is little more that we can do. Fortunately, the phenomenon of insight has been studied with pigeons in greater detail than was possible with chimpanzees. By carefully controlling the components of his pigeons' repertoires, Epstein[52] has been able to provide a plausible moment-to-moment account of their insightful behavior.

The difficulty of interpreting the insight experiments with chimpanzees is that the components of the terminal performance—i.e., pushing boxes, climbing on boxes, reaching for bananas, manipulating sticks, etc.—are responses that are likely to be well-practiced before the experiment. Pigeons, however, engage in none of these behaviors; if insightful performance can be "generated" in the pigeon, we can interpret the behavior of chimpanzees and humans with more confidence.

At a minimum, components of the behavior said to show insight must be in the organism's repertoire. In the simplest insight experiments, Epstein and his colleagues trained pigeons on one or more of the following components of Köhler's box-and-banana problem: (1) Climbing on a stationary box and pecking a miniature "banana" was reinforced with food. (2) Pecking a small box toward a green target at the edge of the chamber was reinforced with food. (3) Attempts to jump or fly up to the banana were extinguished. The pigeons were then presented with a novel situation: The green target was removed, and, for the first time, the box was placed some distance away from the banana. The pigeons were now in a situation analogous to that of Köhler's chimpanzees; they possessed the requisite repertoire to solve the problem, but they had never encountered the particular problem before.

The performance of the three birds who had been trained on all of the constituent behaviors was remarkably similar to that of Köhler's chimps. All of the birds solved the problem within two minutes, their performance appearing almost human:

> At first each pigeon appeared to be 'confused;' it stretched and turned beneath the banana, looked back and forth from banana to box, and so on. Then each subject began rather suddenly to push the box in what was clearly the direction of the banana. Each subject sighted the banana as it pushed and readjusted the box as necessary to move it towards the banana. Each subject stopped pushing in the appropriate place, climbed and pecked the banana.[53]

Pigeons that had not had all of the constituent training displayed predictably ineffective behavior. For example, one bird, which had not been put on extinction for jumping and flying up toward the banana, solved the problem eventually, but only after a prolonged period of unreinforced jumping toward the banana. Birds that had been reinforced for pecking the box, but not toward the green target, pecked the box aimlessly about the chamber. (See **Figure 10.10**.)

Epstein, et al. proposed a moment-to-moment account of the pigeons' behavior: The birds' apparent confusion arose from the fact that they were in a novel situation in which several powerful discriminative stimuli were simultaneously present for the first time. There was no clearly prepotent response. Eventually one repertoire became prepotent, possibly as a consequence of a trivial variable. For example, simply turning the head toward the box would dramatically alter the stimulus configuration as experienced by the bird, and would presumably make the box-elicited repertoire more likely. Once the pigeon made its first peck to the box, the box-pecking repertoire would be quite strong, for the stimulus conditions would be very similar to those of training. Pecking the box toward the banana rather than aimlessly about the chamber could perhaps be explained by the fact that both the target and the banana had, when approached, been paired with food, and both presumably elicited salivation and other food-elicited responses.[54] Once the box approached the banana, the stimulus configuration became more similar to that in which climbing and pecking had been reinforced, and

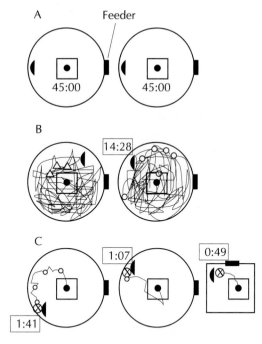

Climbs and Pecks Banana
Starting Position of Box
Climbs and Stretches Toward Banana
Perches

FIGURE 10.10 *Paths along which the box was pushed by seven pigeons in the "insight" experiment of Epstein, et al. (1984)*

The black crescent represents the location of the banana, the square indicates the initial location of the box in the chamber, and the line shows the path of the box as it was pushed by the pigeon. The two pigeons in the top frame had been reinforced for climbing and pecking but never for pushing the box. In a 45 minute test session they never pushed the box at all. The performance of birds reinforced for climbing and pecking and for pushing the box aimlessly is shown in the second frame. One of the pigeons pecked the banana after about 14.5 minutes of pecking the box randomly around the chamber. The pigeons represented in the bottom frame had been taught to climb and peck and to push the box toward a green spot on the floor. These pigeons all solved the problem quickly and with little wasted effort. Boxed times represent the time to a solution in minutes and seconds.

Source: From Epstein, Kirshnit, Lanza, & Rubin. Reprinted with permission from *Nature* (1984, 308, pp. 61-62). Copyright 1984 Macmillan Magazines Ltd.

when that became the prepotent response, the problem was solved.

Epstein was subsequently able to demonstrate insight in the pigeon in a more complex task that required the interaction of four repertoires; climbing and pecking were trained separately, and the pigeon had to retrieve the box from behind a closed door. While the pigeon did solve the problem, its smooth performance was disrupted in predictable ways as the four repertoires interacted with one another. For example, the pigeon climbed on the box prematurely, and only when this had extinguished was progress made toward solving the problem. Lest this seem to vitiate the parallel with insight in chimpanzees, recall that Sultan committed, in Köhler's words, "a great stupidity" by fetching a box when assembling bamboo rods was required to solve the problem. Epstein's experiments suggest that Sultan's errors were as lawful as his insight.

How well do Epstein's pigeons explain insightful performance in human beings? It is premature to say, but we feel that these simulations have brought us much closer to an understanding of insight in humans, for they show how the interplay of only a few repertoires can lead to novel and adaptive performance, requiring that we invoke only a handful of well-established behavioral principles. Humans presumably emit sequences of covert behavior and respond to those sequences. Thus humans can "look ahead" from the moment of insight to the solution of the problem; there is little to suggest that pigeons do so. This covert behavior is not available for study given our current technology. However, there is no reason to believe that the interaction of repertoires cannot occur covertly and so give rise to the euphoria we experience as insight. Human behavior is immeasurably more complex than the few responses established in the pigeons in these insight studies; adult humans have extraordinary repertoires and many years of experience solving problems. Is it not possible that remarkable human insights arise from the richness of our repertoires rather than from the action of qualitatively different principles? To reject the possibility assumes that one can predict how the many components of an individual's repertoire would interact in a complex environment, and that the principles have been found wanting. However, as Epstein has noted,[55] tracking the simultaneous changes in probability of just a few responses in a pigeon, invoking only four behavioral principles, far exceeds the abilities of an unaided human. It is possible that we may do so through formal interpretation, that is, with computer simulation, as Epstein has done with the two-string problem, but work in this domain is just in its infancy.

CONCLUSION

We have attempted to provide an outline of a behavioral interpretation of one of the most complex facets of human behavior. There are some aspects of reasoning and problem solving that we have not had space to discuss—hypothesis testing, analogical reasoning, inferences of probability, induction, syllogistic reasoning, to name a few. The interpretation of these phenomena must be left to the reader, with the reminder that, given the constraints on working with humans, providing an interpretation that invokes only known principles of behavior is often the best we can do.

It is no coincidence that our interpretation of problem solving has many parallels with evolution through natural selection. In a changing environment, structures that were adaptive in the past may be ineffective now, and new forms are selected. But in order for a lineage to be represented in succeeding generations, there must be variability of form among the offspring so that at least one will be selected by the new contingencies of survival. In problem solving, we are faced with novel contingencies; otherwise there would be no problem. In order for us to solve the problem, our repertoire must be varied enough that the prevailing contingencies can select a solution. Throughout this chapter we have seen many examples of the deleterious effects of inflexibility, stereotypy, and mental set, and of successful problem solving through variation and selection.

A complete account of human problem solving remains elusive. We can only vaguely speculate about the moment-to-moment events that account for certain extraordinary feats of problem solving. Consider the mathematical prowess of Zerah Colburn, the "American lightning-calculating boy." Born in rural Vermont in 1804, he became famous as a child for his ability to perform mental calculations, and he toured the United States and Europe, displaying his powers. He quickly solved a famous problem that no one had had the patience to solve before. Fermat, the famous 17th century mathematician, had speculated that a certain series, namely,

$$2^{2^{n}} + 1$$

would produce only prime numbers. What led Fermat to this intuition is unclear, but it is extremely difficult to test, since the numbers get huge very quickly, and it is very tedious to determine if a large number is prime. It appears to be necessary to divide the number by every prime number smaller than the number's square root.[56] The first five numbers of the series had been shown to be primes, but the status of the sixth number, 4,294,967,297, was unknown. The number was shown to Colburn, who replied, after thinking for a minute or two, that it is not a prime; it has the divisor 641.[57]

It is pointless to try to explain the behavior of the hero of an anecdote, dead these 150 years, but it serves as a reminder of how extraordinary human behavior can be. Curiously, Colburn was unable to explain his own performance, but the Irish mathematician, William Hamilton, studied Colburn at length and concluded that his techniques were unremarkable and largely a matter of memory. This conclusion is little help, but we can assume that for Colburn, constantly thinking about numbers as he did, 641 was, at least, a familiar prime.

Hamilton's appraisal of Colburn recalls the modest assessments that Gauss and Newton held of themselves. When asked to explain how he was able to make so many original contributions to mathematics, Gauss replied, "If others would but reflect on mathematical truths as deeply and as continuously as I have, they would make my discoveries." Newton was more succinct; asked how he solved problems opaque to everyone else, he replied, "By always thinking about them."[58]

These replies are undoubtedly too modest, but they remind us that the repertoire these extraordinary men brought to bear on the problems they faced was vastly different from our own. To a pigeon on a city sidewalk, Epstein's birds would appear to be remarkable geniuses, yet their insightful performances were a function of a special repertoire interacting in a unique environment. It is at least a plausible hypothesis that the achievements of our greatest thinkers are also the results of lawful interactions of unusual repertoires in unique circumstances.

STUDY AIDS

Technical Terms

> intraverbal response
> prepotent response
> trial-and-error problem solving
> functional fixedness
> mental set
> two-string problem
> resurgence
> automatic chaining
> means-end analysis

Text Questions

1. What are the three characteristic properties of a problem as defined in the text? Show how the definition applies to a problem in your own experience.

2. Problems cannot be defined by formal properties alone. Explain why a particular situation might be defined as a problem for one person but not another. Make use of the technical definition in your answer.

3. What is meant by "supplementary stimuli"? Are all such stimuli external events? Give an ex-

ample of a supplementary stimulus for your problem in Question 1.

4. How does a target response serve to halt problem-solving behavior? That is, how do we know that we have solved a problem?

5. What are some of the variables that decrease or increase response variability? Relate the concepts of "mental set" and "functional fixedness" to response variability.

6. How do the experiments on the two-string problem illustrate the role of stereotypy and response variability on problem-solving performance?

7. Identify a problem and show how acquired reinforcers can play a role in the solution to the problem.

8. How do data from chained schedules in non-human animals shed light on problem solving in humans?

9. What is meant by "insight"? Why is attributing the solution of a problem to insight unsatisfactory?

10. Consider an example of problem solving from your own experience that illustrates insight, and try to interpret it in light of the experimental data of Schiller and Epstein.

Discussion Questions

11. In its discussion of covert responses, the text warns against unconstrained speculation in accounting for complex behavior. How does a scientific interpretation differ from mere speculation?

12. What is meant by the claim that the observability of a behavior depends upon the observer and not on the behavior itself?

13. In what sense is response variability central to problem solving?

14. What makes an individual an especially good problem solver? Are these characteristics always helpful, or do they sometimes interfere with effective problem solving?

ENDNOTES

1. Rules usually serve functions other than discriminative ones; they alter the functions of other stimuli. See Schlinger & Blakely, 1987; Blakely & Schlinger, 1987; Schlinger, 1990.

2. Skinner, 1957. We will discuss verbal operants frequently and in greater detail in subsequent chapters. We introduce several of them here to remind the reader that a response of a particular topography can have many controlling variables.

3. When we say that a question "indicates" that reinforcement will follow, we mean only that in the past our responses have tended to be reinforced under similar circumstances; reinforcement need not be inevitable. Although reinforcement may be intermittent and inconspicuous, it plays a crucial role in our account of problem-solving behavior. In a perverse world in which correct responses were punished, there would presumably be little problem-solving behavior.

4. The reciprocal of 243, for example.

5. The manipulation of supplementary stimuli can strengthen not only single responses, but whole repertoires, or classes of related responses, a process called *contingency adduction* by Andronis, 1983; Layng and Andronis, 1984.

6. Abstemiously and facetiously are the only two we know of.

7. Palmer, 1991.

8. Collateral overt behavior may well be relevant—we stop what we are doing, avert our eyes, and so on, minimizing competing operants and reflexive orienting responses.

9. Hefferline & Keenan, 1963.

10. Branch (1977) may have been the first to point out that all behavior lies on a "continuum of observability," a consideration that discourages the tendency to regard private events as qualitatively different from behavior that is easily measured. (See Palmer, 1991 for a development of this argument.)

11. e.g., Köhler, 1925.

12. Thorndike, 1898.

13. Donahoe & Wessells, 1980.

14. cf. Campbell, 1974.

15. The two words are "hotcakes" and "somersault" respectively. Technically, an anagram is one word or phrase whose letters can be rearranged to form other words or phrases. The term is now more loosely applied to any sequence of letters that can be rearranged to form a word or phrase, perhaps because of the ubiquitous puzzles of this sort in newspapers and magazines.

16. Staddon & Simmelhag, 1971.

17. Vogel & Annau, 1973.

18. Schwartz, 1980, 1981a, 1981b. In Schwartz's experiments, the pattern of a pigeon's key pecks was guided, in part, by a visual display: a five-by-five matrix of lights. At the beginning of a trial, the upper left light was on. A peck to one key would move the light to the right one column; a peck to the other would move the light down one row. When the light reached the lower right of the display, food would be delivered. While each of the 70 paths was equally effective in producing food, it is clear that some routes require more switching between keys than others.

19. Schwartz, 1982.

20. Schwartz, 1980, 1982.

21. Antonitis, 1951.

22. Notterman, 1959, Notterman & Block, 1960.

23. Mechner, 1958.

24. Carlton, 1962.

25. Cole, 1965.

26. Blough, 1966; Machado, 1989; Schoenfeld, Harris, & Farmer, 1966.

27. Pryor, Haag, & O'Reilly, 1969.

28. Neuringer, 1986, 1991; Page & Neuringer, 1985.

29. Skinner, 1966a.

30. Baron & Galizio, 1983; Baron, Kaufman, & Stauber, 1969; Galizio, 1979; Harzem, Lowe, & Bagshaw, 1978; Hayes, Brownstein, Zettle, Rosenfarb, & Korn, 1986; LeFrancois, Chase, & Joyce, 1988; Matthews, Shimoff, Catania, & Sagvolden, 1977.

31. LeFrancois, Chase, & Joyce, 1988.

32. LeFrancois, Chase, & Joyce, 1988.

33. For those with no patience for such puzzles, the first problem can be solved by adding the integers, 1, 2, 3, etc., to successive terms. The second problem requires adding 2, 4, 8, 16, etc., to successive terms. In the third problem, successive terms are generated by the series, $1(X) + 1, 2(X) + 2, 3(X) + 3$, etc. In the fourth problem, each number represents its corresponding letter in the alphabet and the resulting sequence spells a word. Because the third problem eventually yields to a numerical solution, we are likely to persevere for a long time looking for a quantitative solution to the fourth.

34. Dunker, 1945.

35. Brown, 1989.

36. Naturally, the children treated their solutions as if they were immediately available to individual moths, not as features that would need to develop slowly over generations. One child suggested that the moth turn into a gorilla, a solution of unparalleled effectiveness and no less feasible to an individual moth than developing a mottled pattern on its wings.

37. Maier, 1931.

38. Birch & Rabinowitz, 1951.

39. Epstein, 1985a.

40. Epstein, 1991.

41. Epstein, 1983; 1985b.

42. Newell & Simon, 1972.

43. See Schlinger & Blakely, 1987; Blakely & Schlinger, 1987; Schlinger, 1990 for a discussion of the function-altering effect of certain classes of verbal constructions, viz. "contingency-specifying" verbal behavior.

44. Findley & Brady, 1965.

45. Gollub, 1977; Kelleher & Fry, 1962.

46. Kelleher & Fry, 1962.

47. Findley, 1962.

48. Köhler, 1925.

49. Köhler, 1925, pp. 130–132, passim.

50. Birch, 1945.

51. Schiller, 1958.

52. Epstein, 1985a; Epstein, Kirshnit, Lanza, & Rubin, 1984.

53. Epstein, Kirshnit, Lanza, & Rubin, 1984.

54. The banana was the object that was, on the whole, most similar to the target. If another salient object were present, say, a black target several inches off the floor, we might see the box pecked toward it rather than toward the banana.

55. Personal communication.

56. Some shortcuts are possible, of course. A number ending in 7 can only be evenly divided by numbers ending in 1, 3, 7, or 9, but the number of possibilities is still prodigious.

57. Bell, 1965, p. 66.

58. Bell, 1965, p. 254.

CHAPTER 11

VERBAL BEHAVIOR

In our last chapter we attempted to show that problem solving, quintessentially intelligent behavior, could be interpreted in light of familiar selectionist principles, and the argument was rendered more plausible by evidence that these principles appear to operate to produce problem-solving behavior in nonhuman organisms. Interpreting verbal behavior seems to be a more formidable task, however, for there is little evidence that other organisms, with the possible exception of our closest anthropoid cousins, engage in behavior that is at all comparable to human verbal behavior. It appears that the principle of natural selection will play an important role in our account, for, while our children soon become fluent speakers, the home environment does not have a comparable effect on the family pets.

It is not our purpose here to survey the central topics of verbal behavior. The literature, both theoretical and empirical, is immense, and we could not hope to cover the topic from even a single perspective. It will not have escaped the reader that the paradigm that we have adopted—selectionism—lies outside the mainstream of contemporary psychology. Even so, the topic is too broad for a survey. Rather, we will attempt to examine ways in which verbal behavior is unique and requires special treatment. It is sometimes claimed that a selectionist approach is inadequate, in principle, to account for the remarkable verbal abilities of human beings.[1] Needless to say, we do not endorse this view, but the claims that additional principles are required in a complete account of language cannot be ignored. In this chapter we attempt to identify critical problems in verbal behavior and point to the kind of solutions a selectionist view might provide. We do not claim that our particular interpretations are true or complete—indeed a selectionist account necessarily varies from one case to the next; rather, we hope to illustrate that solutions to the problems are not beyond the scope of selectionist principles.[2]

We will consider, in turn, five aspects of verbal behavior that appear to set it apart from nonverbal behavior, suggesting that it requires special treatment. As will appear below, we accept the premises of the following claims but dispute the conclusions. Nevertheless, we feel that the points must be addressed.

1. Verbal behavior is served by unique physical structures and perceptual mechanisms. Consequently, we must ask if the verbal system constitutes a mental "module" with its own idiosyncratic principles.

2. Speech cannot be considered a chain of responses in which each word or sound evokes the next. Therefore a science of behavior, with its focus on environment-behavior relations, may be of limited use in the analysis of verbal behavior.

3. Verbal behavior is novel, apparently without limit. This suggests that it cannot be understood as a product of selection principles, for selection implies the replication of stable units.

4. Verbal behavior conforms to rules, suggesting that it cannot be understood without reference to a grammar, a system of rules that generates well-formed sentences.

5. Skilled verbal behavior is acquired with extraordinary speed and with little evidence of differential reinforcement from parents. This suggests that there may be special innate adaptations for language learning.

PHYSIOLOGICAL AND ANATOMICAL CONTRIBUTIONS TO VERBAL BEHAVIOR

At the outset, we must note that there are physical structures relevant to speech that are unique to humans. First, adult humans have a specialized vocal apparatus and can manipulate it with exquisite subtlety. Even chimpanzees, our closest relatives, lack the coordinated dexterity of humans in the lips, tongue, palate, and vocal cords.[3] Human evolution exploited the respiratory system to provide the power for sustained vocal expression. Since the respiratory system evolved to serve other purposes, it is not surprising that some modifications were necessary for it to serve this additional function. Speech is produced during the expiratory phase of respiration, and the ability to produce a prolonged utterance of modulated pitch and intensity requires the coordinated action of a particular configuration of the muscles of the rib cage and the abdomen to regulate the volume of the lungs. Human adults—but not newborns—share these adaptations with the anthropoid apes who can also make prolonged, modulated vocalizations; however, apes apparently lack the neural structures necessary for the automated motor patterns of the vocal apparatus so conspicuous in fluent human speech.[4] Expiration contributes to the organization of speech, and vice versa. Our expirations typically coincide with verbal units—usually the sentence—and the chemoreceptors that would ordinarily initiate inspiration may be overridden if the end of a sentence has not been reached.[5]

In adult humans the **pharynx** (the cavity behind the nose and mouth) is elongated relative to that of a chimpanzee or even a newborn human. In newborns and chimpanzees the **larynx** (the upper part of the windpipe, containing the vocal cords) opens just below the oral cavity. By the time the human infant is about two years old, the pharyngeal cavity has developed considerably, while there is little change in the anatomical structures of the chimpanzee. The elongated pharynx serves as a resonating chamber that is necessary for the production of certain sounds common in human speech.[6] (See **Figure 11.1**.) Thus neither the infant

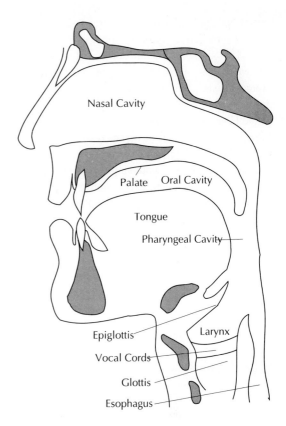

FIGURE 11.1   *The pharynx in the adult human is elongated, providing a resonating chamber that permits a range of speech sounds unavailable to the chimpanzee or even the newborn human*

nor the chimpanzee is capable of making the full range of human speech sounds.

Arduous attempts to teach a chimpanzee spoken language have been conspicuous failures; one chimp, after several years of training, was able to utter only three words: *mama, papa,* and *cup.*[7] However, recognition of the articulatory deficits of chimpanzees has inspired relatively successful attempts to teach them sign language. Chimpanzees are nearly as dexterous as humans and have little trouble making many of the signs of American Sign Language (ASL). Washoe, the first chimp to receive prolonged, systematic training in ASL under controlled conditions, eventually learned some 130 signs and often combined them into two-word, and sometimes longer, sequences.[8] Moreover, she could generate novel sequences of signs: Having been trained to sign *More tickle*, she would later sign *More juice* or *More swing*, which were presumably requests for the respective items. Washoe's use of signs was, in some respects, remarkably human. She would sign *Quiet!* to herself when she was trying to evade notice, or *Hurry!* when she was bustling off somewhere in haste. When signing to a human less fluent in ASL than she, Washoe would sign slowly, in apparent consideration for her unskilled companion. She was observed to invent signs for items for which she knew no name, and she combined signs creatively.

Other researchers have used tangible objects (such as plastic plates of various shapes) as symbols and have found that chimpanzees can follow rather complicated directions, such as, *Sarah insert banana in pail*.[9] They can apply a category name such as *food* or *tool* to novel instances of the category, to pictures of instances of the category, and even to previously learned symbols for items in that category.[10] Woodruff, Premack, and Kennel[11] even showed that a chimpanzee could use symbols to demonstrate "conservation of volume" in a classic Piagetian conservation task: The chimp, after having witnessed the relevant transformation, would place a token meaning "same" between two vessels of different size but containing the same quantity of liquid.

As impressive as these achievements are, chimpanzees show little sensitivity to sign order, and do not progress much beyond two-word phrases, while deaf children typically move on to more and more complicated and elaborate combinations of signs. Fine control of the vocal musculature and unique articulatory mechanisms are not the only human adaptations contributing to adult verbal behavior.

Chimpanzees in language studies are usually given tangible reinforcers and physical contact, and, speaking loosely, much of their signing seems designed to get them what they want. Two-sign phrases are usually sufficient for this. It is possible, of course, that chimpanzees are simply incapable of long integrated sequences of signing behavior, but their fluent locomotor behavior suggests otherwise. It is equally possible that chimpanzees are simply insensitive to those contingencies that control long verbal responses in older children and adults. Humans are especially sensitive to secondary reinforcement and to reinforcement by subtle social stimuli. Money, fame, hearing oneself praised or denigrated, a curt word, an impassive expression, a blip on the stock exchange, hearing that the Celtics have lost, or jingoistic slogans can delight us, arouse us, drive us to despair, or make our blood boil. Most of these powerful events reach us through perfectly arbitrary stimuli only remotely related to events of biological importance. Many nonhuman animals are clearly sensitive to species-specific social stimuli, and to arbitrary stimuli that are typically followed by primary reinforcers, but they cannot be whipped into a frenzy over such trivial events as the burning of a flag, a scurrilous comment, or the death of a religious leader. Human beings stand alone in our sensitivity to arbitrary events. Verbal stimuli, if we except cries of disgust, anger, glee, and so on, are perfectly arbitrary, and the contingencies which regulate such dimensions of verbal behavior as word order, intonation, and stress pattern are exquisitely subtle. It is a tenable hypothesis that a crucial ingredient of the human language faculty is not some language-specific adaptation but, rather, a greater sensitivity to contingencies of conditioned reinforcement, arising perhaps from some general property of the nervous system or possibly from some dimension of the reinforcement mechanism, such as a greater domain of the diffuse reinforcement signal or of the richness of recurrent connections that permit responses to serve discriminative and conditioned reinforcement functions.

Lateralization of Brain Function

In most humans, the detailed motor differentiations and sensory discriminations necessary for verbal behavior are mediated primarily by regions in the left hemisphere. This appears to provide support for those who believe in the modularity of language—that is, that language is a separate domain with its own structures, principles, and evolutionary origins. While the importance of these regions to verbal behavior in the typical human is beyond dispute, we question their relevance to the hypothesis of modularity. First, the left-hemisphere control of fine sensory discrimination and motor differentiation is not confined either to verbal behavior or to humans. In monkeys and birds, discriminating intraspecific calls is largely a left-hemisphere function.[12] Moreover, relative to damage to the right hemisphere, damage to the left hemisphere impairs complex nonverbal motor sequences as well as those involved in speech.[13] It appears that the left hemisphere is specialized for discriminating and mediating sequences of events or responses, be they verbal or nonverbal.[14]

Note that the vocal apparatus, while symmetrical, is a single effector system, unlike the limbs. If control of the vocal tract were bilateral, like the control of other effectors, coordinated movements would require long interconnections between hemispheres with a resulting loss of efficiency. Since our hands often act independently of one another, control of a fine hand movement is relatively efficient, as it is mediated by a single hemisphere. Lateralization may have developed, then, partly from the demands of coordinated action of the musculature of the mouth, tongue and throat. Lateralization would have served ingestive functions as well as speech functions, though the rapid coordination of movements necessary to produce speech sounds would be especially well served.

That verbal behavior is typically mediated by the left hemisphere does not mean that there are unique, innate language centers there with a special architecture that somehow explains speech and speech comprehension. If an infant receives damage to the left hemisphere, verbal functions will eventually be carried out by the right hemisphere, and the child may come to speak essentially normally.[15] Indeed, some victims of congenital hydrocephalus speak normally despite the loss of most of the cerebral cortex in both hemispheres.[16] If special structures are indeed necessary for verbal behavior, they must be widely distributed.

Speech Centers: Evidence from the Aphasias

Clearly, spoken language must be mediated in part by those areas of the nervous system that control the vocal apparatus and that receive input from the auditory system. That there are regions serving such functions and that damage to these areas disrupts speech and comprehension does not suggest that verbal behavior is discontinuous with other behavior, or that it is mediated by structures that embody special linguistic principles. Evidence from subjects with brain damage suggests, to the contrary, that the role of different structures in the nervous system depends greatly upon one's individual experiences.

For example, damage to **Wernicke's area**, in the auditory association cortex of the left temporal lobe, commonly disrupts a variety of language functions including discrimination of speech sounds and writing. However, a lesion to Wernicke's area does not affect the writing abilities of a deaf person.[17] Curiously, if the deaf person is a lip-reader the effect of the lesion is more typical.[18] This finding is not surprising, of course, for control of verbal behavior in deaf people is evidently independent of auditory stimuli; however, it suggests that the specific structures underlying verbal behavior are less important than the contingencies that establish relationships between response classes and discriminative stimuli.

Damage to Wernicke's area in Chinese patients underlines this point. These patients suffer impairments typical of Western patients and, among other things, have difficulty discriminating similar-sounding words. However, like deaf people, they have no trouble writing.[19] Of course, the Chinese do not write in phonetic characters but in pictographs. Evidently their writing behavior is not under the control of auditory stimuli. The Japanese have two classes of written symbol, one of which (**kana symbols**) is phonetic, like Western alphabets, and one of which (**kanji symbols**) is pictorial, like Chinese. Damage to Wernicke's area in a Japanese patient will impair the ability to write kana symbols but not kanji symbols, while other lesions can have the opposite effect.[20]

In conventional treatments of language it is common to speak of a **lexicon**, a repository where words and their meanings are stored. While the lexicon is intended as a metaphor, it is often invoked as if it were real, though no physical structures are ever proposed as possible candidates. The notion that words are appropriate units of behavior and that words have meanings is seldom questioned. From a behavioral perspective, however, the formal properties of a response are an inadequate basis for classification; we must specify the controlling variables as well. A response of a particular topography—say, *paper*—can appear in many reliable three-term contingencies and will consequently be a member of many response classes. To illustrate, the response *paper* can be evoked by reading the word, by repeating it after another, by the sight of a sheet of paper, by wall coverings, written reports, wasps' nests, news sheets, and many other stimuli or events. While *paper* is a single word, it is a member of many response classes, each of which must be analyzed separately. This view of verbal units is supported by neuropsychological data. When people suffer brain lesions they sometimes become unable to name objects. In the traditional formulation this is a loss of lexical access; the word can no longer be retrieved. However, it appears that a more accurate statement of the case is that the stimulus control of a particular response class has been disrupted by the lesion.

For example, Kolb and Whishaw[21] report showing an aphasic patient a picture of a ship's anchor. The patient was unable to name it but responded, "I know what it does . . . You use it to anchor a ship." *Anchor* may be a single word, but it is a member of a number of response classes and not all of them were disrupted by the lesion. Similarly, when Margolin and Carlson[22] showed a subject a picture of a pistol, he was unable to name it. However, after a moment or two he began to pull his "trigger finger" as if firing a gun; he noticed his own response, and replied, "Oh! It's a gun . . . a pistol!" Here, the visual stimulus no longer controlled the verbal response *pistol*, but it did control the behavior of the hand. The tactile and visual stimuli arising from the subject's own behavior were sufficient to evoke the "appropriate" verbal response.

In some cases stimulus control will be lost by one modality but retained by another. One patient, upon meeting a friend, could not recall his name until the friend spoke.[23] Another subject was unable to identify a hammer by sight, but named it promptly upon picking it up.[24] Sometimes, however, within a single modality, the control of some responses is lost while that of others is spared. One subject who could not read words could nevertheless point out that they were misspelled. Carlson[25] gave her a list of eighty word pairs in which one word of the pair was misspelled. She was able to read only five words but picked out the misspelling in 95% of the cases. Another subject could complete the poem "Roses are red, violets are blue. . ." but could not name *sugar* when its definition was read aloud to her.[26]

Thus neuropsychological data suggest that the metaphor of the lexicon is a poor one. Verbal responses, like all other behavior, are evidently controlled by specific antecedents and can best be understood by considering the selecting contingencies in the history of the individual. Some verbal functions may be localized, but considering the diversity of variables that control verbal responses, it is likely that the physical mechanisms mediating verbal behavior are widely distributed in the nervous system.

Categorical Perception

There is some evidence that the human nervous system is specially adapted to perceive human speech sounds. Speech sounds (**phonemes**) are considerably more complicated physically than pure tones, and typically consist of two or more bands of frequencies, sometimes rising or falling, and sometimes interrupted by slight pauses. Tiny variations in the properties of the signal are sufficient for the speech sound to be heard as a different phoneme. For example, the phrase the *gray ship* will be heard as the *gray chip* or the *great ship* depending on slight changes in the length of both the *sh* sound and the preceding brief interval of silence.[27] (See **Figure 11.2**.)

Speech sounds can be simulated mechanically, permitting experimenters to manipulate the physical properties of the sound precisely, sometimes with surprising results. For example, when the initial speech sound of a syllable such as *ga* is presented alone, it does not sound like a consonant or any other speech sound; rather, it sounds like a chirp or whistle. When followed by different vowel sounds, the same chirp will sometimes be heard as two different consonants. In contrast, different chirps followed by different vowels can be heard as the same consonant.

If the consonant portion of a syllable (the chirp) is played through an earphone to one ear, and the vowel portion is simultaneously presented to the other ear, a listener will hear two overlapping sounds—the whole syllable, apparently integrated from its two components, and a chirp.[28] Thus, one hemisphere apparently integrated the two stimuli into a speech sound while the other responded to the raw stimuli. There need be no special act of integration, of course. The auditory input was sufficient to evoke a particular perceptual response in the listener; whether it would do so for a perfectly naive subject is unclear.

When speech sounds are systematically varied along some physical dimension, the perceived sound changes. For example, it is possible to change a *b* sound to a *d* sound to a *g* sound simply by modifying the rise or fall in frequency of the

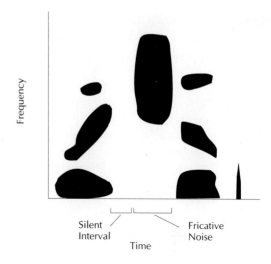

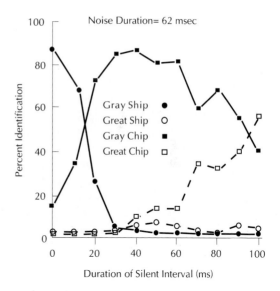

FIGURE 11.2 *A schematic speech spectrogram of the phrase, "gray ship" (top)*
By varying the length of the fricative, "sh," and the preceding silent interval, experimenters altered the words that the subjects heard. With the fricative held constant at 62 milliseconds, subjects predominantly reported hearing "gray ship," "gray chip," and "great chip" as the silent interval was lengthened.
Source: From Repp, B. H., Liberman, A. M., Eccardt, T., & Pesetsky, D. (1978). Perceptual integration of acoustic cues for stop, fricative, and affricative manner. *Journal of Experimental Psychology; Human Perception and Performance, 4,* 621–637. Copyright © 1978 by the American Psychological Association. Reprinted by permission.

initial part of the signal. If the physical properties of the signal are changed in even increments, the perceived sound does not change except at phoneme boundaries, where it changes abruptly. For example, five successive presentations of the stimulus, slightly different from one another, will all be heard as a *d* sound. The next stimulus in the sequence will be heard as a *g* sound, even though it is quite close physically to the previous *d* sound.[29] Thus, slight physical differences at phoneme boundaries are sufficient to evoke different perceptual responses, while large differences within a phoneme are not noticed. (See **Figure 11.3**.) This abrupt shift in phoneme identification is called **categorical perception** and has been cited as an example of a speech-specific adaptation of the human nervous system. Habituation studies with very young infants have demonstrated the phenomenon, suggesting that it does not depend on one's experience in discriminating verbal stimuli.

Categorical perception may, in fact, be important in speech perception, but it is easy to exaggerate its significance with respect to speech-specific adaptations of the human nervous system. First, it is possible that categorical perception is an accidental property of the human auditory system. Incremental changes in the physical properties of stimuli need not affect our receptors in equal increments.[30] If our auditory system were differentially sensitive to certain phonemic boundaries, it would hardly be surprising to find that these boundaries are respected in human speech. After all, we could not communicate in a language whose sounds could not be discriminated.

Not all speech sounds are perceived categorically, and the phenomenon of categorical perception appears to vary somewhat with experimental procedures.[31] Furthermore, phonemic distinctions are not constant across cultures. The Japanese, for example, perceive *l* and *r* categorically, while English-speakers do not. There is some evidence that nonspeech sounds are perceived categorically,[32] and there is even evidence of categorical perception in the chinchilla,[33] an organism with an auditory system similar to our own.

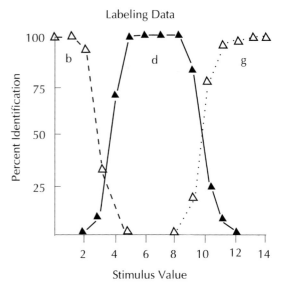

FIGURE 11.3 *Categorical perception*
Continuous changes in the physical properties of the speech signal produce discontinuous changes in what we hear. Stimuli 5 and 9 are physically more dissimilar than stimuli 9 and 10, yet stimuli 5 through 9 are all heard, predominantly, as "d" while stimulus 10 is heard as "g." Subjects make fine discriminations at phoneme boundaries but are unable to detect relatively large differences between stimuli within the boundaries of a phoneme. Some instances of categorical perception appear to arise from properties of our auditory system; some depend on the discriminations honored in the verbal community in which we were raised.
Source: From Liberman, A. M. The grammars of speech and language. *Cognitive Psychology, 1*, 301–323.

Finally, there is evidence suggesting that special perceptual mechanisms for classes of verbal stimuli are unnecessary. Blough[34] has shown that when responses in the presence of two classes of stimuli are differentially reinforced, the discrimination is sharpest at the boundary between the two stimulus classes. This phenomenon, called an edge effect (see Chapter 3), is a kind of categorical perception and follows in a straightforward way from the reinforcement principle: Outcomes which are "surprising" alter the stimulus control of behavior more than outcomes that are "predicted," since, in the former case, there is a relatively large discrepancy between the responses conditioned to the stimulus and the responses elicited by the outcome. In categorical perception, as in edge-effect experiments, slight differences in stimulus properties lead to large differences in outcome (being told that you have won a million bucks is considerably more satisfying than being told that you have won a million ducks); hence, the outcome, after a stimulus boundary is crossed, is relatively surprising, and stimulus control is sharpened. If sharp discrimination between categories follows from the reinforcement principle, then an innate tendency to categorize verbal stimuli is not a dramatic contribution of the genetic endowment to the language faculty.

It is possible, of course, that categorical perception is critical for infants learning their language, and that an innate tendency to perceive phonemes categorically facilitates language acquisition. By the time the infant matures, however, the long years of experience with phoneme perception can override an innate perceptual tendency. Consider the following experiment by MacDonald & McGurk.[35]

Adult subjects were shown a film of a person facing the camera and repeatedly uttering the syllable *ga*. The sound track for the film, however, did not correspond with the picture. The syllable repeatedly presented over the sound track, synchronous with the movements of the mouth, was *ba*. Subjects reported hearing *ga*, the syllable suggested by the visual stimulus, or *da*. (Neither *da* nor *ga* can be formed with closed lips, but *da* is acoustically closer than *ga* to *ba*.) If subjects closed their eyes, they immediately heard the stimulus "correctly" as *ba*. In this case, the perceptual response of the subjects was more powerfully guided by the visual stimuli than by the auditory stimuli. The subjective effect was found to increase with age: 98% of adults, but only 80% of young children, reported hearing something other than the auditory stimulus.

How are we to explain these results? Phonemes carry the burden of semantic distinctions. We respond one way to *boat*, another way to *goat*. Under normal conditions the visual stimuli arising from a speaker's movements correspond to the acoustic stimuli entering our ear. Either complex of stimuli will enable us to differentiate *boat* and *goat* and to respond appropriately. Under noisy conditions, or when the acoustic stimulus is degraded, however, the visual stimulus is more reliably correlated with what is being said than the acoustic stimulus; we cannot make a *b* sound without closing our lips. From what we know of the reinforcement principle, we would expect the more reliable predictor of an event to block control by other, simultaneously presented, stimuli, and it follows that the visual stimulus may, in some cases, for some subjects, control the perceptual response even if it is inconsistent with what is heard. We would not expect to find this effect for most pairs of phonemes, of course. *B* and *g* happen to be formed in ways that are visually distinct; moreover, as we saw above, they are acoustically quite similar. In fact, MacDonald and McGurk found no anomalies in subjects' reports when pairs of syllables were not visually distinct, as in *ga* and *da*.

While our interpretation of the MacDonald and McGurk experiment is necessarily tentative, it is evident that we do not perceive phonemes as we do solely because of a special, speech-specific adaptation of our auditory system. What we perceive is, in part, a product of our experiences. As in all other aspects of human behavior, contingencies of natural selection and contingencies of reinforcement contribute jointly to our perception of speech sounds.

Babbling

For the first year or two of life, children typically emit a wide variety of speech sounds, including not only those sounds found in their native verbal community but those of all other cultures as well. This unsystematic **babbling** is unique to human infants and is undoubtedly important in language acquisition. First, it exercises the vocal apparatus and presumably facilitates the coordination of effectors which will eventually produce speech. Second, it provides a variable pool of responses from which contingencies of selection can shape verbal units. Recall that variability in the units to be replicated is a prerequisite for selection processes. The exploratory behavior of the naive organism in an operant chamber provides the variability from which target behaviors are shaped or selected. Similarly, the variability in the infant's vocalizations provides an appropriate substrate for the selection of speech sounds and larger units in the child's verbal community.

That contingencies of selection can alter the probability of babbling responses was demonstrated in a study by Routh.[36] Infants who were clucked at and tickled following certain classes of speech sound (vowels or consonants) showed a considerable increase in the frequency of the target classes relative to baseline levels, to the unreinforced class of sounds, and to their respective control groups. The reinforcement contingency differentiated the highly variable behavioral substrate into at least two response classes.

The physical mechanisms underlying babbling are unknown, but that babbling is found in all verbal communities and even in deaf children suggests that there is a large innate component to the phenomenon. Moreover, the adaptive significance of babbling is clear. The human infant utters a variety of sounds from which a repertoire of complex verbal operants can be shaped by contingencies of selection.

In conclusion, there are certain physical structures (the pharynx, the respiratory system), certain perceptual mechanisms (categorical perception), certain behavioral dispositions (babbling), and perhaps even a special sensitivity to reinforcement (secondary reinforcement, social reinforcement) that facilitate verbal behavior in human beings; whether they were originally selected because they served that function or are just being exploited by contingencies of verbal behavior is not clear, but the role of the genetic endowment is evident: These features appear to set our species apart from even our closest relatives. However, we are aware of no evidence that there is a "language organ," a neural structure with special properties dedicated solely to the task of generating grammatical sentences. The available physiological evidence suggests that verbal behavior is qualitatively similar to other human behavior.

PARALLEL PROCESSES IN VERBAL BEHAVIOR

Under some conditions we pick our words one by one, as when we try to speak in a foreign tongue of which we have only a crude mastery, or when we are attempting to be precise, as when we are on a witness stand, or when we are trying to achieve a particular effect, as when we are composing a phrase for a fastidious audience. It is more commonly the case, however, that our verbal behavior cannot be considered a chain of discrete operants, each operant a speech sound or a word, comparable to a chain of responses that we might build, step by step, with a rat in an experimental chamber. In writing, one word necessarily follows another in its turn, but in speech there is often no clear boundary between words either in the articulatory movements of the speaker, in the acoustic signal, or in the effect on the listener.

In fluent speech, phonemes overlap, a phenomenon called **parallel transmission**. When the physical properties of a sample of speech are analyzed, one finds that the acoustic signal characteristic of a particular phoneme is often emitted simultaneously with that of nearby phonemes.[37] In the word *bag*, for example, analysis of the acoustic signal reveals that the portion of the signal characteristic of the vowel sound pervades the entire utterance, overlapping completely with the sounds characteristic of *b* and *g*. More striking, perhaps, even the consonant sounds partially overlap one another. (See **Figure 11.4**.) Moreover, the topography of response corresponding to a particular speech sound varies depending on what other speech sounds precede or follow it. The *d* sound in

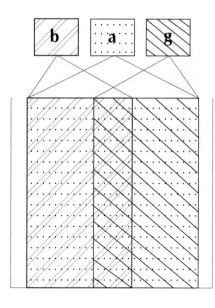

Time

FIGURE 11.4 *Parallel transmission*
A child learning to read sounds out the letters one by one, and we do much the same thing when we encounter a long chemical name or other unfamiliar term. However an analysis of the physical properties of fluent speech reveals that there is considerable overlap of speech sounds. In the word "bag," for example, the physical properties characteristic of the letter "b" overlap the "a" and even the "g" sounds, while the vowel sound pervades the entire utterance.
Source: After Liberman, 1972.

the syllable *di* is slightly different from the *d* sound in the syllable *du*, as shown in physical analyses of the speech signal.[38]

Fluent speech is interspersed with slight pauses in the auditory signal, but the pauses often do not correspond to word boundaries. Rather, the pauses tend to occur at transitions between consonant sounds that may or may not occur at a word boundary.[39] Consider the speech spectrogram (**Figure 11.5**) showing the physical properties of a fragment of speech and the corresponding speech sounds as represented by letters. The most conspicuous pauses in the signal occur within words.

The articulatory movements of the fluent speaker, then, cannot be divided into a sequence of discrete responses, each corresponding to a written letter or word. Clearly, then, the listener does not hear a sequence of discrete, invariant speech sounds. In fact, experienced listeners are remarkably forgiving of defects in the auditory signal. Warren[40] showed that missing speech sounds are seldom detected by listeners, provided that some noise is substituted. He spliced a fragment of white noise (a coughing sound) in the place of speech sounds in samples of recorded speech. For example, in the following sentence,

The state governors met with their respective legi*latures convening in the capital city.

the cough replaced the *s* sound in *legislatures*. Virtually none of his subjects detected the anomaly. Depending on the context, the spliced cough was heard as a variety of different speech sounds.

It was found that the *eel was on the axle.

It was found that the *eel was on the shoe.

It was found that the *eel was on the orange

It was found that the *eel was on the table.

Subjects heard *wheel, heel, peel,* or *meal,* depending on the context.[41]

The fact that speech is not produced or perceived as a sequence of discrete sounds disposes of the simple-minded notion that speech is nothing more than a simple response chain, in which each word or each sound is a response which serves as the controlling stimulus for the next. It does not follow, however, that an analysis of verbal behavior in terms of stimulus and response classes is invalid. We may train a rat, step by step, to run through a tube, climb some stairs, press a bar and so on, but that does not mean that the response chain so established is a model of all response sequences. All behavior, not just spoken sounds, occurs in parallel with other behavior. We gesture, speak, glance around us, walk, and flick bits of lint off of our shirt sleeve, all in parallel. (It is necessary, of course, that the responses be physically compatible with one another.)

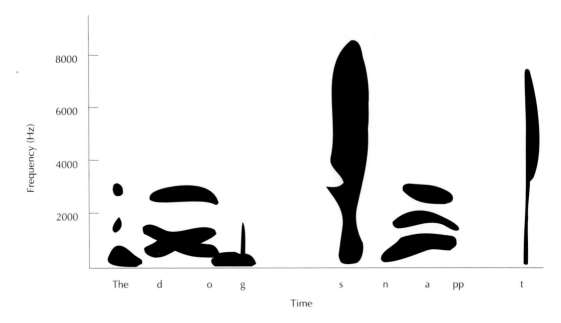

FIGURE 11.5   *A schematic speech spectrogram of a portion of the fluent utterance, "John said that the dog snapped at him."*

Note that the pauses in the physical signal do not always correspond to word boundaries, nor does the signal seem to map onto the sounds as we hear them. For example, we do not hear the breaks in the word "snapped" as pauses, but those breaks contribute to the sounds that we do perceive, as we saw in Figure 11.2.

Source: From Foss, Donald J., & Hakes, David T., *Psycholinguistics,* © 1978, p. 77. Reprinted by permission of Prentice Hall, Englewood Cliffs, New Jersey.

Once the discriminative stimuli controlling a response are present, the probability of the response increases. It can be emitted if no incompatible responses are stronger. If incompatible responses are stronger, the target response can be emitted when the other response has terminated. Many speech sounds are mutually compatible, as the phenomenon of parallel transmission demonstrates. Consequently, it is not surprising that speech sounds overlap. The fact that verbal behavior can be represented as written characters favors the interpretation that there is a one-to-one correspondence between letters and speech sounds, and that speech sounds occur in an orderly sequence. But speech preceded writing, and it is merely a deficiency in our system of transcription that leads us to suppose that responses occur in the order of letters in words.

Jordan, simulating speech production in an adaptive network, has demonstrated that parallel transmission can occur where there is no response competition.[42] He represented eight distinctive features of speech production (voicing, place of articulation, etc.) by different output patterns of a recursive network, and he set the network the task of producing the phrase *sinistre structure*. Using the discrepancy between the actual output and the required output to modify the connection weights, he was able to demonstrate that the network would produce a sequence of articulatory responses comparable to that of a human speaker. Moreover, some of the responses occurred in parallel. The rounding of the mouth required to produce the first vowel sound in *structure* occurred earlier in the pattern than suggested by the position of the *u* in *struct—*. The critical point is that as soon as the rounding of the mouth was free to vary, that distinctive feature appeared. Thus, there is nothing remarkable about parallel transmission once we recall that the utterance *as spoken* is our primary datum; written words are only crude representations.

Under some conditions, of course, verbal responses *are* chained like operants in an experimental chamber. When we attempt to learn a long, unfamiliar name, or a long word in another language, we piece the word together, syllable by syllable, until we can repeat the whole thing. Similarly, when we learn a poem, we learn it phrase by phrase, or line by line, or even word by word. In these cases, response chaining appears to be relevant. We might still see parallel transmission *within* segments, but individual segments appear to be chained together in sequence. Overlapping responses may be common among fluent speakers, but for young children, people speaking haltingly in a foreign tongue, and even adults who anticipate being ridiculed, we might expect responses to be emitted in sequence, perhaps because of a tendency toward self-editing.

The size of the relevant verbal unit is clearly important to whether or not we observe segmentation. The lack of segmentation between word boundaries may be a problem in traditional formulations, but in a selectionist interpretation of verbal behavior, the word is not always an appropriate unit of analysis. If the most orderly unit is a phrase or a frame,[43] we should not necessarily expect to see pauses between individual words. We will examine the issue of appropriate units of analysis in the next section.

NOVELTY IN VERBAL BEHAVIOR

A conspicuous feature of verbal behavior is its novelty. When we consider large units of verbal behavior we rarely find two samples that are identical. This fact has been interpreted as evidence of the inadequacy of principles derived from the study of nonverbal behavior to explain language:

Linguistic creativity automatically rules out all extant associationist theories of language learning, for they cannot, because of the limitations of the principles they employ, account for the infinite number of sentences that every speaker-hearer is potentially capable of understanding (with no previous "learning" history).[44]

The context makes it clear that the term "associationist theories" embraces the selectionist approach that we endorse.

The notion that humans are able to speak and understand an infinite number of grammatical sentences is central to most modern positions in linguistics and in much of psychology. This view has led to the position that a productive grammatical system lies at the heart of language, and that approaches that attempt to account for verbal behavior in terms of environmental contingencies without including a provision for a productive mechanism are likely to be superficial. Indeed, if the sentence were an appropriate unit of verbal behavior, a selectionist account would be inadequate, for selectionist principles account for the emergence and persistence of stable forms, be they physical structures or behaviors. Moreover, in the selectionist's view the first appearance of an adaptive form is due to blind variation: A genetic mutation is more likely to produce a more poorly adapted individual than a better adapted one, and the exploratory behavior of a pigeon in an experimental chamber or of a child with a ring puzzle is more likely to be "incorrect" than to lead to reinforcement. A stream of sentences, each one uttered for the first time, and each one "correct," that is, each one followed by an appropriate response by the verbal community, is clearly not the direct product of blind variation and selection.

For many students of language it is axiomatic that the sentence is an appropriate unit of analysis, but there is no empirical justification for this assumption. First of all, the sentence is a formal unit and has a definition within the formal apparatus of linguistics; it does not have an agreed behavioral or operational definition. We noted above that sentences usually coincide with the expiratory phase of respiration, but this fact appears to bear no relationship to the linguistic concept of the sentence. Furthermore, to the extent that a sentence has a common-sense definition—you know one when you hear one—it is clear that much verbal behavior fails to qualify. "On the top shelf—on the left," "Not if I can help it," and "Maybe, if he hurries" are three examples (gathered within a few minutes) of perfectly clear but elliptical utterances that can be forced into our common-sense mold for sentences only by supplying additional material. Much casual conversation consists of a stream of run-on fragments woven together with conjunctions, gestures, pauses, and meaningless fillers; the linguist can usually dip into this verbal salad and extract a sentence, but that is an exercise in interpretation. Finally, there are many utterances that just don't make any sense; there are verbal slips, nervous prattle, and so on, that no one would defend as sentences. A friend once queried, "Is it still raining outside yet, or what?" While this was presumably merely the blend of two incompatible utterances of roughly equal probability, no such charitable interpretation can be provided for the following testimony of Ron Ziegler, President Nixon's Press Secretary. Asked by a senator whether a set of Watergate tapes were all intact, a question that required only a simple "Yes" or "No," he replied:

> *I would feel that most of the conversations that took place in those areas of the White House that did have the recording system would in almost their entirety be in existence, but the special prosecutor, the court, and, I think, the American people are sufficiently familiar with the recording system to know where the recording devices existed and to know the situation in terms of the recording process, but I feel, although the process has not been undertaken yet in preparation of the material to abide by the court decision, really what the answer to that question is.*[45]

It is customary to dismiss such irregularities as the product of "performance" variables: All verbal utterances begin as grammatically correct sentences in the head, but they get garbled or abbreviated in execution. Clearly this is simply an attempt to salvage the sentence as a unit of analysis. In our view the attempt is misguided. First, it removes the analysis of the central features of language to an unobservable domain—in the head—and second, it requires us to abandon selectionist principles in favor of unknown generative mechanisms, mechanisms that have been inferred from the very data that they are invoked to explain.

An adequate account of verbal behavior must indeed account for its novelty, but it must account for irregular utterances as well as those that most people consider grammatically correct. However, the problem of novelty in verbal behavior is no different from the problem of novelty in nonverbal behavior. If it is true that a child can, in principle, utter an infinite number of sentences, then a child can, in the same sense, climb an infinite number of trees, skip an infinite number of stones across the surface of a pond, or whistle an infinite number of tunes. *All* behavior is novel if we look closely enough; even a rat pressing a bar in an operant chamber will vary the force and position and duration of its presses and the posture of its body from one occasion to the next. The problem of novelty is partly a problem of identifying appropriate units of analysis.

The concept of the response class, or operant, is central to a selectionist account of behavior. It is the operant, not the individual response, that is reinforced and that increases or decreases in frequency. The operant is an empirically defined class of responses that is relatively stable over time—hence not novel—but concatenations or combinations of operants will often be novel. The appropriate unit of analysis in language, then, is the **verbal operant**, and an utterance will be unique if it is composed of a unique combination of verbal operants, just as a sentence will be unique if it is composed of a unique combination of words. One will utter as many unique utterances as there are unique constellations of controlling variables. To say that this is an infinite number is meaningless.

From the foregoing comments it would be natural to assume that words are verbal operants, for they appear to be the stable building blocks from which larger utterances are constructed. We must be cautious, however, in attempting to match units of behavior with the formal units of a grammatical or linguistic analysis. Response classes depend in detail on the specific contingencies of reinforcement for the organism in question; there is no general answer to the question of what a verbal operant is, just as there is no general answer to what constitutes an operant in an experimental chamber. For example, the sarcastic question, "Where's the fire?" is, for most of us, a unitary response, presumably a single operant, evoked by a familiar person or subordinate in a conspicuous but apparently unnecessary hurry. For a fire marshal the same utterance may also be a unitary response, but under the control of the sound of an alarm, and hence a different operant. For the loiterer on a street corner, hearing the wailing of the fire engines, the utterance may be the combination of two or more operants, *fire* and the **grammatical frame**, *Where's the X—?* To one who happens to be reading this text aloud, the utterance is presumably three operants under control of the three printed words. To the six-year-old beginning reader, sounding out the words letter by letter, or trigram by trigram, the utterance is more than three operants, while her younger brother may run about, repeating the phrase as a unitary response, simply in imitation of adults around him. Thus, we cannot begin to understand behavior by considering its formal properties alone.

Verbal Operants

There are, of course, contingencies of verbal behavior that pervade a culture; that is what we mean by a verbal community. An American child will learn to speak English and can get along reasonably well anywhere English is spoken. Even so, the child's verbal repertoire will be unique. It will differ somewhat from that of other people in the verbal community, and it will differ from his own repertoire later in life. Nonetheless, it is possible to analyze typical contingencies of reinforcement in a verbal community to illustrate a variety of verbal operants, as Skinner[46] has done. As we will see,

the validity of this classification of verbal operants is underscored by neuropsychological data. The following examples are but a sample—we only present those classes that will feature in subsequent discussions—but they will give the reader a sense of the variety of variables controlling verbal behavior. We do not present an exhaustive list, for we wish to discourage the reader from equating the classification of verbal operants with Skinner's entire analysis of verbal behavior.

Textual responses. When we read, our verbal behavior is guided by a pattern of visual stimuli. As young children we acquire units of textual behavior[47] initially corresponding to letters, but extending to words and phrases as we become skilled readers. We can even read foreign languages passably, without the slightest understanding of what we are saying. Since the form and sequence of such verbal behavior are controlled by the text, with little relation to context or content, textual responses are quite different from most other verbal operants. Nevertheless, textual responses can be intermixed with other verbal operants as when a politician gives a speech, glancing occasionally at note cards or a prepared text. Under such conditions it would be hopeless to try to interpret the speaker's behavior solely from its topography.

Some persons who have suffered brain damage display a peculiar disorder called **alexia**, or the loss of the ability to read.[48] While this disorder commonly occurs in conjunction with other deficits, it can occur alone. From the present perspective, this poses no special problem; the stimulus control of textual operants is disrupted by a lesion, but other verbal operants remain intact.

Echoic responses. A child also acquires a repertoire of echoic operants, and can repeat sounds, words, phrases, and longer utterances after a model. While this repertoire is probably crucial for the child's learning his language, echoic responses are common in adult speech. We rehearse a name or a phone number until we can write it down or ring up our party, and we recite our vows after the parish vicar or swear to uphold the laws of the commonwealth after the justice of the peace. Often we repeat a phrase from a previous utterance, particularly when we are trying to "buy time." A student who is asked, "What is the capital of Senegal?" may respond, perhaps quite slowly, "The capital of Senegal is . . ." Echoic control apparently supplements other variables to produce a common phenomenon: When a speaker uses a picturesque or slightly unusual word, like *astounding* or *undeniable*, the word is subsequently used throughout the conversation by all parties, possibly in spite of deliberate attempts to avoid it. It is only under such conditions that we are apt to notice the effect of the stimulus word; echoic control is probably far more pervasive than we realize. Like textual responses, echoics are often intermixed with other verbal operants, and an interpretation of verbal behavior must take them into account.

As was the case with textual operants, brain lesions can cause a selective loss of echoic operants. To quote Kolb and Whishaw:

> *Disorders of repetition may result . . . from a selective dissociation between auditory-input and speech-output systems. In this latter case, of selective dissociation, the disorder of repetition may be the only significant language disturbance, and may go unnoticed except through special testing.*[49]

Other lesions can cause a disorder called **transcortical aphasia**, which in some cases is manifested by patients who can repeat words but cannot speak spontaneously. In some cases they can repeat words but not even understand them.[50] Here it appears that mechanisms serving echoic operants have been preserved while others have been lost. Again, these findings are compatible with Skinner's classification of verbal operants but not with morphemes, words, sentences, and other traditional units of analysis.

Tacts.   Another class of verbal behavior (the **tact** in Skinner's terminology) is that class of discriminated operants controlled by some property or object in the nonverbal world. Stimulus control is maintained by the generalized reinforcement of the verbal community, which profits from precise stimulus control of verbal behavior. We are said to tact an object when we name or describe it, but tacts include other kinds of responses to stimuli as well. We say, "Quarter to four" in the presence of the kitchen clock, or "German measles" when confronted by a particular constellation of physical symptoms. Tacts increase in probability in the presence of relevant stimuli, but, like other verbal operants, whether or not they are emitted depends on many other factors as well.

The concepts of reference and naming are clearly related to the concept of the tact, but, as with many traditional terms, they do not map neatly onto units derived from an operant analysis. Operants must be defined in terms of their antecedents and typical consequences as well as the orderliness of the relation among these events. Tacts can be any length: Many tacts are words, but some are phrases or whole sentences: *on the table, in the box, The mail's here!* and so on. In some cases a tact can be a verbal frame: Having learned *on the chair, on the table, on the bed,* the child may say *on the bench* without special training. The frame *on the X—* is a tact controlled in part by the physical relationship of one thing on top of another. *On the news, on the TV,* and *on the radio* presumably include frames of the same topography but under different stimulus control. Tacts need not be whole words; certain **inflections**, such as the terminal *-s* in nouns and present-tense verbs, are presumably controlled by those features of a situation that cause us to speak of plurality, possession, or currency of action. Similarly, parts of words, such as word roots, can, over time, emerge as tacts. When we see a pile of things thrown haphazardly on the floor we might be inclined to call it a *con—* and then grope unsuccessfully for a suitable ending for our word. *Congregation, consortium, confabulation, congeries, convulsion, conglomeration, conjunction, contraption, confection, convocation,* all suggest things thrown together, and *con* may emerge as a unit controlled by that property.

Since tacts are controlled by objects, properties and events, novelty in verbal behavior can be explained, in part, by novel circumstances. Since the verbal community has little interest in hearing the same thing over and over again, we are differentially reinforced for reporting changes, making distinctions, and identifying unique events; consequently, we develop a fine-grained repertoire of tacts and can usually report events quite precisely.[51]

While textual and echoic responses are controlled by visual and auditory stimuli respectively, tacts are controlled by stimuli of every sort. Consequently, it would be remarkable if there were classes of brain lesion that disrupted tacts uniquely. Moreover, since the classification of verbal operants is largely unknown to neuropsychologists, such a lesion would likely go unreported as such. Some neuropsychological data do seem to be relevant, however. Some patients suffer **anomia**, or the inability to name objects; as we have noted above, it is often the case that patients who appear to be unable to name an object can in fact do so under different stimulus conditions. A subject who cannot name a spoon when looking at it may be able to do so when the spoon is picked up. The response *spoon* is a member of a variety of response classes; one class may be disrupted by the lesion while others survive. While there is but a single name for *spoon*, there are many tacts of that topography.

Tacts often provide much of the "content" of what we say. We can get along in a foreign country with a crude repertoire of tacts and with very little understanding of grammatical distinctions. Some frontal-lobe lesions produce **aphasias** in which the patient is able to produce only content words with few, if any, **function words**, such as articles, conjunctions, and prepositions. In these patients it appears that mechanisms underlying tacts were spared while operants evoked by relationships among tacts suffered. (Such operants are called **autoclitics** in Skinner's terminology.)

Intraverbal responses.   The last class of verbal operants that we will mention here is the intraverbal. Intraverbal responses, like echoic responses, are evoked by antecedent verbal stimuli, but there is no point-to-point correspondence between the stimulus and the response in intraverbals. When one particular verbal expression is commonly followed by another, the first one will tend to become a controlling stimulus for the second. Having heard on many occasions *Give me liberty, or give me death!* we are virtually certain to respond *death* to the verbal stimulus *Give me liberty or give me —.* Moreover, even when the antecedent stimulus is simply *liberty, or give me —* the probability of saying *death* presumably increases. Memorized poetry, prose, and "facts" are typically intraverbal chains, which we demonstrate by giving ourselves a "running start" when we falter. When we are interrupted in the middle of Hamlet's soliloquy, we may be unable to continue without going back a line or two. Word associations and much of what passes for knowledge can be interpreted in terms of intraverbal control. The verbal stimulus *Battle of Hastings* increases the probability of a variety of intraverbal responses including *William the Conqueror, ten sixty-six, Harold, Norman invasion,* and *Anglo-Saxons.* Which of them, if any, is actually emitted will depend on many collateral variables. Intraverbal control is clearly relevant to the phenomenon of priming discussed in Chapter 9.

For experienced speakers, intraverbal control contributes strength to virtually everything we say. In some cases intraverbal control will be the dominant variable in determining a response, but in many others the control will be shared with other variables; for example, our choice among synonymous expressions may be largely a function of intraverbal relations. Perhaps the most important role of intraverbals is their contribution to grammatical frames. For example, when we begin a sentence with *He, She* or *It*, the grammatical tag *-s* is strengthened and, if other variables are suitable, can contribute to the proper inflection of present-tense verbs. We have many stock expressions and still more standard constructions with which we pepper our speech. We can see the effect of intraverbal control in grammatical frames most clearly in cases where it leads to grammatical errors. If a singular subject happens to be followed by a prepositional phrase ending in -*s*, we often fall into the error of inflecting the verb as if the subject were plural. For example, we might say *That bunch of idiots cruising our streets make me furious!* Here the intraverbal control exerted by *idiots* and perhaps *streets* was apparently stronger than that of *bunch.*

Some examples of brain lesions have been reported that destroyed all verbal functions except intraverbals and echoics. A victim of a gas leak suffered massive damage to her cerebral cortex, but **Broca's area** and Wernicke's area were preserved. She lost all appropriate spontaneous language but could repeat what was said to her, and if given the beginning of a poem or a phrase, she could complete it. Perhaps most revealing, if an ungrammatical sentence were read to her, she would repeat it with the grammar corrected, suggesting that grammatical tags are indeed, in some cases, a matter of intraverbal control.

In this section, we have attempted to show that words, sentences, and other formal units of grammar have little place in a behavioral analysis. The concept of the verbal operant captures far better the dynamic and idiosyncratic properties of verbal behavior. The extraordinary novelty of verbal behavior emerges from the unlimited number of combinations of orderly units. Novelty arises, not from some hidden lagoon of free will, but from the interplay of controlling variables in an ever-changing and complex world.

VERBAL BEHAVIOR CONFORMS TO RULES

Language is said to be different from nonverbal behavior in that it conforms to rules. Studies of language acquisition reveal that children appear to be following rules in defiance of prevailing contingencies of reinforcement. Consider the phenomenon of **overregularization** or **overgeneralization**. A young child will often learn the correct past tense of irregular verbs such as *go* and *break* and say, "I

went," or "I broke." Somewhat later, the child appears to have learned a rule for forming past-tense verbs and will add a *d* or *ed* sound to the end of the verb and say "followed" and "painted." The child is said to have learned a rule that the past tense of verbs is formed by adding *ed*. He has not simply learned individual past-tense forms one by one, for he will sometimes apply the rule to irregular verbs such as *come, go,* and *get,* and say "I comed" and "I goed" and even, sometimes, "I wented" or "I got upped." These incorrect irregular verbs may even persist in the child's repertoire for years.[52] The child has presumably not heard these words before and undoubtedly has not been differentially reinforced for uttering them.

Berko[53] found further evidence that children appear to extend grammatical rules to new instances despite the absence of these instances in the verbal community. In English, some nouns are made plural by adding an *s* sound, others by adding *ez* and others by adding *z*, e.g., *rock—rocks, glass—glasses,* and *pig—pigs.* Berko showed children drawings of little amoeboid creatures with nonsense-syllable names. She found that children could give the "correct" plural of the nonsense-syllable name most of the time. For example she might say, "This is a 'wug.' Here is another wug. Now we have two ——." The child would correctly reply, "wugz." It is untenable to suppose that the children had been previously reinforced for uttering such words; it appears that they were able to apply a rule when supplied with a novel example.

Children often overregularize plurals in revealing ways. Children will often say "foots" rather than "feet," apparently from having learned to form plurals by adding *s.* Somewhat later, perhaps having learned to add *ez* to words ending in *s* (e.g., fox—foxes), children will sometimes say "footses." Analogous overgeneralizations are found in many other languages, particularly highly inflected languages such as Russian.[54]

These findings are commonly held to be problematic from a behavioral perspective and suggest that the acquisition of language involves the generation and testing of hypotheses about rules.[55]

There is no disputing the apparent obedience to rules in children's verbal behavior, but it does not follow that the rules are actively formulated or sought by children, consciously or unconsciously. The three-term contingency of reinforcement is a rule—in the presence of the discriminative stimulus, a response will be followed by reinforcement—and all discriminated operant behavior is rule-following in this sense.[56] A pigeon who pecks a red key but not a white key can be said to be following a rule, but we do not invoke an active search for regularities or a drive to seek order, nor need we do so with children who overgeneralize the formation of plurals or past tenses.

Skinner discusses verbal discriminated operants at great length[57] and specifically addresses the present issue: Of roots and affixes, he writes:

> They are functional units in the behavior of the speaker only insofar as they correspond with particular features of a stimulating situation. The evidence is clearest when a speaker composes new forms of response with respect to new situations. Having developed a functional suffix -ed with respect to that subtle property which we speak of as action-in-the-past, the suffix may be added for the first time to a word which has hitherto described only action in the present. The process is conspicuous when the speaker composes a form which is not established by the practices of a particular community. He singed is obviously composed from separate elements, because the community reinforces the form He sang. He walked may also have been composed, but since the form is also separately reinforced, the evidence is not so clear.[58]

That the nonstandard form *singed* should displace the previously acquired *sang* should cause no concern. When two responses are incompatible, only the stronger, or prepotent, response will be emitted. The other response is still in the repertoire and continues to fluctuate in probability with changes in controlling variables; it has not been eliminated or erased. Under some conditions we will see the standard form emerge, and, in fact, children often mix correct and incorrect forms of the same verb for months.[59] Ultimately, of course, the nonstandard form loses strength relative to the

standard form, and the child's verbal practices more closely approximate those of the verbal community.

When we grasp the fact that all discriminated operants are rule-following in the sense used here, the prevalence of rules in verbal behavior is unremarkable. More importantly, it reveals that there are rules governing verbal behavior that are not grammatical in nature. Consider Skinner's discussion of verbal fragments:

> Some apparent minimal units have no respectable genealogy, and they have tended to be neglected by those concerned with historical and comparative data. Many examples have long been familiar, however. An initial sp is characteristic of many words in English having to do with emanation from the mouth (spit, speak, spew) or from some other point (sputter, sprinkle, spray) or with radiation from a point (spoke, spire, spur). It would appear, therefore, that the response sp has functional unity under the control of a particular geometric pattern common to many stimuli. . . . The basic fact is that a stimulus involving emanation or radiation from a point commonly evokes the response sp. The response only rarely occurs alone—and even then only in inchoate behavior under stress, in which a novel pattern showing radiation from a point might lead the speaker to stammer sp without completing a standard verbal form. . . .
>
> Although we may demonstrate a functional unit of verbal behavior in which a response of a given form is controlled by a given stimulus, it does not follow that every instance of a response having that form represents the same operant, nor that every instance of a response evoked by that property has that form. It does not follow, for example, that every instance of sp is an instance of the unit just described or that every case of radiation will evoke a response containing sp. (And it does not follow, of course, that the functional unity of a minimal operant in the behavior of a speaker corresponds to the practices of any community. A child of six took the terminal -nese, in Chinese and Japanese, to refer to the shape of the eyes.)[60]

Thus, the mere fact that verbal behavior can be characterized by a system of rules does not, by itself, have any implications about the adequacy of selectionist principles to account for it. However, in our task of accounting for its enormous complexity in selectionist terms, we have made little progress since Skinner's work in 1957, and much remains to be done. We must ask, for example, how it is that *-ed* is merged with *brood* to form *brooded* and not with *gloomy* to form *gloomied*. What in fact are the discriminative stimuli that control the ending *-ed*? Skinner mentions "the subtle property we speak of as action-in-the-past," and no doubt this is relevant. However, current behavior is always guided by current variables, and it is unclear how action-in-the-past is represented in the present constellation of controlling variables. Moreover, the same variables might plausibly evoke either *He brooded* or *He was gloomy* but not *He was brood* or *He gloomied*. Two different syntactical constructions could be evoked by the same set of conditions; we have to ask why the constructions are not parallel and why we do not get blends. To say that *brood* is a verb and *gloomy* is an adjective evades the issue. To put it loosely, how does the speaker know that the one is a verb and the other an adjective, and what place do these terms have in a behavioral account? Answering these questions goes to the very heart of the controversy between those who view language as a qualitatively unique module of the mind with peculiar rules largely constrained by innate mechanisms and those who view it as behavior, behavior mediated by some unique structures, but subject to the same principles as nonverbal behavior. The elaborate systems of rules devised by the linguist to characterize the linguistic competence of the speaker specify relationships among abstract formal entities such as nouns, verbs, prepositions, as well as hidden markers and other terms unfamiliar to the layman. To the selectionist, these rules and concepts are empty unless they can be operationalized, or translated into physical or behavioral terms.

It would be convenient to argue that traditional grammatical concepts cannot be operationalized and can therefore be dismissed from our analysis. It may well be the case that traditional terms carry extra baggage that will be useless in our account, but it appears that some grammatical distinctions refer to real variables that must be considered in an adequate explanation of verbal behavior. Suppose we present someone with the following nonsense (with apologies to Lewis Carroll):

> *The tove gimbles in the wabe*

Our subject may respond, whimsically, with any of the following utterances:

> *How long has the tove been gimbling in the wabe?*
> *Did the tove really gimble?*
> *I gimbled for several hours last night myself.*
> *It takes two toves to gimble.*
> *Will he still gimble after he's seen Paree?*

One might infer that we recognize that *gimbles* is a verb, *tove* a noun, and that they can be used in any of a variety of constructions accordingly. We do not do so because *gimbles* is an activity and *tove* a thing. We know nothing about these words except how they have been used in the passage. Perhaps on the analogy of *The frog sits in the pond* we are able to generalize to novel, but consistent, utterances. The example suggests that the variables guiding inflection are, at least sometimes, wholly verbal or syntactic rather than semantic.

We should be cautious in drawing this conclusion, however. People have been exposed to countless utterances of the form *The tove gimbles*, and it is likely to suggest a meaning to us, however vague. For example, we may perhaps think of some creature gamboling somewhere. In any case, the expression has a familiar form, *The X—Ys*, a frame that we have often seen in modified form: *Two Xs Y—* or *X— needs to Y—* or *Yesterday X— Yed* or *Will X— Y—*? Note that there is no truth to the matter; *gimbles* is not "really" a verb. Our subject has just responded in a way consistent with that interpretation. Another subject might have responded, "Are there other kinds of gimbles in the wabe?" on the analogy of "The fat birds in the tree." Here *tove* is treated as an adjective and *gimbles* as a plural noun.

It appears then, that we say *He brooded* partly because we have heard, or have said, *I was brooding* or *He broods a lot* or any of a number of other constructions in which brood is given the grammatical tags of a verb. In contrast we have never heard or used *gloomy* in such constructions, but we have heard it in adjectival constructions: *A gloomy day; my cousin and her gloomy husband; he is gloomy and dyspeptic;* and so on. Using, or hearing a word used, in a particular kind of frame or construction appears to alter the probability of using it in a variety of related constructions without explicit experience. The stimulus control appears to be mainly intraverbal, although, as we pointed out above, our own responses to a verbal stimulus (our interpretation of it) may be relevant.

We must also entertain the possibility that the individual word is not the appropriate unit of analysis in the examples cited. We may learn *be gloomy* and its variants as units and *a gloomy day, a gloomy man*, etc., as units. The frame *He was X*— may be strong under the same conditions that *He Xed* is strong. The variables disposing the speaker to one rather than the other construction might be trivial, but once embarked on the former frame, there would be intraverbal support for completing it with *gloomy*, but not *brood*.

The task of identifying the appropriate units in such an utterance and the task of specifying the variables controlling grammatical tags is a formidable one. Unfortunately, if, as we believe, human behavior is the product of countless instances of selection, there will be no general solution to the problem. The controlling variables will almost certainly differ somewhat from person to person. However, that does not absolve us from showing that the control is plausible, that there are *some* conditions that can reasonably be invoked to account for a particular construction. Postulating *ad hoc* frames to account for every grammatical puzzle we confront is the weakest form of support for a selectionist position, in the absence of any independent evidence that such frames are, in fact, operants. However, it is likely that fluent speakers have in their repertoire many overlapping operants of different sizes, and that, because of intraverbal control among elements, countless grammatical frames are among these units.

The concept of a grammatical frame is analogous to a response chain in which some elements are free to vary depending on prevailing conditions. For example, we might teach a pigeon the following response chain: A peck to the center key of a three-key display produces either a high-pitched or a low-pitched tone; if high, the pigeon pecks the left key; otherwise it pecks the right key. Finally, a third peck, to the center key, is followed by food. After sufficient practice, we might get fluent performance in which the pigeon rapidly pecks out an appropriate sequence. The "frame" would be *center X— center*. The third peck, to the center key, would be controlled partly by the stimuli arising from the first peck and partly by the temporal and tactile properties (but not the location) of the second peck, while *X*— is a variable that would be controlled in part by "situational" stimuli, in this case, the pitch of a tone. Similarly, in the frame *It's a X— day, isn't it?* the variable term, e.g., *dismal, fine, splendid, lousy*, is controlled partly by the earlier elements of the frame, but partly by the weather. The controlling stimuli for *day* include the specific verbal elements of the first part of the frame, *It's a*, plus the temporal and prosodic elements (but not the phonetic elements) of the variable term.

Similarly, consider the problem of "nonadjacent dependencies." In the utterance *I called him up to ask about getting a ride to Boston*, or *I called Julie up to ask about getting a ride to Boston*, the word *up* follows a variable term. It appears to be part of a frame *call X— up*, where *X*— has certain temporal and prosodic properties. In accounting for the fact that *up* occurs where it does, and not, say, two words later, we appeal to the control by the first element in the frame, *call*, and the temporal and prosodic properties of the variable term. That these latter properties are important, and not just invoked *ad hoc*, is demonstrated by considering different examples of the variable *X*—. There is no *syntactic* reason why we should not include a long subordinate clause in our variable term, but note the weakening effect on the word *up* when we do so:

I called the dentist that did such a good job on your bicuspids up.

Here *up* has lost all of its force. We see the same weakening effect if we are interrupted in the middle of the frame:

I called the dentist that you recommended—No! It wasn't you; it was Eric—up.

If we are determined to use this construction we can maintain some of the force of *up* by uttering the variable term in a rapid monotone:

I called *thefamousbrainsurgeonyourecommended-butnolongerlike* up.

Thus there appears to be anecdotal evidence, at least, that frames have a certain unity regardless of their variable terms.

While we suspect that a careful evaluation of the units of analysis is essential in understanding any given sample of verbal behavior, we must acknowledge that remaining difficulties are formidable. Some grammatical distinctions respected by fluent speakers are subtle, implausible, and not at all self-evident. For one example among many, note that the first three examples are standard but that the fourth is irregular:

I called the doctor up.
I called up the doctor.
I called him up.
I called up him.

There is no communicative or logical reason why the fourth example should be irregular. Similarly, in the first three, but not in the fourth, of the following examples, note the ambiguity in the referent of the pronoun *he.*

Hank dropped his keys when he was leaving.
When he was leaving, Hank dropped his keys.
When Hank was leaving, he dropped his keys.
He dropped his keys when Hank was leaving.

We interpret the fourth example to mean that someone other than Hank dropped his keys. In the first three examples "he" could refer to Hank or to someone else. Again, whatever the reason for this distinction, we cannot appeal to clarity or simplic-

ity—otherwise we would not tolerate the ambiguity of reference in the first three examples. Nor can we appeal to control by situational variables—each of the four constructions might be occasioned by the same circumstances. It is such subtleties as these that motivate many linguists to argue that language is too complex and its rules too arcane to be learned in a few short years by nearly all children in all cultures; children must get a substantial head start from the genetic endowment. They postulate that humans are endowed with a **universal grammar**, and a **language acquisition device** that extracts the relevant elements of the grammar from the restricted and mistake-ridden snatches of speech that children hear. This grammar is used, in turn, to generate sentences.

This hypothesis has a superficial appeal; it sidesteps all of the difficulties of accounting for the acquisition of verbal behavior in terms of principles of learning. Moreover, by invoking the genetic endowment, the hypothesis appears to fall within a selectionist framework. However, we feel that it poses problems far more serious than those it sweeps away. First, there are no plausible contingencies of natural selection that could account for the postulated universal grammar; it strains credibility to suppose that the survival of our forebears hinged on obscure grammatical rules such as the ambiguity of pronoun reference or the interpretation of reflexive expressions. Second, no one has specified how a language acquisition device might actually work. As we have argued elsewhere, such a device can make no use of the physical signal since the phonetic properties of each language are wholly arbitrary. The input to the device must be, not raw stimuli, but a grammatical representation of the stimuli. Unfortunately, this presupposes the very ability to extract a grammar that the language acquisition device was postulated to explain.[61]

While the proffered nativist explanation for syntactical niceties may be implausible and incomplete, we are not relieved of the task of explaining them in selectionist terms. The task must remain a major challenge for future investigators, for there are countless examples requiring interpretation.[62]

We believe that we have identified important variables that will feature in such interpretations; in particular, we suspect that the concept of the intraverbal frame is central to many subtle grammatical distinctions. For example, with regard to the last example, we have heard and said countless utterances of the form *When he did this, So-and-so did that*, and *He did this when So-and-so did that*. The control exerted by *When he X—* over the subsequent form and interpretation of what follows cannot be dismissed.[63]

The fact that verbal behavior conforms to rules has been overinterpreted. It does not follow that rules are "in the head" or that they are somehow "used" to generate verbal behavior. As we have argued, all discriminated behavior can be interpreted as rule-following in the same sense. The subtle regularities in language deserve explanation, but to describe the rule is not to explain the behavior. We must turn to the history of the individual, both as a speaker and a listener, and examine the contingencies responsible for the behavior from which the rule has been inferred.

THE ROLE OF EXPLICIT REINFORCEMENT IN LANGUAGE ACQUISITION

Most children learn to speak their language within a few years, but few receive formal training. The extent to which they receive explicit reinforcement from their parents remains controversial. Brown & Hanlon[64] examined the interactions of parents with their children in an attempt to evaluate the extent to which the parents reinforced grammatical utterances or punished or corrected ungrammatical utterances. They concluded that parents provided very little explicit feedback one way or the other: They tolerated a wide range of deviant utterances and did not praise instances of proper grammar; when parents did correct their children it was typically for content, not errors of grammar. For example, *Mama isn't boy, he a girl*, was followed by *That's right*, while *And Walt Disney comes on Tuesday*, was followed by *No. He does not*. However, Moerk, [65] analyzing the same data, found that there was indeed a high frequency of reinforcement, modeling, and correction by parents. Brown and Hanlon counted only instances in which a response was followed by an explicit expression of approval or disapproval such as *Very good*, or *That's wrong*. Moerk observed that other parental responses can have the same effect; for example, the parent simply repeating the child's utterance can serve a reinforcing function.

Brown and Hanlon's observation that adults provide only the most perfunctory and sporadic feedback to children about the grammatical correctness of their verbal behavior has been influential; it has been cited widely as evidence that contingencies of reinforcement play a relatively unimportant role in language acquisition. Reinforcement, in this view, is seen as the deliberate arrangement of educational contingencies by solicitous parents. However, no one would maintain that explicitly arranged reinforcement is adequate to explain the acquisition of a fluent verbal repertoire. The sheer number of such contingencies that would have to be arranged is staggering. Moreover, many children grow up to be fluent speakers in environments where parents, if present at all, are far from solicitous.

These observations do not force us to retreat to the position that language somehow unfolds in the child, like the petals of a rose, as the product of a genetic plan, nor do they even suggest that reinforcement plays a secondary role in a child's acquisition of a verbal repertoire. Only a very small proportion of the contingencies of reinforcement in human affairs is explicit, and verbal contingencies are no exception, as Moerk's analysis reminds us. When a child speaks, adults usually orient to the child and almost invariably respond appropriately in some way. Verbal behavior provides children with tremendous power, which they learn to wield more and more effectively as their repertoire develops. Virtually every instance of verbal behavior is charged with reinforcement of some sort, and very little of it is explicitly arranged.

Of course, this does not explain how children acquire subtle grammatical discriminations. Discrimination requires, not just reinforcement, but differential reinforcement. Adults respond to children's speech regardless of its grammatical form, and children can control their world quite effectively with the imperfectly developed grammar of the three-year-old. Many aspects of verbal behavior can be accounted for in terms of the reinforcers that follow from effective communication—turn-taking, requesting, naming, verbal game-playing, imitation, learning songs and nursery rhymes, and so on; however, these contingencies appear to be insufficient to account for some of the fine-grained patterns of adult verbal behavior. We should note, in passing, that most adults make every attempt to model language at a level that is appropriate for the child. That is, adults and older siblings speak slowly, emphatically, and distinctly when speaking to a child, eventually fading to adult speech as the child matures, thus providing implicit graded lessons to the child.[66] As important as this modeling undoubtedly is, it still does not explain the acquisition of the subtle verbal operants typical of an adult repertoire, for it does not specify any differentially reinforcing events. While Moerk's analysis showed that reinforcement is prevalent in parent-child interactions, he did not contradict Brown and Hanlon's finding that many grammatically deviant utterances are implicitly and explicitly reinforced as well.

How, then, do we account for the exquisite verbal repertoire of most adults? The answer appears to lie in a seemingly arbitrary characteristic of verbal behavior—the fact that, under typical conditions, it is vocal. In our view, this fact is crucial, not accidental. Auditory stimuli faithfully reach all listeners within earshot with only a small role played by the orientation of receptors. Gestures and signs, however, require that "listeners," or receivers, look at the "speaker," or the signer. Moreover, the pattern of visual stimuli will vary from one receiver to the next. That is, if I make the ASL sign for "work," it will appear slightly different to a person on my right than to a person on my left, and most importantly, it will appear different to me, the "speaker," for I see the gesture from the back, as it were. With vocal behavior, however, the speaker hears his own speech at least as faithfully and as quickly as any other listener.[67] As a consequence, one's own speech is not only a response, it is a stimulus, comparable, as a stimulus, to the speech of others.

Children become discriminating listeners long before they become fluent speakers. As evidence of this, note that they respond appropriately to utterances that are far more complex than those they produce. Furthermore, they can identify irregularities in their own speech as "errors" when those irregularities are mimicked by adults. This is particularly common in the case of phonological irregularities. If an adult says 'top for stop a child might object, even though the child himself pronounces the word that way. Furthermore, children who are initially unable to make the initial s sound in stop, stick, and so on, will often generalize to a wide variety of instances when they first become able to do so,[68] suggesting that their receptive repertoire preceded their productive repertoire.

The significance of these observations is that children (and other speakers) are given immediate feedback about the "correctness" of their speech. That is, the person-as-speaker is provided with differential reinforcement by the stimuli reaching the person-as-listener. We are not able to pronounce *Köhler* or *trompe l'oeil* like a native, and we know it. We "hear" that we have made a mistake even though we cannot, at the moment, say the word correctly. The child cannot say *Larry is very tall*, but may object when his father, imitating him, says, *Larry tall*. The frame *X—is very Y—*, with its particular temporal and prosodic properties, appears to be a perceptual unit in the child-as-listener, but not an intraverbal unit in the child-as-speaker.

Because each speaker is also a listener, verbal distinctions remain relatively sharp across cultures and from generation to generation. In a gestural language it is harder to maintain the same sharp distinctions. We must rely, in part, on feedback from others to know whether we are following the norms of the verbal community. With vocal behavior we do not need to be told. As Skinner pointed out:

> When a sound pattern has been associated with reinforcing events, it becomes a conditioned reinforcer. . . The young child alone in the nursery may automatically reinforce his own exploratory vocal behavior when he produces sounds which he has heard in the speech of others. The self-reinforcing property may be merely an intonation or some other idiosyncrasy of a given speaker or of speakers in general. . . The process is important in shaping up standard forms of response.[69]

Thus, while an occasional contingency of reinforcement may be arranged by parents, countless contingencies of reinforcement are implicit in the acts of speaking and hearing oneself speak. Moreover, the feedback is virtually instantaneous, as reinforcement must be if it is to be very effective. Consider, as an analogy, a boy learning to whistle. The boy is envious of his older brother who can whistle like a flute, but he purses his lips as if he were blowing out candles, and the only sound produced is a decidedly unmusical *Whoosh*. At length, accidentally perhaps, the boy relaxes his lips slightly and produces a tone, his first note. He is electrified! Nothing could be more reinforcing, and he quickly repeats his performance, slightly modifying the topography of his responses. Eventually, he too becomes an adept whistler. No one need stand by and nod approval. The reinforcement is immediate, powerful, automatic, and mediated entirely by repertoires of the boy-as-whistler and the boy-as-listener. We need not embroil ourselves in a controversy as to whether reinforcement can "really" be automatic or self-mediated. It is obvious that it can.

Children learning to speak are in a comparable position. They can recognize the cadence and unity of complex verbal operants but cannot produce them. If, eventually, they succeed in doing so, they need not be congratulated by well-meaning parents; the achievement itself is a powerful and much more immediate reinforcement.[70]

CONCLUSION

Many questions about verbal behavior remain unanswered, particularly those about the acquisition of some of the more subtle grammatical distinctions. However, we feel that selectionist principles are equal to the task, and if the task remains largely unfinished, it is perhaps because of its daunting complexity. Most of these obscure grammatical distinctions have been identified by linguists, to their credit, but linguists are usually committed to a formal analysis and have shown little interest in a selectionist account. On our side, we feel that the formal rules of the linguist do not in any sense provide an explanation of verbal behavior, for they cannot, so far as we can see, be translated into the coin of physical structures or stimulus and response classes, nor can they be reconciled with principles of selection, either phylogenetic or ontogenetic. The formal world of the linguist may be very pure and elegant, but it needs to be related, in detail, to human behavior and human structures before it can be considered as a candidate for an explanation of verbal behavior. Nevertheless, we must be grateful to the linguist for more clearly defining the task with which we are faced.

Skinner, a thoroughgoing selectionist, dedicated several chapters of Verbal Behavior to the problems of grammar and syntax. We feel that his analyses, so far as they go, are sound, but his work preceded most of modern linguistics, and he consequently did not address some of the puzzling questions that have since come to light. He did, however, provide a remarkable framework for the analysis of verbal behavior, and we have no doubt that the remaining problems will eventually yield to analyses within the paradigm that he created virtually single-handedly.

In our review of some of the problems in a selectionist account of verbal behavior, we have found little evidence for a modular view. It appears to us that verbal behavior is not a unitary phenomenon with well-defined principles unique to its domain; rather, it is behavior exquisitely sensitive to many different kinds of stimulus control, drawing on structures that evolved for other functions, and richly interconnected with nonverbal phenomena.

STUDY AIDS

Technical Terms

pharynx
larynx
Wernicke's area
kana symbols
kanji symbols
lexicon
phonemes
categorical perception
babbling
parallel transmission
verbal operant
grammatical frame
alexia
transcortical aphasia
tact
inflection
anomia
aphasias
function words
autoclitic
Broca's area
overregularization (overgeneralization)
universal grammar
language acquisition device

Text Questions

1. Identify physical structures unique to humans that appear to play an important role in verbal behavior.

2. Identify behavioral and perceptual features of humans that appear to play an important role in verbal behavior.

3. Cite evidence for and against the hypothesis that humans perceive speech sounds as we do because of speech-specific adaptations of our auditory system.

4. Cite evidence that human speech cannot be divided into a sequence of discrete responses like letters in a word. Does this mean that an analysis of response chains is unhelpful in understanding verbal behavior?

5. How does the verbal operant differ from traditional grammatical units such as words, phrases, or phonemes?

6. Comment on the following statement: To understand language, we must first analyze the structure or form of language. (To what extent can we understand behavior only by considering the topography of the behavior?)

7. Cite evidence from language acquisition in children that people follow rules when they speak. Does this mean that verbal behavior cannot be understood in terms of elementary selectionist principles?

8. The hypothesis that there is an innate language acquisition device appears to resolve many puzzling questions about the acquisition of a complex verbal repertoire. What are some of the difficulties that face such a proposal?

9. What advantages follow from the fact that language is typically vocal rather than gestural?

Discussion Questions

10. Some researchers hold that the signing repertoire of chimpanzees is not "true language." How would you decide if a repertoire is "truly" language? If you programmed a computer to generate acceptable sentences, would you conclude that it "had language"? Is the question worthwhile? Why or why not?

11. As a consequence of reinforcement, behavior tends to be repeated. If this is so, how can we explain novelty in human behavior, verbal or otherwise? Is the problem of the novelty of verbal behavior different from that of the novelty of nonverbal behavior?

12. The text suggests that learning to speak, like learning to whistle, is acquired partly through "automatic" reinforcement. What other skills might be acquired through automatic reinforcement? Do you think a pigeon or a rat can learn a response through automatic reinforcement? Why or why not?

ENDNOTES

1. See Chomsky, 1959, 1965, 1980, and elsewhere, for strong statements to this effect.

2. The reader who wishes a comprehensive account of verbal behavior from a selectionist perspective should read Skinner's *Verbal Behavior* (1957). Having heard that the book was scrutinized and caustically dismissed by Noam Chomsky in a 1959 review, most psychologists have chosen not to read it. Nevertheless, the review is seriously flawed, and the book remains a masterpiece of selectionist interpretation. We will not rehearse the debate here; the reader is referred to MacCorquodale, 1970 for a review of the review and to Palmer, 1986 for a critique of Chomsky's alternative proposals.

3. Lieberman, 1984.

4. Lieberman, 1967, 1984.

5. Lieberman, 1984. Lenneberg, 1967 points out that we can speak for hours without experiencing any discomfort from the modification of our normal respiration that speech requires. In contrast, other voluntary deviations from normal breathing usually quickly cause distress; e.g., breathing through a tube, voluntary panting, and (for the novice) playing a wind instrument.

6. Lieberman, 1973.

7. Hayes, 1951.

8. Gardner & Gardner, 1971, 1974, 1975.

9. Premack, 1976.

10. Savage-Rumbaugh, Rumbaugh, Smith, & Lawson, 1980.

11. Woodruff, Premack, & Kennel, 1978.

12. Peterson, Beecher, Zoloth, Moody, & Stebbins, 1978.

13. Kimura & Archibald, 1974.

14. Kimura, 1979.

15. Under these conditions, there may be a detectable loss in performance of those functions normally mediated by the right hemisphere relative to a normal adult.

16. Lewin, 1980.

17. Luria, 1970.

18. Cameron, Currier, & Haerer, 1971.

19. Luria, 1970.

20. Sasanuma, 1975.

21. Kolb & Whishaw, 1985.

22. Margolin & Carlson, 1982.

23. Kolb & Whishaw, 1985.

24. Margolin & Carlson, 1982.

25. Carlson, 1984.

26. Geschwind, Quadfasel, & Segarra, 1968.

27. Repp, Liberman, Eccardt, & Pesetsky, 1978; cited in Glass & Holyoak, 1986.

28. Rand, 1974.

29. Liberman, Harris, Hoffman, & Griffith, 1957.

30. For example, certain combinations of auditory stimuli might set up harmonics in the basilar membrane that would render the received stimulus qualitatively different from physically similar stimuli.

31. Pisoni & Lazarus, 1974.

32. E.g., Jusczyk, Rosner, Cutting, Foard, & Smith, 1977; Kopp & Lane, 1968; Pisoni, 1977.

33. Kuhl & Miller, 1975.

34. Blough, 1975.

35. MacDonald & McGurk, 1978; see also McGurk & MacDonald, 1976. We report here only one experimental condition as an illustration of their general findings.

36. Routh, 1969.

37. Liberman, Mattingly, & Turvey, 1972.

38. Liberman, Mattingly, & Turvey., 1972.

39. Foss & Hakes, 1978.

40. Warren, 1967.

41. Warren & Warren, 1970.

42. Jordan, 1986.

43. A frame is a verbal operant in which some components can vary. *Donate the money to the United Way* is an example of the frame *donate X— to Y—. X—* and *Y—* can vary in topography but must be uttered with certain temporal properties and a particular cadence.

44. Weimer, 1973.

45. Cited in Walter, 1982.

46. Skinner, 1957.

47. Skinner's term.

48. Kolb & Whishaw, 1985.

49. Kolb & Whishaw, 1985., p. 350.

50. Kolb & Whishaw, 1985, p. 352.

51. A conspicuous exception is the description of *private events*. Each person has unique access to stimuli originating within the skin. Since the verbal community must use indirect evidence to evaluate the extent of our pain, the depth of our despair, or the volume of our euphoria, a fine-grained repertoire is difficult to estab-

lish, and the language of emotion remains vague and metaphorical. Curiously, it is the inner world that we know the least. We will discuss this topic at greater length in Chapter 12.

52. Slobin, 1979.

53. Berko, 1958.

54. Braine, 1971; Ferguson & Slobin, 1973.

55. E.g., Ashcraft, 1989; Slobin 1979. The argument is buttressed with many more complicated examples but in these cases it is not clear exactly what the rules are. The characterization of the rules is informed by a particular theoretical commitment in linguistics. The overgeneralization examples are widely cited because they are relatively unambiguous.

56. The term *rule-governed behavior* has a restricted technical meaning in the operant literature—a repertoire of behavior under the control of verbal instructions or contingency-specifying stimuli. (See Chapter 5.) Here, we are concerned with all discriminated operant behavior. The role of rules in verbal behavior has been the focus of debate between traditional linguists and those who champion adaptive networks as a model of cognitive processes. Rumelhart and McClelland, 1986 showed that a relatively simple, two-layer network was able to learn by induction to form the correct past tense for many irregular and regular verbs and to generalize to novel cases with no explicit representation of the rules built into the network. They claim: "We have, we believe, provided a distinct alternative to the view that children learn rules of English past-tense formation in any explicit sense. We have shown that a reasonable account of the acquisition of past tense can be provided without recourse to the notion of a 'rule' as anything more than a description of the language." (p. 267) This interpretation was disputed by Pinker and Prince, 1988 who pointed out that there were many crucial differences between the behavior of the network and the behavior of children, that the network failed to capture important generalizations about English past tense formation, and that it could model rules not found in English or any other language. While Rumelhart and McClelland's network was undoubtedly a poor model of a child learning English, it illustrates the important point that a system that can be described by rules need not use the rules to generate orderly behavior. The rules can be in the contingencies, not in the mechanism.

57. Skinner, 1957; pp. 81–146.

58. Skinner, 1957, p. 121.

59. Maratsos, 1983.

60. Skinner, 1957; p. 121–122.

61. See Palmer, 1986, for a more detailed exposition of these points and other difficulties with the nativist position.

62. See Stemmer, 1990, for a good example of such an interpretation. Stemmer discusses, among other things, the role of relational terms in accounting for our sensitivity to grammatical structures. In our terminology, a relational term is an example of a fixed element of a grammatical frame. For example, the word *holds* in the frame *X— holds Y—* specifies the relation between *X—* and *Y—*.

63. Owing to the importance of historical variables and the practical and ethical constraints on working with people, we must usually be content with merely providing plausible interpretations of verbal phenomena. An experimental analysis is usually out of the question. Perhaps as a result, most examples in the literature of puzzling syntactical constructions are hypothetical. When posing a grammatical conundrum, it is standard practice to provide a textual stimulus as the datum to be explained. For example, the following widely-cited sentence is said to be ambiguous:

The shooting of the hunters was awful.

However, our task is to explain verbal behavior, not a carefully constructed arrangement of symbols. If someone actually said such a thing we must know who said it, under what conditions, and with what history. (A glance at the guiding variables of the utterance would dispel any ambiguity.) Textbook examples are usually offered *as if* they were examples of spontaneous verbal behavior; however, they are usually hackneyed examples from the literature or are carefully crafted by the writer to illustrate some grammatical construction. It is an easy task to explain the behavior of the textbook writer, but to "explain" the behavior of a hypothetical speaker is more formidable. Our discussion of such examples can never be more than an interpretation; since the example was invented, the guiding variables must be invented as well.

64. Brown & Hanlon, 1970.

65. Moerk, 1983, 1990.

66. Snow, 1972; Snow & Ferguson, 1977.

67. Under unusual circumstances, as when the speaker is listening to music with earphones, the speaker experiences unique auditory input, and may not hear his own words as clearly as do other listeners. Conversation is difficult and sometimes comical under these conditions.

68. Smith, 1973.

69. Skinner, 1957, p. 58.

70. See Vaughan & Michael, 1982, for a discussion of automatic reinforcement and Sundberg, 1980, for relevant empirical study. Sundberg found that establishing a word as a conditioned reinforcer by pairing it with a strong reinforcer increased the rate at which the word was uttered by a toddler.

CHAPTER 12

REMEMBERING

In the Humphrey Bogart film *Casablanca,* the cynical hero feels a rush of powerful emotions on hearing a few chords of a song—a song last heard years before, when he was passionately in love with a beautiful woman. In Proust's *Remembrance of Things Past,* the contemplative narrator is brought back vividly to scenes of his childhood by the taste of a tea-cake—a special treat of his youth. We have all had similar experiences; a particular stimulus or complex of stimuli—a whiff of talcum powder, an old Beatles song, a voice on the phone, a glimpsed face in the crowd—evokes a strong feeling or a vivid reminiscence of long ago. These are dramatic instances of a commonplace phenomenon. Every day we have countless similar but less striking experiences as we respond to the myriad sights, sounds, and smells with which we are bombarded. The stimulus *reminds us* of an event, an action, or an emotion. As we noted in Chapter 8, memory phenomena of this sort exemplify the discriminative and eliciting function of stimuli. The selecting effect of our experiences alters environment-behavior relations so that future environments are likely to evoke feelings, images, and tendencies to behave in particular ways.

When an experience alters an environment-behavior relation we speak of learning, and when we see evidence that the new relation endures over time, we speak of memory. When used in this sense, memory does not imply a special process or activity; learning and memory are just different aspects of a single biobehavioral phenomenon: the changes brought about by the three-term contingency of environment, behavior, and reinforcer.

When we speak of *remembering,* however, something more is implied. When a stimulus *reminds* us of something, we are passive; feelings,

thoughts, images, and actions come to us unbidden. Remembering something, however, suggests activity. When we see an acquaintance, we falter as we struggle to remember her name. As she approaches, we feverishly run through the alphabet, or recite the names of mutual friends, or rehearse our previous encounters. When we finally blurt out her name, we are responding not just to the sight of our friend, but to our own attempts to recall her name. We use the term remembering for those memory phenomena that comprise not just a single discriminated operant occasioned by its discriminative stimulus, but a complex series of environmental and behavioral events whose combined effect is to occasion the response. In explaining the occurrence of a discriminated operant, it is enough to refer to the three-term contingencies that established the response class. In accounting for an instance of remembering, however, we must explain the interaction of many variables that, in all likelihood, have never occurred together before.

In some cases of remembering—as in the example of our approaching friend—a discriminative stimulus is present that, for some reason, is insufficient to evoke its corresponding discriminated response. When we toil through a final exam in zoology we find that facts that came easily the night before somehow elude us now, even though the nominal discriminative stimuli may be the same. Often it takes hard work to "make the responses come back." Here our task is to determine the role of those activities that supplement the discriminative stimuli.

Other examples are even more mysterious; there appears to be no relevant discriminative stimulus at all: When a friend asks us "What did you do last night?" we cannot explain our response,

"Studied zoology," by referring to a particular three-term contingency in our past. It is unlikely that that response has been reinforced in the presence of that question before. To insist that "Studied zoology" is simply a discriminated operant makes it difficult to explain why the very same question, posed a few days later but under otherwise identical conditions, might occasion the response "I rented a video." Clearly, the question is not a sufficient controlling variable. The experience itself—renting a video—appears to play a crucial role. In fact, it doesn't seem to matter *what* we did last night; whatever it was, we will remember today and respond appropriately. While this is an everyday phenomenon, it is also a remarkable performance that requires a special explanation.

We may be inclined to suppose that the past event itself functions as a discriminative stimulus determining our behavior; our earlier experience appears to act at a distance—a temporal distance—reaching forward in time to guide our behavior today. Many people find this notion no stranger than that of gravity—action at a physical distance—a concept that liberated Renaissance scientists from the billiard-ball mechanics of the ancients. However, the analogy is poor. There is no lawful relationship between past events and current performance on a memory task: The past is fixed, and current behavior is variable. Sometimes we speak of the past, and sometimes we don't; sometimes we remember clearly and sometimes vaguely; sometimes we think we remember clearly, only to have events prove us to be mistaken. We cannot appeal to the immutable past to explain our quixotic behavior, for there is no functional relationship between the two. Our task is to explain current behavior as a function of *current* variables. It is here that the laws of behavior, discovered and developed in the laboratory, can be invoked to explain our actions. Since such accounts are necessarily examples of interpretation rather than experimental analysis, it would perhaps be well to remind ourselves of this important distinction.

THE ROLE OF INTERPRETATION IN THE ANALYSIS OF REMEMBERING

As we noted in Chapters 1 and 4, the principles of behavior on which our interpretations rest have arisen from experimental analyses of behavior, from tightly controlled studies of empirically defined, replicable units of behavior. When we try to account for behavior outside the laboratory *solely in terms of the principles derived from an experimental analysis*, we are engaged in interpretation. To the extent that these principles prove insufficient and we are driven to invent supplementary principles, we are engaged merely in speculation. The interpretation of phenomena outside of the laboratory is a part of the scientific enterprise; speculation may suggest lines of inquiry, but it should not be confused with interpretation, as it is not constrained by empirically derived principles. We are often interested in explaining examples of remembering in our everyday lives for which we have no experimental data. In fact, we may have almost no data at all. Usually, methodological and ethical constraints prevent our acquiring sufficient control over our subjects to provide a cogent experimental analysis; under these conditions the best we can do is provide an interpretation.

Some behavioral phenomena are closely analogous to experimental preparations that have been analyzed in detail. When a friend responds "64" to the question "What is eight times eight?" it is easy to see the relevance of a pigeon pecking a disk in the presence of a green light. It seems clear that "64" is a discriminated operant, presumably acquired in elementary school when that response, and no other, was reinforced in the presence of the question. In fact, the analogy is so close that we are apt to forget that our explanation is an interpretation. We have done no analysis; we have merely provided, after the fact, a plausible explanation for a behavior. For all we know, our friend may never have learned the multiplication tables at all, but has learned to add in his head very rapidly. With more complex examples of behavior, it is even more evident that our account must be interpretive.

Of course few, if any, topics in psychology have been the subject of more experimentation than memory. However, owing to methodological difficulties, few experiments have yielded the kind of data necessary to support the molecular analyses that we favor. In our view, we understand behavior to the extent that we can account for it moment-to-moment in time. Much can happen in a second or two: Even the simplest experimental preparations must be interpreted with care. Let us consider two elementary kinds of experiment that we introduced in Chapter 8: Short-term memory procedures and paired-associate procedures. We will see that a moment-to-moment account of a subject's behavior in such experiments must be highly interpretive.

Short-Term Memory Procedures

You will perhaps recall from Chapter 8 the typical procedure for studying short-term memory: A visual stimulus—perhaps three letters, such as MVK—is presented briefly. Immediately thereafter, the subject hears a number, say 384, and is required to count backwards by 3's, a task designed to prevent rehearsal. After an interval that varies from trial to trial, the subject is signaled to recall the letters. Under these conditions a subject can typically recall the letters correctly after delays of only a few seconds, with performance at 18 seconds no better than chance.[1] (See **Figure 12.1**.)

Can performance in this procedure be explained in terms of a three-term contingency? Clearly not. One term—the stimulus—was presented once. No response was reinforced in its presence, and it was not presented at the time of recall. Of course, accurate performance at any retention interval depends on three-term contingencies in the subject's past; if the stimulus were a complex, unfamiliar hieroglyphic, subjects would be unable to reproduce it at all. Our ability to simply recognize the stimulus reveals the enduring effects of earlier conditioning.

However, the task was not designed to test the endurance of past conditioning; it attempts, rather,

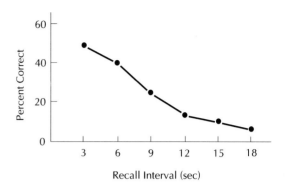

FIGURE 12.1 The relative frequency with which an item was recalled in a short-term memory procedure declined rapidly after a few seconds if rehearsal of the item was prevented.
Note: See also Peterson & Peterson, 1959.

to measure the declining influence of a given stimulus over time. It asks how long a discriminative stimulus can continue to evoke a response without rehearsal, an activity which we can think of as presenting the stimulus over and over again. Answering this question could be an important contribution, analogous to determining the effect of the interstimulus interval in classical conditioning procedures. However, when we examine the procedure moment-to-moment in time, we see that the stimulus and response units are not as simple as they seem.

First, note what it means that the stimulus is *not* an unfamiliar hieroglyphic. When the stimulus is presented, the subject *responds* to it; (at least, the probability of a response increases). That's what we mean when we say that a stimulus is familiar. Most of us, for example, would *read* the letters; that is, we would say the letters to ourselves. The letters might evoke conditioned perceptual behavior. If the stimulus were CVT we might find ourselves visualizing a cat or "feeling" a cut. Someone gifted in sign language might make incipient or even complete signs in response to the stimulus. The subject is next presented with an auditory stimulus (a number) and responds to *that*. Presumably he then complies with the experimenter's request to count backward by threes, a complex performance that requires a particular kind of educational history, problem-solving skills, and a history of interpreting and following arbitrary verbal requests. Finally, a recall signal is given.

The performance of a subject at this point is influenced at least as much by the host of intervening events as by the nominal stimulus. Many questions confront us. Why should the nominal stimulus exert any control at all? When we glance at a set of random letters on a piece of paper, we do not spontaneously say them 15 seconds later. What is the role of the recall signal, and how does it empower the nominal stimulus to exert its effects at this time? It is clear that we are confronted, not with a single stimulus and response class, but with a very complex sequence of interacting events that evoke successful performance, if at all, partly because of unanalyzed experiences in the subject's past and during the retention interval.

As an illustration of the complexity of the procedure, consider the errors that subjects commonly make in the short-term memory task. As we noted in Chapter 7, subjects often erroneously report letters that rhyme with the target letters, but they seldom erroneously report letters that are visually similar. For example, when the target letter is B, subjects are more likely to report having seen a V than an R. This finding confirms that the final performance is affected, at least in part, by the subject's own response to the stimulus, and not just by the nominal physical stimulus itself. Performance in this task depends partly on unspecified events in the retention interval. Note that our hypothetical sign-language expert might perform flawlessly, even after a prolonged retention interval, if he were to maintain his hands in position throughout the distractor task. In any case, we would expect the proprioceptive feedback from signing to be different from that of subvocal speech, with different implications for recall performance. Indeed, Bellugi, Klima, and Siple[2] found that errors made by deaf subjects in a memory task reflect confusions of signing; those deaf subjects who had learned to speak often made errors in letters that are articulated similarly.

We will not attempt to analyze further the variables that influence uttering the correct letters at the time of the recall signal. Because there are so many interacting variables during the retention interval, we believe that every instance of remembering in the short-term memory procedure requires its own interpretation.

Paired-Associate Memory Procedures

A second experimental paradigm we introduced in Chapter 8 is the paired-associate memory task. A subject is presented with pairs of stimuli—perhaps two nonsense syllables, two unrelated words, or combinations of nonsense syllables and words. The stimuli are usually presented sequentially. When the first stimulus is presented, the subject is required to respond with the second. After the subject responds, the second stimulus is presented to confirm or correct his response. For example, when the nonsense syllable *PEM* is presented, the correct response might be *big*. Performance on tasks of this sort has been used to evaluate how retention is affected by prior learning tasks (proactive interference), subsequent learning tasks (retroactive interference), the meaningfulness of stimuli, and many other variables.

At first glance, it appears that performance on this task can be understood entirely in terms of the three-term contingency. In the presence of *PEM* we say the word *big*, and then the written word *BIG* is presented to us; this appears to be analogous to a rat pressing a lever in the presence of a 1000 Hz tone and having a pellet of food roll into a tray: There is a well defined stimulus and a well defined response; when the response occurs in the presence of the stimulus it is reinforced. For the human subject, the reinforcement is simply seeing that the response is correct when the answer is revealed.

However, when we examine the contingency critically, we see that a much more complex interpretation is required. Let us consider the elements of the contingency in turn. The stimulus, we assume, is *PEM*. Is it a neutral stimulus, or does it serve discriminative functions? Is it a unitary stimulus—a member of a well defined stimulus class—or is it a complex stimulus composed of smaller units? Already we have run into difficulty with our analysis. Clearly it is not a neutral stimulus. We *read* the stimulus, either as a syllable or as three separate letters. In the terminology of Chapters 10 and 11, the stimulus is a textual stimulus controlling textual, or reading, responses. The stimulus is not neutral, but whether it serves as a single stimulus or three stimuli surely varies from subject to subject.[3]

Let us now consider the "response." On the first trial, when the second stimulus, *BIG*, appears, we emit a second textual response, either overtly or covertly. Our response, *big*, is not a response to the first stimulus, *PEM*; it is a response to the stimulus *BIG*. So far, our experiment consists of two separate textual operants. This baseline performance is clearly different from the case of the rat pressing a lever in the presence of a tone. Before the first reinforcer, a rat will usually press the lever at a measurable rate, and, if it does not, the experimenter can shape leverpressing by reinforcing successive approximations to the response. However, the baseline probability of saying *big* in the presence of *PEM* is negligible. But the memory experimenter, unlike his colleagues in the animal laboratory, does not shape the response; rather, he simply presents a textual stimulus that already occasions the response, as represented in **Figure 12.2**.

On later trials, when *PEM* is presented, we again read it (we emit the textual response *pem*). If training has been successful, we then respond *big* shortly after the stimulus *PEM* appears; *big* is an intraverbal response, guided either by the written stimulus *PEM*, or by our textual response, *pem*. Finally, when the stimulus *BIG* appears, we emit the textual response *big*. (See **Figure 12.3**.)

What, precisely, is the reinforcer? The stimulus *BIG* is not the reinforcer; nothing in the experiment has established it as such. Rather, reinforcement consists of the formal similarity of our textual

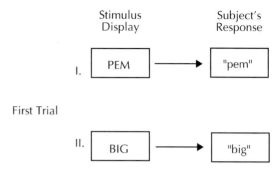

FIGURE 12.2 *On the first trial of a paired-associate procedure the subject is presented sequentially with two textual stimuli, the first of which will serve as the nominal stimulus in later trials*
Both stimuli occasion textual responses, the second of which has the *same form* as the required response in subsequent trials.

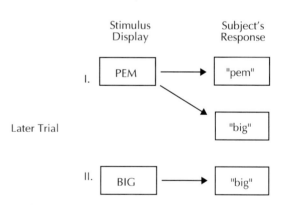

FIGURE 12.3 *On later trials of a paired-associate task two textual stimuli are presented again*
The first, the nominal stimulus, occasions a textual response (usually covert); the stimulus and its textual response together occasion the target response "big." Finally, the second textual stimulus is presented, controlling its corresponding textual response, "big." Reinforcement consists of the formal similarity of the two responses of the subject. The paired-associate procedure entails the acquisition of a discriminated operant—it does not illuminate or even illustrate recall procedures.

response, *big*, to our intraverbal response, *big*. That this similarity serves a reinforcing function depends on a certain kind of history. Most educated people have had long practice in having their "answers" confirmed or refuted under similar circumstances.

The above interpretation of the elements of the two trials is plausible; it appears to explain how correct performance in such an experiment could be maintained. However, it does not explain how correct performance was ever acquired. Our diagrams do not illustrate the *acquisition* of an environment-behavior relation, they illustrate the *transfer* of such a relation. Nothing in our first diagram suggests that correct performance will occur on the second or later trials. In fact, we would expect the stimulus *BIG* to block control of the response *big* by other stimuli; we would not expect control to transfer to *PEM*.

In the laboratory, when we want to transfer control from one stimulus to another, we use a fading procedure. We gradually reduce the intensity of the controlling stimulus and make the stimulus to be conditioned more conspicuous. Presumably something of the kind is occurring here. Most people have learned to use informal fading procedures to learn facts in school or to memorize such things as telephone numbers, poetry, or grocery lists. First we read the item slowly, emphasizing important terms; then we skim, then glance, then shut our eyes, and so on, gradually reducing our exposure to the nominal discriminative stimulus. It is apparent that successful performance on a paired-associate learning task depends on such techniques; thus, even in this apparently simple case, we can only understand performance by considering the history of our subjects. Current performance is a function, not just of a nominal discriminative stimulus, but of the subject's own behavior.

Experimental evidence: The generation effect.

The importance of the relationship between the operant emitted during training and the operant scheduled for reinforcement during testing is dem-

onstrated in a study by Slamecka and Graf.[4] Subjects in the experimental group "generated" appropriate responses after being given a rule (e.g., "synonym"), a stimulus word (e.g., *RAPID*), and the initial letter (e.g., *f*) of a word that is related to the stimulus word by the rule. Control subjects were simply given the stimulus and response words (e.g., *RAPID-FAST*). In cued (stimulus word provided) and uncued tests of recall and recognition, the experimental group performed significantly better than the control group, a phenomenon dubbed the **generation effect**.

These results are consistent with the foregoing analysis. For the experimental group the response was at least partly under the direct control of the stimulus word (e.g., *RAPID*), while for the control group the response was presumably principally controlled by the textual stimulus (e.g., *FAST*). Only for the experimental group were the testing conditions similar to the acquisition conditions.

The curious results of an experiment by Tulving and Thomson[5] can be interpreted in the same light. They found that under some conditions subjects will *recall* items that they will not *recognize* as members of a learned list. Subjects first learned responses to weakly associated stimulus words (e.g., *LADY-queen*). Next they were asked to generate several associates of various common words. For example, a subject presented with *KING* might generate *queen, castle, knight,* and *servant.* In the recognition task, they were asked to scan their list of generated responses and identify any they had encountered in the paired-associate task—in this case *queen* would be correct. Finally, they were presented with the stimulus words of the paired-associate task (e.g., *LADY*) and tested for recall of the response items. In many cases, subjects would fail to recognize that some of the words they had generated had been presented in the earlier condition; however, when prompted with the stimulus word, they would recall the correct response. These results seem strange until we consider that a response of a particular topography may be a member of different response classes, depending on the controlling variables. In this case, the textual response *queen* is different from the intraverbal response *queen*.

The foregoing examples illustrate that even apparently simple examples of human behavior may require complex behavioral interpretations. The tools of our interpretations—the units of analysis and the basic principles—require that we scrutinize examples in fine detail, moment-to-moment in time. We will attempt the same kind of fine-grained analysis of complex examples. We return now to examples of behavior in which a sufficient discriminative stimulus appears to be missing.

MEMORY AS PROBLEM SOLVING

As we noted above, the ease with which we answer a question about our past is difficult to explain. We can assume that the question "What is the capital of Pennsylvania?" is a discriminative stimulus (or complex of discriminative stimuli) that most students have encountered in school or at home, and a correct response to the question at a later time can be understood as the enduring effect of a three-term contingency. However, we can respond correctly to questions about our past that we have never heard before, e.g., "Where were you on the evening of March 12, 1993?" We also respond differently at different times to the same question, e.g., "What did you do last night?" Our answers to such questions cannot be attributed to a single contingency. Rather, they are examples of *problem solving*.

In Chapter 10 we defined a problem as a situation in which three conditions obtain:

1. A target response (or sequence of responses) is in our repertoire; that is, there are some conditions under which a response of the required topography will occur.

2. There are contextual discriminative stimuli present indicating that the target response is currently scheduled for reinforcement.

3. Current discriminative stimuli do not occasion the response directly. More precisely, the target response is not stronger than competing

responses at this time. Often, current variables alter the probability of the response, but not enough for it to be emitted. In network terms, an output unit may be stimulated by other units without reaching its threshold of activation. There may be inhibitory inputs from competing responses, or the excitatory input may not be sufficient for the unit to fire.

It is easy to see how math problems, mechanical problems, logical problems, etc., fall under this definition; it may be less obvious that answering questions about the past and other instances of remembering are also examples of problem solving.

Suppose that a friend asks "What was the last novel you have read?" and suppose further that the last novel you read was *A Tale of Two Cities*. Clearly the utterance "A Tale of Two Cities" is in your repertoire. If the book were in your hand, you could read the title as a sequence of textual responses. If the book had a distinctive cover, you could no doubt emit the title as a tact—a single response occasioned by the physical properties of the book. If someone were to mutter "It was the best of times, it was the worst of times," you might respond, or be inclined to respond, "A Tale of Two Cities!" as an intraverbal response.

Second, the question signals a subtle social contingency: If you say the name of the novel, your friend will behave in a way that is slightly to your advantage, e.g., he will stop repeating the question, he might leave you alone, he might show an interest in your reading habits, he might be impressed with your erudition, and so on. Thus, uttering the target response is scheduled for reinforcement. Like most such questions about your past, the contingency is weak; your friend probably has no independent knowledge of the answer, and you can get away with saying almost anything. Indeed, if the last book you read was a trashy novel from a supermarket display, you are likely to "skip over it" and report a book that is more likely to impress. This hints at a subtle difference between most formal problems (math problems, logical problems, and so on) and remembering. Most formal problems have solutions that can be verified by others; but everyone is uniquely intimate with his or her own past, and reinforcement will usually follow a variety of responses. It is not uncommon for people to "remember" their past in a flattering light, or even to lie outright about their exploits. We will return to this point below in a discussion about whether memories are "real."

The third and final characteristic of a problem is that the response is not directly evoked by the current constellation of stimuli. The question about our last novel does not directly occasion the response "A Tale of Two Cities," as these two events have never occurred together in a three-term contingency. (If the same question is repeated somewhat later, we would not regard it as a problem—you have already responded to the question once and been reinforced for it.) Thus, you are faced with a problem when your friend asks you a question about the last novel you have read; in fact, you would be faced with a problem if you were asked any new question about your past.

Since remembering is a special case of problem solving, our interpretation will draw heavily from that of Chapter 10. However, an analysis of remembering entails special difficulties; each example is idiosyncratic, much relevant behavior is usually covert, and corroboration and evaluation of performance is often impossible. Thus, remembering deserves special analysis.

Recall Procedures: The Role of Supplementary Stimuli

As with problem solving in general, remembering is a process of marshaling supplementary stimuli to augment the effects of the current context so that the target response becomes stronger than competing responses. We can do so in various ways. We might manipulate our relationship to the external environment—we can consult a grocery list while shopping, or look in the dictionary for the correct spelling of a word, or scan the tool room for a misplaced screwdriver. We can engage in covert or overt behavior that directly alters the probability of later behavior—we might imagine what our house

looks like, or recite our schedule, or repeat the sounds of the alphabet to prompt a forgotten name. We will refer to all such activity as **mnemonic behavior**. Although the term *strategy* is widely used in the memory literature, in our view it connotes awareness and deliberation, and is consequently too narrow to encompass all mnemonic behavior.

At any moment we are bombarded with countless stimuli, many of which have both conditioned and unconditioned effects. That is, owing to the contingencies of natural selection and reinforcement, these stimuli affect us in many ways. If every stimulus served every eliciting and discriminitive function possible given our ontogenetic and phylogenetic history, our behavior would be chaotic. In fact, our behavior tends to be organized, fluid, and systematic. In every response system, one response or set of responses tends to be prepotent and is emitted smoothly, without interference from competing responses. There are exceptions, of course; sometimes we falter, stumble, stop, start, and retract, a performance that suggests strong competing contingencies. But these are exceptions that prove the rule—ordinarily our behavior seems to be guided by dominant contingencies. However, the fact that we do not emit a response in a particular context—because a competing response is prepotent—does not mean that the response has no strength in that context. As we saw in the discussion of priming in Chapter 9, a stimulus will strengthen a number of responses, an outcome that can be demonstrated with a priming procedure. When we hear or read the word "straw," the incompatible responses "hay" and "sip"—and other responses, we must assume—will both be strengthened. Note that when we hear the word "straw" we seldom actually say "hay" or "sip." The effect only appears in such measures of strength as the shorter time it takes to identify the word when it is presented.

Thus, one implication of the priming literature is that when we have a rich history with respect to a stimulus—as we do with most everyday words, objects, and events in our lives—the presentation of that stimulus will alter the probability of a wide variety of responses. A second implication is that the strengthening effect of stimuli is additive; that is, if two stimuli separately increase the probability of a response, the two stimuli together increase the probability to a greater extent.[6] This follows from the priming effect in which a measure of response strength, such as speed, is increased when two stimuli are presented (the priming stimulus and the target stimulus). A third implication is that priming effects follow our own covert behavior. Recall from Chapter 9 that some priming effects (e.g., *lion-stripes*) were interpreted as the outcome of mediating covert responses (e.g., *lion—tiger—stripes*).

Remembering is a problem-solving activity that takes advantage of the three effects illustrated by priming studies. First, the nominal discriminative stimuli—e.g., "What was the last novel you have read?"—are not sufficient to occasion the target response, but that does not mean that the stimuli are neutral. Each stimulus element of the question alters the probability of a wide variety of responses. As we noted in Chapter 11, verbal units do not necessarily correspond to words or sentences. A question of this sort might consist of several intraverbal units such as the frames "What was the last X—?" "X— you have Y—" or tacts such as "novel" or perhaps "last novel." We are not in a position to assert what the units are, particularly in a hypothetical example, for units of analysis depend on the particular history of our subjects. However, we can assume that "novel" primes a wide variety of responses, including, perhaps, "A Tale of Two Cities."

As the target response has not been emitted, it is necessary to provide supplementary stimulation, either directly through reafference from covert behavior, from the environmental effects of overt behavior, or from the proprioceptive and exteroceptive stimulation arising from overt behavior. You may, for example, look at your bookcase and scan the titles. If your bookcase is not in view, you may visualize it and covertly scan, i.e., visualize book by book. You may imagine standing at the checkout desk of the library, or opening a wrapped book, or standing at a supermarket or bookstore display. You may recite favorite authors and titles. If you always read in bed, or in an easy chair, or on the bus, you may imagine yourself in your favorite pose, book in hand. You may review facts about your schedule; e.g., "The only time I ever have a chance to read is during vacations. Our last vacation was spring break." The effect of each of these responses is to provide supplementary stimulation that primes relevant responses, including, presumably, the target response. The cumulative effect is to strengthen a class of responses corresponding to book titles or book-related behavior more than competing responses. Eventually the target response itself becomes the prepotent response, and you emit it as the answer to the question.

Note that there is nothing inevitable about your responding with the correct answer. Your technique may strengthen "Wuthering Heights" more than "A Tale of Two Cities." In the case of a math problem, there are codified techniques for providing supplementary stimuli; in an addition problem, for example, we break the problem into smaller parts, systematically modifying the problem until we can read the answer as a textual response. In remembering, however, few people employ codified mnemonic strategies; consequently there is presumably much variability in performance from person to person, and "correct" performance is by no means guaranteed. Nevertheless, some procedures for providing supplementary stimulation seem widespread, and we are often successful.

Many questions about our past require us to report the events of a particular day. If someone asks us "Where were you the night before last? I called, but nobody was home," we are apt to recite the days of the week backward until we arrive at the correct day. If today is Wednesday, we might begin by saying "Wednesday . . . Tuesday . . . Monday . . . The day before yesterday was Monday." In many cultures people often have regular schedules, and stating the day of the week will usually prime relevant responses. For example, "Let's see, Mondays I go to school late . . . then I have a lab in the afternoon . . . it lasts until 4:30 . . . Last Monday I walked back home with Al . . . then we went out for corn dogs." This example illustrates how successive responses prime progressively narrower ranges of responses. Citing the day of the week enables us to identify an activity we typically engage in on that day. This may be enough to remind us of a particular event, perhaps as a conditioned perception (see Chapters 7 and 8). That event, in turn, may prime relevant responses.

Another widespread strategy when we are trying to remember a name, a title, a place, or just a word is to go through the alphabet, "trying out" each sound to see if it triggers the correct response. When we see our acquaintance approaching us, we struggle to remember her name. Her physical appearance is an important variable that we might expect to *remind* us of her name, but for some reason it is insufficient, perhaps because competing responses are strong, or because contextual variables are different from those in which we first learned her name, or perhaps because we never learned her name as a response to her physical appearance to begin with. (Our learning of names is often echoic behavior under the control of prior verbal stimuli: "Dave, I'd like you to meet my friend, Sandra." "Hello, Sandra. Pleased to meet you." A few seconds later—after the echoic stimulus has receded in time—we have no idea what Sandra's name is, and we have to resort to devious and embarrassing circumlocutions.) In this case, her appearance does have an effect on us; we see her as familiar, and we might feel that her name is "on the tip of our tongue." Going through the alphabet provides a second source of control that supplements the physical cues.[7]

Reminiscences

Conditioned perceptions play an important role in our interpretation of remembering. When we are asked about the events of a particular day, we must engage in various mnemonic procedures such as reciting the days of the week, recounting our schedules, and so on. However, such procedures do not seem adequate to explain the subjective impression that we are reliving the original experience. We are likely to feel that our memories are more complex than simply emitting a target response, for the target response does not capture the rich detail of our experience of remembering something. The responses we emit to provide supplementary stimulation do more than prime the target response; often the constellation of stimuli occasions a conditioned perception. We *see* (and perhaps hear, touch, taste, etc.) as we saw in the past. We may *see* the lab on Monday afternoon at 4:30. This conditioned perception provides optimal stimulation to prime conditioned perceptions of later events. Often there is a cascade of conditioned perceptions which we call a reminiscence. It is these conditioned perceptions that provide the unmistakable feeling that we are reliving our experiences.

Conditioned perceptual behavior is usually weak, perhaps because it is ordinarily incompatible with the perceptual behavior guided by current stimulation. To facilitate conditioned perceptions, it is often necessary to reduce the unconditioned effects of current stimulation. When trying hard to remember something we are likely to try to block out stimuli by shutting our eyes, stopping up our ears, looking at the ceiling, unfocusing our eyes, commanding our friends to stop talking for a minute, turning away from the task at hand, and so on.

It follows from this account that the perceptual behavior we experience in a reminiscence must have been conditioned at the time of the original event. Seeing the book *A Tale of Two Cities* was conditioned to contextual events; recalling the context later in a recall strategy evokes the conditioned perception. This suggests that perceptual behavior is continually being conditioned. It is absurd to suppose that the only perceptions conditioned are those that are likely to be useful in future recall strategies. On the other hand, not all conditioned perceptions are genuine; that is, we can imagine experiences that never happened, and we sometimes find ourselves remembering events vividly only to find out later that we were mistaken.

The fact that our reminiscences are sometimes mistaken underscores that conditioned perceptions are *current* perceptual responses under the control of a constellation of *current* variables. They are not past experiences that have been stored. We engage in the behavior anew. It may be true that the conditioned perceptions we experience today are similar, in some sense, to the perceptual responses we engaged in yesterday, but they are evoked by variables in our present environment and thus have the same status as all of our other behavior. When we relive our past, our behavior is no less real than it was in the past.

Sometimes we seem to remember incorrectly. ("I'm positive you told me to meet you here at three o'clock!" "No! I said four!") However, our behavior is never a mistake. A reminiscence may be different in some way from our behavior at an earlier time, but it is not an error. Current variables are different from past variables, and our behavior is an inexorable outcome of these current variables. It is not remarkable that our behavior is different; that is what we would expect. What is remarkable is that our behavior of remembering so often results in behavior that would have been appropriate to past variables as well. The fact that we are so often "right" is all the more surprising when we consider that the general context in which we remember is often quite different from the context of our original experiences. Most adults have become skilled mnemonists, able to quickly and effortlessly supply themselves with the supplementary stimuli necessary to occasion appropriate target responses under a great variety of circumstances.

Recognition of the Target Response

We have argued that remembering is a special case of problem solving, that when faced with a contingency that requires us to behave with respect to stimuli or events no longer present, we engage in mnemonic activities that supplement current stimuli. Thus, in the stream of behavior, an instance of remembering is commonly well defined. It begins with discriminative stimuli signaling such a contingency—perhaps someone asks us the name of a mutual acquaintance—and terminates with the target response—we reply that his name is Ed Kotski. The target response may follow the initial discriminative stimuli almost immediately or after a prolonged period of mnemonic behavior. When the mnemonic activity is covert, we are likely to be relatively inactive; in order to reduce the probability of competing behavior we tend to stop conversing, to orient away from objects of interest, to gaze fixedly at the wall or sky, and so on. Thus the target response serves a special role in terminating mnemonic activity and satisfying the initial contingency.

While the target response serves this special role, and is therefore distinctive to an observer of our behavior, it is not clear how it affects *us* the way it does. How does it serve to alter the cast of our behavior, to terminate mnemonic responses, to reorient us to ongoing activities, to free our fixed gaze? We recognize the target response as such, and we emit it with special emphasis. How do we do so?

It may be difficult to appreciate that this is a formidable question: When we remember something, it is obvious to us. But why is it obvious? What distinguishes the target response from all of the other responses in the stream of behavior? Once again, it may be helpful to consider other examples of problem solving. For arithmetic problems for which we have learned codified procedures, the answer is known by its ordinal and physical relationship to other responses. For example, when we add large numbers with a pencil and paper, we can read the answer as a textual response to the bottom row of numbers after we have summed the leftmost column of digits. There is nothing distinctive about the target response—indeed, our answer may well be wrong. It is only because we have learned a procedure that we are able to emit the response "as the answer."

What are the analogous properties of the "correct" response in remembering? We should note, at the outset, that we sometimes fail to recognize the target response even after we emit it. "Was his name Ed? . . . Or Ted? . . . Let's see, Ed . . . Ted . . . Ned . . . Todd?" Under such conditions, we continue to emit mnemonic responses; the target response does not bring about the changes in behavior characteristic of successful recall. On other occasions we confidently assert an answer and terminate mnemonic behavior, only to find that we are wrong. Clearly there is no necessary and sufficient property distinctive of target responses.

Ordinarily the target response is reinforced, signaling that the contingency has been met. If our friend responds, "That's it! Ed . . . Ed Kotski," we will not engage in further mnemonic activity. But often we are aware at the time we emit our response that it is correct—we utter it with special force, and feel a release of tension or a sense of confident satisfaction before the nominal reinforcer can be delivered. There are variables, then, that affect how we emit the target response and whether we recognize it as "correct."

First, we can often discriminate the strength of our response with respect to its controlling variables. We know when a response is tentative, when it is forceful, when it is "on the tip of our tongue," and so on. We can even say that we were "on the point of saying something" when we were interrupted. Measures of latency and amplitude—and their covert accompaniments—are available to us as discriminative stimuli. The target response will typically be primed slightly by the initial discriminative stimulus (e.g., the question) as well as by many of the mnemonic responses. Speaking loosely, the target response is appropriate to a variety of relevant stimuli, including the question. The mnemonic responses themselves are usually evoked by a much narrower range of stimuli, and most are completely inappropriate to, or very weakly primed by, the question. For example, if, among other mnemonic behavior, we recite the letters of the alphabet to prompt a forgotten name, we are emitting a long intraverbal chain in which each response is largely determined by the preceding response. None of these responses is strong relative to the initial question. The target response,

"Ed," has been primed by both the intitial question and a subset of the mnemonic responses.

Second, the target response primes a wide variety of other responses. Recalling Ed's name may remind us that he was captain of the chess team, or of the amusing incident of the flat tire on Interstate 81. We may see him indistinctly "in our mind's eye." Some of these responses have doubtless been primed by our self-prompting mnemonic behavior. The target response may consequently cause a sudden cascade of related responses, many of which are strong relative to the supplementary stimuli and perhaps even to the initial question.

Thus, the strength of the target response relative to the constellation of stimuli provided by mnemonic responses and the initial question, along with the set of related responses occasioned by the target response, enable us to recognize the target response as "correct." We emit it "as the answer" and terminate problem-solving activity.

MNEMONIC BEHAVIOR: ACQUISITION PROCEDURES

So far, we have considered only mnemonic procedures that we engage in at the time of recall. We have shown that without recall procedures we would be helpless to answer novel questions about past events. However, such procedures would often be ineffective if we did not also engage in mnemonic procedures when environment-behavior relations are first acquired. For example, when we are going to take a quiz on Friday, we will often study Thursday night. "Studying" is an example of an acquisition procedure—it facilitates future recall, commonly by strengthening behavior that will feature in a later recall procedure. We will next consider both general acquisition procedures, such as rehearsal, and specific, codified strategies, such as those that have been shown to be particularly helpful in remembering vocabulary terms or sequences of events.

Rehearsal

Rehearsal is an acquisition procedure that we commonly employ when it is clear that retention intervals will be brief. When we are entrusted to deliver a message, or wish to dial an unfamiliar phone number, or want to remember to stop at the post office on the way to work, we are likely to employ rehearsal. Rehearsal is effective, at the very least, in bridging or reducing temporal gaps. A number in a phone book can serve as an effective stimulus for dialing the number if we are looking at it, but when we put the book down it becomes ineffective almost immediately, unless we rehearse the number: First we respond to the number as a textual stimulus. Our textual response then serves as a stimulus for an echoic response of the same topography. Each echoic response can serve as a stimulus for subsequent echoic responses, overt or covert, in a series that can bridge considerable temporal gaps.

The rehearsed response often has the same topography as the target response. For example, a message has the same form when it is rehearsed as when it is delivered. Consequently, rehearsal facilitates future recall of the target response even when the temporal gap has not been significantly reduced. In many cases, the response required in a recall contingency is a verbal response, even if the original behavior or event was not verbal. Rehearsal of the event can strengthen the verbal behavior that will be required later. For example, we might be asked to recall the items on a table. Here, the responses scheduled for reinforcement might not actually occur, overtly or covertly, at the time of our original exposure to the items. Upon seeing an orange on a table we might salivate or think of lunch, but we might not emit the tact "orange." However, if we have reason to rehearse the items on the table, as we would if we anticipated a recall test, we would almost certainly respond verbally to the orange, perhaps making it more likely that we will be able to respond verbally when asked about the items on the table later.

Rehearsal helps to integrate chains of distinct responses into one or more unitary responses.

When we first encounter an unfamiliar word in German class or an unfamiliar term in a neuroanatomy class, we must sound it out syllable by syllable; when learning a dance routine or a magic trick, we first step through it slowly and awkwardly. With rehearsal these words or movements become fluent. Even a long message or speech can become fluent, as intraverbal chains are established. The task of remembering a response chain is thus greatly simplified, as recalling a single link provides a mnemonic stimulus that may be sufficient to evoke subsequent links in the chain. The integration of discrete responses into unitary chains is an example of what, in the memory literature, is called "chunking." If we are given a set of unrelated items—say, random letters or digits—we are unlikely to immediately recall more than a half dozen or so.[8] If the letters form words in our repertoire, however, we can recall about a half dozen words and hence many more letters. If the words form simple sentences, we can recall several of those, and hence still more letters. (See panel on page 337.) Of course a sentence is not a chain of letters, but recalling a sentence would provide a stimulus from which we could determine a series of individual letters. In general, recall of individual responses is facilitated if they can be integrated into a larger pattern that can be recalled as a unit.

An additional effect of rehearsal is to bring the target response under the control of a variety of stimuli. We might learn someone's name at a friend's house, mention the person the next day in a phone conversation, and hail her in town the following week. We are likely to remember her name in the future, for there are many stimuli that can serve to prime the response. The more contexts in which we emit a response, the more stimuli we can recruit at the time of recall to evoke the response. Our self-prompting procedures and other mnemonic devices are more likely to be successful if there are a variety of events that will evoke the target response. Rehearsal insures that responding is extended in time, increasing the number of antecedent events that can later prime the response.

Chunking: Units of response vary in size, and this is reflected in our performance on immediate recall tasks. Most people can remember about five to nine numbers, letters, or words from a list when tested immediately. For example, if the following 27 letters were read to you at the rate of one each second, you would probably find it difficult to recall more than nine:

R I Y E O I R F S B P U I O E I N R D C T P L N I T I

Each letter is a unit of behavior, an echoic response in our repertoire. However, if letters are arranged into three-letter syllables, each syllable would be an echoic unit. You could probably recall five to nine of the following syllables and reconstruct many more than nine of the letters in the list above.

LIT BIL TIB PER RUP IDE NIF COR SON INN TEE

Similarly, if the syllables were arranged to form a phrase, you could surely recall the entire phrase, and perhaps half a dozen more like it:

INCORRUPTIBILITY PERSONIFIED

From the phrase you could reconstruct the entire list of 27 letters. Thus, the amount of verbal material that we can recall in such a task depends, not on the physical dimensions of the stimuli, but on our responses to the stimuli.

However, we should note that mere repetition of a response need not insure future recall.[9] A response of a particular topography evoked by one stimulus is a different operant from a response of the same topography under the control of a second stimulus. Repeating echoic responses evoked by prior verbal stimuli may be of little use at the time of recall when the verbal model is absent and an intraverbal response is required. Sanford[10] reported that he read aloud the same set of prayers to his family over 5000 times—about once a day for 25 years—but he never learned to recite them "from memory." No doubt he read them fluently at the end of 25 years, but recitation requires control, not by textual stimuli, but by intraverbal stimuli. In the absence of fading procedures, we should expect control by the written text to block control by other stimuli.

If rehearsal is effective partly because it increases the number of contextual events that can evoke the response, simple iteration of a response in a single context is likely to be a less effective procedure than more complex kinds of rehearsal in which we practice, not just the target response itself, but mnemonic procedures as well. This is

necessarily the case when we rehearse in different contexts and at various intervals. For example, we might study for an exam in the library and then quiz ourselves later that day in our room. This is more than simply rehearsing target responses, for in our room we must engage in mnemonic procedures to emit the responses at all. Verbal stimuli are effective in evoking echoic responses only for a minute or two. If we rehearse at longer intervals, we must recruit supplementary stimuli. In general, the more time that elapses between the acquisition of the response and the rehearsal of the response, the fewer shared contextual stimuli there are and the more supplementary stimuli are required. Rehearsing mnemonic behavior and target responses at greater and greater intervals is likely both to maintain a high rate of successful performance and to bring performance under control of a wide variety of stimuli. Moreover, it approaches more and more closely the conditions under which the response is ultimately likely to be required. The superiority of temporally distributed practice over massed practice can be interpreted in this light: Typically, researchers in verbal-learning experiments have found that recall performance is better when trials or stimulus presentations are spread out in time than when they occur sequentially.[11]

Imagery

The "use of imagery" is widely acknowledged to be an effective acquisition mnemonic. However, imagery is difficult to define and difficult to investigate experimentally, since it cannot be studied independently of other variables.[12] Nevertheless, it is a real behavioral phenomenon. If we cannot exert experimental control over it, we must rely heavily on interpretation in our discussion. As a first approximation, we can define imagery as conditioned perceptual behavior. However, "the use" of imagery implies something more than passive conditioned perceptions. Sometimes visualizing is active, constructive and "goal directed," as when we count the windows of our house "in our mind's eye."[13] Thus the use of imagery appears to be like other problem-solving behavior: It is guided partly by the stimuli defining a problem, and partly by other (often covert) responses that provide supplementary stimuli. It terminates when a particular target response has been emitted—that is, when the goal has been reached. For present purposes, then, we can define imagery as conditioned perceptual behavior and the *use* of imagery as perceptual problem-solving behavior—perceptual behavior that occurs when a problem contingency is in effect. It terminates when the target behavior has been emitted—the problem is solved—or when other contingencies become dominant.

Imagery is particularly effective for remembering stories, lists, things to bring on a camping trip, or any other set of concrete items. Narratives lend themselves to imagery, and we often find ourselves following a story or a poem by visualizing the events as they unfold. Our behavior when we hear the story is thus often perceptual rather than verbal. When we repeat the story, it is highly unlikely that we will do so verbatim. We have not acquired a set of intraverbal chains; rather, we have acquired conditioned perceptual behavior which can guide our verbal responses. The gist of the story will be transmitted, but its form will be different. Our version of the story may be rife with distortions and omissions, for our perceptual responses do not stand in a one-to-one relationship to the words in a narrative. Reading a story, in contrast to hearing it, may facilitate verbal recall because we are responding verbally as we read, but a single reading is unlikely to establish long intraverbal chains, as Professor Sanford's prayer illustrates.

In a now-classic study of the recall of narrative material, Bartlett[14] presented subjects with a short story and later asked them to reproduce it. Not surprisingly, the subjects' renditions were distorted and incomplete. Their stories were clearly guided by their perceptual responses to the narrative, not by their textual responses. (See page 339.) In a study by Reder,[15] subjects read stories and were then asked, at various retention intervals, whether certain target sentences had appeared in the stories and whether the sentences were true, given the stories. Recognition of the sentences was poor relative to truth judgments, particularly at retention intervals of 20 minutes or more. It is safe to assume that recall of the sentences would have been much worse. It is worth noting that reaction times to sentences from the stories were shorter than to other sentences, a priming effect that suggests some control by the original textual responses.

Imagery is an effective procedure for recalling lists of unrelated items, particularly when it is used deliberately, i.e., as an explicit mnemonic procedure. For example, to recall the items on a grocery list it is usually helpful to imagine the items interacting in a scene or in a sequence that tells a story. Absurd images or stories are easily discriminated from other images and stories, and are therefore likely to be particularly effective. We might imagine a press conference in which we see the president wearing glasses made of bagels, standing on a soap box, at a podium made from an orange crate, clutching a microphone made of a can of tomato soup, reading from slices of bread rather than note cards; a critic is shouting "Baloney!" while a photographer calls out "Say cheese!"

In Bartlett's investigation of the recall of narrative material, subjects read the following story twice at their normal reading speed. They were then asked, at various retention intervals, to reproduce the story as accurately as possible.

The War of the Ghosts

One night two young men from Egulac went down to the river to hunt seals, and while they were there it became foggy and calm. Then they heard war-cries, and they thought: "Maybe this is a war-party." They escaped to the shore, and hid behind a log. Now canoes came up, and they heard the noise of paddles, and saw one canoe coming up to them. There were five men in the canoe, and they said:

"What do you think? We wish to take you along. We are going up the river to make war on the people."

One of the young men said: "I have no arrows."

"Arrows are in the canoe," they said.

"I will not go along. I might be killed. My relatives do not know where I have gone. But you," he said, turning to the other, "may go with them."

So one of the young men went, but the other returned home.

And the warriors went up the river to a town on the other side of Kalama. The people came down to the water, and they began to fight, and many were killed. But presently the young man heard one of the warriors say: "Quick, let us go home: that Indian has been hit." Now he thought: "Oh, they are ghosts." He did not feel sick, but they said he had been shot.

So the canoes went back to Egulac, and the young man went ashore to his house, and made a fire. And he told everybody and said: "Behold I accompanied the ghosts, and we went to fight. Many of our fellows were killed, and many of those who attacked us were killed. They said I was hit, and I did not feel sick."

He told it all, and then he became quiet. When the sun rose he fell down. Something black came out of his mouth. His face became contorted. The people jumped up and cried.

He was dead.

(Bartlett, 1932, p. 65)

Subjects commonly showed little evidence of control by the precise wording of the original narrative. Two readings would not ordinarily suffice to establish long intraverbal chains. Rather, the subjects' renditions appear to have been guided by their own responses—perceptual, verbal, emotional, and perhaps physical—to the original story. The following performance, at a 15-minute retention interval, is typical:

The Ghosts

There were two men on the banks of the river near Egulac. They heard the sounds of paddles, and a canoe with five men in it appeared, who called to them saying: "We are going to fight the people. Will you come with us?"

One of the two men answered, saying: "Our relations do not know where we are, and we have not got any arrows."

They answered: "There are arrows in the canoe."

So the men went, and they fought the people, and then he heard them saying, "An Indian is killed, let us return."

So he returned to Egulac, and told them he knew they were Ghosts.

He spoke to the people of Egulac, and told them that he had fought with the Ghosts, and many men were killed on both sides, and that he was wounded, but felt nothing. He lay down and became calmer, and in the night he was convulsed, and something black came out of his mouth.

The people said:

"He is dead."

(Bartlett, 1932, p. 87)

Rehearsal of verbal material works, in part, by establishing intraverbal relationships, so that one response serves as a prompt for the next. Visual imagery may work in an analogous way. It appears to establish integrated perceptual responses, so that recalling one serves as a prompt for others. An experiment by Bower[16] appears to confirm this view. He found that recall in a paired-associate task was superior for subjects who were instructed to form compound images of the two words interacting, compared with subjects who were instructed to form two separate images of the two words.

Imagery also facilitates recall by providing one or more additional modalities to be tapped by mnemonic recall procedures.[17] It is commonly found that, in the learning of verbal material in laboratory settings, concrete words such as automobile and sailboat are remembered better than abstract words such as truth and thought.[18] The imagery need not, of course, be restricted to the visual modality. Some words or phrases, such as "coffee" or "chocolate chip cookies," can be imagined in several sense modalities, facilitating a wide variety of recall procedures. We can visualize the coffee being brewed, feel it scald our tongue, smell it, taste it, hear it percolate, even hear the jingle from the television commercial. A wide variety of supplementary stimuli would serve to prompt the target response. Generally, imagery has been found to be a more effective acquisition procedure than rote rehearsal. For example, Bower[19] found that subjects in an imagery condition recalled more than twice as many items as subjects in a rehearsal condition. However, the effect may depend partly on the nature of the material to be learned. Researchers[20] have found little advantage for the use of imagery in the learning of abstract verbal material.

Organization

When the material to be remembered is systematic in some way, an effective mnemonic procedure is to reorganize it to accentuate relationships among its various elements. A newspaper reporter who

wishes to learn the names and districts of the 100 United States senators might list them according to geographic region, beginning with Maine and New Hampshire and working west to the Pacific coast states and Hawaii. This strategy would support a recall procedure of using a real or imagined map of the United States to prompt the state names in order; the state name would, in turn, prompt the name of the corresponding senator.

Similarly, if a heterogeneous list of words is presented in a laboratory task, recall would be facilitated if the items were reorganized into classes, e.g., living organisms, geographical places, structures, abstract nouns, words beginning with "M," etc.[21] In many cases, identifying the class name, or even a single member of the class, would tend to prime other members of the class. Moreover, if items have been organized into classes, one can use systematic recall procedures that are particularly effective. Some classes, such as state names, digits, letters, body parts, colors, and so on, permit mnemonic procedures that exhaustively generate elements of the class; the name of an element in the target set is a particularly effective supplementary stimulus, since it is usually easier to recognize an item than to recall it.

Elaboration

In general, the more we think about something, the more likely we are to remember it.[22] As we noted above, if a wide variety of events reminds us of a target response or primes a target response, mnemonic procedures at the time of recall are more likely to be successful. An important acquisition procedure, then, is to explicitly verbalize or visualize the relationship between a target response and high-probability responses in our repertoire. Consider the example of a subject in a laboratory task who was required to recall a series of unrelated digits. With prolonged practice he increased his performance from about seven to as many as 80 digits. He was an avid runner, and among his mnemonic strategies was an elaboration procedure in which series of digits were related to familiar running times. For example, the digits 3, 5, and 1 became 3'51" which had been a long-standing world record for the mile run.[23] In another study, Bower and Clark[24] instructed subjects to weave lists of unrelated words into stories. In a recall test, these subjects were able to recall nearly all of the 120 words presented in the experiment. Control subjects who were instructed merely to rehearse the words recalled, on average, only 13% of the words.

There are a variety of codified mnemonic procedures that exemplify elaboration. These are general procedures that have been explicitly cultivated and widely publicized. The most venerable procedure is the **method of loci**, which was described by Cicero over 2,000 years ago and attributed by him to Greek poets of several centuries earlier. The method of loci takes advantage of the ease with which we move about familiar surroundings. Each item to be remembered is visualized in a particular location in a familiar setting such as our home. If we are trying to remember items on a grocery list, we picture ourselves walking about our home, placing the items in distinctive places. The hot dogs go in the mailbox, the bag of onions is hung from the front door knob, the carrots are put in a vase on the coffee table, and so on. In recalling the items, we visualize ourselves retracing our steps and finding the items in their various places. The method of loci is particularly effective because it specifies at the time of acquisition what the recall procedure will be. It then attempts to establish strong responses to elements of the recall procedure. It exploits imagery and novelty, and it can be rehearsed as often as needed.

Another well-known procedure is called the **peg-word mnemonic**. Like the method of loci, it specifies a recall procedure in advance and arranges for target responses to be evoked by stimuli generated during recall. It requires first learning a set of rhymes for the numbers one through ten (and beyond if necessary): "One is a bun, two is a shoe, three is a tree, four is a door," and so on. Thus each number is paired with a common concrete object. The items to be recalled are then visualized inter-

acting in some absurd (easily discriminated) way with one of the objects. Our car keys are visualized served up with onions on a hamburger bun; our umbrella is seen fending off a hailstorm of shoes; our briefcase is being carried off by squirrels to a hollow tree; and so on. At the time of recall we can generate the numbers easily as an intraverbal chain. Each number provides intraverbal and echoic stimuli that evoke the corresponding rhyme. The rhyming word serves in turn as a supplementary stimulus for a particular target response.

A third codified mnemonic is known as the **keyword mnemonic**, a procedure designed to facilitate acquisition of vocabulary in foreign languages. Each foreign word is paired with an English word of similar form; the meaning of the English word is then visualized interacting with the meaning of the foreign word. *Jour*, the French word for *day*, might remind us of *jury*; we then might imagine a jury locked in a chamber for many days. At the time of recall, *jour* provides a formal prompt for *jury*, which in turn serves to occasion *day*.

The effectiveness of elaboration mnemonic procedures has been demonstrated experimentally[25] as well as anecdotally. Professional mnemonists routinely use such procedures to astonish audiences, and many students who attempt to employ these mnemonics report success.

Detrimental Effects of Mnemonic Procedures

We sometimes struggle to recall a name or a word only to have it "pop into our heads" effortlessly an hour later when we have "forgotten all about it." Events of this sort seem to belie the utility of mnemonic procedures. How are we to explain them?

We must not forget that recall procedures do not lead us inexorably to the target response. They are more like blind groping than directed searches: Of necessity, we don't know what we're looking for. We use those mnemonic procedures that have been most strongly reinforced in the past under similar circumstances, and there is no guarantee that they will be the most effective ones for the task at hand. Moreover, recall procedures are likely to prime responses related to the target response as well as the target response itself. These responses will compete with the target response and may be prepotent. We find ourselves saying "Todd" instead of "Ed." Further mnemonic behavior may provide supplementary stimuli that only serve to evoke the competing response more strongly. We may be unable to stop emitting the competing response even though we "realize that it is incorrect." The more we repeat the competing response, the more it becomes integrated with other strong responses evoked by the recall context; the recall mnemonic provides rehearsal and elaboration procedures for strengthening the competing response! Our recall procedure has led us into a blind alley; we must back out and start afresh.

Giving up and turning to another activity is effective partly because it reduces the strength of particular competing responses. When we return to the problem in another context, the initial conditions may control a different sequence of mnemonic responses which quickly evoke the target response. Some new contexts may themselves provide enough relevant supplementary stimuli that the response is emitted directly, i.e., without self-prompting procedures. For example, if Ed was a skilled piano player, a context that included a piano might by itself evoke his name.

Mnemonic Procedures: A Summary

Acquisition procedures and recall procedures complement one another. Acquisition procedures strengthen target behavior with respect to a variety of stimuli, some of which are likely to be provided as supplementary stimuli by recall procedures. Clearly this is a complex and flexible performance that must be gradually shaped.

The acquisition mnemonics that we have reviewed require that we behave in special ways today so that we will be reinforced tomorrow. Moreover, they take time and effort. That these mnemonic procedures are prepotent over competing behavior indicates that there are often powerful contingencies in effect for remembering certain kinds of events. We apparently learn to identify those classes of event which we must later recall, and we engage in the mnemonic behaviors discussed above. That these special procedures are acquired at all is testimony to the difficulty of many recall tasks. It appears that some of our experiences are distinctive enough and interrelated enough that we can remember them without employing special acquisition procedures. Other experiences, unrelated to anything else, need to be elaborated with acquisition strategies so that recall procedures can work. For example, we can recall trivial events at a friend's wedding with ease, but are helpless to recall the names of the twelve cranial nerves on an exam, despite our most anguished efforts. There are many things we talk about in our day-to-day lives, and talking about things is an implicit elaboration procedure. We rehearse, talk about, and recall important events over and over again. Perhaps if we were to discuss cranial nerves as often with our friends, we would recall them effortlessly too.

If our account is correct, children will be unable to remember the past until they acquire behavior that generates supplementary stimuli. They will be skilled at remembering the past only when they have acquired a full range of acquisition and recall mnemonic procedures. This is not to say that children never experience conditioned perceptions or respond as if absent stimuli were present; children can be reminded of past events and respond appropriately. We can say to a child "Do you remember the giraffe we saw at the zoo last week?" and the child will perhaps visualize the giraffe and its surroundings as his strongest response to the verbal stimulus "giraffe." However, if we ask "What did we do last week?" the child may be unable to respond that we went to the zoo and saw a giraffe; the question does not evoke that response directly, and the child may not have acquired the requisite problem-solving skills to provide the supplementary stimuli necessary to evoke it. The child can be reminded of the past, but cannot remember it when asked about it. We now turn to the question of how these mnemonic skills are acquired.

THE ACQUISITION OF MNEMONIC BEHAVIOR

Remembering encompasses a variety of skills that are by no means universal. Not only do children differ from adults, but individuals differ from one another according to culture and level of education as well. Generally non-schooled subjects perform worse than their educated counterparts in typical laboratory memory tasks.[26] Much of the discrepancy appears to be due to differences in the use of rehearsal and organizational mnemonic procedures.[27] When tasks are varied to make organizational procedures more explicit, the differences are reduced. The discrepancy may arise in part because the meaningless kinds of memory tests employed in laboratory tasks are not commonly encountered outside of school.[28] In school, memorization is often an explicit goal, and recall techniques may be taught explicitly or implicitly.

However, much implicit training undoubtedly occurs in the home. Parents often model the use of recall procedures by providing young children with supplementary stimuli when they are faced with a recall task: "Tell Grandma what we saw this afternoon. . . Do you remember? We went in the car . . . There was a barn . . . You ran up to the fence . . . Yes, cows! We saw cows." Parents naturally fade these prompts when children provide them for themselves.

Many recall procedures are undoubtedly acquired fortuitously. Recall tasks often involve the whole family, and parents commonly prompt one another, modeling mnemonic procedures for the children. When searching for a mislaid checkbook one parent might say to the other, "When did you last have it? . . . Retrace your steps . . . What did you do when you first came in the house?" and so on. These supplementary stimuli affect the speaker and everyone within earshot, including the chil-

dren, who might find themselves recalling their own behavior or even that of their parents.

Memory research with children reveals the expected trend: Young children typically have very primitive skills, but by adolescence, most children use a wide range of mnemonic procedures. A study by Istomena[29] illustrates differences in the use of a variety of mnemonic procedures in 3-, 4-, and 5-year-old children. Children participated in a game in which they played a number of different roles. One child was required to go to an adjoining room to a "store" to "buy" five items, ostensibly for the purpose of feeding the others. An experimenter told the child what to buy, and sent him on his way. The number of items recalled increased, as a rule, with the age of the child. An analysis of the actual behavior of the children suggests that the increase was a function of the use of acquisition and recall strategies. Three-year-olds engaged in little, if any, mnemonic acquisition or recall procedures. Typically a child would set out for the store without waiting for the experimenter to finish telling him what to buy. Once at the store, the child would improvise, announcing, for example, that candy was required. Thus, competing behavior was strong at the time of acquisition, and the behavior at the time of recall was strongly controlled by the current setting.

Four-year-olds, as a rule, stopped what they were doing and looked at the experimenter when the list was presented. That is, competing responses were terminated, and an orienting response was made which maximized control by the list stimuli and minimized control by competing stimuli. These children then typically rushed to the adjoining room, carefully skirting encounters with "guards," and blurted out as much of the message as they could. That is, the time interval between the presentation of the target stimulus (the experimenter's list) and the recall stimulus (the counter of the store) was minimized, and stimuli controlling competing responses were avoided.

There were exceptions to the rule. One child repeated the items as they were presented and asked the experimenter to repeat several of the items. Another child repeated the items loudly as they were presented. Clearly this is an important advance. What was scheduled for reinforcement was the behavior of emitting the list, not the behavior of listening to it. Repeating items establishes or strengthens, albeit in the wrong setting, the very behavior scheduled for reinforcement. Repeating the items loudly strengthens any intraverbal control by one response on later responses. Once one response was recalled, other responses would have a higher probability of being recalled.

Five- and six-year-olds engaged in more elaborate strategies, both at acquisition and recall. When the list was presented they typically would:

1. Orient toward the speaker and stop competing activity.

2. Repeat items, either in a whisper, aloud, or just by moving their lips. Repetitions were requested.

3. Rehearse the whole list immediately.

4. Rehearse silently on their way to the store (as shown by the fact that several stopped halfway and came back to confirm the last few items.)

5. Elaborate on the items (as shown by the fact that recall errors were often semantic in nature—for example, one child recalled "macaroni" instead of "spaghetti").

At the store, recall strategies were used:

1. Remembered items were repeated, sometimes loudly, thus maximizing intraverbal control of other items.

2. A single item was sometimes repeated again and again, presumably for the same reason.

3. They reduced competing responses by screwing up their eyes, looking down or to one side, and avoiding eye contact with others.

4. There were long pauses during which, presumably, covert mediating responses could occur.

This study illustrates that improvement in recall performance is correlated with specific behavior or procedures, even in preschoolers.

Other researchers have examined differences among children in the use of particular mnemonic procedures. For example, Flavell, Beach, and Chinsky[30] used lip-reading to evaluate the use of rehearsal in 5-, 7-, and 10-year-old children in a picture-recall task. Relatively few 5-year-olds appeared to rehearse at all, while nearly all of the 10-year-olds rehearsed. Further research with subjects ranging from 7-year-olds to adults found differences in the nature of the rehearsal procedure. 7-year-olds tended to simply repeat the most recently presented item, while older subjects tended to rehearse groups of words, thus establishing some intraverbal control among target responses.

Ornstein, Naus, and Liberty[31] presented subjects of various ages with words randomly presented from four categories. An effective acquisition procedure is to rehearse category members together; this strengthens intraverbal control among items, and between items and the category name, making the category name a particularly effective recall cue. Again, only older children (13 years) tended to employ an organizational procedure. Moely, Olson, Halwes, and Flavell[32] found similar results for a picture-recall task in which the pictures could be arranged in categories during the study phase of the experiment.

Kreutzer, Leonard, and Flavell[33] investigated the use of external stimuli as prompts. They asked children of various ages to generate mnemonic procedures for remembering to attend a skating party. Younger children tended to suggest manipulating environmental cues, e.g., by getting out the skates and putting them in a conspicuous place. Older children were more likely to suggest verbal prompts—writing a note, asking a parent to remind them—and covert rehearsal and elaboration.

Some researchers have been successful in improving performance on recall tasks by teaching children to engage in recall and acquisition procedures, or by choosing a task that induced them to engage in such procedures.[34] For example, Turnure, Buium, and Thurlow[35] demonstrated that the poor recall performance of young children can be attributed to failure to employ mnemonic procedures, not to intrinsic developmental limitations. Children were required to learn 21 terms in a paired-associate paradigm. Those in the elaboration group were asked questions that required them to weave the terms into a story. For example, if the terms were *soap-jacket*, subjects might be asked, "Why is the soap hiding in the jacket?" These children recalled an average of 14 items, strikingly more than subjects in a control group who just repeated the stimulus and response terms and presumably did not engage in other mnemonic procedures; subjects in this condition recalled only two items, on average.

Butterfield, Wambold, and Belmont[36] taught a rehearsal procedure to mentally retarded children and greatly improved their performance on a short-term memory task. Subjects were presented with a sequence of six items and asked to identify in which position a target item occurred; they controlled the rate at which items were presented by pressing a button, which allowed the experimenters to assess when they were rehearsing items. Adults with experience in this procedure typically pause and rehearse the first three items in the series, then quickly view the last three items. When the target item is presented, they first recall the last three items; if the target was not among them, they recall the rehearsed items. This procedure exploits both the distinctiveness of responses to recently presented stimuli and the relatively enduring effects of rehearsal. When the rehearsal strategy was taught to the children their performance improved considerably, but only for the first three items in the set. However, when they were given detailed instructions on both the acquisition procedure (rehearsal) and the recall procedure (recalling the recent items first), their performance increased dramatically, from about 35% correct to about 85% correct.

This study illustrates the complexity of performance on a recall task. It is often not enough to employ a stock procedure such as rehearsal or elaboration; one must sometimes employ a combination of acquisition and recall procedures that are effective for a particular problem. Most adults have had long experience with a wide variety of recall tasks; our mnemonic procedures are often integrated units that are occasioned by typical features of familiar problems. We can quickly and effortlessly recall what we did today, whom we saw, and what we said. Under these conditions we are sometimes unaware that we are engaging in any special mnemonic procedures at all; that is, we are unable to describe our own mnemonic behavior. On other occasions, when the task is unfamiliar, relevant supplementary responses may be weak. Under these conditions we are likely to respond verbally to our own covert behavior. We become aware of our mnemonic behavior; furthermore, our verbal responses help guide later mnemonic activity. This evaluation of one's own mnemonic behavior and its effect on subsequent behavior has been called **metamemory**.[37]

Metamemory: Awareness of Mnemonic Behavior

A discussion of our awareness of mnemonic procedures, of probability of successful recall, and of other features of remembering raises the general problem of self-awareness. How is it that we are able to describe covert events—our thoughts, feelings, intentions, and so on? As Skinner[38] points out, "In setting up the type of verbal operant called the tact, the verbal community characteristically reinforces a given response in the presence of a given stimulus. This can only be done if the stimulus acts upon both speaker and reinforcing community." This poses no problem when we learn to describe the external world, but *self*-awareness implies sensitivity to a private world. This is a formidable problem for which Skinner proposes a unique solution. He identifies four ways in which a verbal community can shape verbal behavior guided by covert events.[39] (See panel on page 346.)

1. Some events have both private and public dimensions. For example, if we prick our finger there is a tactile stimulus that is private and a visual

We have a common terminology to describe the external world, and the verbal community reinforces adherence to and punishes deviations from the common standard. The boy who cried "Wolf!" was ostracized because no wolf was present, and Paul Revere was honored because, indeed, the British were coming. Presumably more humdrum contingencies account for the precision with which most of us describe the world. But how do we learn to describe our private world within the skin when no second observer can shape our verbal behavior? Skinner suggests four ways. Let us consider them in the light of a single example: A child who has fallen asleep with his arm hooked awkwardly behind him. When he wakes he finds that his arm is "still asleep." How does the child learn to describe this peculiar sensation?

1. A public stimulus may be typically correlated with the private events. An adult may have noticed the child's awkward position and asks, "Is your arm asleep?" The adult has no access to the private sensation, but a posture that appears to cut off circulation to a limb is public. The term "asleep" may then be acquired by the child, to whom both public and private stimuli are available. In other cases, "tickle" is paired with the brush of a feather, "hurt" with a pin prick, "burn" with contact with a lighted match, and so on.

2. Private events may evoke distinctive public behavior. The child may hold his arm inertly and massage it with his free hand. Here the adult notices the collateral behavior and infers that the child's arm is asleep. In other cases, a frown suggests "angry," laughter suggests "happy," a stagger suggests "dizzy," pressing the temples suggests "headache," and so on.

3. The private event may be similar to some property of a public event. The child may say, as circulation returns, "It feels like pins and needles!" Here the child's vocabulary has already been shaped by the verbal community and no further shaping occurs here. In other cases, the child might describe his feelings as "fluttery," or "depressed," or "jumpy," and so on.

4. Some behavior may be public on some occasions and of such diminished magnitude on others that only the speaker is able to detect it. Thus, the child may report, "I am trying to move my arm!" under the control of proprioceptive stimuli usually accompanied by the movement of his arm. In other cases, we often report covert speech, presumably under the control of events that accompany overt speech.

None of the four ways that we acquire a self-descriptive repertoire guarantees precision. It is ironic that the world within our skin, the world to which we have such intimate and privileged access, should be so difficult to describe precisely.

stimulus—the pin entering the skin, the drop of blood—that is public. "That hurts!" is a response that can be shaped by the verbal community and can be evoked by both stimuli. The community's response is evoked by only the public stimulus, but our behavior can be evoked by either one.

2. Private events sometimes evoke typical overt behavior. If we suddenly jerk our arm away from a dresser, an observer might reply "Oh, you hit your funny bone!" If we hold our jaw and groan, an observer is likely to comment "You have a toothache." We can utter these expressions our-selves later, even when the private event is the only relevant stimulus.

3. Private events may have some conspicuous properties in common with public events. Although there is only partial overlap, the response to the public event is evoked by the private event as well. When we say we feel "agitated" we may be feeling rapidly changing emotions, like the contents of a blender; when we say that we are "ebullient" we may feel "bubbly" inside. Skinner calls this transfer of response "metaphorical extension," and notes that much of our self-descriptive behav-

ior is metaphorical. Note that a term descriptive of a public event might be a prepotent response to a private event even if the two events share only a relatively small number of features, since competing verbal behavior evoked by the private event is likely to be weak.

4. An overt response has private as well as public stimulus properties. Both the speaker and a listener can hear a verbal response uttered, but only the speaker can feel the proprioceptive feedback from the tongue, lips, and throat. The magnitude of a response can diminish to the point where it is no longer observed by the listener, but the private stimulation may be the same, except in magnitude, as for the overt response. Responses shaped in the presence of overt behavior may be emitted even when the behavior has receded to the covert level. Verbal behavior, for example, is shaped as overt behavior, but it can occur covertly; we have no more trouble reporting what we said to ourselves than what we said to others.

The verbal community often has an interest in **private events**, since they often reveal the effect of historical variables that are out of reach. For example, we might ask a guest "Are you hungry?" rather than collecting data on the number of calories he has consumed and the time since his last meal. Thus there are powerful contingencies that shape self-descriptive verbal behavior. However, Skinner notes that none of the four ways in which private events can be shaped by the verbal community guarantees the precision of control possible for external, manipulable stimuli. Thus, self-description is necessarily somewhat imprecise. An implication of Skinner's analysis is that it is the verbal community that teaches us to "know ourselves," and that, ironically, we cannot describe ourselves with the same precision that we can describe the external world.

Responding verbally to one's own covert behavior is, itself, an effective mnemonic procedure that helps select other appropriate mnemonic behavior. For example, when asked for the name of a book, an actor, or our sixth-grade teacher, we may find that no response is strong; but we can't just

stand there in silence. There is a powerful social contingency requiring that we emit the name or other relevant verbal behavior. Our responses are likely to be guided by covert events: "Let's see, sixth grade . . . I can't remember . . . Oh, wait . . . I can picture her now . . . she was old; she used to wear dowdy dresses and rubber-soled shoes . . . 'Fahey' rings a bell . . . or 'Lahey' . . . I think she was Irish . . . Her name's on the tip of my tongue . . ." This temporizing patter satisfies the social contingency and also serves as powerful supplementary stimulation. If the answer is important, our questioner may press us for a more complete account of our mnemonic behavior. Thus, we describe, and hence become aware of, our mnemonic behavior partly because of social contingencies and partly because such self-descriptive behavior has been reinforced by its effect on recall. We can report what we have remembered, what we think we are about to remember, and even those things that we are sure we cannot remember. These self-reports and the contingencies from which they arise can serve to evoke subsequent mnemonic behavior; thus, metamemory itself embraces a set of important mnemonic procedures.

ANTEROGRADE AMNESIA AND MNEMONIC BEHAVIOR

We have seen that remembering is a complex, unreliable, and often difficult task, even in those with unimpaired nervous systems. It is not surprising that persons who have suffered brain injury often show deficits in remembering. Since remembering is a complex behavior requiring the interaction of multiple stimulus and response events—including proprioceptive stimulation and reafference—we can be confident that the neural activity underlying any instance of remembering is widely distributed. Usually the events that cause damage to the nervous system, such as a blow to the head, loss of oxygen to the brain, and even surgical procedures, have widespread effects unique to each victim. Consequently we cannot expect to find simple relationships between brain trauma and recall performance. Nevertheless, experimental analyses of brain lesions in nonhumans, in conjunction with case studies and *post mortem* analyses of brain trauma in humans, point to an important role for the hippocampus in remembering.

In Chapter 9 we discussed the effect of hippocampal lesions on awareness, specifically on verbal responses requiring polysensory integration. Here we will extend the discussion to include what we have learned about acquisition and recall procedures. Bilateral damage to the hippocampus appears to be sufficient (but not necessary) to cause severe anterograde amnesia. As we noted in Chapter 9, subjects with this disorder can usually recall events that occurred before their injury but cannot remember—i.e., are completely unaware of—events following the injury. One subject, whose hippocampus was deliberately lesioned to cure a severe case of epilepsy, has been intensively studied, since apart from his amnesia, he seems to be normal. He can carry on a conversation, recall events from the distant past, and repeat verbal utterances. He has some problem-solving skills and can do arithmetic problems. Moreover, he can emit echoic chains, but if he is interrupted he will be unable to recall the rehearsed response. Each new day is novel to him. He can't name people that he has met since the operation that caused his injury, he can't find his way around new surroundings, and he never gets bored with the same magazine or the same jokes. He can, however, learn visual discriminations and retain acquired motor skills such as a mirror-drawing task.[40] (See **Figure 12.4**.) It appears that new environment-behavior relations can be established and maintained. Moreover, it appears that he can still engage in *recall* mnemonic procedures, since he can generate the supplementary stimuli necessary to discuss the distant past. However, it seems that *acquisition* procedures—either explicit mnemonic procedures or everyday verbal exchanges that implicitly serve the same purpose—are ineffective for him. The responses acquired since his operation remain con-

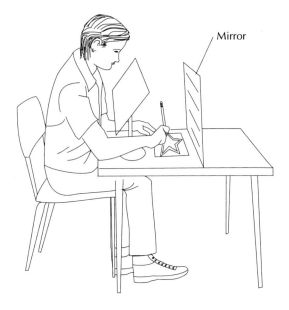

FIGURE 12.4   *The mirror-tracing task*
In the mirror-tracing task, the subject must follow a printed pattern, such as a star, with a pencil line, guided only by the image in a mirror. The subject is prevented from directly viewing his performance by an opaque shield. The task is surprisingly difficult, at first, as the strongest response at any point tends to produce a line going in the wrong direction. With practice most people improve considerably, as new discriminative responses are acquired.
Source: Carlson, N. (1984). *Psychology: The Science of Behavior.* Boston: Allyn & Bacon.

trolled by a very narrow range of stimuli, and are thus out of reach of recall mnemonic procedures.

In Chapter 7 we proposed a stimulus-selection network in which the hippocampus integrates polysensory input in the sensory association cortex. If this system were destroyed, polysensory units controlled by concurrent stimuli could not be established. The relationship among events normally established by acquisition mnemonics would no longer be exemplified in the network, and the subject would suffer impairment in remembering new experiences. Moreover, concurrent stimuli in the environment would not be integrated.

The subject would fail to respond appropriately to novel complexes of stimuli such as faces or places. Polysensory units established before the destruction of the hippocampus might or might not survive the trauma, depending on the extent of the injuries. Those units that survived would presumably still mediate recognition of faces, places, and other complex events. Moreover, those polysensory units which had arisen from earlier acquisition mnemonics might also remain intact, to be tapped by recall procedures.

The role of the hippocampus in the proposed stimulus-selection network provides a plausible interpretation of the amnesia data in light of the present discussion of acquisition and recall procedures. The hippocampus may serve other relevant roles as well. It receives projections from all regions of sensory association cortex, as well as from the motor cortex of the frontal lobe, and is ideally suited to play a role in the rich interplay of responses and stimuli in mnemonic procedures.

THE INTERPRETATION OF EXCEPTIONAL MNEMONIC PERFORMANCES

Some people can recall events—even trivial and arbitrary events—in remarkable detail and over long retention intervals. Some of these people have simply practiced and developed ordinary mnemonic procedures to the point that their performance on typical memory tasks is extraordinary. In at least one well documented case, however, this explanation does not seem to fit the facts. A man known to science simply as S. was studied over a period of years by the Soviet psychologist A. R. Luria, who found that S.'s astonishing recall performances depended, in part, on abnormal perceptual behavior. Let us briefly illustrate his performance, in Luria's words:

I gave S. a series of words, then numbers, then letters, reading them to him slowly or presenting them to him in written form . . . I increased the number of elements in each series, giving him as many as thirty, fifty, or even seventy words or numbers, but this, too, presented no problem for him . . . Usually during an experiment he would close his

eyes or stare into space, fixing his gaze on one point; when the experiment was over, he would ask that we pause while he went over the material in his mind to see if he had retained it. Thereupon, without another moment's pause, he would reproduce the series that had been read to him . . . He could reproduce a series in reverse order just as simply as from start to finish . . . It was of no consequence to him whether the series I gave him contained meaningful words or nonsense syllables . . . Some of the experiments designed to test his retention were performed (without his being given any warning) 15 or 16 years after the session in which he had originally recalled the words. Yet invariably they were successful.[41]

How are we to interpret these remarkable performances? It is tempting to simply assert that S. "has a good memory" or, better, a "photographic memory." However, this provides a label for what we already know, not an explanation. We are not entirely ignorant of relevant facts: He evidently engaged in acquisition mnemonics, for he required a pause of three to four seconds between items, during which he reduced competition from other stimuli, as indicated by the abstracted gaze mentioned above. Moreover, S. reported using the method of loci in order to establish ordinal relations among items. S. also engaged in some routine recall procedures; Luria notes that when recalling a list learned years before, S. would sit with his eyes closed, pause, and then begin to speak:

"Yes, yes . . . This was a series you gave me once when we were in your apartment . . . You were sitting at the table and I in the rocking chair . . . You were wearing a gray suit and you looked at me like this . . . Now, then, I can see you saying . . ." And with that he would reel off the series precisely as I had given it to him at the earlier session. If one takes into account that S. had by then become a well-known mnemonist, who had to remember hundreds and thousands of series, the feat seems even more remarkable.[42]

However, it appears that S.'s mnemonic procedures were considerably more effective for him than they are for most people. An important piece of the puzzle is that S. experienced an unusual degree of **synesthesia**, or multiple perceptual responses to a single stimulus. For S., every sound apparently evoked perceptions of light, color, touch, and taste. Consider his response to a loud, low tone:

> *Presented with a tone pitched at 50 cycles per second and an amplitude of 100 decibels, S. saw a brown strip against a dark background that had red, tongue-like edges. The sense of taste he experienced was like that of sweet and sour borscht, a sensation that gripped his entire tongue.*[43]

For S. the most trivial stimulus evoked unique and complex multimodal responses. No doubt routine acquisition procedures such as elaboration and imagery resulted in larger, integrated responses that were both very distinctive and very complex indeed. The supplementary stimuli supplied by recall mnemonics were also presumably complex. We must suppose that the likelihood that a feature of the recall stimulus would prime at least one feature of the target response would be quite high for S. Thus his remarkable performances appear to arise from the interaction of skilled, but ordinary, mnemonic procedures with extraordinary perceptual behavior. We can only speculate about the origins of S.'s synesthesia. We are all sensitive to polysensory events, and most people report some degree of synesthesia: The smell of ginger evokes an image of our grandmother's kitchen, Beethoven's Sixth evokes a woodland scene, and so on. S. apparently represents one extreme on a continuum. As we noted in Chapter 7, sensitivity to polysensory events is adaptive and is a joint product of phylogenetic and ontogenetic contingencies of selection. However, evoked perceptual experiences can be maladaptive if they compete with perceptual responses directly elicited by external events. While S.'s remarkable synesthesia enabled him to remember things easily, it exacted a heavy price in other domains. It was difficult for him to read a book or carry on a conversation without kaleidoscopic perceptual responses competing with one another. Worse, everything reminded him of something else; a passage or phrase in one book would remind him of an identical phrase in another book, and soon the plot would

become a chaotic melange. Tasks that are simple for most of us were an arduous ordeal for S. His is a rare case and will perhaps remain so; it may be that contingencies of natural selection have favored those who experience synesthesia only as a vague and fleeting phenomenon.

CONCLUSION

Most of our everyday behavior is fluid and coordinated. At any moment an observer of our behavior might conclude that we are "doing something"—mowing the lawn, studying chemistry, chatting with a friend. The apparent unity of our behavior belies the fact that, in a complex world, countless competing responses are also strong. When responses are mutually incompatible, the strongest, or prepotent, response will emerge, to be appraised by our observer as "what we are doing." Our observer will fail to detect that the prevailing conditions have also altered the probability of a wide variety of other behavior. Our behavior may appear to be a linear sequence of responses, but it is better thought of as a bubbling stew: Just below the surface competing responses are simmering, only to appear when a slight change of conditions alters the prevailing contingencies. When a response occurs it, too, becomes an important controlling variable that alters the probability of related behavior. A prepotent class of behavior tends to perpetuate itself—once we have begun mowing the lawn, conditions are optimal for continuing to do so. Thus a pattern of behavior can be prolonged, obscuring the wealth of competing behavior.

When we are asked about a past event, the question establishes a dominant contingency, but relevant behavior is typically weak. It is under these conditions that we engage in those mnemonic activities we call remembering. In the absence of a dominant pattern of responding, subtle self-prompting behavior is sufficient to selectively strengthen, among the pandemonium of competing responses, those that are relevant to the prevailing contingency. Each successive response selectively strengthens other relevant behavior so that, over time, the target response—moments ago no stronger than countless other responses—emerges as the prepotent response. The target response occasions corroboratory related behavior, and we emit it with special emphasis; we say that we "recognize that it is correct."

Some events are important and interesting to us; we discuss them, argue about them, daydream about them, and rehearse them. Such events are particularly easy to recall, for relevant behavior is strong and can be primed by a vast variety of events. We eventually employ such procedures to facilitate recall of events that are less interesting to us, but that we are likely to need to remember some day: schoolwork, traffic laws, dental appointments, and so on. Acquisition procedures and recall procedures complement one another to produce, in the mature individual, remarkably fluent mnemonic behavior.

Our friends and family often ask us about our thoughts and feelings, pleasures and pains, intentions and memories. Through the efforts of this verbal community, we acquire a repertoire of verbal behavior under the control of private events. We become increasingly aware of the variables controlling our behavior, and increasingly able to describe subtle behavior and predict future behavior. Such verbal behavior alters the probability of other behavior in our repertoire. As our verbal responses often precede and alter later behavior, we feel increasingly that we control and direct our own behavior, though the verbal responses are, themselves, presumably controlled by earlier events. Most adults can describe their own mnemonic behavior and predict the likelihood of recalling a target response. No doubt this helps shape and select effective mnemonic procedures suitable to particular tasks, and contributes to the feeling that we are in control of a "memory capacity."

In analyzing mnemonic behavior we are constrained by the nature of our subject matter. Remembering is one of the most complex of human activities and, like all complex behavior, it is a product of a long, varied history of selection. We can inspect the current products of selection, but the history is largely lost to us. Experimental analyses of behavior, physiology, and genetics have provided us with elementary principles and units of analysis. In interpreting complex behavior we must infer a plausible history exploiting these principles and units. Each example is unique and requires a unique interpretation. If such interpretations seem discouragingly tentative, we must remind ourselves that, while the past has left its stamp on our behavior, ephemeral events, crucial to our analysis, have been lost forever.

Principles of selection have provided remarkably parsimonious explanations of complexity in nature. Selectionism remains controversial—it tends to undermine more baroque theories of complexity, and hence is often resisted. However, we find the simplicity, power and apparent scope of selectionist principles to be extraordinarily elegant and exciting. The role of selection in the evolution of physical structures is now beyond dispute, but we are among those who think that its scope is far wider. We have attempted to sketch an outline of the role of selection in some examples of complex behavior; we hope we have encouraged you to wield the same interpretive tools to supplement our account in the light of your own experiences.

STUDY AIDS

Technical Terms

> generation effect
> mnemonic behavior
> prepotent response
> method of loci
> peg-word mnemonic
> keyword mnemonic
> metamemory
> private events
> synesthesia

Text Questions

1. Translate the following statement into behavioral terms: Some memories are automatic whereas

others must be retrieved by cognitive control processes.

2. Why does the text claim that it is a "remarkable performance" to respond correctly when a friend asks, "What did you do last night?" Try to identify your own behavior when asked the following question: What were you doing at 4:30 PM two weeks ago yesterday?

3. In studies of the *generation effect,* why do subjects perform better if they are required to generate the response word than if they are simply given the response word? How does this explanation bear on the results of the experiment by Tulving and Thompson?

4. In what respect is remembering an example of problem solving? What memory phenomena are *not* examples of problem solving?

5. What is meant by the term *prepotent response*? What is the relevance of the term to the interpretation of mnemonic behavior?

6. How does the literature on priming facilitate our interpretation of recall? Illustrate from an example of your own.

7. Comment on the following statement: An image of the accident was stored in his brain, but when he testified at the trial, he must have suffered a retrieval failure, for his memory of the incident was mistaken.

8. Why is it a "formidable question" how we recognize a target response? What are some ways in which we might do so?

9. What is the difference between acquisition and recall mnemonic procedures? Identify and briefly discuss three acquisition procedures.

10. Describe the difference in the use of mnemonic procedures by children in the Istomena study.

11. Identify the four ways in which the verbal community can shape "self-awareness" or verbal behavior descriptive of private events.

12. What is meant by *synesthesia*, and how does it help explain the unusual mnemonic performance of Luria's subject?

Discussion Questions

13. What are some of the advantages and disadvantages of experiencing multiple perceptual responses to simple stimuli? Do you think that typical human responses to stimuli are optimal?

14. Most people find it difficult to discuss memory without alluding to "storage." What is stored? In what sense do neural structures represent behavior?

15. Imagine a computer file comprising ten statements, one of which is "The strawberries will be ripe in a few weeks." It seems legitimate to say that the statements are stored in the computer. Do you think it is possible to program the computer reliably to "retrieve" the target statement when asked a novel but relevant question, such as "Which statement would be of interest to a gourmand?" or "Which statement is about delayed gratification?" Does the storage metaphor help you solve this problem or do you need to resort to supplementary "mnemonic behavior"?

ENDNOTES

1. Peterson & Peterson, 1959.
2. Bellugi, Klima, & Siple, 1975.
3. See Branch, 1977 for a discussion of the importance of identifying empirical units of analysis in memory research. His paper provides a readable and cogent argument against the conceptual carelessness that pervades most discussions of memory. Branch was perhaps the first behaviorist to point out that the field of memory, as traditionally studied, is not a conceptually coherent subject. (See Palmer, 1991 for related arguments.)
4. Slamecka & Graf, 1978.
5. Tulving & Thomson, 1973.
6. See Skinner, 1957, Chapter 9 for an extended discussion of these points.
7. Skinner, 1957 called such stimuli formal prompts, because they have the same form as part of the target response.
8. E.g., Miller, 1956.
9. Cf. Craik & Watkins, 1973.
10. Sanford, 1917/1982.
11. E.g., Melton, 1967; Underwood, 1961.
12. See Reese, 1977 for discussion.

13. See Skinner, 1953, Chapter 17 for a discussion of these points.

14. Bartlett, 1932.

15. Reder, 1982.

16. Bower, 1972.

17. Cf. Paivio, 1971. Paivio proposed a "dual coding hypothesis," namely, that concrete terms can be recalled relatively easily because we can respond to them verbally as well as perceptually and hence have a greater stock of effective recall responses.

18. E.g., Bevan & Steger, 1971; Paivio, 1969.

19. Bower, 1972.

20. E.g., Denis, 1982.

21. E.g., Mandler, 1967.

22. The information processing theorists Craik & Lockhart (1972) refer to "levels of processing" to explain probability of recall. Things we process "deeply" are easily remembered; mere iteration of a target response is "shallow" and leads to poor recall.

23. Chase & Ericsson, 1982.

24. Bower & Clark, 1969.

25. See Atkinson & Raugh, 1975; Bower, 1970; Miller, Galanter, & Pribram, 1960; Roediger, 1980.

26. Cole, Gay, Glick, & Sharp, 1971; Fahrmeier, 1975; Hall, 1972.

27. Cole, Gay, Glick, & Sharp, 1971; Wagner, 1974, 1978.

28. Rogoff & Mistry, 1985.

29. Istomena, 1975.

30. Flavell, Beach, & Chinsky, 1966.

31. Ornstein, Naus, & Liberty, 1975.

32. Moely, Olson, Halwes, & Flavell, 1969.

33. Kreutzer, Leonard, and Flavell, 1975.

34. Belmont & Butterfield, 1977.

35. Turnure, Buium, & Thurlow, 1976.

36. Butterfield, Wambold, & Belmont, 1973.

37. Flavell, 1971; Flavell & Wellman, 1977.

38. Skinner, 1957, p.130.

39. Skinner, 1957, pp. 130–134.

40. Carlson, 1991.

41. Luria, 1980, p. 383.

42. Luria, 1980, p. 384.

43. Luria, 1980, p. 385.

GLOSSARY

acquired reinforcers   stimuli that function as reinforcers as a result of being paired with other reinforcers, i.e., those learned during the lifetime of the organism. (See **conditioned reinforcers** and **higher-order conditioning**.)

activation pattern   a widespread pattern of neural activity in the brain, initiated by stimuli applied to the receptors of an experienced learner.

activity-dependent mechanisms   mechanisms whereby the strengthening of connections during neural development depends on the coactivation of neighboring or adjacent neurons.

affordance   the concept whereby the observer is said to perceive the behavior a stimulus permits or *affords*, in addition to the stimulus itself.

alexia   the loss of the ability to read.

amnesia   an impairment in which the environment can no longer evoke verbal behavior with respect to past stimuli.

anomia   the loss of the ability to name objects.

anterograde amnesia   the inability to recall events that occurred before the brain was damaged.

aphasias   speech disorders resulting from brain damage.

appetitive elicitor   a stimulus that evokes an approach response; i.e., a response that brings the learner into contact with the stimulus.

apraxias   behavioral deficits in movements controlled by verbal stimuli, caused by brain damage.

arbitrary matching   in the matching-to-sample procedure, a contextual discrimination in which the sample and comparison stimuli bear no physical similarity to one another.

autobiographical memories   episodic memories in which the guiding stimulus includes oneself as a salient event; e.g., recalling what you said to someone at a gathering, in contrast to recalling merely who was at the gathering.

autoclitics   verbal operants guided by relationships among other verbal operants.

automatic chaining   the emergence of a sequence of responses with functional unity, in which each response provides stimuli that guide subsequent responses.

aversive elicitor   a stimulus that evokes withdrawal, or escape, responses.

babbling   the unsystematic emission of a wide variety of speech sounds by human infants.

backward chaining   a technique in which the components of a behavioral sequence are added in reverse order to that in which they will ultimately occur.

base-rate neglect   overvaluation of a stimulus believed to be characteristic of an infrequent event.

behavioral chaining   the formation of a sequence of environment-behavior relations in which each relation is maintained by the discriminative stimulus produced by the preceding response.

behavioral discrepancy   a difference between ongoing and elicited behavior.

behavioral engineering   the technology of changing behavior by altering the contemporary environment.

behavioral mixture   a combination of previously selected behaviors that occurs in environments similar to that in which selection originally occurred.

biological constraints on learning   limitations, resulting from natural selection, on the outcome of behavioral selection by reinforcement. (See **taste aversion**.)

blindsight   a condition resulting from brain damage, in which the patient behaves nonverbally as if he can see, but speaks as if he cannot see.

blocking   the phenomenon in which an earlier stimulus paired with an elicitor prevents learning with a later stimulus.

Broca's area a brain region that plays an important role in speech production; see Fig. 9.8.

categorical perception different perceptual responses evoked by slight physical differences at phoneme boundaries.

categorical responding an abrupt change in response strength, even though the stimuli are changing gradually.

classical conditioning the technique of studying learning by presenting an environmental event followed by an eliciting stimulus.

comparative approach comparison of human behavior with that of other species.

comparison stimuli the stimuli that guide the learner's response options in the matching-to-sample procedure.

compound stimulus an environment that includes separable stimulus components, such as a light and a tone.

computer simulation the use of a computer to model relations among real-world events, such as those between the environment and the behavior of an organism.

concurrent-chain procedure an operant procedure in which there are two simultaneously available response options, each of which consists of successive stimuli, with the reinforcer presented after the final stimulus.

concurrent schedules procedures in which more than one response is scheduled for reinforcement.

conditioned reinforcers stimuli that function as reinforcers in operant procedures as a result of having been paired with other reinforcers.

conditioned response the response evoked by the conditioned stimulus in the classical procedure.

conditioned stimulus the stimulus which comes to evoke behavior as a result of being paired with the eliciting stimulus in the classical procedure.

configural conditioning a discrimination task in which responding to a simultaneous compound stimulus and responding to the separate components of the compound are differentially reinforced; e.g., responding to the occurrence of a tone and a light together is reinforced, but not responding to the tone or the light alone.

constructionism a view of perceiving which holds that environmental stimuli are inadequate to fully specify the environment, and that inferred mental processes are required for the organism to "construct" an accurate representation of the world from those impoverished stimuli. (See **direct perception**.)

contextual discrimination a differential training procedure in which the same stimulus guides one response in one stimulus context and a different response in a second context.

contextual stimuli or **context** stimuli that accompany the training stimuli but are not manipulated by the experimenter.

contingency a relation in which the occurrence of one event depends on the occurrence of another event.

contingency-shaped behavior behavior produced by differential reinforcement.

continuous reinforcement the presentation of the reinforcing stimulus after each occurrence of the unconditioned stimulus in the classical procedure, or after each occurrence of the response in the operant procedure.

corpus callosum a very large bundle of axons that connects the right and left hemispheres of the brain.

counterselections selected environment-behavior relations that alter the environment and thereby influence subsequent selection.

critical periods see **sensitive periods**.

cross-modal generalization guidance of the same response by the same stimulus across more than one sensory modality (e.g., sight and touch), without specific reinforcement of the second relation.

cross-modal priming facilitation of the target response when the priming and target stimuli are in different sensory modalities.

cross-sectional studies studies in which different individuals of different ages are observed.

cues the term used for discriminative stimuli in memory research.

cumulative record a graphic record of responding in which responses are cumulated over time, and each response produces an increase in the curve with the passage of time.

decay theory the view that environment-behavior relations weaken with the mere passage of time.

deprivation a reduction in the organism's contact with a stimulus below the level that would occur if it had unlimited access to the stimulus.

derived relations environment-behavior relations that were strengthened by a training procedure even though they were not directly reinforced.

devaluation a change in the strength of an environment-behavior relation produced when the reinforcing stimulus that was used to select the relation is later modified in some way; e.g., a change in the strength of food-reinforced lever-pressing when the food is later independently paired with shock.

developmental approach examination of behavior over the life history of the individual.

dichotic listening procedure a laboratory procedure in which different messages are simultaneously presented to both of the listener's ears through stereophonic earphones.

differential training procedure a training procedure in which the learner is exposed to different environments in which responses have different consequences.

direct perception the view that environmental stimuli fully specify the environment. (See **constructionism**.)

discriminative stimulus an environmental stimulus that has come to guide or control responding through individual selection.

discriminative stimulus class a range of stimuli that bear some physical similarity to one another and control common responses; e.g., members of the class *dog* have similar physical characteristics.

distractor task a task, such as counting backwards by 3's, used to interfere with recall performance during memory research.

divided-attention tasks laboratory procedures that produce interfering interactions among different environment-behavior relations.

dopamine a neuromodulator whose presence in a synapse results in long-lasting increases in the ability of the presynaptic neuron to activate the postsynaptic neuron, and which is released by neurons in the VTA, among other brain regions.

echoic responses vocal responses whose sound is similar to those that one has heard; i.e., repetitions of words spoken by another.

ecologically valid observations observations obtained in the environments in which behavior originated and now normally occurs.

edge effects the enhanced differences in responding that occur near the boundaries between regions of differential reinforcement in a differential training procedure.

electrode a pair of fine wires, insulated from one another except at their tips, that is inserted into a brain region to stimulate neurons or monitor their activity.

eliciting function the ability of an environmental stimulus to reliably evoke behavior.

eliciting stimuli or **elicitors** stimuli that reliably evoke behavior as a result of natural selection.

environment-behavior relations orderly relations between environmental and behavioral events, resulting from either natural selection or selection by reinforcement.

environment-environment relations orderly relations between environmental events, the perception of which results from either natural selection or selection by reinforcement.

environmental chaining the formation of a sequence of environment-behavior relations in which each relation is maintained by the discriminative stimulus following, but not necessarily produced by, the preceding response; the result of a serial compound conditioning procedure.

episodic memory   an environment-behavior relation in which recall is guided by many of the particular stimuli in whose presence selection originally occurred, such as the location where you last met a friend.

equivalence class   a type of functional class in which selection processes directly affecting one member of a stimulus or response class have similar effects on all members of that class; produced by multiple contextual discriminations.

escape   a withdrawal response.

excitatory neurotransmitters   chemical substances that, when released by a presynaptic neuron, tend to activate the postsynaptic neuron.

experimental analysis   the process whereby the antecedents of a phenomenon are manipulated or controlled and their effects are measured. Experimental analysis in biobehavioral science seeks to achieve orderly and precise functional relations from observations of single organisms. This idealized set of conditions is approximated as closely as permitted by available scientific knowledge and technology. Not all experiments meet the demands of experimental analysis (e.g., most experiments with human subjects) and not all experimental analyses are experiments (e.g., some observations in astronomy).

extinction   the weakening of the guidance of a previously reinforced response by a stimulus when the response occurs in the presence of that stimulus but is no longer reinforced.

fading   a discrimination training procedure that begins by using substantially different training stimuli, which are progressively and gradually changed to their final and more similar values.

feed-forward networks   neural networks in which the activity of a unit can only be influenced by the activity of earlier or "upstream" units.

fixed-interval (FI) schedule   a contingency during which a response produces a reinforcer only after a fixed period of time has elapsed since the previous reinforced response.

fixed-ratio (FR) schedule   a contingency during which a response produces a reinforcer only after a fixed number of responses have occurred since the previous reinforced response.

flashbulb memories   instances of episodic memory in which the detailed circumstances surrounding some dramatic event (such as learning of President Kennedy's assassination) are recalled.

formal interpretation   the use of a formal system such as logic or mathematics to systematize the processes held to account for complex phenomena; differs from the use of formal systems in cognitive psychology and artificial intelligence, in which the processes do not result from experimental analysis.

fovea   the area in the center of the retina where the visual receptors are most densely concentrated, and where the light from a fixated object falls.

frontal lobe   the region of the cerebral cortex located at the front of the brain; see Fig. 9.8.

function words   words denoting relationships among other words, phrases, and clauses, such as articles, conjunctions, and prepositions.

functional class   a range of stimuli that may differ physically but have similar uses and control common responses; e.g., members of the class *toy* may differ in appearance, but are all used in play.

functional fixedness   the tendency to neglect secondary properties or uncommon uses of a familiar object.

fuzzy boundary   a characteristic of stimulus classes produced by selection; indicates that no single feature need be present in a complex stimulus to evoke the behavior guided by the complex stimulus.

generalized identity matching   see **reflexive relation**.

generation effect   a phenomenon in which subjects who had, when given certain information, "generated" the response to the stimulus word

performed better on retention tests than subjects trained in the traditional paired-associate
procedure.

genetic engineering the technology that makes
it possible to alter the genetic processes which
have resulted from natural selection.

glutmate an excitatory, amino acid neurotransmitter.

grating a visual stimulus made up of parallel
bands of light and dark, used to study the receptive fields of cortical cells.

grammatical frame a verbal operant containing
one or more variable elements, such as
"Where's the —X—?"

habituation the weakening of an unlearned environment-behavior relation when the environmental event is repeatedly presented without
consequence.

hemispheres the right and left halves of the
brain.

higher-order conditioning environment-behavior relations selected when acquired elicitors are used as reinforcers in classical
procedures.

hippocampal amnesia retrograde amnesia produced by interruption of pathways between the
sensory association cortex and the hippocampus.

identity matching in the matching-to-sample
procedure, a contextual discrimination in
which the response is reinforced if the comparison stimulus is the same as the sample stimulus.

illusion a stimulus array that, as a result of the
prior selection of perceptual invariants or regularities, guides behavior inconsistent with the
"objective" values of the array; e.g., in the
illusion resulting from lateral inhibition, the
organism sees the white space at the intersection of four black squares as darker than the
white space between two black squares.

imagining behavior similar to that guided by
certain stimuli, evoked by stimuli not physically similar to those that usually guide perceiving; i.e., behaving "as if" the absent stimuli
are perceived.

imprinting the attachment a duckling forms by
following a moving object (usually its mother)
shortly after being hatched.

inflections changes of word form that mark case,
gender, number, tense, person, mood, or voice;
e.g., the terminal "s" that denotes plurality in
nouns.

information processing the approach to the
study of behavior in which the structures and
processes of digital computers are used as a
metaphor for inferred structures and processes
thought to intervene between the environment
and behavior.

inhibitory neurons neurons that reduce the activity of the neurons on which they synapse.

inhibitory neurotransmitter a chemical substance that, when released by an inhibitory
neuron, makes it less likely that the postsynaptic neuron will be activated by its excitatory
inputs.

input unit an element of an adaptive neural network, simulating the activity of a neuron or
group of neurons that mediate an environmental event.

instrumental conditioning the technique of
studying learning by presenting an eliciting
stimulus after a behavioral event.

intermittent reinforcement the presentation of
a reinforcing stimulus after fewer than 100% of
the occurrences of the unconditioned stimulus
in the classical procedure, or after fewer than
100% of the occurrences of the response in the
operant procedure.

internal reinforcement activation of the ventral
tegmental area by feedback from neural circuits
in the frontal lobes rather than more directly by
environmental stimuli; dependent on prior
learning.

interpretation see **scientific interpretation**

interresponse times (IRTs) the lengths of time
occurring between measured responses, such as
keypecks or leverpresses, in an operant procedure.

intraverbal response a verbal response guided
by a non-identical spoken or written stimulus;

e.g., the response "67" to the stimulus "64...65...66..."

kana symbols Japanese phonetic written symbols.

kanji symbols Japanese pictorial written symbols.

keyword mnemonic a mnemonic acquisition procedure for foreign vocabulary, in which each foreign word is paired with an English word of similar form and then the two meanings are visualized interacting with one another.

language acquisition device in traditional linguistics, the innate capacity that enables a child to extract the relevant elements of universal grammar from the speech he hears.

larynx the upper part of the windpipe, containing the vocal cords; see Fig. 11.1.

latent learning facilitation of performance in a learning task following unreinforced exposure to the learning environment.

lateral geniculate nuclei nuclei in the thalamus that receive stimulation from retinal ganglion cells and transmit stimulation to the visual cortex.

lateral inhibition inhibition of the cells responding to light from the center of a visual stimulus by the cells responding to light from the sides of the stimulus.

lexicon in conventional treatments of language, a repository where words and their meanings are stored.

longitudinal studies studies in which the same individuals are observed over time.

masking stimulus a stimulus presented within a few ms of the sample stimulus in a modification of the matching-to-sample procedure.

matching principle the principle which states that, during a concurrent schedule, the relative frequency of responding on an alternative matches the relative frequency of reinforcers produced by responding on that alternative.

matching-to-sample procedure a laboratory procedure for studying contextual discriminations, in which the learner's response to a comparison stimulus is reinforced or not, depending on the value of the sample stimulus.

means-end analysis in problem solving, a strategy of minimizing the difference between the present situation and the target situation.

mental set the tendency to approach a problem in a way that has proven successful in the past, even if another approach would be more fruitful under present circumstances.

metamemory the evaluation of one's own mnemonic behavior and its effect on subsequent behavior.

method of loci a mnemonic acquisition procedure in which each item to be remembered is visualized in a particular location in a familiar setting.

methodological behaviorism the approach to the study of behavior which holds that scientific psychology should restrict its attention to observed behavior which can be measured directly.

mnemonic behavior overt or covert activity that produces supplementary stimuli which facilitate remembering.

model preparations artificial and highly simplified experimental situations, such as the rabbit nictitating-membrane preparation, which clearly reveal the effects of the variables being studied.

molar principle a principle, such as the matching principle, that describes the relation between two variables that are defined over a relatively long time interval.

molecular principle a principle, such as the reinforcement principle, that describes the relation between two variables that are defined over a relatively brief time interval.

motivating function the general effect of deprivation on the strength and type of an organism's reaction to a range of stimuli other than those of which it has been deprived.

motivating stimulus or **motivator** a stimulus that functions to establish other stimuli as reinforcers or punishers.

naming task a procedure in which a priming stimulus is presented, followed by a visually presented target word that is to be read aloud.

natural selection   the principle that summarizes the processes which, by influencing the characteristics that affect the survivability of offspring, give rise to biological diversity and organization.

neurons   nerve cells.

neuropsychological approach   examination of the effects of neural damage on behavior, particularly in humans.

neurotransmitters   chemical compounds that allow a neuron to affect the functioning of the neurons on which it synapses.

nominal fallacy   using the name of a phenomenon as if it were an explanation for the phenomenon.

nondifferential training procedure   a training procedure in which the learner is exposed to only a single environment.

observing responses   acquired environment-behavior relations whose primary function is to affect the sensing of stimuli, which then function as conditioned reinforcers for those relations.

occipital lobe   the region of the cerebral cortex located at the rear of the brain; see Fig. 9.8.

operant conditioning   see **instrumental conditioning**.

operants   responses that are less reliably evoked by stimuli than respondents, or for which the stimulus is not well specified.

optic chiasm   the region where half of the axons in the optic nerve cross to the other side of the brain.

optic nerve   the neural pathway from the retina to the optic chiasm.

optic tract   the neural pathway from the optic chiasm to the lateral geniculate nuclei.

organismic interpretation   a laboratory simulation in which an organism is provided with the selection history that experimental-analytic principles indicate is sufficient to produce an environment-behavior relation.

output unit   an element of an adaptive neural network, simulating the activity of a neuron or group of neurons that mediate a behavioral event.

over-expectation   a decline in the ability of individual stimuli to evoke a conditioned response after they have been presented in a simultaneous compound followed by the same elicitor that each had been paired with previously.

overregularization or **overgeneralization**   the extension of grammatical rules to instances not reinforced by the verbal community, such as the treatment of irregular verbs as if they were regular; e.g., "I goed" rather than "I went."

paired-associate learning   a laboratory procedure for studying retention, in which pairs of words are sequentially presented to the subject.

parallel processing   the simultaneous activation of many units in the brain.

parallel transmission   the overlapping of phonemes in fluent speech.

parietal lobe   the region of the cerebral cortex located between the frontal and occipital lobes of the brain; see Fig. 9.8.

partial reinforcement   see **intermittent reinforcement**.

path-dependent   a characteristic of environment-behavior relations, and of the input-output relations of adaptive networks that simulate them, in which the final expression of the relation is influenced by the particular sequence of selecting events that produced it.

peg-word mnemonic   a mnemonic acquisition procedure in which numbers are paired with common concrete objects that rhyme with them, and then each item to be remembered is visualized interacting in some easily discriminated way with one of the objects.

perceptual invariants   relations between environmental events that are constant over evolutionary time.

perceptual regularities   relations between environmental events that change over evolutionary time, but are relatively constant within an individual's lifetime.

persistence   see **resistance to extinction**.

pharynx   the cavity behind the nose and mouth; see Fig. 11.1.

phonemes   speech sounds.

photopigments chemical compounds, contained in the visual receptors, that are sensitive to visible light.

place learning the integration of combinations of environmental cues that specify one's location in relation to them.

polymodal association cortex cortical cells that are activated by inputs from different sensory channels from multiple sensory modalities e.g., auditory and tactile as well as visual stimuli.

polysensory invariants relations between environmental events in different sensory channels that are constant over evolutionary time.

polysensory regularities relations between environmental events in different sensory channels that change over evolutionary time, but are relatively constant within an individual's lifetime.

postsynaptic neuron the neuron receiving the stimulation.

prepotent response the strongest, or most probable, among a set of competing resonses.

presynaptic neuron the neuron transmitting the stimulation.

primacy effect the higher retention of the earlier stimuli in the serial-recognition procedure.

prime to facilitate the performance of the target response in the priming procedure.

priming procedure a laboratory procedure for studying the effect of an earlier stimulus on responding to a stimulus presented immediately thereafter.

priming stimulus the stimulus whose effect on responding is being assessed in the priming procedure.

principle of behavioral selection the principle that summarizes the selecting effect of the individual environment.

principle of reinforcement the principle of behavioral selection.

private events the inner world of the individual; i.e., the stimuli originating within the skin, to which each person has unique access.

proactive facilitation the enhancement of the retention of later learning by earlier learning.

proactive interference the impairment of the retention of later learning by earlier learning.

probe stimulus the stimulus presented following the target stimuli in the serial-recognition procedure.

prototype a typical input pattern for a stimulus class; i.e., the most typical combination of the environmental features that were present during selection, but not necessarily one of the specific patterns used in training the network.

punishing stimulus or **punisher** an elicitor that reduces the strength of the operant that produces it.

punishment an operant procedure in which an environment-behavior relation is followed by an elicitor that reduces the strength of the relation.

radical behaviorism the approach to the study of behavior developed mainly by B. F. Skinner, which holds that the science of behavior embraces all behavior, both private events and publicly observed behavior, and that a common set of principles should be identified through experimental analysis of observed events. (Contrast with **methodological behaviorism** and **information processing**.)

reafference alterations in the activity of units in the sensory component of an activation pattern by activity in the motor component, through recurrent connections.

recency effect the higher retention of the later stimuli in the serial-recognition procedure.

receptive field the region of the visual field from which light activates a given cortical cell.

recurrent connections pathways that permit the activity of later or "downstream" units in a neural network to influence earlier units.

reflex a reliable environment-behavior relation that is largely the result of natural selection.

reflexive relation the relation demonstrated when a subject who has learned identity matching with one set of stimuli (A-A) matches a different set of stimuli (B-B) without additional training; i.e., generalization of identity matching from one set of stimuli to another.

reinforcing stimulus or **reinforcer**   an eliciting stimulus that functions to select environment-behavior relations.

remembering   behavior determined by previously selected environment-behavior relations, but for which the present environment does not contain stimuli sufficient to guide the behavior now scheduled for reinforcement. (See **reminding**.)

reminding   the provision of stimuli that, as a result of past selections, directly guide the behavior currently scheduled for reinforcement; i.e., the present environment *reminds* the learner of responses selected in past environments. (See **remembering**.)

resistance to extinction   the persistence of an environment-behavior relation after the reinforcing stimulus has been omitted; characteristic of relations that have been intermittently reinforced.

respondent conditioning   see **classical conditioning**.

respondents   responses that are reliably evoked by a specific stimulus, such as airpuff-evoked blinking.

response class   a range of behaviors not necessarily confined to the specific responses that were previously selected by reinforcers in that environment.

response-selection network   the component of a selection network that selects connections which mediate environment-behavior relations.

resurgence   the emergence of other responses during the extinction of a dominant response.

retina   a network of complexly interconnected receptors and neurons that cover the back interior surface of the eyeball.

retroactive facilitation   the enhancement of the retention of earlier learning by later learning.

retroactive interference   the impairment of the retention of earlier learning by later learning.

retrograde amnesia   the inability to recall events that have occurred since the brain was damaged.

rule-governed behavior   behavior guided by verbal stimuli such as definitions or instructions.

saccadic eye movements or **saccades**   rapid eye movements which fixate on the fovea objects detected in the periphery of the visual field.

sample stimulus   the stimulus that provides the context in the matching-to-sample procedure.

schedule of reinforcement   a complete description of the environmental and behavioral conditions present when a response is followed by a reinforcer; e.g., a specification of the number of responses emitted or the amount of time elapsed between reinforced responses.

scientific interpretation   the process whereby principles derived from experimental analysis are used to account for observations that, themselves, cannot be subjected to experimental analysis. Most complex behavior, especially human behavior, is the province of the interpretative rather than the experimental-analytic aspects of biobehavioral science.

secondary reinforcers   see **conditioned reinforcers.**

semantic memory   an environment-behavior relation in which recall is guided by a relatively narrow range of stimuli, particularly when the behavior includes verbal responses; e.g., knowledge of a fact, such as a person's name.

sensitive periods   circumscribed time periods in an organism's development, to which the effect of the individual environment on the selection of sensory and polysensory invariants is restricted.

sensitization   the alteration of responding to a range of other stimuli as a result of the presentation of a stimulus, particularly an intense stimulus.

sensory channel   a neural circuit that is activated by one aspect of environmental stimulation, such as variation in color or motion.

serial compound conditioning   a classical procedure in which two or more stimuli are successively presented before a reflexive eliciting stimulus; see **environmental chaining**.

serial-position curve   in the serial-recognition procedure, the function relating the percentage of correct recognition responses to the serial position of the target stimuli.

serial processing   the sequential activation of units in the brain.

serial-recognition procedure   a laboratory procedure for studying retention, in which the learner is asked to recognize whether a probe stimulus appeared in the sequence of target stimuli presented earlier.

shadowing   attending to the auditory stimuli presented to one ear during a dichotic listening procedure, and emitting echoic responses to those stimuli.

shaping   gradual changes in a response-reinforcer contingency to select environment-behavior relations whose component responses progressively approximate some criterion response topography.

spatial frequency   the number of stripes per degree of visual angle in a grating.

state-dependent forgetting   impaired performance resulting from differences in the internal context (e.g., because of drugs) during acquisition and retention.

stimulus class   a range of guiding stimuli whose members are not restricted to the specific stimuli present when the environment-behavior relation was selected.

stimulus discrimination   the process by which unreliable environmental and behavioral events are eliminated from selected environment-behavior relations.

stimulus generalization   the process by which responding comes to be guided by a range of stimuli similar, but not limited, to the original selecting environment.

stimulus generalization gradient   the curve showing the variation in strength of responding as a function of the value of the stimulus dimension.

stimulus-selection network   the component of a selection network that selects connections which mediate environment-environment relations.

superior collicular nuclei   nuclei in the hindbrain, containing cells that respond differentially to visual stimuli, especially movement.

superstitious behavior   an environment-behavior relation that has arisen without true dependencies between the behavior and eliciting stimuli.

symbolic matching   see **arbitrary matching**.

symmetric relation   the relation demonstrated when, after contextual discrimination training (A-B task), the subject responds to the sample and comparison stimuli as if they were interchangeable (B-A task).

synapse   the gap between one neuron and another into which neurotransmitters are released.

synaptic efficacy   the effectiveness with which one neuron activates another.

synesthesia   multiple perceptual responses to a single stimulus, such as perceptions of color and taste, as well as sound, to an auditory stimulus.

tact   a discriminated verbal operant in which the guiding stimulus is some nonverbal property or object.

target response   in the priming procedure, the response evoked by the target stimulus.

target stimuli   in the serial-recognition procedure, the sequence of stimuli initially presented to the subject.

target stimulus   in the priming procedure, the stimulus to which the subject responds.

taste aversion   an environment-behavior relation in which a taste or smell that has been accompanied by nausea is subsequently avoided by the organism.

temporal contiguity   the occurrence of two events with a very short time interval between them.

temporal lobes   the regions of the cerebral cortex located at the sides of the brain; see Fig. 9.8.

textual responses   verbal responses guided by written or printed words; i.e., reading.

theoretically coherent term a technical term, resulting from experimental analysis, that applies to a group of phenomena produced by a common set of consistent, well-defined basic processes.

theoretically incoherent term a nontechnical term, arising from everyday experience, that groups together similar-appearing phenomena that may result from a variety of different processes.

three-term contingency a condition in which the occurrence of a reinforcing stimulus depends on the performance of a specific behavioral response in the presence of a specific environmental stimulus.

threshold of detectability the interval between the sample and masking stimuli at which a subject can accurately judge whether a word has been presented.

threshold of semantic detection the interval between the sample and masking stimuli at which a subject can accurately recognize which word has been presented.

topography the form of a response.

transcortical aphasia a disorder in which patients can repeat words but cannot speak spontaneously, and sometimes cannot even understand the words they repeat.

transfer effect the effect of earlier selection on selection in a later task.

transitive relation the relation demonstrated when, after contextual discrimination training on both A-B and B-C tasks, the subject responds appropriately on an A-C task.

trial-and-error problem solving emitting different responses in a stimulus situation until reinforcement occurs.

two-string problem a task used in problem-solving research, in which the subject is asked to tie together two strings that are hanging from hooks in the ceiling.

unconditioned response the response elicited by the unconditioned stimulus in the classical procedure.

unconditioned stimulus the eliciting stimulus in the classical procedure.

unified principle of reinforcement the reinforcement principle proposed in this book, which incorporates the selection process in the classical and operant procedures and holds that *whenever a behavioral discrepancy occurs, an environment-behavior relation is selected that consists of all stimuli occurring immediately before the discrepancy and all responses occurring immediately before and at the same time as the elicited response.*

universal grammar in traditional linguistics, an innate knowledge of the rules governing language.

variable-interval (VI) schedule a contingency during which a response produces a reinforcer only after a variable period of time has elapsed since the previous reinforced response.

variable-ratio (VR) schedule a contingency during which a response produces a reinforcer only after a variable number of responses have occurred since the previous reinforced response.

ventral tegmental area (VTA) a region of the brain whose stimulation functions as a particularly effective reinforcer.

verbal bias the assumption that everything we know is reflected in our verbal behavior.

verbal interpretation explanation of a phenomenon in terms of processes identified by prior experimental analysis, and the principles that summarize those processes.

verbal operant the unit of analysis in verbal behavior; an empirically defined class of verbal responses that is relatively stable over time.

visual association cortex cortical cells that are activated by neurons from different sensory channels in the visual cortex.

Wernicke's area a region in the auditory association cortex of the left temporal lobe of the brain, damage to which disrupts a variety of speech functions; see Fig. 9.8.

REFERENCES

Ackley, D., & Litman, M. (1991). Interactions between learning and evolution. In C. G. Langton, C. Taylor, J. D. Farmer, & S. Rasmussen (Eds.), *Artificial life II, SFI studies in the sciences of complexity* (pp. 487–507). New York: Addison-Wesley.

Acredolo, L. P. (1979). Laboratory vs. home: The effect of environment on the 9-month-old infant's choice of spatial reference system. *Developmental Psychology, 15*, 666–667.

Alavosius, M. P. (1987). The endurance of health-care routines following schedules of feedback. Unpublished doctoral dissertation, University of Massachusetts.

Albrecht, D. G., & De Valois, R. L. (1981). Striate cortex responses to periodic patterns with and without the fundamental harmonics. *Journal of Physiology (London), 319*, 497–514.

Alkon, D. L. (1980). Cellular analysis of a gastropod (*Hermissenda crassicornis*) model of associative learning. *Biological Bulletin, 159*, 505–560.

Alkon, D. L. (1984). Calcium-mediated reduction of ionic currents: A biophysical memory trace. *Science, 226*, 1037–1045.

Alkon, D. L. (1988). *Memory traces in the brain.* New York: Cambridge University Press.

Allport, D. A. (1980). Patterns and actions. In G. L. Claxton (Ed.), *New directions in cognitive psychology.* London: Routledge & Kegan Paul.

Allport, D. A., Antonis, B., & Reynolds, P. (1972). On the division of attention: A disproof of the single channel hypothesis. *Quarterly Journal of Experimental Psychology, 24*, 225–235.

Amaral, D. G. (1987). Memory: anatomical organization of candidate brain regions. In F. Plum (Ed.), *Handbook of Physiology. Section 1: Neurophysiology, Vol. 5: Higher Functions of the Brain* (pp. 211–294). Bethesda, MD: American Physiological Society.

Ambros-Ingerson, J., Granger, R., & Lynch, G. (1990). Simulation of paleocortex performs hierarchical clustering. *Science, 247,* 1344–1347.

Amsel, A. (1958). The role of frustrative nonreward in noncontinuous reward situations. *Psychological Bulletin, 55*, 102–119.

Amsel, A. (1972). Behavioral habituation, counter-conditioning, and a general theory of persistence. In A. H. Black & W. F. Prokasy (Eds.), *Classical conditioning. II. Current research and theory.* New York: Appleton-Century-Crofts.

Anderson, J. A. (1984). Neural models and a little about language. In D. Caplan, A. R. Lecours, and A. Smith (Eds.), *Biological perspectives on language.* Cambridge, MA: MIT Press.

Anderson, J. R. (1978). Arguments concerning representations for mental imagery. *Psychological Review, 85*, 249–277.

Anderson, J. R. (1983). *The architecture of cognition.* Cambridge, MA: Harvard University Press.

Anderson, J. R. (1985). *Cognitive psychology and its implications* (2nd ed.) San Francisco: Freeman.

Andronis, P. T. (1983). Symbolic aggression by pigeons: Contingency coadduction. Ph.D. dissertation: The University of Chicago.

Antonitis, J. J. (1951). Response variability in the white rat during conditioning, extinction, and reconditioning. *Journal of Experimental Psychology, 42,* 273–281.

Arbuckle, J. L., & Lattal, K. A. (1992). Molecular contingencies in schedules of intermittent reinforcement. *Journal of the Experimental Analysis of Behavior, 58,* 361–376.

Aris, R., Davis, H. T., & Steuwer, R. H. (1983). *Springs of scientific creativity.* Minneapolis, MN: University of Minnesota Press.

Ashcraft, M. H. (1989). *Human memory and cognition.* Glenview, IL: Scott, Foresman & Co.

Ashe, J. H., & Nachman, M. (1980). Neural mechanisms of taste aversion learning. *Progress in Psychobiology and Physiological Psychology, 9,* 233–262.

Aslin, R. N., Alberts, J. R., & Peterson, M. R. (1981). *Development of perception.* New York: Academic.

Aslin, R. R., & Smith, L. B. (1988). Perceptual development. In A. R. Rosenzweig & L. W. Porter (Eds.), *Annual Review of Psychology,* (Vol 39, pp. 435–473). Palo Alto, CA: Annual Reviews, Inc.

Atkinson, R. C., & Raugh, M. R. (1975). An application of the mnemonic keyword method to the acquisition of a Russian vocabulary. *Journal of Experimental Psychology: Human Learning and Memory, 1,* 126–133.

Atkinson, R. C., & Shiffrin, R. M. (1968). Human memory: A proposed system and its control processes. In K. W. Spence & J. T. Spence (Eds.), *The psychology of learning and motivation* (Vol. 2, pp. 89–195). San Francisco: Freeman.

Averbach, E., & Coriell, A. S. (1961). Short-term memory in vision. *Bell System Technical Journal, 40,* 309–328.

Baars, B. J. (1986). *The cognitive revolution of psychology.* New York: Guilford.

Baddeley, A. P. (1986). *Working memory.* New York: Oxford University Press.

Bading, H., & Greenberg, M. E. (1991). Stimulation of protein tyrosine phosphorylation by NMDA receptor activation. *Science, 253,* 912–914.

Bahrick, H. P. (1979). Maintenance of knowledge: Questions about memory we forgot to ask. *Journal of Experimental Psychology: General, 108,* 296–308.

Bahrick, H. P. (1983). The cognitive map of a city—fifty years of learning and memory. In G. H. Bower (Ed.), *The psychology of learning and motivation: Advances in research and theory* (Vol. 17, pp. 125–163). New York: Academic.

Bahrick, H. P. (1984). Semantic memory content in permastore: Fifty years of memory for Spanish learned in school. *Journal of Experimental Psychology: General, 113,* 1–29.

Bahrick, H. P., Bahrick, P. C., & Whittlinger, R. P. (1975). Fifty years of memories for names and faces: A cross-sectional approach. *Journal of Experimental Psychology: General, 104,* 54–75.

Bahrick, H. P., & Phelps, E. (1988). The maintenance of marginal knowledge. In U. Neisser & E. Winograd, (Eds.), *Remembering reconsidered: Ecological and traditional approaches to the study of memory* (pp. 178–192). New York: Cambridge University Press.

Balaz, M. A., Gutsin, P., Cacheiro, H., & Miller, R. R. (1982). Blocking as a retrieval failure: Reactivation of associations to a blocked stimulus. *Quarterly Journal of Experimental Psychology, 34B,* 99–113.

Balota, D. A. (1983). Automatic semantic activation and episodic memory encoding. *Journal of Verbal Learning and Verbal Behavior, 22,* 88–104.

Balsam, P. D. (1984). Bringing the background to the foreground. In M. L. Commons, R. J. Herrnstein, & A. R. Wagner (Eds.), *Quantitative analyses of behavior: Vol. 3, Acquisition* (pp. 145–171). Cambridge, MA: Ballinger.

Balsam, P. D., & Tomie, A. (1985). *Context and learning.* Hillsdale, NJ: Erlbaum.

Banks, M. S., & Salapatek, P. (1983). Infant visual perception. In P. H. Mussen (Ed.), *Carmichael's handbook of child psychology* (Vol. 2, pp. 435–571). New York: Wiley.

Barker, L. M., Best, M. R., & Domjan, M. (Eds.). (1977). *Learning mechanisms in food selection.* Waco, TX: Baylor University Press.

Barnes, J. M., & Underwood, B. J. (1959). "Fate" of first-list associations in transfer theory. *Journal of Experimental Psychology, 58,* 97–105.

Baron, A., & Galizio, M. (1983). Instructional control of human operant behavior. *The Psychological Record, 33,* 495–520.

Baron, A., Kaufman, A., & Stauber, K. A. (1969). Effects of instructions and reinforcement-feedback on human operant behavior maintained by fixed-interval reinforcement. *Journal of the Experimental Analysis of Behavior, 12,* 701–712.

Bartlett, F. C. (1932). *Remembering: A study in experimental and social psychology.* Cambridge, England: Cambridge University Press.

Baum, W. M. (1974). On two types of deviations from the matching law. *Journal of the Experimental Analysis of Behavior, 22,* 231–242.

Bear, M., & Cooper, L. (1989). Molecular mechanisms for synaptic modification in the visual cortex: Interaction between theory and experiment. In M. A. Gluck & D. E. Rumelhart (Eds.), *Neuroscience and connectionist theory* (pp. 64–94). Hillsdale, NJ: Erlbaum.

Bell, E. T. (1965). *Men of mathematics.* New York: Simon & Schuster.

Bellugi, U., Klima, E. S., & Siple, P. (1975). Remembering in signs. *Cognition, 3,* 93–125.

Belmont, J. M., & Butterfield, E. C. (1977). The instructional approach to developmental cognitive research. In R. V. Kail & J. W. Hagen

(Eds.), *Perspectives on the development of memory and cognition* (pp. 437–481). Hillsdale, NJ: Erlbaum.

Beninger, R. J. (1983). The role of dopamine activity in locomotor activity and learning. *Brain Research Reviews, 6,* 173–196.

Berger, T. W., Berry, S. D., & Thompson, R. F. (1986). Role of the hippocampus in classical conditioning of aversive and appetitive behaviors. In R. L. Issacson & K. H. Pribram (Eds.), *The hippocampus* (Vols. III, IV, pp. 203–239). New York: Plenum Press.

Berko, J. (1958). The child's learning of English morphology. *Word, 14,* 150–177.

Bersch, P. J. (1951). The influence of two variables upon the establishment of a secondary reinforcer for operant responses. *Journal of Experimental Psychology, 41,* 62–73.

Berthoz, A., & Jones, G. M. (Eds.) (1985). *Adaptive mechanisms in gaze control.* New York: Elsevier.

Bevan, W., & Steger, J. A. (1971). Free recall and abstractness of stimuli. *Science, 172,* 597–599.

Bhatt, R. S., Wasserman, E. A., Reynolds, W. F., & Knauss, K. S. (1988). Conceptual behavior in pigeons: Categorization of both familiar and novel examples from four classes of natural and artificial stimuli. *Journal of Experimental Psychology: Animal Behavior Processes, 14,* 219–234.

Bickel, W. K., & Etzel, B. C. (1985). The quantal nature of controlling stimulus-response relations as measured in tests of stimulus generalization. *Journal of the Experimental Analysis of Behavior, 44,* 247–270.

Biederman, I., & Cooper, E. E. (1990). Priming contour deleted images: Evidence for intermediate representations in visual object recognition. *Cognitive Psychology, 18,* 121–133.

Bienstock, E. L., Cooper, L. N., & Munro, P. W. (1982). Theory for the development of neuron selectivity: Orientation specificity and binocular interaction in visual cortex. *Journal of Neuroscience, 2,* 32–48.

Billy, A. J., & Walters, E. T. (1989). Long-term expansion and sensitization of mechanosensory receptive fields in *Aplysia* support an activity-dependent model of whole-cell sensory plasticity. *Journal of Neuroscience, 9,* 1254–1267.

Bilodeau, I., & Schlosberg, H. (1951). Similarity in stimulating conditions as a variable in retroactive inhibition. *Journal of Experimental Psychology, 41,* 199–204.

Birch, H. G. (1945). The relation of previous experience to insightful problem-solving. *Journal of Comparative Psychology, 38,* 367–383.

Birch, H. G., & Rabinowitz, H. S. (1951). The negative effect of previous experience on productive thinking. *Journal of Experimental Psychology, 41,* 121–125.

Bisiach, E., & Luzzatti, C. (1978). Unilateral neglect of representational space. *Cortex, 14,* 129–133.

Bisiach, E., Luzzatti, C., & Perani, D. (1979). Unilateral neglect, representational schema, and consciousness. *Brain, 102,* 609–618.

Bjork, R. A., & Richardson-Klavehn, A. (1989). On the puzzling relationship between environmental context and human memory. In C. Izawa (Ed.), *Current issues in cognitive processes* (pp. 313–344). Hillsdale, NJ: Erlbaum.

Blake, R. (1989). A neural theory of binocular rivalry. *Psychological Review, 96,* 145–167.

Blakely, E., & Schlinger, H. (1987). Function-altering contingency-specifying stimuli. *The Behavior Analyst, 10,* 183–187.

Blakemore, C., & Cooper, G. F. (1970). Development of the brain depends on the visual environment. *Nature, 228,* 477–478.

Blakemore, C., & Mitchell, D. E. (1973). Environmental modification of the visual cortex and the neural basis of learning and memory. *Nature, 241,* 467–468.

Blakemore, C., & Tobin, E. A. (1972). Lateral inhibition between orientation detectors in the cat's visual cortex. *Experimental Brain Research, 15,* 439–440.

Bliss, T. V. P., & Lømo, T. (1973). Long-lasting potentiation of synaptic transmission in the dentate area of the anesthetized rabbit following stimulation of the perforant path. *Journal of Physiology, 232,* 331–356.

Bloedel, J. R. (1987). The cerebellum and memory storage. *Science, 238,* 1728–1729.

Blough, D. S. (1966). The reinforcement of least frequent interresponse times. *Journal of the Experimental Analysis of Behavior, 9,* 581–591.

Blough, D. S. (1975). Steady state data and a quantitative model of operant generalization and discrimination. *Journal of Experimental Psychology: Animal Behavior Processes, 1,* 3–21.

Blough, D. S. (1985). Discrimination of letters and random dot patterns by pigeons and humans. *Journal of Ex-*

perimental Psychology: Animal Behavior Processes, 11, 261–280.

Blough, D. S. (1989). Attentional priming and visual search in pigeons. *Journal of Experimental Psychology: Animal Behavior Processes, 15,* 358–365.

Blough, D. S. (1991). Selective attention and search images in pigeons. *Journal of Experimental Psychology: Animal Behavior Processes, 17,* 292–298.

Bobrow, D. G., & Norman, D. A. (1975). Some principles of memory schemata. In D. G. Bobrow & A. Collins (Eds.), *Representation and understanding.* New York: Academic.

Bolles, R. C. (1970). Species-specific defense reactions and avoidance learning. *Psychological Review, 77,* 32–46.

Boothe, R. G. (1981). Development of spatial vision in infant macaque monkeys under conditions of normal and abnormal visual experience. In R. N. Aslin, J. R. Alberts, & M. R. Petersen (Eds.), *Development of perception* (Vol. 2, pp. 217–242). New York: Academic.

Boring, E. G. (1950). *A history of experimental psychology* (2nd ed). New York: Appleton-Century-Crofts.

Bower, G. H. (1970). Analysis of a mnemonic device. *American Scientist, 58,* 496–510.

Bower, G. H. (1972). Mental imagery and associative learning. In L. W. Gregg (Ed.), *Cognition in learning and memory.* New York: Wiley.

Bower, G. H. (1975). Cognitive psychology: An introduction. In W. K. Estes (Ed.), *Handbook of learning and cognitive processes* (Vol. 1, pp. 1–23). Hillsdale, NJ: Erlbaum.

Bower, G. H. (1981). Mood and memory. *American Psychologist, 36,* 129–148.

Bower, G. H., & Clark, M. C. (1969). Narrative stories as mediators for serial learning. *Psychonomic Science, 14,* 181–182.

Bower, G. H., & Morrow, D. G. (1990). Mental models in narrative comprehension. *Science, 247,* 44–48.

Bowlby, J. (1969). *Attachment and loss. Vol. 1. Attachment.* New York: Basic Books.

Bowler, P. J. (1983). *The eclipse of Darwin.* Baltimore, MD: Johns Hopkins University Press.

Bowler, P. J. (1988). *The non-Darwinian revolution.* Baltimore, MD: Johns Hopkins University Press.

Bowles, N. L., & Poon, L. W. (1985). Effects of priming in word retrieval. *Journal of Experimental Psychol-*

ogy: Learning, Memory, and Cognition, 11, 272–283.

Braine, M. D. S. (1971). The acquisition of language in infant and child. In C. Reed (Ed.), *The learning of language* (pp. 7–95). Englewood Cliffs, NJ: Prentice Hall.

Branch, M. N. (1977). On the role of "memory" in the analysis of behavior. *Journal of the Experimental Analysis of Behavior, 28,* 171–179.

Bransford, J. D., & Franks, J. J. (1971). The abstraction of linguistic ideas. *Cognitive Psychology, 2,* 331–350.

Bransford, J. D., McCarrell, N. S., Franks, J. J., & Nitsch, K. E. (1977). Toward unexplaining memory. In R. Shaw & J. D. Bransford (Eds.), *Perceiving, acting, and knowing* (pp. 431–466). New York: Wiley.

Breland, K., & Breland, M. (1961). The misbehavior of organisms. *American Psychologist, 16,* 661–664.

Brennan, P., Kaba, H., & Keverne, E. B. (1990). Olfactory recognition: A simple memory system. *Science, 250,* 1223–1226.

Broadbent, D. E. (1952). Speaking and listening simultaneously. *Journal of Experimental Psychology, 43,* 267–273.

Broadbent, D. E. (1958). *Perception and communication.* London: Pergamon.

Broadbent, D. E. (1973). *In Defence of Empirical Psychology.* London: Methuen.

Broadbent, D. E. (1982). Task combination and selective intake of information. *Acta Psychologica, 50,* 253–290.

Broerse, J., & Crassini, B. (1984). Investigations of perception and imagery using CAEs: The role of experimental design and psychophysical method. *Perception and Psychophysics, 35,* 155–164.

Brooks, D. N., & Baddeley, A. (1976). What can amnesic patients learn? *Neuropsychologia, 14,* 111–122.

Brooks, L. (1978). Nonanalytic concept formation and memory for instances. In E. Rosch and B. B. Lloyd (Eds), *Cognition and categorization.* Hillsdale, NJ: Erlbaum.

Brown, A. (1989). Analogical reasoning and transfer: What develops? In S. Vosniadov & A. Ortony (Eds.), *Similarity and analogical reasoning* (pp. 369–412). Cambridge, England: Cambridge University Press.

Brown, I. D., & Poulton, E. C. (1961). Measuring the spare mental capacity of car drivers by a subsidiary task. *Ergonomics, 4,* 35–40.

Brown, J. A. (1958). Some tests of the decay theory of immediate memory.

Quarterly Journal of Experimental Psychology, 10, 12–21.

Brown, J. W. (1988). *Neuropsychology of visual perception.* Hillsdale, NJ: Erlbaum.

Brown, J. W. (1989). *Neuropsychology of visual perception.* New York: Erlbaum.

Brown, R., & Hanlon, C. (1970). Derivational complexity and order of acquisition in child speech. In J. R. Hayes (Ed.), *Cognition and the development of language.* New York: Wiley.

Brown, R., & Kulik, P. (1977). Flashbulb memories. *Cognition, 5,* 73–99.

Bruce, C., Desimone, R., & Gross, C. G. (1981). Visual properties of neurons in a polysensory area in superior temporal sulcus of the macaque. *Journal of Neurophysiology, 46,* 369–384.

Bruner, J. (1988). *In search of mind.* New York: Harper & Row.

Brunswik, E. (1956). *Perception and the representative design of experiments.* Berkeley, CA: University of California Press.

Bruyer, R. (1986). *The neuropsychology of face perception and facial expression.* Hillsdale, NJ: Erlbaum.

Buonomano, D. V., & Byrne, J. H. (1990). Long-term synaptic changes produced by a cellular analog of classical conditioning in *Aplysia. Science, 249,* 420–423.

Butter, C. M. (1963). Stimulus generalization along one and two dimensions in pigeons. *Journal of Experimental Psychology, 65,* 339–346.

Butter, C. M., Mishkin, M., & Rosvold, H. E. (1965). Stimulus generalization in monkeys with inferotemporal and lateral occipital lesions. In D. I. Mostofsky (Ed.), *Stimulus generalization* (pp. 119–133). Stanford, CA: Stanford University Press.

Butterfield, E. C., Wambold, C., & Belmont, J. M. (1973). On the theory and practice of improving short-term memory. *American Journal of Mental Deficiency, 77,* 654–669.

Cameron, R. F., Currier, R. D., & Haerer, A. F. (1971). Aphasia and literacy. *British Journal of Disorders of Communication, 6,* 161–163.

Campbell, D. T. (1966). Pattern matching as an essential in distal knowing. In K. R. Hammond (Ed.), *The psychology of Egon Brunswik* (pp. 81–105). New York: Holt, Rinehart, & Winston.

Campbell, D. T. (1974). Evolutionary epistemology. In P. A. Schlipp (Ed.), *The philosophy of Karl Popper. The library of living philosophers* (Vol.

14–1, pp. 413–463). LaSalle, IL: Open Court Publishing Co.

Campbell, F. W., Kulikowski, J. J., & Levison, J. (1966). The effect of orientation on the visual resolution of gratings. *Journal of Physiology (London), 187*, 427–436.

Campbell, F. W., & Robson, J. G. (1968). Application of Fourier analysis to the visibility of gratings. *Journal of Physiology (London), 197*, 551–566.

Capaldi, E. J. (1966). Partial reinforcement: A hypothesis of sequential effects. *Psychological Review, 73*, 459–477.

Capaldi, E. J. (1971). Memory and learning: A sequential viewpoint. In W. K. Honig & P. H.R. James (Eds.), *Animal memory* (pp. 111–154). New York: Academic.

Carew, T. J., Abrams, T. W., Hawkins, R. D., & Kandel, E. R. (1984). The use of simple invertebrate systems to explore psychological issues related to associative learning. In D. L. Alkon & J. Farley, (Eds.), *Primary neural substrates of learning and behavioral change* (pp. 169–183). New York: Cambridge University Press.

Carew, T. J., Hawkins, R. D., & Kandel, E. R. (1983). Differential classical conditioning of a defensive withdrawal reflex in *Aplysia californica. Science, 219*, 397–400.

Carlson, N. (1984). *Psychology: The Science of behavior.* Boston: Allyn & Bacon.

Carlson, N. R. (1991). *Physiology of behavior.* Boston: Allyn and Bacon.

Carlton, P. L. (1962). Effects of deprivation and reinforcement magnitude on response variability. *Journal of the Experimental Analysis of Behavior, 5*, 481–486.

Carpenter, P. A., & Eisenberg, D. (1978). Mental rotation and the frame of reference in blind and sighted individuals. *Perception and Psychophysics, 23*, 117–124.

Carr, T. H. (1986). Perceiving visual language. In K. R. Boff, L. Kaufman, & J. P. Thomas (Eds.), *Handbook of human performance.* (Vol. 2, pp. 319–338). New York: Wiley.

Carr, T. H., & Dagenbach, D. (1990). Semantic priming and repetition priming from masked words: Evidence for a center-surround attentional mechanism in perceptual recognition. *Journal of Experimental Psychology: Learning, Memory, and Cognition, 16*, 341–350.

Case, D. A., Fantino, E., & Wixted, J. (1985). Human observing: Maintained by negative informing stimuli only if correlated with improvement in response efficiency. *Journal of the Experimental Analysis of Behavior, 43*, 289–300.

Case, D., Ploog, B. O., & Fantino, E. (1990). Observing behavior in a computer game. *Journal of the Experimental Analysis of Behavior, 54*, 185–200.

Catania, A. C. (1975). The myth of self-reinforcement. *Behaviorism, 3*, 192–199.

Catania, A. C. (1987). Some Darwinian lessons for behavior analysis: A review of Bowler's: *The eclipse of Darwinism. Journal of the Experimental Analysis of Behavior, 47*, 249–257.

Cegarvske, C. F., Thompson, R. F., Patterson, M. M., & Gormezano, I. (1976). Mechanisms of efferent neuronal control of the reflex nictitating membrane response in the rabbit. *Journal of Comparative and Physiological Psychology, 90*, 411–423.

Cerella, J. (1980). The pigeon's analysis of pictures. *Pattern Recognition, 12*, 1–6.

Cermak, L. S. (1982). *Human memory and amnesia.* Hillsdale, NJ: Erlbaum.

Changeux, J. P., Heidman, T., & Pattle, P. (1984). Learning by selection. In P. Marler & H. S. Terrace (Eds.), *The biology of learning* (pp. 115–133). New York: Springer-Verlag.

Chase, W. G., & Ericsson, K. A. (1972). Skill and working memory. In J. R. Anderson (Ed.), *Cognitive skills and their acquisition* (pp. 141–189). Hillsdale, NJ: Erlbaum.

Cherry, E. C. (1953). Some experiments on the recognition of speech with one and with two ears. *Journal of the Acoustical Society of America, 31*, 373–395.

Chomsky, N. (1959). Review of *Verbal Behavior* by B. F. Skinner. *Language, 35*, 26–58.

Chomsky, N. (1965). *Aspects of a theory of syntax.* Cambridge, MA: MIT Press.

Chomsky, N. (1980). *Rules and representations.* New York: Columbia University Press.

Church, R. M. (1969). Response suppression. In B. A. Campbell & R. M. Church (Eds.), *Punishment and aversive behavior* (pp. 111–156). New York: Appleton-Century-Crofts.

Clarke, S. C., & Trowill, J. A. (1971). Sniffing and motivated behavior in the rat. *Physiology and Behavior, 6*, 49–52.

Clifton, R. K., Morrongiello, B. A., Kulig, J. W., & Dowd, J. M. (1981). Newborns' orientation toward sound: Possible implications for cortical development. *Child Development, 52*, 833–888.

Clifton, R. K., Siqueland, E. R., & Lipsett, L. P. (1972). Conditioned headturning in human newborns as a function of conditioned response requirements and states of wakefulness. *Journal of Experimental Child Psychology, 13*, 43–57.

Cohen, L. R., Looney, T. A., Brady, J. H., & Aucella, A. F. (1976). Differential sample response schedules in the acquisition of conditional discriminations by pigeons. *Journal of the Experimental Analysis of Behavior, 26*, 301–312.

Cohen, N., & Squire, L. R. (1980). Preserved learning and retention of pattern analyzing skill in amnesia: Dissociation of knowing how and knowing what. *Science, 210*, 207–209.

Cohen, N., & Squire, L. R. (1981). Retrograde amnesia and remote memory impairment. *Neuropsychologia, 119*, 337–356.

Cohen, S. L., & Branch, M. N. (1991). Foodpaired stimuli as conditioned reinforcers: Effects of *d*-amphetamine. *Journal of the Experimental Analysis of Behavior, 56*, 277–289.

Cole, J. L. (1965). Force gradients in stimulus generalization. *Journal of the Experimental Analysis of Behavior, 8*, 231–242.

Cole, M., Gay, J., Glick, J. A., & Sharp, D. W. (1971). *The cultural context of learning and thinking.* New York: Basic Books.

Coleman, S. (1981). Historical context and systematic functions of the concept of the operant. *Behaviorism, 9*, 207–226.

Coleman, S. (1984). Background and change in B. F. Skinner's metatheory from 1930 to 1938. *Journal of Mind and Behavior, 5*, 471–500.

Coleman, S. R., & Gormezano, I. (1979). Classical conditioning and "the law of effect": Historical and empirical assessment. *Behaviorism, 7*, 1–33.

Collingridge, G. L., & Bliss, T. V. P. (1987). NMDA receptors—their role in long-term potentiation. *Trends in Neuroscience, 10*, 288–293.

Collins, J. P. (1974). Generalization and decision theory. Unpublished doctoral dissertation, University of Massachusetts-Amherst. Described in J. W. Donahoe and M. G. Wessells, *Learning, language, and memory.* New York: Harper & Row, 1980.

Colombo, J., Mitchell, D. W., Coldren, J. T., & Atwater, J. D. (1990). Discrimination learning during the first year: Stimulus and positional cues. *Journal of Experimental Psychology: Learning, Memory, and Cognition, 16,* 98–109.

Colonnier, M. (1968). Synaptic patterns on different cell types in the different laminae of the cat visual cortex. An electron microscope study. *Brain Research, 9,* 268–287.

Colwill, R. M., & Rescorla, R. A. (1985). Post-conditioning devaluation of a reinforcer affects instrumental responding. *Journal of Experimental Psychology: Animal Behavior Processes, 11,* 120–132.

Colwill, R. M., & Rescorla, R. A. (1986). Associative structures in instrumental learning. In G. H. Bower (Ed.), *The psychology of learning and motivation* (Vol. 20, pp. 55–104). New York: Academic.

Conrad, R. (1964). Acoustic confusions in immediate memory. *British Journal of Psychology, 55,* 75–84.

Constantine-Paton, M., Cline, H. T., & Debski, D. (1990). Patterned activity, synaptic convergence, and the NMDA receptor in developing visual pathways. *Annual Review of Neuroscience, 13,* 129–154.

Cooper, L. A., & Shepard, R. N. (1973). Chronometric studies of the rotation of mental images. In W. G. Chase (Ed.), *Visual information processing* (pp.75–176). New York: Academic.

Corballis, M. C. (1989). Laterality and human evolution. *Psychological Review, 96,* 492–505.

Corteen, R. S., & Dunn, D. (1974). Shock-associated words in a nonattended message: A test of momentary awareness. *Journal of Experimental Psychology, 102,* 1143–1144.

Corteen, R. S., & Wood, B. (1972). Autonomic responses to shock-associated words in an unattended channel. *Journal of Experimental Psychology, 94,* 308–313.

Costall, A. P. (1984). Are theories of perception necessary? A review of Gibson's *The ecological approach to perception. Journal of the Experimental Analysis of Behavior, 41,* 109–115.

Cotman, C. W., & Monaghan, D. T. (1988). Excitatory amino acid neurotransmission: Receptors and Hebb-type synaptic plasticity. *Annual Review of Neuroscience, 11,* 61–80.

Cowley, B. J., Green, G., & Braunling-McMorrow, D. (1992). Using stimulus equivalence procedures to teach name-face matching to adults with brain injuries. *Journal of Applied Behavior Analysis, 25,* 461–475.

Craik, F. I. M., & Lockhart, R. S. (1972). Levels of processing: A framework for memory research. *Journal of Verbal Learning and Verbal Behavior, 11,* 671–684.

Craik, F. I. M., & Tulving, E. (1975). Depth of processing and the retention of words in episodic memory. *Journal of Experimental Psychology: General, 104,* 268–294.

Craik, F. I. M., & Watkins, M. J. (1973). The role of rehearsal in short-term memory. *Journal of Verbal Learning and Verbal Behavior, 12,* 599–607.

Creese, I. (1981). Dopamine receptors. In H. I. Yamamura & S. J. Enna (Eds.), *Neurotransmitter receptors: Part 2, Biogenic amines* (pp. 129–183). London: Chapman & Hall, Ltd.

Crick, F. H. C. (1984). The function of the thalamic reticular spotlight: The searchlight hypothesis. *Proceedings of the National Academy of Sciences, USA, 81,* 4586–4590.

Crick, F. H. C., & Asanuma, C. (1986). Certain aspects of the anatomy and physiology of the cerebral cortex. In J. L. McClelland, D. E. Rumelhart, & The PDP Research Group (Eds.), *Parallel distributed processing* (Vol. 2, pp. 333–371). Cambridge, MA: MIT Press.

Crowder, R. G. (1976). *Principles of learning and memory.* Hillsdale, NJ: Erlbaum.

Crowder, R. G. (1982). The demise of short-term memory. *Acta Psychologica, 50,* 291–323.

Crowley, M. A. (1979). The allocation of time to temporally defined behaviors: responding during stimulus generalization. *Journal of the Experimental Analysis of Behavior, 32,* 191–197.

Crowley, M. A. (1981). The acquisition and generalization of matching. Unpublished doctoral dissertation, University of Massachusetts, Amherst, MA.

Cumming, W. W., & Berryman, R. (1965). The complex discriminated operant: Studies of matching-to-sample and related problems. In D. I. Mostofsky (Ed.), *Stimulus generalization* (pp. 284–330). Stanford, CA: Stanford University Press.

Dagenbach, D., Carr, T. H., & Barnhardt, T. M. (1990). Inhibitory semantic priming of lexical decisions due to failure to retrieve weakly activated codes. *Journal of Experimental Psychology: Learning, Memory, and Cognition, 16,* 328–340.

D'Agostino, P. R., O'Neill, B. J., & Paivio, A. (1977). Memory for pictures and words as a function of levels of processing. Depth or dual coding? *Memory and Cognition, 5,* 252–256.

Dallery, J., & Baum, W. M. (1991). The functional equivalence of operant behavior and foraging. *Animal Learning and Behavior, 19,* 146–152.

D'Amato, M. R., Salmon, D. P., Loukas, E., & Tomie, A. (1985). Symmetry and transitivity of conditional relations in monkeys (*Cebus apella*) and pigeons (*Colomba livia*). *Journal of the Experimental Analysis of Behavior, 44,* 35–47.

Darwin, C. (1859). *The origin of species by means of natural selection.* London: John Murray.

Darwin, C. (1871). *The descent of man.* London: John Murray.

Darwin, C. (1872). *The expression of emotions in man and animals.* London: John Murray.

Davenport, R. K., Rogers, C. M., & Russell, I. S. (1973). Cross-modal perception in apes. *Neuropsychologica, 11,* 21–28.

Davies, G. M., & Thomson, D. M. (1988). *Memory in context: Context in memory.* New York: Wiley.

Davis, M. (1970). Effects of interstimulus interval length and variability on startle-response habituation in the rat. *Journal of Comparative and Physiological Psychology, 72,* 177–192.

Davis, M. (1992). The role of the amygdala in conditioned fear. In P. Aggleton (Ed.), *The amygdala: Neurobiological aspects of emotion and mental dysfunction* (pp. 255–305). New York: Wiley-Liss.

Dawes, R. M., Faust, D., & Meehl, P. E. (1989). Clinical versus actuarial judgment. *Science, 243,* 1668–1674.

Dawkins, R. (1976). *The selfish gene.* New York: Oxford University Press.

Dawkins, R. (1986). *The blind watchmaker.* New York: Norton.

Day, W. F. (1983). On the difference between radical and methodological behaviorism. *Behaviorism, 11,* 89–102.

Deadwyler, S. A., West, M. O., & Robinson, J. H. (1981). Entorhinal and septal inputs differentially control sensory-evoked responses in the rat dentate gyrus. *Science, 211,* 1181–1183.

Denis, M. (1982). Imagine while reading text: A study of individual differences. *Memory and Cognition, 10,* 540–545.

Dennett, D. (1981). *Brainstorms.* Cambridge, MA: MIT Press.

Dennett, D. C. (1984). *Elbow room.* Cambridge, MA: MIT Press.

Desmond, N. L., & Levy, W. B. (1983). Synaptic correlates of associative potentiation/depression: An ultrastructural study in the hippocampus. *Brain Research, 265,* 21–30.

Deutsch, J. A., & Deutsch, D. (1963). Attention: Some theoretical considerations. *Psychological Review, 70,* 80–90.

De Valois, K. K., De Valois, R. J., & Yund, E. W. (1979). Responses of striate cortex cells to grating and checkerboard patterns. *Journal of Physiology (London), 291,* 483–505.

De Valois, R. L., & De Valois, K. K. (1988). *Spatial vision.* New York: Oxford University Press.

Devaney, J. M., Hayes, S. C., & Nelson, R. O. (1986). Equivalence class formation in language-able and language-disabled children. *Journal of the Experimental Analysis of Behavior, 46,* 243–257.

de Villiers, P. A. (1977). Choice in concurrent schedules and a quantitative formulation of the law of effect. In W. K. Honig & J. E. R. Staddon (Eds.), *Handbook of operant behavior.* Englewood Cliffs, NJ: Prentice Hall.

Diamond, R., & Rozin, P. (1984). Activation of existing memories in anterograde amnesia. *Journal of Abnormal Psychology, 93,* 98–105.

Dick, M., Ullman, S., & Sagi, D. (1987). Parallel and serial processes in motion detection. *Science, 237,* 400–402.

Dickerson, R. E. (1978). Chemical evolution and the origin of life. *Scientific American, 239,* 70–86.

Dickinson, A. (1988). Intentionality in animals conditioning. In L. Weiskrantz (Ed.), *Thought without language* (pp. 305–325). Oxford: Claredon Press.

DiLollo, V., Lowe, D. G., & Scott, J. P., Jr. (1973). Backward masking and interference with the processing of brief visual displays. *Journal of Experimental Psychology, 103,* 934–940.

Dinsmoor, J. A. (1950). A quantitative comparison of the discriminative and reinforcing functions of a stimulus. *Journal of Experimental Psychology, 40,* 458–472.

Disterhoft, J. F., Quinn, K. J., Weiss, C., & Shipley, M. T. (1985). Accessory abducens nucleus and conditioned eye retraction in rabbit. *Journal of Neuroscience, 5,* 941–950.

Ditchburn, R. W., & Ginsborg, B. L. (1952). Vision with a stabilized retinal image. *Nature, 170,* 36–37.

Domjan, M. (1980). Ingestional aversion learning: Unique and general processes. In J. S. Rosenblatt, R. A. Hinde, C. Beer, & M. Busnel (Eds.), *Advances in the study of behavior* (Vol. 11). New York: Academic.

Domjan, M. (1983). Biological constraints on instrumental and classical conditioning: Implications for general process theory. *Psychology of learning and motivation* (Vol. 13). New York: Academic.

Domjan, M., & Galef, B. G. (1983). Biological constraints on instrumental and classical conditioning: Retrospect and prospect. *Animal Learning & Behavior, 11,* 151–161.

Donahoe, J. W. (1977). Some implications of a relational principle of reinforcement. *Journal of the Experimental Analysis of Behavior, 27,* 341–350.

Donahoe, J. W. (1984). Commentary: Skinner—The Darwin of ontogeny. *The Behavioral and Brain Sciences, 7,* 287–288.

Donahoe, J. W. (1991). The selectionist approach to verbal behavior: Potential contributions of neuropsychology and connectionism. In L. J. Hayes & P. N. Chase (Eds.), *Dialogues on verbal behavior* (pp. 119–150). Reno, NV: Context Press.

Donahoe, J. W., Burgos, J. E., & Palmer, D. C. (1993). Selectionist approach to reinforcement. *Journal of the Experimental Analysis of Behavior, 58,* 17–40.

Donahoe, J. W., & Burns, R. (1984). Unified reinforcement principle: Shock as reinforcer. Paper presented to the Psychonomic Society, San Antonio, TX.

Donahoe, J. W., Crowley, M. A., Millard, W. J., & Stickney, K. A. (1982). A unified principle of reinforcement. *Quantitative models of behavior* (Vol. 2, 493–521). Cambridge, MA: Ballinger.

Donahoe, J. W., & Marrs, D. P. (1982). 12-year retention of stimulus and schedule control. *Bulletin of the Psychonomic Society, 19,* 184–186.

Donahoe, J. W., & Palmer. D. C. (1988). Inhibition: A cautionary tale. *Journal of the Experimental Analysis of Behavior, 50,* 333–341.

Donahoe, J. W., & Palmer, D. C. (1989). The interpretation of complex human behavior: Some reactions to Parallel Distributed Processing. *Journal of the Experimental Analysis of Behavior, 51,* 399–416.

Donahoe, J. W., & Wessells, M. G. (1980). *Learning, language, and memory.* New York: Harper & Row.

Donegan, N. H., & Wagner, A. E. (1987). Conditioned diminution and facilitation of the UR: A sometimes opponent-process interpretation. In I. Gormezano, W. F. Prokasy, & R. F. Thompson (Eds.), *Classical conditioning III: Behavioral, neurophysiological, and neurochemical studies in the rabbit* (pp. 339–369). Hillsdale, NJ: Erlbaum.

Dube, W. V., Green, G., & Serna, R. W. (1993). Auditory successive conditional discrimination and auditory stimulus equivalence classes. *Journal of the Experimental Analysis of Behavior, 59,* 103–114.

Dube, W. V., McIlvane, W. J., Mackay, H. A., & Stoddard, L. T. (1987). Stimulus class membership established via stimulus-reinforcer relations. *Journal of the Experimental Analysis of Behaviors, 47,* 159–175.

Dunker, K. (1945). On problem-solving. *Psychological Monographs, 270,* pp. 1–112.

Dupree, A. H. (1988). *Asa Gray.* Baltimore, MD: Johns Hopkins University Press.

Durso, F. T., & Johnson, M. K. (1980). The effects of orienting tasks on recognition, recall, and modality confusion of pictures and words. *Journal of Verbal Learning and Verbal Behavior, 19,* 416–429.

Eckerman, D. A., Hienz, R. D., Stern, S., & Kowlowitz, V. (1980). Shaping the location of a pigeon's peck: Effect of rate and size of shaping steps. *Journal of the Experimental Analysis of Behavior, 33,* 299–310.

Edelman, G. M. (1987). *Neural Darwinism.* New York: Basic Books.

Egeland, B. (1975). Effects of errorless training on teaching children to discriminate letters of the alphabet. *Journal of Applied Psychology, 60,* 533–536.

Ehri, L. C. (1976). Do words really interfere in naming pictures? *Child Development, 47,* 502–505.

Eich, J. M. (1985). Levels of processing, encoding specificity, elaboration, and CHARM. *Psychological Review, 92,* 1–38.

Eichenbaum, H., & Otto, T. (1992). The hippocampus—What does it do? *Behavioral and Neural Biology, 57,* 2–36.

Eickelboom, R., & Stewart, J. (1982). The conditioning of drug-induced physiological responses. *Psychological Review, 89,* 507–528.

Eldredge, N. (1984). Individuals, hierarchies, and processes. Toward a more complete evolutionary theory. *Paleobiology, 10,* 146–171.

El-Wakil, F. (1975). The nature of memory impairment in Korsakoff patients. Unpublished master's thesis.

University of Massachusetts, Amherst, MA.

Engberg, L. A., Hanson, G., Welker, R. L., & Thomas, D. R. (1972). Acquisition of key-pecking via autoshaping as a function of prior experience: "Learned laziness?" *Science, 178,* 1002–1004.

Epstein, R. (1983). Resurgence of previously reinforced behavior during extinction. *Behavior Analysis Letters, 3,* 391–397.

Epstein, R. (1984). Simulation research in the analysis of behavior. *Behaviorism, 12,* 41–59.

Epstein, R. (1985a). Extinction induced resurgence: Preliminary investigations and possible applications. *Psychological record, 35,* 143–153.

Epstein, R. (1985b). Animal cognition as the praxist views it. *Neuroscience & Biobehavioral Reviews, 9,* 623–630.

Epstein, R. (1991). Skinner, creativity, and the problem of spontaneous behavior. *Psychological Science, 2,* 362–370.

Epstein, R., Kirshnit, C., Lanza, R., & Rubin, L. (1984). "Insight" in the pigeon: Antecedents and determinants of an intelligent performance. *Nature, 308,* 61–62.

Estes, W. K. (1955). Statistical theory of spontaneous recovery and regression. *Psychological Review, 62,* 145–154.

Estes, W. K. (1956). The problem of inference from curves based on group data. *Psychological Bulletin, 53,* 134–140.

Estes, W. K. (1958). Stimulus-response theory of drive. In M. R. Jones (Ed.), *Nebraska Symposium of Motivation.* (pp.35–69). Lincoln, NE: University of Nebraska Press.

Estes, W. K., & Skinner, B. F. (1941). Some quantitative properties of anxiety. *Journal of Experimental Psychology, 29,* 390–400.

Fahrmeier, E. D. (1975). The effect of school attendance on intellectual development in northern Nigeria. *Child Development, 46,* 282–285.

Fallon, J. H., & Loughlin, S. E. (1987). Monoamine innervation of cerebral cortex and a theory of the role of monoamines in cerebral cortex and basal ganglia. In E. G. Jones & A. Peters (Eds.), *Cerebral cortex. Vol. 6. Further aspects of cortical function, including hippocampus* (pp. 41–127). New York: Plenum.

Farah, M. J. (1985). The neurological basis of mental imagery: A componential analysis. In S. Pinker (Ed.), *Visual cognition* (pp. 245–271). Cambridge, MA: MIT Press.

Farah, M. J. (1988). Is visual imagery really visual? Overlooked evidence from neuropsychology. *Psychological Review, 95,* 307–317.

Farah, M. J. (1989). The neural basis for mental imagery. *Trends in Neuroscience, 10,* 395–399.

Farah, M. J., & Kosslyn, S. M. (1982). Concept development. In H. W. Reese & L. P. Lipsitt (Eds.), *Advances in Child Development* (Vol 16, pp. 125–167). New York: Academic.

Farah, M. J., Peronnet, F., Gonon, M. A., & Giard, M. H. (1988). Electrophysiological evidence for a shared representational medium for visual images and visual percepts. *Journal of Experimental Psychology: General, 117,* 248–257.

Feniello, K. B. (May, 1988). Cross-modal transfer of stimulus equivalence. Paper presented at the 14th annual convention of the Association for Behavior Analysis, Philadelphia, PA.

Ferguson, C. A., & Slobin, D. I. (Eds.) (1973). *Studies of child language development.* New York: Holt, Rinehart, & Winston.

Ferster, C. B., & Skinner, B. F. (1957). *Schedules of reinforcement.* New York: Appleton-Century-Crofts.

Fields, L., Adams, B. J., Verhave, T., & Newman, S. (1990). The effects of modality on the formation of equivalence classes. *Journal of the Experimental Analysis of Behavior, 53,* 345–358.

Fields, L., & Verhave, T. (1987). The structure of equivalence classes. *Journal of the Experimental Analysis of Behavior, 48,* 317–332.

Findley, J. D. (1962). An experimental outline for building and exploring multi-operant behavior repertoires. *Journal of the Experimental Analysis of Behavior, 5,* 113–166.

Findley, J. D., & Brady, J. D. (1965). Facilitation of large ratio performance by use of conditioned reinforcement. *Journal of the Experimental Analysis of Behavior, 8,* 125–129.

Fisk, A. D., & Schneider, W. (1983). Category and word search: Generalizing search principles to complex processing. *Journal of Experimental Psychology: Learning, Memory, and Cognition, 9,* 177–195.

Flavell, J. H. (1971). First discussant's comments: What is memory development the development of? *Human Development, 14,* 272–278.

Flavell, J. H., Beach, D. R., & Chinsky, J. M. (1966). Spontaneous verbal rehearsal in a memory task as a function of age. *Child Development, 37,* 283–299.

Flavell, J. H., & Wellman, H. M. (1977). Metamemory. In R. V. Kail & J. W. Hagen (Eds.), *Perspectives on the development of memory and cognition* (pp. 113–175). Hillsdale, NJ: Erlbaum.

Foss, D. J. (1988). Experimental psycholinguistics. *Annual Review of Psychology, 39,* 301–348.

Foss, D. J., & Hakes, D. T. (1978). *Psycholinguistics: An introduction to the psychology of language.* Englewood Cliffs, NJ: Prentice Hall.

Fox, J. L. (1984). The brain's dynamic way of keeping in touch, *Science, 225,* 820–821.

Fox, P. T., Mintun, M. A., Raichle, M. E., & Miezin, F. M. (1986). Mapping human visual cortex with positron emission tomography. *Nature, 323,* 806–809.

Frazier, L., & Rayner, K. (1990). Taking on semantic commitments: Processing multiple meanings vs. multiple senses. *Journal of Memory and Cognition, 29,* 181–200.

Frazier, T. W., & Bitetto, V. E. (1969). Control of human vigilance by concurrent schedules. *Journal of the Experimental Analysis of Behavior, 12,* 591–600.

Freedman, J. L., & Loftus, E. F. (1971). Retrieval of words from long-term memory. *Journal of Verbal Learning and Verbal Behavior, 10,* 107–115.

Freud, S. (1904). The psychopathology of everyday life. In A. A. Brill, (Ed.), *The basic writings of Sigmund Freud.* (Trans. by A. A. Brill). New York: Modern Library, 1938.

Freud, S. (1920). *Introduction to psychoanalysis.* New York: Boni & Liveright.

Frey, U., Huang, Y.-Y., & Kandel, E. R. (1993). Effects of cAMP simulate a late stage of LTP in hippocampal CA1 neurons. *Science, 260,* 1661–1664.

Friedhoff, A. J., & Chase, T. N. (Eds.). (1982). Gilles de la Tourette syndrome. *Advances in neurology* (Vol. 35). New York: Raven.

Friedman, A., Polson, M. C., Dafoe, C. G., & Gaskill, S. J. (1982). Dividing attention within and between hemispheres: Testing a multiple resources approach to limited-capacity information processing. *Journal of Experimental Psychology: Human Perception and Performance, 8,* 625–650.

Friedman, R. P., & Weinstein, F. A. (1977). Hemi-inattention and hemisphere specialization: Introduction and historical review. In E. A.

Weinstein & R. P. Friedman (Eds.), *Advances in neurology* (Vol. 18, pp. 1–31). New York: Raven.

Frost, B. J., & Nakayama, K. (1983). Single visual neurons code opposing motion independent of direction. *Science, 220,* 744–745.

Fujita, K., Blough, D. S., & Blough, P. M. (1991). Pigeons see the Ponza illusion. *Animal Learning and Behavior, 19,* 283–293.

Fuster, J. M. (1989). *The prefrontal cortex.* New York: Raven.

Galizio, M. (1979). Contingency-shaped and rule-governed behavior: Instructional control of human loss avoidance. *Journal of the Experimental Analysis of Behavior, 31,* 53–70.

Gallistel, C. R. (1990). *The organization of learning.* Cambridge, MA: MIT Press.

Garcia, J., Erwin, F. R., & Koelling, R. A. (1966). Learning with prolonged delay in reinforcement. *Psychonomic Science, 5,* 121–122.

Gardiner, J. H., Craik, F. I. M., & Birtwistle, J. (1972). Retrieval cues and release from proactive inhibition. *Journal of Verbal Learning and Verbal Behavior, 11,* 778–783.

Gardner, B. T., & Gardner, R. A. (1971). Two-way communication with an infant chimpanzee. In A. M. Schrier and F. Stollnitz (Eds.), *Behavior of nonhuman primates* (Vol. 4, pp. 117–184.) New York: Academic.

Gardner, B. T., & Gardner, R. A. (1974). Comparing the early utterances of child and chimpanzee. In A. D. Pick (Ed), *Minnesota symposia on child psychology,* Vol. 8. Minneapolis: The University of Minnesota Press.

Gardner, B. T., & Gardner, R. A. (1975). Evidence for sentence constituents in the early utterances of child and chimpanzee. *Journal of Experimental Psychology: General, 104,* 244–267.

Gazzaniga, M. S. (1970). *The bisected brain.* New York: Appleton-Century-Crofts.

Geffen, G., & Sexton, M. A. (1978). The development of auditory strategies of attention. *Developmental Psychology, 15,* 11–17.

Geoders, N. E., & Smith, J. E. (1983). Cortical dopaminergic involvement in cocaine reinforcement. *Science, 221,* 773–775.

Georgopoulos, A. P. (1990). Neurophysiology of reaching. In M. Jeannerod (Ed.), *Attention and performance XIII* (pp. 227–263). Hillsdale, NJ: Erlbaum.

Georgopoulos, A. P., Lurito, J. T., Petrides, M., Schwartz, A. B., & Massey, J. T. (1989). Mental rotation of the neuronal population. *Science, 243,* 234–236.

Georgopoulos, A. P., Schwartz, A. B., & Ketner, R. E. (1986). Neuronal population coding of movement direction. *Science, 233,* 1416–1419.

Gerall, A. A., & Obrist, P. A. (1962). Classical conditioning of the pupillary dilation responses in normal and curarized cats. *Journal of Comparative and Physiological Psychology, 55,* 486–491.

Geschwind, N. (1965). Disconnexion syndromes in animals and man: Part I. *Brain, 88,* 237–293.

Geschwind, N. (1972). Language and the brain. *Scientific American, 226,* 76–83.

Geschwind, N., Quadfasel, F. A., & Segarra, J. M. (1968). Isolation of the speech area. *Neuropsychologica, 6,* 327–340.

Gewirtz, J. L. (1971). The roles of overt responding and extrinsic reinforcement in "self" and "vicarious-reinforcement" phenomena and in "observational learning" and imitation. In R. Glaser (Ed.), *The nature of reinforcement* (pp. 279–309). New York: Academic.

Gibbon, J. J., & Balsam, P. (1981). Spreading association in time. In C. M. Locurto, H. S. Terrace, & J. Gibbon (Eds.), *Autoshaping and conditioning theory* (pp. 219–253). New York: Academic.

Gibbs, C. M., Latham, S. B., & Gormezano, I. (1978). Classical conditioning of the rabbit nictitating membrane response: Effects of reinforcement schedule and resistance to extinction. *Animal Learning and Behavior, 6,* 209–215.

Gibson, E. J. (1971). Perceptual learning and the theory of word perception. *Cognitive Psychology, 2,* 351–358

Gibson, E. J. (1982). The concept of affordances in development: The renascence of functionalism. In W. A. Collins (Ed.), *The concept of development (Minnesota Symposium on Child Psychology,* vol. 15). Hillsdale, NJ: Erlbaum.

Gibson, E. J. (1988). Exploratory behavior in the development of perceiving, acting, and the acquiring of knowledge. *Annual review of psychology* (pp. 1–41). Palo Alto: CA: Annual Reviews, Inc.

Gibson, E. J., & Spelke, E. (1983). The development of perception. In P. H. Mussen (Ed.), *Carmichael's handbook of child psychology* (Vol. 3, pp. 1–76). New York: Wiley.

Gibson, E. J., & Yonas, A. (1966). A developmental study of visual search behavior. *Perception and Psychophysics, 1,* 169–171.

Gibson, J. J. (1950). *The perception of the visual world.* Boston, MA: Houghton-Mifflin.

Gibson, J. J. (1966). *The senses considered as perceptual systems.* Boston, MA: Houghton-Mifflin.

Gibson, J. J. (1979). *The ecological approach to visual perception.* Boston: Houghton Mifflin.

Gillund, G., & Shiffrin, R. M. (1984). A retrieval model for both recognition and recall. *Psychological Review, 91,* 1–67.

Gimpl, M. P., Gormezano, I., & Harvey, J. A. (1979). Effect of haloperidol and pimozide (PIM) on Pavlovian conditioning of the rabbit nictitating membrane response. In E. Usdin, I. Kopin, & J. Barchas (Eds.), *Catecholamines: Basic and clinical frontiers* (Vol. 2, pp. 1711–1713). New York: Permagon.

Gingrich, K. J., & Byrne, J. H. (1987). Single-cell neuron model for associative learning. *Journal of Neurophysiology, 57,* 1705–1715.

Ginsburg, A. P. (1971). Psychological correlates of a model of the human visual system. M.A. Thesis GE/EE/715–2, Wright-Patterson AFB, Ohio, Air Institute of Technology.

Glanzer, M., & Cunitz, A. R. (1966). Two storage mechanisms in free recall. *Journal of Verbal Learning and Verbal Behavior, 5,* 351–360.

Glass, A. L., & Holyoak, K. J. (1986). *Cognition* (2nd ed.). New York: Random House.

Gleick, J. (1987). *Chaos: Making a new science.* New York: Viking.

Glickman, S. E., & Schiff, B. B. (1967). A biological theory of reinforcement. *Psychological Review, 74,* 81–109.

Gluck, M. A. (in press). Stimulus sampling and distributed representations in adaptive network theories of learning. In A. Healy, S. Kosslyn, & R. Shiffrin (Eds.), *Festschrift for W. K. Estes.* Hillsdale, NJ: Erlbaum.

Gluck, M. A., & Bower, G. H. (1988). From conditioning to category learning: An adaptive network model. *Journal of Experimental Psychology: General, 117,* 227–247.

Gluck, M.A., & Thompson, R.F. (1987). Modeling the neural substrates of associative learning and memory: A computational approach. *Psychological Review, 94,* 176–191.

Goeders, N. E., & Smith, J. E. (1983). Cortical dopaminergic involvement in cocaine reinforcement. *Science, 221,* 773–775.

Goldiamond, I. (1962). Perception. In A. J. Bachrach (Ed.), *Experimental foundation of clinical psychology* (pp. 280–340). New York: Basic Books.

Goldiamond, I. (1976). Self-reinforcement. *Journal of Applied Behavior Analysis, 9,* 509–514.

Gollub, L. (1977). Conditioned reinforcement: Schedule effects. In W. K. Honig & J. E. R. Staddon (Eds.), *Handbook of operant behavior* (pp. 288–312). Englewood Cliffs, NJ: Prentice Hall.

Gormezano, I. (1966). Classical conditioning. In J. B. Sidowski (Ed.), *Experimental methods and instrumentation in psychology* (pp. 385–420). New York: McGraw-Hill.

Gormezano, I., & Kehoe, E. J. (1981). Classical conditioning and the law of contiguity. In P. Harzem & M. D. Zeiler (Eds.), *Predictability, correlation, and contiguity* (pp. 1–45). New York: Wiley.

Gormezano, I., Kehoe, E. J., & Marshall, B. S. (1983). Twenty years of classical conditioning research with the rabbit. *Progress in psychobiology and physiological psychology* (Vol. 10, pp. 197–275). New York: Academic.

Gormezano, I., Schneiderman, N., Deaux, E. B., & Fuentes, I. (1962). Nictitating membrane: Classical conditioning and extinction in the albino rabbit. *Science, 138,* 33–34.

Gould, J. L., & Gould, C. G. (1981). The instinct to learn. *Science 81, 2,* 44–50.

Gould, S. J. (1982). Darwin and the expansion of evolutionary theory. *Science, 216,* 380–387.

Graf, P., Shimamura, A. P., & Squire, L. R. (1985). Priming across modalities and priming across category levels: Extending the domain of preserved function in amnesia. *Journal of Experimental Psychology: Learning, Memory, and Cognition, 11,* 386–396.

Graham, N., & Nachmias, J. (1971). Detection of grating patterns containing two spatial frequencies: A comparison of single channel and multichannel models. *Vision Research, 11,* 251–259.

Grant, D. A. (1972). A preliminary model for processing information conveyed by verbal conditioned stimuli in classical conditioning. In A. H. Black and W. F. Prokasy (Eds.), *Classical conditioning II. Current research and theory.* Englewood Cliffs, NJ: Prentice Hall.

Grau, J. W., & Rescorla, R. A. (1984). Role of context in autoshaping. *Journal of Experimental Psychol-*

ogy: Animal Behavior Processes, 10, 324–332.

Gray, C. M., Konig, P., Engel, A. E., & Singer, W. (1989). Oscillatory responses in cat visual cortex exhibit inter-column synchronization which reflect global stimulus properties. *Nature, 338,* 334–337.

Green, G. (1991). Everyday stimulus equivalences for the brain-injured. In W. Ishaq (Ed.), *Human behavior in today's world.* New York: Praeger.

Greeno, J. G., James, C. T., DaPolito, F., & Polson, P. G. (1978). *Associative learning: A cognitive analysis.* Englewood Cliffs, NJ: Prentice Hall.

Gregory, R. L., & Gombrich, E. H. (1973). *Illusion in nature and art.* New York: Scribner.

Grice, G. R. (1948). The relation of secondary reinforcement to delayed reward in visual discrimination learning. *Journal of Experimental Psychology, 38,* 1–16.

Grosch, J., & Neuringer, A. (1981). Self-control in pigeons under the Mischel paradigm. *Journal of the Experimental Analysis of Behavior, 35,* 3–22.

Grossberg, S. (1982). *Studies of mind and brain.* Dordrecht, Holland: Reidel.

Groves, P. M., & Thompson, R. F. (1970). Habituation: A dual-process theory. *Psychological Review, 77,* 419–450.

Guan, X.-M., & McBride, W. J. (1989). Serotonin microinfusion into the ventral tegmental area increases accumbens dopamine release. *Brain Research Bulletin, 23,* 541–547.

Guthrie, E. R. (1935). *The psychology of learning.* New York: Harper & Row.

Guthrie, S. (1989). Retinal axon guidance: near or far? *Trends in Neuroscience, 12,* 481–482.

Guttman, N., & Kalish, H. I. (1956). Discriminability and stimulus generalization. *Journal of Experimental Psychology, 51,* 79–88.

Haber, R. N. (1983). The impending demise of the icon: A critique of the concept of iconic storage in visual information processing. *The Behavioral and Brain Sciences, 6,* 1–54.

Hall, G. (1991). *Perceptual and associative learning.* New York: Oxford University Press.

Hall, J. W. (1972). Verbal behavior as a function of amount of schooling. *American Journal of Psychology, 85,* 277–289.

Hanson, H. M. (1959). Effects of discrimination training on stimulus generalization. *Journal of Experimental Psychology, 58,* 321–334.

Harasi, F. I., & Hashimoto, Y. (1983). Ultraviolet visual pigment in a vertebrate: A tetrachromatic cone system in the Dace. *Science, 222,* 1021–1023.

Harlow, H. F. (1959). Learning set and error factor theory. In S. Koch (Ed.), *Psychology: A study of a science* (pp. 492–537). New York: McGraw-Hill.

Harris, C. E. (1980). Two examples of perceptual plasticity in the human adult In C. E. Harris, (Ed.), *Visual coding and adaptability* (pp. 95–149). Hillsdale, NJ: Erlbaum.

Hart, J. T. (1965). Memory and the feeling-of-knowing experience. *Journal of Educational Psychology, 56,* 203–216.

Hartline, H. K., & Ratliffe, F. (1957). Inhibitory interaction of receptor units in the eye of *Limulus. Journal of General Physiology, 40,* 357–376.

Harzem, P. (1986). The language trap and the study of pattern in human action. In T. Thompson & M. D. Zeiler (Eds.), *Analysis and integration of behavioral units* (pp. 45–53). Hillsdale, NJ: Erlbaum.

Harzem, P., Lowe, C. F., & Bagshaw, M. (1978). Verbal control in human operant behavior. *The Psychological Record, 18,* 405–423.

Hawkins, R. D., Carew, T. J., & Kandel, E. R. (1986). Effects of interstimulus interval and contingency on classical conditioning of *Aplysia* siphon-withdrawal reflex. *Journal of Neuroscience, 6,* 1695–1701.

Hayes, C. (1952). *The ape in our house.* London: Gollancz.

Hayes, S. C. (1989). Nonhumans have not yet shown stimulus equivalence. Journal of the *Experimental Analysis of Behavior, 51,* 385–392.

Hayes, S. C., Brownstein, A. J., Zettle, R. D., Rosenfarb, I., & Korn, Z. (1986). Rule-governed behavior and sensitivity to changing consequences of responding. *Journal of the Experimental Analysis of Behavior, 45,* 237–256.

Hayes, S. C., Rosenfarb, I., Wulfert, E., Munt, E. D., Korn, Z., & Zettle, R. D. (1985). Self-reinforcement effects: An artifact of social standard setting? *Journal of Applied Behavior Analysis, 18,* 201–214.

Hearst, E., & Franklin, S. R. (1977). Positive and negative relation between a signal and food: Approach-withdrawal behavior to the signal. *Journal of Experimental Psychology: Animal Behavior Processes, 3,* 37–52.

Hebb, D. O. (1949). *The organization of behavior.* New York: Wiley.

Hefferline, R. F., & Bruno, L. J. J. (1971). The psychophysiology of private events. In A. Jacobs & L. B. Sachs (Eds.), *The psychology of private events* (pp. 163–192). New York: Academic.

Hefferline, R. F. & Keenan, B. (1963). Amplitude-induction gradient of a small-scale (covert) operant. *Journal of the Experimental Analysis of Behavior, 6*, 307–315.

Hefferline, R. F., Keenan, B., & Harford, R. A. (1959). Escape and avoidance conditioning in human subjects with and without their observation of the response. *Science, 130*, 1338–1339.

Heilman, K. M., & Valenstein, E. (Eds.). (1979). *Clinical neuropsychology.* New York: Oxford University Press.

Hein, A. (1980). The development of visually guided behavior. In C. E. Harris, (Ed.), *Visual coding and adaptability* (pp. 51–67). Hillsdale, NJ: Erlbaum.

Hein, A., & Held, R. (1962). A neural model for labile sensorimotor coordinations. In E. E. Bernard & M. R. Kare (Eds.), *Biological prototypes and synthetic systems* (Vol. 1). New York, Plenum.

Hein, A., Held, R., & Gower, E. (1970). Development and segmentation of visually controlled movement by selective exposure during rearing. *Journal of Comparative and Physiological Psychology, 73*, 181–187.

Hein, A., & Jeannerod, M. (1983). *Spatially oriented behavior.* New York: Springer-Verlag.

Heinnemann, E. G., & Rudolph, R. L. (1963). The effect of discrimination training on the gradient of stimulus generalization. *American Journal of Psychology, 76*, 653–656.

Held, R. (1980). The rediscovery of adaptability in the visual system: Effects of extrinsic and intrinsic chromatic dispersion. In C. E. Harris, (Ed.), *Visual coding and adaptability* (pp. 69–94). Hillsdale, NJ: Erlbaum.

Held, R. (1981). Development of acuity in infants with normal and analogous visual experience. In R. N. Aslin, J. R. Alberts, & M. R. Petersen (Eds.), *Development of perception* (Vol. 2, pp. 279–296). New York: Academic.

Held, R., & Hein, A. V. (1958). Adaptation of disarranged eye-hand coordination contingent on reafferent stimulation. *Perceptual and Motor Skills, 8*, 87–90.

Hendry, D. P. (Ed.). (1969). *Conditioned reinforcement.* Homewood, IL: Dorsey Press.

Henik, A., Friedrich, F. J., & Kellogg, W. A. (1983). The dependence of semantic relatedness upon prime processing. *Memory and Cognition, 11*, 366–373.

Hernandez, L., & Hoebel, B. G. (1990). Feeding can enhance dopamine turnover in the prefrontal cortex. *Brain Research Bulletin, 25*, 975–979.

Herrnstein, R. J. (1966). Superstition: A corollary of the principles of operant conditioning. In W. K. Honig (Ed.), *Operant conditioning: Areas of research and application* (pp. 33–51). New York: Appleton-Century-Crofts.

Herrnstein, R. J. (1970). On the law of effect. *Journal of the Experimental Analysis of Behavior, 13*, 243–266.

Herrnstein, R. J. (1982). Meliorationas behavioral dynamicism. In M. L. Commons, R. J. Herrnstein, & H. Rachlin (Eds.), *Quantitative analyses of behavior: Vol. 2. Matching and maximizing accounts of behavior* (pp. 433–458). Cambridge, MA: Ballinger.

Herrnstein, R. J. (1984). Objects, categories, and discriminative stimuli. In H. L. Roitblat, T. G. Bever, & H. S. Terrace (Eds.), *Animal cognition.* Hillsdale, NJ: Erlbaum.

Herrnstein, R. J., & Loveland, D. H. (1964). Complex visual concept in the pigeon. *Science, 146*, 549–551.

Herrnstein, R. J., & Loveland, D. H. (1975). Maximizing and matching on concurrent variable ratio schedules. *Journal of the Experimental Analysis of Behavior, 24*, 107–116.

Herrnstein, R. J., Loveland, D. H., & Cable, C. (1976). Natural concepts in pigeons. *Journal of Experimental Psychology: Animal Behavior Processes, 2*, 285–302.

Hill, R. T. (1970). Facilitation of conditioned reinforcement as a mechanism of psychomotor stimulation. In E. Costa & S. Garattini (Eds.), *Amphetamines and related compounds.* New York: Raven.

Hind, J. E., Rose, J. E., Davies, P. W., Woolsey, C. N., Benjamin, R. M., Welker, W. I., & Thompson, R. F. (1961). Unit activity in the auditory cortex. In C. L. Rasmussen and R. F. Thompson (Eds), *Neural mechanisms of the auditory and vestibular systems* (pp. 201–210). Springfield, IL: Thomas.

Hineline, P. N. (1980). The language of behavior analysis: Its community, its functions, and its limitations. *Behaviorism, 8*, 67–86.

Hinson, J. M., & Staddon, J. E. R. (1983). Hill-climbing by pigeons.

Journal of the Experimental Analysis of Behavior, 39, 25–48.

Hinton, G. E., & Anderson, J. A. (Eds.). (1981). *Parallel models of associative memory.* Hillsdale, NJ: Erlbaum.

Hinton, G. E., McClelland, J. L., & Rumelhart, D. E. (1986). Distributed representations. In D. E. Rumelhart, & the PDP Group (Eds.), *Parallel distributed processing* (Vol. 1, pp. 77–109). Cambridge, MA: MIT Press.

Hinton, G. E., & Nowlan, S. (1986). How learning can guide evolution. *Technical Report No. CMU-CS-86-128.* Computer Science Department, Carnegie-Mellon University, Pittsburgh, PA.

Hirsch, H. V. B., & Spinelli, D. N. (1970). Visual experience modifies distribution of horizontally and vertically oriented receptive fields in cats. *Science, 168*, 869–871.

Hirst, W. (1986). The psychology of attention. In J. E. LeDoux & W. Hirst (Eds.), *Mind and brain: Dialogues in cognitive neuroscience* (pp. 105–141). New York: Cambridge University Press.

Hirst, W., & Kalmar, D. (1987). Characterizing attentional resources. *Journal of Experimental Psychology: General, 116*, 68–81.

Hirst, W., Spelke, E., Reaves, C. C., Caharack, G., & Neisser, U. (1980). Divided attention without alternation or automaticity. *Journal of Experimental Psychology: General, 109*, 98–117.

Hocherman, S., Benson, D. A., Goldstein, M. H., Jr., Heffner, H. E., & Hienz, R. D. (1976). Evoked unit activity in auditory cortex of monkeys performing a selective attention task. *Brain Research, 117*, 51–68.

Hoebel, B. G. (1988). Neuroscience and motivation: Pathways and peptides that define motivational systems. In R. A. Atkinson (Ed.), *Stevens' handbook of experimental psychology* (pp. 547–625). New York: Wiley.

Hoeler, F. K., Kirshenbaum, D. S., & Leonard, D. W. (1973). The effects of overtraining and successive extinctions upon nictitating membrane conditioning in the rabbit. *Learning and Motivation, 4*, 91–101.

Hoffman, H. S., & Ratner, A. M. (1973). A reinforcement model of imprinting: Implications for socialization in monkeys and men. *Psychological Review, 80*, 527–544.

Holland, P. C. (1983). "Occasion-setting": In Pavlovian feature-positive discriminations. In M. L.Commons, R. J. Herrnstein, & A. R. Wagner

(Eds.), *Quantitative analyses of behavior: Vol 1. Discrimination processes* (pp. 183–206). Cambridge, MA: Ballinger.

Hollis, K. (1984). Cause and function of animal learning processes. In P. Marler & H. S. Terrace (Eds.), *The biology of learning* (pp. 357–371). New York: Springer-Verlag.

Holmes, P. W. (1979). Transfer of matching performance in pigeons. *Journal of the Experimental Analysis of Behavior, 31,* 101–114.

Holt, P. E., & Kehoe, E. J. (1985). Cross-modal transfer as a function of similarities between training tasks in classical conditioning of the rabbit. *Animal Learning and Behavior, 13,* 51–59.

Holtzman, J. D., & Gazzaniga, M. S. (1982). Dual task interactions due exclusively to limits on processing resources. *Science., 218,* 1325–1327.

Honig, W. K. (1969). Attentional factors governing stimulus control. In R. Gilbert & N. S. Sutherland (Eds.), *Discrimination learning* (pp. 35–62). New York: Academic.

Horel, J. A. (1976). The neuroanatomy of amnesia: A critique of the hippocampal memory hypothesis. *Brain, 101,* 403–445.

Horton, D. L., & Kjeldegaard, P. M. (1961). An experimental analysis of associative factors in mediated generalizations. *Psychological Monographs, 75* (Whole No. 515), pp. 1–26.

Hubel, D. H., & Livingstone, M. S. (1987). Segregation of form, color, and stereopsis in primate area 18. *Journal of Neuroscience, 7,* 3378–3415.

Hubel, D. H., & Wiesel, T. N. (1959). Receptive fields of single neurons in the cat's striate cortex. *Journal of Physiology (London), 148,* 574–591.

Hubel, D. H., & Wiesel, T. N. (1962). Receptive fields, binocular interaction and functional architecture in the cat's visual cortex. *Journal of Physiology (London), 160,* 106–154.

Hubel, D. H., & Wiesel, T. N. (1968). Receptive fields and functional architecture of monkey striate cortex. *Journal of Physiology (London), 195,* 215–243.

Hubel, D. H., & Wiesel, T. N. (1972). Laminar and columnar distribution of geniculo-cortical fibers in the macaque monkey. *Journal of Comparative Neurology, 146,* 421–450.

Hubel, H., Henson, C. O., Rupert, A., & Galambos, R. (1959). "Attention" units in the auditory cortex. *Science, 129,* 1279–1280.

Hull, C. L. (1934). The concept of the habit-family hierarchy and maze learning. *Psychological Review, 41,* 33–54.

Hull, C. L. (1943). *Principles of behavior.* New York: Appleton-Century-Crofts.

Hull, D. L. (1973). *Darwin and his critics.* Cambridge, MA: Harvard University Press.

Hummel, J. E., & Biederman, I. (1990). Dynamic binding in a neural network for shape recognition. *Report 90–5.* Minneapolis, MN: Department of Psychology, University of Minnesota.

Hunt, E., & Lansman, M. (1986). Unified model of attention and problem-solving. *Psychological Review, 93,* 446–461.

Hunt, R. R., & Elliot, J. M. (1980). The role of nonsemantic information in memory: Orthographic effects on retention, *Journal of Experimental Psychology: General, 109,* 49–74.

Imperato, A., Honore, T., & Jensen, L. H. (1990). Dopamine release in the nucleus caudatus and in the nucleus accumbens is under glutaminergic control through non-NMDA receptors: A study in freely-moving rats. *Brain Research, 530,* 223–228.

Intons-Peterson, M. J. (1983). Imagery paradigms: How vulnerable are they to experimenter expectations? *Journal of Experimental Psychology: Human Perception and Performance, 9,* 394–412.

Iriki, A., Pavlides, C., Keller, A., & Asanuma, H. (1989). Long-term potentiation in the motor cortex. *Science, 245,* 1385–1387.

Istomena, Z. M. (1975). The development of voluntary memory in preschool age children. *Soviet Psychology, 13,* 5–64.

Ito, M. (1984). *The cerebellum and motor control.* New York: Appleton-Century-Crofts.

Ittelson, W. H. (1952). *The Ames demonstrations in perception.* Princeton, NJ: Princeton University Press.

Itzkoff, S. W. (1983). *The form of man: The evolutionary origins of human intelligence.* Ashfield, MA: Paideia Publishers.

Jacobs, K. M., & Donoghue, J. P. (1991). Reshaping the cortical motor map by unmasking latent intracortical connections. *Science, 251,* 944–946.

Jacobs, R. A. (1988). Initial experiments on constructing domains of expertise and hierarchies in connectionist networks. Technical Report. Department of Computer and Information Science, University of Massachusetts, Amherst, MA.

Jacoby, L. L., (1988). Memory observed and memory unobserved. In U. Neisser, U. & E. Winograd (Eds.), *Remembering reconsidered: Ecological and traditional approaches to the study of memory* (pp. 145–177). New York: Cambridge University Press.

Jacoby, L. L., & Hayman, C. A. (1987). Specific visual transfer in word identification. *Journal of Experimental Psychology: Learning, Memory, and Cognition, 9,* 478–485.

Jacoby, L. L., & Witherspoon, D. (1982). Remembering without awareness. *Canadian Journal of Psychology, 36,* 300–324.

Jarvis, M. J., & Ettinger, G. (1977). Cross-modal recognition in chimpanzees and monkeys. *Neuropsychologica, 15,* 499–506.

Jenkins, H, M., & Harrison, R. H. (1960). Effects of discrimination training on auditory generalization. *Journal of the Experimental Analysis of Behavior, 5,* 434–441.

Jenkins, J. J. (1965). Mediation theory and grammatical behavior. In S. Rosenberg (Ed.), *Directions in psycholinguistics* (pp. 66–96). New York: Macmillan.

Jenkins, J. J. (1980). Can we have a fruitful cognitive psychology? In J. H. Flowers (Ed.), *Nebraska Symposium on Motivation,* Lincoln, NE: University of Nebraska Press.

Jenkins, J. G., & Dallenbach, K. H. (1924). Obliviscence during sleep and waking. *American Journal of Psychology, 35,* 605–612.

Johanson, I. B., & Hall, W. G. (1979). Appetitive learning in 1-day old rat pups. *Science, 205,* 419–421.

Johansson, G., von Hofsten, C., & Jansson, G. (1980). Event perception. *Annual Review of Psychology, 31,* 27–66.

John, E. R., Bartlett, F., Shimokochi, M., & Kleinman, D. (1973). Neural readout from memory. *Journal of Neurophysiology, 36,* 893–924.

John, E. R., Tang, Y., Brill, A. B., Young, R., & Ono, K. (1986). Double-labeled metabolic maps of memory. *Science, 233,* 1167–1175.

Johnson, R. E. (1980). Memory-based rehearsal. In G. H. Bower (Ed.), *The psychology of learning and motivation* (Vol. 14, pp. 263–307). New York: Academic.

Joncich, G. (1968). *The sane positivist: A biography of Edward L. Thorndike.* Middletown, CT: Wesleyan University Press.

Jones, E. E., & Nisbett, R. E. (1971). *The actor and the observer: Divergent perceptions of the causes of behav-*

ior. Morristown, NJ: General Learning Press.

Jones, J. E. (1962). Contiguity and reinforcement in relation to CS-UCS intervals in classical aversive conditioning. *Psychological Review, 69,* 176–186.

Jonides, J., & Gleitman, H. (1972) A conceptual category effect in visual search: "O" as letter or digit. *Perception and Psychophysics, 20,* 289–298.

Jordan, M. I. (1986). *Serial order: A parallel distributed processing approach.* Institute for Cognitive Science Technical Report No. 8604, University of California, San Diego, CA.

Julesz, B. (1980). Spatial-frequency channels in one-, two-, and three-dimensional vision: Variations on an auditory theme by Bekesy. In C. S. Harris (Ed.), *Visual coding and adaptability* (pp. 263–316). Hillsdale, NJ: Erlbaum.

Jusczyk, K. P., Rosner, B., Cutting, J., Foard, C., & Smith, L. (1977). Categorical perception of nonspeech sounds by two-month-old infants. *Perception and Psychophysics, 21,* 50–54.

Kahneman, D. (1973). *Attention and effort.* Englewood Cliffs, NJ: Prentice-Hall.

Kahneman, D., & Chajczyk, D. (1983). Tests of the automaticity of reading: Dilution of Stroop effects by color-irrelevant stimuli. *Journal of Experimental Psychology: Human Perception and Performance, 9,* 497–509.

Kahneman, D., & Henik, A. (1981). Perceptual organization and attention. In M. Kubovy & J. R. Pomerantz (Eds.), *Perceptual organization* (pp. 181–211). Hillsdale, NJ: Erlbaum.

Kahneman, D., Slovic, P., & Tversky, A. (1982). *Judgments under uncertainty: Heuristics and biases.* Cambridge: Cambridge:University Press.

Kahneman, D., & Treisman, A. (1984a). Changing views of attention and automaticity. In E. Donchin (Ed.), *Cognitive psychophysiology: Event-related potentials and the study of cognition* (pp. 29–61). Hillsdale, NJ: Erlbaum.

Kahneman, D., & Treisman, A. (1984b). Changing views of attention and automaticity. In R. Parasuraman & D. R. Davies (Eds.), *Varieties of attention* (pp. 29–61). New York: Academic.

Kahneman, D., & Tversky, A. (1973). On the psychology of prediction. *Psychological Review, 80,* 237–251.

Kalaska, J. F., & Crammond, D. J. (1992). Cerebral cortical mechanisms of reaching movements. *Science, 255,* 1517–1523.

Kamin, L. J. (1968). Attention-like processes in classical conditioning. In M. R. Jones (Ed.), *Miami symposium on the prediction of behavior* (pp. 9–31). Miami, FL: University of Miami Press.

Kamin, L. J. (1969). Predictability, surprise, attention and conditioning. In B. A. Campbell & R. M. Church (Eds.), *Punishment and aversive behavior* (pp. 279–296). New York: Appleton-Century-Crofts.

Kandel, E. R. (1976). *Cellular basis of behavior.* San Francisco: Freeman.

Kaplan, E., & Velis, D. C. (1983). The neuropsychology of 10 after 11. Paper presented at the International Neuropsychological Meeting. Mexico City.

Karen, R. L. (1974). *An introduction to behavior theory and its applications.* New York: Harper & Row.

Kehoe, E. J. (1982). Conditioning with serial compound stimuli. *Experimental Animal Behavior, 1,* 30–65.

Kehoe, E. J. (1986). Summation and configuration in conditioning of the rabbit's nictitating membrane response to compound stimuli. *Journal of Experimental Psychology: Animal Behavior Processes, 12,* 186–195.

Kehoe, E. J. (1988). A layered network model of associative learning: Learning to learn and configuration. *Psychological Review, 95,* 411–433.

Kehoe, E. J., Feyer, A., & Moses, J. L. (1981). Second-order conditioning of the rabbit nictitating membrane response as a function of the CS2-CS1 and CS1-US intervals. *Animal Learning and Behavior, 9,* 304–315.

Kehoe, E. J., Gibbs, C. M., Garcia, E., & Gormezano, I. (1979). Associative transfer and stimulus selection in classical conditioning of the rabbit's nictitating membrane response to serial compound CSs. *Journal of Experimental Psychology: Animal Behavior Processes, 5,* 1–18.

Kehoe, E. J., & Gormezano, I. (1980). Configuration and combination laws in conditioning with compound stimuli. *Psychological Bulletin, 87,* 351–378.

Kehoe, E. J., & Napier, R. M. (1991). Real-time factors in the rabbit's nictitating membrane response to pulsed and serial conditioned stimuli. *Animal Learning and Behavior, 19,* 195–206.

Kelleher, R. T. (1958a). Stimulus-producing responses in chimpanzees.

Journal of the Experimental Analysis of Behavior, 1, 87–102.

Kelleher, R. T. (1958b). Fixed-ratio schedules of conditioned reinforcement with chimpanzees. *Journal of the Experimental Analysis of Behavior, 9,* 475–485.

Kelleher, R. T. (1966). Chaining and conditioned reinforcement. In W. K. Honig (Ed.), *Operant behavior: Areas of research and application* (pp. 160–212). Englewood Cliffs, NJ: Prentice Hall.

Kelleher, R. T., & Fry, W. T. (1962). Stimulus functions in chained fixed-interval schedules. *Journal of the Experimental Analysis of Behavior, 5,* 167–173.

Keller, F. S., & Schoenfeld. W. N. (1950). *Principles of psychology.* New York: Appleton-Century-Crofts.

Kelley, A. E., & Delfs, J. M. (1991). Dopamine and conditioned reinforcement. II. Contrasting effects of amphetamine microinjections into the nucleus accumbens with peptide microinjection into the ventral tegmental area. *Psychopharmacology, 103,* 197–203.

Kelso, S. R., & Brown, T. H. (1986). Differential conditioning of associative synaptic enhancement in hippocampal brain slices. *Science, 232,* 85–87.

Kendrick, K. M., & Baldwin, B. A. (1987). Cells in temporal cortex of conscious sheep can respond preferentially to the sight of faces. *Science, 236,* 448–450.

Keppel, G., & Underwood, B. J. (1962). Proactive inhibition in short-term retention of single items. *Journal of Verbal Learning and Verbal Behavior, 1,* 153–161.

Kettlewell, H. B. D. (1955). Selection experiments on industrial melanism in *Lepidoptera. Heredity, 9,* 323–343.

Kety, S. S. (1970). The biogenic amines in the central nervous system: Their possible role in arousal, emotion, and learning. In F. O. Schmidt (Ed.), *Neuroscience second study program* (pp. 324–336). New York: Rockefeller University Press.

Killeen, P. (1972). The matching law. *Journal of the Experimental Analysis of Behavior, 17,* 489–496.

Killeen, P. R., & Fantino, E. (1990). Unification of models for choice between delayed reinforcers. *Journal of the Experimental Analysis of Behavior, 53,* 189–200.

Kimura, D. (1979). Neuromotor mechanisms in the evolution of human communication. In H. D. Steklis and M. J. Raleigh (Eds.), *Neurobiology* of social communication in primates (pp. 197–219). New York: Academic.

Kimura, D., & Archibald, Y. (1974). Motor functions of the left hemisphere. *Brain, 97*, 337–350.

Kinchla, R. A. (1980). The measurement of attention. In R. S. Nickerson (Ed.), *Attention and performance VIII* (pp. 231–238). Hillsdale, NJ: Erlbaum.

King, H. J., Huthings, M. E., Moore, D. R., & Blakemore, C. (1988). Developmental plasticity in the visual and auditory representations in the mammalian superior colliculus. *Nature, 332*, 73–76.

Kinsbourne, M., & Hicks, R. E. (1978). Functional cerebral space: A model for overflow, transfer and interference in human performance. In J. Requin (Ed.), *Attention and performance* (Vol. VII). New York: Academic.

Kintsch, W., & Mross, E. F. (1985). Context effects in word identification. *Journal of Memory and Language, 24*, 336–349.

Kintsch, W., & Witte, R. S. (1962). Concurrent conditioning of bar press and salivation responses. *Journal of Comparative and Physiological Psychology, 55*, 963–968.

Kitai, S. T., Sugimori, M., & Kocsis, J. D. (1976). Excitatory nature of dopamine in the nigrocaudate pathway. *Experimental Brain Research, 24*, 351–363.

Klopf, A. H. (1982). *The hedonistic neuron.* Washington, DC: Hemisphere Publishing Corp.

Knapp, A. G., & Anderson, J. A. (1984). Theory of categorization based on distributed memory storage. *Journal of Experimental Psychology: Learning, Memory, and Cognition, 10*, 616–637.

Knudsen, E. I.(1984). The role of auditory experience in the development and maintenance of sound localization. *Trends in the Neurosciences, 7*, 326–330.

Knudsen, E. I. (1983). Early auditory experience aligns the auditory map of space in the optic tectum of the barn owl. *Science, 222*, 939–942.

Knudsen, E. I., & Brainard, M. S. (1991). Visual instruction of the neural map of auditory space in the developing optic tectum. *Science, 253*, 85–87.

Knudsen, E. I., & Knudsen, P. F. (1985). Vision guides the adjustment of auditory localization in young barn owls. *Science, 230*, 545–548.

Kohlenberg, B. S., Hayes, S. C., & Hayes, L. J. (1991). The transfer of contextual control over equivalence classes through equivalence classes: A possible model of social stereotyping. *Journal of the Experimental Analysis of Behavior, 56*, 505–518.

Köhler, W. (1925). *The mentality of apes.* London: Routledge & Kegan Paul.

Kohonen, T. (1977). *Associative memory—a system-theoretical approach.* New York: Springer-Verlag.

Kohonen, T., Lehtio, P., & Oja, E. (1981). Storage and processing of information in distributed associative memory systems. In G. Hinton & J. A. Anderson (Eds.), *Parallel models of associative memory* (pp. 105–143). Hillsdale, NJ: Erlbaum.

Kohonen, T., Oja, E., & Lehtio, P. (1985). A model of cortical associative memory. In W. B. Levy, J. A. Anderson, & S. Lehmkule (Eds.), *Synaptic modification, neuron selectivity, and nervous system organization* (pp. 209–221). Hillsdale, NJ: Erlbaum.

Koichi, O. (1987). Superstitious behavior in humans, *Journal of the Experimental Analysis of Behavior, 47*, 261–271.

Kolata, G. (1984). Studying learning in the womb. *Science, 225*, 302–303.

Kolb, B., & Whishaw, I. Q. (1985). *Fundamentals of human neuropsychology.* San Francisco: Freeman.

Kolers, P. A. (1973). Remembering operations. *Memory and Cognition, 1*, 347–355.

Kolers, P. A. (1979). A pattern analyzing basis of recognition. In L. S. Cermak & F. I. M. Craik (Eds.), *Levels of processing in human memory* (pp. 353–384). Hillsdale, NJ: Erlbaum.

Kolers, P. A., & Roediger, H. L. (1984). Procedures of the mind. *Journal of Verbal Learning and Verbal Behavior, 23*, 425–449.

Kolers, P. A., & Smythe, W. E. (1984). Symbol manipulation: Alternatives to the computational view of mind. *Journal of Verbal Learning and Verbal Behavior, 23*, 289–314.

Konorski, J. (1948). *Conditioned reflexes and neuron organization.* Cambridge, England: Cambridge University Press.

Konorski, J. (1967). *Integrative activity of the brain.* Chicago: University of Chicago Press.

Kopp, J., & Lane, H. L. (1968). Hue discrimination related to linguistic habits. *Psychonomic Science, 11*, 61–62.

Kossan, N. E. (1981). Developmental differences in concept acquisition strategies. *Child Development, 52*, 290–298.

Kosslyn, S. M. (1983). *Ghosts in the mind's machine.* New York: Norton.

Kosslyn, S. M., Pick, H. L., Jr., & Fariello, G. R. (1974). Cognitive maps in children and men. *Child Development, 45*, 707–716.

Kosslyn, S. M., & Pomerantz, J. P. (1977). Imagery, propositions, and the form of internal representations. *Cognitive Psychology, 9*, 52–76.

Kremer, E. F. (1978). The Rescorla-Wagner model: Losses in associative strength in compound conditioned stimuli. *Journal of Experimental Psychology: Animal Behavior Processes, 4*, 22–36.

Kreutzer, M. A., Leonard, C., & Flavell, J. H. (1975). An interview study of children's knowledge about memory. *Monographs for the Society for Research in Child Development, 40* (1, Serial No. 159), pp. 1–60.

Krieckhaus, E. E., Donahoe, J. W., & Morgan, M. A. (1992). Paranoid schizophrenia may be caused by dopamine hyperactivity of CA1 hippocampus. *Biological Psychiatry, 31*, 560–570.

Kucharski, D., Burka, N., & Hall, W. G. (1990). The anterior limb of the anterior commissure is an access route to contralaterally stored olfactory memories. *Psychobiology, 18*, 195–204.

Kuhl, P. K., & Meltzoff, A. N. (1982). The bimodal perception of speech in infants. *Science, 218*, 1138–1141.

Kuhl, P. K., & Miller, J. D. (1975). Speech perception by the chinchilla: Voiced-voiceless distinction in alveolar plosive consonants. *Science, 190*, 69–72.

LaBerge, D., & Brown, V. (1989).Theory of attentional operations in shape identification. *Psychological Review, 96*, 101–124.

Lachner, J. R., & Garrett, M. F. (1972). Resolving ambiguity: Effects of biasing context in the unattended ear. *Cognition, 1*, 359–372.

Lal, R., & Friedlander, M. J. (1989). Gating of retinal transmissions by afferent eye position and movements signals. *Science, 243*, 93–96.

Landfield, P. W., & Deadwyler, S. A. (Eds.) *Long-term potentiation: From biophysics to behavior.* New York: Liss.

Lashley, K. S. (1938). Conditional reactions in the rat. *Journal of Psychology, 6*, 311–324.

Lattal, K. A. (1972). Response-reinforcer independence and conventional extinction after fixed-interval and variable-interval schedules. *Journal of the Experimental Analysis of Behavior, 18*, 133–140.

Layng, T. V. J., & Andronis, P. T. (1984). Toward a functional analysis of delusional speech and hallucinatory behavior. *The Behavior Analyst, 7,* 139–156.

LeDoux, J. E. (1978). *The integrated mind.* New York: Plenum.

LeDoux, J. E., Thompson, M. E., Iadecola, C., & Reis, D. J. (1983). Local cerebral blood flow increases during emotional processing in the conscious rat. *Science. 221,* 576–577.

LeFrancois, J. R., Chase, P. N., & Joyce, J. H. (1988). The effects of a variety of instructions on human fixed-interval performance. *Journal of the Experimental Analysis of Behavior, 49,* 383–393.

Lehrman, D. L. (1970). Semantic and conceptual issues in the nature-nurture problem. In L. R. Aronson, E. Tobach, D. S. Lehrman, & J. S. Rosenblatt (Eds.), *Development and evolution of behavior* (pp. 17–52). San Francisco: Freeman.

Lehrman, D. S., Hinde, R. A., & Shaw, E. (Eds.) (1972). *Advances in the study of behavior,* New York: Academic.

Lenneberg, E. H. (1967). *Biological foundations of language.* New York: Wiley.

Levinthal, C. F., Tartell, R. H., Margolin, C. M., Fishman, H. (1985). The CS-US interval (ISI) function in rabbit nictitating membrane response conditioning with very long intertrial intervals. *Animal Learning and Animal Behavior, 13,* 228–232.

Levy, W. B. (1985). Associative changes at the synapse: LTP in the hippocampus. In W. B. Levy, J. A. Anderson, & S. Lehmkuhle (Eds.), *Synaptic modification, neuron selectivity, and nervous system organization* (pp. 5–33). Hillsdale, NJ: Erlbaum.

Levy, W. B., & Steward, O. (1979). Temporal contiguity requirements for long-term associative potentiation/depression in the hippocampus. *Neuroscience, 8,* 791–797.

Lewandowsky, S. (1991). Gradual unlearning and catastrophic interference: A comparison of distributed architectures. *Cognitive Processes Laboratory Technical Report.* Norman, OK: University of Oklahoma.

Lewin, R. (1980). Is your brain really necessary? *Science, 210,* 1232–1234.

Lewin, R. (1986). RNA catalysis gives fresh perspective on the origin of life. *Science, 231,* 545–546.

Lewis, J. (1970). Semantic processing of unattended messages using dichotic listening. *Journal of Experimental Psychology, 85,* 225–228.

Leyland, C. M., & Mackintosh, N. J. (1978). Blocking of first- and second-order autoshaping in pigeons. *Animal Learning and Behavior, 6,* 392–394.

Li, H., & Graur, D. (1991). *Fundamentals of molecular evolution.* Sunderland, MA: Sinauer.

Liberman, A. M. (1970). The grammars of speech and language. *Cognitive Psychology, 1,* 301–323.

Liberman, A. M., Harris, K. S., Hoffman, H. S., & Griffith, B. C. (1957). The discimination of speech sounds within and across phoneme boundaries. *Journal of Experimental Psychology, 54,* 358–368.

Liberman, A. M., Mattingly, I. G., & Turvey, M. T. (1972). Language codes and memory codes. In A. W. Melton & E. Martin (Eds.), *Coding processes in human memory* (pp. 307–334). New York: Holt, Rinehart, & Winston.

Liddell, H. S., James, W. T., & Anderson, O. D. (1935). The comparative physiology of the conditioned motor reflex. *Comparative Psychology Monographs, 11:1,* Serial No, 51.

Lieberman, P. (1967). *Intonation, perception and language.* Cambridge, MA: MIT Press.

Lieberman, P. (1973). On the evolution of language: A unified view. *Cognition, 2,* 59–94.

Lieberman, P. (1984). *The biology and evolution of language.* Cambridge, MA: Harvard University Press.

Lipkens, R., Kop, P. F. M., & Matthijs, W. (1988). A test of symmetry and transitivity in the conditional discrimination performance of pigeons. *Journal of the Experimental Analysis of Behavior, 49,* 395–409.

Lipsitt, L. (1987). Learning in children. Colloquium presentation, University of Massachusetts, May 12, 1986. Amherst, MA.

Lisberger, S. G., & Pavleko, T. A. (1988). Brain stem neurons in modified pathways for motor learning in the primate vestibulo-ocular reflex. *Science, 242,* 771–773.

Little, A. H. (1970). Eyelid conditioning in the human infant as a function of the interstimulus interval. Unpublished master's thesis, Brown University. Providence, RI.

Littman, D., & Becklen, R. (1976). Selective looking with minimal eye movements. *Perception and Psychophysics, 20,* 77–79.

Livingstone, M. S., & Hubel, D. H. (1987). Psychophysical evidence for separate channels for the perception of form, color, movement, and depth. *Journal of Neuroscience, 7,* 3416–3468.

Logan, F. A. (1965). Decision making by rats: Delay vs. amount of reward. *Journal of Comparative and Physiological Psychology, 59,* 1–12.

Loggie, R. H., & Baddeley, A. D. (1990). Imagery and working memory. In J. Richardson, D. Marks, P. Hampson (Eds.), *Imagery: Current developments* (pp. 103–108). London: Routledge & Kegan Paul.

Logothetis, N. K., Schiller, P. H., Charles, E. R., & Hurlburt, A. C. (1990). Perceptual deficits and the activity of the color-opponent and broadband pathways at isoluminance. *Science, 247,* 214–217.

Logue, A.W. (1988). Research on self-control: An integrating framework. *Behavioral and Brain Sciences, 11,* 665–710.

LoLordo, V. M. (1979). Selective associations. In A. Dickinson, L. W. Tucker, & R. A. Boakes (Eds.), *Mechanisms of learning and motivation* (pp. 367–398). Hillsdale, NJ: Erlbaum.

Long, J. B. (1966). Elicitation and reinforcement as separate stimulus functions. *Psychological Reports, 19,* 759–764.

Lowel, S., & Singer, W. (1992). Selection of intrinsic horizontal connections in the visual cortex by correlated neuronal activity. *Science, 255,* 209–212

Lubow, R. E., Weiner, I. & Schnur, P. (1981). Conditioned attention theory. In G. H. Bower (Ed.), *The psychology of learning and motivation* (Vol. 15, pp. 1–49). New York: Academic.

Luce, R. D. (1991). *Response times: Their role in inferring elementary mental organization.* New York: Oxford University Press.

Luria, A. R. (1970). The functional organization of the brain. *Scientific American, 222,* 66–79.

Luria, A. R. (1976). *The man with a shattered world.* Chicago: Regnery.

Luria, A. R. (1980). The mind of a mnemonist (excerpts). In U. Neisser (Ed.), *Memory observed* (pp. 382–389). San Francisco: Freeman.

Lyford, G. L., & Jarrad, L. E. (1991). Effects of the competitive NMDA antagonist CPP on performance of a place and cue radial maze. *Psychobiology, 19,* 157–160.

Lynch, G., & Baudry, M. (1984). The biochemistry of memory: A new and specific hypothesis. *Science, 224,* 1057–1063.

MacDonald, J., & McGurk, H. (1978). Visual influences on speech perception processes.*Perception and Psychophysics, 24,* 253–257.

Mace, W. M. (1977). James J. Gibson's strategy for perceiving: Ask not what's inside your head, but what your head's inside of. In R. F. Shaw & J. Bransford (Eds.), *Perceiving, acting, and knowing* (pp. 43–65). Hillsdale, NJ: Erlbaum.

MacFarlane, D. A. (1930). The role of kinesthesis in maze learning. *University of California Publications in Psychology, 4*, 277–305.

Machado, A. (1989). Operant conditioning of behavioral variability using a percentile reinforcement schedule. *Journal of the Experimental Analysis of Behavior, 52*, 155–166.

MacKay, D. (1973). Aspects of the theory of comprehension, memory, and attention. *Quarterly Journal of Experimental Psychology, 25*, 22–40.

Mackintosh, N. J. (1974). *The psychology of animal learning*. New York: Academic Press.

Mackintosh, N. J. (1975). A theory of attention: Variations in the associability of stimuli with reinforcement. *Psychological Review, 82*, 276–298.

Mackintosh, N. J. (1977). Stimulus control: Attentional factors. In W. K. Honig & J. E. R. Staddon (Eds.), *Handbook of operant behavior* (pp. 481–513). Englewood Cliffs, NJ: Prentice Hall.

Mackintosh, N. J. (1983). *Conditioning and associative learning*. New York: Oxford University Press.

Mackintosh, N. J., & Dickinson, A. (1979). Instrumental (Type II) conditioning. In A. Dickinson & R. A. Boakes (Eds.), *Mechanisms of learning and motivation* (pp. 143–169). Hillsdale, NJ: Erlbaum.

Macko, K. A., Jarvis, C. D., Kennedy, C., Miyako, M., Shinohara, M., Sokoloff, L., & Mishkin, M. (1982). Mapping the primate visual system with $[2–^{14}]$deoxyglucose. *Science, 218*, 394–396.

Madison, D. V., Malenka, R. C., & Nicoll, R. A. (1991). Mechanisms underlying long-term potentiation of synaptic transmission. *Annual Review of Neuroscience, 14*, 379–397.

Maffei, L., Morrone, C., Pirchio, M., & Sandini, G. (1979). Responses of visual cortical cells to periodic and nonperiodic stimuli. *Journal of Physiology (London), 296*, 27–47.

Maier, N. R. F. (1931). Reasoning and learning. *Psychological Review, 38*, 332–342.

Malott, R. W., & Siddall, J. W. (1972). Acquisition of the people concept in pigeons. *Psychological Reports, 31*, 3–13.

Malpass, R. S., & DeVine, P. G. (1981). Eyewitness identification: lineup instructions and the absence of an offender. *Journal of Applied Psychology, 66*, 482–489.

Mandler, G. (1962). From association to structure. *Psychological Review, 61*, 415–427.

Mandler, G. (1967). Organization and memory. In K. W. Spence & J. T. Spence (Eds.), *The psychology of learning and motivation* (Vol. 1, pp. 328–372). New York: Academic.

Mandler, G. (1981). What is cognitive psychology? What isn't? Paper presented at the meeting of the American Psychological Association, Los Angeles.

Maratsos, M. (1983). Some current issues in the study of the acquisition of grammar. In P. H. Mussen (Ed.), *Handbook of child psychology*. (Vol. 3, pp. 707–786). New York: Wiley.

Marcel, A. J. (1983a). Conscious and unconscious perception: Experiments on visual masking and word recognition. *Cognitive Psychology, 15*, 197–237.

Marcel, A. J. (1983b). Conscious and unconscious perception: An approach to the relations between phenomenal experience and perceptual processes. *Cognitive Psychology, 15*, 238–300.

Marchant, H. G., III, & Moore, J. W. (1973). Blocking of the rabbit's conditioned nictitating membrane response in Kamin's two-stage paradigm. *Journal of Experimental Psychology, 101*, 155–158.

Marcucella, H., & MacDonall, J. S. (1977). A molecular analysis of multiple schedule interactions: negative contrast. *Journal of the Experimental Analysis of Behavior, 28*, 71–82.

Marder, E. (1991). Modulating a neural network. *Nature, 335*, 296–297.

Margolin, D. I., & Carlson, N. R. (1982). Common mechanisms in anomia and alexia. Paper presented at the twentieth Annual Meeting of the Academy of Aphasia, Lake Mohonk, NY.

Maricq, A. V., Peterson, A. S., Brake, A. J., Myers, R. M., & Julius, D. (1991). Primary structure and functional expression of the 5HT$_3$ receptor, a serotonin-gated ion channel. *Science, 254*, 432–437.

Marmor, G. S., & Zaback, L. A. (1976). Mental rotation by the blind: Does mental rotation depend on visual imagery? *Journal of Experimental Psychology: Human Perception and Performance, 2*, 515–521.

Marr, M. J. (1992). Behavior dynamics: One perspective. *Journal of the Experimental Analysis of Behavior, 57*, 249–266.

Marshall-Goodell, B., & Gormezano, I. (1991). Effects of cocaine on conditioning of the rabbit nictitating membrane response. *Pharmacology, Biochemistry, and Behavior, 39*, 503–507.

Martin, E. (1971). Verbal learning theory and independent retrieval phenomena. *Psychological Review, 75*, 421–444.

Matthews, B. A., Shimoff, E., Catania, A. C., & Sagvolden, T. (1977). Uninstructed human responding: Sensitivity to ratio and interval contingencies. *Journal of the Experimental Analysis of Behavior, 43*, 155–164.

Maxwell, T., Giles, C. & Lee, Y. (1986). Nonlinear dynamics of artificial neural systems. In J. Denker (Ed.), *AIP Conference Proceedings 151: Neural Networks for Computing* (pp.299–304). New York: American Institute for Physics.

Maynard-Smith, J. (1982). *Evolution and the theory of games*. Cambridge, England: Cambridge University Press.

Mayr, E. (1982). *The growth of biological thought: Diversity, evolution, and inheritance*. Cambridge, MA: Harvard University Press.

Mayr, E. (1988). *Toward a new philosophy of biology*. Cambridge, MA: Harvard University Press.

Mazur, J. E. (1981). Optimization theory fails to predict performance of pigeons in a two-response situation. *Science, 214*, 823–825.

McClelland, J. L., & Elman, J. L. (1986). The TRACE model of speech perception. *Cognitive Psychology, 18*, 1–16.

McClelland, J. L., & Rumelhart, D. E. (1985). Distributed memory and the representation of general and specific information. *Journal of Experimental Psychology: General, 114*, 159–188.

McClelland, J. L., Rumelhart, D. E., & The PDP Group (Eds.). (1986). *Parallel distributed processing* (Vol. 2). Cambridge, MA: MIT Press.

McCloskey, M., & Cohen, N. J. (1989). Catastrophic interference in connectionist networks: The sequential learning problem. In G. H. Bower (Ed.), *The psychology of learning and motivation* (Vol. 24, pp. 109–164). New York: Academic.

McCloskey, M., Wible, C. G., & Cohen, N. J. (1988). Is there a special flashbulb-memory mechanism? *Journal of Experimental Psychology: General, 117*, 171–181.

McCorquodale, K., & Meehl, P. E. (1948). On a distinction between hypothetical constructs and intervening variables. *Psychological Review, 55,* 95–107.

McCorquodale, K. (1970). On Chomsky's review of Skinner's *Verbal Behavior. Journal of the Experimental Analysis of Behavior, 13,* 83–99.

McDaniel, M. A., & Masson, M. E. J. (1985). Altering memory representation through retrieval. *Journal of Experimental Psychology: Learning, Memory, and Cognition, 11,* 371–385.

McDowell, J. J. (1991). Irreconcilable differences and political reality in these dark ages. *Behavior Analyst, 14,* 29–33.

McGeoch, J. A., & Irion, A. L. (1952). *The psychology of human learning* (2nd ed.). New York: McKay.

McGuigan, F. J. (1978). *Cognitive psychophysiology: principles of covert behavior.* Englewood Cliffs, NJ: Prentice Hall.

McGurk, H., & MacDonald, J. (1976). Hearing lips and seeing voices. *Nature, 264,* 746–748.

McIlvane, W. K., & Dube, W. V. (1992). Stimulus control shaping and stimulus control topographies. *Behavior Analyst, 15,* 89–94..

McIntire, K. D., Cleary, J., & Thompson, T. (1987). Conditional relations by monkeys: Reflexivity, symmetry, and transitivity. *Journal of the Experimental Analysis of Behavior, 47,* 279–285.

McKoon, G., & Ratcliff, R. (1980). Priming in item recognition: The organization of propositions in memory for text. *Journal of Verbal Learning and Verbal Behavior, 19,* 369–386.

McNamara, T. P., & Healy, A. F. (1988). Semantic, phonological, and mediated priming in reading and lexical decisions. *Journal of Experimental Psychology: Learning, Memory, and Cognition, 14,* 398–409.

Mechner, F. (1958). Sequential dependencies of the lengths of consecutive response runs. *Journal of the Experimental Analysis of Behavior, 1,* 229–233.

Medin, D. L., & Smith, E. E. (1984). Concepts and concept formation. *Annual Review of Psychology, 35,* 113–138.

Melton, A. W. (1967). Repetition and retrieval from memory. *Science, 158,* 532.

Meridith, M. A., & Stein, B. E. (1986). Spatial factors determine the activity of multisensory neurons in the cat superior colliculus. *Brain Research, 365,* 350–354.

Mervis, C. B. (1980). Category structure and the development of categorization. In R. J. Spito, B. C. Bruce, &

W. F. Brewer (Eds.), *Theoretical issues in reading comprehension: Perspectives from cognitive psychology, linguistics, artificial intelligence, and education* (pp. 279–307). Hillsdale, NJ: Erlbaum.

Mervis, C. B. (1987). Child-basic object categories and early lexical development. In U. Neisser (Ed.), *Concepts and conceptual development: Ecological and intellectual factors in categorization* (pp. 201–233). New York: Cambridge University Press.

Mervis, C. B., & Mervis, C. A. (1988). Role of adult input in young children's category evolution. I. An observational study. *Journal of Child Language, 15,* 257–272.

Merzenich, M. M., & Kaas, J. H. (1980). Principles of organization of sensory-perceptual systems in mammals. In J. M. Sprague & A. N. Epstein (Eds.), *Progress in Psychobiology and Physiological Psychology* (Vol. 9, pp. 1–42). New York: Academic.

Mesiter, M., Wong, R. O. L., Baylor, D. A., & Shatz, C. J. (1991). Synchronous bursts of action potentials in ganglion cells of the developing mammalian retina. *Science, 252,* 939–943.

Meyer, D. E., & Schvaneveldt, R. W. (1971). Facilitation in recognizing pairs of words. Evidence of a dependence between retrieval operations. *Journal of Experimental Psychology, 90,* 227–234.

Meyer, D. E., & Schvaneveldt, R. W. (1976). Meaning, memory structures, and mental processes. In C. Cofer (Ed.), *The structure of human memory* (pp. 54–89). San Francisco: Freeman.

Michaels, C. F., & Carello, C. (1981). *Direct perception.* Englewood Cliffs, NJ: Prentice Hall.

Migler, B. (1964). Effects of averaging data during stimulus generalization. *Journal of the Experimental Analysis of Behavior, 7,* 303–307.

Migler, B., & Millenson, J. R. (1969). Analysis of response rates during stimulus generalization, *Journal of the Experimental Analysis of Behavior, 12,* 81–87.

Mignard, M., & Malpeli, J. G. (1991). Paths of information flow through visual cortex. *Science, 251,* 1249–1251.

Miller, G. A. (1956). The magical number seven, plus or minus two: Some limits on our capacity for processing information. *Psychological Review, 63,* 81–97.

Miller, G. A., Galanter, E., & Pribram, K. H. (1960). *Plans and the struc-*

ture of behavior. New York: Holt, Rinehart, & Winston.

Miller, K. D., Keller, J. B., & Stryker, M. P. (1989). Ocular dominance column development: Analysis and simulation. *Science, 245,* 605–615.

Miller, N. E. (1959). Liberalization of basic S-R concepts: Extensions to conflict behavior, motivation, and social learning. In S. Koch (Ed.), *Psychology: Study of a science* (Vol. II, pp. 196–292). New York: McGraw-Hill.

Miller, N. E., & Carmona, A. (1967). Modification of a visceral response, salivation in thirsty dogs, by instrumental conditioning with water reward. *Journal of Comparative and Physiological Psychology, 63,* 1–6.

Miller, N. E., & DeBold, R. C. (1965). Classically conditioned tongue-licking and operant bar pressing recorded simultaneously in the rat. *Journal of Comparative and Physiological Psychology, 59,* 109–111.

Miller, R. R., & Matzel, L. D. (1988). The comparator hypothesis: A response rule for the expression of associations. In G. H. Bower (Ed.), *The psychology of learning and motivation* (Vol. 22, pp. 51–92). New York: Academic.

Miller, R. R., & Schachtman, T. R. (1985). Conditioning context as an associative baseline: Implications for response generation and the nature of conditioned inhibition. In R. R. Miller & N. E. Spear (Eds.), *Information processing in animals: Conditioned inhibition* (pp. 51–88). Hillsdale, NJ: Erlbaum.

Milner, B. (1962). Les troubles de la memoire accompangant des lesions hippocampiques bilaterales. *Physiologie de l'hippocampe* (pp. 257–272). Paris: Centre National de la Recherche Scientifique.

Milner, B. (1972). Disorders of learning and memory after temporal lobe lesions in man. *Clinical Neurosurgery, 19,* 421–466.

Milner, B., Corkin, S., & Teuber, H. L. (1968). Further analyses of the hippocampal amnesiac syndrome: 14-year follow-up study of H. M. *Neuropsychologia, 6,* 215–234.

Mimura, K. (1986). Development of visual pattern discrimination in the fly depends on light experience. *Science, 232,* 83–85.

Mineka, S. (1979). The role of fear in theories of avoidance learning, flooding, and extinction. *Psychological Bulletin, 86,* 985–1010.

Minsky, M. L., & Papert, S. A. (1969). *Perceptrons.* Cambridge, MA: MIT Press.

Minsky, M. L., & Papert, S. A. (1988). *Perceptrons* (expanded edition). Cambridge, MA: MIT Press.

Mischel, W., & Bakler, N. (1975). Cognitive transformations of reward objects through instructions. *Journal of Personality and Social Psychology, 74,* 46–51.

Mishkin, M. (1978). Memory in monkeys severely impaired by combined but not separate removal of amygdala and hippocampus. *Nature, 273,* 297–298.

Mishkin, M. (1979). Analogous neural models for tactual and visual learning. *Neuropsychologica, 17,* 139–151.

Mishkin, M. (1982). A memory system in the monkey. *Philosophical Transactions of the Royal Society of London: Series B Biological Sciences, 298,* 85–92.

Mitchell, D. E. (1980). The influence of early visual experience on visual perception. In C. E. Harris (Ed.), *Visual coding and adaptability* (pp. 1–50). Hillsdale, NJ: Erlbaum.

Mitchell, D. E. (1981). Sensitive periods in visual development. In R. N. Aslin, J. R. Alberts, & M. R. Petersen (Eds.), *Development of perception* (Vol. 2, pp. 3–43). New York: Academic.

Mitchell, D. E., & Ware, C. (1974). Interocular transfer of a visual aftereffect in normal and stereoblind humans. *Journal of Physiology, 236,* 707–721.

Moely, B. E., Olson, F. A., Halwes, T. G., & Flavell, J. H. (1969). Production deficiency in young children's clustered recall. *Developmental Psychology, 1,* 26–34.

Moerk, E. L. (1983). A behavioral analysis of controversial topics in first language acquisition: Reinforcements, corrections, modeling, input frequencies, and the three-term contingency. *Journal of Psycholinguistic Research, 12,* 129–155.

Moerk, E. L. (1990). Three-term contingency patterns in mother-child verbal interactions during first language acquisition. *Journal of the Experimental Analysis of Behavior, 54,* 293–305.

Montgomery, G. (1991). The mind in motion. *Discover,* Special issue, 12–19.

Moonen, C. T. W., van Zil, P. C. M., Frank, J. A., Le Bihan, D., & Becker, E. D. (1990). Functional magnetic resonance imaging in medicine and physiology. *Science, 250,* 53–61.

Moran, N. J., & Desimone, R. (1985). Selective attention gates visual processing in the extrastriate cortex. *Science, 229,* 782–784.

Moran, T. H., Lew, M. F., & Blass, E. M. (1981). Intracranial self-stimulation in 3-day-old rat pups. *Science, 214,* 1366–1368.

Moray, N. P. (1959). Attention in dichotic listening: Affective cues and the influence of instructions. *Quarterly Journal of Experimental Psychology, 11,* 56–60.

Moray, N. P., & O'Brien, T. (1967). Signal detection theory applied to selective listening. *Journal of the Acoustical Society of America, 42,* 765–772.

Morgan, C. L. (1894). *An introduction to comparative psychology.* London: W. Scott.

Morris, E. K., Higons, S. T., & Bicker, W. K. (1982). Comments on cognitive science in the experimental analysis of behavior. *Behavior Analyst, 5,* 109–125.

Morris, R. G. M. (1983). An attempt to disassociate "spatial mapping" and "working-memory" theories of hippocampal function. In W. Seifert (Ed.), *Neurobiology of the hippocampus.* New York: Academic.

Morse, E. K. (1982). Comments on cognitive science in the experimental analysis of behavior. *Behavior Analyst, 5,* 109–125.

Morse, W. H. (1966). Intermittent reinforcement. In W. K. Honig (Ed.), *Operant behavior: Areas of research and application* (pp. 52–108). Englewood Cliffs, NJ: Prentice Hall.

Morse, W. H., & Kelleher, R. T. (1977). Determinants of reinforcement and punishment. In W. K. Honig & J. E. R. Staddon (Eds.), *Handbook of operant behavior* (pp. 174–200). Englewood Cliffs, NJ: Prentice Hall.

Morse, W. H., & Skinner, B. F. (1957). A second type of superstition in the pigeon. *American Journal of Psychology, 70,* 308–311.

Morton, J. (1980). The logogen model and orthographic structure. In U. Frith (Ed.), *Cognitive processes in spelling.* London: Academic Press.

Movshon, J. A., Chambers, B. E. I., & Blakemore, C. (1972). Interocular transfer in normal humans and those who lack stereopsis. *Perception, 1,* 483–490.

Moyer, R. S. (1973). Comparing objects in memory: Evidence suggesting an internal psychophysics. *Perception and Psychophysics, 13,* 180–184.

Mueller, K. L., & Dinsmoor, J. A. (1984). Testing the reinforcing properties of S-: A replication of Lieberman's procedure. *Journal of the Experimental Analysis of Behavior, 41,* 17–25.

Mueller, K. L., & Dinsmoor, J. A. (1986). The effect of negative stimulus presentations on observing-response rates. *Journal of the Experimental Analysis of Behavior, 46,* 281–291.

Munro, P. W. (1986). State-dependent factors influencing neural plasticity: A partial account of the critical period. In J. L. McClelland, D. E. Rumelhart, & the PDP Group (Eds.). *Parallel distributed processing* (pp. 471–502). Cambridge, MA: MIT Press.

Murdock, B. B., Jr. (1982). A theory for the storage and retrieval of item and associative information. *Psychological Review, 89,* 609–626.

Murdock, B. B., Jr. (1987). Serial-order effects in a distributed memory model. In D. S. Gorfein & R. R. Hoffman (Eds.), *Memory and learning: The Ebbinghaus centennial conference* (pp. 277–310). Hillsdale, NJ: Erlbaum.

Myers, N. A., & Myers, J. L. (1965). A test of a discrimination hypothesis of secondary reinforcement. *Journal of Experimental Psychology, 70,* 98–101.

Nadel, L., Willner, J., & Kurz, E. M. (1985). Cognitive maps and environmental context. In P. D. Balsam, & A. Tomie (Eds.), *Context and learning* (pp. 385–406). Hillsdale, NJ: Erlbaum.

Navon, D. (1977). Resources—a theoretical soupstone. *Psychological Review, 91,* 216–234

Neely, J. H. (1977). Semantic priming and retrieval from lexical memory: Evidence for facilitatory and inhibitory processes. *Memory and Cognition, 4,* 648–654.

Neisser, U. (1964). Visual search. *Scientific American, 210,* 94–102.

Neisser, U. (1976). *Cognition and reality.* San Francisco: Freeman.

Neisser, U., & Becklen, R. (1975). Selective looking: attending to visually-specified events. *Cognitive Psychology, 7,* 480–494.

Nelson, T. O., Gerler, D., & Narens, L. (1984). Accuracy of feeling-of-knowing judgments for predicting perceptual identification and relearning. *Journal of Experimental Psychology: General, 113,* 282–300.

Nelson, T. O., & Rothbart, R. (1972). Acoustic savings for items forgotten from long-term memory. *Journal of Experimental Psychology, 93,* 357–360.

Neuringer, A. (1986). Can people behave "randomly"?: The role of feedback. *Journal of Experimental Psychology: General, 115,* 62–75.

Neuringer, A. (1991). Operant varibility and repetition as functions of inter-response time. *Journal of Experimental Psychology: Animal Behavior Processes, 17*, 3–12.

Nevin, J. A. (1973). Conditioned reinforcement. In J. A. Nevin & G. S. Reynolds (Eds.), *The study of behavior* (pp. 154–198). Glenview, IL: Scott, Foresman & Co.

Nevin, J. A. (1988). Behavioral momentum and the partial reinforcement effect. *Psychological Bulletin, 103*, 44–56.

Nevin, J. A. (1992). An integrative model for the study of behavioral momentum. *Journal of the Experimental Analysis of Behavior, 57*, 301–316.

Nevin, J. A., Mandell, C., & Atak, J. (1983). The analysis of behavioral momentum. *Journal of the Experimental Analysis of Behavior, 39*, 49–60.

Newell, A. (1973a). You can't play 20 questions with nature and win: Projective comments on the papers of this symposium. In W. G. Chase (Ed.), *Visual information processing* (pp. 283–308). New York: Academic.

Newell, A. (1973b). Production systems. Models of control structures. In W. G. Chase (Ed.), *Visual information processing* (pp. 463–526). New York: Academic Press.

Newell, A., Rosenbloom, P. S., & Laird, J. E. (1984). *Symbolic architectures for cognition.* Cambridge, MA: MIT Press.

Newell, A., & Simon, H. A. (1972). *Human problem solving.* Englewood Cliffs, NJ: Prentice Hall.

Norman, D. A. (1969). Memory while shadowing. *Quarterly Journal of Experimental Psychology, 21*, 85–93.

Norman, D. A. (1986). Reflections on cognition and parallel distributed processing. In J. L. McClelland, D. E. Rumelhart, & The PDP Group (Eds.), *Parallel distributed processing* (pp. 531–546). Cambridge, MA: MIT Press.

Norman, D. A., & Bobrow, D. G. (1975). On data-limited and resource-limited processes. *Cognitive Psychology, 7*, 44–64.

Notterman, J. M. (1959). Force emission during bar pressing. *Journal of Experimental Psychology, 58*, 341–347.

Notterman, J. M., & Block, A. H. (1960). Note on response differentiation during a simple discrimination. *Journal of the Experimental Analysis of Behavior, 3*, 289–291.

Novak, L., Bregestovski, P., Ascher, P., Herbert, A., & Prochiantz, A. (1984). Magnesium gates glutamate-activated channels in mouse central neurons. *Nature, 307*, 462–465.

Nur, U., Werren, J. H., Eickbush, D. G., Burke, W. D., & Eickbush, T. H. (1988). A "selfish" B chromosome that enhances its transmission by eliminating the paternal genome. *Science, 231*, 512–514.

O'Keefe, J., & Nadel, L. (1978). *The hippocampus as a cognitive map.* Oxford, England: Oxford University Press.

Olds, J., & Milner, P. (1954). Positive reinforcement produced by electrical stimulation of the septal and other regions of rat brain. *Journal of Comparative and Physiological Psychology, 47*, 419–427.

Olton, D. S. (1983). Memory functions and the hippocampus. In W. Seifert (Ed.), *Neurobiology of the hippocampus* (pp. 335–373). London: Academic.

O'Mara, H. (1991). Quantitative and methodological aspects of stimulus equivalence. *Journal of the Experimental Analysis of Behavior, 55*, 125–132.

Onifer, W., & Swinney, D. A. (1981). Accessing lexical ambiguities during sentence comprehension: Effects of frequency of meaning and contextual bias. *Memory and Cognition, 9*, 225–236.

Optican, L. M., & Richmond, B. J. (1987). Temporal encoding of two dimensional patterns by single units in primate inferior temporal cortex. III. Information theoretic analysis. *Journal of Neurophysiology, 57*, 162–178.

Ornstein, P. A., Naus, M. J., & Liberty, C. (1975). Rehearsal and organizational processes in children's memory. *Child Development, 46*, 818–830.

Osgood, C. E. (1949). The similarity paradox in human learning: A resolution. *Psychological Review, 56*, 132–143.

Osgood, C. E. (1953). *Method and theory in experimental psychology.* New York: Oxford University Press.

Ostry, D., Moray, N. & Marks, G. (1976). Attention, practice, and semantic targets. *Journal of Experimental Psychology: Human Perception and Performance, 2*, 326–336.

Overton, D. A. (1985). Contextual stimulus effects of drugs and internal states. In P. D. Balsam & A. Tomie (Eds.), *Context and learning* (pp. 357–384). Hillsdale, NJ: Erlbaum.

Page, S., & Neuringer, A. (1985). Variability is an operant. *Journal of Experimental Psychology: Animal Behavior Processes, 11*, 429–452.

Paivio, A. (1969). Mental imagery in associative learning and memory. *Psychological Review, 76*, 241–263.

Paivio, A. (1971). *Imagery and verbal processes.* New York: Holt, Rinehart, & Winston.

Palmer, D. C. (1986). Chomsky's nativism: A critical review. In P. N. Chase & L. J. Parrott (Eds.), *Psychological aspects of language* (pp. 49–60). Springfield, IL: Charles Thomas.

Palmer, D. C. (1986). The blocking of conditioned reinforcement. Unpublished doctoral dissertation. University of Massachusetts, Amherst, MA.

Palmer, D. C. (1991). A behavioral interpretation of memory. In L. J. Hayes & P. N. Chase (Eds.) *Dialogues on verbal behavior* (pp. 261–279). Reno, NV: Context Press.

Palmer, D. C., & Donahoe, J. W. (1993). Essentialism and selectionism in cognitive science and behavior analysis. *American Psychologist, 47*, 1344–1358.

Parkinson, J. K., Murray, E., & Mishkin, M. (1988). A selective mnemonic role for the hippocampus in monkeys: Memory for the location of objects. *Journal of Neuroscience, 8*, 4159–4167.

Parnevelas, J. G., & Papadopoulos, G. C. (1989). The monoaminergic innervation of the cerebral cortex is not diffuse and nonspecific. *Trends in Neuroscience, 12*, 315–319.

Parsons, L. M. (1987). Imagined spatial transformation of one's body. *Journal of Experimental Psychology: General, 116*, 172–191.

Pavlov, I. P. (1927). *Conditioned reflexes.* New York: Oxford University Press. Reprint. New York: Dover, 1960.

Pear, J. J. (1985). Spatiotemporal patterns of behavior produced by variable-interval schedules of reinforcement. *Journal of the Experimental Analysis of Behavior, 44*, 217–231.

Pear, J. J., & Legris, J. A. (1987). Shaping by automated tracking of an arbitrary operant response. *Journal of the Experimental Analysis of Behavior, 47*, 241–247.

Pearce, J. M., & Hall, G. (1980). A model of Pavlovian learning: Variations in the effectiveness of conditioned but not unconditioned stimuli. *Psychological Review, 87*, 532–552.

Pearce, J. M., Montgomery, A., & Dickenson, A. (1982). Contralateral transfer of inhibitory and excitatory eyelid conditioning in the rabbit. *Quarterly Journal of Experimental Psychology, 33*, 45–61.

Petersen, S. E., Fox, P. T., Posner, M. I., Mintun, M. A., & Raichle, M. E. (1988). Positron emission tomographic studies of the processing of single words. *Journal of Cognitive Neuroscience, 1*, 153–170.

Petersen, S. E., Fox, P. T., Snyder, A. Z., & Raichle, M. E. (1990). Activation of extrastriate and frontal cortical areas by visual words and word-like stimuli. *Science, 249*, 1041–1044.

Petersen, S. E., Robinson, D. L., & Keys, W. (1985). Pulvinar nuclei of the behaving monkey: Visual responses and their modulation. *Journal of Neurophysiology, 54*, 867–886.

Peterson, L. R., & Peterson, M. J. (1959). Short-term retention of individual verbal items. *Journal of Experimental Psychology, 58*, 193–198.

Peterson, M. R., Beecher, S. R., Zoloth, D. B., Moody, D. B., & Stebbins, W. C. (1978). Neural lateralization: Evidence from studies of the perception of species-specific vocalizations by Japanese macaques (*Macada puscata*). *Science, 202*, 324–326.

Peterson, N. (1960). Control of behavior by presentation of an imprinted stimulus. *Science, 132*, 1395–1396.

Pettigrew, J. D. (1974). The effect of visual experience on the development of stimulus specificity by kitten cortical neurons. *Journal of Physiology (London), 237*, 49–74.

Pettigrew, J. D. (1985). Some constraints operating on the synaptic modifications underlying binocular competition in the developing visual cortex. In W. B. Levy, J. A. Anderson, & S. Lehmkule (Eds.), *Synaptic modification, neuron selectivity, and nervous system organization* (pp. 79–87). Hillsdale, NJ: Erlbaum.

Pillemer, D. B., Goldsmith, L. R., Panter, A. T., & White, S. H. (1988). Very long-term memories of the first year in college. *Journal of Experimental Psychology: Learning, Memory, and Cognition, 14*, 709–715.

Pinker, S., & Prince, A. (1988). On language and connectionism: Analysis of a parallel distributed processing model of language acquisition. *Cognition, 28*, 73–193.

Pisoni, D. B. (1977). Identification and discrimination of the relative onset time of two-component tones: Implications for voicing perception in stops. *Journal of the Acoustical Society of America, 61*, 1352–1361.

Pisoni, D. B., & Lazarus, J. H. (1974). Categorical and non-categorical modes of speech perception along the voicing continuum. *Journal of the Acoustical Society of America, 55*, 328–333.

Platt, J. R. (1979). Interresponse-time shaping by variable-interval-like interresponse-time reinforcement contingencies. *Journal of the Experimental Analysis of Behavior, 31*, 3–14.

Pollen, D. A., & Ronner, S. F. (1982). Spatial computations performed by simple and complex cells in the visual cortex of the cat. *Visual Research, 22*, 101–118.

Pons, T. P., Garraghty, P. E., Ommaya, A. K., Kaas, J. H., Taub, E., & Mishkin, M. (1991). Massive cortical reorganization after sensory deafferentation in adult macaques. *Science, 252*, 1857–1860.

Poole, R. (1990). Pushing the envelope of life. *Science, 247*, 158–160.

Popper, K. (1957). *The poverty of historicism.* Boston: Beacon Press.

Popper, K. (1978). Natural selection and the emergence of mind. *Dialectica, 32*, 339–355.

Posner, M. I. (1978). *Chronometric explorations of mind.* Hillsdale, NJ: Erlbaum.

Posner, M. I. (1982). Cumulative development of attentional theory. *American Psychologist, 37*, 168–179.

Posner, M. I. (1984). Current research in the study of selective attention. In E. Donchin (Ed.), *Cognitive psychophysiology: Event-related potentials and the study of cognition* (pp. 37–50). Hillsdale, NJ: Erlbaum.

Posner, M. I., & Keele, S. W. (1968). On the genesis of abstract ideas. *Journal of Experimental Psychology, 77*, 353–363.

Posner, M. I., & Petersen, S. E. (1990). The attention system of the human brain. In W. Maxwell Cowan (Ed.), *Annual review of neurosciences* (Vol. 13, pp. 25–42). Palo Alto, CA: Annual Reviews, Inc.

Posner, M. I., Petersen, S. E., Fox, P. T., & Raichle, M. E. (1988). Localization of cognitive operations in the human brain. *Science, 240*, 1627–1631.

Posner, M. I., & Snyder, C. R. R. (1975). Facilitation and inhibition in the processing of signals. In P. M. A. Rabbitt & S. Dornic (Eds.), *Attention and performance V* (pp. 669–682). New York: Academic.

Postman, L. (1971). Transfer, interference, and forgetting. In J. W. Kling & L. A. Riggs (Eds.), *Woodworth and Schlosberg's experimental psychology* (3rd ed., pp. 1019–1132). New York: Holt, Rinehart, & Winston.

Postman, L., & Underwood, B. J. (1973). Critical issues in interference theory. *Memory and Cognition, 1*, 19–40.

Potter, M. C. (1975). Meaning in visual search. *Science, 187*, 965–966.

Premack, D. (1976). Language and intelligence in ape and man. *American Scientist, 64*, 674–683.

Pritchard, F. H. (1953). *The world's best essays: From Confucius to Mencken,* London: MacMillan.

Pritchatt, D. (1968). An investigation in some of the underlying verbal processes of the Stroop color-word task. *Quarterly Journal of Experimental Psychology, 20*, 351–359.

Pryor, K. W., Haag, R., & O'Reilly, J. (1969). The creative porpoise: Training for novel behavior. *Journal of the Experimental Analysis of Behavior, 12*, 653–661.

Raaijmakers, J. G. W., & Shiffrin, R. M. (1980). SAM: A theory of probabilistic search of associative memory. In G. H. Bower (Ed.), *The psychology of learning and motivation* (Vol. 14, pp. 208–262). New York: Academic.

Raaijmakers, J. G., & Shiffrin, R. M. (1981). Search of associative memory. *Psychological Review, 88*, 93–134.

Rabacchi, S., Bailly, Y., Delhaye-Bouchaud, N., & Mariani, J. (1992). Involvement of the N-methyl D-aspartate (NMDA) receptor in synapse elimination during cerebellar development. *Science, 256*, 1823–1825.

Rachlin, H., & Burkhard, B. (1978). The temporal triangle: Response substitution in instrumental conditioning. *Psychological Review, 85*, 22–47.

Rachlin, H., & Green, L. (1972). Commitment, choice, and self-control. *Journal of the Experimental Analysis of Behavior, 17*, 15–22.

Ramoa, A. S., Campbell, G., & Shatz, C. J. (1987). Transient morphological features of identified ganglion cells in living fetal and neonatal retina. *Science, 237*, 522–525.

Rand, T. C. (1974). Dichotic release from masking for speech. *Journal of the Acoustic Society of America, 55*, 678–680.

Rasmussen, M., Barnes, C. A. & McNaughton, B. L. (1989). A systematic test of cognitive mapping, working-memory, and temporal discontiguity theories of hippocampal function. *Psychobiology, 17*, 335–348.

Ratcliff, R. (1990). Connectionist models of recognition memory: Constraints imposed by learning and forgetting functions. *Psychological Review, 97*, 285–308.

Ratcliff, R., & McKoon, G. (1988). A retrieval theory of priming in memory. *Psychological Review, 95*, 385–408.

Rawlins, J. N. R. (1985). Associations across time: The hippocampus as a temporary memory store. *Behavioral and Brain Sciences, 8*, 479–496.

Rayner, K., & Frazier, L. (1989). Selection mechanisms in reading lexically ambiguous words. *Journal of Experimental Psychology: Learning, Memory, and Cognition, 15*, 779–790.

Real, P. G., Iannazzi, R., & Kamil, A. C. (1984). Discrimination and generalization of leaf damage by blue jays (*Cyanocitta cristata*). *Animal Learning and Behavior, 12*, 202–208.

Reason, J. (1984). Lapses of attention in everyday life. In A. Parasuraman & D. R. Davies (Eds.), *Varieties of attention* (pp. 515–549). New York: Academic.

Reder, L. M. (1982). Plausibility judgments versus fact retrieval: Alternative strategies for sentence verification. *Psychological Review, 89*, 250–280.

Reese, H. W. (1977). Imagery and associative memory. In R. V. Kail & J. W. Hagen (Eds.), *Perspectives on the development of memory and cognition* (pp. 113–175). Hillsdale, NJ: Erlbaum.

Reeve, L., Reeve, K. F., Brown, A. K., Brown, J. L., & Poulson, C. L. (1992). Effects of delayed reinforcement on infant vocalization rate. *Journal of the Experimental Analysis of Behavior, 58*, 1–8.

Reeves, A., & Sperling, G. (1986). Attention gating in short-term visual memory. *Psychological Review, 93*, 180–206.

Reinhold, D. B., & Perkins, C. C., Jr. (1955). Stimulus generalization following different methods of training. *Journal of Experimental Psychology, 49*, 423–427.

Repp, B. H., Liberman, A. M., Eccardt, T., & Pesetsky, D. (1978). Perceptual integration of acoustic cues for stop, fricative, and affricative manner. *Journal of Experimental Psychology: Human Perception and Performance, 4*, 621–637.

Rescorla, R. A. (1968). Conditioned inhibition of fear. In N. J. Mackintosh & W. K. Honig (Eds.), *Fundamental issues in associative learning* (pp. 65–89). Halifax, Nova Scotia: University of Dalhousie Press.

Rescorla, R. A. (1970). Reduction in the effectiveness of reinforcement after prior excitatory conditioning. *Learning and Motivation, 1*, 372–381.

Rescorla, R. A. (1971). Variation in effectiveness of reinforcement following prior inhibitory conditioning. *Learning and Motivation, 2*, 113–123.

Rescorla, R. A. (1973). Evidence for "unique stimulus" account of configural conditioning. *Journal of Comparative and Physiological Psychology, 85*, 331–338.

Rescorla, R. A. (1976). Stimulus generalization: Some predictions from a model of Pavlovian conditioning. *Journal of Experimental Psychology: Animal Behavior Processes, 2*, 88–96.

Rescorla, R. A. (1980). *Pavlovian second-order conditioning.* Hillsdale, NJ: Erlbaum.

Rescorla, R. A. (1985a). Pavlovian conditioning analogues to Gestalt perceptual principles. In F. R. Brush & J. B. Overmeir (Eds.), *Affect, conditioning, and cognition: Essays on the determinants of behavior* (pp. 113–130). Hillsdale, NJ: Erlbaum.

Rescorla, R. A. (1985b). Conditioned inhibition and facilitation. In R. R. Miller & N. E. Spear (Eds.), *Information processing in animals:* Conditioned inhibition (pp. 299–326). Hillsdale, NJ: Erlbaum.

Rescorla, R. A. (1988). Behavioral studies of Pavlovian conditioning. *Annual Review of Neuroscience, 11*, 329–352.

Rescorla, R. A. (1991). Associative relations in instrumental learning: The eighteenth Bartlett memorial Lecture. *Quarterly Journal of Experimental Psychology, 43B*, 1–23.

Rescorla, R. A., & Colwill, R. M. (1989). Associations with anticipated and obtained outcomes in instrumental learning. *Animal Learning and Behavior, 17*, 291–303.

Rescorla, R. A., & Solomon, R. L. (1967). Two-process learning theory: Relationship between Pavlovian conditioning and instrumental learning. *Psychological Review, 74*, 151–182.

Rescorla, R. A., & Wagner, A. R. (1972). A theory of Pavlovian conditioning: Variations in the effectiveness of reinforcement and nonreinforcement. In A. H. Black & W. F. Prokasy (Eds.), *Classical conditioning II* (pp. 64–99). New York: Appleton-Century-Crofts.

Revusky, S. H., & Garcia, J. (1970). Learned associations over long delays. In G. H. Bower & J. T. Spence (Eds.), *The psychology of learning and motivation* (Vol. 4, pp. 1–84). New York: Academic.

Richardson, W. K., & Warzak, W. J. (1981). Stimulus stringing by pigeons. *Journal of the Experimental Analysis of Behavior, 36*, 267–276.

Richelle, M. (1986). Variation and selection: The evolutionary analogy in Skinner's theory. In S. Modgil & C. Modgil (Eds.), *B. F. Skinner: Consensus and controversy* (pp. 127–137). New York: Falmer.

Richmond, B. J., & Optican, L. M. (1987). Temporal encoding of two-dimensional patterns by single units in primate inferior temporal cortex. II. Quantification of response waveform. *Journal of Neurophysiology, 57*, 147–161.

Riggs, L. A., Ratliff, F., Cornsweet, J. C., & Cornsweet, T. N. (1953). The disappearance of steadily fixated visual test objects. *Journal of the Optical Society of America, 43*, 495–501.

Rilling, M. E. (1977). Stimulus control and inhibitory processes. In W. K. Honig & J. E. R. Staddon (Eds.), *A handbook of operant conditioning.* Englewood Cliffs, NJ: Prentice-Hall.

Rilling, M. E., & LaClaire, T. L. (1989). Visually guided catching and tracking skills in pigeons: A preliminary analysis. *Journal of the Experimental Analysis of Behavior, 52*, 377–385.

Roberston, A. (1989). Multiple reward systems and the prefrontal cortex. *Neuroscience and Biobehavioral Reviews, 13*, 163–170.

Roberts, W. A. (1991). Testing optimal foraging theory on the radial maze: The role of learning in patch sampling. *Animal Learning and Behavior, 19*, 305–316.

Roberts, W. A., & Mazmanian, D. S. (1988). Concept learning at different levels of abstraction by pigeons, monkeys, and people. *Journal of Experimental Psychology: Animal Behavior Processes, 14*, 247–260.

Roe, A. W., Pallas, S. L., Hahn, J. O., & Sur, M. (1990). A map of visual space induced in primary auditory cortex. *Science, 250*, 818–820.

Roediger, H. L. (1980). The effectiveness of four mnemonics in ordering recall. *Journal of Experimental Psychology: Human Learning and Memory, 6*, 558–567.

Roediger, H. L., III. (1979). Implicit and explicit memory models. *Bulletin of *the Psychonomic Society, 6,* 339–342.

Roediger, H. L., (1990a). Implicit memory: Retention without remembering. *American Psychologist, 45,* 1043–1056.

Roediger, H. L., III. (1990b). Implicit memory: A commentary. *Bulletin of the Psychonomic Society, 28,* 373–380.

Roediger, H. L., III, & Challis, B. H. (1989). Hyperamnesia: Improvements in recall with repeated testing. In C. Izawa (Ed.), *Current issues in cognitive processes* (pp. 175–200). Hillsdale, NJ: Erlbaum.

Roediger, H. L., III, Neely, J. H., & Blaxton, T. A. (1983). Inhibition from related primes in semantic memory retrieval: A reappraisal of Brown's (1979) paradigm. *Journal of Experimental Psychology: Learning, Memory, and Cognition, 9,* 478–485.

Rogoff, B., & Mistry, J. (1985). Memory development in cultural context. In M. Pressley & C. J. Brainerd (Eds.), *Cognitive learning and memory in children* (pp. 117–142). New York: Springer-Verlag.

Roland, P. E., & Friberg, L. (1985). Localization of cortical areas activated by thinking. *Journal of Neurophysiology, 53,* 1219–1243.

Rosch, E., & Mervis, C. B. (1975). Family resemblances: Studies in the internal structures of categories. *Cognitive Psychology, 7,* 573–605.

Rosch, E., Mervis, C. B., Gray, W. D., Johnson, D. M., & Boyes-Braem, P. (1976). Basic objects in natural categories. *Cognitive Psychology, 8,* 332–349.

Rose, S. A., & Ruff, H. A. (1987). Cross-modal abilities in human infants. In J. Osofsky (Ed.), *Handbook of infant development* (pp. 318–362). New York: Wiley.

Rosenbaum, D. A. (1991). *Human motor control.* San Diego, CA: Academic.

Rosenfeld, H. M., & Baer, D. M. (1970). Unbiased and unnoticed verbal conditioning: The double-agent robot procedure. *Journal of the Experimental Analysis of Behavior, 14,* 97–107.

Routh, D. (1969). Conditioning of vocal response differentiation in infants. *Developmental Psychology, 1,* 219–225.

Rovee, C. K., & Rovee, D. T. (1969). Conjugate reinforcement of infant exploratory behavior. *Journal of Experimental Child Psychology, 8,* 33–39.

Rovee-Collier, C. K., & Gekoski, M. J. (1979). The economics of infancy: A review of conjugate reinforcement. In H. W. Reese & L. P. Lipsitt (Eds.), *Advances in Child Development and Behavior* (Vol. 13, pp. 195–225). New York: Academic.

Rovee-Collier, C. K., & Lipsitt, L. P. (1983). Learning, adaptation, and memory in the newborn. In P. Stratton (Ed.), *Psychobiology of the human newborn* (pp. 147–190). New York: Wiley.

Rovee-Collier, C. K., Morrongiello, B. A., Aron, M., & Kuperschmidt, J. (1978). Topographical response differentiation and reversal in 3-month-old infants. *Infant Behavior and Development, 1,* 323–333.

Rozin, P., & Kalat, J. W. (1971). Specific hungers and poison-avoidance as adaptive specializations of learning. *Psychological Review, 7,* 459–486.

Rubin, D. C. (1988). Go for the skill. In U. Neisser & E. Winograd (Eds.), *Remembering reconsidered* (pp. 374–383). Cambridge, England: Cambridge University Press.

Rudolph, R. L., & Van Houten, R. (1977). Auditory stimulus control in pigeons: Jenkins and Harrison (1960). *Journal of the Experimental Analysis of Behavior, 27,* 327–330.

Rudy, J. W. (1974). Stimulus selection in animal conditioning and paired-associate learning: Variations in the associative process. *Journal of Verbal Learning and Verbal Behavior, 13,* 282–296.

Rudy, J. W., & Keith, J. R. (1990). Why NMDA-receptor-dependent long-term potentiation may not be a mechanism of learning and memory: Reappraisal of the NMDA-receptor strategy. *Psychobiology, 18,* 251–257.

Rumelhart, D. E., Hinton, G. E., & Williams, R. J. (1986). Learning internal representations by error propagation. In D. E. Rumelhart, J. L. McClelland, & The PDP Group (Eds.), *Parallel distributed processing* (Vol. 1, pp. 318–362). Cambridge, MA: MIT Press.

Rumelhart, D. E., & McClelland, J. L. (1986). On learning the past tense of English verbs. In D. E. Rumelhart, J. L. McClelland, & The PDP Group (Eds.), *Parallel distributed processing* (Vol. 2). Cambridge, MA: MIT Press.

Rumelhart, D. E., McClelland, J. L., & The PDP Group (Eds.). (1986). *Parallel distributed processing* (Vol. 1). Cambridge, MA: MIT Press.

Rumelhart, D. E., Smolensky, P., McClelland, J. L., & Hinton, G. E. (1986). Schemata and sequential thought processes in PDP models. In J. L. McClelland, D. E. Rumelhart, & the PDP Group (Eds.) *Parallel distributed processing* (Vol. 2, pp. 7–57). Cambridge, MA: MIT Press.

Rumelhart, D. E., & Zipser, D. (1986). Feature discovery by competitive learning. In D. E. Rumelhart, J. L. McClelland, & the PDP Group (Eds.), *Parallel distributed processing* (Vol. 1, pp. 151–193). Cambridge, MA: MIT Press.

Sacks, O. (1987). *The man who mistook his wife for a hat and other clinical tales.* New York: Simon & Schuster.

Sahley, C., Rudy, J. W., & Gelperin, A. (1981). An analysis of associative learning in a terrestrial mollusc. *Journal of Comparative and Physiological Psychology, 144,* 108–113.

Sakitt, B. (1975). Locus of short-term visual storage. *Science, 190,* 1318–1319.

Salamone, J. D. (1991). Behavioral pharmacology of dopamine systems: A new synthesis. In P. Willner & J. Scheel-Kruger (Eds.), *The mesolimbic dopamine system: From motivation to action.* New York: Wiley.

Saltzman, I. J. (1949). Maze learning in the absence of primary reinforcement. *Journal of Comparative and Physiological Psychology, 42,* 161–173.

Sands, S. F., & Wright, A. A. (1980). Serial probe recognition performance by a Rhesus monkey and a human with 10- and 20-item lists. *Journal of Experimental Psychology: Animal Behavior Processes, 6,* 386–396.

Sanford, E. C. (1917/1982). Professor Sanford's morning prayer. In U. Neisser (Ed.), *Memory observed* (pp. 176–177). San Francisco: Freeman.

Santi, A. (1978). The role of physical similarity of the sample and correct comparison stimulus in matching-to-sample paradigms. *Journal of the Experimental Analysis of Behavior, 29,* 511–516.

Sasanuma, S. (1975). Kana and kanji processing in Japanese aphasics. *Brain and Language, 2,* 369–383.

Saunders, R. R., Wachter, J., Spradlin, J. E. (1988). Establishing auditory stimulus control over an eight-member equivalence class via conditional discrimination procedures. *Journal of the Experimental Analysis of Behavior, 49,* 95–115.

Savage-Rumbaugh, E. S., Rumbaugh, D. M., Smith, S. T., & Lawson, J. (1980). Reference: The linguistic essential. *Science, 210,* 922–925.

Scaife, M., & Bruner, J. S. (1975). The capacity for joint visual attention in the infant. *Nature, 253,* 265–266.

Schacter, D. L . (1985). Multiple forms of memory in humans and animals. In N. Weinberger, G. Lynch, & J. McGaugh (Eds.), *Memory systems of the brain: Animal and human cognitive processes* (pp. 351–379). New York: Guilford Press.

Schacter, D. L. (1987). Implicit memory: History and current status. *Journal of Experimental Psychology: Learning, Memory, and Cognition, 13,* 501–518.

Schacter, D. L., Cooper, L. A., Delaney, S. M., Peterson, M. A., & Tharan, M. (1991). Implicit memory for possible and impossible objects: Constraints on the construction of structural descriptions. *Journal of Experimental Psychology: Learning, Memory, and Cognition, 17,* 3–19.

Schiller, P. H. (1958). Innate motor action as a basis of learning: Manipulative patterns in the chimpanzee. In C. H. Schiller (Ed.), *Instinctive behavior: The development of a modern concept* (pp. 264–287). New York: International Universities Press.

Schlaggar, B. L., & O'Leary, D. D. M. (1991). Potential of visual cortex to develop an array of functional units unique to somatosensory cortex. *Science, 252,* 1556–1560.

Schlinger, H. (1990). A reply to behavior analysts writing about rules and rule-governed behavior. *The Analysis of Verbal Behavior, 8,* 77–82.

Schlinger, H., & Blakely, E. (1987). Function-altering effects of contingency-specifying stimuli. *The Behavior Analyst, 10,* 41–46.

Schmidt, S. R., & Bohannon, J. N., III (1988). In defense of the flashbulb-memory hypothesis: A comment on McCloskey, Wible, and Cohen (1988). *Journal of Experimental Psychology: General, 117,* 332–335.

Schneider, W., Dumais, S. T., & Shiffrin, R. M. (1984). Automatic and control processing and attention. In R. Parasuraman & D. R. Davies (Eds.), *Varieties of attention* (pp. 1–27). New York: Academic.

Schneider, W., & Shiffrin, R. M. (1977). Controlled and automatic human information processing. I. Detection, search, and attention. *Psychological Review, 84,* 1–66.

Schoenfeld, W. N. (Ed.). (1970). *The theory of reinforcement schedules.* Englewood Cliffs, NJ: Prentice-Hall.

Schoenfeld, W. N., Cole, B. K., Blaustein, J., Lachter, G. D., Martin, J. M., & Vickery, C. (1972). *Stimulus schedules: The t-τ systems.* New York: Harper & Row.

Schoenfeld, W. N., & Farmer, J. (1970). Reinforcement schedules and the "behavior stream." In W. N. Schoenfeld (Ed.), *The theory of reinforcement schedules* (pp. 215–245). New York: Appleton-Century-Crofts.

Schoenfeld, W. N., Harris, A. H., & Farmer, J. (1966). Conditioning response variability. *Psychological Reports, 19,* 551–557.

Schwartz, B. (1980). Development of complex, stereotyped behavior in pigeons. *Journal of the Experimental Analysis of Behavior, 33,* 153–166.

Schwartz, B. (1981a). Control of complex sequential operants by systematic visual information in pigeons. *Journal of Experimental Psychology: Animal Behavior Processes, 7,* 31–44.

Schwartz, B. (1981b). Reinforcement creates behavioral units. *Behavior Analysis Letters, 1,* 33–41.

Schwartz, B. (1982). Reinforcement-induced behavioral stereotypy: How not to teach people to discover rules. *Journal of Experimental Psychology: General, 111,* 23–59.

Segal, S. J., & Fusella, V. (1970). Influence of imagined pictures and sounds on detection of visual and auditory signals. *Journal of Experimental Psychology, 8,* 458–464.

Seidenberg, M. S., Tanenhaus, M. K., Leiman, J. M., & Bienkowski, M. (1982). Automatic access of the meanings of ambiguous words in context: Some limitations of knowledge-based processing. *Memory and Cognition, 10,* 489–537.

Sejnowski, T. J. (1986). Open questions about computation in cerebral cortex. In J. L. McClelland, D. E. Rumelhart, & The PDP Research Group (Eds.), *Parallel distributed processing* (Vol. 2, pp. 372–389). Cambridge, MA: MIT Press.

Selfridge, O., Sutton, R. S., & Barto, A. G. (1985). Training and tracking in robotics. *Proceedings of the ninth international conference on artificial intelligence.* Los Angeles, CA.

Seligman, M. E. P. (1970). On the generality of the laws of learning. *Psychological Review, 77,* 406–418.

Seligman, M. E. P., & Hager, J. L. (Eds.) (1972). *Biological boundaries of learning.* Englewood Cliffs, NJ: Prentice Hall.

Sewall, W. B., & Kendall, S. B. (1965). A note on interresponse time distributions during generalization testing. *Psychonomic Science, 3,* 95–96.

Shaffer, L. H. (1975). Multiple attention in continuous verbal tasks. In P. Rabbit & S. Dornic (Eds.), *Attention and performance* (Vol. V). New York: Academic.

Shank, R. C., & Abelson, R. P. (1977). *Scripts, plans, goals, and understanding.* Hillsdale, NJ: Erlbaum.

Shapiro, M. M. (1960). Respondent salivary conditioning during operant lever pressing in dogs. *Science, 132,* 619–629.

Shapiro, M. M. (1962). Temporal relationship between salivation and leverpressing with differential reinforcement of low rates. *Journal of Comparative and Physiological Psychology, 5,* 556–571.

Shapiro, M. M., & Miller, T. M. (1965). On the relationship between conditioned and discriminative stimuli and between instrumental and consummatory responses. In W. F. Prokasy (Ed.), *Classical conditioning* (pp. 269–301). New York: Appleton-Century-Crofts.

Sharp, P. E. (1991). Computer simulation of hippocampal place cells. *Psychobiology, 19,* 103–115.

Sheffield, F. D. (1965). Relation between classical conditioning and instrumental learning. In W. F. Prokasy (Ed.), *Classical conditioning* (pp. 302–322). New York: Appleton-Century-Crofts.

Shepard, R. N. (1984). Ecological constraints on internal representation: Resonant kinematics of perceiving, imagining, thinking, and dreaming. *Psychological Review, 91,* 417–447.

Shepard, R. N., & Metzler, J. (1971). Mental rotation of three-dimensional objects. *Science, 153,* 642–654.

Sherry, D. F., & Schacter, D. L. (1987). The evolution of multiple memory systems. *Psychological Review, 94,* 439–454.

Shettleworth, S. J. (1983). Function and mechanism in learning. In M. D. Zeiler & P. Harzem (Eds.), *Biological factors in learning* (pp. 1–40). New York: Wiley.

Shettleworth, S. J., & Juergensen, M. R. (1980). Reinforcement and the organization of behavior in golden hamsters: Brain stimulation reinforcement for seven action patterns. *Journal of Experimental Psychology: Animal Behavior Processes, 6,* 352–375.

Shiffrin, R. M. (1975). The locus and role of attention in memory systems. In P. M. A. Rabbitt & S. Dornie (Eds.), *Attention and performance* (Vol. V). London: Academic.

Shiffrin, R. M., & Grantham, D. W. (1974). Can attention be allocated to sensory modalities? *Perception and Psychophysics, 15,* 460–474.

Shiffrin, R. M., & Schneider, W. (1977). Controlled and automatic human information processing. II. Perceptual learning, automatic attending, and a general theory. *Psychological Review, 84,* 127–190.

Shimamura, A. P., & Squire, L. R. (1984). Paired-associate learning and priming effects in amnesia: A neuropsychological study. *Journal of Experimental Psychology: General, 113,* 556–570.

Shimp, C. P. (1969). Optimal behavior in free-operant experiments. *Psychological Review, 76,* 97–112.

Shizgal, P., Bielajew, C., & Rompre, P-P. (1988). Quantitative characteristics of the directly stimulated neurons subserving self-stimulation of the medial forebrain bundle: Psychophysical inference and electrophysiological measurement. In M. L. Commons, R. M. Church, J. R. Stellar, & A. R. Wagner (Eds.), *Quantitative analyses of behavior: Vol. 7. Biological determinants of reinforcement* (pp. 59–85). Hillsdale, NJ: Erlbaum.

Sidman, M. (1960). *Tactics of scientific research.* New York: Basic Books.

Sidman, M. (1969). Generalization gradients and stimulus control in delayed matching-to-sample. *Journal of the Experimental Analysis of Behavior, 33,* 285–289.

Sidman, M. (1980). A note on the measurement of conditional discrimination. *Journal of the Experimental Analysis of Behavior, 33,* 285–289.

Sidman, M. (1986). Functional analysis of emergent verbal classes. In T. Thompson & M. D. Zeiler (Eds.), *Analysis and integration of behavioral units* (pp. 213–245). Hillsdale, NJ: Erlbaum.

Sidman, M., & Cresson, O. (1973). Reading and crossmodal transfer in severe retardation. *American Journal of Mental Deficiency, 77,* 515–523.

Sidman, M., Cresson, O., Jr., & Willson-Morris, M. (1974). Acquisition of matching to sample via mediated transfer. *Journal of the Experimental Analysis of Behavior, 22,* 261–272.

Sidman, M., Rauzin, R., Lazar, R., Cunningham, S., Tailby, W., & Carrigan, P. (1982). A search for symmetry in the conditional discriminations of rhesus monkeys, baboons, and children. *Journal of the Experimental Analysis of Behavior, 37,* 23–44.

Sidman, M., & Stoddard, L. T. (1967). The effectiveness of fading in programming a simultaneous form discrimination for retarded children. *Journal of the Experimental Analysis of Behavior, 10,* 3–15.

Sidman, M., & Tailby, W. (1982). Conditional discrimination vs. matching to sample: An expansion of the testing paradigm. *Journal of the Experimental Analysis of Behavior, 37,* 5–22.

Sidman, M., Wynne, C. K., Macquire, R. W., & Barnes, T. (1989). Functional classes and equivalence relations. *Journal of the Experimental Analysis of Behavior, 56,* 261–274.

Siegel, S. (1977). Morphine tolerance acquisition as an associative process. *Journal of Experimental Psychology: Animal Behavior Processes, 3,* 1–13.

Siegel, S. (1983). Classical conditioning drug tolerance and drug dependency. In A. Smart (Ed.), *Research advances in alcohol and drug problems* (Vol. 7). New York: Plenum.

Siegel, S. (1985). Psychopharmacology and the mystery of the Moonstone. *American Psychologist, 40,* 580–581.

Siegel. S., Allan, L. G., & Eisenberg, T. (1992). The associative basis of contingent color after-effects. *Journal of Experimental Psychology: General, 121,* 79–94.

Sieroff, E., & Michel, A. (1987). Verbal visual extinction in right/left hemisphere patients and the problem of lexical access. *Neuropsychologia, 25,* 807–818.

Sieroff, E., Pollatsek, A., & Posner, M. I. (1988). Recognition of visual letter strings following injury to the posterior visual spatial attention system. *Cognitive Neuropsychology, 5,* 427–449.

Sieroff, E., & Posner, M. I. (1988). Cueing spatial attention during processing of words and letters strings in normals. *Cognitive Neuropsychology, 5,* 451–472.

Silberberg, A., Hamilton, B., Ziriax, J. M., & Casey, A. C. (1978). The structure of choice. *Journal of Experimental Psychology: Animal Behavior Processes, 4,* 368–398.

Silberberg, A., Thomas, J. R., & Berendzen, N. (1991). Human choice in concurrent variable-interval variable-ratio schedules. *Journal of the Experimental Analysis of Behavior, 56,* 575–584.

Silberberg, A., & Ziriax, J. M. (1982). The interchange-over time as a molecular dependent variable in concurrent schedules. In M. L. Commons, R. J. Herrnstein, & H. Rachlin (Eds.), *Quantitative analyses of behavior: Vol. 2. Matching* *and maximizing accounts of behavior* (pp. 111–130). Cambridge, MA: Ballinger.

Sillito, A. M. (1975). The contribution of inhibitory mechanisms in the receptive field properties of neurons in the cat's visual cortex. *Journal of Physiology, 250,* 304–330.

Simpson, G. B. (1984). Lexical ambiguity and its role in models of word recognition. *Psychological Bulletin, 96,* 316–340.

Simpson, G. G. (1984). *Tempo and mode in evolution.* New York: Columbia University Press.

Singer, W. (1985). Hebbian modification of synaptic transmission as a common mechanism in experience-dependent maturation of cortical functions. In W. B. Levy, J. A. Anderson, & S. Lehmkule (Eds.), *Synaptic modification, neuron selectivity, and nervous system organizatio* (pp. 35–64). Hillsdale, NJ: Erlbaum.

Singer, W., & Rauschecker, J. P. (1982). Central core control of developmental plasticity in the kitten visual cortex: II. Electrical activation of mesencephalic and diencephalic projections. *Experimental Brain Research, 47,* 223–233.

Skinner, B. F. (1931). The concept of the reflex in the description of behavior. *Journal of General Psychology, 5,* 427–458.

Skinner, B. F. (1935). The generic nature of the concepts of stimulus and response. *Journal of General Psychology, 12,* 40–65.

Skinner, B. F. (1937). Two types of conditioned reflex: A reply to Konorski and Miller. *Journal of General Psychology, 16,* 272–279.

Skinner, B. F. (1938). *The behavior of organisms.* New York: Appleton-Century-Crofts.

Skinner, B. F. (1945). The operational analysis of psychological terms. *Psychological Review, 52,* 270–277.

Skinner, B. F. (1948). "Superstition" in the pigeon. *Journal of Experimental Psychology, 38,* 168–172.

Skinner, B. F. (1950). Are theories of learning necessary? *Psychological Review, 57,* 193–216.

Skinner, B. F. (1953). *Science and human behavior.* New York: Macmillan.

Skinner, B. F. (1957). *Verbal behavior.* New York: Appleton-Century-Crofts.

Skinner, B. F. (1963). Behaviorism at fifty. *Science, 140,* 951–958.

Skinner, B. F. (1964). Behaviorism at fifty. In T. W. Wann (Ed.), *Behaviorism and phenomenology* (pp. 79–

96). Chicago: University of Chicago Press.

Skinner, B. F. (1966a). An operant analysis of problem solving. In B. Kleinmuntz (Ed.), *Problem solving: Research, method, teaching* (pp. 225–257). New York: Wiley.

Skinner, B. F. (1966b). The ontogeny and phylogeny of behavior. *Science, 153*, 1203–1213.

Skinner, B. F. (1971). *Beyond freedom and dignity.* New York: Knopf.

Skinner, B. F. (1974). *About behaviorism.* New York: Random House.

Skinner, B. F. (1977). Why I am not a cognitive psychologist. *Behaviorism, 1*, 1–10.

Skinner, B. F. (1981). Selection by consequences. *Science, 213*, 501–504.

Slamecka, N. J., & Graf, P. (1978). The generation effect: Delineation of a phenomenon. *Journal of Experimental Psychology: Human Learning and Memory, 4*, 592–604.

Slobin, D. L. (1979). *Psycholinguistics.* Glenview, IL: Scott, Foresman & Co.

Smith, D. A., & Graesser, A. C. (1981). Memory for actions in scripted activities as a function of typicality, retention interval, and retrieval task. *Memory and Cognition, 9*, 550–559.

Smith, J. M. (1978). The evolution of sex. Cambridge, England: Cambridge University Press.

Smith, M. C. (1968). CS-US interval and US intensity in classical conditioning of the rabbit's nictitating membrane response. *Journal of Comparative and Physiological Psychology, 69*, 226–231.

Smith, M. C., Coleman, S. P., & Gormezano, I. (1969). Classical conditioning of the rabbit's nictitating membrane response at backward, simultaneous, and forward CS-US intervals. *Journal of Comparative and Physiological Psychology, 69*, 226–231.

Smith, N. V. (1973). *The acquisition of phonology: A case study.* Cambridge England: Cambridge University Press.

Smith, S. M., Glenberg, A., & Bjork, R. A. (1978). Environmental context and human memory. *Memory and Cognition, 6*, 342–353.

Smolensky, P. (1986). Neural and conceptual interpretation of PDP models. In J. L. McClelland, D. E. Rumelhart, & The PDP Research Group (Eds.), *Parallel distributed processing* (Vol. 2, pp. 372–389). Cambridge, MA: MIT Press.

Smolensky, P. (1987). On variable binding and the representation of symbolic structures in connectionist systems. Institute of Cognitive Science, University of Colorado.

Smolensky, P. (1988). On the proper treatment of connectionism. *The Behavioral and Brain Sciences, 11*, 324–353.

Snodgrass, J. G. (1989). How many memory systems are there really?: Some evidence from the picture fragment completion task. In C. Izawa, (Ed.), *Current issues in cognitive processes* (pp. 135–174). Hillsdale, NJ: Erlbaum.

Snow, C. E. (1972). Mothers' speech to children learning language. *Child Development, 43*, 549–565.

Snow, C. E., & Ferguson, C. A. (Eds.) (1977). *Talking to children: Language input and acquisition.* Cambridge, England: Cambridge University Press.

Sober, E. (1984). *The nature of selection: evolutionary theory in philosophical focus.* Cambridge, MA: MIT Press.

Solomon, R. L., & Corbitt, J. D. (1974). An opponent-process theory of motivation: I. Temporal dynamics of affect. *Psychological Bulletin, 81*, 119–145.

Solomon, R. L., & Turner, L. H. (1962). Discriminative classical conditioning in dogs paralyzed by curare can later control discriminative avoidance responses in the normal state. *Psychological Review, 69*, 202–219.

Solomon, R. L., & Wynne, L. (1953). Traumatic avoidance conditioning: Acquisition in normal dogs. *Psychological Monographs*, Vol. 67, No. 4 (Whole no. 354).

Spear, N. E. (1973). Retrieval of memory in animals. *Psychological Bulletin, 80*, 163–194.

Spelke, E. (1976). Infants' intermodal perception of events. *Cognitive Psychology, 8*, 553–560.

Spelke, E., Hirst, W., & Neisser, U. (1976). Skills of divided attention. *Cognition, 4*, 215–230.

Spelke, E., Reaves, C., Hirst, W., & Neisser, U. (1977). Skills of divided attention II: A sentence copying experiment. Unpublished manuscript cited in Neisser, 1976.

Spence, D. P. (1988). Passive remembering. In U. Neisser & E. Winograd, (Eds.), *Remembering reconsidered: Ecological and traditional approaches to the study of memory* (pp. 311–325). New York: Cambridge University Press.

Spence, K. W. (1936). The nature of discrimination learning in animals. *Psychological Review, 43*, 427–449.

Spence, K. W. (1947). The role of secondary reinforcement in delayed reward learning. *Psychological Review, 54*, 1–8.

Spence, K. W. (1956). *Behavior theory and conditioning.* New Haven: Yale University Press.

Sperling, G. (1960). The information available in brief visual presentations. *Psychological Monographs*, No. 498.

Sperry, R. W. (1968). Hemisphere disconnection and unity in conscious awareness. *American Psychologist, 23*, 723–733.

Sperry, R. W. (1974). Lateral specialization in the surgically separated hemispheres. In F. O. Schmitt and F. G. Worden (Eds.), *Neurosciences: Third study program* (pp. 714–722). Cambridge, MA: MIT Press.

Spillman, L., & Werner, J. S. (1990). *Visual perception. The neurophysiological foundations.* New York: Wiley.

Spivey, J. E. (1967). Resistance to extinction as a function of the number of N-R transitions and percentage of reinforcement. *Journal of Experimental Psychology, 75*, 43–48.

Spradlin, J. E., Cotter, V. W., & Baxley, N. (1973). Establishing a conditional discrimination without direct training: A study of transfer with retarded adolescents. *American Journal of Mental Deficiency, 77*, 556–566.

Spradlin. J. E., & Saunders, R. R. (1984). Behaving appropriately in new situations: A stimulus class analysis. *American Journal of Mental Deficiency, 88*, 574–579.

Squire, L. R. (1989). On the course of forgetting in very long-term memory. *Journal of Experimental Psychology: Learning, Memory, and Cognition, 15*, 241–245.

Squire, L. R. (1992). Memory and the hippocampus: A synthesis from findings with rats, monkeys, and humans. *Psychological Review, 99*, 195–231.

Squire, L. R., & Cohen, N. J. (1984). Human memory and amnesia. In G. Lynch, J. L. McGaugh, & N. M. Weinberger (Eds.), *Neurobiology of learning and memory* (pp. 3–64). New York: Guilford.

Squire, L. R., Cohen, N. J., & Nadel, L. (1984). The medial temporal region and memory consolidation: a new hypothesis. In H. Weingartner & E. Parker (Eds.), *Memory consolidation* (pp. 185–210). Hillsdale, NJ: Erlbaum.

Squire, L. R., Shimamura, A. P., & Amaral, D. G. (1989). Memory and the hippocampus. In J. Byrne & W. Berry (Eds.), *Neural models of plas-*

ticity (pp. 208–239). New York: Academic.

Squire. L. R., & Zola-Morgan, S. (1983). The neurology of memory: The case for correspondence between the findings of human and non-human primates. In J. A. Deutsch (Ed.), *The physiological basis of memory* (pp. 199–268). San Diego, CA: Academic.

Squire, L. R., & Zola-Morgan, S. (1988). Memory: brain systems and behavior. *Trends in Neuroscience, 11*, 170–175.

Staats, A. W. (1968). *Learning, language, and cognition.* New York: Holt, Rinehart, and Winston.

Staddon, J. E. R. (1977). Behavioral competition in conditioning situations: Notes toward a theory of generalization and inhibition. In H. Davis & H. M. B. Hurwitz (Eds.), *Operant-Pavlovian interactions* (pp. 103–131). Hillsdale, NJ: Erlbaum.

Staddon, J. E. R. (1983). *Adaptive behavior and learning.* Cambridge, England: Cambridge University Press.

Staddon, J. E. R., & Hinson, J. M. (1983). Optimization: A result or a mechanism? *Science, 221*, 976–977.

Staddon, J. E. R., & Simmelhag, V. L. (1971). The "superstition" experiment: A reexamination of its implications for the principles of adaptive behavior. *Psychological Review, 78*, 3–43.

Staddon, J. E. R., & Zhang, Y. (1993). On the assignment-of-credit problem in operant learning. In M. L. Commons, S. Grossberg, & J. E. R. Staddon (Eds.), *Quantitative analyses of behavior. Vol. 14, Neuronal networks of conditioning and action* (pp. 279–292). Hillsdale, NJ: Erlbaum.

Starkey, P., Spelke, E. S., & Gelman, R. (1983). Direction of intermodal numerical correspondence in human infants. *Science, 222*, 179–181.

Stein, B. E., & Gordon, B. (1981). Maturation of the superior colliculus. In R. N. Aslin, J. R. Alberts, & M. R. Petersen (Eds.), *Development of perception* (Vol. 2. pp. 157–196). New York: Academic.

Stein, B. E., Honeycutt, W. S. & Meridith, M. A. (1988). Neurons and behavior: the same rules of multisensory integration apply. *Brain Research, 448*, 355–358.

Stein, L., & Belluzzi, J. D. (1988). Operant conditioning of individual neurons. In M. L. Commons, R. M. Church, J. R. Stellar, & A. R. Wagner (Eds.), *Quantitative analyses of*

behavior (Vol. VII, pp. 249–264). Hillsdale, NJ: Erlbaum.

Stein, L., & Belluzzi, J. D. (1989). Cellular investigations on behavioral reinforcement. *Neuroscience and Biobehavior Reviews, 13*, 69–80.

Stemmer, N. (1990). Skinner's *Verbal Behavior,* Chomsky's review, and mentalism. *Journal of the Experimental Analysis of Behavior, 54*, 307–315.

Stephens, D. W., & Krebs, J. R. (1986). *Foraging theory.* Princeton, NJ: Princeton University Press.

Stetter, K. O., Lauerer, G., Thomm, M., & Neuner, A. (1987). Isolation of extremely thermophilic sulfate reducers: Evidence for a novel branch of archaebacteria. *Science, 236*, 822–824.

Stickney, K., & Donahoe, J. W. (1983). Attenuation of blocking by a change in US locus. *Animal Learning and Animal Behavior, 11*, 60–66.

Stiles-Davis, J., Kritchevsky, M., & Bellugi, U. (1987). *Spatial cognition: Brain bases and development.* Hillsdale, NJ: Erlbaum.

Stoddard, L. T., & Sidman, M. (1967). The effects of errors on children's performance on a circle-ellipse discrimination. *Journal of the Experimental Analysis of Behavior, 10*, 261–270.

Stoffregen, T. A., & Becklen, R. C. (1989). Dual attention to dynamically structured naturalistic events. *Perceptual and Motor Skills, 69*, 1187–1201.

Stokes, T. F., & Baer, D. M. (1977). An implicit technology of generalization. *Journal of Applied Behavior Analysis, 10*, 349–367.

Stone, G. O. (1986). An analysis of the delta rule and the learning of statistical associations. In D. E. Rumelhart, J. L. McClelland, & the PDP Group (Eds.). *Parallel distributed processing* (Vol. 1, pp. 444–459). Cambridge, MA: MIT Press.

Stromer, R. (1986). Control by exclusion in arbitrary matching-to-sample. *Analysis and Intervention in Developmental Disabilities, 6*, 59–72.

Strong, G. W., & Whitehead, B. A. (1989). A solution to the tag-assignment problem for neural networks. *Behavioral and Brain Sciences, 12*, 381–433.

Stroop, J. R. (1935). Studies of interference in serial verbal reactions. *Journal of Experimental Psychology, 18*, 643–662.

Stryker, M. P., Sherk, H., Leventhal, A. G., & Hirsch, H. V. B. (1978). Physiological consequences for the cat's visual cortex of effectively restrict-

ing visual experience with oriented contours. *Journal of Neurophysiology, 41*, 896–909.

Sundberg, M. L. (1980). The role of automatic reinforcement in early language development. *Western Michigan University Behavioral Monograph #2*, Kalamazoo, MI.

Suppes, P. C. (1969). *Studies in the methodology and foundations of science.* Dordrecht, Germany: Reidel.

Sur, M., Garraghty, P. E., & Roe, A. W. (1988). Experimentally induced visual projections into auditory thalamus and cortex. *Science, 242*, 1437–1441.

Sussman, H. M. (1989). Neural coding of relational invariance in speech: Human language analogs to the barn owl. *Psychological Review, 96*, 631–642.

Sutherland, N. S., & Mackintosh, N. J. (1971). *Mechanisms of animal discrimination learning.* New York: Academic.

Sutherland, R. J., & Rudy, J. W. (1989). Configural association theory: The role of the hippocampal formation in learning, memory, and amnesia. *Psychobiology, 17*, 129–144.

Sutton, R. S., & Barto, A. G. (1981). Toward a modern theory of adaptive networks: Expectation and prediction. *Psychological Review, 88*, 135–171.

Swanson, L. W. (1982). The projections of the ventral tegmental area and adjacent regions: a combined fluorescent retrograde tracer and immunofluorescent study in the rat. *Brain Research Bulletin, 9*, 321–353.

Swindale, N. V. (1979). How ocular dominance stripes may be formed. In R. D. Freeman (Ed.), *Developmental neurobiology of vision* (pp. 267–273). New York: Plenum.

Terrace, H. S. (1966). Stimulus control. In W. K. Honig (Ed.), *Operant behavior: Areas of research and application* (pp. 271–344). New York: Appleton-Century-Crofts.

Teuber, H. L. (1963). Space perception and its disturbances after brain injury in man. *Neuropsychologia, 1*, 47–57.

Thomas, D. R. (1970). Stimulus selection, attention, and related matters. In J. H. Reynierse (Ed.), *Current issues in animal learning* (pp. 311–356). Lincoln, NE: University of Nebraska Press.

Thomas, D. R. (1985). Contextual stimulus control of operant responding in pigeons. In P. D. Balsam & A. Tomie (Eds.), *Context and learning* (pp. 295–321). Hillsdale, NJ: Erlbaum.

Thomas, D. R., & Caronite, S. C. (1964). Stimulus generalization of a positive conditioned reinforcer. II. Effects of discrimination training. *Journal of Experimental Psychology, 68*, 402–406.

Thomas, D. R., Miller, J. T., & Svinicki, J. G. (1971). Nonspecific transfer effects of discrimination training in the rat. *Journal of Comparative and Physiological Psychology, 74*, 96–101.

Thompson, R. F. (1965). The neural basis of stimulus generalization. In D. I. Mostofsky (Ed.), *Stimulus generalization* (pp. 154–178). Stanford, CA: Stanford University Press.

Thompson, R. F. (1986). The neurobiology of learning and memory. *Science, 233*, 941–947.

Thompson, R. F. (1990). Neural mechanisms of classical conditioning in mammals. *Philosophical Transaction of the Royal Society, 306*, London, 161–170.

Thompson, R. F., McCormack, D. A., & Lavond, D. G. (1991). Localization of the essential memory trace system for a basic form of associative learning in the mammalian brain. In S. Hulse (Ed.), *G. Stanley Hall Centennial Volume*. Baltimore, MD: Johns Hopkins Press.

Thomson, D. M., & Tulving, E. (1970). Associative encoding and retrieval: Weak and strong cues. *Journal of Experimental Psychology, 86*, 255–262.

Thorndike, E. L. (1898). Animal intelligence: An experimental study of the associative processes in animals. *The Psychological Review Monograph Supplements, 2:8*, 1–74.

Thorndike, E. L. (1932). *The fundamentals of learning*. New York: Columbia University Press.

Timberlake, W. (1980). A molar equilibrium theory of learned performance. In G. H. Bower (Ed.), *The psychology of learning and motivation* (Vol. 14, pp. 1–58). New York: Academic.

Timberlake, W., & Lucas, G. A. (1985). The basis of superstitious behavior: Chance contingency, stimulus substitution, or appetitive behavior? *Journal of the Experimental Analysis of Behavior, 44*, 279–299.

Timberlake, W., & Lucas, G. A. (1989). Behavior systems and learning: From misbehavior to general principles. In S. B. Klein & R. R. Mowrer (Eds.), *Contemporary learning theories: Instrumental conditioning and the impact of biological constraints on learning* (pp. 237–275). Hillsdale, NJ: Erlbaum.

Tinbergen, N. (1952). "Derived" activities: Their causation, biological significance, origin, and emancipation during evolution. *Quarterly Review of Biology, 27*, 1–32.

Tinbergen, N. (1964). The evolution of signaling devices. In W. Etkin (Ed.), *Social behavior and evolution among vertebrates* (pp. 206–230). Chicago, IL: University of Chicago Press.

Tolman, E. C. (1932). *Purposive behavior in animals and men*. New York: Appleton-Century-Crofts.

Tolman, E. C., & Honzik, C. H. (1930). "Insight" in rats. *University of California Publications in Psychology, 4*, 215–232.

Tootell, R. B. H., Silverman, M. S., Switkes, E., & De Valois, R. L. (1982). Deoxyglucose analysis of retinotopic organization in primate striate cortex. *Science, 218*, 902–904.

Townsend, J. T. (1971a). A note on the identifiability of parallel and serial processes. *Perception and Psychophysics, 10*, 161–163.

Townsend, J. T. (1971b). Theoretical analysis of an alphabetic confusion matrix. *Perception and Psychophysics, 9*, 40–50.

Townsend, J. T. (1972). Some results on the identifiability of serial and parallel processes. *British Journal of Mathematical and Statistical Psychology, 25*, 168–199.

Townsend, J. T. (1974). Issues and models concerning the processing of a finite number of inputs. In B. H. Kantowitz (Ed.), *Human information processing: Tutorials in performance and cognition*. Hillsdale, NJ: Erlbaum.

Townsend, J. T., & Evans, R. (1983). A systems approach to parallel-serial testability and visual feature processing. In H. G. Geissler (Ed.), *Modern issues in perception* (pp. 166–192). Berlin: VEB Deutscher Verlag der Wissenschaften.

Tranel, D., & Damasio, A. R. (1985). Knowledge without awareness: An autonomic index of facial recognition by prosopagnosics. *Science, 228*, 1453–1454.

Trapold, M. A., & Overmier, J. B. (1972). The second learning process in instrumental learning. In A. H. Black & W. F. Prokasy (Eds.), *Classical conditioning II: Current research and theory*. Englewood Cliffs, NJ: Prentice Hall.

Trehub, A. (1977). Neuronal models for cognitive processes: Networks for learning, perception, and imagination. *Journal of Theoretical Biology, 65*, 141–169.

Trehub, A. (1987). Visual-cognitive neural networks. In M. A. Arbib & A. R. Hanson (Eds.) *Vision, Brain, and Cooperative Communication* (pp.623–664). Cambridge, MA: MIT Press.

Trehub, A. (1991). *The cognitive brain*. Cambridge, MA: MIT Press.

Triesman, A. M. (1960). Contextual cues in selective listening. *Quarterly Journal of Experimental Psychology, 12*, 242–248.

Treisman, A. M., & Davies, A. (1973). Divided attention to eye and ear. In S. Kornblum (Ed.), *Attention and performance* (Vol. IV). New York: Academic.

Treisman, A. M., Squire, R., & Green, J. (1974). Semantic processing in dichotic listening? A replication. *Memory and Cognition, 2*, 641–646.

Trowill, J. A., Panksepp, J., & Gandelman, R. (1969). An incentive model of rewarding brain stimulation. *Psychological Review, 76*, 264–281.

Tulving, E. (1972). Episodic and semantic memory. In E. Tulving & W. Donaldson (Eds.), *Organization of memory* (pp. 361–403). New York: Academic.

Tulving, E. (1974). Cue-dependent forgetting. *American Scientist, 62*, 74–82.

Tulving, E. (1985). Ebbinghaus' memory: What did he learn and remember? *Journal of Experimental Psychology: Learning, Memory, and Cognition, 11*, 485–490.

Tulving, E., & Psotka, J. (1971). Retroactive inhibition in free recall: Inaccessibility of information available in the memory store. *Journal of Experimental Psychology, 87*, 1–8.

Tulving, E., & Schacter, D. L. (1990). Priming and human memory systems. *Science, 247*, 301–306.

Tulving, E., & Thomson, D. M. (1973). Encoding specificity and retrieval processes in episodic memory. *Psychological Review, 80*, 352–373.

Turnure, J., Buium, N., & Thurlow, M. (1976). The effectiveness of interrogatives for promoting verbal elaboration productivity in young children. *Child Development, 47*, 851–855.

Turvey, M. T. (1978). Visual processing and short-term visual memory. In W. K. Estes (Ed.), *Handbook of learning and cognitive processes* (pp. 91–142). Hillsdale, NJ: Erlbaum.

Turvey, M. T., & Shaw, R. E. (1979). The primacy of perceiving: An ecological reformulation of perception for understanding memory. In L. G. Nilsson (Ed.), *Perspectives on memory research: Essays in honor of*

Uppsala University's 500th anniversary (pp. 167–222). Hillsdale, NJ: Erlbaum.

Turvey, M. T., Yosel Solomon, H., & Burton, G. (1989). Knowing by wielding. *Journal of the Experimental Analysis of Behavior, 52,* 387–408.

Underwood, B. J. (1957). Interference and forgetting. *Psychological Review, 64,* 48–60.

Underwood, B. J. (1961). Ten years of massed practice on distributed practice. *Psychological Review, 68,* 229–247.

Underwood, B. J. (1972). Are we overloading memory? In A. W. Melton & E. Martin (Eds.), *Coding processes in human memory* (pp. 1–23). Washington, DC: Winston.

Underwood, G. (1974). Moray vs. the rest: The effects of extended shadowing practice. *Quarterly Journal of Experimental Psychology, 26,* 368–372.

Ungerleider, L. G., & Mishkin, M. (1982). Two cortical visual systems. In D. J. Ingle., M. A. Goodale, & R. J. Mansfield (Eds.), *Analysis of visual behavior* (pp. 549–586). Cambridge, MA: MIT Press.

Urcuioli, P. J. (1991). Retardation and facilitation of matching acquisition by differential outcomes. *Animal Learning and Behavior, 19,* 29–36.

Valenstein, E. S., Cox, V., & Kakolewski, J. W. (1969). The hypothalamus and motivated behavior. In J. T. Tapp (Ed.), *Reinforcement and behavior* (pp. 242–285). New York: Academic.

Van Hoesen, G. W., & Damasio, A. R. (1987). Neural correlates of cognitive impairment in Alzheimer's disease. In F. Plum (Ed.), *Handbook of physiology. Section I: The nervous system. Vol. 5. Higher functions of the brain* (pp. 871–989). Philadelphia: F. A. Davis.

van Hof, M. W., & van der Mark, F. (1976). Monocular pattern discrimination in normal and monocularly light-deprived rabbits. *Physiology and Behavior, 16,* 775–781.

Van Willigen, F., Emmett, J., Cotte, D., & Ayres, J. J. B. (1989). CS modality effects in one-trial forward and backward excitatory conditioning as assessed by conditioned suppression in rats. *Animal Learning and Behavior, 17,* 481–485.

Vaughan, M. E., & Michael, J. L. (1982). Automatic reinforcement: An important but ignored concept. *Behaviorism, 10,* 217–227.

Vaughn, W., Jr. (1981). Melioration, matching, and maximizing. *Journal of the Experimental Analysis of Behavior, 36,* 141–150.

Vaughn, W., Jr. (1988). Formation of equivalence sets in pigeons. *Journal of Experimental Psychology: Animal Behavior Processes, 14,* 36–42.

Vigilant, L., Stoneking, M., Harpending, H., Hawkes, K., & Wilson, A. C. (1991). African populations and the evolution of human mitochondrial DNA. *Science, 253,* 1503–1507.

Vogel, R., & Annau, Z. (1973). An operant discrimination task allowing variability of response patterning. *Journal of the Experimental Analysis of Behavior, 20,* 1–6.

vom Saal, W., & Jenkins, H. M. (1970). Blocking the development of stimulus control. *Learning and Motivation, 1,* 52–64.

von der Malsburg, C. (1973). Self-organizing or orientation sensitive cells in the striate cortex. *Kybernetik, 14,* 85–100.

von der Malsburg C. (1981). The correlation theory of brain function. *Report 81–2.* Munich, Germany: Department of Neurobiology, Max Planck Institute of Biophysical Chemistry.

von der Malsburg, C. (1987). Synaptic plasticity as a basis of brain organization. In J. P. Changeux & M. Konishi (Eds.), *The neural and molecular basis of learning* (pp. 411–432). New York: Wiley

von Wright, J. M., Anderson, K, & Stenman, U. (1975). Generalization of conditioned GSRs in dichotic listening. In P. M. A. Rabbitt & S. Doric (Eds.), *Attention and performance* (Vol. V). London: Academic.

Wachtershauser, G. (1990). Evolution of the first metabolic cycles. *Proceedings of the National Academy of Science, U. S. A., 87,* 200–204.

Wagner, A. R. (1976). Priming in STM: An information-processing mechanism for self-generated depression in performance. In T. J. Tighe & R. N. Leaton (Eds.), *Habituation: Perspectives from child development, animal behavior, and neurophysiology* (pp. 95–128). Hillsdale, NJ: Erlbaum.

Wagner, A. R. (1981). SOP: A model of automatic memory processing in animal behavior. In N. E. Spear & R. R. Miller (Eds.), *Information processing in animals: Memory mechanisms* (pp. 5–47). Hillsdale, NJ: Erlbaum.

Wagner, A. R., & Donegan, N. H. (1989). Some relationships between a computational model (SOP) and a neural circuit for Pavlovian (rabbit eyeblink) conditioning. In R. D. Hawkins & G. H. Bower (Eds.), *The psychology of learning and motivation: Computational models of learning in simple neural systems* (Vol. 23, pp. 157–303). New York: Academic.

Wagner, A. E., Mazur, J. E., Donegan, N. H., & Pfautz, P. L. (1980). Evaluation of blocking and conditioned inhibition to a CS signaling a decrease in US intensity. *Journal of Experimental Psychology: Animal Behavior Processes, 6,* 376–385.

Wagner, A. R., & Rescorla, R. A. (1972). Inhibition in Pavlovian conditioning. In R. A. Boakes & M. S. Halliday (Eds.), *Inhibition and learning.* New York: Academic.

Wagner, D. A. (1974). The development of short-term and incidental memory: A cross-cultural study. *Child Development, 45,* 389–396.

Wagner, D. A. (1978). Memories of Morocco: The influence of age, schooling and environment on memory. *Cognitive Psychology, 10,* 1–28.

Waldrop, M. M. (1992). Finding RNA makes proteins gives "RNA world" a big boost. *Science, 256,* 1396–1397.

Wallman, J., Gottlieb, M. D., Rajaram, V., & Fugate-Wentzek, L. A. (1987). Local retinal growth regions control local eye growth and myopia. *Science, 237,* 73–77.

Walter, C. (Ed.) (1982). *Winners: The blue-ribbon encyclopedia of awards.* New York: Facts on File.

Wang, L.-Y., Salter, M. W., & MacDonald, J. F. (1991). Regulation of kainate receptors by cAMP-dependent protein kinase and phosphatases. *Science, 253,* 1132–1135.

Warren, R. M. (1967). Perceptual restoration of missing speech sounds. *Science, 167,* 392–393.

Warren, R. M., & Warren, R. P. (1970). Auditory illusions and confusions. *Scientific American, 223,* 30–36.

Warrington, E. K., & Weiskrantz, L. (1982). Amnesia: A disconnection syndrome? *Neuropsychologia, 20,* 233–248.

Washburn, M. F. (1908). *The animal mind.* New York: Macmillan.

Watanabe, S. (1988). Failure of visual prototype learning in the pigeon. *Animal Learning and Behavior, 16,* 147–152.

Watkins, J. E. (1990). Mediationism and the obfuscation of memory. *American Psychologist, 45,* 328–335.

Watkins, M. J., & Tulving, E. (1975). Episodic memory: When recognition fails. *Journal of Experimental Psychology: General, 104,* 5–20.

Watson, J. B. (1913). Psychology as the behaviorist views it. *Psychological Review, 20,* 158–177.

Waugh, N. C., & Norman, D. A. (1965). Primary memory. *Psychological Review, 20,* 158–177.

Weichselgartner, E., & Sperling, G. (1987). Dynamics of automatic and controlled visual attention. *Science, 238,* 778–780.

Weimer, W. B. (1973). Psycholinguistics and Plato's paradoxes of the *Meno. American Psychologist, 28,* 15–33.

Weiskrantz, L. (1986). *Blindsight: A case study and implications.* New York: Oxford University Press.

Weiskrantz, L. (1988). *Thought without language.* Oxford, England: Clarendon Press.

Weiskrantz, L., & Warrington, E. K. (1979). Conditioning in amnesic patients. *Neuropsychologia, 17,* 187–194.

Weiskrantz, L., Warrington, E. K., Sanders, M. D., & Marshall, J. (1974). Visual capacity in the hemianopic field following a restricted occipital ablation. *Brain, 97,* 709–728.

Weiss, K. M. (1978). A comparison of forward and backward procedures for the acquisition of response chains in humans. *Journal of the Experimental Analysis of Behavior, 29,* 255–259.

Weiss, S. J. (1972). Stimulus compounding in free-operant and classical conditioning. *Psychological Review, 78,* 189–208.

Weiss, S. J., & Schindler, C. W. (1985). Conditioning history and inhibitory instrumental stimulus control: Independent-groups and within-groups measures. *Animal Learning and Behavior, 13,* 215–222.

Weisstein, N., & Harris, C. S. (1980). Masking and unmasking of distributed representations in the visual system. In C. Harris (Ed.), *Visual coding and adaptability* (pp. 317–364). Hillsdale, NJ: Erlbaum.

Welker, R. L., & McAuley, K. (1978). Reductions to resistance to extinction and spontaneous recovery as a function of changes in transportational and contextual stimuli. *Animal Learning and Behavior, 6,* 451–457.

Werbos, P. J. (1974). *Beyond regression: New tools for prediction and analysis in the behavioral sciences.* Unpublished Doctoral Dissertation, Applied Mathematics, Harvard University, Cambridge, MA.

Wetherill, G. W. (1991). Occurrence of earth-like bodies in planetary systems. *Science, 252,* 535–538.

Wickens, C. (1980). The structure of attentional processes. In R. S. Nickerson (Ed.), *Attention and performance* (Vol. VIII, pp. 239–257). Hillsdale, NJ: Erlbaum.

Wickens, C. (1984). Processing resources in attention. In R. Parasuraman & D. R. Davies (Eds.), *Varieties of attention* (pp. 63–102). New York: Academic.

Wickens, D. D. (1972). Characteristics of word encoding. In A. W. Melton & E. Martin (Eds.), *Coding processes in human memory* (pp. 191–215). New York: Winston.

Widrow, B., & Hoff, M. E. (1960). Adaptive switching circuits. *WESTCON Convention Record, Part IV,* 96–104.

Wiesel, T. N. (1982). Postnatal development of the visual cortex and the influence of the environment. *Nature, 299,* 583–591.

Williams, B. A. (1981). The following schedule of reinforcement as a fundamental determinant of steady-state contrast in multiple schedules. *Journal of the Experimental Analysis of Behavior, 35,* 293–310.

Williams, B. A. (1988). The effects of stimulus similarity of different types of behavioral contrast. *Animal Learning and Behavior, 16,* 206–216.

Williams, B. A. (1990a). Enduring problems for molecular accounts of operant behavior. *Journal of Experimental Psychology: Animal Behavior Processes, 16,* 213–216.

Williams, B. A. (1990b). Absence of anticipatory contrast in rats trained on multiple schedules. *Journal of the Experimental Analysis of Behavior, 53,* 395–407.

Williams, B. A. (1991). Choice as a function of local versus molar reinforcement contingencies. *Journal of the Experimental Analysis of Behavior, 56,* 455–473.

Williams, B. A., & Dunn, R. (1991a). Substitutability between conditioned and primary reinforcers in discrimination acquisition. *Journal of the Experimental Analysis of Behavior, 55,* 21–36.

Williams, B. A., & Dunn, R. (1991b). Preference for conditioned reinforcement. *Journal of the Experimental Analysis of Behavior, 55,* 37–46.

Williams, D. R., & Williams, H. (1969). Auto-maintenance in the pigeon: Sustained pecking despite contingent nonreinforcement. *Science, 12,* 511–520.

Williams, G. C. (1966). *Adaptation and natural selection.* Princeton, NJ: Princeton University Press.

Wilson, E. O. (1975). *Sociobiology.* Cambridge, MA: Harvard University Press.

Winograd, E. (1988). Continuity between ecological and laboratory approaches to memory. In U. Neisser & E. Winograd, (Eds.), *Remembering reconsidered: Ecological and traditional approaches to the study of memory* (pp. 11–20). New York: Cambridge University Press.

Wise, R. A. (1989). The brain and reward. In J. M. Liebman & S. J. Cooper (Eds.), *The neuropharmacological basis of reward* (pp. 377–424. New York: Oxford University Press.

Wise, R. A., & Bozarth. M. A. (1987). A psychomotor stimulant theory of addiction. *Psychological Review, 94,* 469–492.

Witcher, E. S., & Ayres, J. J. B. (1984). A test of two methods for extinguishing Pavlovian conditioned inhibition. *Journal of Experimental Psychology: Animal Behavior Processes, 12,* 149–156.

Wolfe, J. B. (1936). Effectiveness of token rewards for chimpanzees. *Comparative Psychology Monographs, 12* (No. 60), 1–72.

Wolff, P. H., & White, B. L. (1965). Visual pursuit and attention in young infants. *Journal of the American Academy of Child Psychiatry, 4,* 473–484.

Woodbury, C. B. (1943). Learning of stimulus patterns by dogs. *Journal of Comparative Psychology, 35,* 29–40.

Woodruff, G., Premack, D., & Kennel, K. (1978). Conservation of liquid and solid quantity by the chimpanzee. *Science, 202,* 991–994.

Wright, A. A. (1972). The influence of ultraviolet radiation on the pigeon's color discrimination. *Journal of the Experimental Analysis of Behavior, 17,* 325–338.

Wright, A. A. (1989). Memory processing by pigeons, monkeys, and people. In G. H. Bower (Ed.), *Psychology of learning and motivation* (Vol. 24, pp. 25–70). New York: Academic.

Wright, A. A., Cook, R. G., Rivera, J. J., Shyan, M. R., Neiworth, J. J., & Jitsumori, M. (1990). Naming rehearsal, and interstimulus interval effects in memory processing. *Journal of Experimental Psychology: Learning, Memory, and Cognition, 16,* 1043–1059.

Wright, A. A., & Cumming, W. W. (1971). Color-naming functions for the pigeon. *Journal of the Experimental Analysis of Behavior, 15,* 7–18.

Wright, A. A., Santiago, H. C., Sands, S. F., Kendrick, D. F., & Cook, R. G. (1985). Memory processing of serial lists by pigeons, monkeys, and people. *Science, 229*, 287–289.

Wright, A., & Watkins, M. J. (1987). Animal learning and memory and their relation to human learning and memory. *Learning and Memory, 18*, 131–146.

Wurtz, R. H., Goldberg, M. E., & Robinson, D. L. (1980). Behavioral modulation of visual responses in the monkey: Stimulus selection for attention and movement. In J. M. Sprague & A. N. Epstein (Eds.), *Progress in Psychobiology and Physiological Psychology* (Vol. 9, pp. 43–83). New York: Academic.

Wyckoff, L. B., Jr. (1952). The role of observing responses in discrimination learning: Part I. *Psychological Review, 59*, 431–442.

Wyckoff, L. B., Jr. (1969). The role of observing responses in discrimination learning. In D. P. Hendry (Ed.), *Conditioned reinforcement* (pp. 237–260). Homewood, IL: Dorsey Press.

Yarbus, A. L. (1967). *Eye movements and vision*. New York: Plenum.

Yeomans, J. S. (1975). Quantitative measurement of neural post-stimulation excitability with behavioral methods. *Physiology and Behavior, 15*, 593–602.

Yeomans, J. S. (1982). The cells and axons mediating medial forebrain bundle reward. In B. G. Hoebel & D. Novin (Eds.), *The neural basis of feeding and reward* (pp. 405–417). Brunswik, ME: Haer Institute.

Yeomans, J. S. (1988). Mechanisms of brain stimulation reward. In A. N. Epstein & A. R. Morrison (Eds.), *Progress in Psychobiology and Physiological Psychology, 13*, 227–266.

Yeomans, J. S. (1989). Two substrates for medial forebrain bundle self-stimulation: Myelinated axons and dopamine neurons. *Neuroscience and Biobehavioral Reviews, 13*, 91–98.

Yeomans, J. S., Kofman, O., & McFarlane, V. (1988). Cholinergic involvement in hypothalamic and midbrain rewarding brain stimulation. In M. L. Commons, R. M. Church, J. R. Stellar, & A. R. Wagner (Eds.), *Quantitative analyses of behavior: Vol. 7. Biological determinants of reinforcement* (pp. 87–102). Hillsdale, NJ: Lawrence Erlbaum.

Yonas, A., & Granrud, C. E. (1984). The development of sensitivity to kinetic, binocular and pictorial depth information in human infants. In D. Ingle, D. Lee, & M. Jeannerod (Eds.), *Brain mechanisms and spatial vision* (pp. 113–145). Amsterdam: Martinus Nijhoff.

Yonas, A., & Owsley, C. (1987). Development of visual space perception. In P. Salapatek & L. Cohen (Eds.), *Handbook of infant perception* (Vol. 2, pp. 79–122). New York: Academic.

Young, M. P., & Yamane, S. (1992). Sparse population coding of faces in the inferotemporal cortex. *Science, 256*, 1327–1331.

Yuste, R., Peinado, A., & Katz, L. C. (1992). Neuronal domains in developing neocortex. *Science, 257*, 665–669.

Zeiler, M. D. (1972). Superstitious behavior in children: An experimental analysis. In H. W. Reese (Ed.), *Advances in child development and behavior* (Vol. 7, pp. 1–29). New York: Academic.

Zimler, J., & Keenan, J. M., (1983). Imagery in the congenitally blind: How visual are visual images? *Journal of Experimental Psychology: Learning, Memory, and Cognition, 9*, 269–282.

Zimmer-Hart, C. L., & Rescorla, R. A. (1974). Extinction of Pavlovian conditioned inhibition. *Journal of Comparative and Physiological Psychology, 86*, 837–845.

Zola-Morgan, S., & Squire, L. R. (1990). Neuropsychological investigations of memory and amnesia: Findings from humans and nonhuman primates. In A. Diamond (Ed.), *The development and neural bases of higher cognitive functions* (pp. 434–456). New York: New York Academy of Sciences.

Zola-Morgan, S., Squire, L. R., & Amaral, D. G. (1986). Human amnesia and the medial temporal region: Enduring memory impairment following a bilateral lesion limited to field CA1 of the hippocampus. *Journal of Neuroscience, 6*, 2950–2967.

NAME INDEX

SUBJECT INDEX